£20·00

MANAGING GLOBAL MARKETING

MANAGING GLOBAL MARKETING

Cases and Text

KAMRAN KASHANI

Professor of Marketing
International Institute for Management Development
Lausanne, Switzerland

PWS-KENT PUBLISHING COMPANY, BOSTON

PWS-KENT
Publishing Company

Sponsoring Editor: Al Bruckner
Editorial Assistant: Laurie Rosatone
Production Editor: Eve Mendelsohn Lehmann
Manufacturing Coordinator: Marcia Locke
Production Service: The Book Department
Interior Designer: The Book Department
Cover Designer: Eve Mendelsohn Lehmann
Compositor: The Clarinda Company
Cover Printer: Henry N. Sawyer Co., Inc.
Text Printer and Binder: R.R. Donnelley & Sons Company

PWS-KENT Publishing Company is a division of Wadsworth, Inc.

 This book is printed on acid-free, recycled paper.

Printed in the United States of America.
1 2 3 4 5 6—95 94 93 92

Library of Congress Cataloguing-in-Publications Data

Kashani, Kamran.
    Managing global marketing : cases and text / Kamran Kashani.
        p.   cm.
    Includes bibliographical references.
    ISBN 0-534-92977-X
    1. Export marketing—Management—Case studies.   I. Title.
    HF1416.K37 1992   91-48363
    658.8′48—dc20   CIP

International Student Edition ISBN: 0-534-97211-X

To Nini,
Niloufar and Nissa.

CONTENTS

vii

PREFACE

This book responds to two growing concerns in American management education: Insufficient student exposure to the challenges of doing business in markets other than one's own, and the need for more managerial relevance in what is taught and learned. Both of these concerns bear directly on the quality of education the students receive.

Although the perceived need for more international content in business curricula is not new, its actual urgency is. As the list of industries in which U.S. companies have lost their global competitiveness grows, so do the voices of critics who put the blame partly on an inward-looking business education concerned more with the familiar domestic market than with the unfamiliar international markets. From high tech to low tech, from tangible goods to intangible services, companies need to learn new skills to operate in an increasingly global marketplace. The critics charge the business schools with not doing enough to develop these skills. There is more than a grain of truth in what these critics say.

Similarly, managerial relevance in business education has come under increased scrutiny in recent years. The issue centers on the balance between the theory and practice of management in business curricula. A number of recent studies have revealed that emphasis on elegant models of management has come at the expense of useful insights in dealing with the often less than elegant reality of the practictioner.[1] The critics maintain that the pendulum in business education has swung too far from a healthy balance between the science and the art of managing. Once again, there is more than an element of truth in such criticism.

Managing Global Marketing introduces the student of mangement to the reality and the challenges of globalized markets and offers a managerially oriented context in which to learn about global marketing. The book's introductory text is meant to acquaint the student with the issues of strategy making and implementation and is written with many recent examples of successes and failures, good and bad practices, in global marketing. The examples, almost all taken from the author's extensive field-based research project, help to illustrate many of the key

1. See, for example, "Leadership for a Changing World," a study conducted by Graduate Management Admission Council and published in 1990.

points in the text in terms that are easy to understand. In addition, the text is complemented with an extensive list of suggested readings for optional in-depth study of issues.

The main body of this book is devoted to a wide selection of management cases as vehicles to develop insights and skills in problem analysis and decision making in global marketing. The cases put the student at the center of the learning process and provide a chance to encounter the complexity and the thrills of global marketing as experienced by real managers in real companies. The case problems take the student around the world to more than twenty different countries, markets, and cultural environments. The case sites range from North America to Europe and the Far East. A distinguishing feature of these cases is their multicountry, truly *global* coverage; no single nation dominates the cases. The student develops a genuinely global perspective by seeing the world not only through the eyes of U.S. companies but also through those of other nationalities. In this respect, European companies and markets get special attention due to the rising economic convergence on the continent and its growing impact on global trade in the 1990s. Many of the cases examine issues that are the direct result of Europe's continuing progress toward a single, borderless market.

All cases are recently researched and written for easy reading. While the cases present comprehensive background data for analysis and decision making, they are not unduly long or complex. An early chapter in the book is devoted to introducing the student to the art and techniques of analyzing cases.

The book is divided into three main parts and an appendix. *Part One* is an introduction to global marketing. It defines the topic, and its cases give an overview of managerial issues in global marketing.

Part Two takes the student deeper into a discussion of global marketing strategy, its analysis and decisions. Part Two's introductory chapter and cases deal with the topics of opportunity analysis in global markets, product policy, marketing communication, distribution channels, pricing, and marketing program formulation—all in a multimarket, global setting.

Part Three addresses the important and often ignored subject of global strategy implementation. It introduces the student to the different elements of implementation, from "hard" to "soft," from structure to process, and from cross-cultural to individual managerial skills.

Finally, the *Appendix* consists of twenty country facts sheets that give the student a quick, yet informative, look at the economic, social, and political facts and life-styles of each of the international markets covered in the book. The Appendix helps to add to the student's knowledge of world markets and the depth of analysis of case problems.

Managing Global Marketing offers instructors of international marketing maximum flexibility in designing a course of high educational value. The teacher can build a curriculum from introductory chapters, cases, and suggested readings to fit any course requirements or preferred areas of emphasis. The selection and sequence of cases may also be adapted to the teacher's own objectives for the course. Sufficient diversity in the material allows such "customizing." It is the author's own experience that the combination of case discussions, background readings, and instructor's own complementary lectures makes for a rich and stimulating learning experience for students. This book is designed to facilitate such learning.

ACKNOWLEDGMENTS

A book in global marketing would not be true to its title if it were the product of a single individual from a single part of the world. *Managing Global Marketing* is true to its title. This publication can claim to be a truly global product thanks to a long list of contributors from different parts of the world who have enriched its content by either contributing their cases or otherwise helping with its realization. My first thanks go to those international colleagues, representing seven nationalities, who have generously allowed me to complement my own cases with theirs. I have worked with all of them at one point or another in my career and have come to respect them as dedicated teachers who care immensely about the quality of their students' learning. The high caliber of their cases is the best testimony to this fact. Given the special nature of their contribution, I have listed them separately under Contributors.

Many others have been instrumental in helping me to develop the ideas for the book and bring them to life. Because this space is too small to name them all, I will mention only those who have had the most impact, even if indirectly. My gratitude goes to my former dean, Derek Able, who kept nudging me toward developing a field of study in international marketing and provided the means to undertake my initial research in the area. Bob Buzzell, my good friend and former mentor, deserves a special mention for offering me intellectual and physical space at Harvard Business School to think and write during my sabbatical leave. With his critical reviews, he helped greatly with my early writings on global marketing. Norman Govoni of Babson College kindly hosted me in his department during part of my stay in Massachusetts. I am grateful to him and his marketing faculty.

Four colleagues at my school, IMD in Lausanne, Switzerland, deserve special words of thanks for their direct contributions to the book. They include three research associates, James Henderson, Bob Howard, and David Hover, in addition to Faith Towel, our editor. The research associates helped to collect the data for my cases and for the country facts sheets. They have done a fine job. Faith was most helpful with reading and suggesting changes for the first drafts of cases and text.

I would also like to thank the following reviewers for their helpful comments and criticisms: Roberto Friedmann, University of Georgia; Salah A. Hassan, George Washington University; Stan Palidowa, University of Calgary; and Milton M. Pressley, University of New Orleans.

Finally, I have appreciated the assistance and advice I have received from Al Bruckner and Laurie Rosatone, the editorial staff at PWS-KENT. Without their constant attention to details and insistence on important editorial matters, my book would have never reached a happy ending.

Kamran Kashani

International Institute for
Management Development (IMD)
Lausanne, Switzerland

CONTRIBUTORS

Joseph R. D'Cruz, Associate Professor, Faculty of Management, University of Toronto, Toronto, Canada.

Terry H. Deutscher, Associate Dean and R.A. Barford Professor of Marketing Communications, Western Business School, London, Canada.

H. Michael Hayes, Professor of Marketing and Strategic Management, University of Colorado at Denver, Denver, Colorado, United States.

Jacques Horovitz, founder and President of Management of Strategic Resources and former Professor at ESSEC, France, and at International Institute for Management Development, Lausanne, Switzerland.

Per V. Jenster, Professor of Marketing, International Institute for Management Development, Lausanne, Switzerland.

Jean-Jacques Lambin, Dean of Lovanium International and Professor at the Institut d'Administration et de Gestion, Louvain University, Louvain, Belgium.

Christian Pinson, Professor of Marketing at INSEAD, Fontainbleu, France.

Kurt Schaer, Professor of Finance, International Institute for Management Development, Lausanne, Switzerland.

Dominique Turpin, Professor of Marketing, International Institute for Management Development, Lausanne, Switzerland.

Sandra Vandermerwe, Professor of Marketing and Services Management, International Institute for Management Development, Lausanne, Switzerland.

Robert F. Young, Associate Professor of Management, Northeastern University, Boston, Massachusetts, United States.

CASE ABSTRACTS

have failed to produce tangible results so far. Is the problem different Japanese tastes or product standards or ways of doing business? Should management persist or forget Japan altogether?

5. Club Med Sales, Inc. (A)

The company's globally successful packaged vacation concept is not meeting its sales targets in the United States. Management is considering commissioning market research to understand the American customer better. What type(s) of research should be considered, if any?

6. Club Med Sales, Inc. (B)

Management is analyzing the findings from several research studies it has commissioned. How useful are the reuslts, and what should management do to remedy the sales decline problem?

Product Policy

7. Colgate-Palmolive: Cleopatra

A soap product that has been highly successful in France flops in Canada. Headquarters management believes the international transfer of the concept was a good idea but it was implemented poorly. Some local Canadian managers are ready to scrap the product. Is the product truly global, or is it a one-market concept suitable only for France?

8. Nabisco Brands, Inc.–Cipster

Regional headquarters is looking at some branding options for a new snack product to be introduced in one market, Italy. Management may take the opportunity presented by the new product to begin streamlining branding practices across the company's autonomous local units in Europe. Should headquarters press for the adoption of a pan-European brand? What are the costs or benefits, if any?

Communication

9. Hertz Autovermietung GmbH (A)

Hertz's advertising agency in Germany is asked to make recommendations that would help improve the car and truck rental company's sales and profits. The agency is studying the highly competitive rental market to better assess the threats and opportunities. What could the agency recommend to its client?

10. Hertz Autovermietung GmbH (B)

The agency is reviewing its prize-winning and highly successful campaign for Hertz. What elements in the campaign have contributed most to its success?

11. Grasse Fragrances SA

A global marketer of industrial fragrances is reexamining its sales force management in light of changes that are taking place among its international clients and markets. How should the current management practices be changed, if at all?

Distribution

12. Leykam Mürztaler AG

An Austrian producer of high quality paper is reacting to international trends in its channels of distribution. To compensate for the growing power of middlemen, who also market their own private labels, management is considering strengthening the corporate identity and brand. Will the strategy work or backfire?

13. Jordan A/S

A small Norwegian exporter of mechanical oral hygiene products is finding itself squeezed internationally between large global competitors and ever-concentrating wholesale and retail trade. Management is wondering if a change in the company's successful past strategy of thinking small is called for. What should the company do to survive the international market consolidation?

Pricing

14. Pharma Swede: Gastirup

A medium-sized Swedish drug company is facing the prospects of massive parallel trade or significant losses in revenues if the divergent local prices of a major product are not harmonized across Europe. Management is examining several options, including some drastic measures to deal with the pricing issue. Which option, if any, makes most sense?

15. Philip Morris KK

Two global tobacco giants are fighting for market share in the small but growing imported segment of the Japanese market. The company's dominant position in this segment is being threatened by a new, low-priced product from the competition. Should management retaliate and risk a potentially costly price war?

Global Marketing Programs

16. Swatch

An innovator in the global watch market is deciding how to modify its proven strategy for continued international success. In the face of growing competition in its original lines, management is debating issues related to product line extension and brand positioning and communciation. Should the brand concept be broadened to incorporate other products, including fashion wear?

17. Volvo Trucks Europe

The world's second largest producer and marketer of heavy trucks is facing changes in its number one market, Europe. Management is considering more panregional coordination of marketing decisions currently delegated to semi-independent country organizations. What decisions should now be coordinated centrally, and what steps are needed to help with implementing a unified international marketing strategy?

PART THREE   **IMPLEMENTING GLOBAL STRATEGY:**
From Global Vision to Management Action

18. Maschinenfabrik Meyer AG (A)

A small Swiss-based company is planning its future in the growing and increasingly competitive membrane-based industrial filters market. Its entrepreneurial management is lobbying for financial and logistics help from its large parent to gain a viable share of this global market. The vehicle for seeking the parent's support is a five-year business plan. What should the plan contain, and how could management build support for its case?

19. Maschinenfabrik Meyer AG (B)

Management has prepared a five-year plan for the membrane-based industrial filters business. How good is the plan? Should the parent company give the resources asked for the plan's implementation?

20. Kao in Singapore

A newly appointed country head is given the job of turning around the Japanese company's loss in the soap-making and toiletries business in Singapore. He soon finds himself torn between two managers with conflicting strategies for a turnaround: his Japanese boss in headquarters and a senior manager in the local company. To whom should he listen, and how should he resolve the dilemma?

21. Alto Chemicals Europe (A)

A new marketing manager for this North American company's operations in Europe is planning a major strategy revision for a line of commodity-like chemicals. However, he runs into stiff opposition from country-level sales managers who label his strategy unworkable and call him dictatorial. Should he retreat or persist toward implementation?

22. Alto Chemicals Europe (B)

Six months later the marketing manager is still insisting on his strategy but at some cost. His working relationship with country sales managers has deteriorated into shouting matches, and sales results are mixed. Can he still salvage something, possibly even his job? What should he do now?

HOW TO ANALYZE A CASE

The cases included in this book are about real managers, real problems, and real companies. This is true even for those firms that are presented under disguised names to respect the wishes of their management for anonymity. Each case is thus a snapshot of the business and marketing reality faced by a company and its management. Cases typically focus on certain issues and provide the background data available to the managers at the time. Cases allow the student to experience the challenges of real-life managers and learn their craft by simulated problem solving and decision making. Learning by doing—that is what using management cases is all about.

Case analysis, like problem solving in management, is an art. Like any other art form, it has certain techniques, requires a great deal of creativity, and improves with practice. Some of the more useful techniques of case analysis are highlighted here. These techniques should help improve the efficiency and effectiveness of the case analysis process. When combined with inquisitive analysis and inventive thinking, the techniques should lead to good solutions to case problems—solutions that could possibly make the difference between success and failure in the real world.

GETTING STARTED

A good place to start the analysis of a case is with a quick look at the case and an identification of its main issues. This exercise can save much time later by helping to focus the in-depth reading and examination of case data in those sections relevant to the analysis. A quick look could mean reading the first and last pages of the case and skimming the sections in between. Exhibits are best left for a later, more in-depth examination of the case. On the other hand, when discussion questions are assigned, they should be consulted at this stage. Depending on the length or complexity of the case, 10 to 15 minutes should be sufficient for this first glance. By then, the student should have a good idea about the problems the case deals with and also some of the background data available in the document. Having this knowledge will enable the student to proceed to the next step.

DELVING DEEPER

The primary task of case analysis is to define the problems that underlie the issues with which the company is grappling. For example, management may be concerned with the increase in the level of competition in its markets worldwide and the resulting erosion in profitability. The real problem, however, may lie elsewhere. Low profits may be only a symptom of more fundamental problems. An in-depth look at the case may well reveal that declining profitability is not uniformly present in all geographic markets. The presence of low profits may be associated with a number of underlying factors: declining investment in product innovation, out-dated production facilities, and insufficient expenditure on brand advertising. These more profound problems surface only after the student delves deeper into the analysis. With this insight, the student can now focus the rest of the analysis on ways to resolve the real problems.

Delving deeper into case analysis involves a careful reading of the case, with particular emphasis on those sections earlier identified as pertinent to the issues. It means examining the exhibits and identifying relevant information from both the exhibits and the text. At this point, the student should note on a page or two the relevant facts that are often scattered throughout the case. Once assembled, these facts begin to reveal patterns that point to underlying problems. At this stage the

student must be warned to fight the common temptation to arrive at quick conclusions before all the relevant pieces of the puzzle have been examined. That means the student should not be misled by management's own views of what the problems might be. They must bear in mind that in real life managers can also be wrong!

Here are a few useful tips on problem analysis for students:

■ In your first reading of the whole case, underline or highlight passages that you believe are relevant to the analysis. Your review of case facts will thus be more focused later on.

■ Insightful interpretation of case data is part of effective analysis. For this reason, it is at times necessary to "read between the lines" in order to better understand a problem and further the analysis. That often means putting your own interpretations on case facts and what the company management or the case writer is saying or hinting. Your interpretations are an essential and integral part of your analysis.

■ When a case includes figures on sales, profits, margins, and so forth, it is appropriate to take a few minutes to consider how they might be used to further the analysis. At the same time, "numbers crunching" for its own sake can be a waste of time. Before devoting much time to this exercise, it is wise to ask: "How might the numbers help the analysis?"

■ At times, you may believe that a piece of information not included in the case could help advance analysis. In such circumstances, make an assumption regarding the missing information, and proceed with the analysis. Any such assumption should be consistent with other case facts and, in addition, defensible. Defensibility means that you can offer convincing arguments as to why the assumption is valid and probably not far from reality.

■ There are many dead-ends in analyzing a complex management problem. Yet all avenues must be pursued before the analyst discovers those that lead to a clear problem definition. In presenting your analysis, include only those pieces of the analysis, qualitative as well as quantitative, that help with problem definition. By implication, exclude all other pieces of information that do not directly bear on the analysis, regardless of the amount of time you have spent studying them.

PLANNING ACTION

Problem identification is at the core of case analysis, but it is only the first step toward a solution. Complete case analysis includes a recommended plan of action that, when implemented, would lead to problem resolution.

Before deciding what course of action to recommend, the student must look at a number of alternative ways in which a problem could be tackled. A common mistake at this phase of the analysis is to focus on one course of action and ignore others. The student should be reminded that there is always more than one solution to most management problems, especially those in marketing. Therefore, it is important that a number of alternative courses of action are evaluated before one is selected. This exercise requires objectively assessing each course of action against certain explicit criteria that the student believes to be keys to an effective resolution of the problem. In the earlier example, the student may argue that any action designed to return low-profit countries to higher profitability must have a long-term impact to be acceptable. Actions that cannot be sustained for long, for budgetary reasons or otherwise, are thus rejected. This criterion, of course, needs to be made explicit and defended, but once done, it becomes a dimension along which alternative courses of action are evaluated.

For a thorough analysis, the student should examine the pros and cons of all the alternatives, along the chosen criteria and possibly other less important considerations, before choosing one to recommend. For each alternative the student may use a two-column T-bar—one column for pros and the other for cons—to highlight the trade-offs. Such an exercise can narrow the action options to a subset of original alternatives. Because "perfect" solutions to management problems rarely emerge, even after narrowing the options, a good deal of judgment is still called for in selecting the most promising course of action. At a minimum, the chosen plan should satisfy all or most of the decision criteria set forth earlier. But viable action plans must do better than this bare minimum. In addition, they must be *consistent* with the market environment of the firm, *persuasive* in their promise to solve the problem, and *implementable*. This latter quality becomes critical in global marketing, where implementation is a complex process that involves many markets and cultures, widespread organizational units, and distant managers.

Here are other tips to define action plans:

■ In preparing action alternatives, do not initially discard any option without evaluating it at some length. At this first stage, the aim should be to prepare a long list of alternatives before later reducing the list to a short one.

■ Decision criteria used to evaluate action alternatives must be few in number and critically important to the company or the problem at hand. Avoid making a long list that does not distinguish between more important and less important criteria.

■ Before finalizing your plan of action, try to think through the mechanics of how it is supposed to work. It is too tempting, and dangerous, to assume that all the details will take care of themselves once the plan is put into motion. Ask yourself: What are the critical steps and how will they help solve the problem? How practical are they?

■ Once you have decided on the "best" course of action, it is wise to give some thought to possible criticisms the plan could encounter. This advance mental preparation will help you defend the plan and make it more convincing—to your colleagues in the classroom or, later on, to your management audience.

LIKE THE REAL WORLD

In-depth case analysis, which is about synthesizing hard and soft data into meaningful inferences, can be a frustrating exercise. The student is often under time constraints to finish the analysis and move on to other projects; the data are incomplete and yet a plan of action must be recommended; the facts at times are contradictory and rarely presented in a useful form; and key information has to be extracted from among volumes of seemingly useless data. These frustrations are common in case analysis, and yet they are also present in the managerial world, which is similarly characterized by decision making under the pressure of deadlines and without the benefit of consistent and complete information in a concise and clear form. These "imperfections" are inherent to managerial decision making, but they do not necessarily hamper the process of making effective decisions. Good decisions are made in spite of them. Cases, because they are vehicles for learning by experiencing and doing, prepare students not only for the challenges of the subject matter, marketing or otherwise, but also for the hurdles they are likely to face as future managers and decision makers.

PART ONE

INTRODUCTION:

Global Markets and Marketing

World markets are merging, and many traditional market boundaries are disappearing. The 1970s and 1980s witnessed the acceleration of a trend toward convergence among dispersed national markets, a process that had started years earlier and is continuing today. The "globalization" of markets, as some have referred to this trend,[1] has had profound implications for business in general and marketing in particular. Firms in sectors as diverse as processed foods, packaged consumer goods, durable consumer products, and industrial products and services are discovering that the traditional rules of international competition have changed dramatically in their now globalized markets. In industry after industry, from commodity chemicals to fast food, and from pharmaceuticals to disposable baby diapers, new rules for survival are deciding the winners and losers. In these global markets, past success is no guarantee for the future. Firms that have adapted to the requirements of converged world markets have outperformed those that have not. In the breakneck competition for world customers, there is little mercy for the half-hearted and the slow mover.

What distinguishes a global market? The process of globalization manifests itself differently in different industries. Yet many of the following patterns are generally present:

- Disappearing "national" market boundaries as competitors and customers cross traditional geographic borders to buy and to sell.

- Declining number of competitors and increasing size of the remaining players as the

5

smaller firms, unable to compete because of their suboptimal size or narrow geographic focus, are absorbed by the larger ones or forced out.

- Competition among the same group of world-class players in every national market.
- Increasing interdependence among national or regional markets as developments or marketing strategies in one location impact markets elsewhere.
- Growing similarity among segments of customers worldwide as gaps in their life-styles, tastes, and behavior narrow.

Exhibit 1.1 portrays the contrasting pictures of local and global markets. As markets evolve from local fragmentation to global integration, major shifts take place along the parameters shown in the exhibit.

FORCES OF CHANGE

Before examining the implications of the trend toward globalization for marketing, let us examine some of the forces responsible for the trend itself. Indeed, several powerful forces are at work bringing about a progressive change toward convergence of world markets, among them economies of combined size, rising investments, communication, convergence of consumer behavior, and integration of economies.

Economies of Combined Size More and more companies are discovering the potential for huge savings in purchasing and manufacturing when these functions are combined and integrated on a regional or worldwide basis. To illustrate, Philips, the Netherlands-based electronics giant, was traditionally managed as a federation of powerful national companies, each operating autonomously and performing all functions independently. Under pressure from the low-priced Japanese competition in consumer electronics, a new team of top managers at Philips began to stream-

line and modernize the procurement and manufacturing operations—initially in Europe and later on a worldwide scale. The aims of the undertaking, which centralized many of the functions previously performed on a country-by-country basis, were to reduce duplication; reach a world scale in plant size; invest in manufacturing automation, which could only be done once production units reached a minimum scale; and exploit savings in high-volume purchasing of raw materials and manufacturing of standardized products.

Philips's response to the global competitive challenge paid off handsomely in that it resulted in a streamlined operation in consumer electronics and enabled the company to confront the Japanese, who were themselves serving the world market from centralized and highly efficient manufacturing sites. In one product line alone, the color TV operation, Philips was able to reduce the labor content of an average set from 22 hours under previously fragmented local production to less than 30 minutes. Despite Philips's recent problems, the consumer products business remains profitable thanks to the restructuring that took place in the 1980s.

Rising Investments The ever-rising expenditures for R&D and manufacturing are responsible for a decline in the number of players in many industries. To cite a few examples, in the pharmaceuticals industry, the cost of discovering a useful molecule has been steadily rising worldwide. The low "hit ratio" in drug research, estimated to be one usable molecule in 10,000 discoveries, has boosted the average "molecule-to-market" cost of new products to nearly $200 million. In telecommunications, the estimated cost of developing a new generation of computer-based telephone exchange systems is nearly $1 billion. Similarly, a new passenger car model could cost its developer upward of $1,200 million in design and production machinery.

Considering that these are up-front expenditures before a single product reaches the market,

EXHIBIT 1.1 Local vs. Global Markets: Key Differences

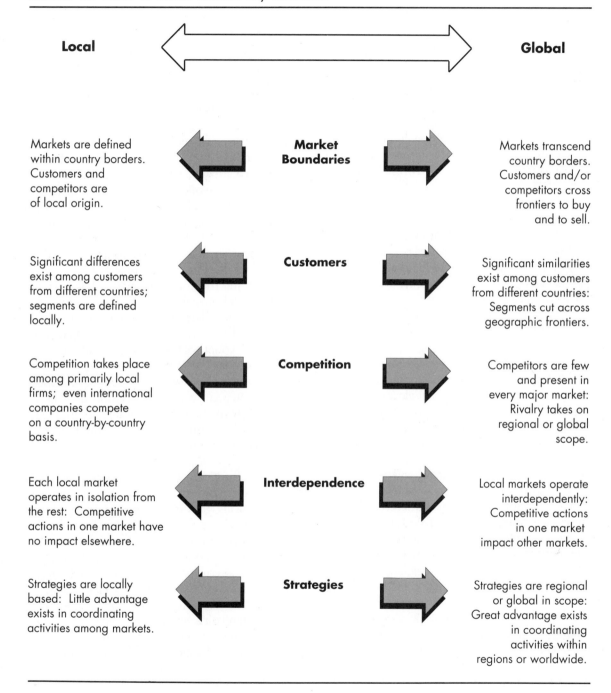

Local ⟷ **Global**

Local		Global
Markets are defined within country borders. Customers and competitors are of local origin.	**Market Boundaries**	Markets transcend country borders. Customers and/or competitors cross frontiers to buy and to sell.
Significant differences exist among customers from different countries; segments are defined locally.	**Customers**	Significant similarities exist among customers from different countries: Segments cut across geographic frontiers.
Competition takes place among primarily local firms; even international companies compete on a country-by-country basis.	**Competition**	Competitors are few and present in every major market: Rivalry takes on regional or global scope.
Each local market operates in isolation from the rest: Competitive actions in one market have no impact elsewhere.	**Interdependence**	Local markets operate interdependently: Competitive actions in one market impact other markets.
Strategies are locally based: Little advantage exists in coordinating activities among markets.	**Strategies**	Strategies are regional or global in scope: Great advantage exists in coordinating activities within regions or worldwide.

the high and rising investments have had two powerful implications for their industries. First, not every company can afford the financial burden of such investments. Hence the decline in the number of competitors through mergers and acquisitions and a growing trend toward alliances in product development and manufacturing among hitherto competing firms. Second, no single national or even regional market has the needed size to pay back such expenditures alone. The investments could only be justified if they were amortized on the basis of a worldwide market.

Communication The spread of communication is rapidly shrinking the global marketplace. This development is taking place at both the consumer and corporate levels. With the assistance of satellite communication technology, and also the emergence of a worldwide market for TV productions, viewers worldwide are being linked to overlapping networks of information and entertainment. Satellite transmissions are facilitating instantaneous broadcasts from anywhere in the world to potentially everywhere. Recent worldwide broadcasts of live sports and newsworthy events have attracted audiences approaching one billion people. Also, TV entertainment is leapfrogging across national and cultural barriers. Viewers in Europe and elsewhere are watching TV productions made in places all over the world, including Brazil, Japan, and the United States; American serials such as "Dallas" and "Dynasty" have been popular wherever they are shown, including many Third World countries.

One manifestation of the impact of global communication at the consumer level is the emergence of the so-called "global brands"—brands that have transcended their country of origin to become household names around the world. The list in Exhibit 1.2 identifies top-ranking global brands based on a recent survey of nearly 10,000 consumers in 11 countries in North America, Europe, and the Far East.

As for communication at the corporate level, an increasing number of companies are integrat-

EXHIBIT 1.2 The World's Best-Known Brands

1. Coca-Cola	6. Toyota
2. McDonald's	7. Nestlé
3. Pepsi-Cola	8. Disney
4. Sony	9. Honda
5. Kodak	10. Ford

Source: The Landor ImagePower Survey, 1990.

ing their previously geographically dispersed and isolated information systems into worldwide networks. At Citibank, for example, a global communication network allows access to banking information from any location around the world. Managers can also use the system to send messages electronically from any desk in Citibank's worldwide corporate structure to any other Citibank office. Benetton, the global fashion house, utilizes an information network that links manufacturing and inventory control operations to points of sales. The network links around-the-clock sales data from more than 5,000 Benetton stores in 35 countries to the company's headquarters in the village of Ponzano, Italy. Such worldwide information networks as these have helped firms to integrate corporate decision making at the center with those in the distant local operations. Physical distances are thus no longer a barrier to global integration.

Convergence of Consumer Behavior The increase in international communication, combined with narrowing gaps in consumer demographics, has brought about a trend toward convergence in consumer behavior worldwide. Increasing urbanization, rising disposable incomes, similar product ownership patterns (such as cars, TVs, and refrigerators), and a surge in foreign travel are some of the elements responsible for the visible and growing similarity among segments of world consumers in how they live, what they want, and how they buy. The global spread of such diverse products and brands as Nescafé, the Sony Walkman, Perrier mineral water, Marlboro cigarettes, Pampers disposable diapers, Levis jeans, and

McDonald's fast foods, just to name a visible few, has been made possible by the convergence of segments of consumers on a global scale.

A company that has successfully taken advantage of the global convergence among consumers is IKEA, the world's largest marketer of household furniture and furnishing products. The Swedish-based company has identified a "global niche" of consumers with similar needs and tastes who buy the same way whether they are in North America, Europe, or the Far East. With more than 70 company-owned stores worldwide, IKEA's unique concept of retailing reasonably priced, ready-to-assemble products to young couples in combination warehouse-showrooms is no more Scandinavian than European or American. The concept is as much at home in Philadelphia or Hong Kong as in its original hometown, Almhult, Sweden. IKEA is a truly global concept with a world-wide appeal. Exhibit 1.3 highlights the key elements of IKEA's winning global marketing strategy.

Integration of Economies The convergence of world markets has been aided by a number of intergovernmental agreements toward regional economic integration. Perhaps the most ambitious of such pacts is the one governing the creation of a unified market in Western Europe by 1992. The Single Market Act, signed in 1986, calls for the free movement of goods, services, labor, and capital in a frontierless European Community (EC).[2] The 12-member EC represents a market of 325 million consumers and a combined gross domestic production (GDP) of about $4.8 trillion.[3] With increasing political resolve, the member states have taken significant steps toward removing major barriers to the creation of a unified market. As the rendezvous with "1992" becomes a reality, firms operating across the continent are reexamining their structure and realigning their strategies to take advantage of one of the world's largest single markets. Exhibit 1.4 compares data on EC members, as well as the United States and Japan.

The EC is expected to expand its 12-state membership by the mid-1990s. Pressure to incorporate a larger number of economies is building up on the community from nonmember European states that wish to share in the benefits of a single market. One source of pressure is coming from the 7-nation European Free Trade Association, EFTA.[4] Aiming to create a greater "European Economic Area" (EEA), EFTA negotiated with the EC the mechanisms by which its membership could influence the Community's decisions and benefit from many of the privileges enjoyed by its members, without full-fledged economic, monetary, and political union. Despite the difficulties in EC-EFTA negotiations, an accord was reached in late 1991 which sets 1993 as the target date for the creation of a 19-member free trade zone. When the accord is ratified by the parliaments of all the countries concerned, it will create the world's largest integrated economic block. Another source of pressure is from the newly reformed economies of Eastern Europe. Former East Germany has become a defacto member of the EC, thanks to its unification with West Germany. But the initial bottlenecks of integrating East Germany, which happened to be the most developed among the East European economies, are indicative of the problems that will inhibit for years to come the EC's expansion eastward.

A more recent and less ambitious economic pact in another part of the world is the Free Trade Agreement between the United States and Canada. The agreement, which came into effect in 1989, envisages free movement of goods and services through a step-by-step removal of trade barriers between the two countries. Spread over a ten-year horizon, the pact covers in the first round such goods as computer hardware, vending machines, skis, and motorcycles. Future rounds will include other products such as paper, telecommunication equipment, and chemicals. By 1998, the remaining tariffs would be lifted on such products as most agricultural goods, textiles and apparel, steel, appliances, and tires.[5] The U.S.-Canada

EXHIBIT 1.3   IKEA's Global Marketing Strategy

Segmentation	Young urban couples with mid-range but rising incomes: They lead a casual life-style and prefer modern designs and one-stop shopping.
Product and Service	Wide variety of products with functional designs often sold in "knocked-down" kits ready to be taken home and assembled; in-store services include a restaurant, baby-sitting, and a playroom for kids.
Pricing	"Affordable" and "value for money" prices targeted at or below traditional retailers' prices.
Distribution	Large combination warehouse-showrooms located outside urban centers and accessible by car.
Communication	Annual catalogues with extensive coverage of all products; projected store image: "A warm and friendly place to shop."

Free Trade Agreement is likely to expand its coverage to include Mexico in the first stage and other Central and South American countries in future stages.

Still another regional accord is ASEAN, a loose economic alliance of six South-East Asian countries: Brunei, Indonesia, Malaysia, Philippines, Singapore, and Thailand. Dating back to 1967, the agreement provides a framework for cooperation among member states in economic and industrial development projects. An important element in the agreement provides for reduced tariffs on products manufactured within the group of six. Companies producing in one location would enjoy preferential access to the other ASEAN markets.

With varying speeds, the regional trade agreements such as the ones just highlighted are helping to break down artificial barriers and create unified markets out of fragmented economies. They represent one more force in the continuing fusion of world markets.

EXHIBIT 1.4 Comparative Data: EC Members, United States, and Japan

Country	Population (1989 est.) (millions)	GDP* (1989 est.) ($ billions)	Per capita GDP (1989 est.) ($)
Belgium	9.88	151.23	15,306.68
Denmark	5.13	99.59	19,413.25
France	56.10	939.53	16,747.42
Germany**	61.30	1,194.74	19,490.04
Greece	10.01	54.27	5,421.58
Ireland	3.54	32.34	9,135.59
Italy	57.50	858.90	14,937.39
Luxembourg	0.37	6.54	17,675.68
Netherlands	14.84	219.07	14,762.13
Portugal	10.47	46.89	4,478.51
Spain	39.20	340.84	8,694.90
U.K.	57.20	846.67	14,801.92
Total EC	325.54	4,790.61	14,715.89
U.S.	248.00	5,235.00	21,108.87
Japan	123.30	2,829.71	22,949.80

Source: Economist Intelligence Unit, Country Profiles, 1989–1990.
*Gross domestic production.
**Before reunification with East Germany.

THE DUAL TASKS OF GLOBAL MARKETERS

How a firm markets its products in its home market or internationally ought to take into account the fact that national markets are no longer islands of opportunity operating in isolation from one another. Marketers, as members of the most outward-looking function in business, have a special responsibility in this respect. They must not only define a *strategy* that reflects the global shifts in their industry; they must also bring about a change of *perspectives* within the larger organization so that decisions made elsewhere, at the headquarters or national subsidiaries, are consistent with the reality of globalization. Both tasks are important to the success of the firm.

Defining the Strategy The first task is about strategy making or, broadly speaking, defining *who* the target segment is and *how* the members of the segment are served. Market segmentation and marketing mix decisions are the outputs of the strategy-making process. Indirectly and by implication, marketing decisions also define the competitive arena in which the firm operates—that is, where and with whom the firm competes and how it plans to *outperform* the competition. Defined as such, marketing strategy is at the heart of a firm's broader business strategy. For this reason it must play a leading role in consolidating a firm's operations in a global setting, from fragmented country-by-country strategies toward worldwide integration.

As national markets converge, marketing management needs to reexamine some of the fundamental assumptions that have traditionally led to "multidomestic" strategies, where each of the firm's local subsidiaries devised its own marketing scheme with a great deal of autonomy from the headquarters and in almost total isolation from the rest of the organization.[6] With a narrowing of differences among segments of customers worldwide and the emergence of a handful of competitors as global contenders, such a country-by-country approach to strategy making may prove suboptimal, if not fatal.

For example, in the 1980s, Procter & Gamble (P&G) discovered that its decades-old policy of almost total local autonomy for its national companies was running counter to the heightened need for speedy worldwide rollout of new products. With competition closely watching P&G's new product launches in the "prime-mover" markets and preempting P&G elsewhere with competing lines, more central coordination among national subsidiaries was called for. In the case of Pampers, the company's brand of disposable baby diapers, the product was introduced in Germany as a first step toward a country-by-country rollout on the continent. But due to differing local management priorities, and despite a successful launch in Germany, it was not until years later that the brand made its appearance in other countries. In this span of time, competition had entered these markets with similar products and, in some cases, even with marketing strategies identical to that of Pampers. As a latecomer, P&G faced an uphill battle for a share of the European market it had helped to create.[7]

Although strategy making in an international setting is concerned with market features that cut across different country markets, global marketing is far more complex than treating the world as one homogeneous marketplace. That would be simplistic and far from reality in most industries. The complexity of global marketing lies in the need to formulate strategies that identify and exploit cross-border market *commonalities,* while allowing sufficient flexibility to deal locally with individual market *differences.* To arrive at this delicate balance, three key questions have to be asked:

- Are there significant commonalities among local markets to justify the development of

a regional or even a truly global marketing strategy in which key elements are standardized across different countries?

- What are the significant differences among local markets that may stand in the way of a common marketing strategy?

- What advantages could be gained over competition by centralizing certain decisions at headquarters or by coordinating otherwise independent local marketing activities?

Informed answers to these questions provide the basis for formulating strategies that exploit international market commonalities on the one hand, while respecting individual market differences on the other. They also lead to strategies that leverage the firm's size or geographic scope for creating tangible competitive advantage.

Changing Perspectives   The second task of global marketers has to do with changing internal perspectives. Pioneers in global thinking often have to contend with management's traditional ways of thinking about world markets. Habits die hard, especially those that have in the past brought prosperity to the firm. Many assumptions regarding differences among local customers, the local nature of competition, and the like are rooted in what has worked well in years gone by. But change is the only constant in the global market environment. Management perspectives both at the headquarters and the local level may well lag behind some of the fundamental but insidious shifts taking place in the marketplace. For all these reasons, it is not enough to make strategies that take advantage of the broad changes in the business environment. In the absence of an appreciation in the larger organizations for the global dimensions of the proposed strategies, these plans would never lead to management commitment and actions—the exact ingredients the strategies need for implementation. Global marketing is famous for having more than its fair share of "good and well-intended" strategies that have flopped.

Consider the following story of Parker Pen, a company that tried to "go global" a few years ago. Under a new management team, the world's best-known pen company embarked on a major strategy overhaul whereby key marketing decisions were taken away from the company's 154 local operations and were centralized at the head office in Jamesville, Wisconsin.[8] The architects of Parker's global strategy, referred to by some as "the best and brightest minds in international marketing," pruned the product line everywhere, centralized the manufacturing, and standardized many marketing decisions, including packaging, pricing, promotions, and advertising. Country managers who had traditionally controlled all advertising decisions locally were expected under the new regime to follow tight standards on positioning, slogan, layout, graphics, logo, and typeface. They also had to work with only one centrally appointed agency worldwide.

Local managers who had traditionally enjoyed autonomy in running their own affairs did not like the new direction. They objected to the revamped and standardized product line and top management's assumption that, similar to Marlboro cigarettes (their model of streamlined global marketing), Parker pens were purchased the same way around the world. Perhaps most important, the local managers objected to being left out of the global marketing decision making. So they fought back!

Only two years into the job, the company's CEO and his top management team were forced to resign. The local management's unhappiness with the global scheme, combined with losses from operations, finally led to the downfall of these global marketers. A new top management team subsequently reversed many of the global decisions, thereby returning to country management their lost autonomy. Reflecting on the demise of their worldwide scheme, the deposed executives placed the blame primarily on their failure to elicit the support of the rest of the organization. "We tried to take massive leaps [but] people weren't brought into it," said one former manager. Another commented, "We should have talked more with those people in the field. We should have gotten their support."[9]

FROM GLOBAL VISION TO LOCAL ACTION

Parker Pen's fiasco demonstrates the complexity of global marketing: Marketers must not only reckon with the external market forces but also with the internal organizational realities. The problem is not helped by the fact that the strategists rarely have direct authority over all those managers, often in local organizations scattered around the world, on whose day-to-day decisions the success of the strategies depends.

It is the paradox of global marketing that a global vision needs to be translated into local action if it is to materialize. In this respect, it is useful to distinguish among management vision, strategy, and action.

Vision—that is, defining the management's planning horizon—must be broad enough to encompass a market's global dimensions. A narrow local or even regional vision risks being too parochial to take account of the worldwide forces and opportunities that cross borders. This global perspective, however, is rarely present in local subsidiaries; it is sometimes absent even in the regional or worldwide headquarters where it belongs. Yet it is an indispensable starting point for global marketing.

Strategy—that is, defining the parameters of marketing action—is global only to the extent that it is the output of a global vision. It is the management's game plan to survive and prosper in its global market. But global marketing does not necessarily lead to standardized decisions for all individual markets. As mentioned earlier, a centrally formulated global strategy may leave many decisions to local discretion because, due to inherent diversity in these markets or otherwise, those decisions are best made close to local markets. A balanced strategy only capitalizes on the commonalties to build competitive advantage; it does not monopolize decision making.

The *actions* that managers take throughout the larger organization are what ultimately decide the fate of a strategy. In other words, it is the combined activities undertaken in individual markets by local managers that can help or hinder reaching the strategic objectives. If vision and strategy making are centrally driven and global in their scope, actions are by their nature primarily local. As stated earlier, a constant challenge of global marketing lies in bringing dispersed local actions in line with the reality of a global vision and the aims of a global strategy.

The translation of a global vision into effective strategies and actions does not take place automatically: It needs to be managed at all levels. To illustrate this point with an example, consider the case of International Products Corporation (IPC), a disguised name for the personal care division of a major U.S.-based corporation. Faced with market maturity and increasing competition in its markets worldwide, the top management aimed to improve the division's ability to compete through a program of global rationalization. IPC's executive vice president spearheaded a so-called "5% Program," designed to improve the overall profit margin through adoption of a number of measures: eliminating duplication of activities in each of the company's four regions around the world, centralizing manufacturing for a number of countries whenever possible, and reducing unnecessary product diversity among different countries. This new vision in managing the corporation went counter to the history of IPC, which was characterized by strong local management operating with almost total autonomy.

As expected, the global program ran into immediate opposition from the country organizations. "The idea is a good one, but not for my market," was a typical local reaction. As a result, the process of implementation was initially slow and difficult. But, in time, the global program became a success as the vision was finally translated into regional strategies and specific country action plans—actions that fulfilled the broad objectives of the vision. For example, in Europe, country-by-country marketing plans were abandoned in favor of regionwide planning with the aim of harmonizing marketing practices across the continent. To this end, Europe's regional director appointed the area director for the northern countries to head a fact-finding task force with the mission of identifying for all of Europe where production could be centralized and what products or brands offered the most opportunity for standardization.

The task force, made up of functional managers from the regional headquarters and some country organizations, soon realized that their mission would not be accomplished if country heads were left out of the deliberations. Country managers had traditionally held the veto power at IPC. By forming a "Strategic Committee" of the country general managers, and by presenting the results of their study to the committee, members of the task force achieved what was most essential: a local "buy-in" for central manufacturing, product rationalization, and pan-European marketing standardization.

The hard work of deciding which brands to keep, or which of several package designs and product formulations should become the standard for central manufacturing in "Europlants," still remained. Those issues were given to a team of product group managers drawn from country organizations for resolution. By the time the team was assigned to the job, the rest of the organization, namely the regional and country general management, had come to accept the global perspective. The specific actions taken by the product group managers, who had to consider not only their own countries but also the impact of their decisions on the other markets, added substance to the vision. These decisions transformed into concrete reality a vision that had been formulated a few years earlier, then a long physical and organizational distance away. The payoffs in Europe were great and long lasting: a streamlined product line, longer production runs of standardized products, up to 15% reduction in cost of goods sold, and a more cohesive organization better able to think globally while still acting locally. Exhibit 1.5 highlights the transformation of IPC's global vision into local action plans and traces the sequence of management decisions in the European region.

MANAGING GLOBAL MARKETING

This book addresses the strategic as well as the managerial issues in global marketing. Experienced global marketers know only too well how intertwined both sets of issues are in reality. To separate them here would be to mislead the student of global marketing. However, for the purposes of sequencing the topics, and in the interest of in-depth discussion, the book is structured into three parts. Part One is an introduction to global markets and marketing. It provides an overview of globalization and offers insights into strategy making in such a context. The cases in Part One deal with issues from the often divergent perspectives of headquarters and local management. They provide a useful map of the territory and a flavor of the managerial challenges involved.

Part Two is devoted to a discussion of global marketing strategy. The introductory chapter provides an overview of key decisions and elements of analysis in formulating global strategy. The process of decision making in a corporate context and the respective contributions of the head office and local management to strategy making are also explored. Guidelines are offered to help delineate center-dominated and subsidiary management decisions—typically an area of much corporate tension. Part Two cases are organized around decision-oriented topics and focus on the elements of marketing strategy from local, regional, and global angles. Together, the chapter and the cases provide a comprehensive treatment of strategy-related topics in global marketing.

Part Three examines the managerial challenges facing global marketers. The introductory chapter and the cases deal with issues of implementing a global scheme through the labyrinth of a worldwide organization. The pitfalls and pathways of transforming a global vision into local action are highlighted. Together with the strategic topics covered earlier, this section prepares the student for the challenges that global marketers routinely encounter.

CASES IN PART ONE

The two introductory cases in Part One provide a useful overview of global marketing before the topic is dealt with in more detail and depth later on. The cases highlight the strategic and organizational dynamics of decision making in global markets. The first case, Libby's Beverages, is about an experienced international, if not global, marketer of food products. The case demonstrates a typical decision situation where the headquarters and local management are in disagreement. This rather "routine" scenario centers on the opportunities and the obstacles of implementing in the United States a strategy that seems to have worked well in Europe. The second case, Nokia Data, is about a relatively small newcomer to the international computer market. The management is planning to overcome the company's size and late-entry disadvantage by adopting a multidomestic approach that is contrary to the regional and global strategies adopted by its larger and more established competitors.

The student can expect the following learning points from analyzing the cases in Part One:

- Understanding of the fundamental differences between global and multidomestic strategies.
- Practice in comparative country market analysis.
- Exposure to and general familiarity with the strategic and organizational dimensions of global marketing.

EXHIBIT 1.5 IPC: From Global Vision to Local Action

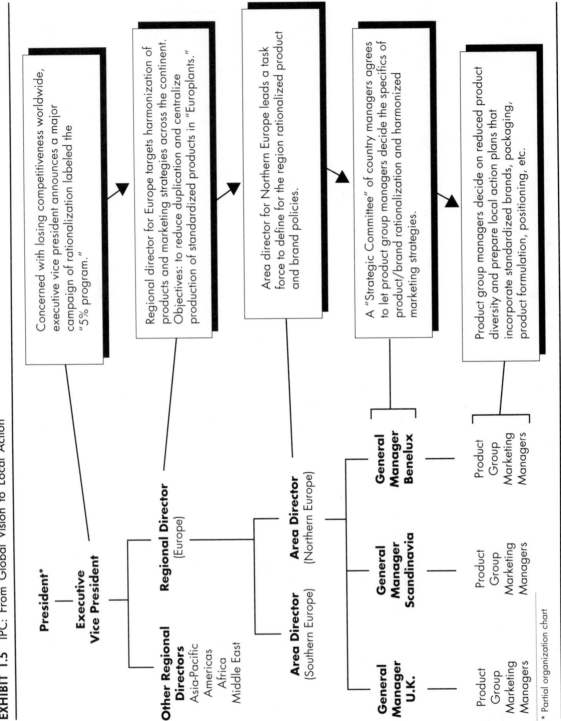

Concerned with losing competitiveness worldwide, executive vice president announces a major campaign of rationalization labeled the "5% program."

Regional director for Europe targets harmonization of products and marketing strategies across the continent. Objectives: to reduce duplication and centralize production of standardized products in "Europlants."

Area director for Northern Europe leads a task force to define for the region rationalized product and brand policies.

A "Strategic Committee" of country managers agrees to let product group managers decide the specifics of product/brand rationalization and harmonized marketing strategies.

Product group managers decide on reduced product diversity and prepare local action plans that incorporate standardized brands, packaging, product formulation, positioning, etc.

President*

Executive Vice President

Regional Director (Europe)

Other Regional Directors
Asia-Pacific
Americas
Africa
Middle East

Area Director (Southern Europe)

Area Director (Northern Europe)

General Manager U.K.

General Manager Scandinavia

General Manager Benelux

Product Group Marketing Managers

Product Group Marketing Managers

Product Group Marketing Managers

* Partial organization chart

- Appreciation for the often divergent global and local perspectives on marketing issues.
- Insight into the challenges that are specific to newcomers to global markets and marketing.

Endnotes

1. See Theodore Levitt, "Globalization of Markets," *Harvard Business Review* (May-June 1983): 92–102.

2. As of 1990, membership in the EC consists of Belgium, Denmark, France, Germany, Greece, Italy, Ireland, Luxembourg, Netherlands, Portugal, Spain, and the United Kingdom.

3. Estimates are based on *Country Profiles* (London: Economist Intelligence Unit, 1989). They exclude changes brought about by German reunification.

4. EFTA, founded in 1959, is a free trade agreement that has led to a gradual reduction of tariffs on nonagricultural products among its member states, which include Austria, Finland, Iceland, Liechtenstein, Norway, Sweden, and Switzerland. Denmark, Portugal, and the United Kingdom also belonged to EFTA but lost their membership when they joined the EC.

5. *Source: Canada-United States Free Trade Agreement—Securing Canada's Future* (Ottawa: Department of External Affairs, 1987).

6. For an elaborate definition of "multidomestic" strategies, see Michael E. Porter, *Competition in Global Industries* (Boston: Harvard Business School Press, 1986), pp. 18–19.

7. A full account can be read in "P&G Europe," a 1983 Harvard Business School case study by Christopher A. Bartlett (case no. 9-384-139).

8. Parker Pen's encounter with the hazards of global marketing can be found in J. M. Winski and L. Wentz, "Parker Pen: What Went Wrong," *Advertising Age* (June 2, 1986): 1, 71.

9. Ibid.

Further Readings

Cateora, Philip R. *International Marketing,* 6th ed. Homewood, Ill.: Irwin, 1987, chap. 1.

Hamel, Gary, and C. K. Prahalad. "Do You Really Have a Global Strategy?" *Harvard Business Review* (July-August 1985): 139–148.

Henzler, Herbert, and Wilhelm Rall. "Facing Up to the Globalization Challenge." *The McKinsey Quarterly* (Winter 1986): 52–68.

"The Honda Way: Battling for Global Markets." *Time,* September 8, 1986, pp. 26–28, 33–36.

Hout, Thomas, Michael E. Porter, and Eileen Rudden. "How Global Companies Win Out." *Harvard Business Review* (September-October 1982): 98–108.

Jain, Subhash C. *International Marketing Management,* 3d ed. Boston: PWS-KENT, 1990, chaps. 1–2.

Keegan, Warren J. *Global Marketing Management,* 4th ed. Englewood Cliffs, N.J.: Prentice-Hall, 1989, chap. 1.

Levitt, Theodore. "Globalization of Markets." *Harvard Business Review* (May-June 1983): 92–102.

"Multinationals vs. Global." *The Economist,* May 5, 1984, p. 67.

Ohmae, Kenichi. "Becoming a Triad Power: The New Global Corporation." *International Marketing Review* (Autumn 1986): 7–20.

Porter, Michael E. "Competition in Global Industries: A Conceptual Framework." In *Competition in Global Industries.* Boston: Harvard Business School Press, 1986, pp. 15–60.

Shanks, David C. "Strategic Planning for Global Competition." *Journal of Business Strategy* (Winter 1985): 80–89.

Terpstra, Vern. *International Dimensions of Marketing.* Boston: Kent, 1982, chaps. 1–3.

"When to Adopt a Global Strategy." *Strategic Direction* (January 1987): 18–20.

1 LIBBY'S BEVERAGES

Um Bongo is a success story in the U.K., Portugal and Spain and we think the U.S. market should also be ready for it.

—A headquarters beverage executive at Nestlé, Vevey, Switzerland

Um Bongo has strange flavors, unfamiliar to the American child's taste buds, and a very unusual commercial with jungle drums and animals and lots of activity all over the place. . . . In tests it lost to Hawaiian Punch, a leading competitor, so the project died right there.

—A Libby's executive, Purchase, New York

In 1989, managers at Libby's American operation and its parent Nestlé were debating the future of Um Bongo in the United States. Um Bongo was a fruit-based drink with 25% juice content, specifically developed for children. It was originally introduced by Libby's U.K. company but later also marketed by the Spanish and Portuguese organizations. Nestlé executives considered the Um Bongo concept of combining "fun and health" a significant product and marketing innovation with broad international appeal. As proof, they pointed to the success of the brand in three different European markets. Libby's U.S. managers were less convinced of Um Bongo's general appeal. Initial consumer tests had pointed to potential problems with its taste and TV commercials used in Europe. Besides, the U.S. managers claimed they were busy with another children's brand, Juicy Juice, a 100% fruit juice product. Juicy Juice had been relaunched two years ago with great success. U.S. management now intended to consolidate Juicy Juice's gains for further growth and improved profitability. The addition of Um Bongo to the product line, these managers argued, would only detract from the tasks ahead.

All names have been disguised.
This case was developed by Professor Kamran Kashani, with assistance from Research Associate Robert C. Howard. Copyright © 1989 by the International Institute for Management Development (IMD), Lausanne, Switzerland. Not to be used or reproduced without the author's permission.

COMPANY BACKGROUND

Libby's was a division of Nestlé, the world's largest food company. With more than $24 billion in sales and 428 factories in five continents, Nestlé and its wholly owned divisions marketed a large variety of products, including evaporated milk and infant foods, chocolate, coffee, beverages, culinary products (such as sauces, mixes, soups, etc.), and refrigerated and frozen products. Nestle's flagship products, such as its 50-year old Nescafé, were sold in more than 100 countries.

Since the early 1970s, Nestlé had pursued an active acquisition policy in the international food business. In 1970, Nestlé acquired Libby's, one of the largest fruit and vegetable processors in the United States. Other major acquisitions that followed were Stouffer (U.S., 1973), Chambourcy (France, 1978), Carnation (U.S., 1985), Buitoni-Perugina (Italy, 1989), and Rowntree (U.K., 1989). In most cases the acquired companies, including Libby's activities around the world, were integrated into Nestlé's local operations.

In 1989, less than 3% of the company's total turnover came from nonfood activities, including cosmetics and pharmaceuticals. (See Exhibit 1 for a breakdown of sales by product category and geographic region.)

Each Nestlé country operation was run by a country manager who had full responsibility for profitability and for overseeing all functions, including marketing, manufacturing, and finance. Many country managers were local nationals who had risen through the marketing function.[1]

Nestlé's corporate structure was organized along five geographic zones and nine product groups. The zones were Europe; Asia, Australia, and New Zealand; South and Central America; United States and Canada; and Africa and the Middle East. The product groups consisted of beverages, including coffee, mineral water, fruit juices, and drinks; cereals, milks, and dietetic products; culinary products; frozen foods and ice cream; chocolate and confectionaries; refrigerated products; pet foods; pharmaceuticals and cosmetics; and food services.

Zone managers who were located in the company's headquarters in Vevey, Switzerland, worked with individual country managers for setting overall sales and profit targets and monitoring performance. Product directors, along with teams of product managers who reported to them, were also in Vevey. They interfaced with their respective country product managers, who reported to their local executives, to implement global or regional product strategies, to search for new products, and to maximize cross-fertilization of marketing practices internationally. In the beverages group, for example, four product managers looked after Nestlé's worldwide activities in roast and ground coffee, instant coffee, chocolate and malt drinks, and tea and liquid beverages, including fruit juices and drinks. In Nestlé's matrix of staff product groups and line geographic zones, zone management wielded considerably more influence on local matters. (See Exhibit 2 for a partial organization chart.)

Nestlé had traditionally been run as a decentralized organization, giving much autonomy to country management. Country heads, evaluated on overall results,

1. Certain information on Nestlé's organization are based on Harvard Business School case study Nestlé S.A.

were thought of as "pillars of the organization" and allowed freedom to run their "one-man shows." Marketing, more than other functions, was considered to be a local activity aimed at capitalizing on the particularities of each market.

Recently, more attention was being paid to global branding and looking for marketing opportunities that cut across traditional market boundaries. Helmut Maucher, Nestlé's CEO, was explicit on this point:

> [Our] aim is to identify market groups and build global brands. These can be sold to the same groups of people all over the world—single households, the health conscious, old people, oriental food lovers, instant coffee drinkers. The idea is to target these segments clearly for maximum sales, and hence become the lowest-cost producer.[2]

Nevertheless, Nestlé believed there were limits to how far a food company could go global and satisfy consumers in five continents. The company aimed to stay close to local markets.

WORLD FRUIT AND JUICE MARKET

In 1988, the world's total consumption of fruit juices and juice-based drinks[3] amounted to an estimated 27 billion liters, representing a value of $23 billion at manufacturer prices. Included in these figures were all forms of industrially processed juices and drinks, including nectars, ready-to-drink preparations, concentrates, and frozen juices and drinks. Orange juice and orange-based drinks were the best-selling flavors, accounting for nearly one-half of all consumption. Apple was the second most popular flavor with 15%, followed by grapefruit, pineapple, and grape. The fruit juice and drinks consumption had grown by about 8% per year since the early 1980s.

Unlike the world market for soft drinks, the world market for fruit juices and drinks was fragmented. No competitor appeared dominant internationally, although Coca-Cola held the leading position with an estimated worldwide share of 15%. Coca-Cola's brands were Hi-C, Minute Maid, Five Alive, and Sprite (a carbonated soft drink with 10% of fruit juice content). Other major competitors were Pepsi-Cola (Slice), Procter & Gamble (Citrus Hill), Seagram's (Tropicana), U.K.-based Cadbury Schweppes (Sunkist), and Melitta (Granini) headquartered in Germany.

Three countries accounted for more than 60% of the world's volume of juices and drinks: United States, 41%; Japan, 13%; and Germany, 9%. Consumption volumes and patterns differed internationally. For example, one study showed that although per capita consumption in the United States surpassed 70 liters annually, the volume in the other Anglo-Saxon countries was in the 20–25 liters range, and in the Latin countries it was below 10 liters. The same study highlighted other differences in how juices and drinks were consumed:

2. *Management Europe,* January 16, 1989.

3. "Drinks" was a term used to refer to fruit-based beverages whose juice content was less than 100%. Most drinks contained between 10% and 50% fruit juices, with the rest consisting of water, sugar, color, and flavoring.

	Occasions of consumption	
	Anglo Saxon	Latin
Breakfast	35%	10%
Lunch/dinner	25	10
During the day	40	80
At home	70%	55%
Out of home	30	45

Source: Company records.

In spite of national and cultural differences, Nestlé's management identified a number of trends that were influencing the juice and drinks industry worldwide:

■ *Health.* Among the industrialized countries, consumers were paying unprecedented attention to their own and their family's health and diet. Fruit juices and drinks were benefiting from this trend as "healthy" alternatives to modern soft drinks or traditional coffee and tea.

■ *Quality.* In major markets internationally, a growing segment of consumers was turning to premium quality fruit juices. This factor explained the growth of premium-priced, ready-to-drink brands marketed under "like freshly squeezed" taste platforms.

■ *Value.* In large markets, an increasing percentage of fruit juices and drinks were accounted for by the low-priced "value for money" segment. The rise in the number and volume of private brands marketed by large food chains in Europe and North America had helped this trend.

■ *Advertising.* Media advertising for fruit juices and drinks was on the rise. In some markets it had already surpassed relative expenditure levels of soft drinks, historically a media-intensive category. In 1987, for example, the U.S. media expenditure for fruit juices approached $200 per 10,000 liters versus $100 for soft drinks.

U.S. FRUIT JUICE AND DRINKS MARKET

Overview

In 1988, the U.S. market for fruit juices and drinks was approximately $9.4 billion at manufacturer prices. This volume represented only a small portion of a much larger beverage market estimated at more than $112 billion in that year. (See Exhibit 3.)

Libby's management divided the juice and drinks products into frozen, shelf-stable, and refrigerated segments. The ready-to-drink, shelf-stable products were by far the largest segment, accounting for close to one-half the market. The refrigerated products, typically citrus flavors, accounted for 26% of the market in 1988. These products had increased their market share by nearly 10 points over the last five years at the expense of the frozen segment.

The juice and drinks market was also segmented by flavor. In the shelf-stable category, blended juices and drinks were leading with about two-thirds share of the dollar volume, followed by apple (17%), grapefruit (5.2%), grape (5.6%), and orange (3.3%). Orange juice was the dominant flavor in both frozen and refrigerated segments, with 61% and 72%, respectively.

A variety of packaging was used for fruit juices and drinks. Glass was by far the most dominant form among shelf-stable products, accounting for 47%, followed by cans (31%), aseptic brik packs (16%), and plastic containers (6%). In recent years, both glass and brik packs had grown in relative terms, while cans had declined. In the refrigerated and frozen segments, paper and plastic cartons were the most common forms of packaging.

The overall fruit juice and drinks market had grown by nearly one-third since 1982 and was projected to reach $11 billion by 1990. The annual growth rates had doubled since the mid-1970s, reaching 7% by 1988. Since 1982, dollar sales in the refrigerated segment had grown 104%, and frozen product sales had actually declined 6%. With 36% growth in this period, the shelf-stable segment had slightly outgrown the industry average. Among the flavors, orange and blended flavors were the fastest growing varieties in the refrigerated and shelf-stable segments, respectively.

Industry analysts attributed the continued U.S. market growth to health and fitness concerns of consumers, the growing popularity of new aseptic packaging, and the impact of new products such as blended fruit juices. These factors combined had contributed to a rise in per capita juice and drinks consumption from 11.5 gallons (52 liters) in the mid-1970s to 15.7 gallons (71 liters) in the mid-1980s.[4]

Competition

Three firms dominated the U.S. fruit juice and drinks market: Coca-Cola Foods, Seagrams, and Ocean Spray. Coca-Cola Foods was the largest juice and drinks marketer, with total 1988 sales of $1.3 billion and a market share of 14%. The company's Minute Maid brand, an orange juice in shelf-stable and frozen forms, accounted for slightly more than $1 billion of sales. Another major brand was Hi-C, a shelf-stable fruit drink, with sales of $203 million. Seagrams was the second largest producer in the industry. The firm's 10% market share was almost entirely from its highly successful and fast-growing Tropicana brand of refrigerated and shelf-stable orange juice. Ocean Spray, the industry's third largest producer, had sales of $700 million and a market share of 9%. The company's wide variety of cranberry-based and other fruit drinks made it the largest player in the shelf-stable segment.

Besides the three largest, more than 10 other producers, including divisions of such large firms as Procter & Gamble (P&G), Campbell Soup, RJR/Nabisco, and Nestlé competed in the industry. Private labels represented a growing segment of the U.S. juice and drinks market, accounting for an estimated 16% in 1988. (Exhibit 4 provides data on competitors and products in the shelf-stable segment, including Libby's brand, Juicy Juice.)

4. U.S. population: 247 million.

According to Libby's management, a number of juice and drinks companies had recently entered the 100% blended fruit juice segment, where Juicy Juice was the leading brand. The newcomers had been attracted by the segment's growth, which was estimated to be the highest in the industry. Starting with a modest size of $10 million in the mid-1970s, the blended juice market had reached $145 million in 1988. Among the new entrants were Coca-Cola Food's Hi-C 100, Seagram's Tropicana Twisters, Motts, and Dole. However, in the opinion of Libby's management, despite "strong introductions and megabuck expeditures," none of the "Big Boys" had seriously damaged Juicy Juice's leadership in the segment. Nevertheless, the management believed that directly or indirectly all fruit-based beverages competed with one another, and Juicy Juice's competition came not only from the 100% blended juice products but also the single-flavor juices as well as the lower-priced fruit drinks. (See Exhibit 5 for major brands' sales and market shares.)

JUICY JUICE BY LIBBY'S: "100% REAL FRUIT JUICES"

We turned a "corporate dog" into a success story, and we did it by following the good old recipe of effective product management.

—A Nestlé fruit juice and drinks executive in Vevey, Switzerland

We went to market at a time when the juice content of products was becoming more top of mind for parents. . . . A lot of people thought Hi-C and Hawaiian Punch were good products; they felt they were giving their kids something that was healthy. Well, we came along and said no. That's 10% juice and we are 100%. And a lot of people were not aware of that fact.

—A Libby's executive in Purchase, New York

History of Juicy Juice

The above comments refer to the turnaround of Juicy Juice, a brand acquired by Libby's in 1984 from Fruitcrest, a regional producer. The brand had been launched by Fruitcrest in 1978 and was distributed in the eastern part of the United States. With five different blended flavors[5] targeted at children, from "Real Red" to "Yummy Yellow" to "Golden Good," the Juicy Juice brand enjoyed a sales level of $34 million in 1984. Each product was made up of a blend of 100% fruit juices, including apple, grape, and cherry, to give it a distinctive taste and color. Libby's management believed the brand was not profitable for Fruitcrest.

Libby's own products in 1984 included Libby's Nectars, a range of drinks with 50% juice content, and Hearts Delight, a private-label drink with less than 50% juice. Both were targeted at adults and families. In the opinion of many Nestlé executives, prior to the launch of Juicy Juice, Libby's beverage range was "imbalanced" toward the price-oriented segment of the market. "Libby's was trying to fight the big brands like Del Monte or Minute Maid in the volume business," explained one

---

5. A blended flavor was made of a mixture of concentrates from different fruits. In manufacturing, only water and natural fruit flavor were added to restore the juices to their original strength.

such executive in Vevey, "but with their small share, they had no chance." In the early 1980s, the company's annual losses amounted to nearly 10% of sales.[6]

In 1985, Libby's launched Juicy Juice nationally, with a "100% juice" taste platform targeting children, and spending $2.5 million on media (70%) and promotions (30%). A year later, due to what management diagnosed as "inferior" taste and a "weak marketing program," the line was withdrawn from national distribution. Juicy Juice continued to be marketed in its core market, eastern United States, representing 48% of the United States. By the end of 1986, the brand's sales were $13 million, or 60% below the 1985 level.

In 1986, Juicy Juice was given to Robert Mead, the newly appointed group vice president for beverages, and his management team to turn around. (See Exhibit 6 for Libby's partial organization chart in the United States.) The appointment came when, in Mead's words, "the whole damn Libby's beverage business was going to hell." In his opinion, the product had failed because of poor taste, its "1950s image" labels, and a positioning that did not differentiate it from competition. Although constrained by limited funds, Mead's team was expected to put new life into Juicy Juice and relaunch it, initially in its core markets and later, nationally.

Juicy Juice was relaunched in 1987 following a number of changes. First, with help from Nestlé's research facilities in the United States and outside, the formulation and taste of the product were improved dramatically. Consumer research showed Juicy Juice had a taste superior to the major blended juice brands Tree Top and Hi-C 100. Next, the labels were changed to show real fruits and to substitute fruit names (e.g., "Cherry") for what had been color names (e.g., "Real Red"). The new labels clearly identified Libby's as the parent behind Juicy Juice. Also, while flavors were expanded from four to six (cherry, grape, punch, tropical, berry, and apple), the pack sizes were reduced from four to two (a 1.4-liter can and a new .250 liter brik pack).[7] (See Exhibit 7 for sample labels.)

According to Libby's management, the most important change from the past was repositioning Juicy Juice from good taste and "100% juice" to "We are 100% juice and they're not." Explained Dennis Scott, the general manager for beverages:

> There is a lot of confusion out there. Some say they are "100% natural," or "a blend of ten different juices." Yet they all contain 50% or less of real fruit juice. So when we come along and say "we are 100% and they are not," that stays in the consumer's mind. Juicy Juice became a point of reference for the consumer against which to compare all others.

Exhibit 8 shows a positioning map used by management for locating the repositioned Juicy Juice and its competitors.

The Juicy Juice brand carried a significant price premium over other drinks, leading to relatively higher trade margins. Juicy Juice's $1.59 retail price for its 1.4-liter can, for example, compared with a $.79 to $.99 price range for similar sizes of Hi-C and Hawaiian Punch. The premium prices were thought by management to

---

6. By 1984, Nestlé had sold off Libby's other operations and kept only the beverages.
7. A glass option for packaging was dropped initially because of its higher costs.

reinforce the superior quality positioning: "When you bring something that's unique or with high value added, you ought to be able to get a price for it," argued Mead.

In 1987, the company spent $3 million on media to relaunch the product in its core market but stayed away from excessive price-oriented promotions common in the industry. (Exhibit 9 shows a 15-second TV commercial storyboard for Juicy Juice.)

Juicy Juice's positioning was thought to have contributed to its strength against recent competitive entries such as Coca-Cola's Hi-C 100, a 100% blended juice brand extension from Hi-C. "They came at us with all kinds of ad dollars," recalled Mead. "But when they raised their prices for the juice, the consumers refused to pay. They said 'you are a drink, a price brand and I won't buy what you are selling.' "

Results to Date

The results of the relaunch were dramatic. "With this improved product, improved label, improved positioning, and improved everything else," Mead recalled, "we went to war." By the end of 1987, a full year later, Juicy Juice sales in its core market had increased by 82% to $23 million. In 1988, when the product was reintroduced to new markets representing an additional 21% of the United States, sales increased by another 32% to $31 million. (Between 1986 and 1988, the total shelf-stable blended segment had grown by 20% to $145 million.) Currently, Juicy Juice was being sold in cans (73% of dollar shipment) in addition to brik packs (24%) and the newly introduced glass (3%). It was distributed through more than 28 thousand grocery stores in 42 states representing 80% of the national market. Libby's management projected sales of nearly $50 million from a nationwide coverage in 1989. (See Exhibit 10 for a consumer profile drawn by management for the relaunched Juicy Juice. Exhibit 11 shows highlights of the brand's 1989 marketing plan.)

UM BONGO BY LIBBY'S: THE "JUNGLE JUICE"

The success of Um Bongo is due to its concept: a product developed specifically for kids. It's not a me-too this or a me-too that which anybody can imitate. It's UM BONGO from nose to tail!
—A Nestlé beverage executive in Vevey, Switzerland

Um Bongo was one of the few juice drinks targeted at children with a fun overtone; its advertising was very instrumental in getting the product off to a good start.
—A Libby's marketing manager in Croyden, United Kingdom

History of Um Bongo

Um Bongo was introduced in 1984 by Libby's U.K. beverages division. It was the company's newest entry in a growing but also highly competitive local market for fruit juices and drinks, where price-oriented private brands held more than 50% share. Libby's other products included a line of fruit and vegetable juices and drinks targeted primarily at adults. The company was also producing under private labels. In the early 1980s the U.K. company was losing annually approximately 2% on a stagnating turnover of about $15 million. (See Exhibit 12 for data on the U.K. market and shares.)

Before Um Bongo's introduction, company-sponsored research had shown that while per capita consumption of traditional beverages such as tea (290 liters), milk (110 liters), and beer (100 liters) had declined over the years, those of soft drinks (100 liters) and fruit juices and drinks (14 liters) had risen constantly. Research also showed that 45% of all soft drinks were consumed by children aged 15 years or younger, a segment accounting for only 20% of the population.[8] Furthermore, focus group discussions revealed that fruit juices and drinks, though considered by children as "good for you," suffered from an old and traditional image when compared with the younger and more contemporary soft drinks. Mothers indicated they wanted a healthier alternative to soft drinks, which they thought to be artificial and "not good for you." "All those facts led to the conclusion that there was a marketing opportunity for a product especially developed for children," recalled Paul Lawrence, the U.K. marketing manager for Libby's beverages. "Thus was born Um Bongo."

Um Bongo was a blended drink with 25% juice content. It was launched under Libby's umbrella with one flavor, a mixture of nine juices, and in two brik pack sizes (1 liter and 2 liter). Its extraordinary "jungle name" and its "jungle juice" positioning were decidedly unique to stand out and offer a "balance of fun and health." Almost every aspect of the product, including its tropical flavor, color, packaging, and cartoon advertising, had been designed for and tested with children and their mothers. The "jungle juice" concept had been developed by Libby's advertising agency to project the "fun overtone" that management considered important. (See Exhibits 13 and 14, respectively, for samples of packaging and a TV commercial storyboard. Exhibit 15 shows U.K. consumer research data on Um Bongo.)

Um Bongo carried a premium price, which was 32% over private brand drinks but 10% below equivalent volumes of 100% fruit juices. The launch was supported in its first year by $1.5 million in advertising and $1 million in consumer and trade promotions. The company subsequently introduced new flavors (Apple Um Bongo and Orange Um Bongo), thus capitalizing on the largest flavor segments in the juice and drinks category. The company also added a new package incorporating three single-serve briks. In 1988, $230,000 was spent on advertising and $152,000 on promotions.

Results to Date

Um Bongo's factory sales in its first year of introduction reached $2.1 million. The brand had grown to $3.9 million by 1988, accounting for 20% of Libby's total sales in beverages. In 1989, sales were expected to grow by about 40%. Um Bongo's performance was a key factor behind the U.K. division's growth in total sales and significantly improved profitability since 1984.

8. U.K.'s population: 57 million.

Um Bongo's success had led to the entry of what management considered imitative drinks brands, such as Kia Ora from Cadbury Schweppes in 1986 and Fruit Troop from Del Monte, a division of RJR/Nabisco, in 1989. Both brands had targeted children and their mothers and, like Um Bongo, used cartoon characters on packaging and in TV commercials. In mid-1989, Libby's management carefully watched Del Monte's launch of Fruit Troop, which was being supported with heavy advertising.

Um Bongo's performance in the United Kingdom had not gone unnoticed by Libby's other European divisions. Since 1987, the Spanish and Portuguese companies had introduced Um Bongo in their markets. The brand concept, including its communication, had been kept intact, and only product taste and language on the label were adapted locally. The drinks were produced from imported concentrates. Both countries had used the U.K. TV commercials, dubbing in the local language.

In Spain, the per capita consumption of processed fruit juices and drinks (less than two liters) had traditionally been limited due to the availability of freshly prepared varieties at relatively low prices.[9] The market was also characterized by low marketing activities and poor quality products. (See Exhibit 16 for data on the Spanish market.)

Libby's produced a line of fruit juices and drinks targeted at families in Spain. Sales had declined by about 25% in volume since the early 1980s to $3.5 million in 1986, or less than 3 million liters. Nestlé executives attributed the decline to poor packaging, unfocused positioning, and the absence of advertising support.

Libby's beverage sales in Spain received a boost with the 1987 test introduction of Um Bongo in the Valencia region, which represented 25% of the national market. Supported by $100,000 in TV advertising, the brand's sales reached $110,000 in the test area, a level several times its target. In 1988, sales in the region had grown to $350,000 and 300,000 liters. The increased marketing activities related to Um Bongo had helped to pull the rest of Libby's business up to a total of $4.5 million and 4.2 million liters in 1988. The management projected an additional 90% growth for Um Bongo in 1989 after national introduction.

In Portugal, a smaller market than Spain but similar in features, Um Bongo had been introduced nationally in the Spring of 1988.[10] Nestlé's local management had recently concluded that significant growth opportunities existed in the beverages sector where Libby's had not been present. Previously, sales had been limited to only Nestle's dry grocery products such as coffee and cereals. (Exhibit 17 provides data on the Portuguese juice and drinks market.)

In the words of Patrick Martin, the Nestlé headquarters product manager for juices and drinks, Um Bongo's introduction in Portugal "blew up the market." With an advertising support of $1.2 million, Um Bongo's national sales for the year reached $4.7 million or 4.8 million liters. The first year sales were 240% of budget. By early 1989, with less than one year in the market, Um Bongo had reached what management believed was a significant market position and accounted for close to

9. Spain's population: 39 million.
10. Portugal's population: 10.5 million.

5% of total Nestlé sales in the country. The company expected a doubling of Um Bongo sales in 1989.

U.S. REACTIONS TO UM BONGO

Convinced that Um Bongo was a global concept with a universal appeal, executives at Vevey had prodded Libby's U.S. management to examine the opportunities for the brand's introduction in the American market. According to one headquarters executive, "We have a winner and it would be a pity if we couldn't transfer it to the world's largest market—the U.S."

Research Results

Recently, the U.S. management had commissioned a study to test the acceptance of Um Bongo by the American consumer. The research consisted of a taste test and interviews with 300 children between the ages of 8 and 18 in four states: Ohio, New York, Arizona, and Florida. Imported Um Bongo from the U.K. was tested against the leading drink, Hawaiian Punch. The research also aimed to evaluate the effectiveness of Um Bongo's "jungle" commercial used in the U.K., Spain, and Portugal.

The study's overall conclusion stated that "Um Bongo could be a viable entry in the U.S. fruit juice/drinks market given certain refinements." The refinements had to do primarily with making the flavor less "sour/tangy" and to changing the commercial to communicate the product concept more clearly. On most dimensions the product had rated equal to Hawaiian Punch except for purchase interest and taste, the latter's ratings in these areas being significantly higher. (See Case 1 Appendix for a summary of the study's findings and conclusions.)

Management Priorities

"It's hard for Um Bongo to make the jump to the U.S. marketplace because food habits are so culturally dependent," explained Dennis Scott in giving his reactions to the brand's performance during test marketing. He went on:

> To give you a fresh example on how cultural food is, we tested a one-liter (32-oz.) brik pack, which is so popular in Europe but doesn't exist here. We thought it made inherent sense to the American consumer. We put Juicy Juice into it, made big supermarket displays with special prices and the American consumer said "I don't know what that is. So I am not going to venture out." People are just resistant to change.

A change in Um Bongo's flavor had been considered by U.S. management, but according to Scott: "We just don't have the time or manpower to focus on it right now. We have our hands full."

At the time, Scott and his colleagues were preoccupied with Juicy Juice's performance on a national level. "Our aim is to make Juicy Juice a $100 million business in five years," explained Jean Graham, Juicy Juice's marketing director. Among short- and medium-term actions being planned were completion of the national rollout, introduction of new concentrated and refrigerated forms, expansion into nongrocery outlets, and addition of glass packaging. Improved household penetration was a prime medium-term objective. With 7.8% penetration, Juicy Juice was trailing Hi-C (16%) and Ocean Spray (34%).

Profitability remained another issue of immediate concern. "Our biggest challenge is to make this business profitable," explained Graham. "We have high costs in a low-margin industry. Our current gross margin is 35%—which is the number off the production line and before any distribution costs or marketing expenses. That's pitiful compared with other grocery categories such as 65% on tea or 85% on corn chip snack."

In 1989, management was looking at ways of reducing the raw material and packaging costs. A target date of 1990 was set for breaking even on Juicy Juice.

Other projects preoccupying Libby's management included a new children's beverage product made from a combination of milk and fruit juices. "We are looking at 'Moo Juice' or some such brand name for a milkshake-like product which means fun to kids and health to moms," explained Graham. The product was in an early phase of development.

Management believed that timing was another factor in favor of innovative new products such as milk-juice mix and against a drink like Um Bongo. "Um Bongo idea has severe competition today in the United States from companies like Coca-Cola, General Foods, Ocean Spray and RJR/Nabisco," argued Scott. "If we had introduced a product like it a few years ago, it might have had a chance. But Um Bongo would be entry number five at this point."

CONCLUSION

Vevey was aware of U.S. management's views on Um Bongo. "There is no secret about our different views on Um Bongo's potential in the United States," confirmed the worldwide juice and drinks product manager Patrick Martin. He added:

> While we are totally convinced that it's a good product concept, we also understand their hesitation to take on ideas from outside. It's natural. Even the management in Portugal were initially resistant to the Um Bongo idea, and look what happened there when they tried it. So our attitude is: "Give it a try and prove the idea wrong." Meanwhile, all we could do from here is to build confidence in the product by telling them what is going on elsewhere.

Martin and his colleagues in Vevey advocated test marketing of Um Bongo as the next step in the United States. "We would like to see a real market test and not just a consumer taste test," Martin explained. Estimated costs of undertaking such a test in the United States ranged from $500 thousand to $1 million per city, including advertising and promotional expenses. A minimum of two major cities, representing at least 2% of the U.S. consumption, was considered necessary for representative results.

On the U.S. side, meanwhile, attention was focused on the future of Juicy Juice. Mead described his views on the next steps:

> My challenge is to identify the three biggest ideas and make sure we execute those. Therefore I tell my people I don't want to hear about product extensions. You've got big, big opportunities still with Juicy Juice that need to be fulfilled. Once you've the important piece in place we can always add another. We can always circle back.

EXHIBIT 1   Nestle's 1988 Sales Breakdown
(Sales: 40 billion Swiss Francs)

Product category (%)		Geographic regions (%)	
Beverages	27	Europe	46
Dairy	15	North America	26
Chocolate/ confectionary	12	Asia	12
Culinary	12	Latin America	10
Frozen foods/ ice cream	10	Africa	3
Refrigerated products	9	Oceania	3
Infant foods	6		
Pet foods	5		
Pharmaceuticals/ cosmetics	2		
Others	2		
	100		100

Source: Company records.

EXHIBIT 2 Partial Corporate Nestlé Organization Chart

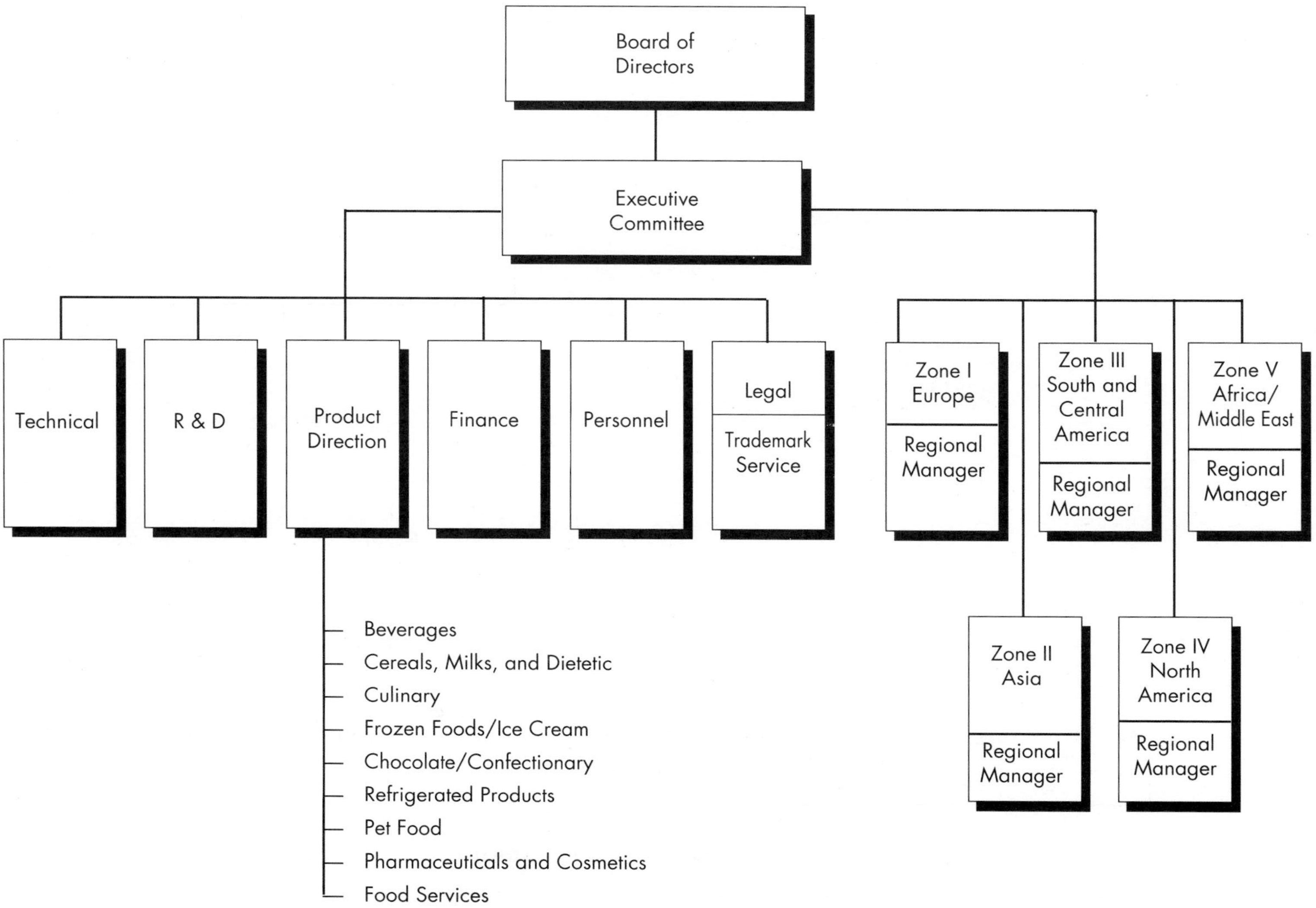

Board of Directors

Executive Committee

Technical

R & D

Product Direction
- Beverages
- Cereals, Milks, and Dietetic
- Culinary
- Frozen Foods/Ice Cream
- Chocolate/Confectionary
- Refrigerated Products
- Pet Food
- Pharmaceuticals and Cosmetics
- Food Services

Finance

Personnel

Legal | Trademark Service

Zone I Europe | Regional Manager

Zone II Asia | Regional Manager

Zone III South and Central America | Regional Manager

Zone IV North America | Regional Manager

Zone V Africa/Middle East | Regional Manager

EXHIBIT 3 Segmentation of the U.S. Beverage Market (1988)

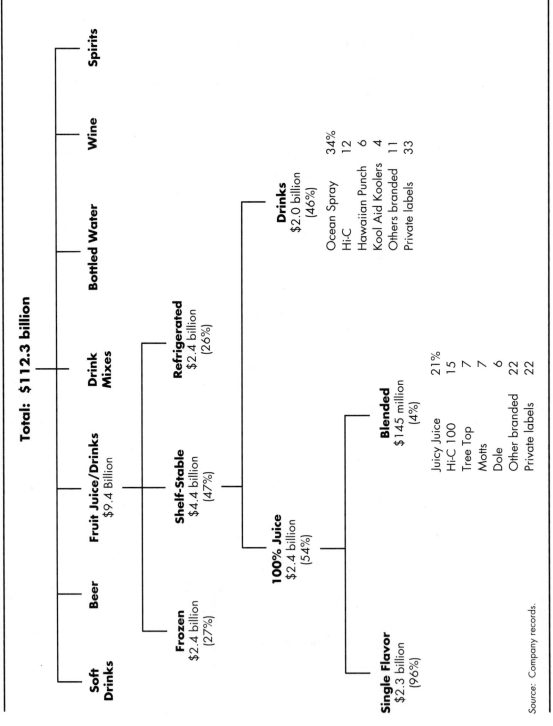

Total: $112.3 billion

Soft Drinks · **Beer** · **Fruit Juice/Drinks** $9.4 Billion · **Drink Mixes** · **Bottled Water** · **Wine** · **Spirits**

Frozen $2.4 billion (27%) · **Shelf-Stable** $4.4 billion (47%) · **Refrigerated** $2.4 billion (26%)

100% Juice $2.4 billion (54%) · **Drinks** $2.0 billion (46%)

Drinks	
Ocean Spray	34%
Hi-C	12
Hawaiian Punch	6
Kool Aid Koolers	4
Others branded	11
Private labels	33

Single Flavor $2.3 billion (96%) · **Blended** $145 million (4%)

Blended	
Juicy Juice	21%
Hi-C 100	15
Tree Top	7
Motts	7
Dole	6
Other branded	22
Private labels	22

Source: Company records.

EXHIBIT 4 U.S. Competitive Overview: Who Is Who in Shelf-Stable Juice

Manufacturer/ brand	1988 Sales* ($ millions)	Positioning	Product	Retail price	Packaging	1988 Ad spending* ($ millions)
Ocean Spray- All brands	695	Refreshment for adults (cranberry juice and grapefruit)	Line of cranberry juice cocktails (27% juice) incl. concentrates	$1.89–$2.29 (48 oz)	92% glass; 8% brik	21.9
cranberry line	562					
Mauna Lai	41	Exotic taste (Mauna Lai)	Grapefruit juice cocktail Mauna Lai drinks	$0.99–$1.29 (brik)		
grapefruit juice	51		Crantastic			
Splash	1		Testing Splash			
concentrate	40		(carbonated juice drink)			
Coke Foods	239					
Hi-C	203	Fun and good taste targeted to kids	10% fruit juice	$0.79–$0.99 (46 oz) $0.79–$0.99 (brik)	34% cans; 61% brik 4% glass	2.8
Hi-C 100	14	Family and kids	100% fruit juice	$1.19	100% brik	N/A part of $25mm umbrella campaign
Minute Maid	22	Wholesome juice for kids	Brik pak is only shelf-stable item. Offer 100% juice and drinks	$0.99–1.29 (brik)	brik	
RJR/Nabisco	195					
Hawaiian Punch	114	Great taste for kids	10% juice	$0.79–$0.99 (46 oz) $0.79–0.99 (brik)	60% cans 23% brik 14% glass 3% plastic	1.8
Del Monte fruit blends	81	Great tasting fruit drink for adults	50% juice	$1.79–$1.99 (48 oz)	glass brik	0.1

(continued)

EXHIBIT 4 (continued)

Manufacturer/ brand	1988 Sales* ($ millions)	Positioning	Product	Retail price	Packaging	1988 Ad spending* ($ millions)
General Foods Kool-Aid Koolers	73 / 57	The wacky, "cool" juice drink for kids	20% juice	$0.79–0.99 (brik)	100% brik	4.6
Tang	16	100% natural w/ great taste and variety targeted to kids	10% juice	$0.79–0.99 (brik)	100% brik	2.5
Nestlé Juicy Juice	73 / 38	100% juice and they're not	100% juice for kids	$1.59 (46 oz) $1.19 (brik)	76% can 21% brik 3% glass	2.5
Other Libby's	35					
Tree Top	177	100% pure fruit juices targeted to adults	100% juice blends based largely on apple juice; product inferior due to the absence of natural flavors	$1.79–$1.99 (48 oz) $1.39–$1.49 (cans) $0.99–1.29 (brik)	glass, brik, can	3.2
Seagrams Tropicana Twisters	13	Unusual taste	Line of 6 citrus-based juice drinks with 30–40% juice	$1.79–$1.99 (46 oz)	100% glass	7.9
Welch's Welch's Orchard All others	268 / 200 58 10	Heritage campaign (100 yrs)	50% juice	$1.79–$2.09 (40 oz glass) $0.99–$1.19 (brik)	glass, (brik)	2.7 umbrella campaign

Source: Company records.
*A. C. Nielsen, 1988

EXHIBIT 5 1988 Dollar Volume and Share Trends Total U.S. Juice/Drinks Category (in million dollars)

Manufacturer	Brand	1988 volume	Vs. last year (%)	Share	% National distribution
Coke Foods	Total company	$1,255	+ 6.7	16.5	
	Minute Maid	1,038	+ 7.3	13.7	100
	HI-C	203	+ 4.6	2.7	100
	HI-C 100	14	−10.8	0.1	89
Seagrams	Total company	$ 748	+24.2	9.8	
	Tropicana	735	+22.5	9.7	99
	Tropicana Twisters	13	+++	0.1	71
Ocean Spray	Total Ocean Spray	$ 696	+ 4.8	9.2	100
Procter & Gamble	Total Citrus Hill	$ 342	+36.1	4.5	98
Campbell Soup	Total company	$ 268	+20.4	3.5	
	Campbells	50	+ 3.3	0.7	100
	V-8	218	+25.3	2.8	100
Welch Foods	Total company	$ 268	+ 9.9	3.5	
	Welch's	200	+12.5	2.6	100
	Welch's Orchard	58	− 2.0	0.8	84
	All other	10	+45.3	0.1	
Quaker Oats	Gatorade	$ 221	+36.0	2.9	100
RJR/Nabisco	Total company	$ 195	+ 7.7	2.6	
	Hawaiian punch	114	+ 0.6	1.5	100
	Del Monte	81	+19.9	1.1	99
Tree Top	Total Tree Top	$ 177	+12.5	2.3	78
Nestlé	Total company	$ 73	+28.1	1.0	
	Juicy Juice	38	+51.3	0.6	45
	Libby Nectars	25	+ 7.5	0.3	63
	Hearts Delight	10	+17.5	0.1	34
General Foods	Total company	$ 73	+10.2	0.9	
	Kool-Aid Koolers	57	−12.6	0.8	99
	Tang	16	+++	0.1	89

Source: A. C. Nielsen, 1988.

EXHIBIT 6 Libby's U.S. Division's Reporting Structure

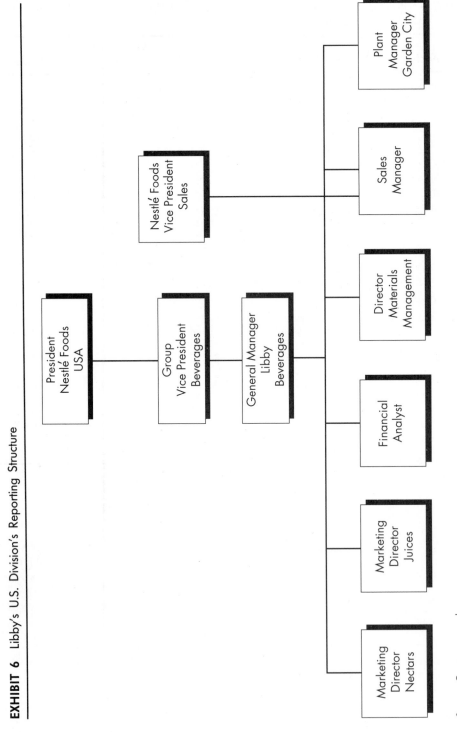

Source: Company records.

EXHIBIT 7 Juicy Juice: Sample Labels

EXHIBIT 8 Juicy Juice Positioning
               (based on 1987 creative)

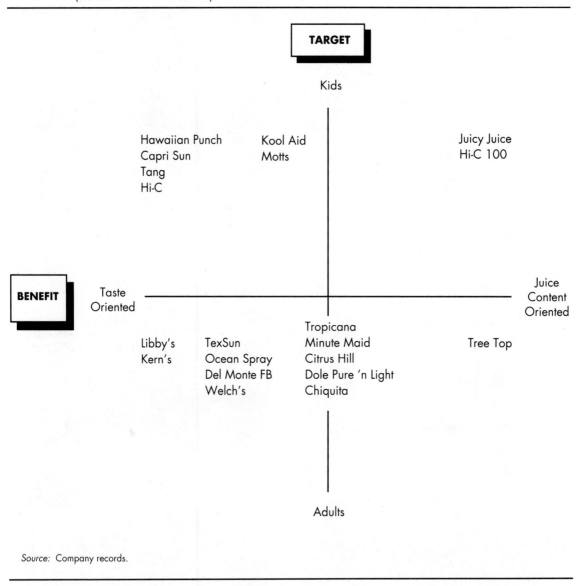

TARGET

Kids

Hawaiian Punch	Kool Aid		Juicy Juice
Capri Sun	Motts		Hi-C 100
Tang			
Hi-C			

BENEFIT

Taste   Juice
Oriented   Content
                                                         Oriented

		Tropicana	
Libby's	TexSun	Minute Maid	Tree Top
Kern's	Ocean Spray	Citrus Hill	
	Del Monte FB	Dole Pure 'n Light	
	Welch's	Chiquita	

Adults

Source: Company records.

EXHIBIT 9 Juicy Juice Storyboard

"Trick Glass"

NEJJ-6025   :15   Oct., 1986

KID #1: You'll never get more than 10% real juice out of those drinks.

No matter how much you pour.

But Juicy Juice from Libby's is 100% real fruit juice.

KID #2: Wow.

ANNCR: Juicy Juice is a juicer juice.

KID #1: It's 100%.

EXHIBIT 10   Juicy Juice Consumer Profile

Demographics	Purchasing patterns

Heavy users
  Income: +$25M/YR.
  Female head under 35 and full time
  housewife/mother
  Household size 3+
  Users age: 2–11
	Juice purchase cycle is short
	  Purchased every 2 weeks
	  Comparatively, coffee is purchased every
	  9 weeks
	Juice is a high impulse item
	  Planned purchase for juice: 39%
	  Planned purchase for coffee: 64%

Source: Company records.

EXHIBIT 11   Highlights of 1989 Juicy Juice Marketing Plan

1. *Long-term strategy:*
   Increase sales to $100mm+ via expansion of product into multiple store locations (shelf-stable and refrigerated) and through multiple distribution outlets (grocery stores, nonfood, convenience stores, vending, food service).

2. *Short-term strategies:*
   - Increase household penetration
   - Increase product usage
   - Continue to steal share from juice drinks and 100% juices
   - Continue to improve profitability

3. *Target sales:* $39 million
   Target spending: $9 million (+ 13% over 1988)
   - Ads   3 million
   - Consumer promotion   1.3 million
   - Trade promotion   4.7 million

4. *Pricing:* Price at significant premium to kid's 10% drinks, but not at a premium which risks volume; parity with other 100% juices

5. *Advertising:* To create awareness in new markets; maintain awareness in core markets

6. *Positioning:*
   - Juicy Juice is the 100% juice blend alternative to kids' 10% juice drinks.
   - Target audience: Moms age 25–49 with kids 2–11
                       $20,000+ household income

7. *Promotions:*
   - Consumer
     to maintain current heavy user base
     to increase household penetration
   - Trade
     to increase listings in core market and new expansion markets
     to focus on gaining displays at reduced price

8. *New products:* continue work on new flavors, packaging, and form (concentrate).

EXHIBIT 12 1988 Segmentation of the U.K. Beverage Market ($ millions)

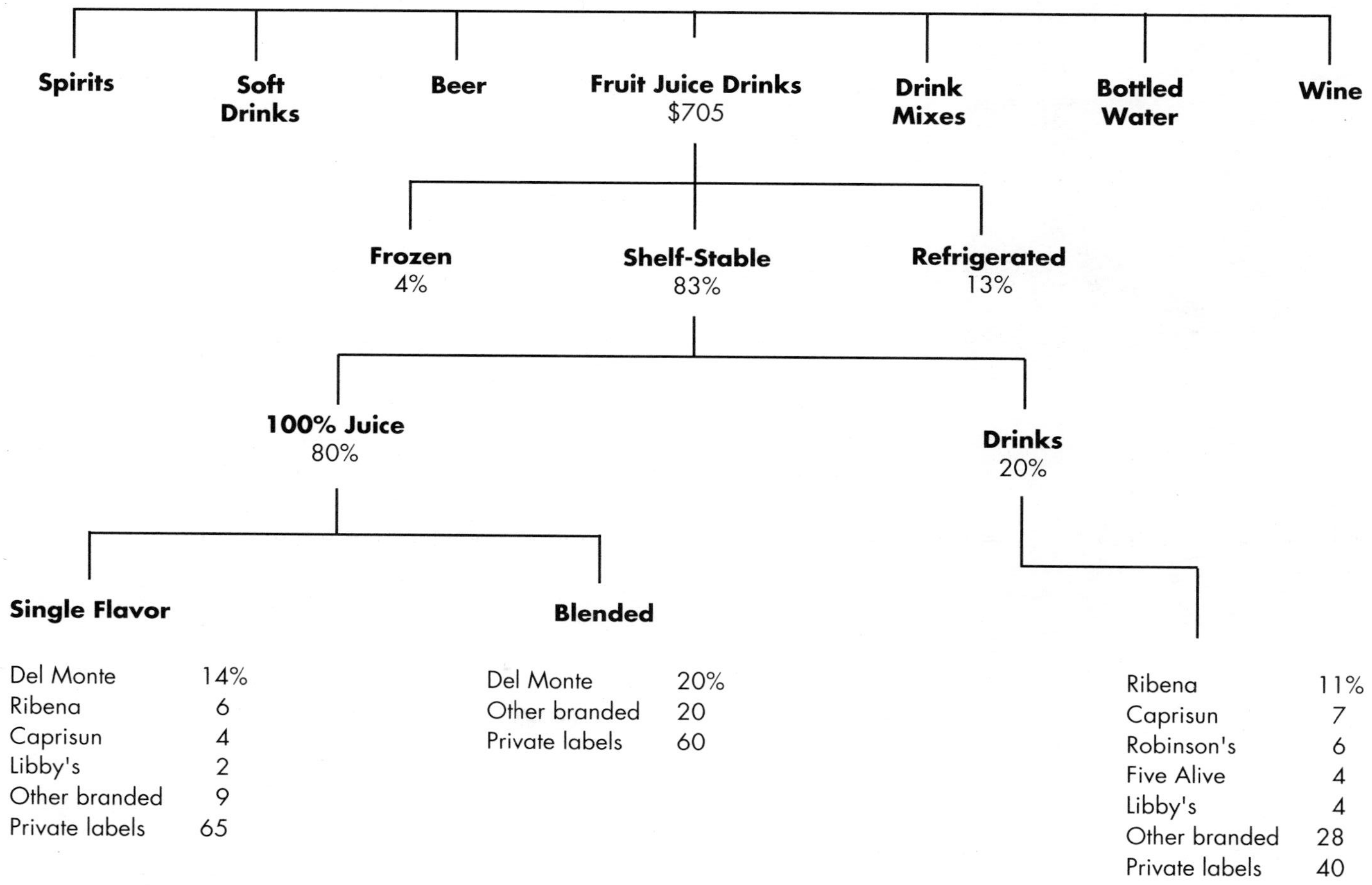

Spirits

Soft Drinks

Beer

Fruit Juice Drinks $705

Drink Mixes

Bottled Water

Wine

Frozen 4%

Shelf-Stable 83%

Refrigerated 13%

100% Juice 80%

Drinks 20%

Single Flavor

Del Monte	14%
Ribena	6
Caprisun	4
Libby's	2
Other branded	9
Private labels	65

Blended

Del Monte	20%
Other branded	20
Private labels	60

Ribena	11%
Caprisun	7
Robinson's	6
Five Alive	4
Libby's	4
Other branded	28
Private labels	40

EXHIBIT 13   Um Bongo Brik Packs

EXHIBIT 14   Um Bongo Commercial Storyboard

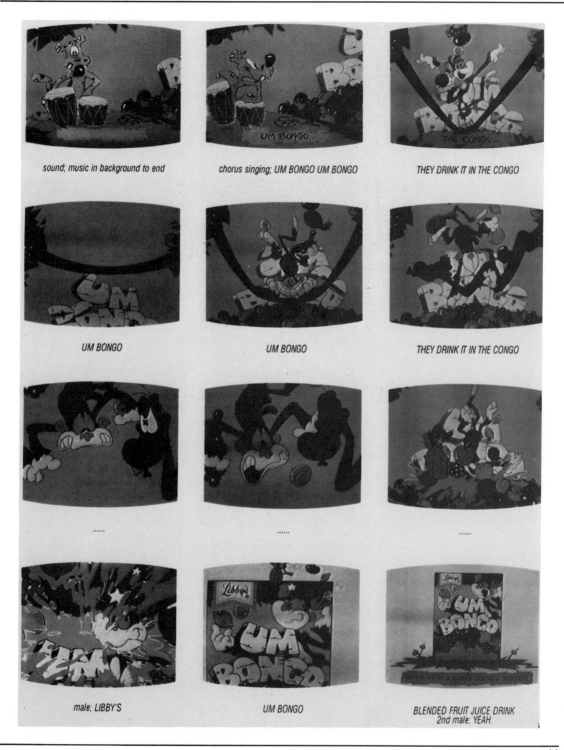

sound; music in background to end

chorus singing; UM BONGO UM BONGO

THEY DRINK IT IN THE CONGO

UM BONGO

UM BONGO

THEY DRINK IT IN THE CONGO

......

......

......

male; LIBBY'S

UM BONGO

BLENDED FRUIT JUICE DRINK
2nd male; YEAH.

EXHIBIT 15 U.K. Consumer Data on Um Bongo

Children's opinion		Children's agreement with attributes*		Mothers' agreement with attributes*	
Like it a lot	53%	Fun	81%	Fun	93%
Like it quite well	34	Something I would buy	79	Children would ask for it	92
		Exciting flavor	84	High quality	80
Don't like it very much	7	Good for me	86	Full of goodness	70
Don't like it at all	3	Something mother would buy for me	65		
No opinion	3				
	100				

Note: Responses given after product trial and exposure to video of TV commercial.
*Percentages do not add up to 100 due to multiple responses.

EXHIBIT 16 Spanish Fruit Juice and Drinks Market,* 1988

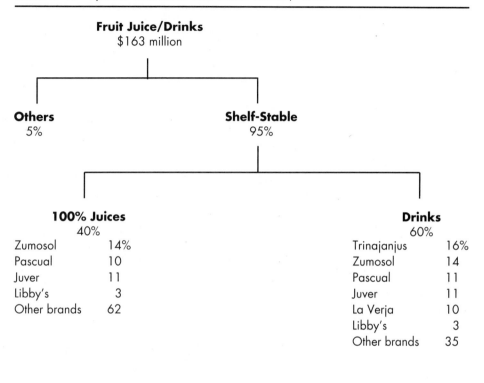

Fruit Juice/Drinks
$163 million

| **Others** | **Shelf-Stable** |
| 5% | 95% |

100% Juices		**Drinks**	
40%		60%	
Zumosol	14%	Trinajanjus	16%
Pascual	10	Zumosol	14
Juver	11	Pascual	11
Libby's	3	Juver	11
Other brands	62	La Verja	10
		Libby's	3
		Other brands	35

* Excludes fresh juices
Source: Company records.

EXHIBIT 17 Portuguese Fruit Juice and Drinks Market,* 1988

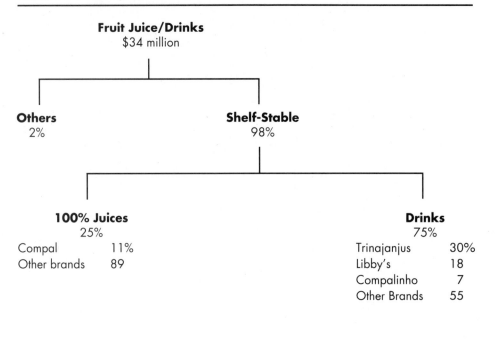

Fruit Juice/Drinks
$34 million

Others
2%

Shelf-Stable
98%

100% Juices		**Drinks**	
25%		75%	
Compal	11%	Trinajanjus	30%
Other brands	89	Libby's	18
		Compalinho	7
		Other Brands	55

* Excludes fresh juices
Source: Company records.

CASE 1 APPENDIX

INTERPRETATIVE SUMMARY AND SELECTED FINDINGS

Background and Purpose

The ready-to-drink fruit juice and fruit drink markets continue to be among the fastest-growing segments of the overall U.S. beverage market.

Nestlé has offered Libby's USA the opportunity to market Um Bongo, a ready-to-drink fruit juice presently being successfully marketed by Libby's in the U.K.

Management wishes to evaluate the acceptability of the product to the American consumer, specifically to determine:

- The acceptance of the Um Bongo product vs. Hawaiian Punch (the market leader) on a blind taste basis.
- The incremental value of the Um Bongo concept (in video form) in heightening the appeal of the product.
- How well the Um Bongo product lives up to the expectations generated by the concept.
- The communication ability of the Um Bongo commercial.

Conclusions/Recommendations

Based on the research results, it appears that Um Bongo could be a viable entry in the U.S. fruit juice/drink market given certain refinements.

The strength of the Um Bongo product itself lies in the specific fruit flavors and the strength of those flavors. However, a "sour/tangy" taste seems to pull down the product's acceptance and would need to be reduced to improve acceptance.

From a conceptual standpoint, the current commercial enhances the product's acceptance and the perception that the product is unique—definitely a plus in the vast sea of fruit juice/drink beverages. However, the commercial needs to communicate the concept in a clearer manner. It is hypothesized that after viewing the commercial consumers are not sure of what to expect, and when they taste the product they are pleasantly surprised. A more focused and clear explanation of the product in the commercial with-

out diminishing the uniqueness would aid in enhancing the product's acceptance overall.

KEY FINDINGS

1. The Um Bongo commercial generated limited interest in trying the product. After trial, however, consumers were more receptive to the product.

2. Positioning the product prior to trial enhanced the product's perception of being unique, as well as its acceptance overall.

3. On a blind basis, Um Bongo performs similarly to Hawaiian Punch in terms of overall rating and total purchase interest. However, when directly compared, Hawaiian Punch is significantly preferred.

4. Um Bongo's product advantages are seen in its specific fruit flavors and the strength of those flavors. However, its "sour/tangy" aspect was the major focus for rejection.

SUMMARY OF FINDINGS

Video Impact

1. Within the context of a single viewing, the Um Bongo video produces limited enthusiasm for product trial.

2. The video succeeds in communicating the brand name and places the product squarely in the fruit juice and drinks market.

3. Consumers who are reluctant to try Um Bongo have ill-defined concerns apparently based on their difficulty in understanding words in the commercial.

4. Despite these reservations, concept positioning via the video ultimately appears to aid in the actual product's acceptance.

Product Acceptance after Commercial Exposure

1. The product fosters significantly greater buying interest than was considered before trial; it was better than expected.

2. Um Bongo is judged best in terms of its uniqueness—providing a good overall taste through a combination of strong, tangy fruit flavors.

3. Acceptance/rejection, although often expressed in terms of sweetness/tartness levels, ultimately translates into the impact of these physical attributes on beverage benefits—that is, taste satisfying, refreshing.

Blind Acceptance of Um Bongo vs. Hawaiian Punch

1. In absolute terms, the Um Bongo product produces ratings approximate to those given Hawaiian Punch.

2. They are not equal, however. Purchase interest in Hawaiian Punch is significantly higher, and when directly compared, Hawaiian Punch is overwhelmingly preferred to Um Bongo.

3. The sweeter, not too tart flavor of Hawaiian Punch is the dominant reason for its preference.

4. Tanginess is the major point of focus in rejecting Um Bongo.

Selected Tables

Impact of Video

1. *The Um Bongo commercial, albeit after a single exposure, produces only limited enthusiasm for product trial.* Just 5% of children 8 to 18 years of age express a definite commitment to buy. The overwhelming reaction appears to be one of cautious reserve, with 81% indicating a "probably buy" to "might or might not buy" purchase interest. (See Table A.1.)

2. *The video succeeds in communicating the brand name and places the product squarely in the fruit juice/drink market.*

- 86% recall Um Bongo as the brand name.

- 84% believe product will be most similar to other fruit juice/drinks, particularly Hawaiian Punch. (See Table A.2.)

3. *Commercial also positions Um Bongo as most appropriate for pre-teenage children, at other than the formal meal occasions of dinner and breakfast.* Regardless of age, Um Bongo is perceived as most suitable for young children, particularly those under 8. Few teenagers (19%) see the product directed at them, while 2 of 3 pre-teens (67%) indicate they would be likely to use the product. Non meal, at-home occasions are considered best for Um Bongo. (See Table A.3.)

4. *In spite of these reservations, the video, as the tool for presenting the Um Bongo concept, appears to alter favorably ultimate product acceptance.* Actual product ratings and interest in buying Um Bongo are uniformly higher when consumers are previously shown the video than when tasting the product occurs without concept positioning. (See Table A.4.)

Product Acceptance after Commercial Exposure With product trial, the uncertainties that existed after only concept exposure are clarified, producing a significantly broader base of favorably disposed purchasers.

Tasting the product engenders significantly greater buying interest than was considered before the trial. (See Table A.5.)

Product Acceptance Blind vs. Hawaiian Punch Um Bongo overall and specific product characteristic ratings closely parallel those elicited by Hawaiian Punch. Only in the specific area of fruit taste does Hawaiian Punch garner a higher satisfaction rating.

Nevertheless, in spite of this seemingly similar level of acceptance, purchase interest is significantly greater for Hawaiian Punch. (See Table A.6.)

TABLE A.1 Postvideo Purchase Intent

Total respondents	(150)
Definitely would buy	5%
Probably would buy	50
Might or might not buy	31
Probably would *not* buy	7
Definitely would *not* buy	7%

TABLE A.2 One Beverage Most Similar

Total respondents	(150)
Hawaiian Punch	45%
Juicy Juice	22
Hi-C	17
Orange juice	7
Kool-Aid	4%

TABLE A.3 Use/Occasions Appropriateness

	Total	8- to 13-year-olds	14- to 18-year-olds
Total respondents	(150)	(76)	(74)
Would be likely to use:			
Children under 8	89%	88%	89%
Children 8–12	73	67	78
Teenagers 13–19	21	24	19
Adults 20 and over	13	17	10
With breakfast	47	51	42
"On the go" occasions	58	54	62
Drink at home	79	87	70
With a snack	79	83	76
With lunch	64	68	60
With dinner	23	29	16
Away from home	60%	66%	54%

☐ = significant difference at the 90% level of confidence.

TABLE A.4 Video Impact on Product Evaluation

	Um Bongo		
	With video	Without video	Difference
Total respondents	(150)	(75)	
	%	%	±
Purchase intent			
% Definitely would buy	25	15	− 10
Total positive	67	60	− 7
Overall rating			
% Excellent/extremely good	44	33	− 11
Mean	3.97	3.80	−.17
Attribute ratings (% excellent/ extremely good)			
Is tangy	50	36	− 14
Is refreshing	47	39	− 8
Has a strong fruit taste	56	49	− 7
Is sweet tasting	46	43	− 3
Is satisfying	44	40	− 4
Is bitter tasting	27	20	− 7
Is a good combination of flavors	49	45	− 4
Has a good overall flavor	51	41	− 10
Leaves a pleasant taste in your mouth	46	43	− 3
Has an appealing color	45	43	− 2
Is different	59	56	− 3
Is a beverage for me	44	41	− 3
Is fun to drink	43	33	− 10

☐ = significant difference at the 90% level of confidence.

TABLE A.5 Purchase Intent

	Postvideo exposure	Postproduct trial	Difference
Total respondents	(150)	(150)	
	%	%	±
Definitely would buy	5	25	+ 20
Probably would buy	50	42	− 8
(Total Positive)	(55)	(67)	+ 12
Might or might not buy	31	15	− 16
Probably would *not buy*	7	7	±
Definitely would *not buy*	7	11	+ 4

☐ = significant difference at the 90% level of confidence.

TABLE A.6 Blind Test—Um Bongo and Hawaiian Punch

	Um Bongo	Hawaiian Punch
Total respondents	(75)	(75)
	%	%
Purchase intent		
% Definitely would buy	15	29
Total positive	60	72
Overall rating		
% Excellent/extremely good	33	36
Mean	3.80	4.04
Attribute ratings (% excellent/ extremely good)		
Is tangy	36	27
Is refreshing	39	43
Has a strong fruit taste	49	48
Is sweet tasting	43	49
Is satisfying	40	45
Is bitter tasting	20	11
Is a good combination of flavors	45	45
Has a good overall flavor	41	41
Leaves a pleasant taste in your mouth	43	41
Has an appealing color	43	56
Is different	56	43
Is a beverage for me	41	44
Is fun to drink	33	37
Directional ratings (% just right)		
Sweetness	77	80
Color	79	79
Fruit taste	68	84
Too strong	17	11
Too weak	15	5

☐ = *significant difference at the 90% level of confidence.*

2 NOKIA DATA

Early in 1989, the top management of Nokia Data was mapping the key elements of the firm's strategy for growth and international expansion through the mid-1990s. In the previous year, as a first step toward becoming a major player in the European market for information technology, the Finnish computer company had acquired the Data Systems Division of Sweden's L.M. Ericsson. In spite of the acquisition, however, less than a quarter of Nokia Data's $1.2 billion sales was generated outside of the Nordic market,[1] where it now held the leading position. The management intended to improve the company's spotty international presence by aggressively expanding into the large but also highly competitive markets of the rest of Europe.

A cornerstone of Nokia Data's European growth strategy was what management referred to as a "multidomestic" approach. Management believed that in the fast-maturing European market for computers, the key to competitive advantage in each European country lay in customer orientation achieved through a strong local identity and domestically tailored marketing programs. Thus, local hardware and software customization, local branding, local marketing, and local sales and support services constituted the main elements of Nokia Data's multidomestic approach.

Top executives were keenly aware that their planned approach went counter to industry practices, which increasingly emphasized pan-European integration and marketing. In fact, some Nokia Data managers had expressed doubts regarding the wisdom of the multidomestic approach. Explained Kalle Isokallio, the president of Nokia Data:

> We have a different view of the industry than what one reads in the papers. Our industry is no longer high growth or high tech. Both sales and technology are maturing. In this competitive market, we can't compete with majors like IBM or Siemens in volume or new technology. We don't have the resources.

This case was prepared by Research Associate Robert C. Howard under the direction of Professor Kamran Kashani. Copyright © 1989 by the International Institute for Management Development (IMD), Lausanne, Switzerland. Not to be used or reproduced without permission.

1. The Nordic market consisted of the three Scandinavian countries (Sweden, Norway, and Denmark), plus Finland.

Where we can outperform them is by being closer to the computer buyer who prefers to buy from a domestic supplier. In every country in which we compete, therefore, we want to be considered as one of the top domestic vendors. Pan-European identity and integration doesn't make sense for us. We are too small for that.

THE NOKIA GROUP

Nokia was founded in 1865 in the village of Nokia, Finland, as a timber and paper company. In the subsequent 100 years, Nokia grew and diversified into tires, power transmission, radio, telecommunications, electronics, and computer technology. In 1988, the Nokia Group of companies had sales of $5,500 million, earned a net profit of $215 million, and spent 5% of net sales on research and development. With its 44,000 employees, Nokia conducted operations in 32 countries, 17 of which had manufacturing facilities. By 1988, the Nokia Group of companies was Finland's largest publicly traded industrial enterprise. In addition to being listed on the Helsinki stock exchange, Nokia shares were listed on the stock exchanges in Stockholm, London, Paris, and Frankfurt. (See Exhibit 1 for information on the Nokia Group of companies.)

Nokia Information Systems (NIS)

Nokia's experience with computers dated from 1962, the year in which Nokia Electronics was formed to capitalize on the company's recent purchase of its first mainframe. At this time, Nokia implemented a time-sharing system with outside companies to handle bookkeeping and other data processing activities. In the late 1960s, Nokia began serving as a sales agent for Honeywell, marketing its complete product line of mainframes, terminals, and printers to the Finnish market. During this period, Nokia management combined their increasing knowledge of hardware with their data processing know-how from time-sharing. In the early 1970s, Nokia developed, manufactured, and sold its own minicomputer.

Throughout the 1970s, the Honeywell product line represented a main source of revenue at Nokia Electronics. However, in 1977, prompted by the growth of its customer base in the banking and retailing sectors, Nokia formed a separate department for its own products. In 1981, Nokia expanded its product offering further with its first personal computer, the Mikro Mikko 1. In 1985, Nokia Electronics split into four divisions: Information Systems, Telecommunications, Mobile Telephones, and Consumer Electronics.

As of 1987, the Honeywell line accounted for 40% of Nokia Information Systems' revenues in Finland. Honeywell's role was limited to manufacturing, performed in the United States, Italy, or Scotland, and providing operating system software. Aside from adding its own terminals to Honeywell's computers, Nokia was responsible for all applications software and after-sales services. In 1987, Nokia Information Systems enjoyed the leading market share in Finland, where it generated 75% of its total sales.

Nokia Data

With limited growth opportunities in the small Finnish market, Nokia management began searching for an acquisition in the Nordic countries. In 1988, Nokia Information Systems purchased the Data Systems unit of the Ericsson Group in Stockholm and merged the two operations to form Nokia Data. Data Systems produced and marketed a range of minicomputers, personal computers, telephone exchanges, and printers throughout Europe, in addition to Hong Kong and Australia. Aside from keeping sales offices in North America and other overseas markets, the Ericsson Group retained a 20% share ownership in Nokia Data. Nokia, on the other hand, was able to strengthen its share of the Nordic countries' market and gained the opportunity to expand into Germany, France, Britain, and other European markets. Management believed that increased geographic coverage translated into greater credibility among Nokia's customers and helped ensure the company's survival in the Nordic countries at a time of industry consolidation. By the end of 1988, with sales of $1.2 billion, Nokia Data was the largest computer company in the Nordic countries. The firm employed 8,500 employees, had subsidiaries in 10 European countries, and a European-installed base of over 700,000 terminals and personal computers. (See Exhibit 2 for the Nokia Data reporting structure.)

THE INFORMATION TECHNOLOGY INDUSTRY

In its broadest sense, information technology (IT) was defined as the industry that combined the data processing and storage power of computers with the distance-transmission capabilities of telecommunications. The industry included all types of computers, word processors, printers, plotters, disk drives, telephones, telephone networks, public databases, and related software. Virtually all organizations used these products. In Western Europe, the manufacturing, finance, retail, and public sectors accounted for the largest expenditures. In 1987, the worldwide market for IT was valued at $407 billion, with volume distributed heavily among three geographic markets: North America, 38%; Europe, 26%; and Japan, 30%. For 1989, total industry sales were forecast to reach $505 billion.

Nokia's Data Business

In the vast information technology field, Nokia Data management defined their core business as the sector of the computer industry focused on terminals, personal computers, and related networks. In 1987, the total European computer industry was valued at $86 billion; Nokia Data management estimated that their industry sector accounted for $20 to $22 billion.

Nokia Data's product offering included terminals, personal computers, minicomputers, local area networks (hardware connected to share and exchange information among a group of users), and the related communication links for connecting different brands and classes of computers. In addition to hardware, Nokia Data provided application software and services tailored to meet the needs of its five primary customer segments in retailing, banking and insurance, manufacturing, government, and general business. Typical examples of general business applications included materials administration, purchasing, order handling, invoicing, database management, word processing, graphics, and spreadsheets. Across Europe, the five segments in which Nokia Data competed were forecast to grow between 7 and 10% per year through the early 1990s.

Markets and Competition

In Europe, Nokia Data competed directly and indirectly with a large number of firms. Exhibit 3 shows the top 25 manufacturers in the European data processing market, ranked by their total volume of business in the region. Nokia Data's management believed that such rankings were misleading because not all firms competed in the sector of the market that Nokia defined as terminals, personal computers, networks, and related products and services.

Instead, to delineate the competition, management used the diagram shown in Exhibit 4, which clustered industry participants around four product/system zones: terminals, personal computers, local area networks, and systems. The four zones differed in their volume potential and product/system configuration. (See Exhibit 5 for a summary of Nokia Data's key competitors and their product offerings along the four zones.)

Terminals The European terminal market, consisting of keyboards and screens, represented approximately 6% of the European sector in which Nokia Data competed and was valued at $2.2 billion. Terminals had no data processing power of their own and, hence, had to be connected to a host computer. Sales were divided between add-on terminals (90–95%), where customers expanded an existing system by adding new terminals, and upgrades (5–10%), where customers substituted new terminals for old. The terminal market was contested by mainframe and minicomputer suppliers, such as IBM and DEC, which were able to sell their own terminals on the strength of their computers, and by a large number of component suppliers. Among these were Memorex Telex of U.S. origin and SEL of Germany, which made terminals compatible with existing computers as well as disk drives, cassettes, and other computer accessories. Across Europe, Nokia Data management considered IBM, Memorex Telex, and Olivetti their primary competitors in the terminal market.

Typical customers for terminals included large organizations, such as banks and insurance agencies, that processed data with a large central computer and a score of dispersed terminals. Customers purchasing terminals from component suppliers rather than from the large computer companies cited price as an important factor. More recently, ergonomics had become a criterion, as it was believed to contribute to improved employee comfort and productivity. Since the terminal market was primarily an add-on market, functions performed for the customer were installation and, when necessary, after-sales repair.

According to Nokia Data management, keys to success in the terminal market were compatibility with hardware from the major computer companies, competitive pricing, and credibility as a terminal supplier. Credibility, a sales manager clarified, meant a supplier was known for dependable products and was large enough to survive any industry shakeout.

In unit sales, the terminal market was projected to remain stagnant through the early 1990s and decline thereafter. In 1989, the market was becoming increasingly competitive. The average terminal prices in Europe had declined by about 8% in recent months.

Personal Computers   In 1988, the European personal computer market was valued at $11 billion and was expected to reach $18 billion by 1993. Competitors in this zone were well-known personal computer manufacturers such as IBM, Olivetti, Siemens, Amstrad, Apple, and Compaq. These firms were further classified by Nokia Data management according to their origin and historic customer base. More specifically, IBM, Siemens, and Olivetti, for example, had begun with and enjoyed established reputations in the business community and were described by Nokia Data management as having an "institutional" market background. On the other hand, Amstrad, Apple, and Compaq, unlike most of the large companies, were originally associated with the mass market and were said by management to have a "consumer" background.

From 1984 to 1987, the share of all personal computers sold by the institutional group in Europe had declined from 45 to 35%, with the balance of sales accounted for by the consumer group. Nokia Data considered itself as having more of an institutional than a consumer background.

Regardless of their original customer base, by the late 1980s, competitors from both groups offered stand-alone personal computers direct to large accounts and via retail outlets to the medium-sized and small business and consumer markets. Typically, larger accounts relied on the manufacturer for installation and after-sales services. Smaller accounts, as well as individual buyers, relied on the manufacturer's dealer or repair network for help—a practice considered less reliable.

According to Goran Hermannson, a marketing manager in Sweden, to succeed in marketing personal computers to large accounts, a hardware supplier had to be known for reliable products and perceived by the customer as large enough to survive the computer industry's eventual consolidation. Companies from the institutional group had an advantage, as they already enjoyed a reputation as suppliers of mainframes and minicomputers. More recently, compatibility with hardware from multiple vendors had become an important factor for supplying personal computers to large accounts. Major institutional companies, such as IBM, that had traditionally employed their own proprietary systems were now facing increasing pressure to abandon these in favor of industry standards and multiple vendor compatibility.

Nokia Data management believed, on the other hand, that to succeed in the mass market a supplier needed low manufacturing cost, extensive retail distribution, and a favorable price-performance image in the eyes of the customer. Examples of such companies included Amstrad, Commodore, and Compaq.

Local Area Networks (LANs) LANs were a collection of computers, printers, cables, and other communications links that allowed a network of users to process data and to communicate with one another. In addition to hardware, LANs were equipped with operating systems software, applications software, and sophisticated LAN management software that allocated data processing among the computers in a network.

As a concept in computing, LANs were relatively new to the industry, represented $670 million of the $20 to $22 billion segment in which Nokia Data competed, and were expected to grow between 20 and 30% per annum through the mid-1990s. Although LANs could include mainframes and mini-computers, they were built primarily using personal computers. One advantage of LANs was their attractive cost-performance ratio. An independent estimate showed that it cost less than $10,000 per employee to set up a network of personal computers versus $12,000 for a seat at a minicomputer and $14,000 at a mainframe. In addition to lower hardware costs, networks eliminated the inefficiencies of multiple training staffs, multiple software packages, and data transmission costs.

Typical customers in the LAN segment, according to Goran Hermannson, were companies or departments with fewer than 100 personal computer users. He explained that it was technically easier to implement LAN solutions in smaller companies than in those with hundreds of personal computers. In addition, he believed that the LAN technology was less popular with central data processing management in larger companies because it allowed individual departments to decide on their own systems independently.

Due to the complexity associated with the design, installation, and maintenance of a LAN, services accounted for a large portion of the purchase price. In addition, customers were keenly aware of the importance of vendor support in the early phases of a LAN's installation. In the words of one Nokia Data customer, it was important to have "someone to shoot" if something went wrong.

According to Nokia Data management, to be successful as a LAN supplier, a company had to enjoy the same qualifications as a personal computer vendor—namely, reliable products, hardware compatibility in a multivendor environment, and customer-perceived longevity. In addition, the successful company had to have the technical know-how to act as a systems integrator, connecting products from one or many vendors. Most important, a LAN supplier had to be willing to service a network that contained products from vendors other than itself and guarantee against a network failure.

Because LANs were built primarily with personal computers, competitors came from both the institutional and the consumer groups. In the institutional group, Nokia Data's largest competitor in Europe was IBM, although companies such as Olivetti and Philips were strong in their local markets. The largest competitor in the consumer group was Compaq.

Systems   At Nokia Data, a system was defined as a set of hardware and software products tailored to meet a specific need within an industry or industry segment. A system could consist of terminals sold with tailor-made software utilizing a client's existing mainframe or minicomputer. Alternatively, a system could be based on LAN products, complemented by customized software. In 1988, the European systems business was estimated to be $7 billion and projected to grow 10 to 15% annually through the early 1990s.

As with the personal computer market, systems competitors were categorized by Nokia Data management into the institutional and consumer groups. The distinguishing feature between these groups, according to a Nokia Data sales executive, was the knowledge of their customers' industries. He explained that companies like IBM and Siemens had accumulated a vast base of experience in such industries as insurance, banking, and manufacturing, in which centralized data processing using mainframes and terminals had been practiced for over two decades. On the other hand, newcomers with a consumer background, such as Compaq and Amstrad, relied more on the industry knowledge of third parties, including value-added resellers (VARs), to compete in the systems market. (See page 60 for more information about VARs).

Systems customers were typically large organizations seeking to decentralize their data processing activities to a department or work-group level. Decentralized data processing was attractive because it eliminated users' dependency on a single computer, of particular importance in organizations such as banks where a computer breakdown might force shutdown of operations.

Leif Lindfors, a sales manager for Sweden, believed that as in the LAN market, success in systems required reliable hardware and software. However, he explained, the most important requirement for success in systems was to have a sales force with industry-specific knowledge, assisted by a technical support staff capable of developing customized software. Nokia Data management identified their primary systems competitor as IBM, followed by other institutional companies such as Unisys, Siemens, Olivetti, Nixdorf, and Philips.

Industry Trends

Industry observers, as well as Nokia Data executives, believed several trends were influencing the level and nature of competition in the European data processing market. Among these trends were slowing growth, improved price-performance ratio of hardware, growth of decentralized computing, emergence of industry standards, proliferation of VARs, and the anticipated European integration toward a single market after 1992.

Slowing Growth   In the late 1980s, the overall growth in the European computer industry was slowing down to single digits. As of 1988, annual growth for the first time had declined below 10%, and some analysts were predicting only 6% yearly growth through 1992. Mainframes and minicomputers had experienced the greatest decline in growth rates, as customers shifted to lower-cost computing alternatives such as personal computers and LANs. In fact, analysts expected mainframe and minicomputer sales to grow at only 8% and 3%, respectively, into the early 1990s. Demand for personal computers, however, was expected to remain strong, with 10% growth forecast through 1992.

Price-Performance Ratio   Advances in the computer chip technology had substantially reduced the cost of computing power during the 1980s—a trend that was expected to continue into the 1990s. For example, in 1981, a mainframe capable of processing one million instructions per second cost over $400,000; by the early 1990s, a hardware with similar performance was expected to be priced around $50,000. More important, the computing power associated with some earlier mainframes was available by 1988 in a desktop computer at a fraction of the cost—a trend referred to in the industry as "downsizing." Furthermore, as more and more processing power was provided to end users, analysts believed that powerful personal computers would replace terminals connected to mainframes and minicomputers.

Decentralized Computing   In the early days of computing, companies needed a mainframe and a multitude of dumb terminals to perform all data processing centrally. The first step toward decentralization occurred with minicomputers, allowing users to process up to 95% of their data within their own department. The next step in decentralization came with the personal computer, placing data processing capability directly on the end user's desk. Personal computers, however, were limited in their computing capacity; as stand-alone hardware, they did not allow communication among users.

The recent arrival of LAN technology provided an alternative means to decentralize computing by distributing data processing among a work group's or a department's interconnected computers. Employing primarily personal computers in a network of users, LANs had computing capacity similar to minicomputers but at a fraction of their cost. In the opinion of many analysts, downsizing and distributed data processing were together substantially changing the way companies competed in the computer industry. One analyst believed that decentralization was providing end users with more say in computer purchase decisions, leading to an increasing number of specialized narrow segments. The net result, according to another observer, was that the more expensive minicomputer and mainframes would lose sales to the less costly, personal computer-based LANs.

Industry Standards   Through the 1980s, minicomputer and mainframe manufacturers such as IBM, DEC, and Siemens, sold their hardware with proprietary software, thus locking customers into a specific data handling method. Having made a substantial investment in hardware and software, few customers were willing to purchase new systems from other manufacturers—a decision that could entail difficult and expensive tasks of rewriting old programs.

In contrast to proprietary systems, the U.S.-based AT&T developed and licensed UNIX, a nonproprietary operating system that allowed different brands of computers to communicate with each other. Preferred by an increasing number of computer buyers, UNIX-based hardware and software were increasingly being used worldwide. Industry observers believed that interconnectivity would become an important buying criterion in the 1990s.

Proliferation of VARs   During the 1980s, the focus of competition in the computer industry had shifted from hardware toward software and services. Staffan Simberg, vice president of Group Europe, attributed this trend to the "commoditization" of computers, where substantive technological differences in hardware were narrowing among different manufacturers. Another factor was what many in Nokia Data management referred to as the "declining technical sophistication of the average buyer." Increasingly, computer decisions in small- to medium-sized companies were being made by noncomputer people who were more concerned with the quality of "solutions" than with the technicalities of the "black box."

The two trends combined had given rise to VARs—independent companies that filled a gap between manufacturers on the one hand, and small- to medium-sized clients on the other. Typically, VARs bought hardware from a variety of producers and added customized software and services for narrow vertical user segments such as the legal and medical professions, specialized retailers, plumbing, and farming. VARs competed among themselves and with computer manufacturers in the LANs and systems markets. From modest levels in the 1970s, the number of VARs in Europe had grown in recent years to several hundred. Together they accounted for an estimated $3 billion in industry sales.

To use a VAR for competitive advantage, explained one Nokia Data sales executive, a company had to provide hardware with an attractive price and encourage the resellers to develop applications in their special end-user segments. In an average installation, 65% of the price paid by a customer was accounted for by the cost of hardware to the reseller; the rest went to cover expenses, including costs associated with application development and margins.

European Integration   The European Community (EC) had chosen 1992 as the date to integrate its internal market by liberalizing trade and removing barriers among its 12 member states. Increased competition among manufacturers in an open market implied that government procurement could no longer favor a local vendor over another vendor from the EC. Hence, 1992 posed a serious challenge to national computer companies that sold up to 50% of their sales to their local governments. Increased competition was also expected to lead to concentration in the industry, as companies strived to achieve critical mass and economies of scale. Recent examples of such activities included Alcatel, formed through the merger of ITT's European business and the French CGE group, and Memorex Telex, formed by the merger of Memorex International and the U.S. Telex organization.

Also, in anticipation of 1992, companies such as Apple, IBM, Siemens, and Olivetti were integrating regional operations toward a "European" posture and identity. In the case of Apple, its management had recently created a European research and development center in Paris: "We want to form a strong European identity so that we are able to be part of the European economy."[2] By adopting a regional profile, both European and non-European companies wanted to be better positioned to compete for local government bids after 1992 when procurement policies were no longer biased toward domestic suppliers. In this respect, Olivetti's executive vice president, Elserino Piol, maintained that the "European companies that remain 'national champions' are going to suffer after 1992." The same article concluded: "Europe's computer makers have all opted for the same survival strategy: Each is scrambling to go pan-European as fast as possible."[3]

NOKIA DATA'S EUROPEAN STRATEGY

Current Position

At the end of 1988, Nokia Data manufactured its products in Sweden and Finland and operated wholly owned sales and service branches in all four Nordic countries (Sweden, Norway, Denmark, and Finland), in addition to Germany, the Netherlands, Spain, the United Kingdom, France, and Switzerland. In Germany, Nokia Data's largest non-Nordic countries' operation, the company employed a total of 450 people in sales and service. Nokia Data also sent sales agents who had previously sold Nokia Information Systems or Ericsson Data Systems products to Finland, Sweden, Belgium, Austria, Italy, Portugal, Hong Kong, and Australia.

The company assembled most of its products in its own facilities; a minor share of total production was subcontracted to third parties in the Nordic countries as well as in the Far East. Management saw definite advantages to sourcing internationally and using its own facilities for assembly. Components purchased as far away as the United States and the Far East accounted for 70% of the total cost of production; the rest of the cost was divided equally between labor and plant overhead. Efficient sourcing and materials management were considered critical to overall cost performance. A recent estimate indicated that well-run procurement and manufacturing operations, including rationalized purchasing and investment in modern assembly, could potentially save the company as much as 40% on the production costs of terminals and PCs. One-half of the projected savings would have come from reduced materials cost. Some Nokia Data executives believed that while potential for savings existed, it probably was less than the estimated 40%.

Nokia Data marketed what management called its "horizontal products"— terminals, personal computers, and LAN-based hardware—in all markets. With minor exceptions, these products were based on nonproprietary technologies. "Vertical systems," as management called them, were sales of hardware and software to target segments in banking/insurance, retailing, manufacturing, government, and general business. Nokia Data did not use VARs in a market until management believed the company had a strong local presence. Hence, as of 1988, VARs were

---

2. *Business Marketing,* September 1988.
3. *Business Week International,* September 12, 1988.

used only in Finland and Sweden. Less than 3% of the company's sales were generated through sales agents or VARs.

In Finland, Nokia Data used the Mikko brand for its entire line. In all other markets, Nokia Data used the Alfaskop brand name that it had acquired from Ericsson Data Systems.

Although Nokia Data products were sold as far away as Hong Kong and Australia, 95% of Nokia Data's sales were concentrated in Europe, with Finland, Sweden, and Germany representing 40%, 25%, and 11%, respectively, of total sales. (Exhibits 6, 7, and 8 summarize Nokia Data's sales by country, segment, and product.)

Senior managers thought of their company as a sales-driven organization. Although major strategic decisions were made by product groups in the headquarters, the regions and country management in larger markets wielded significant influence on short-term policies and sales action. For example, although product design was a headquarters' decision, a local sales operation could ask for the development of a special terminal and keyboard for a large order. Local managers in new and "strategic" markets, such as Germany, France, and Spain, were measured and rewarded based on sales performance. In the more established markets, such as Finland and Sweden, both sales and profitability were considered in performance evaluation.

Competitive Standing

Top management at Nokia Data believed that they enjoyed a number of competitive advantages in their sector of the computer industry. In particular, they believed that the large institutional competitors had been slow to respond to the growing customer demand for multivendor connectivity and were, consequently, up to one year behind Nokia Data in developing the necessary LAN expertise. Companies from the consumer group, on the other hand, were believed to be even further behind in developing networking expertise and, in addition, lacked the industry knowledge of the institutional companies, including Nokia Data. One Nokia Data executive commented that the company's two decades of experience in the banking and retail sectors and its ability to design solutions around hardware from other vendors were important factors in achieving the 35% and 25% market shares in the Nordic countries' banking and retail segments, respectively.

Nokia Data's other competitive strengths were believed to include the financial backing of a large parent, the Nokia Corporation, the company's small size, and its industry reputation as an ergonomic trend setter. Because of its smaller size, the company was thought to be more able to keep pace with the evolving industry trends than its larger competitors such as IBM. Furthermore, ergonomics, translated into improved user comfort and productivity, was proving to be a distinct advantage against smaller manufacturers as well as larger competitors from the institutional group. As an example, Goran Hermannson pointed to the fact that Ericsson, although not a technological forerunner, had pioneered the separate keyboard and the tilt-and-swivel screen on personal computers. A more recent innovation was

Nokia Data's positive display screen with sharp black characters on a paper-white background, designed to reduce eye strain.

Despite these advantages, Yrjänä Ahto, vice president of marketing communication, believed that Nokia Data was not sufficiently known outside the Nordic countries—meaning in some customers' opinion that it was "a risky company" to do business with. Furthermore, although top management considered Nokia Data's size to be an asset, some European country managers believed the company was too small and lacked the critical mass and resources to compete with big players like IBM.[4]

Future Strategy

Nokia Data's top management aimed to make the company a leading supplier of terminals, personal computers, LANs, and systems for the European business community. Management wanted to achieve this goal within the next five years and without acquisitions. The targeted turnover for 1993 was set at $2.5 billion, equally distributed between the Nordic countries and the rest of Europe. The targeted revenues represented an annual growth rate of 6% in the Nordic countries and 35% outside.

For the next three years, the company planned to concentrate on non-Nordic markets where it operated wholly owned subsidiaries. With the exception of minicomputers, Nokia Data planned to sell its full line in each market. Management believed that the company's own minicomputer, based on a proprietary operating system, was not competitive in a market that increasingly demanded multivendor connectivity.

Management also aimed to increase Nokia Data's presence outside the Nordic countries in its five target segments by following the product pathway shown in Exhibit 4, starting with the sale of terminals. Company executives believed that because customers had already made substantial investments with other companies in hardware, software, and training, any purchases from Nokia Data had to build on a client's existing systems. Also, because Nokia Data was not well known outside the Nordic countries, management believed that the first step had to be a perception by the customer that little, if any, risk was involved. Consequently, explained Yrjänä Ahto, terminals were the logical entry point with new clients, as they were far less complex than a LAN or a system and were considered less of a risk. "Thereafter," he explained, "as the company becomes better known and as customers upgrade terminals to personal computers and LANs, Nokia Data can move up the product line, growing in size and perceived ability to deliver at the upper end."

Within its five end-user segments, management planned to target the larger organizations with over 500 terminals tied to minicomputers or mainframes but with few personal computers. According to management, sales to large customers were the fastest way to generate volume and, when the client was a public organization like a local telephone company, for example, to build Nokia Data's image as a reliable supplier of computer products and services.

---

4. IBM Europe's operations included 15 plants in 6 countries, in addition to 9 R&D facilities, 7 scientific centers, and sales and service units in all markets. The company claimed a high degree of European content (92%) in its products and integrated manufacturing across the continent.

Since 1988, the company had undertaken an extensive European advertising campaign in local as well as international media, with the aim of improving its awareness level and consolidating its corporate image. Costing $14 million in 1988, the press advertisements promoted the company's products as "built by Europeans for Europeans." Headlined "For the European Generation," the standardized series of color advertisements promoted the company's Alfaskop brand. They appeared in the international editions of such magazines as *The Economist, Time, Newsweek,* and *Fortune.* (See Exhibit 9 for sample advertisements.)

Multidomestic Implementation

Nokia Data's senior management believed that a strong local identity and presence in each major European country was crucial to achieving the company's ambitious strategic goals. More specifically, top management aimed to decentralize decision making by adopting what they referred to as a "multidomestic" approach. This approach contrasted with pan-European integration and implied strong country management voice in local activities. According to senior managers, a multidomestic implementation of the company's expansion strategy would affect many aspects of its operations.

For example, activities such as product development, production, and marketing were to be delegated to the local organizations that had reached a minimum size. Local branding, in particular, was believed essential for a favorable local identity. Management believed that companies that used the same brand in every market did so to their detriment. "A local image," commented Ahto, "is simply not possible without a local brand—even for companies like IBM who manufacture in almost every European country." Similarly, local manufacturing was to allow the company to differentiate itself from the competition by more closely reflecting local tastes. Commented a top executive, "Ultimately, I only care about what the customer wants, whether that's a red terminal or a blue keyboard."

The main elements of the multidomestic approach are highlighted in the Case 2 appendix and are summarized in Exhibit 10. Nokia Data's multidomestic approach went counter to strategies adopted by others in the industry. For example, in 1988, Apple Computer began to integrate its European operations under the control of a stronger Paris headquarters. According to the company, Apple's national subsidiaries would continue to look after their own local markets while Paris looked for pan-European customers and transferred effective strategies regionwide. In the words of an Apple executive, "When one Apple company comes up with an excellent marketing scheme, it will be up to the Paris headquarters to try and get it introduced into other EC countries."[5]

Siemens also had recently restructured its operations for improved competitiveness outside of its home market, Germany. Referring to Siemens' aim to become a "true global player," one member of the top management was quoted as saying, "In five years, Siemens will be a completely different company. Among Europeans, we

5. *Business Marketing,* September 1988.

will be one of the most aggressive."[6] In recent advertisements, shown in Exhibit 11, the company had billed itself as "the top European computer company in the world market." On another front, IBM was recently capitalizing on the 1992 European integration issue by promoting the concept of integrated operations for a single European market. In a company-sponsored publication called "1992 Now," IBM Europe's president was quoted as saying, "in IBM, we manage our European manufacturing activities as if it were 1992."

Nokia Data's outspoken president, Kalle Isokallio, believed that a pan-European approach was "nonsense," as it assumed homogeneous European markets. He thought that the 1992-related harmonization might bring uniform technical standards, but buyer behavior would still be nationally oriented. To illustrate, Isokallio described a typical German customer as someone "who never buys a proto-type and signs nothing but a lengthy and detailed contract." In sharp contrast, he pointed to a typical French customer, "who is willing to try new, innovative products and sign a contract on the back of a Gauloise cigarette pack." The president ex-plained that in a nonhomogeneous EC, characterized by trends toward decentralized computing and narrow market segments, a manufacturer had to get close to its cus-tomer. Therefore, he emphasized, "local identity" was the key and required a mini-mum level of local production, some local development, and strong local brands.

As of early 1989, the company's local presence varied among markets. In Finland and Sweden, for example, management believed they were rightfully a "domestic" company because of local production, local development, and most important, local brands. "Yet," explained Ahto, "before we can claim to be domestic in the non-Nordic countries, we must reach a minimum size. After that we can start local production and introduce a local brand. But before we reach that critical mass, we will try to be 'European.'"

Management Discussions

Although Nokia Data management at all levels agreed with the strategic goal of long-term viability through rapid growth, there was less consensus on the specifics of how that might be achieved. For example, concerns were expressed at both the head-quarters and country organizations as to whether the company in the near future would be able to take advantage of the growth in the LANs and vertical systems. For one thing, some argued, the company did not enjoy the needed name recognition in most European markets to be considered a credible supplier of highly technical LANs or sophisticated vertical systems. Furthermore, others argued that, even where the company had an established reputation, as in most of the Nordic countries, it was more for terminals and personal computers than the more advanced LANs and systems. "We have too much of an ordinary hardware supplier image," complained Nils Wilborg, head of the Information Department in the Swedish country organization. On a related point, Ingvar Persson, vice president of product planning, explained that while competition centered on hardware in the 1970s and on software

6. *Business Week International*, February 20, 1989.

in the 1980s, the distinguishing feature in the future would be in services. "Yet," he emphasized, "the market views us as a hardware vendor, not a service provider."

Doubts were also expressed regarding the practicality of and the rationale behind the multidomestic approach. Jürgen Olschewski, the German managing director, believed that Nokia Data's small size in his country was a big obstacle to the company's becoming a full-fledged manufacturing, marketing, and service operation. Nevertheless, he agreed with top management that a strong German identity would be an asset in competing against firms with a nonlocal image such as IBM or Compaq. A few others wondered, on the other hand, if a multidomestic approach might not fragment the company too much for it to compete effectively against larger and more integrated competitors.

CONCLUSION

Nokia Data's top management were aware of the concerns among some of their colleagues regarding the company's future direction. Yet, they believed that Nokia Data's fortunes in a maturing industry depended on innovative thinking and quick action close to customers—elements they thought were inherent in their overall strategy for growth and a multidomestic approach. Explained Ahto, "Our plans for the future are in line with the corporate culture which we want to establish within Nokia Data—a culture which emphasizes profit performance, business orientation, speedy decision making and fast action. Doing business under tough conditions has always been fun at Nokia. We want to continue having fun in the future."

EXHIBIT 1 The Nokia Group of Companies

	Group sales (in $ millions)		
Industry segment	1988	1987	1986
Electronics			
Information Systems	1,170*	459	336
Telecommunications	359	364	197
Mobile Telephones	271	214	178
Consumer Electronics	1,432	678	441
Cables and Machinery			
Cables	557	529	438
Machinery	255	188	163
Electrical Wholesaling	245	180	75
Paper, Power, and Chemicals			
Paper	628	589	447
Chemicals	130	110	81
Rubber and Floorings			
Rubber Products	342	337	271
Floorings	75	64	51
Group Total*	5,237	3,500	2,519

Source: Company records.
*Less inter-division sales and sales between industry segments.

EXHIBIT 2 Nokia Data: Partial Organization Chart

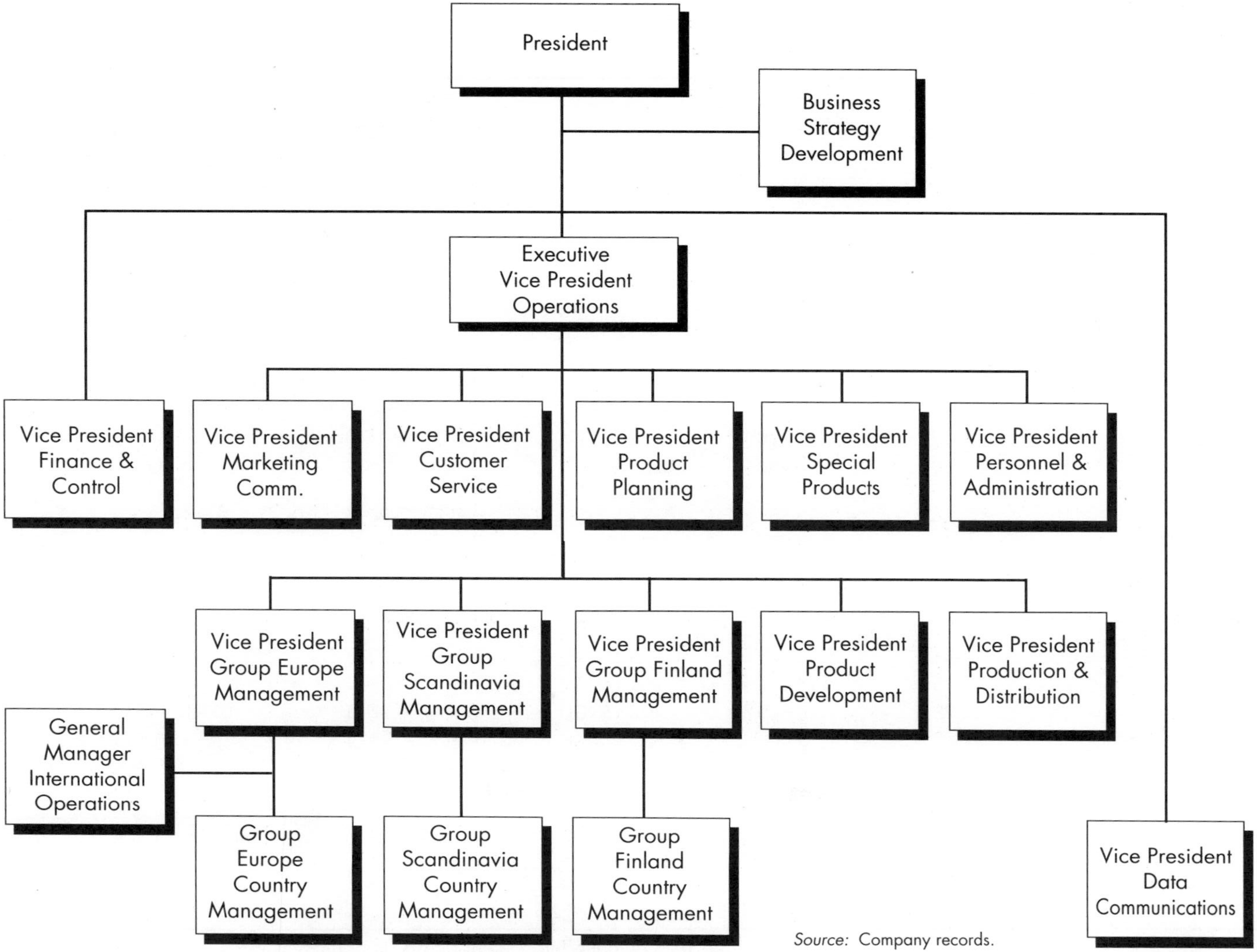

President

Business Strategy Development

Executive Vice President Operations

Vice President Finance & Control

Vice President Marketing Comm.

Vice President Customer Service

Vice President Product Planning

Vice President Special Products

Vice President Personnel & Administration

Vice President Group Europe Management

Vice President Group Scandinavia Management

Vice President Group Finland Management

Vice President Product Development

Vice President Production & Distribution

Vice President Data Communications

General Manager International Operations

Group Europe Country Management

Group Scandinavia Country Management

Group Finland Country Management

Source: Company records.

EXHIBIT 3 The 25 Largest Computer Companies Competing in Europe

1987 Rank	Company	Origin	Total revenue ($ millions, 1987)	European revenue ($ millions, 1987)	Europe as % of total	Estimated revenues from Nokia Data's industry sector[a]	Major European markets
1	IBM	United States	50,485.7	18,332.5	36	3520	F, D, I, UK
2	Siemens	Germany	5,703.0	4,961.6	87	357	D
3	Olivetti	Italy	4,637.2	3,802.5	82	1041	I, D, F
4	Digital (DEC)	United States	10,391.3	3,533.0	34	73	F, D, I, UK
5	Nixdorf	Germany	2,821.5	2,652.2	94	266	D, F, UK
6	Groupe Bull	France	3,007.5	2,345.8	78	30	F, E, UK
7	Unisys	United States	8,742.0	2,272.9	26	28	F, CH
8	Philips	Netherlands	2,601.6	2,055.2	79	271	NL, D, B, L
9	Hewlett-Packard	United States	5,000.0	1,800.0	36	0	F, D, I, UK
10	STC	UK	2,123.9	1,720.4	81	40	UK
11	NCR Corp.	United States	5,075.7	1,583.6	31	144	D, F, UK, NL
12	LM Ericsson[b]	Sweden	1,511.6	1,284.9	85	—	S, D, DK
13	Alcatel NV	France	2,052.1	1,272.3	62	229	F
14	Inspectorate	Switzerland	1,225.0	1,033.0	84	0	CH
15	Société Générale	France	970.1	970.1	100	0	F
16	Atlantic Computers	UK	959.7	892.7	93	0	UK
17	Honeywell Bull	United States	2,059.0	885.4	43	21	F, E, I, UK
18	Memorex Intl	Netherlands	1,041.1	832.9	80	54	D, NL
19	Wang Laboratories	United States	3,045.7	822.3	27	49	F, D, I, UK
20	Mannesmann AG	Germany	686.0	617.0	90	90	D
21	Apple Computer	United States	3,041.2	547.4	18	204	F, S
22	Cap Gemini Sogeti	France	682.3	545.8	80	0	F
23	Econocon Intl	Netherlands	674.3	525.9	78	0	NL
24	Amstrad plc	United Kingdom	533.0	501.0	94	250	UK, F, E
25	Amdahl Corp.	United States	1,505.2	493.1	33	0	F, D, I, UK

Source: Datamation, company records.

[a]Nokia Data's industry sector is defined as terminals, personal computers, LANs, and vertical systems installed in the company's five end-user segments.

[b]Figures are for year-end 1987, prior to Nokia Information System's acquisition of the Ericsson Data Systems Division. Following the acquisition by Nokia Data in 1988, parts of the company were sold off.

Country Codes:
B = Belgium
CH = Switzerland
D = Germany
DK = Denmark
E = Spain
F = France
I = Italy
L = Luxembourg
NL = Netherlands
S = Sweden
UK = United Kingdom

EXHIBIT 4 Nokia Data's Industry Sector: Product/Service Zones

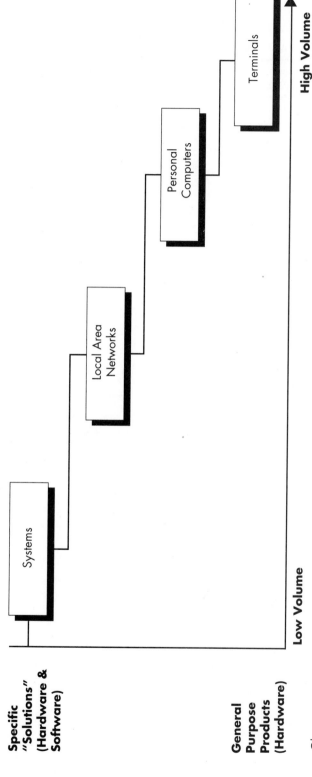

Glossary:

- All terminals and personal computers contained a keyboard plus a video screen.

- Terminals had no data processing ability of their own, were connected to a host computer, either a minicomputer or a mainframe, and were used primarily for entering, retrieving, or manipulating data.

- Personal computers had their own data processing capabilities and were used primarily on a "stand alone" basis but could also be connected to other computers.

- A local area network (LAN) was a connection of terminals and/or personal computers that allowd communication among users in the same "network."

- A system was a set of hardware to which tailor-made software had been added.

Source: Company records.

69

EXHIBIT 5 Nokia Data's Main Competitors

Company/product	Systems*	LANs	Personal computers	Terminals
IBM	All	X	X	X
Siemens	M, G, GB, I	X	X	X
Olivetti	B, R, GB	X	X	X
Digital (DEC)		X		X
Nixdorf	All	X		X
Bull	GB, M	X	X	X
Unisys	GB, M	X	X	X
Philips	B, I, M, GB	X	X	X
STC	GB, M	X		X
NCR	B, R	X	X	X
Alcatel				X
Memorex				X
Wang	GB	X	X	X
Mannesmann	All	X	X	
Apple	GB	X	X	
Amstrad				
Compaq		X	X	
Commodore			X	

Source: Company management.

*Nokia Data management defined systems competitors as those offering "solutions" in the company's five end-user segments. Yet, because management viewed the competition in terms of industry standards, proprietary systems, and horizontal product offerings, a number of the companies listed in Exhibit 3 were not seen as direct competitors.

Systems Code:
B = Banking
I = Insurance
R = Retail
M = Manufacturing
G = Government
GB = General Business

EXHIBIT 6 Nokia Data Sales Summary by Segment
($ millions, 1988)

Country	SF	S	DK	N	D	NL	E	UK	Others	Total	% Total
Retail	34.4	12.1	21.1	2.7	3.0	0	8.3	0	0	81.6	7
Banking/insurance	199.8	144.3	4.5	14.5	23.5	2.7	19.4	0.7	6.0	415.4	35
Manufacturing	75.4	92.3	9.7	11.0	25.0	15.9	13.6	24.5	9.4	276.8	24
Government	88.1	50.4	23.7	6.8	74.5	17.2	7.7	0.6	1.5	270.5	23
General business	106.0	3.3	4.3	4.1	5.3	1.2	1.5	0	0	125.7	11
Total	503.7	302.4	63.3	39.1	131.3	37.0	50.5	25.8	16.9	1,170.0	100
% Total	43	26	5	3	11	3	4	2	2	100	

Source: Company records.

Country Codes:
SF = Finland   NL = Netherlands
S = Sweden   E = Spain
DK = Denmark   CH = Switzerland
N = Norway   Others = Belgium, Italy, Austria, Portugal, Hong Kong, Australia
D = Germany

EXHIBIT 7 Nokia Data Sales Summary by Product and Service Category ($ millions, 1988)

Country	SF	S	DK	N	D	NL	E	UK	F	CH	Others	Total	% Total
Terminals	56.3	103.6	34.8	10.2	67.0	13.9	24.1	8.6	5.2	10.4	15.5	349.6	29.9
Personal computers	117.2	137.3	14.2	18.8	54.5	18.0	12.1	6.7	9.0	5.3	7.9	401.0	34.3
Peripherals	8.4	10.2	0.2	1.1	0	0.6	4.0	0	0	0	0	24.5	2.1
Minicomputers	56.0	30.2	8.6	7.5	2.1	2.2	5.8	8.6	2.2	0.3	2.9	126.4	10.8
LANs	10.7	13.7	2.9	0.6	3.5	0.9	1.2	0.9	0.2	0	0	34.6	2.9
Service and miscellaneous	226.2	1.5	1.2	0.3	1.2	0.9	2.4	0.2	0	0	0	233.9	20.0
Total	474.8	296.5	61.9	38.5	128.3	36.5	49.6	25.0	16.6	16.0	26.3	1,170.0	100
% Total	40.6	25.4	5.3	3.3	11.0	3.1	4.2	2.1	1.4	1.4	2.2	100	

Source: Company records.

Notes:
1. The service and miscellaneous figure for Finland includes sales of a large number of turnkey systems projects estimated at around $200 million in total.
2. Peripherals included specialized banking printers, plotters, and personal identification number (PIN) keyboards.

Country Codes:
SF = Finland
S = Sweden
DK = Denmark
N = Norway
D = Germany
NL = Netherlands
E = Spain
UK = United Kingdom
F = France
CH = Switzerland
Others = Belgium, Italy, Austria, Portugal, Hong Kong, Australia

EXHIBIT 8 Nokia Data Sales by Products Category (1988)

	$ Millions	Units	$ Average price
Terminals	349.6	161,106	2,170
Personal computers	401.0	125,312	3,200
Peripherals	24.5	21,993	1,114
Minicomputers	126.4	1,973	64,065
LANs	34.6	245	141,224*

*Includes related terminals, central processing equipment, and connections.

EXHIBIT 9

Alfaskop 386.
For the European Generation.

You know that 386 in the computer world means the same as a 3.8 litre engine in a 2.0 litre auto world.

You are a European business professional who has outgrown the standard PCs and is looking for the superior processing power and speed that only a 386 workstation can provide.

Alfaskop TT/386 and Alfaskop WS/386 are two new Scandinavian entries in the turbo class. Both of them super-fast PCs and powerful workstations in Local Area Networks.

Alfaskop workstations. Built by Europeans for Europeans.

NOKIA DATA

Nokia Data is a Scandinavian information technology group specializing in business computers, workstations and networks for the European business community. With more than 600,000 workstations already installed we rank among the biggest suppliers in Europe.

For the business professional, it is the opportunity to access and process the facts with a speed that can't be overestimated.

The ambitious curiosity of the increasingly well-educated young Europeans will change the world.

EXHIBIT 9 (continued)

Alfaskop Thinking.
For the European Generation.

Their thoughts about the future are of vital importance. And they will demand more power and influence than ever in the fulfilment of their ambitions.

You are an important individual.

You need a workstation that makes your job simpler, faster and more fun.

Alfaskop ergonomics.

And you need a workstation that can communicate with the other workstations in your company.

Alfaskop networking.

Alfaskop thinking is that ergonomics and networking is the best way to stimulate your individual creativity and ambitions.

The European solution for the European generation.

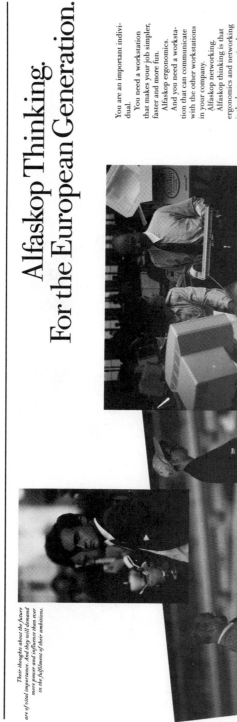

You'll be making result-oriented teams where individuality provides the motivation force.

What is happening is that today's personalities are already outpacing yesterday's professionals.

NOKIA DATA

Nokia Data is a Scandinavian information technology group specializing in business computers, workstations and networks for the European business community. With more than 600.000 workstations already installed we rank among the biggest suppliers in Europe.

Call Nokia Data: *Denmark* (02) 84 84 84 *Finland* (0) 5671 *France* (01) 4740 7107 *The Netherlands* (03480) 70810 *Norway* (02) 64 84 80 *Spain* (91) 457 1311 *Sweden* (08) 784 0000 *Switzerland* (01) 823 6310 *UK* (01) 409 2710 *West Germany* (0203) 60100

EXHIBIT 9 (continued)

Alfaskop Workstations.
For the European Generation.

They come in all sizes,
shapes and ages. Ambitious, creative, demanding.

Released individuality can be an elevating force in any business
organization.

Give them workstations
perfectly adapted to their taste, needs and demands.
And wonderful things will happen.

Don't accept dull conformity!
The result of your work depends on your competence, fantasy, creativity, individuality and ambition.

Your workstation is your workmate.

It should make everything easier, faster and more fun.

Alfaskop workstations are built by Europeans for Europeans.

There is one for every system environment and every individual need.

There is one for you.

NOKIA DATA

Nokia Data is a Scandinavian information technology group specializing in business computers, workstations and networks for the European business community. With more than 600,000 workstations already installed we rank among the biggest suppliers in Europe.

EXHIBIT 9 (continued)

Alfaskop Networking.
For the European Generation.

Your company is changing. The decisionmaking process is decentralized. The pace is mounting. The competition grows.

You must act!

The solution is networking. More and more people in your company will be able to share essential information. And fast information access and interchange may turn into your company's most competitive weapon.

Use it!

Alfaskop networks. A European solution made for European needs. Use it!

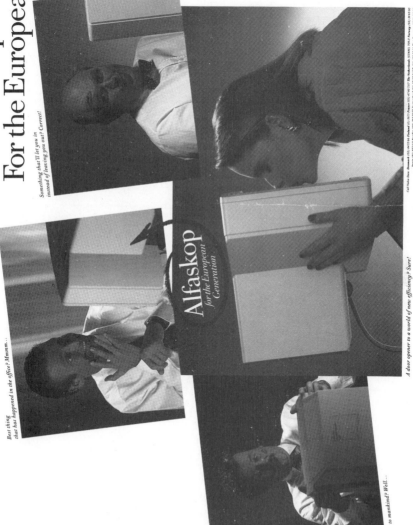

Something that'll let you in instead of leaving you out? Correct!

Best thing that has happened in the office? Mmmm...

Alfaskop *for the European Generation*

A door opener to a world of new efficiency? Sure!

A gift to mankind? Well...

EXHIBIT 10 Areas of Primary Management Responsibility*
A Multidomestic Approach

	Central	Local
R & D:		
Basic product design	X	
Applications software		X
Production:		
Procurement	Coordination	Purchasing
Manufacturing		X
Marketing:		
Advertising: general framework	X	
execution		X
Branding		X
Segmentation		X
Sales force		X
Distribution		X
Pricing (end-user price)		X
Servicing		X

Source: Company records.

*This chart refers to future division of responsibilities under a multidomestic approach.

EXHIBIT 11

SIEMENS

It's official:
Once again Siemens
ranks as Europe's No.1
in Computers

Every year the international computer magazine
"Datamation" publishes a table of the world's
leading Information Systems companies.
For the fourth year in succession, Siemens is No.1
in the European league and, as such, the top
European computer company in the world market.

This success can be attributed to four major
product groups:

● the BS2000 computers, which run under a single
  operating system – from small departmental computers right through to the largest mainframes.
● the SINIX™ multi-user system, Europe's best-
  selling UNIX™ computers.
● the Siemens Personal Computers – made in
  Europe, with a continually increasing share of the
  market.
● the digital office communications systems, which
  are at home throughout the world.

Each of these systems is the result of an intensive,
ongoing program of research and development.

Moreover, Siemens itself manufactures the
key components, being the sole European source,
of the Megabit chip – a chip for both the
world electronics market and Siemens computers.

If you would like to know more about
Siemens Computing, please write to Siemens AG,
Infoservice 134/Z560, P.O.Box 23 48,
D-8510 Fürth, Federal Republic of Germany.

Leading European-Based IS Companies

	Company	World IS Rev ($mil)
1	Siemens AG	$5,703.0
2	Ing. C. Olivetti & Co. SpA	4,637.2
3	Groupe Bull	3,007.5
4	Nixdorf Computer AG	2,821.5
5	NV Philips Gloeilampenfabrieken	2,601.6
6	STC plc	2,123.9
7	Alcatel NV	2,052.1
8	LM Ericsson	1,511.6
9	Inspectorate Intl. Ltd.	1,225.0
10	Memorex Intl.	1,041.1

Source: Datamation, August 1988

SINIX is the UNIX System derivative of Siemens.
UNIX is a registered trademark of AT&T.

**There's a Siemens Computer
for every business.**

CASE 2 APPENDIX

ELEMENTS OF NOKIA DATA'S MULTIDOMESTIC APPROACH

Research and Development

As Nokia Data implemented its multidomestic approach across Europe, management planned to consolidate basic product development such as video display and keyboards in Sweden. Market-specific development, such as language translation and application software, however, would all be performed locally.

Production

Management believed local manufacturing was one of the conditions needed for a local identity. Hence, Nokia Data planned to set up production facilities in each market once the company had achieved an economically viable minimum sales volume, estimated at around 50,000 personal computers or terminals annually. Sourcing of components was to be centralized in Sweden.

Segmentation

As of 1989, Nokia Data's penetration in each of its five primary segments varied considerably across different national markets. As part of local say in local strategies, country management would decide which of the five segments to concentrate on. Local management could also decide to develop a share of its business in segments not considered primary by Stockholm.

Branding

Management believed that the Mikko name in Finland and the Alfaskop name in Norway, Sweden, and Denmark were viewed by those markets as local brands with a local image. Outside of Scandinavia, management planned to introduce local brands but not until Nokia Data's corporate identity became better established. In each country, local brands were perceived to offer Nokia Data a decided advantage, especially over nonlocal international brands.

Communication

At the end of 1988, Nokia Data's subsidiaries used the same pictures, advertisements, and brochures, localized only through text translation. In the future, however, each subsidiary would work from a general framework defined in Stockholm, taking responsibility for local execution. Aside from local campaigns designed to promote local brands, Nokia Data headquarters would continue a Europe-wide, English-language corporate advertising campaign in international publications.

Distribution

Decisions regarding the use of VARs or sales agents and the extent of their contribution to local marketing were made at headquarters. In the future, as sales through such channels increased, local organizations would play a primary role in such decisions.

Pricing

As in the past, future pricing decisions at Nokia Data would be the responsibility of country managers. Aside from pricing in accordance with market conditions, local organizations were to pay Stockholm a transfer price set at their market price, less the local margin of 30 to 40%. However, no central control on local pricing was foreseen.

Customer Service

In the past, Nokia had maintained more service points than sales offices in a local market—a factor that management believed helped to reassure customers of speedy availability of help when needed. In the future, that policy would not change. But, under local management, the customer services concept was to be broadened to incorporate "Careware," a comprehensive package designed to meet the total needs of most clients.

The Careware Concept, formulated in Stockholm for implementation in local organizations, went beyond normal after-sales service and included presales consulting, planning and testing, installation, and technical and educational services. Careware was divided into six groups of "Customer Service Products." The following list represents the content of Careware Services.

NOKIA DATA'S CUSTOMER CAREWARE

Operational Services

Education and Training
Systems Evaluation
Network Services
On-site Service Representative
Total Customer Service Responsibility
System Security Services
Standby Customer Service
Safety Tests and Checkups
Terminal Cleaning

Installation Services

Project Management and Administration
Cabling
Product Installation
Customizing

Nokia On-Site/Remote Services

Customer Carry-In Services

Nokia Software Services

Nokia Time and Material Service

PART TWO

FORMULATING GLOBAL MARKETING STRATEGY

In a world characterized by isolated country markets, strategy making is a relatively simple process: Each subsidiary management is responsible for developing a marketing strategy that reflects the peculiarities of its local market and delivers the financial returns the parent expects from its investment in that country. As a relatively self-sufficient group, local managers decide what products to market, to whom, and how. Typically, as long as the financial targets are met, headquarters stays out of the picture, their rationale being that the local managers know what is best for their market.

This oversimplified picture is still true for many firms that operate internationally. The forces that were highlighted in the introduction to Part One, however, are changing the dynamics of many markets and complicating the strategy-making process. Both country-by-country and decentralized decision making are less and less appropriate for companies that are operating in markets with disappearing boundaries. For example, major computer firms are having to deal with an increasing number of multinational customers who aim to buy from one vendor worldwide and expect special discounts on volume purchases, a consistent level of service everywhere, and coordinated vendor contacts around the world. Nothing short of a central strategy for such global accounts and a closely knit network of local sales and service operations worldwide can satisfy the needs of this segment.

Many manufacturers have learned the hard way that uncoordinated local pricing can provoke transshipments of trade stocks from low-price countries to high-price ones. This is true for many product categories where the cost of transportation relative to the price is small and where information regarding local prices can be readily obtained. Such "parallel trade" or the "gray market," as the phenomenon is often called, is a growing problem for a variety of firms in such diverse sectors as chemicals, photographic equipment and supplies, consumer electronics, and car and truck tires. The rise in multinational wholesale establishments, central procurement by customers, and improved international communication are the engines behind the "gray market."

In response to forces of globalization, companies are reexamining their strategy-making process and proactively taking advantage of the opportunities that lie in internationally coordinated or standardized marketing practices. When done well, such global strategies build competitive advantage. Consider the following two success stories:

- The American company Johnson Wax was able to improve its European standing in the highly competitive household cleaning market through a major program that reduced and standardized brands and product variety across the continent. Savings of as much as 15% in manufacturing and inventory handling costs resulted from unifying product ingredients. In one area alone, more than 20 perfume varieties were reduced to 7. The payoffs were bigger discounts in raw materials purchases, longer production runs, and lower finished goods inventory levels. The rationalization program also made it possible to operate the company's main European plant with about one-half the personnel.

- Unilever's best-selling Cif, a liquid abrasive cleaner, was a wonderful technical discovery but without a market before the company's management in France found an effective way to position the product and communicate its unique customer benefit. Previous attempts by the Dutch-British company to emphasize the "cleaning" power of the product had failed to draw enough users away from the dominant powder cleaners. The French company discovered that a "scratch-free" positioning was appealing to a large segment of customers who normally abstained from using powder to clean polished surfaces such as ceramics and stainless steel. A TV commercial showing a rotating skater scratching the surface of the ice was instrumental in making the product a major success in France.

Following the French triumph, and using the same positioning and communication strategy, Unilever's U.K.-based headquarters led a rollout of the brand throughout the rest of Europe and as far away as Japan. There was no need to reinvent a good wheel. To management's delight, the initial success repeated itself everywhere, making Cif one of Unilever's most profitable brands.

These two examples show how a streamlined marketing strategy or a well-coordinated implementation can save millions in costs (Johnson Wax) or can earn millions in improved market acceptance (Unilever). Either way, through improved *efficiency* or enhanced marketing *effectiveness,* a firm can upgrade its posture vis-à-vis the competition.

In this introduction to Part Two, we will examine the strategic issues in global marketing from a variety of vantage points. First, we will review the elements of strategy by focusing on issues salient to global marketing decisions. The aim is to explore decision areas in which a firm might build competitive advantage by improving its internal efficiency or enhancing its external effectiveness. Next, we will examine several components of marketing analysis that can help in formulating well-informed strategic decisions. Then, we will deal with the process of decision making in a global corporate context by introducing a framework for delineating central and local management contributions to marketing strategy. Here, we highlight the importance of a flexible corporate "decision-making map" that is responsive to changing market forces. Finally, we will offer a number of guidelines that can help in arriving at a productive balance between center-dominated and subsidiary management decisions.

GLOBAL MARKETING DECISIONS

The strategic issues facing a global marketer are of two kinds: (1) issues that are "generic" to marketing decision making in general and (2) others that are special to marketing in a global context. The issue of skimming versus penetration pricing for a new product is an example of the "generic" category. The choice of one or the other could have a limited single-country focus or a wide-spread international scope. On the other hand, the issue of developing standard global products versus modified local adaptations is specific to marketing in an international context. Single-country decisions follow only after these global choices.

This section deals with decisions that are specific to global marketing. They are organized around the five building blocks of a marketing strategy: segmentation, product line, communication, distribution, and pricing. Our aim is not to be exhaustive but selective, highlighting only those dimensions that have a particular relevance to marketing decisions in a global context.

Segmentation   The issues of segmentation have to do with grouping dispersed countries into meaningful clusters and with the desirability or practicality of targeting in different country markets groups of customers who have similar profiles and/or behavior:[1] The questions to be addressed include the following:

- What criteria (such as per capita income, size, culture, climate, etc.) should be used to group countries into meaningful clusters for strategy making?
- What are the relevant dimensions for segmenting the market within a country or across several countries?

- To what extent should these dimensions be country-specific, regional, or even global?
- If the dimensions are country-specific, are the segments large enough to be served economically?
- If the dimensions are regional or global, is it practical or economical to carve out segments that cut across many country markets?

Product Line   Issues in product policy deal with the opportunities that might exist in a unified approach to different country markets. The broad choice of global standardization versus local adaptation is at the core of these issues. Product-line decisions are based on answers to the following questions:[2]

- Should new product development be centrally directed or managed by individual subsidiaries?
- If new product development is centrally directed, to what extent should resources be channeled to product concepts with a global appeal as opposed to country-specific features?
- To what extent do global product designs offer an advantage, economic or otherwise, over local products?
- What are the benefits or risks of leaving branding and packaging decisions in the hands of local management?
- How much would an internationally standard policy on support services improve the customer-perceived value of the product or service offering?

Communication   Communication through media advertising or personal selling is often transmitted to the target audiences locally. However, relevant questions remain as to the need or practicality of having some degree of central direction concerning what is communicated and how communication is executed.[3]

The following key issues in *advertising* have to be addressed:

- Are the customer-perceived benefits derived from the product or service the same everywhere?
- If so, should the advertising message be essentially the same internationally, emphasizing similar themes or customer benefits?
- Can a successful campaign in one market be transferred elsewhere?
- What are the opportunities or risks in locally led advertising?
- Are there advantages in using a single advertising agency internationally, or should agency selection be left to the subsidiaries?

The following key issues in *personal selling* also have to be addressed:

- Are buying and selling processes essentially the same in different countries?
- If so, can the role of the sales force within the marketing strategy, leading to specific prescribed selling activities, be defined the same way everywhere?
- Can sales force performance be improved by adopting similar sales management policies (such as in recruitment and training, sales force organization, compensation, performance evaluation, etc.) in different subsidiaries?
- What are the advantages and drawbacks in centralizing the personal selling function for multinational accounts?
- What are the opportunities and problems in centralizing certain aspects of sales support functions, such as technical assistance or defining product specifications for customized solutions?

Distribution Issues in distribution revolve around several concerns, including speed and cost of market entry, concentration and growth among multinational channels of distribution, the level of channel power, and the quality of customer service.[4] More specifically, the following issues have to be examined:

- In entering new markets, what are the trade-offs between establishing one's own distribution network versus utilizing existing local channels of distribution? Which provides a faster coverage or a less costly distribution?
- What are the implications of trends in internationalization of wholesaling and retailing for marketing decisions in general, and the cost and effectiveness of distribution in particular?
- How is the balance of channel control vis-à-vis wholesale or retail establishments changing regionally or globally? What are the implications of such trends for a global marketer?
- What are the benefits or risks in acquiring local agents as a move to upgrade the distribution function or as a defense against similar actions by local or global competitors?
- How important is the customer service function to the activities performed by local distributors? Should a standard global policy toward such services be adopted, or should such decisions be delegated to local management?

Pricing With an immediate impact on profitability, pricing remains at the forefront of marketing decisions that preoccupy global marketers. Issues in this area involve trade-offs between centrally administered policies and local decisions, risks and impacts of parallel trade, and administration of regional or global price coordination, including policies on transfer prices, pricing for multinational clients, and the use of price as an offensive or defensive tool.[5] The following represent the more specific issues that have to be addressed:

- Given regional or global trends among customers, distributors, and competitors, what are the opportunities or drawbacks of coordinating local prices centrally?

- If prices are set to fit local conditions, what are the risks and costs of potential parallel trade from low-price to high-price countries?

- What should be the pricing policy toward multinational clients, with or without a central buying function?

- If some degree of regional or global price coordination is deemed desirable, what should be the mechanisms for administering such coordination? When the product is centrally manufactured, what policies on transfer pricing are most appropriate?

- In competition against key rivals, should aggressive local pricing be used selectively to improve share position one market at a time? On the other side, how should a company defend itself against the predatory pricing of a local or global competitor in key markets?

GLOBAL MARKETING ANALYSIS

Effective marketing decisions—that is, those that help firms fulfill their customers' needs and improve their competitive standing—follow from insightful analysis. Such analysis enables managers at the outset to shape a strategy that reflects the forces operating in the market and allows managers over time to adapt the strategy to the changing dynamics of these forces. It is through insightful analysis that a firm can identify opportunities for upgrading its internal efficiency and/or external market effectiveness—the two dimensions of strategic advantage. Systematic marketing analysis, both at the center as well as at the local market level, is thus indispensable to decision making in complex, competitive environments. Without it, the marketer is embarking on a hazardous journey lacking adequate preparation.

As with global marketing decisions, it is useful to classify marketing analysis into certain analytical modes for further examination. For this reason, we have grouped the different areas of strategic analysis into five analytical modes: customers, competitors, company (own firm), trade, and government. A thorough understanding of these areas contributes to strategy making that is in line with market and corporate realities. Exhibit 2.1 graphically depicts the strategic marketing decisions and their analytical underpinnings. To appreciate the contribution that insights from sound analysis can make to management decisions, we will briefly examine each of the five modes of global marketing analysis.

Customers A safe place to start any marketing analysis is at the customer level. A good analyst often tries to "creep" into the mind of the potential customer to see the world—including the marketer's own firm and its offerings, as well as those of competition—through the customer's eyes. A global marketer must by necessity perform this analysis through the vantage points of several customer groups in different parts of the world. Neither their differences nor their similarities can be taken for granted: Each group of customers must first be understood on its own right before any generalizations can be made. For example, household detergent companies have learned that in theory, while product concepts, formulation, and packaging might be transferable from one market to another, in practice, strong cultural preferences for different types of fragrances make transfers of finished products nearly impossible. Likewise, makers of coffee have had to deal with major or minor differences among their consumers internationally. Nescafé, a global brand of coffee from Swiss-based Nestlé, is formulated in more than 70 different flavors to accommodate the different local consumer preferences around the world. At the other extreme, IKEA, the furniture company mentioned in the introduction to Part One, has succeeded in carving out around the world a more or less uniform segment of

EXHIBIT 2.1 Global Marketing Strategy: Decisions and Analysis

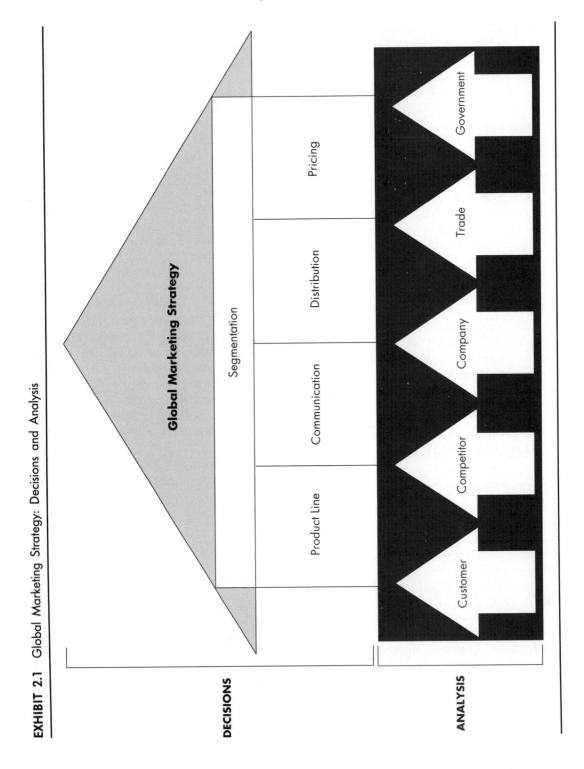

consumers whose similar needs and purchasing behavior outweigh their demographic or cultural differences.

The following questions raised in global consumer analysis are examples of those that have to do with understanding customer characteristics, purchasing behavior, and attitudes in each local market and across markets:

- What are the consumer demographics in target countries? How does consumer purchasing power differ from one market to another?

- How often do consumers buy our products? How and when do they use them? Are there significant similarities among national markets in the way our products are purchased or used?

- What cultural norms might help or hinder our marketing practices?

- How open are potential consumers to innovations coming from the outside? How open are they to purchasing from foreign companies? How do they see us vis-à-vis local competitors?

- For industrial goods, what local organizational buying practices should be taken into account? How do buyers compare global vendors with local competitors?

Competitors In highly contested markets, a strategy must reflect the nature and intensity of the competition. The acid test of a sound strategy is not only how well it meets the target customers' needs—as central as this first test is—but also how effectively it enables the firm to *outperform* the other players in the marketplace. Informed competitor analysis can lead to shrewd strategies that exploit a rival's vulnerabilities. To illustrate, MCL, a disguised name for a U.S.-based manufacturer of medical diagnostic products, was able to drive its main Japanese rival for sonar fetal scanning equipment out of international markets thanks to a highly insightful analysis of the competitor's

strengths and weaknesses. The Japanese firm had been challenging the U.S. company's global dominance in this product category by selling its equipment worldwide to hospitals and clinics at significant discounts below MCL's prices. An analysis of the Japanese product and service records conducted by MCL management showed that the competitor's technology was less reliable and had a product failure rate several times that of MCL's scanner. MCL's high price, the analysts concluded, could be justified *if* the reliability feature were made more apparent to the quality-sensitive customers. Accordingly, a decision was made to increase the product's warranty period from one year, which was the standard in the industry, to an unprecedented five years. The assumption underlying this unheard of action was that the Japanese rival could neither match the longer warranty period, as it was too expensive to do so for its less reliable product, nor reduce prices any further, as it was already selling at narrow margins. The results proved that the analysts were right. Two years after the adoption of the new policy, MCL had regained its lost market share worldwide, forcing the Japanese competitor into receivership.

Questions in competitor analysis have to do with understanding the strategies and the relative posture of rivals, both locally and globally:

- Who are our direct and indirect competitors? Who competes with us locally? Regionally? Globally? How is this picture likely to change in the future?

- What are the main features of the strategies pursued by the competition? Or, expressed differently, how does the competition try to win orders and outperform others, including us?

- For local competitors, what are their strengths vis-à-vis us or other global players? Are there significant advantages to being locally owned? Are there weaknesses?

- For regional or global competitors, how integrated are their strategies across national markets? Are they taking advantage of their regional or global network to outdistance themselves from us or from local rivals? How?

- How can we exploit the weaknesses of our competitors? Can we realistically match their strengths? Based on what we know about their history and current management, how are they likely to react to our moves?

Company The other side of the spectrum in customer and competitor analysis is an assessment of one's own relative standing in the market. The aim of such an analysis is to base the firm's marketing strategy on areas of corporate strength and avoid taxing areas of weakness. MCL's strategy was built precisely on the company's unique strength—that is, its superior product technology translated into client-perceived reliability. As another example, Del Monte, the U.S.-based marketer of canned fruits and juices, was able to formulate a highly successful international advertising campaign based on a multicountry consumer survey that highlighted the brand's strengths and weaknesses in the canned fruit category. The research had discovered that while consumers used canned fruits differently in different markets (e.g., with cream topping in the U.K.; without it, elsewhere), Del Monte was a known brand and uniformly acknowledged to be among the best in the category. The research also revealed that despite its reputation the brand's consumer loyalty was low and that consumers were increasingly opting for price-oriented private labels. To build on the brand's high levels of international awareness and consumer franchise, and also to explain why Del Monte "deserved" a premium price, a TV advertising campaign that communicated the freshness of Del Monte's canned products *without* showing how they were actually used was formulated. Called "The Man from Del Monte," the commercial emphasized the same-day packing of fruits under the uncompromising control of a Del Monte inspector. A highly successful commercial, it was shown in several countries in Europe and

the Middle East, with only the words translated into local languages. The communication strategy proved effective because it was built on important insights from factual self-analysis.

Lead questions in company analysis attempt to portray an objective picture of the firm:

- What is our current competitive profile vis-à-vis local and global rivals? What unique areas of competence do we enjoy? What other strengths do we have? In what areas are we weak?

- How are we perceived by our customers or members of the trade in local markets? Is the "global" nature of our company perceived as an advantage or a disadvantage?

- Is our current global strategy in line with our competitive posture in individual markets? Is the strategy building on areas of verified strength and shoring up on weaknesses?

- How can we turn our global scope into competitive advantage? Are there areas in which we are not exploiting the economies of scale that come with our global size? How well and how fast do we transfer innovations globally? What are the areas in which we can still do better by improving internal efficiency or external market effectiveness?

- How does the current profile of our management compare with those of our competitors? Do we have the skills needed locally and in headquarters to implement our chosen strategy? Is our organizational structure in line with the strategy? How can it be improved to help with implementation?

Trade Members of the channel of distribution are another market force that must be dealt with in strategy making. Like customers or competitors, they cannot be taken for granted. Rather, they must be understood in every market in which the firm is operating. Many otherwise successful global companies, for example, have failed in Japan because they did not understand or adapt to the intricacies of that country's fragmented and complex distribution channels. Or, in Europe, more and more consumer goods manufacturers are observing with justified apprehension a regionwide consolidation in retailing. The resulting decrease in the number of retail chains and the corresponding increase in the remaining chains' bargaining power are forcing firms to reexamine many elements of their marketing strategies, including branding policies, pricing, and allocation of funds to consumer advertising and trade promotion. A correct analysis of the implications of this evolving distribution picture would place companies in a far superior position competitively. As still another example, Apple Computer's success in Europe is due largely to its strategy of building a strong franchise network at the retail level. While many of the company's larger rivals have struggled with the distribution of their personal computers, Apple correctly understood from the beginning the important role that members of the local trade could play in achieving rapid market penetration. Others have only recently reached the same conclusion.

Questions in trade analysis have to do with understanding the role, the influence, and the impact that members of the distribution channel might have on a firm's marketing performance:

- What is the structure of distribution channels in local markets? How fragmented or concentrated is the volume of trade among members? How "open" is the trade to a new source of supply?

- What functions do existing members of the trade perform for the manufacturers? At what cost? Can a manufacturer perform some of these functions at less cost or more effectively?

- How is the customer's decision influenced by the local retailer for consumer goods or by sales agents for industrial products? How can a manufacturer help to improve

customer-distributor interaction to its advantage?

- What is the relative power of brand holders (manufacturers) vis-à-vis members of the trade? How is this balance changing? How could brand holders gain added bargaining power? How can we best transfer our experience with the local trade from one market to other markets?

- Are members of the trade becoming multinational or even global? Are there advantages to be gained over local or global competitors by dealing with the multinational trade on a centralized basis?

Government Although, generally speaking, world economies have been moving toward greater liberalization of commerce and trade, the trend has not always meant a diminished role of national governments in the local economy. Indeed, in some sectors the active role of public authorities has remained unchanged or has been on the rise. These sectors include certain agricultural products and basic foods, as well as pharmaceuticals, air transportation, banking, and arbitrarily designated "strategic industries"—for example, energy and telecommunication—to name a few. Besides being affected by the continuing role of the state in the economy, global companies have traditionally been easy targets for local government policymakers. Motivated by nationalism or by a desire to protect locally owned firms from the threat of global competition, host governments in both developed and developing countries have often intervened in the affairs of foreign concerns with relative impunity. To illustrate, a few years ago the French government came to the aid of local manufacturers of home video machines by creating a nearly impossible entry barrier for their Japanese rivals. The government's policy tool was deceivingly simple and innocuous: French customs announced that all imports of video equipment had to pass through a small and understaffed customs office, a process that would easily consume months before any imported goods could be released. The order was lifted several months later, however, when the Japanese agreed to a self-imposed quota on their exports to France. In addition to such tactics of protectionism, governments are also known to aid local firms—through straight subsidies, tax breaks, or other incentives—in getting and maintaining a foothold in foreign markets. Japan's Ministry of International Trade and Industry (MITI) has often been accused of materially assisting Japanese firms in their global expansion—an accusation that MITI, as well as the companies, has consistently denied.

For the reasons just cited, the influence of national governments on a firm's global strategy or its implementation in local markets cannot and should not be ignored. Through an analysis of the real or potential impact of government policies and actions, global firms can be better prepared for dealing with this powerful force.

Lead questions of analysis focus on a country's political climate, the government's policy objectives, and the means of resolving potential conflicts:

- What is the current political climate in the country? What is the official attitude toward foreign companies and their activities? How are local politics likely to change? What impact are such changes likely to have on our operation in the country?

- What policy objectives are driving the government's actions? Protection of local companies? Promotion of economic development? Increasing local value added? Protection of local consumers? Expanding tax revenues or reducing public expenditures? Other objectives?

- How can our local operation help the authorities to meet some or all of their objectives? Are there areas of overlapping interest where our strategies and their objectives coincide? In what areas can we reach a compromise? Where should we stand firm on our position and objectives?

- When entering into negotiations with the authorities, is there an ideal outcome we should aim for? What is a minimum acceptable outcome that we would be satisfied with? Who should lead the negotiations— local management or headquarters? If local management, what assistance can we provide from the center? If headquarters, what should be local management's role? What lessons have we learned from dealings with governments in other markets that might help in this case?

- What other organizations—private or public, inside or outside of the country—might be interested in the outcome of our discussions with the government? What assistance might these interested bodies give us in advancing our objectives vis-à-vis the policy-makers?

DECISION-MAKING MAP

It should be evident by now that strategy making in the complex global environment involves more than treating the world as one homogeneous marketplace. What makes global marketing a much more complex process than multidomestic marketing—where key decisions are for the most part left in the hands of local management—is the fact that not all industries or marketing decisions lend themselves to direction by headquarters management. In many markets where significant differences still exist among different countries, as in indigenous food product categories, the room for headquarters-dominated and internationally coordinated marketing is limited. Even where opportunities for coordination or standardization are present, as in many consumer or industrial goods, not all marketing decisions lend themselves equally well to international streamlining. Many decisions, such as those requiring rapid response to customer demands or those involving local tactics, are still best made locally by managers close to those markets. Global marketing thus involves important choices as to *who* decides *what* and *where*.

Exhibit 2.2 graphically depicts the key choices for a global marketer. Simplified to highlight the key dimensions, the horizontal axis shows the decisions related to a marketing program—for example, branding, positioning, pricing, and so forth. This axis includes all the elements from major and strategic to minor and tactical. The vertical axis, on the other hand, defines where and by whom those decisions are made, whether centrally by regional or worldwide headquarters, or locally by country management. The decision-making space defined by the two axes is further divided by a line delineating the degree of influence that local and central management, respectively, exert on individual decisions. The shaded area above this "strategy line" defines the "global" influence where central coordination plays a role. The area below the line defines the extent of "local" influence on decisions. In the example shown, branding and product development are "global" decisions, primarily influenced by central management. On the other hand, such tasks as pricing and sales promotions are delegated primarily to local management. Positioning and advertising fall into the "joint decision" area, where final decisions are the outcome of dialogue and discussion between central and local management and where both country-specific as well as international considerations come into play. In this example, no single decision is strictly global or local: Both local and headquarters management are involved; only the extent of their influence on the various decisions is different.

Using the above model to illustrate other scenarios, Exhibit 2.3 contrasts a multidomestic decision-making map of a consumer packaged goods firm with that of a global approach adopted by a major computer company. In the former case, the internationally coordinated or standardized decisions are few: Only branding has to conform to a worldwide policy; other marketing decisions are left largely to local considerations. In contrast, the computer firm insists on tight coordination of many decisions among its subsidiaries. Sales and service operations are the only areas in which the local management exerts high influence. As these two examples show, the sequence of individual decisions on the horizontal axis, combined with the location and slope of the strategy line, determines the degree to which a strategy is essentially locally based, hence multidomestic or global.

As a strategy evolves over time, so does the decision-making map of the marketer. To illustrate, Nestlé, the world's largest food company, has traditionally followed a multidomestic approach, allowing local managers to enjoy a great deal of freedom in designing and implementing their own local marketing strategies. In the unwavering opinion of management, due to the local nature of the competition, as well as to diverse national market conditions, the company was best served by leaving key strategic and tactical decisions in the hands of those closest to the markets—the local managers. Except in a few areas, such as branding and packaging, headquarters stayed out of local activities and saw its primary roles as "cross-fertilizing" and "persuading" local managers to adopt certain common practices. For almost all decisions, however, local management had the final say. Nestlé's traditional approach to decision making is depicted by strategy line A in Exhibit 2.4.

Strategy making at Nestlé is slowly undergoing change. Recently, regional and corporate managers are exerting more influence on key decisions, due to a number of factors, including a consolidation in international competition, the appearance of "global niches" of food consumers with similar profiles and behavior, and a perceived need to rationalize manufacturing operations within Europe and other regions. As such, the multidomestic line A of Exhibit 2.4 is gradually shifting downward toward line B, thus signaling more headquarters say on issues. The shift to more integration symbolizes Nestlé's response to its changing global environment and is likely to continue for years to come.

EXHIBIT 2.2 Decision-making Map: Global vs. Local Influence

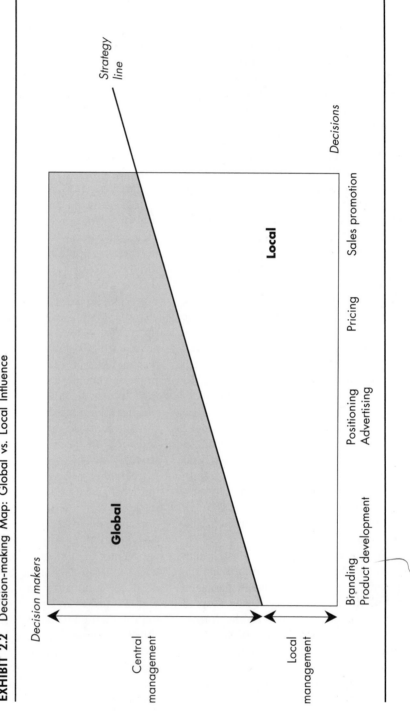

EXHIBIT 2.3 Contrasting Scenarios in Marketing Strategy

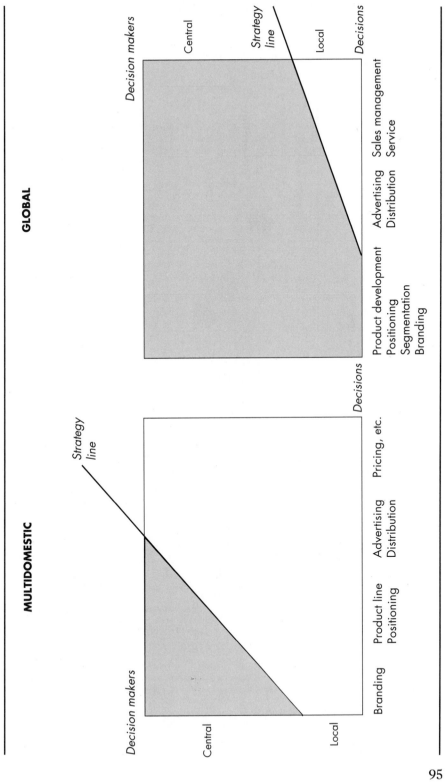

EXHIBIT 2.4 Evolving Strategy Making at Nestlé

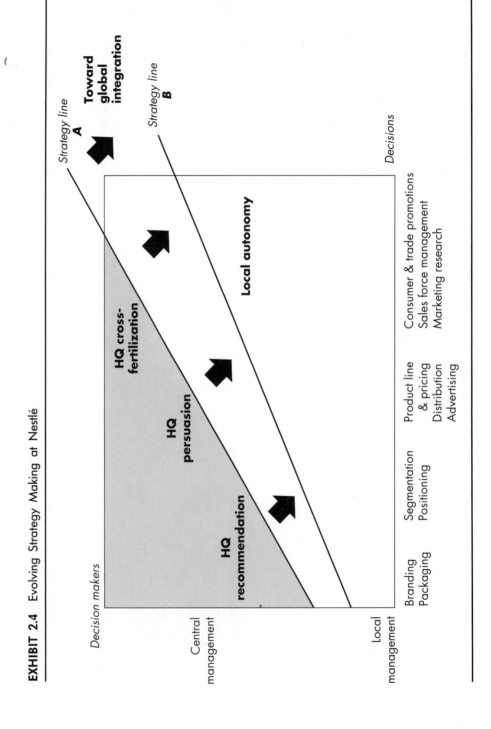

LOCAL VERSUS GLOBAL DECISIONS

In designing a strategy-making process that best fits the competitive and market requirements of a firm, the global marketer must make an assessment as to the extent that commonalities among national markets can be exploited. Where there are important commonalities and where these can be leveraged for improved efficiency or effectiveness, there is room for centrally driven marketing. Where no such commonalities are present, a locally driven approach is most appropriate.

Even when there are significant commonalities that can potentially be exploited, a global marketer must still discriminate between those decisions that should be made centrally and those that are best left to the discretion of subsidiary management. This last distinction is critical to the success of the overall strategy, as it addresses a typical headquarters dilemma—how to benefit from central strategy making without losing local market responsiveness.

What decision areas best lend themselves to central direction? What areas do not? Although it is impossible to make a general rule that applies in all cases, one may attempt to group decisions into high- and low-potential categories, depending on their general propensity for benefiting from central direction. Exhibit 2.5 lists some of the more important dimensions of the high- and low-potential decision areas. These are described below.[6]

HIGH-POTENTIAL DECISION AREAS

Decision areas that enjoy one or more of the following features are likely to benefit from central direction:

- *Savings*. Where significant economies of scale exist in combining individual country activities, as might be the case in manufacturing of similar products, new product development, or advertising production costs for an international brand.

- *Size*. Where relatively large critical mass is prerequisite to quality and productivity, as in certain R&D activities, marketing research, or training.

- *Spillover*. Where practices in one individual market impact others, as might be the case in pricing of an internationally branded product or advertising with cross-border reach, as in satellite broadcasts.

- *Expertise*. Where a core of highly specialized know-how critical to the activity cannot be duplicated in every country, as in the case of major overhauls of highly sophisticated machinery like jet engines or gas turbines.

- *Global Accounts*. Where the activity impacts the same customer in different locations around the world, as in the case of major international clients of a bank with an extensive international network of branches.

LOW-POTENTIAL DECISION AREAS

Decision areas that are characterized by one or more of the following features are *unlikely* to benefit from central direction; they are better candidates for local decision making:

- *Speed*. Where the speed of reaction to customer needs or competitive action is critical to success, as in quick repair services for industrial machinery or pricing in highly volatile local market conditions.

- *Customization*. Where much of the value added is through customization of the product or service to specific client needs, as in systems definition and application development for computers.

- *Service*. Where personal service is a major part of the activity, as in consultative selling that combines gaining in-depth knowledge of the customer problem with sales of tailored solutions.

EXHIBIT 2.5 Global Decisions

High Potential	Low Potential
Major economies of scale	Response time critical
Critical mass important	Value added close to the customer
High cross-border impact	High service content
Special know-how or expertise	Short-lived tactics
Multinational account management	Local trade activities

- *Tactics.* Where short-lived measures are used to address specific local issues, such as in consumer promotions.
- *Trade.* Where activities are carried out in conjunction with local channels of distribution, as in cooperative advertising or trade promotions.

BALANCE AND ADAPTATION

The previous discussion has advanced a number of points that need to be underscored. First, global strategy combines *both* centrally directed and locally initiated decisions. What sets global marketing apart from multidomestic marketing is not the presence or absence of headquarters influence, but its degree of impact on the strategy. The line separating the two forms of strategy is a fine one indeed. Second, global strategy making is a selective process and focuses on those decisions that exploit market commonalities and can be leveraged to yield competitive advantage. The truth is that in any marketing context not all decisions are equally critical to building and sustaining competitive advantage. Global strategy identifies those decisions that are pivotal and exploits their potential. Third, global marketing does not always lead to standardized practices across local markets. Where simple harmonization of local practices offers the desired results, such as in regional coordination of pricing for a commodity chemical, standardization would be unnecessarily burdensome and even counterproductive. Finally, not all marketing activities are good candidates for central decision

making. Global marketing strategy can still benefit from many activities that are initiated and implemented by local management.

Thus, the success of global marketing depends on the balance it maintains among different but interrelated elements—the balance between central and local management influence on individual decisions, between centrally controlled pivotal decisions and others, between tight standardization and loose coordination, and between headquarters-led activities and local initiatives. The success of global marketing also depends on how well this delicate balance is adapted over time to the changing market and competitive conditions. If trade promotions, for example, are handled in a decentralized manner, the growth in multinational channels may make such locally decided practices less and less appropriate. Similarly, but going in the opposite direction, a regionally coordinated pricing policy may have to be selectively sacrificed to counter the predatory pricing attacks of a competitor in a key subsidiary market. An effective global strategy, therefore, is a moving target: It requires constant vigilance to ensure that it stays in line with the changes in the local and global environments.

CASES IN GLOBAL MARKETING STRATEGY

The issues in global marketing strategy are vast in scope. They involve an array of decisions, from single-market situations to those that cut across a number of countries simultaneously. Global strategy issues also involve decision making from a variety of perspectives—from global or regional management concerns down to those of individual subsidiaries. Needless to say, the differences in the organizational location and the outlook of decision makers strongly influence the final decisions.

The cases that follow this introduction to Part Two represent a wide spectrum of issues in global marketing, from single-market to multicountry contexts, and from subsidiary management concerns to regional and worldwide perspectives. Together, they allow the student to explore the strategic issues from a diversity of perspectives and to undertake different modes of marketing analysis in arriving at sound managerial decisions.

Part Two cases are organized in sections that address the elements of marketing strategy: opportunity analysis, product policy, communication, distribution, and pricing. A final section deals with global marketing programs, or the integration of various decisions in shaping marketing strategy. More than two-thirds of the cases covered in these sections deal with multicountry or global perspectives; the remainder deal with issues from a single-country angle. Even single market situations often embody the impact of global decisions on one country. The cases cover a wide geographic area. Although the companies that are subjects of the case studies are headquartered in various locations in Europe and North America, the managers and central decision makers in these cases are located in about a dozen countries in Europe, North America, and the Far East.

Endnotes

1. For an in-depth discussion of international segmentation, see Subhash C. Jain, *International Marketing Management*, 3d ed. (Boston: PWS-KENT, 1990), chapter 11.

2. For an in-depth discussion of global product policy, see Philip R. Cateora, *International Marketing*, 6th ed. (Homewood, Ill.: Irwin, 1987), chapters 12–13.

3. For an in-depth discussion of international advertising and sales management, see Subhash C. Jain, *International Marketing Management*, 3d ed. (Boston: PWS-KENT, 1990), chapters 15–16.

4. For an in-depth discussion of international distribution, see Warren J. Keegan, *Multinational Marketing Management*, 3d ed. (Englewood Cliffs, N.J.: Prentice-Hall, 1984), chapter 14.

5. For an in-depth discussion of international pricing, see Subhash C. Jain, *International Marketing Management*, 3d ed. (Boston: PWS-KENT, 1990), chapter 13.

6. Michael E. Porter and Hirotaka Takeuchi have employed another approach to the issues of centralization and coordination by focusing on specific marketing *activities* such as advertising, selling, etc. See Michael E. Porter, *Competition in Global Industries* (Boston: Harvard Business School Press, 1986), pp. 121–125.

Further Readings

Boddewyn, J.J., Robin Soehl, and Jacques Picard. "Standardization in International Marketing: Is Ted Levitt in Fact Right?" *Business Horizons* (November–December 1986): 69–75.

Buzzell, Robert D. "Can You Standardize Multinational Marketing?" *Harvard Business Review* (November–December 1968): 102–113.

Cateora, Philip R. *International Marketing*, 6th ed. (Homewood, Ill.: Irwin, 1987), chs. 11–17.

Doz, Yves L. "Government Policies and Global Industries." In *Competition in Global Industries*, edited by Michael E. Porter, pp. 225–266. Boston: Harvard Business School Press, 1986.

Farley, John U. "Are There Truly International Products—And Prime Prospects for Them?" *Journal of Advertising Research* (October–November 1986): 17–20.

Farrell, Pia. "Global Marketing Is Not a Black and White Affair." *International Herald Tribune*, October 18, 1989, pp. 18–19.

Grosse, Robert, and Duane Kujawa. *International Business* (Homewood, Ill.: Irwin, 1988), ch. 20.

Hill, John S., and Richard R. Still. "Adopting Products to LDC Tastes." *Harvard Business Review* (March–April 1984): 92–101.

Jain, Subhash C. *International Marketing Management*, 3d ed. (Boston: PWS-KENT, 1990), chs. 12–17.

Johansson, Johny K. "Japanese Marketing Failures." *International Marketing Review* (Autumn 1986): 33–46.

Keegan, Warren J. *Global Marketing Management,* 4th ed. (Englewood Cliffs, N.J.: Prentice Hall, 1989), chs. 12–15.

Kotler, Philip. "Global Standardization—Courting Danger." *The Journal of Consumer Marketing* (Spring 1986): 13–15.

McIntyre, David R. "Your Overseas Distributor Action Plan." *Journal of Marketing* (April 1977): 88–90.

Quelch, John A., and Edward J. Hoff. "Customizing Global Marketing." *Harvard Business Review* (May–June 1986): 59–68.

Sanchez, Jesus. "A 19-Country Campaign for Gillette's New Razor." *International Herald Tribune,* October 4, 1989, p. 18.

Sorenson, Ralph Z., and Ulrich E. Wiechman. "How Multinationals View Marketing Standardization." *Harvard Business Review* (May–June 1975): 38–44, 48–50, 54, 166.

Terpstra, Vern. *International Dimensions of Marketing.* (Boston: Kent Publishing Company, 1982), chs. 4–8.

Van Mesdag, Martin. "Winging It in Foreign Markets." *Harvard Business Review* (January–February 1987): 71–74.

Ward, J. "Product and Promotional Adaptation by European Firms in the U.S." *Journal of Business Studies* (Spring 1973): 74–85.

Wentz, Laurel. "1992 to Breed Global Brands." *Advertising Age,* April 24, 1989, p. 44.

Opportunity Analysis

Marketing strategy, whether local or global in scope, follows only after thorough market assessment in which the opportunities for profitable market entry and penetration are fully analyzed. In this respect, a prerequisite of strategy making is opportunity analysis in which diverse forces in the market are brought into focus and their potential impact evaluated. Good strategic decisions can only build on the insights gained from such analysis.

The importance of front-end opportunity analysis to global marketing cannot be overestimated. Global markets are full of opportunities but also full of threats: A highly successful product concept in one part of the world can easily succumb to different local customer preferences elsewhere. Or, seemingly comparable competitive conditions across a number of national markets may hide significant differences that become apparent only upon closer examination. By necessity, effective opportunity analysis in a global context has to make sharp distinctions between market conditions that provide the firm with a sound platform for entry and growth and those whose dynamics preclude viable operations.

ISSUES

The issues covered in this section of the book relate to market assessment for a number of products and services with worldwide potential. The first case, The Skisailer, examines the global opportunities and obstacles for a new product concept, with an eye toward discovering the problems hampering the product's sales and revitalizing the firm's marketing strategy. In the second case, Lestra Design, the failure of a producer of down pillows to export to Japan

becomes the basis for analyzing the peculiarities of the Japanese market and understanding some of the difficulties foreign companies often face when marketing in Japan. The next two cases, Club Med Sales, Inc. (A) and Club Med Sales, Inc. (B), reexamine the opportunities and problems inherent in exporting to the United States a proven global concept in packaged vacations. Here, management is undertaking market research to better understand the American customer.

LEARNING POINTS

The student can expect the following learning points from the analysis and class discussion of the cases in this section:

- Competence in assessing overall market attractiveness based on an analysis of data from diverse sources.

- Appreciation for marketing opportunities that cut across national market boundaries.

- Heightened sensitivity to real differences among national markets that prevent the export of some product or service concepts without genuine adaptation to local market conditions.

- Insight into the opportunities and obstacles of marketing to Japan.

- Skills in formulating marketing research designed to help with informed opportunity analysis.

3 THE SKISAILER

Early in 1987, David Varilek received bad news about the worldwide sales of his invention, the Skisailer. The management at Mistral, the company that had invested in Varilek's innovation, informed him that the first-year sales of Skisailer had failed to match the target and that the future of the product was in doubt. Only 708 Skisailers had been sold during the first season the product was on sale. Mistral, who manufactured and marketed the product worldwide, had already invested more than half a million dollars in the project. Management was seriously considering dropping the product from its line next year.

Realizing that such a setback could jeopardize the future of his four-year-old invention, Varilek, in March 1987, asked a group of MBA students to study the market potential for the Skisailer and to recommend what needed to be done to revive sales. The students had recently completed the first phase of the project. They had presented him with their findings, and the 23-year old inventor was reviewing the information.

THE INVENTION

The Skisailer was based on a concept that combined downhill skiing and windsurfing in a new sport: skisailing. As a Swiss native, David Varilek considered himself "born on skis." However, he had always been frustrated by not being able to ski on the flat snowfields that surrounded his home in the winter season.

In 1983, in his own garage, Varilek invented a connection bar that could be fixed onto regular skis and still allow them to be directed with great flexibility. A windsurfing rig, consisting of a connecting bar and a sail, could then be installed on the connection bar; with enough wind, flat snow surfaces could become great fun for skiing. The idea was subsequently patented under Swiss law. A major feature of the invention was that the Skisailer's unique design also allowed "windskiers" to use regular downhill skis and almost any type of windsurfing rig—an innovation that

This case was written by Professors Dominique Turpin and Kamran Kashani. Copyright © 1990 by the International Institute for Management Development (IMD), Lausanne, Switzerland. Not to be used or reproduced without permission.

limited the buyer's expense. The connection bar and the sail were easy to install. Lateral clamps used for attaching the connection bar to the skis did not damage them in any way except for small grooves on the side of each ski. Only 5 cm (2 inches) of the ski's length were held rigid, and the rest retained normal flexibility. Safety had also been an important consideration in the development of the Skisailer; three self-releasing safety mechanisms were installed on the product. (See Exhibit 1 for an illustration of the skisailer.)

The Skisailer could be used on either smooth slopes or flat surfaces, but the ideal surface for skisailing was the hard-packed snow usually found on groomed ski slopes. The Skisailer could also be used on ice where it could achieve speeds of up to 100km/h.* Skisailing in deep snow or on a slight incline required stronger wind. For use at high speeds, a safety helmet was recommended.

According to Varilek, skisailing was as much fun as windsurfing, even though it had to be done in cold weather:

> For identical sensations, skisailing is easier to learn and handle than windsurfing. You can get on and get off the Skisailer easily, and you are always on your feet. Another great thing with the Skisailer is that you can take advantage of the terrain to perform the same kind of loopings as on sea waves. The Skisailer is a great vehicle for discovering variety in the surroundings.

COMPANY BACKGROUND

In 1987, Mistral Windsurfing AG was a company affiliated with the ADIA Group. ADIA, a $1-billion conglomerate with headquarters in Lausanne, Switzerland, had its activities revolve around ADIA Interim, a company that provided temporary personnel to companies around the world.

In 1980, ADIA had acquired Mistral as part of its diversification strategy. The acquisition was seen as an opportunity to enter a rapidly growing industry. Consistency in marketing and product policy over the past 10 years had made Mistral a leader in the worldwide windsurfing industry. This success was grounded in technological competence, permanent innovation, high-quality standards, a selective international distribution policy, and strong financial backing. Thus, in a fiercely competitive market for windsurfing equipment, characterized by the rise and fall of brands and manufacturers, Mistral was occupying a leading position. To Martin Pestalozzi, the president of ADIA, the Skisailer represented a good opportunity to extend Mistral's product line at a time when Mistral management was increasingly concerned about the future of the windsurfing market.

THE WINDSURFING EQUIPMENT MARKET

The fathers of modern windsurfing were two Californians, Hoyle Schweitzer and James Drake. They had developed the concept and registered the Windsurfer brand.

*1 kilometer = .62 mile.

In 1970, they had applied for and received a patent for their device, a cross between a surfboard and a sailboat.

In the early 1970s, Schweitzer bought out Drake and developed his own firm, Windsurfing International, taking it from a living-room operation to a multimillion dollar corporation with branches in six countries. Due to its North American patents, Windsurfing International was able to hold a virtual monopoly in the United States and Canada until 1979, when a number of other firms entered the market.

Meanwhile, competition in the European windsurfing equipment market was years ahead of that in North America. First introduced to the European market by Ten Cate, a Dutch firm, windsurfing enjoyed an unprecedented growth, particularly in France and Germany. Even as the industry matured during the mid-1980s, it maintained growth in terms of dollar volume, though not in units. Interest in windsurfing had grown from a small pool of enthusiasts to a large and growing population, estimated at between 2 and 3 million people internationally.

Established in 1976 in Bassersdorf near Zurich, Switzerland, Mistral rapidly won an international reputation among windsurfers. Its success was enhanced by two promotional strategies. First, from the start, Mistral had signed up Robby Naish, a young Californian who had won all the major distinctions and titles in this sport to endorse the product. Using Mistral windsurfing equipment, Robby Naish had become the 1977 world champion at age 12 and had dominated the sport ever since. In 1986, Naish won the world title for the 10th time in a row. Mistral's second promotional strategy was to supply several hundred windsurfing rigs gratis to such leisure organizations as Club Méditerranée, giving the brand visibility around the world.

Mistral also enjoyed an advantage over other windsurfing equipment manufacturers by concentrating on the upper-price and quality range of the market. Worldwide, Mistral's equipment was considered the best. Robby Naish's name and the high quality and reliability of Mistral's products had helped build an extensive network of distributors in 30 countries. In 1980, the company had its own subsidiary in the United States where it generated about one-third of its global sales and had market share. Mistral was also directly represented in a number of European countries, such as France, Germany, and Benelux. For the rest of the world, Mistral used exclusive agents who were responsible for selling Mistral products in specific regions.

Recently, a number of factors had combined to dampen the sales of windsurfing equipment in the U.S. market. Patent infringement fights had led to the forced withdrawal of Bic and Tiga, two French manufacturers, from the market. With a total sales of 16,000 units, the two companies were among the major brands in the United States. Meanwhile, a number of European manufacturers had gone bankrupt, thus reducing even further the supply of and marketing expenditures on windsurfing equipment. Market saturation had also contributed to the decline of sales from 73,000 units in 1985 to 62,000 in 1986.

In Europe, where windsurfing had grown at spectacular rates over the years, the market was showing signs of a slowdown. According to the French market research group ENERGY, windsurfing equipment sales in France had risen from less than

600 units in 1974 to more than 115,000 units in the early 1980s. However, cool weather conditions, as well as general market saturation, had reduced French sales to 65,000 units in 1986. In Germany, the second largest market after France, sales had also declined to below 60,000 units from the high levels of the early 1980s. Sales had leveled off in Italy at around 35,000 units, in Holland at 45,000 units, and in Switzerland at 15,000 units.

European sales were dominated by European brands. In France, for example, Bic and Tiga together accounted for 45,000 sales. Mistral was the top imported brand. In Germany, Klepper was the leading local brand; Mistral was a distant fourth in market share. In 1986, Mistral's global sales of 45,620 units were distributed as follows: 25% in the United States, 30% in Europe, and 45% throughout the rest of the world. Windsurfing equipment accounted for 60% of the company's $52 million sales. The rest was accounted for by sportswear (20%) and spare parts and accessories (20%).

THE SKISAILER AND MISTRAL'S DIVERSIFICATION POLICY

Mistral Windsurfing AG had contacted David Varilek at the beginning of 1984 after ADIA management learned about the Skisailer from a four-page article in a major Swiss magazine. Varilek was interested in establishing a relationship with Mistral, as the company was the world leader in windsurfing equipment.

The Skisailer seemed an appropriate product diversification for Mistral. The Skisailer could also fit in with the new line of winter sportswear and other ski-related products that Mistral's management was planning to develop. Mistral had full support from ADIA to launch the project.

In spring 1984, a contract for development, manufacturing, and distribution of the Skisailer was formally signed between David Varilek and Mistral. For the duration of the agreement, all Skisailer patent and trademark rights would be transferred to Mistral, but Varilek would serve as technical adviser to the company and in return would receive 2% royalties on sales. It was also agreed that Varilek would demonstrate the Skisailer in competitions and exhibitions in which Mistral was participating. Should total sales fall short of 5,000 units by the end of 1986, either party could terminate the agreement, with trademarks and patents reverting back to David Varilek. Mistral could also counter any competitive offer made to Varilek, a so-called first right of refusal.

INTRODUCING THE SKISAILER

During the summer of 1984, two prototypes of Skisailer were developed at Mistral for presentation in November at ISPO, the largest European sports exhibition held annually in Munich, Germany. Between May and November 1984, Mistral engineers developed several innovations that were added to the Skisailer. For example, the connecting bar and mounting blocks were strengthened to resist shocks and low temperatures. The equipment was also modified to accommodate the Mistral windsurfing sailing rig.

In Munich at ISPO, the Skisailer was widely acclaimed as a truly innovative product that would certainly win public enthusiasm. At this early stage of development, however, the product still lacked promotional support. No pamphlet, video, or pictures had been developed to present the product and educate potential users. Varilek thought that the pictures used to introduce the product to Mistral's distributors were not attractive enough to trigger interest and buyers. Nevertheless, some distributors liked the product and placed immediate orders.

The formal launch of Skisailer got under way in 1986. Mistral produced 2,000 Skisailers, consisting of a mast foot, a sail (available from its standard windsurfing line), and the connecting bar. The Skisailers were to be distributed worldwide through the company's network of wholesalers and independent sports shops in large- and medium-sized cities. For example, in Lausanne, Switzerland, a city of 250,000 inhabitants, with 30 ski shops and 3 windsurfing equipment stores, Skisailer was sold in three locations. Of the three stores, two specialized in ski equipment and the third sold windsurfing products.

Skisailer was priced $410 at retail; the price included the bar connection and its mounting blocks but excluded the sail and its mast, which cost an additional $590. Retail margins on Skisailer and its rig were set at 35%. The wholesale margins were also 35%. Skisailer cost Mistral $85 per unit to produce and ship to distributors; the cost for the sailing rig was around $200.

The 1986 promotional budget of $15,000 set for Skisailer was deemed by Varilek as too little. Mistral management had already turned down a $35,000 proposal from Varilek to produce a promotional video showing Skisailer in action. Nevertheless, Varilek had decided to arrange for shooting of such a video on his own at Mammoth Lake, California. Mistral later refunded Varilek the $10,000 that the video had cost him.

As of early 1987, Mistral had invested more than half a million dollars in Skisailer:

Development costs		
Engineering and tooling		$214,000
Other costs		74,000
		$288,000
Inventory – assembled and spares		
At central warehouse		$180,000
At distributors		68,000
		$248,000
	Total	$536,000

MARKET RESEARCH FINDINGS

Concerned with the future of Skisailer, David Varilek in the spring of 1987 had commissioned a group of MBA students at a leading international school of management in Switzerland to study the global market for Skisailer and to report on their findings. By early fall, the students had completed the first phase of their study, which dealt with the market potential for Skisailer, competing products, ski market developments, and a survey of buyers, retailers, and wholesalers. A summary of the findings follows.

Potential Market

Based on interviews with buyers of Skisailer, the research team had learned that potential customers were likely to be those who did *both* skiing and windsurfing. Building on industry reports suggesting a total worldwide population of 2 million windsurfers and 30 million skiers, the team estimated that a maximum of 60% of windsurfers, or a total of 1.2 million individuals, were also skiers. The "realizable market" for Skisailer, according to the MBA students, was far below this maximum, however. They identified at least 4 "filters," which together reduced the realizable market potential to a fraction of the maximum:

Filter 1: Customer Type   As a relatively new sport, skisailing appealed to a group of enthusiasts whom the MBA students referred to as "innovators." Their study had suggested that these buyers were in the 15- to 25-year-old age bracket, liked sports, but for the most part could not afford the price tag of the Skisailer. The next most likely group of buyers, called "early adopters," was older, less sporty, and more image conscious. For this segment, price was not a major factor. The team believed that sufficient penetration of the first segment was necessary before the second group showed any interest in the new product.

Filter 2: Location   Users of Skisailer reported that ideal skisailing conditions, such as flat ice- or snow-covered fields, were not always accessible. This location factor, the team believed, tended to reduce the potential for the product.

Filter 3: Climate   Climate, according to the MBA students, was another inhibiting factor. Skisailer required not only suitable snow or ice, but also a good wind. The minimum required wind speed was around 20 kilometers/hour. The study identified a number of regions as meeting both the needed snow and wind conditions: Scandinavia and central Europe, certain parts of North America, and parts of Southern Australia.

Filter 4: Competing Products   Four similar products were identified but, according to the student report, all lacked brand image, wide distribution, and product sophistication. Although information on competing products was scanty, the students had assembled the following information from different sources:

Brand (origin)	Retail price	Total units sold	Main sales area
Winterboard (Finland)	$395	4,000	Finland, U.S.
Ski Sailer (Australia)	$ 90	3,500	Australia, U.S.
ArcticSail (Canada)	$285	3,000	Canada, U.S.
Ski Sailer (U.S.)	$220	300	U.S.

Based on their initial estimate of the maximum size of the potential market, as well as the limiting effects of the four "filters," the students had arrived at an estimate of 20,000 units as the total realizable market for Skisailer. This volume, they believed, could grow by as much as 10% per year. Exhibit 2 contains an estimate of the market potential. Exhibit 3 shows what the students believed were achievable levels of sales for Skisailer over the next five years.

Competing Products

Winterboard   Winterboard, a light windsurfing board with skis, had been invented in Finland. It could be used on both ice and snow, and its performance was said to be impressive. Some rated the Winterboard as the best performing windski after the Skisailer. In terms of sales, Winterboard had been the most successful windski product. Over the last five years, 4,000 units had been sold, mainly in Scandinavia and in the United States, in regular sports shops. Winterboard was being sold at a retail price of $395, excluding the sailing rig. Retail margins were at 40%. The skis were already integrated into the board and did not need to be purchased as an extra.

According to the research team, Winterboard's management believed that prices, retail margins, and advertising expenditures were relatively unimportant in their marketing strategy. The key to their success was organizing windskiing events. Winterboard's management realized that people wanted sportive social gatherings on weekends in the winter, but if they went snowsailing in the cold by themselves, they quickly lost interest.

Australian-made "Ski Sailer"   This product was essentially a simple bar with a mastfoot that could be attached to normal ski boots and used with either conventional skis or roller skates. The Ski Sailer had an equalizing slide and joint mechanism, so maneuvers such as parallel turns, jump turns, and snow-plowing were possible. Any sailing rig could be fitted to the Ski Sailer's mast post.

The U.S. distributor for this product reported cumulative sales of about 3,000 units (30% through ski shops, 70% through surf shops) at a retail price of $90 each. But the distributor admitted that he had lost interest in the product when he realized that only customers who were tough and resistant to the cold enjoyed windsurfing in the wintertime. This meant a much smaller customer base than for his other leisure/sportswear products.

"ArcticSail Board"   This product was essentially a W-shaped surfboard for use on snow, ice, or water. It was distributed by Plastiques L.P.A. Ltd. in Mansonville, Quebec, Canada, approximately 50 miles from the U.S.-Canadian border.

The ArcticSail was especially designed for snow and ice, but it could also be used on water, in which case the rear filler plates would be replaced by two ailerons, also supplied with the board. Adjustable footstraps, included with the board, also had to be repositioned for use on water. The product was made of special plastic, usable at both normal *and* very low temperatures. The producer warned users to watch for objects that could damage the underside of the sled.

The company reported cumulative sales of approximately 3,000 units (600 estimated for the 1987/88 winter), mostly in Canada at the retail price of $285 (including 38% retail margin). Promotion expenses were approximately 15% on Canadian and U.S. sales, mainly spent on a 2-man team demonstrating at ski resorts.

American-made Ski Sailer   Yet another "Ski Sailer" had been invented by a young Californian, Carl Meinberg. The American Ski Sailer also used a small board mounted on skis and was similar to the product developed by David Varilek. On his own, the inventor had sold about 50 Ski Sailers, retailing at $220 each. During the winter season, Meinberg toured a number of ski resorts, demonstrating the Ski Sailer; he spent the rest of the year selling his invention.

Recent Developments in the World Ski Market

As background to their study, the research team had also obtained information on the ski market. The total world alpine skiing population was estimated at 30 million people in 1987. Competition in the ski market was intensive, and production capacity exceeded demand by an estimated 25 to 30% in 1987. Prices for skis were under pressure, and retailers used discounts to build traffic. Retail profits were mostly made on sales of accessories and skiwear. The 1986 sales of downhill (also called alpine) and cross-country skis are given in Exhibit 4.

In distribution, specialty shops were losing market share to the large chains. Production was concentrated, with seven manufacturers controlling 80% of the market. The falling exchange rate for the U.S. dollar had put the large European producers such as Fischer and Kneissel at a disadvantage in the U.S. market.

Marketing skis depended heavily on successes in world championships and the image associated with the winning skis. In the mid-1980s, customers in the United States appeared to be losing interest in skiing, but these signs had not been observed in Europe and Japan, where the sport remained popular and at a stable level.

An innovation in skiing was the snowboard, a product gaining popularity among younger winter sports enthusiasts. The snowboard was essentially a single large ski with two ski bindings positioned in a similar way as the footstraps on a windsurfing rig.

The snowboard had been in existence in the United States for many years but had only recently been introduced in Europe.

Worldwide sales of snowboards had doubled every year, reaching an estimated 40,000 in the 1986 season. One U.S. manufacturer, Burton, accounted for 50% of the market.

Many manufacturers of winter products had taken advantage of the increasing popularity of the snowboard and had started producing their own versions. The product was very popular in the European distribution channels, and expectations for further growth were high.

Buyers' Survey

The research team had interviewed a small number of Skisailer buyers in Germany, Austria, Benelux, the United States, and Canada. Highlights of their comments on advantages and disadvantages of Skisailer follow:

Advantages of the Product

- Sure, skisurfing in winter is great; it's a lot of fun.
- You can do quick maneuvers, nice turns, beautiful power turns, and fast changes of the grips. It [the Skisailer] gives a good opportunity to train for windsurfing, as you have to drive the way you surf—with the pressure on the inner ski.
- I did not have any problem with turns.
- It is not difficult to learn if you have some feeling for sailing.
- It simulates surfing in your backyard.
- It is the right device if you want to do something on Sunday afternoon (with no time to drive somewhere in your car).
- Fun, different, new, good.
- It is the only thing with a mountain touch that you can use on the plain.
- It turns. That makes it much more fun than the other products on the market. You can do jives, curve jives, jumps. . . . It is close to sailing a shore boat. . . . It's a lot of fun.
- If the conditions are ideal, it's a lot of fun."

Disadvantages of the Product

- Your feet get twisted; sailing on the wind requires exceptional twisting of the legs and knees.
- Both of the white caps at the end of the bar came off, and it was virtually impossible to get spare parts.

- Difficult in heavy snow.
- Difficult to find the perfect conditions.
- You use it three to four times a season. For this, the price is too high.
- It is uncomfortable to use. You have to loosen up your boots; otherwise, the rim of the shoe cuts into your twisted leg.
- If the snow is too deep, you cannot use it. What you want is strong wind.
- The price is too high.
- My problem is that there is hardly any wind in winter.
- In the beginning, I was getting stiff in the unnatural position and my knees hurt, but later I got more relaxed . . . and with time you have a lot of fun.
- In high winter, it is too cold to use it; spring is ideal.

Retailers' Opinions of the Mistral Skisailer

A dozen retailers of Skisailer were also surveyed in Germany, Canada, Austria, and France. Highlights of their comments follow:

Advantages of the Product

- You could sell a lot of them in the first year, but I do not see it as the absolute "barnstormer."
- It is a first-year novelty.
- It is a lot of fun in the snow . . . and for people with a lot of money. It is a new gimmick.
- It combines two favorite sports—skiing and windsurfing.
- It is better than all self-built products—you have full movability.
- Easy to use. It is an original idea.
- You can use your skis, it is flexible and easy to store.
- Very thoroughly constructed, very stable.

Disadvantages of the Product

- Unhappy product—usable only under specific weather conditions.
- It is only a fad.
- You just don't drive with your skis to a lake and try it on the ice.
- Maybe it sells better in a winter shop.
- Your position on the skis is abnormal—the snowboard is a better alternative.
- We do not think that it will be *the* fast turning product.
- Impossible to sell—nobody's tried it.
- In my environment, there is no space to do it—no lakes, no fields.
- For a backyard product, the price is too high. Even Mistral's good image doesn't help. Maybe this will change if the product is better known.

- Customers watched the video with enthusiasm, but when they learned the price, enthusiasm was nil. We are offering our last piece now at a discount of 40%.
- If you ski *and* windsurf, your hobbies cost you a lot of money.
- Often the early user is the sportive freak with low income. How will you convince him about the product?

Distributors' Comments

The research team interviewed Mistral distributors in ten different countries in Europe and North America. Highlights of comments from five distributors follow:

- We first learned about the Skisailer at ISPO in Munich and ordered some.
- From Mistral we got some folders and the video. If you see it on the video, you want to use the Skisailer right away.
- We did not support the retailers very much because we felt that the Skisailer's marketing was not done professionally from the beginning. For instance, Skisailer deliveries were late.
- The product would have potential if the price were lowered and the promotion were done professionally all the way through.
- We bought the Skisailer, which is good for use in our winter climate, after Mistral contacted us in 1985.
- The product is expensive and not really functional.
- Promotion was not good at all—only a few folders and a video which was not free of charge. When there were product breakdowns, spare parts were not available.
- A Finnish competitor has now captured the market with a product that looks like a surfboard with two skis fitted into it. We have the right places for ski-sailing here!
- We used all our contacts and spent approximately $7,500 in mid-1987 to promote this product on television.
- The retail price is too high for a product to be used only a few weekends in the winter.
- The snowboard, especially made for surfing on ski slopes, is much more fashionable.
- Surf and ski shops make higher margins on clothing and accessories that are sold in larger quantities.
- You don't create a product first and then look for the market; this is the wrong way around. The Skisailer is more a product for Scandinavia and similar regions in America or Canada.

France

- We didn't know the product but found the demonstration film to be convincing. Therefore, we organized ski resort demonstrations in the French

Alps at racing events where there are many spectators. We also pushed about 40 Skisailers in several retail shops.

- For this product, finding suitable locations where you can have a training session with wind and snow is necessary.
- We estimate that the retailers have sold about half their inventory, but we do not want to get more involved and have the rest sent back to us. Retailers are looking for customer demand which is lacking.

Canada

- I cannot see further sales of the Skisailer without more product support. At low temperatures the rubber joints failed, but when we asked for replacements, there was no reply from Mistral. In the end we had to strip other Skisailers to get the spare parts.
- We have good skisailing conditions (in South Ontario/Quebec) and a group of interested enthusiasts here. The product has been promoted to thousands of people! The folder and video are very good.
- At a trade show in Toronto, the product was well received except for the price, which is a problem.

CONCLUSION

In reviewing the research team's report, David Varilek was searching for clues that could explain Skisailer's poor performance in its first selling season. Was it the product design that needed further refinement? Or the skisailer's price, which was perceived by some as being high? Was the absence of high promotional support, which he always suspected to be a problem, a key factor? Or maybe Mistral's selective distribution was the core issue. What else could explain why his invention had failed to match everybody's expectations?

An additional piece of information had heightened the need for immediate action. Varilek had just received the final sales and inventory figures for Skisailer from Mistral indicating that while 708 units had been sold to the trade, only 80 units had been bought at retail.

| | Unit sales | | |
Country	To distributors	To retailers	To end-users
U.S./Canada	233	98	45
Germany	250	50	10
Switzerland	42	30	1
France	56	40	20
Benelux	60	0	0
Others	67	12	4
Total Shipped	708	230	80

Varilek knew that Mistral management was soon to review the future of Skisailer. He feared that in the absence of a convincing analysis and action plan from him, the Skisailer would be dropped from Mistral's line. He was therefore impatiently waiting for the MBA research team's recommendations based on the data already collected.

EXHIBIT 1   Illustration of Skisailer from Product Brochure

The SKISAILER™

Invented by David Varilek and developed in conjunction
with Mistral Windsurfing AG, Bassersdorf, Switzerland

Contact

Mistral Windsurfing A.G.
CH - 8303 Bassersdorf/Zürich
Switzerland
Telephone 01/836-8922
Telex 59 266 MWAG CH

EXHIBIT 1 (continued)

FREEDOM : With the Skisailer, Mistral has developed the ultimate marriage of wind and snow, ski and sail. All the thrills of skiing without the need of mountains or ski-lift passes. More sport and pleasure per hour invested. The boring, grey, winter afternoons,when all you can do is gaze at surf photos in the magazines and remember the sunny days on your funboard, are over. Mistral Skisailer - That's funboard surfing in the snow and ski-holidays hanging on the boom.

EASE : Once you have fixed the small rails to your skis in front of the toe-bindings, you are free at any time to "fly" across the snow-covered countryside, simple and easy to assemble, the equipment stores neatly in a back-pack, leaving you free to ski,should you wish to switch from wind-power to gravity-power.

FUNCTION : The principal advantages of the Skisailer derive from the basic concept and the light, strong construction of the equipment. The multidirectional freedom of movement of the mast-foot plate allows for all normal ski manoevers (edging, turning etc.) while the optimum positioning of the mast in relation to the skier allows the manoevers of sailboarding (jibing, jumping, snow-starts !).

SAFETY : There is no limit to your striving for always more speed, longer jumps and more radical manoevers. The security of the sport is assured by the triple release security system: the conventional ski bindings, the mast-foot plate connectors and the mast-foot.

FREEDOM : Mit dem Skisailer lässt Mistral den Traum vom Windsurfen im Pulverschnee Wahrheit werden. Vergessen Sie endlose Warteschlangen am Lift und überfüllte Pisten. Die langweiligen, grauen Winternachmittage, an denen die Erinnerungen an die Surferlebnisse des letzten Sommers nur noch beim Betrachten der Fotos in den Magazinen wach werden, sind vorbei. Mistral Skisailer - Fundboardfahren im Pulverschnee, Skivergnügen am Gabelbaum.

IT'S SO EASY : Montieren Sie einfach die Funktionsteile vor Ihrer Skibindung. Und los geht's: Snowstart, Raumshots über verschneite Wiesen, Take-Off an einer Bodenwelle, weiche Landung, Slalom zwischen den Schneeflocken, Duck-Jibe, ... Hawaii ist vergessen. Wenn der Wind nachlässt, schalten Sie um von Windkraft auf Schwerkraft, und gehen normal skifahren. Die nicht mehr benötigten Teile passen in Ihren Rucksack.

THE CONCEPT : Der Vorteil des Mistral Skisailers liegt in der superleichten, robusten Konstruktion der Funktionselemente und in der Wirkungsweise des Prinzips. Die allseitige Bewegungsfreiheit der Mastfussplatte ermöglicht Kanteneinsatz und Schwungauslösung wie beim normalen Skilauf. Durch die optimale Positionierung des Riggs auf den Skiern, funktionieren die Funboardmanöver im Schnee bald genauso gut wie auf dem Wasser.

SAFETY FIRST : Ihrem Drang nach immer mehr Speed, noch weiteren Sprüngen und noch heisseren Manövern können Sie freien Lauf lassen. Selbst bei spektakulären Stürzen schützt Sie ein dreifaches Sicherheitssystem: Ihre Skibindung, der Mastfuss und die Mastfussplatten-Verbinder sind auslösende Konstruktions - elemente.

LIBERTE : Avec le Skisailer, Mistral réalise enfin le mariage du vent et de la neige, du ski et de la voile. Tous les avantages du ski, sans les inconvénients de la foule et des remontées mécaniques, donnent un rapport plaisir/temps investi incomparable. Fini l'ennui des gris après-midi d'hiver où la seule distraction était de lire des magazines de surf et de se souvenir. Le Skisailer de Mistral c'est du funboard sur neige, des vacances d'hiver accroché au wishbone.

FACILITE : Une fois les petits rails de fixation installés à l'avant des butées, plus rien ne peut vous empêcher de "voler" à travers les plaines enneigées, de jiber sur une bosse de neige ou si le vent vous lâche, de ranger votre matériel dans un sac à dos et de skier comme tout le monde.

TECHNICITE : La conception même du Skisailer en est son atout majeur. Les articulations multidirectionnelles de la plaque de soutien du mât permettent une totale liberté de mouvement des skis (prise de carre, virage etc...). D'autre part, la position optimale du mât sur les skis permet de faire toutes les manoeuvres de funboard (snow starts, jibes, sauts).

SECURITE : Celle-ci est assurée en cas de choc par un déclanchement à trois niveaux: aux fixations de ski conventionnelles, aux articulations de la plaque de soutien et au pied de mât. Ainsi toutes craintes dissipées, vos progrès en saut, vitesse et manoeuvres seront encore plus rapides.

EXHIBIT 2 Skisailer Market Potential

Market	Unit Size	%	"Filters"
Potential market	1.2 million	100	
			• Customer type
Available market	800K	66	
			• Location • Climate
Qualified market	80K	7	
			• Indirect competition (monoski,skates, etc.)
Served market	40K	3.5	
			• Direct competition (Winterboard, ArcticSail, etc.)
Realizable market	20K	1.7	
			• Customer type

EXHIBIT 3   Skisailer Achievable Sales Estimate

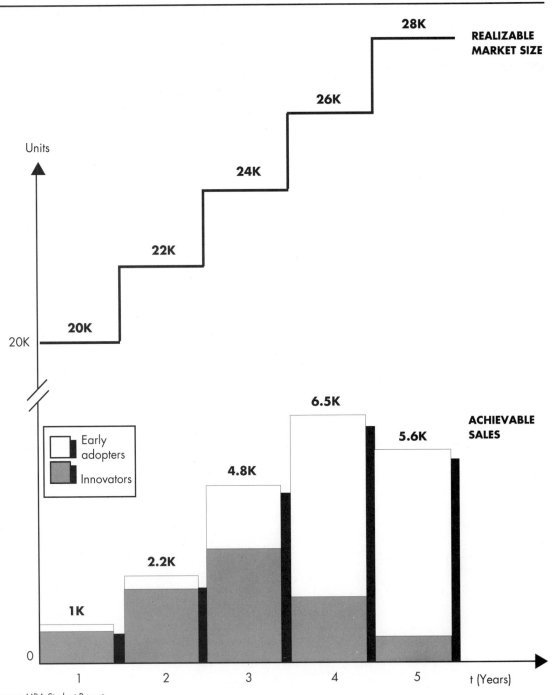

Source: MBA Student Report.

EXHIBIT 4 World Market of Alpine and Cross-Country Skis

1985/86 season	Pairs sold
Alpine ski sales	
Austria, Switzerland, Germany	1,450,000
Rest of Europe	1,550,000
United States and Canada	1,600,000
Japan	1,100,000
Other countries	300,000
Total	6,000,000
Cross-country ski sales	
Austria, Switzerland, Germany	700,000
Scandinavia	800,000
Rest of Europe	400,000
United States and Canada	750,000
Other countries	150,000
Total	2,800,000

4 LESTRA DESIGN

In May 1985, Mr. Claude Léopold, president of Lestra Design, was wondering what action he should take regarding the Japanese market. For several years, Lestra Design had been trying to enter the Japanese market for duvets (comforters) and eiderdowns (down-filled comforters). The Japanese market for these products was certainly the largest in the world, but Lestra Design had faced a number of obstacles that had cooled Claude Léopold's enthusiasm. Then recently, he had met again with Daniel Legrand, a French consultant in Tokyo, who had been supervising Lestra Design activities in Japan for the last two years. Daniel Legrand had explained that despite the earlier difficulties experienced by Lestra Design, the company had several alternatives which could enable it to be successful in Japan.

COMPANY BACKGROUND

Lestra Design was a subsidiary of Léopold & Fils, a family business established in Amboise, France, a medium-sized town about 250 kilometers southwest of Paris. Claude Léopold's father had established the parent company as a feather and down company in the early 1930s. At first the company was mainly trading in down and feathers, but Léopold & Fils soon became a major French manufacturer of feather- and down-filled cushions, pillows, bolsters, and eiderdowns. In 1971, when Claude Léopold took over the business from his father, he decided to establish two new companies: (1) Lestra Design to produce and distribute feather and down duvets, and (2) Lestra Sport to manufacture and distribute feather and down sleeping bags (see Exhibits 1 and 2). By using more aggressive sales management and the talents of Claude Léopold's wife Josette, a renowned French fashion designer, Lestra Design rapidly became the leading duvet company in France. Josette Léopold's creative ideas for using innovative fabric designs with attractive prints helped Lestra Design and Lestra Sports quickly establish an international reputation for high-class, fashionable products. Although in 1985, Léopold & Fils, together with its two

This case was written by Professor Dominique Turpin. Copyright © 1989 by the International Institute for Management Development (IMD), Lausanne, Switzerland. Not to be used or reproduced without permission.

subsidiaries (Lestra Sports and Lestra Design), had only 128 employees for revenues of FF 72 million,[1] Claude Léopold believed that the prospect of growth in international markets was extremely promising.

Sales over the past five years had experienced double-digit growth, and exports to England, West Germany, and other European countries, representing 20% of Lestra Design sales, had recently started to boom. A few years earlier, Lestra Design had also placed an order in Japan through Kanematsu-Gosho Ltd., a "sogo shosha" (large trading company) affiliated with the Bank of Tokyo and traditionally strong in textiles. However, the Japanese trading company had not reordered any product from Lestra Design since 1979.

LESTRA DESIGN CONSIDERS THE JAPANESE MARKET

In 1978, Georges Mekiès, general manager, and Claude Léopold, president of Lestra Design, had met with Daniel Legrand, a French consultant established in Tokyo. That same year, Legrand had conducted a market survey for Léopold, which clearly indicated that a major opportunity for growth existed in Japan. With close to 120 million inhabitants and half of the population using duvets, Japan was clearly the largest market for duvets in the world.

In 1978 and 1979, Léopold had been preoccupied with developing Lestra Design sales in Europe. As a result, he had not taken any immediate action to investigate further the potential of the Japanese market for Lestra Design products. Léopold wanted first to provide the French and other European markets with good service before addressing any other market in either the United States or Japan. In autumn 1979, during the ISPO exhibition in Frankfurt, West Germany, Léopold and Mekiès were approached by a manager from Ogitani Corporation, a Japanese trading company based in Nagoya. Hiroshi Nakayama, the representative of Ogitani Corporation, wanted to import and distribute Lestra Design products in Japan. He especially liked the unique designs of Lestra Design's duvets and eiderdowns. He told Léopold and Mekiès that the innovative designs, as well as the French image with the "Made in France" label, would be the two strongest selling points in Japan.

The Trademark Issue

In December 1979, Ogitani ordered 200 duvets to be delivered to Nagoya. However, after the goods were shipped, Georges Mekiès heard nothing from his Japanese distributor. By chance, on a trip to Japan in April 1980, Mekiès discovered that Ogitani had registered the two trademarks, Lestra Sport and Lestra Design, under the Ogitani name. Mekiès decided to call Hiroshi Nakayama and request a meeting in Nagoya to discuss the trademark issue. Nakayama responded that he was too busy. Mekiès then insisted that another executive from the trading company talk with him, but he received only a rebuff.

1. In 1985, FF 7.10 = US $1.

That same day, a furious Georges Mekiès called Yves Gasquères, the representative of the French Textile Manufacturers Association in Tokyo, for advice. Gasquères, who also represented the well-known Lacoste shirts in Japan, explained that Lestra Design was not the only such case. The best advice he could give Mekiès was to contact Koichi Sato, a Japanese lawyer specializing in trademark disputes.

Mekiès also saw Daniel Legrand, who confirmed Gasquères's advice. Legrand said that, although trademark disputes were rapidly disappearing in Japan, there were still some recent disputes between Western and Japanese firms, especially with several big French fashion houses like Cartier, Chanel, Dior, and so forth. Legrand also mentioned the recent example of Yoplait, a major French yogurt producer. A few years ago, Yoplait had signed a licensing agreement with a major Japanese food company to manufacture and distribute yogurt in Japan. While negotiating the contract, executives at Yoplait discovered that the Yoplait name had been registered by another Japanese food company under different Japanese writing transcriptions.[2] Although the French company decided to fight the case in court, Yoplait finally decided to use another name ("Yopuleito" using the Katagana transcription) for its products in Japan.

Before going back to France, Mekiès arranged for Legrand to supervise the trademark dispute with Ogitani. A few weeks later, Legrand learned from Hiroshi Nakayama at Ogitani that the Japanese firm had registered the Lestra Design and Lestra Sports brands under its own name only to prevent other Japanese competitors from doing so. Mekiès was not fully convinced, however, about the sincerity of this answer. One month later, he learned from Legrand that the legal department of the French Embassy in Tokyo was going to intervene in Lestra Design's favor. Finally, at the end of 1982, Legrand informed Léopold & Fils that Ogitani had agreed to give up the two trademarks in exchange for full reimbursement of the registration fees paid by Ogitani to the Tokyo Patent Office.

Finding a New Distributor

During his short stay in Japan, Georges Mekiès was able to size up the many business possibilities offered by the Japanese market. Despite the bad experience with Ogitani, Claude Léopold and Georges Mekiès believed that Lestra Design had a major opportunity for business development in Japan. The Lestra Design trademark was now fully protected by Japanese law. In April 1983, Léopold commissioned Daniel Legrand to search for and select a new Japanese partner. To shorten the traditional distribution chain and reduce costs (see Exhibits 3 and 4), Legrand decided to use his personal contacts at some of the major Japanese department stores. Stores such as Mitsukoshi, Takashimaya, and Seibu enjoyed considerable prestige in Japan for selling luxurious products. Moreover, the major department stores had branches all over Japan, enabling Lestra Design to cover the entire Japanese market. Most of these department stores were already carrying competitive duvets from West Germany and France, including prestigious brands like Yves Saint

---

2. The Japanese use three different types of transcription, together with the occasional use of the Roman alphabet. In addition to Chinese ideograms ("Kanji"), "Katagana" is used for the exclusive transcription of foreign words and names. "Hiragana" is used for all other words not written in "Kanji."

Laurent and Pierre Cardin. Legrand thought that department stores would be the right outlet for Lestra Design to position its products in the upper segment of the Japanese duvet and eiderdown market. However, the idea had been rejected because most Japanese department stores worked on consignment (i.e., at the end of the season, the store would count the number of duvets it sold, pay the supplier, and return the unsold goods). Legrand also went to various Japanese companies in the bed and furniture industry, as well as to several large trading companies such as Mitsui & Co., Mitsubishi Corporation, and C. Itoh. He also visited Mr. Inagawa, in charge of the Home and Interior Section of Kanematsu-Gosho, which used to import from Léopold & Fils. But Inagawa said that his company did not intend to import any more duvets from Lestra Design because its products were too highly priced.

The general reaction from potential Japanese buyers was that Lestra Design's colors (red, green, and white) were not appropriate for the Japanese market. However, most of these buyers agreed that, with some modifications to accommodate the Japanese market, the "Made in France" image was a great asset for selling Lestra Design products in Japan. Duvets and eiderdowns under names like Yves Saint Laurent, Courrèges, and Pierre Cardin were being manufactured in Japan under license and were sold successfully because Japanese distributors and potential customers tended to view French interior textiles as fashion products for which France was so famous.

To attract distributors, Legrand had advised Léopold & Fils to participate in the annual Home Fashion Show held in Tokyo. However, Léopold and Mekiès had not responded to this suggestion. By June 1983, some potential distributors had already been identified, but most of them wanted to license the design and then manufacture in Japan rather than import the final products from France. Léopold preferred to export directly from France and thus create more jobs for his own employees.

In July 1983, Legrand met with Akira Arai, president of Trans-Ec Co. Ltd. Japan, a firm specializing in importing and exporting down and feathers. Arai, 41 years old, had started his own company six years earlier after working for a large trading company since his graduation from Keio University.

Arai was enthusiastic about French duvets and quilts and the Lestra Design products mainly because of the "Made in France" label and the prestige attached to French textiles. Like most of the potential distributors Legrand had talked to, Arai also perceived Lestra Design products as French fashion products similar to the duvets and quilts sold in Japan under prestigious fashion names like Yves Saint Laurent, Cardin, and Courrèges. Some French fashion designers almost unknown in France had built a very strong reputation in Japan. Both Arai and Legrand believed there was room in Japan for Lestra Design to achieve very strong brand recognition. Arai had had some experience working with other French firms. In the past, he had imported down and feathers from Topiol, a French company that was an indirect competitor of Léopold & Fils. Legrand thought that Arai, who had already heard about Lestra Design, could be a potential partner for the French company. Arai knew the down and feather industry thoroughly, and he had good connections in the complex distribution system of the Japanese duvet industry. Arai had also been highly recommended by Eiko Gunjima, in charge of fashion items at the Commercial Section of the French Embassy in Tokyo.

THE OBSTACLES

The Design Problem

In July 1983, Legrand and Arai met again in Roppongi, a fashionable district of Tokyo where Arai's office was located. Arai explained that it would be difficult to sell Lestra Design duvets in Japan as they appeared in the current Lestra Design catalogue. In his opinion, Lestra Design would have to adapt its products for the Japanese market. Arai proposed that Lestra Design send him a sample that would meet the market requirements (i.e., sizes, colors, fillings, etc.). In particular, he thought that the choice of colors was very important. Although Arai liked the innovative motifs and the colors of Lestra Design products, he told Legrand that Japanese customers would rarely buy a red, pink, or black duvet. Most duvets sold in Japan were in soft colors with many flowers in the design. Legrand emphasized that Lestra Design was introducing something really new to the Japanese market, but Arai insisted that most Japanese customers would prefer floral motifs on their duvets. Indeed, Legrand had noticed that almost all the Japanese duvets displayed in Tokyo stores had designs with floral motifs.

Arai also recommended that Lestra Design duvets be smaller than French duvets and be paving-blocked (quilted) to prevent the down from moving too freely inside the duvet. Arai suggested these requirements, including all the technical details needed to manufacture the duvet, so that Lestra Design could meet the Japanese trade expectations. Arai's specifications were quite different from those of Lestra Design, but Legrand was confident that the French company had the flexibility to adapt its products to the Japanese market. Arai also requested that Lestra Design deliver the sample within a month. Legrand had trouble explaining to Arai that Lestra Design, like most French firms, would be closed during the whole month of August for its summer holidays. Arai joked about the French taking so much holiday in summer, but he agreed to wait until the beginning of September.

The Dust Problem

At the beginning of October 1983, Legrand went to Arai's office with the sample he had just received from France. With almost no hesitation, Georges Mekiès had agreed to redesign a duvet to meet the Japanese customer's expectations. The fabric was printed with floral motifs, paving-blocked, and exactly the requested size. Arai seemed pleased when he first saw the product. Then, as Legrand watched, Arai picked up the sample, carried it to the window, folded it under his arm, and then slapped it vigorously with his hands. Both men were surprised to see a small cloud of white dust come from the duvet. Arai put the sample down on his desk, shook his head in disappointment, and stated, "This is not a good product. If Lestra Design wants to compete against the big Japanese, German, and other French brands, the product must be perfect."

Legrand immediately telexed Arai's reaction to Georges Mekiès. In Arai's opinion, the problem had to do with washing the duvet. Although Mekiès was surprised by the result of Arai's test, he agreed to send a new sample very soon.

Just after New Year's Day, Legrand arrived at Arai's office with a new sample. Mr. Naoto Morimoto, in charge of the Bedding and Interior Section of Katakura Kogyo,[3] a major textile trading company, had also been invited by Arai to examine the new sample. Morimoto was an old friend of Arai, as well as a potential customer for Lestra Design products. After the ritual exchange of business cards between Legrand and Morimoto, Arai proceeded to perform the same dust test. Again, some dust came out, although less dust than last time. Arai and Morimoto decided to open the duvet and look inside for an explanation to the problem. In their opinion, the feathers had not been washed in the same way as in Japan. Morimoto suspected that the chemicals used to wash the duvet were very different from those traditionally used in Japan. Moreover, Arai found that the duvet was filled with both grey and white down. He asked Legrand to recommend that Lestra Design use only new white down and no feathers at all, not even very small ones. In front of Legrand, Arai also demonstrated the same test with several Japanese- and German-made duvets. No dust came out. As a result, Legrand and Arai decided to send two Japanese- and German-made samples to Mekiès so that he could test the dust problem himself. With the two samples, Arai attached a note emphasizing that to compete successfully in Japan, "Lestra Design products must be perfect, especially since the Japanese customers generally believe that textiles and fashion products from France are of great quality."

At the end of March 1984, a third sample arrived in Tokyo. Mekiès had phoned Legrand beforehand, emphasizing that the utmost care had been given to this sample. But again this time, the sample failed Arai's test. Legrand immediately phoned Mekiès to inform him of the situation. Arai was frustrated, and from the sound of the telephone conversation between Legrand and Mekiès, it seemed as if Léopold & Fils was about to give up on the Japanese market. Mekiès could not fully understand Arai's rejection of the samples, because in his whole career at Lestra Design he had never heard any complaint about dust coming out of Lestra Design duvets.

Legrand thought that the only way to save the Japanese business would be for Georges Mekiès to visit Tokyo. Legrand emphasized again the considerable opportunities offered by the Japanese market and thus convinced Mekiès and Jacques Papillault, Lestra Design's technical director, to board the next flight for Tokyo. Mekiès said they would only be able to stay 48 hours in order to meet with Akira Arai.

The Retail Price Problem

A few days later, Mekiès and Papillault arrived in Tokyo. Arai claimed that he was genuinely interested in selling Lestra Design products in Japan, but he explained that in order to compete with existing Japanese duvets, Lestra Design products had to meet the local standards of quality. Arai and his friend Morimoto insisted that, since French textile products carried such a high image in Japan, they should be of the finest quality. Arai also stressed that only new white goose down should be used to

---

3. In 1982, Katakura Kogyo had profits of US $5.5 million on sales of US $2.8 billion and employed 1,852 people.

fill the duvet. In side conversation with Daniel Legrand, Georges Mekiès asked if this requirement came directly from the final customer. Legrand replied that it did not seem to be the case. He himself had interviewed Japanese customers in down and duvet shops and had found that the average customer did not know about different qualities of down; nor did customers seem to care whether the down was grey or white. Mekiès was therefore a bit surprised by Arai's requirement. In France, as in most European countries, the customer was usually concerned only about price and design. Legrand explained that Arai wanted to use "new white goose down only" as a major selling point to market Lestra Design duvets as a high-quality product to the distributors and the retailers. From previous conversations with both wholesalers and retailers, Legrand explained that "new white goose down only" was indeed a reasonable expectation, consistent with the upper positioning of European products in Japan, as well as with the high quality associated with French fashion items. According to the trade, the "new white goose down only" argument would also justify the premium price charged by the retailers for Lestra Design products. Retail prices for Lestra Design products in Japan were expected to range between ¥60,000 and ¥110,000[4] and compared similarly with competitive high-quality products imported from West Germany. However, prices varied greatly according to the quality of the down and feathers and the mix of the two from a 100 to a 300 retail price index. In fact, some stores, both in Japan and in Europe, offered customers the option of choosing the filling they wanted for their duvets and eiderdowns, giving a lot of pricing flexibility to the customer.

Retail prices for Lestra Design in Japan would have to be more than twice those in France. Such a difference could be explained by the lengthy distribution system, typical of Japan, which inflated the price of imported goods (see Exhibit 4). For an ex-factory price index of 100, cost, insurance, and freight would add 4%, and duties, an additional 6%. Then, Arai would price the goods to enjoy a 12% markup on his selling price to Morimoto, who would take a 10% commission when selling to smaller wholesalers. In turn, small wholesalers would enjoy a 20% markup on their selling price to retailers, who would finally sell Lestra Design products at a price that would allow them a 40 to 60% markup. On a retail price basis, Lestra Design products in Japan would be about 30 to 50% more expensive than most local products of similar quality. Cheap models (either locally made or imported from China) would sell for ¥40,000. On the other hand, Nishikawa, the market leader, offered many models in the Lestra Design price range, as well as a few prestigious models over the ¥1,000,000 mark. Competitive products from West Germany were sold in Japan with a strong emphasis on the German tradition for making duvets. Advertising for these products would often carry the German flag, emphasize the "Made in Germany" label, and include a commercial slogan in German.

The Dust Problem Again

The conversation between Arai and Mekiès then moved to the dust problem. Arai explained that, in his view, the problem lay with the composition of the chemical

4. In 1985 ¥240 = US $1.

formula used to wash the down. Arai had already made arrangements for Mekiès and Papillault to visit a Japanese duvet and eiderdown manufacturer in the afternoon. To get this Japanese company to open its doors, Arai had simply told the plant manager that a group of French importers was interested in buying his products. As a result, the Japanese manufacturer was quite willing to let the French group visit the factory. Mekiès and Legrand were impressed by the state-of-the-art equipment used by the Japanese firm. Papillault noticed that the Japanese were using microscopes and some very expensive machines that he had never seen in Europe to measure, for example, the greasiness of the down. Mekiès was amazed to observe three Japanese employees in white smocks separating down from small feathers with medical tweezers. According to Papillault, not a single Western manufacturer was as meticulous as this Japanese company. During the visit, Mekiès also picked up some useful information about the chemical formula used by the Japanese manufacturer to wash the down and feathers.

The next day, Mekiès and Papillault flew back to France, fully aware that much remained to be done to crack the Japanese market. Before leaving, Mekiès told Arai that this trip had been extremely useful, and that Léopold & Fils would work hard to make a new sample that would meet the Japanese quality standards. Arai also promised Mekiès that he would try to get more information about the chemical formula used by the Japanese company they had visited.

The Fabric Problem

Two weeks later, Arai sent Léopold & Fils some additional information on the chemical formula. Mekiès then contacted a large French chemical company that immediately produced an identical formulation for Lestra Design. At the end of April, Arai told Legrand that Lestra Design should hurry with its new samples. Most wholesalers would be placing orders in May for late October delivery to the retail shops. Arai also indicated that Morimoto from Katakura Kogyo had already selected some designs and had basically agreed to order 200 duvets at the FOB (free on board) price of FF 900 each, provided that Lestra Design solved the dust problem.

In late May 1984, three new duvet samples arrived in Japan. Arai found them much better than the previous ones. However, he still felt that the dust problem was not completely solved. Arai and Morimoto decided to have the fabric inspected in the laboratories of the Japanese Textile Association in Osaka. Legrand was informed that the fabric used by Lestra Design did not have the same density of threads per square inch as most Japanese duvet fabrics had. Legrand reported this latest development to Mekiès, who was obviously upset by this new complaint from the Japanese. Legrand was also worried that the time required to have the fabric inspected would further delay the manufacturing of the 200 duvets that Morimoto was planning to order. In the meantime, Lestra Design had been obliged to order the fabric with the printed design selected by Morimoto in order to get exclusivity from its French supplier.

"GOKAI" (MISUNDERSTANDINGS)

At the end of June 1984, Takeshi Kuroda, an executive from Katakura Kogyo, was on a business trip in the southern part of France and visited Georges Mekiès and Claude Léopold in Amboise. Mekiès had trouble communicating with the Japanese executive because of Kuroda's limited fluency in English. However, Mekiès understood from Kuroda that Lestra Design had the green light to manufacture 200 duvets using the fabric selected by Morimoto. Mekiès communicated the good news to Legrand, who phoned Morimoto to thank him for the order. Morimoto was surprised by D. Legrand's call because he personally had not taken any steps to confirm the order. Morimoto had first wanted to have the results of the test being conducted in Osaka. Finally, in early July, the report from the Japanese Textile Association brought bad news for Lestra Design. The Japanese laboratories found that the density of Lestra Design's fabric was far below that of most Japanese duvet fabrics.

The test results confirmed the fears of Arai and Morimoto that the fabric problem created a major obstacle for selling Lestra Design duvets in Japan. Although the test could not legally prevent Lestra Design from selling on the Japanese market, Arai and Morimoto insisted that the French products had to be perfect to be sold in Japan. Thus, Morimoto told Legrand that he would not be able to proceed with importing the 200 duvets. Legrand tried to counter with the argument that the test was merely a nontariff barrier for Lestra Design products in Japan. However, Morimoto insisted that Lestra Design had to meet the market requirements to succeed in Japan.

When Legrand phoned the Lestra Design office in Amboise, Georges Mekiès was very upset. As far as he knew, the Japanese were the only ones in the world to conduct this kind of investigation, which he believed was a nontariff barrier to prevent non-Japanese products from entering the Japanese market. Mekiès' exasperation was increased because, following Kuroda's visit, the 200 duvets for Katakura Kogyo had already been manufactured. Because the duvets had been made to fit Japanese specifications, they could be sold only in Japan. Legrand replied that he would explain the situation to Morimoto and that he would try to convince him to do something about it. During the following days, Legrand tried hard to persuade Morimoto to accept the order. It seemed to him that Kuroda was directly responsible for the misunderstanding. But Morimoto remained inflexible and said that he could not buy products inferior in quality to those sold by Japanese competitors.

During the latter half of 1984, little communication took place between the French and the Japanese. Claude Léopold and Georges Mekiès were upset by the attitude of the Japanese. On the Japanese side, Akira Arai and Naoto Morimoto said that it was too late to meet with the distributors, as most of their orders had already being placed in late July for the winter season. However, Legrand and Arai stayed in touch. At the end of February 1985, Arai said that he was still interested in importing Lestra Design products. Both Legrand and Arai were convinced that despite all the setbacks there was still hope for Lestra Design to grasp a share of the huge Japanese market for duvets. Legrand had learned that Lestra Design's major French competitor had faced similar problems in Japan and had decided to give up the Japanese market. On the other hand, he knew that several German competitors were operating successfully in Japan.

In April 1985, Legrand took advantage of a business trip to France to visit Léopold and Mekiès in Amboise. He was aware that Lestra Design was making a successful start in the United States. In fact, Léopold was just back from an exhibition in New York where a major order had been placed. Legrand emphasized again the great potential of the Japanese market and the need to take a long-term view of this market. Legrand recognized that, although Japan was a tough market to crack, persistence would eventually pay off. Claude Léopold said that he had already tried hard and confessed that he was still quite disappointed by the Japanese market. However, at the end of the meeting, Léopold said that he would consider one last try.

THE ALTERNATIVES

In early May 1985, Legrand again met with Arai and Morimoto. Morimoto mentioned that he would be interested in buying the original designs from Josette Léopold and then having the duvets manufactured in Japan under license. Claude Léopold was not keen about this idea. He knew that Yves Saint Laurent, Lanvin, and Courrèges duvets were manufactured this way in Japan. Léopold also knew that Lacoste shirts, although considered a universal product, had been completely adapted to suit the Japanese market. The colors, shape, and even the cotton material of Lacoste shirts sold in Japan were different from the Lacoste products sold in the rest of the world. Bernard Lacoste, the son of the famous tennis player and a personal friend of Claude Léopold, ran the Lacoste business around the world. A few months earlier, Léopold had heard from Lacoste himself that in the previous year, the Lacoste company had had trouble with its Japanese licensee. Yves Gasquères, the French consultant in Tokyo who was monitoring Lacoste's operations in Japan, had discovered that the licensee had at one point in time "forgotten" to pay the full amount of royalties due to Lacoste in France. Léopold was therefore wondering if licensing would be the best solution.

Arai had also proposed that Lestra Design buy some Japanese fabric and manufacture the duvets in France. He argued that this would definitively solve the dust problem. Moreover, Lestra Design products could still carry the "Made in France" label that was so appealing to Japanese customers.

Another alternative recommended to Mekiès was to buy fabric for the duvets from West Germany where textile standards were similar to the ones in Japan. Lestra Design could then print Josette Léopold's designs on the German cloth and still manufacture the duvets in France. Because the Japanese insisted on floral motives, Lestra Design could even buy fabric with floral prints in West Germany. Arai had found that many Japanese companies like Nishikawa (the leading duvet manufacturer in Japan) were already buying a lot of German fabric for duvets. However, in order to be granted the design exclusivity, Mekiès needed to buy a minimum amount of fabric, the equivalent of 300 duvets.

As he was reviewing these different alternatives for Lestra Design, Claude Léopold wondered if he should continue trying to gain a foothold in the Japanese market, or should he simply forget about Japan and focus more on Europe and the United States.

EXHIBIT 1

EXHIBIT 2

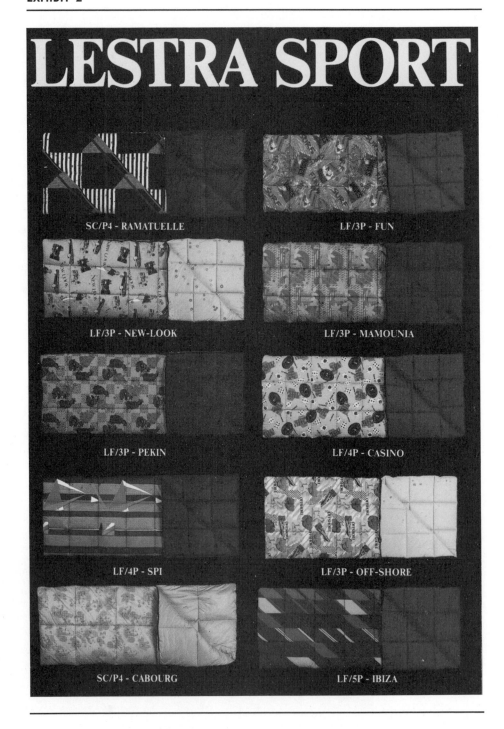

EXHIBIT 3 Comparative Distribution Channels for Duvets and Interior Textiles

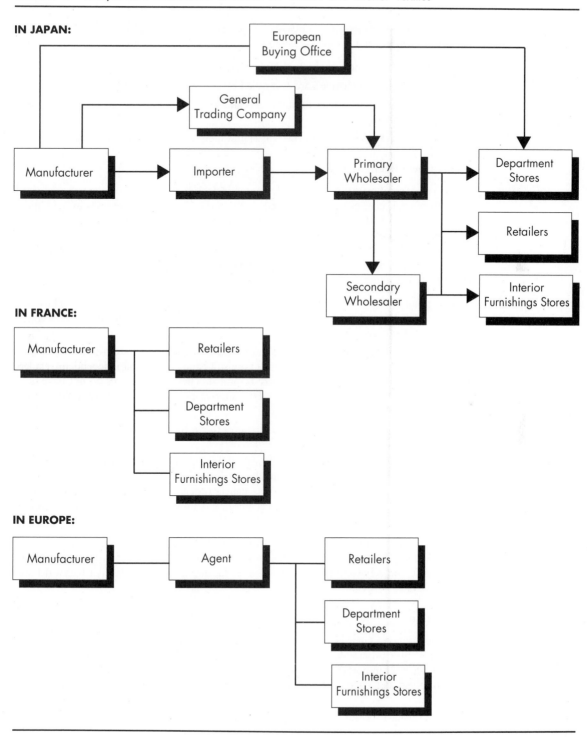

EXHIBIT 4 Short Note on Distribution in Japan

In the early 1980s, many foreign businesspeople were commenting that Japan's distribution system was lengthy and complex. Common criticisms included the following:

- Distribution channels are long and complex.
- Some distribution channels are controlled by large manufacturers.
- Some import agents prefer high margins and low volume, leading to high prices for imported goods.
- The costs of setting up one's own distribution are high and time consuming.

The Japanese Retail Market

The Japanese retail market was extremely fragmented. In 1984, independent stores accounted for 57% of retail sales in Japan, compared to 3% in the United States and 5% in the United Kingdom. Japan had 1,350 shops for every 100,000 persons—twice as many as in most European countries.

According to a publication by the Japan External Trade Organization (JETRO),[5] the reasons for the fragmentation of retailing were closely related to Japan's social, cultural, and economic environment:

- *Shopping patterns* The typical Japanese housewife usually shops once a day. This custom is directly related to the size of the average home in Japan, which cannot accommodate large quantities of food.
- *Economics* The price of land in Japan precludes establishing Western-style supermarkets. Most retail sales in Japan are still handled by small independent retailers who own the land on which the store is located. These family stores do not have to consider return on investment as would a supermarket setting up a large-scale operation on the same site.
- *Regulation* Opening a supermarket requires that a company make 73 applications for 26 separate approvals under 12 different laws.
- *Service* Smaller stores are located near one's home and give housewives a place to socialize. Small retail stores also have longer business hours, making it easier to shop at night. Independent retailers will also deliver orders for their customers and extend credit. The neighborhood shopping center near a subway or train station is a firmly established institution in Japan.

In the same publication, JETRO also predicted that the number of small retail stores would continue to rise. In conclusion, the report stated that, given the Japanese preference for more convenience and service, the retailing sector in Japan was not necessarily a backward and underdeveloped system.

Implications

The implications of greater fragmentation in retailing were that either the manufacturer or the wholesaler must provide for small stores the services that they cannot provide themselves. Some of the most important services are finance, collection of bills, inventory, risk absorption, marketing and merchandising, and marketing feedback.   (continued)

5. "Planning for Distribution in Japan," Jetro Marketing Series, Tokyo, 1983.

EXHIBIT 4 (continued)

Trade Practices

- *Margins* For duvets, the margin for the primary wholesaler (as a percentage of retail price) is approximately 15%, and that of the secondary wholesaler, about 10%.

- *Rebates* Payments from the manufacturer to the wholesaler and from the wholesaler to the retailer on such factors as sales performance are a common practice in Japan.

- *Physical distribution* Construction of delivery centers has been encouraged to modernize physical distribution. When a distribution center has been constructed, typically the merchandise flows directly from the manufacturer to the center and then to retail outlets, even though orders and other information may pass through wholesaler intermediaries.

- *Payment terms* Payment periods run from 60 to 180 days after delivery of goods.

- *Consignment sales* Sales on consignment is the rule in most Japanese industries. Retailers and wholesalers can reserve the right to return unsold goods to the manufacturer.

- *In-channel sales promotion* Wholesalers engage in sales promotion activities similar to those of manufacturers.

5 CLUB MED SALES, INC. (A)

It was still raining in New York on May 31, 1983, when Serge Trigano, chairman and CEO of Club Med Sales, Inc. (CMI), returned to his office. He sat and went over in his mind the events of the meeting he had just attended. When CMI's bookings for summer 1983 had gone 3% below those of the previous summer, a meeting with CMI's advertising agency had been called to examine the situation.

The advertising agency's suggested response to the dip in sales was to send a discount coupon for September vacations to people who had been to Club Med in the recent past. Club Med's immediate reaction had been, "Was a discount suitable for the Club Med customer?" It became clear during the meeting that no detailed definition of the Club Med customer had been formalized. No formal market research had yet been done on the American consumer. Did Club Med need to do this research? If so, what kind of research should be done and where? What could be done in the short term to help boost sales? Were there other, more important issues that should be addressed? Some in Club Med management believed a variety of questions needed to be answered to find out why this successful global vacation concept was running into difficulties in the United States.

COMPANY BACKGROUND

From its inception as a nonprofit venture in 1950, Club Méditerranée (Club Med), CMI's parent, had been a unique enterprise. Lodging for vacationers was furnished in a way never before seen in France. Gilbert Trigano, part-owner of a family tent-making business, rented the required tents to Club Med with no down payment.

In 1954, Gilbert Trigano formally joined Club Med and turned it into a profit-making business. The unique concept of the straw hut village was born. The idea was to create a Polynesian, "back-to-nature" atmosphere. The huts were bare of any luxury, and showers were shared. Outdoor activities were the main focus of daily

This case was written by Professor Jacques Horovitz, European School of Management; Terry Deutscher of IMD and University of Western Ontario; and Research Associate Juli Dixon. Copyright © 1987 by the International Management Development Institute (IMD), Lausanne, Switzerland, and EAP, Paris, France. All rights reserved.

life. From this type of village came the image that Club Med has represented to this day—sun, sea, and sport.

Club Med expanded quickly, frequently adding one or two resorts per year. In 1956, the first ski resort opened in Switzerland. Club Med moved into what would become known as the American zone in 1968. Europe, however, continued to be its main target. By 1982, Club Med was represented in 24 countries by 98 villages (one-fifth of which were ski resorts), 58 residences, and 6 resort hotels. Financially, Club Med was very profitable (see Exhibit 1). Another indication of Club Med's success was that it had become a household word in France, where it was known simply as "le Club."

The Club Med Concept

The Club Med concept was unique. Any package vacation that Club Med offered had the same basics: a prepaid, fixed-price holiday, including air fare, meals (with unlimited wine and beer), sports, sports instruction, and other activities such as a discotheque, arts and crafts, classical concerts, and cabaret shows at night. Sports were varied and included activities such as archery, snorkeling, deep-sea diving, horseback riding, and yoga, as well as standard favorites like swimming, tennis, sailing, golf, and many others. Vacationers could choose either to take part or not take part in these activities. The villages also contained other facilities such as a shop, car rentals, and an excursions office, all of which were within walking distance. Club Med was famous for selecting the best available beach areas in every country where it had summer villages.

A no-hassle, relaxed atmosphere was created, since Club Med arranged meals and leisure time. Each village staff member (called a *gentil organisateur* or GO) had responsibilities in an area such as applied arts, sports, excursions, food, bar, or receptions. There were about 80 to 100 of these organizers per village. They would move to a different village every six months. The GOs were encouraged to mix with the vacationers (called GMs for *gentils membres*) and performed the various roles of hosts, friends, teachers, and entertainers rather than staff.

Another aspect of the Club Med concept was the absence of clocks, phones, radios, money, tips, and rigid dress code; people could dress casually or more formally as they wished. Extra drinks were purchased using prepaid bead necklaces.

Club Med had ensured that it was fundamentally different from other packaged tours. First, the homogeneity of the villages provided a predictable fantasy within a Club Med world anywhere, so that Club Med was not really selling a destination as were other tour groups. Second, the informal way of life in the village, along with the absence of money, broke down the established barriers of class and wealth among vacationers.

Furthermore, Club Med had overcome the seasonality problem by opening some resorts all year round and by providing both winter and summer vacation locations. Also, Club Med had been operating for a long time and had built up much goodwill—70% of its European vacationers had been on a Club Med vacation before.

International Business Week (September 27, 1982) called Club Med "the innovative French vacation specialist." The company earned this reputation by refusing to sit back and let its proven formula work. It was continually adjusting and adding to its offerings. In fact, its success was so great that it received the compliment of having the "capacity to anticipate the needs of [its] clients" (*International Business Week,* August 3, 1981).

The Gentil Membre

Broadly speaking, a whole spectrum of vacationers was represented among the Club Med customers. However, there was a larger representation of office workers, executives, and professional people. Club Med had not yet examined its customer base in detail.

THE AMERICAN MARKET AND CMI

The Economic Climate

According to the *Economist,* (October 1982), despite the worsening recession, the number of tourists had increased (see Exhibit 2). One point that favored Club Med in the travel industry was that packaged tours generally remained popular; however, people were starting to take less expensive or shorter vacations or were staying closer to home.

Deregulation in the United States airline industry in 1979 had brought about substantial changes in the packaged tour business. The ensuing price war had slashed travelers' costs, uncovering a new mass market for inexpensive air travel. The number of travel agents had increased from 7,000 in 1970 to over 22,000 in 1983. Travel agents demanded higher commissions when group selling became a large part of their business. With the subsequent increase in commissions, it became even more attractive to set up an agency. As in Europe, travel agents were the primary channel for sales in the travel business.

Club Med believed that it occupied a unique position in the market and had no major competitors. Its closest competition, however, did come from other packaged tour operators.

As a result of deregulation, some prices for airline tickets had recently dropped by 30%. Club Med had not yet incorporated these decreases into its prices. Table 1

TABLE 1 One-Week Club Med Vacation vs. Packaged Tour

	Club Med	Competitor
Before decrease	$799[a]	$505[b]
After decrease	$799	$399

[a]Includes air fare of $400, lodging, all meals, all sports, and other activities.
[b]Includes air fare, hotel, and breakfast.

gives an example of the price structure, comparing a Club Med trip from Los Angeles to Puerta Vallarta, Mexico, with a competitive package sold by an airline.

It was estimated that some 4.5 million residents of the United States had gone on packaged tours in 1982, including about 1.5 million who had taken cruises. Many others took vacations to "sun destinations" without using packaged tours. For example, it was projected that in 1983 about 1.5 million people from the U.S. mainland would go to Puerto Rico, a destination that was within the same geographical area as five Club Med villages. Another 2.5 million were expected to go to the Caribbean islands, and 500,000 to Bermuda. (Exhibit 2 gives a breakdown by destination of U.S. travelers abroad during 1980–1982.)

Targeting North America

In the mid-1970s, Club Med started to target the North American market specifically. In 1980, Club Med was restructured so that marketing and operations were more closely linked. North and South America made up the American zone, which had its own profit responsibilities. By 1983, North Americans represented 15% of the GMs worldwide, but less than half of 1% of the North American population were Club Med clients. Total sales in North America were almost $140 million in 1981–1982, representing some 120,000 GMs.

In 1980, Serge Trigano took charge of the American zone. Improving Club Med's image in the North American market was his first priority, as there was a feeling in the organization that an image of sexual permissiveness was deterring many Americans from patronizing Club Med. Club Med believed that the North American market represented a sound base for growth.

By the beginning of 1983, Serge Trigano was convinced he was well on the way to achieving the goals he had set. Revenues had grown by 6% over the previous year, and profits had exceeded his expectations. He also believed that substantial progress had been made in improving Club Med's image. A new campaign—the Antidote for Civilisation—had set Club Med apart from other travel advertisers. Club Med spent several million dollars a year on this image-oriented consumer advertising, emphasizing the uniqueness of the concept. The campaign had generated considerable favorable public relations for the organization, and it had been nominated for a prestigious CLIO award in the advertising industry.

CMI'S MARKETING STRATEGY

Organization

The organization of CMI in the American zone was such that Serge Trigano, as CEO, had about 25 people reporting to him directly in the following areas: public relations, transportation, operations, advertising agency coordinator, finance, sales promotion, and so forth. In the sales promotion area, 7 regional sales managers (about 35 years old) supervised 14 district sales managers. In contrast, a single airline had 40 sales representatives for the New York market alone.

All of CMI's regional and district sales managers were former GOs. They were expected to make sales calls to the travel agents, give them brochures, and talk to them about the Club Med concept. No formal system had been set up regarding which agents to visit at what time. As a result, each representative performed his or her job differently. Each one also operated independently in developing creative ideas to boost sales. Some representatives had consumer shows at which people could hear about the Club Med concept. Others participated in professional travel shows or ran cooperative advertising with their own copy. This arrangement was consistent with the company's management style that allowed the GOs running a Club Med village to be their own masters in designing enjoyable vacation programs.

Regional representatives were earning over $50,000 a year, with an additional bonus of up to 25%; district representatives earned a straight $25,000 a year. These figures did not include expenses, which were approximately $500,000 for all representatives, including travel.

Sales Promotion and Advertising

Serge Trigano was the final decision maker for sales promotion and advertising. The total marketing budget for 1983 is presented in Table 2.

TABLE 2 CMI's Total Marketing Budget (1983)

Advertising (5.7% of sales)	$ 8 million[a]
"Push"[b]	2
Brochures	2
Reservation center (Toll-free, 800 number)	4
Travel agents' commission (10% of sales)	12
Miscellaneous	1
	$29 million

[a]Advertising in 1980 had been $2.5 million.
[b]Sales managers' salaries and expenses, trade advertising, travel agents' familiarization trips, and promotional material directed at travel agents.

Club Med used the words "tactical" and "image" to distinguish between its two types of advertising. Image advertising intended to build up in people's minds a long-term concept of Club Med and what it represented. Television, magazines, and sometimes billboards were considered the most effective media for this type of advertising. Tactical advertising, on the other hand, was a call for action in the short term that would generate revenue the following week. Club Med used radio and newspaper for this type of sales-oriented advertisement. One-third of the advertising budget was currently allocated to tactical advertising. (See Exhibit 3 for an example of a tactical advertisement.)

Travel agents accounted for 86% of CMI's sales. CMI had a reservation center in Phoenix from which 100 reservations employees serviced the public as well as the bookings from travel agents. In contrast, only 35% of Club Med sales were from travel agents in the French market.

American travel agents received a 10% commission from Club Med, the usual rate given for business travel (such as airplane tickets). Packaged tour competitors, however, frequently raised commissions with special promotions. For example, if a travel agent's volume exceeded a certain level, the commission would be increased, or a travel agent who sold packages during certain periods earned more. Sometimes a direct cash bonus was offered for selling certain packages. Large travel agencies that did a sizable volume of business for a competitor often got a higher base commission. The net effect of these programs was that travel agents could sometimes earn 15% commissions and, on rare occasions, even as much as 20%. Club Med did not offer such incentives.

ADVERTISING AGENCY MEETING, MAY 31, 1983

The climate of the meeting was tense because Serge Trigano was not pleased that bookings had dropped to 3% below the sales of the previous summer, after an annual growth averaging 5 to 6% (before inflation) in recent years. The advertising agency had reserved a conference room in the Hotel Meridien in New York City and had asked its own CEO to make an elaborate presentation (booklet, overhead, and past TV spots shown on video, as well as current summer newspaper advertising). The ten representatives from the agency were anxious to appease Serge, who they sensed was very concerned. Jean Rambaud, who had recently agreed to become assistant to the chairman and CEO of CMI, with major responsibilities in sales and marketing, had also been invited to the meeting to be briefed on CMI's advertising strategy.

One of the main ideas presented by the advertising agency was to send recent Club Med members a gift certificate for a $100 discount on a September holiday. Otherwise, despite the dip, the agency proposed to continue the same newspaper advertising campaign that it had started in April.

When asked for his opinion about the discount idea, Jean Rambaud replied:

> The advertisements you just showed me on video, used mostly in the winter, appear to be targeted at an upscale customer. If Club Med is attracting that kind of person, how will they react to a discount on the same holiday they paid full price for last year? I'd worry that they might wonder just who will start coming to Club Med. We might lose this upscale customer and attract another kind. Is that what we want?

Trigano thought that the present newspaper advertising campaign was not aggressive enough and would not attract sales in the short term. Also, because September was the end of the season, Trigano questioned waiting that long before attempting to remedy an immediate problem.

The agency indicated that it believed Club Med was overreacting and that business would pick up. "Don't worry, our plan will work" was the agency's response. The agency also suggested that bookings would increase if the agency sweetened the sales opportunities for the travel agents.

Rambaud returned to his concern about the Club Med customer:

> You seem sure that the Club Med customer will rush to the villages because of a $100 discount. But, who is the Club Med customer?

Taken aback, the agency admitted that without any recent formal market research it could not accurately describe the Club Med customer. This answer strengthened Rambaud's resolve to examine the discount suggestion more closely. He remarked that it would be a good idea to do some market research. The agency agreed.

After the meeting, Trigano and Rambaud talked about the potential for market research. Trigano encouraged Rambaud to develop a research proposal and to offer other suggestions that would address the problem. Both agreed that in the short run it was important to stay within the current $29 million marketing budget (see Table 2).

Rambaud returned to his hotel and thought through the situation. There were several important questions. What should Club Med do in the short term to improve its bookings? Was a market research study necessary, and if so, what kind and where? What did management need to know, and what would they do with the results when they got them? Rambaud was aware that CMI had not done formal market research before and that for results to be used effectively the project would have to be carefully implemented in the organization.

After making preliminary inquiries the next day, Rambaud drew up a list of the different types of research and their associated costs (see Exhibit 4).

EXHIBIT 1 Club Med Financial Statements

	1980/1981[a]	1981/1982[b]
	(000's FF)	(000's FF)
Gross income	3,180,523	3,953,812
Gross margins	1,994,388	2,486,948
	(62.7%)	(62.9%)
Earnings	142,128	174,331
Consolidated earnings per share	43.99	50.46
Hotel Days Spent in Zone (000) (winter and summer)	1980/1981 (000)	1980/1981 (000)
North America	1,279	1,464
All other zones	5,635	5,693
Average Bed Occupancy Rate (%)	1980/1981 (%)	1981/1982 (%)
Total	71.51	71.27
Europe/Africa	76.66	75.76
South America	50.44	44.33
North and Central America	59.24	61.93
Asia, South Pacific, Indian Ocean	65.18	68.21

Source: Club Méditerranée Annual Report 1982/83.
[a]U.S. $1 = FF 5.67.
[b] U.S. $1 = FF 7.25.

EXHIBIT 2 Destinations of U.S. Travelers Abroad

	1980	1981	1982
	(in thousands)		
Canada[a]	11,171	11,374	10,974
Mexico[b]	3,442	3,432	3,580
Europe and Mediterranean	3,934	3,931	4,144
Caribbean and Central America	2,624	2,453	2,637
South America	594	567	529
Other Areas	1,011	1,089	1,200
Total	22,421	22,846	23,064

Source: U.S. Department of Commerce, Bureau of Economic Analysis.
Note: Includes business travel; exclude cruises and travel by military personnel and other government employees stationed abroad.
[a]Visitors staying one or more nights in Canada.
[b]Visitors staying one or more nights in Mexico.

EXHIBIT 3 Club Med Advertisement

CLUB MED PRESENTS THE SUMMER CLUBS.

Club Med serves up Intensive Tennis for players at all levels. There'll be 2½-hour daily lessons, ball machines, closed-circuit video and training films. Paradise Island, Bahamas, May 1 to Oct. 31. From $790 to $885 (depending on date) for one week, including air fare from New York.*

Professional artists and performers at our Fine Arts and Music Festival will exhibit their talents and help you develop yours in special classes and workshops. Magic Haiti, Haiti, July 1 to July 31. Special 10-day package, only $980 including air fare from New York.* Week-long packages also available.

Aerobics, jogging, running, yoga, gymnastics and more are the components of our special Fitness Month vacations. They'll prove to you that shaping up really can be fun. Caravelle, Guadeloupe, Oct. 1 to Oct. 31. From $900 to $940 (depending on date) for one week, including air fare from New York.*

This year's International Bridge Festival bids to be the best ever. Enjoy the camaraderie of players from around the world, in team and mixed-doubles competitions. Punta Cana, Dominican Republic, Sept. 4 to Sept. 11. Only $880 for one week, including air fare from New York.*

Learn how to harness the wind and the sea during our Windsurfing Weeks. Intensive teaching will help you master the techniques of the masters. And you'll find yourself competing in our grand regattas. Magic Haiti, Haiti, June 5 to June 19. Only $790 for one week, including air fare from New York.*

Our French Immersion vacations feature daily audiovisual language labs, French film classics and tables where only French is spoken at mealtimes. So you'll learn a new language almost effortlessly. Caravelle, Guadeloupe, July 1 to Aug. 31. Special 11-day package, only $1135 including air fare from New York.* Week-long packages also available.

DAYS ARE LONGER. ACTIVITIES ARE BROADER. PRICES ARE LOWER. AND GOOD-BYES ARE HARDER.

There is a vacation that is far removed from the petty annoyances of ordinary vacations.

A week full of sports like tennis, waterskiing and sailing. And gourmet meals. And glittering entertainment.

At a special vacation village designed only for your amusement. On an exquisite beach lapped by cool tropical waters.

It is Club Med.

At Club Med villages all year round, you can enjoy this unique vacation for one very reasonable all-inclusive price.

But in the summer there's even more to enjoy: a range of sports and unusual activities that will make your vacation more of a celebration than ever before. At lower prices than in the wintertime.

Our Summer Club special events are described in greater detail above. But what's almost indescribable is the feeling of relaxation and harmony you will discover at Club Med this summer.

You see, we've done everything possible to make sure that at Club Med the living is easy. So only the leaving for home is not.

CLUB MED®
The antidote for civilization.℠
Call your travel agent or 1-800-528-3100.

*Per person double occupancy. Does not include $25 annual membership fee. All prices subject to change. Activities vary from village to village. © 1982 Club Med, Inc. 40 West 57th St., New York, NY 10019

Source: Ammirati & Puris Inc.

EXHIBIT 4 Comparative Direct Costs per Completed Interview

Data collection method	Approximate cost ($)
1. Mail survey (costs depend on return rate, incentives, and follow-up procedure).	5–10
2. Telephone interviews 7-minute interview with head of household in metropolitan area	8–10
15-minute interview with small segment of national population from central station	15–25
3. Personal interviews: 10-minute personal interview in middle-class suburban area (2 callbacks and 10% validation)	20–30
40- to 60-minute interview of national probability sample (3 callbacks and 10% validation)	40–50
Executive (VIP) interviews (1 to 2 hours)	150
One focus group of 15 people (includes analysis and a report on the session)	3,000–4,000

Note: Includes travel and telephone charges, interviewer compensation, training, and direct supervision expenses.

6 CLUB MED SALES, INC. (B)

Club Méditerranée (Club Med) offered packaged vacations all over the world. It had been concentrating on the American market in recent years because it considered North America to be a growth market. When, in the spring of 1983, bookings for summer vacations in the American zone had dipped 3% below sales of the previous summer, an urgent meeting with the advertising agency for Club Med Sales, Inc. (CMI) had been called by Serge Trigano, the CEO of the American zone. Jean Rambaud, a former associate of Trigano, had attended the meeting because he was going to join the company in July 1983 to do a six-month project on the work methods of the sales organization.

At this meeting, the advertising agency suggested offering a discount to customers in order to increase sales. However, there was some doubt as to whether or not a discount was suitable for the type of customer who took a Club Med vacation. The agency was unable to provide an adequate description of the Club Med customer, and thus it was agreed that market research was needed. Jean Rambaud was to take the lead by identifying Club Med's needs, designing the research, and implementing the results.

For background information on CMI, see Case 5, Club Med Sales, Inc. (A).

ADVERTISING MEETING, MAY 31, 1983: CMI'S RESPONSE

Club Med did not follow its advertising agency's suggestion to introduce a customer discount. It did, however, immediately drop prices in the California market where Club Med air travel prices were 30% higher than those offered by competing package tours. Also, the advertising was changed to emphasize all the activities, meals, and other extras that were included in Club Med's price, and not available in other tours (see Exhibit 1). These advertisements demonstrated that Club Med

This case was prepared by Jacques Horovitz, visiting professor from EAP (European School of Management) and Terry Deutscher, visiting professor from the University of Western Ontario, with the assistance of research associate Juli Dixon. Copyright © 1987 by the International Management Development Institute (IMD), Lausanne, Switzerland, and EAP, Paris, France. Not to be used or reproduced without permission.

provided good value for the money in a market where airline deregulation was enabling many inexpensive packages to be offered.

Data from Club Med's own computer revealed that 12,000 of the 22,000 travel agents in the United States had sold at least one Club Med trip in the past year. Half of Club Med's sales were generated in 2,000 of these agencies, but half of these top sellers were different from year to year.

THE RESEARCH

Five studies were done to help Club Med learn more about its customers and its market. The first study was a demographic profile study of the Club Med customer (see Exhibit 2). The second study compared the profile of Club Med vacationers to a cluster of 40 groups representing all U.S. residents. This information, available from a data bank called PRIZM, helped determine what "types" of people were interested in Club Med and where they came from. After the major "types" were identified, detailed data (on media habits, activities, interests, and opinions of a panel of 20,000 people) from the Simmons Market Research Bureau were correlated with the "types" in order to distinguish likely tastes of Club Med customers. (See Exhibits 3, 4, and 5.)

In the next stage, a detailed two-phase study of the consumer market was conducted for Club Med. Phase One, called Focus Groups (see Exhibit 6), consisted of an in-depth discussion with small groups of Club Med members and nonmembers to elicit hypotheses for a thorough survey of members and prospective members. Phase Two, called the Quantitative Study (see Exhibit 7), was a survey that was designed to elicit the following information:

- Members' and prospects' opinion of Club Med (see Exhibit 8).
- A picture of Club Med members and prospects (see Exhibit 9).
- Members' and prospects' expectations of vacations (see Exhibits 10 and 11).
- The impression Club Med members were communicating (see Exhibit 12).
- Members' booking behavior (see Exhibit 13).
- Prospective customers' cost perception of a Club Med vacation (see Exhibits 14 and 15).
- Key Prospects' interest in particular vacation activities and services (see Exhibit 16).

Most of the findings presented in Exhibits 2–16 represent the responses of "Key Prospects" and "Key Members." (To be designated as "key," a person must have responded that he or she would probably or definitely consider a Club Med vacation in the near future, either as a repeat purchase or as an initial trial.) A summary of how "Other Members" responded to the survey is also given (see Exhibit 17). Exhibits 7–17 are a condensation of more than 400 pages of research results.

The fourth research study looked at U.S. travel agents to determine their attitude toward Club Med so that Club Med could improve its working relationship with the agents (see Exhibit 18). The fifth and last study, the Destination Study, determined the number of inhabitants from selected cities who traveled to particular geographical locations (see Exhibit 19).

After the data were collected, Club Med had another set of decisions to make. Did the company's current strategy fit with the findings? If not, what changes should be made in positioning, communications, product, pricing, and distribution? CMI had to decide who should be its customer and how to persuade this potential customer to patronize Club Med's villages.

EXHIBIT 1   Club Med Tactical Advertising, 1983

THE CLUB MED SUMMER VACATIONS. FOR PEOPLE WHO WANT EVERYTHING FOR PRACTICALLY NOTHING.

THE ALL-INCLUSIVE VACATION.

Club Med in the Caribbean. The Bahamas. Mexico. And Tahiti. Where all your sports, all your meals, your airfare and accommodations are all included for one extraordinary price that's less than what many hotels charge for a mere room. How much less? Simply glance at the list of daily activities on the right and compare the price of a day at Club Med to any equivalent hotel vacation. And once that's convinced you what an exceptional value Club Med truly is, call us or your travel agent for reservations.

$00

KIDS 4-7 STAY FREE*

Rest assured, the price you see above isn't a misprint. At Club Med, kids 4-7 stay absolutely free. Kids 8-11 stay for half price. And every kid stays fully occupied at our Mini Club in the Ixtapa village in Mexico (open June 11th through September 10th). Children can stay for an hour or an entire day. They can enjoy a wide range of sports. Attend magic classes. Even attend video workshops where they can direct and star in their own productions. All of which lets you enjoy your vacation while your kids are enjoying theirs.

PLAYA BLANCA

$60

PER DAY
Room
Breakfast
Lunch (With Wine)
Dinner (With Wine)
Snorkeling/Scuba
Sailing
Tennis
Yoga
Arts and Crafts
French Language Labs
Sports Instruction
Discotheque
Cabaret Shows

Since the value of the dollar has gone up in Mexico and airfares are lower, the price of a Club Med Vacation has gone down. We've been able to lower the cost of a week in Playa Blanca to just $599† from Houston, our lowest rate this summer.

CLUB MED
The antidote for civilization™
Call 1-800-528-3100 or your travel agent.

NEW LOW SUMMER PRICE

$599

All prices are per person, double occupancy, do not include $30 annual membership fee and are subject to change. Activities vary from village to village. *When accompanied by a parent at villages with a Mini-Club. †Effective May 29-Dec. 17, 1983. Add $50 week of Nov. 19. © 1983 Club Med, Inc. 40 West 57th St., NY, NY 10019.

Source: Ammirati & Puris Inc.

EXHIBIT 2 Demographic Profile Study (July 1983)

Cost: $7,000

Purpose: To determine major characteristics of Club Med customers.

Sample: 1000 people who booked Club Med vacations in the summer of 1982 (506 calls) or in the winter 1982–1983 (494 calls) in a North American village.

Methodology: Telephone interviews

Data: Forty percent of the Gentils Membres (GMs) interviewed had been to Club Med more than once.

Age	Winter vacations (%)	Summer vacations (%)
35+	60	44
25–30	32	50
less than 25	8	6

Marital status	(%)
Married	51
Single	36
Separated	1
Divorced	11
Widowed	1

Education	(%)
Graduate school	38
College graduate	40
Some college	13
High school or less	9

Community of residence	(%)
City	43
Suburb	49
Rural	7

Number in party	(%)
One	25
Two	52
Three or more	24

Household income	(%)
Less than $30,000	16
$30,000–$39,999	20
$40,000–$49,999	14
$50,000–$59,999	12
$60,000–$79,999	16
Greater than $80,000	22

Sources of information* about Club Med Vacation	(%)
Friends/associates	62
Travel agent	25
Advertising—TV	7
—magazine	4
—news	7
Brochure	6
Direct from Club Med	1

*Sum to more than 100 because multiple answers were allowed.

(continued)

EXHIBIT 2 (continued)

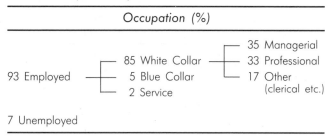

| | Occupation (%) | |

EXHIBIT 3 The Prizm Study (Fall 1983)

Produced by an organization named Claritas, PRIZM is a database used for postal code marketing. The use of PRIZM is based on the hypothesis that the same kind of people tend to live in the same postal codes (called zip codes in the United States).

Cost: $3,700

Purpose: The study was to help determine "group types" of people most likely to be interested in Club Med. The company planned to use the information for direct response purposes (mailing lists of people fitting the appropriate profile could be purchased), to determine the choice of message and the way in which the message would be written for the Club Med consumer, and to help choose appropriate media.

Sample: In the PRIZM database, census data from 36,000 zip codes were clustered into 44 homogeneous neighborhood groups, based on education, income, mobility, ethnicity, housing stock, degree of urbanization, age, family composition, and so forth. Club Med compared the zip codes of its customers with the clusters obtained from the PRIZM database to identify what kinds of people went to Club Med.

Data: Index of Concentration (See Exhibit 4)

Definition of Index of Concentration

The index of concentration is calculated by dividing the percentage of Club Med members whose addresses (i.e., zip codes) would place them in a given PRIZM cluster by the percentage of population in the PRIZM cluster and multiplying by 100.

Take, for example, Urban Gold Coast, the first cluster listed in Exhibit 4. The zip codes of 5.41% of Club Med members fall in this cluster, but the membership of the cluster itself is only 0.31% of the U.S. population.

Then, the index of concentration
= 5.41 divided by 0.31 times 100
= 1745

Therefore, the percentage of Club Med members from Urban Gold Coast is 17.45 times higher than the percentage of Urban Gold Coast people in the United States.

EXHIBIT 4 The Prizm Study: Analysis, Total Members

Cluster	Index of concentration
Urban Gold Coast	1,745
Blue Blood Estates	637
Bohemian Mix	556
Money and Brains	437
Furs and Station Wagons	291
Two More Rungs	279
Young Influentials	269
Pools and Patios	214
Sun Belt Singles	186
Blue to White	150
Young Suburbia	135
Old Melting Pot	134
God's Country	114
Blue Collar Catholics	80
Blue Chip Blues	74

Note: Only the 15 highest clusters on index of concentration are shown in this exhibit. They collectively represent 39.64% of the U.S. population and 81.18% of U.S. Club Med members. To illustrate the PRIZM analysis, the top five clusters are described below.

Of all 44 PRIZM clusters, the *Urban Gold Coast* cluster has the highest concentration of income, is the most densely populated, and has the highest percentage of young adults, singles, professionals, renters, childless house holders, and residents of New York City.

The *Blue Blood Estates* cluster has the most affluent people and the most well traveled. Also included are a large number of young adults living with their parents.

The *Bohemian Mix* cluster can be described as "high-rise singles."

The *Money and Brains* cluster are heavy consumers of adult luxuries in apparel, restaurants, and travel.

The *Furs and Station Wagons* cluster consists of well-educated, mobile professionals.

EXHIBIT 5 The Prizm Study: Market Potential Index and Activity and Media Analysis

Market Potential Index

This part of the study ranked various cities according to the prevalence of PRIZM clusters with a high proportion of Club Med members (relative to 100).

Washington	241
New York	207
San Francisco	195
Miami	151
Chicago	149
Los Angeles/Palm Springs	147

Activity and Media Analysis: In this analysis, data from the Simmons Market Research Bureau were used. This information has been collected in the United States every year from a sample of 20,000 people who were asked detailed questions about their media habits (television, radio, magazines, and newspapers) and life-styles. When these data were combined with the PRIZM data, it was possible to determine the tastes of the clusters full of Club Med members. An index measuring how frequently each cluster did an activity was correlated with the index of concentration. This correlation was done for income, education, marital status, sports tastes, tastes in reading, and media preferences.

Results: It was determined that the total Club Med membership was upscale in income and education and more likely to be single, not to have children, to travel a lot, to be sports-oriented (racquetball, jogging, sailing, tennis), and to own an American Express Green Card. As far as media were concerned, newspapers and magazines were better cluster fits than TV or radio. Tennis viewers were the only TV watchers with a profile similar to members' profiles. Radio did have some high correlations: classical, 0.867; all news, 0.822; and talk show stations, 0.802 (in contrast, country music, -0.681).

Magazines and Newspapers

New York Times Magazine	0.889*
New Yorker	0.856
New York Times, daily edition	0.782
Gentlemen's Quarterly	0.777
Time	0.764
Wall Street Journal	0.737
Harper's Bazaar	0.733

*This number is the correlation coefficient between a measure of clusters' readership of the *New York Times Magazine* and the index of concentration for each cluster. Each of the following correlation coefficients is created in the same way.

EXHIBIT 6 A Study of the Consumer Market Using Focus Groups (Summer 1983)

Cost: $15,000

Purpose: To develop hypotheses to be tested in the quantitative research to follow. CMI wanted to be sure it did not miss any important questions and that the questions were asked in the consumer's language.

Sample: Four groups of 15 people each: two groups from New York and two from San Francisco; two male groups, two female groups; 60% members, 40% nonmembers.

Methodology: CMI subcontracted this research to another firm that made up a list of questions relating to the subject of vacations in general. Questions such as "Where did you go on your vacation?" "What did you get out of your vacation?" and "Why did you choose this vacation?" were asked. Each group, which met in a room for two hours, was led by the head of the research group, a trained psychologist, and was watched by Jean Rambaud (and sometimes Serge Trigano and regional sales managers) from behind a one-way glass partition. Club Med could identify its members since their name tags were different from those of nonmembers. The group did not know that Club Med was sponsoring the research. After the focus groups were finished, the psychologist did a content analysis on the sessions. This last part helped to build the questions (as it highlighted important themes such as attitudes toward vacations and expectations from vacations), and it also helped to build the scales for the questions (on a scale of one to ten, like/dislike, etc.).

Results: Club Med made a list of questions or hypotheses that it could use for quantitative research. Each question and element was something that had been mentioned in the focus groups. The quantitative study would test from a larger group whether these hypotheses were true.

EXAMPLE
In the focus group, one person might say, "When I'm on vacation, I like to take tours through museums." To test if people really do like museum tours on vacation, Club Med asked (in the section on Interest in Activities and Services) whether people wanted this service offered.

During the focus groups, respondents were asked, "Where did you go on vacation?" It was interesting to note that people gave an actual destination (e.g., Hawaii) unless it was a Club Med vacation. In the latter case, they simply answered "Club Med."

EXHIBIT 7 Description of the Quantitative Study of the Consumer Market (September 21 to October 3, 1983)

Cost: $50,000

Purpose:
1. To serve as the foundation for a new consumer marketing approach by providing information on past Club Med vacationers (prospective repeat customers) and prospective new Club Med members;
2. To identify Key Prospects, and where they could best be found;
3. To position Club Med;
4. To develop Club Med's communication strategy by determining what should be communicated and how it should be communicated (e.g., in what tone and manner);
5. To identify how the distribution strategy could be refined (e.g., how to make the best use of travel agents);
6. To determine what the optimal pricing policy should be;
7. To determine if and how the Club Med "product" should be modified.

Sample: Six markets in three regions (see table below)

	Sample Sizes		
Region	Club Med member sample[a]	Prospect sample[b]	Total
North	167	130	297
Southeast	123	93	216
West	170	129	299
Total	460	352	812

[a]Members: random sample of U.S. residents who visited in the past year
[b]Prospects: a 1 was added to the last digit of Club Med members' phone numbers to create a parallel universe of nonmembers in the same neighborhoods.

Definition of a Prospect: The person had to be between 25 and 49 years old. If married, the individual had to earn at least $35,000 a year; if single, the person had to earn at least $25,000 a year. Furthermore, the person must have taken a vacation at least one week long within the past year (or intend to take one within the next year) and have had prepaid accommodations, either on a cruise ship or plane.

Methodology: A 40-minute phone interview was then followed by immediate mailing of a survey. Though refusal rates among both members and prospects were low, it took many calls to generate the prospect sample—only 7% of those called qualified as prospects.

EXHIBIT 8   Quantitative Study: Panel A and Panel B

Panel A: Likelihood of considering a Club Med vacation in next year or so

Question 10 (phone): Thinking about the next year or so, how likely are you to consider a vacation at Club Med—definitely, probably, probably not, or definitely not?

	Members %		Prospects %	
Definitely will not	8		20	
Probably will not	18		35	
Probably will	40	key members	39	key prospects
Definitely will	34		6	

Key Members and Key Prospects are defined as those people falling in the lower two sections.

Panel B: Overall opinion of Club Med among Key Members/Prospects vs. others

Question 7 (phone): Thinking of everything you know about Club Med, what is your overall opinion of Club Med as a place at which to have a wonderful vacation—poor, fair, good, very good, or excellent?

	Members		Prospects	
	Key %	Others %	Key %	Others %
Fair, poor	1	27	7	27
Good	7	27	31	41
Very good	37	32	49	29
Excellent	55	14	13	3

EXHIBIT 9 Quantitative Study: Demographic Profile of Key Prospects vs. Key Members

	Key prospects (%)	Key members (%)	Compared to key prospects, key members are (%)
Education			
Some college or less	42	24	−18*
College graduate	41	40	− 1
Postgraduate	17	36	+19*
Income			
Under $30,000	8	23	+15*
$30,000 to $39,999	23	19	− 4
$40,000 to $59,999	40	29	−11*
$60,000 or more	29	29	0
Occupation			
Professional/semi-prof.	24	35	+11*
Proprietor/manager	32	31	− 1
Clerical/sales	21	19	− 2
Full time homemaker	7	2	− 5
Sex			
Male	45	60	+15*
Female	55	40	−15*
Age			
Under 30 years	28	24	− 4
30 to 34	26	25	− 1
35 to 39	19	22	+ 3
40 and over	27	29	+ 2
AVERAGE	35	36	+ 1
Marital Status			
Married/couples	55	43	−12*
Singles	32	36	+ 4
Ex-married	13	21	+ 8
Have children at home	36	23	−13*
Under 12 years	23	17	− 6

*Indicate a difference of at least 10 percentage points. These differences were also maintained on every item when all members were compared with all prospects.

EXHIBIT 10 Quantitative Study: Differences Between Key Prospects and Key Members

Key Prospects rate these items[a] to be of:	Compared to Key Prospects, Key Members rate the importance of the item to be:		
	Higher	Similar[c]	Lower
Very high importance[b]			
I make my own decisions.		X	
Vacation is an escape from everyday life.		X	
My goal in life is to experience as many things as I can.			X
Vacation is a reward for hard work.			X
I have fun doing things with others.		X	
High importance[d]			
I like to live to the fullest.			X
I like to be pampered on vacation.			X
I prefer a beach vacation.	X		
I like doing things my way.			X
I am anti singles bars and vacations.			X
I do my own thing despite others.		X	
I want peace and quiet on vacation.		X	
Moderate importance[e]			
There is no worry re vacation cost.		X	
I feel free since I won't see people again.			X
I am anti going/doing things by myself.		X	
I enjoy planning my vacation.			X
I don't like being surrounded by people who talk to each other in a foreign language.		X	

[a]*Question asked:* I would like to know how you feel generally about vacations. I am going to read you a list of phrases. Could you rate on a scale of one to ten (with one being the lowest) how much this phrase describes you and how you feel about vacations?

[b]At least 50% of Key Prospects chose 9 or 10 on the ten-point importance scale.

[c]Key Members and Key Prospects are categorized "similar" if their importance scores (% choosing 9 or 10 on the ten-point importance scale) are within ten percentage points of each other.

[d]From 30 to 49.9% chose 9 or 10 on the importance scale.

[e]From 10 to 29.9% chose 9 or 10 on the importance scale.

EXHIBIT 11 Quantitative Study: Vacation Benefits

Benefits	Importance ratings[a]		Rating of Club Med[b]	
	Key Prospects[c]	Key Members vs Key Prospects[d]	Key Prospects[c]	Key Members vs Key Prospects[d]
Everything works right	Very high[c]	—[d]	Moderate[c]	Similar[d]
Can do what/when you want	Very high	Similar	High	+
Allows you to relax	Very high	Similar	High	+
Good value for money	Very high	Similar	High	+
No hassles/problems	Very high	Similar	High	Similar
Beautiful location	Very high	Similar	Very high	Similar
Good, interesting food	Very high	—	High	Similar
Activities you like	High	Similar	High	+
Well-managed	High	Similar	Moderate	+
Can be spontaneous	High	Similar	Moderate	Similar
Easy to arrange	High	—	High	+
Lots of fun	High	Similar	High	+
Lot or little contact	High	Similar	Moderate	+
See variety of places	High	—	Moderate	—
Status, $ unimportant	High	—	Low	+
Explore local area	Moderate	Similar	Moderate	+
Very exciting	Moderate	Similar	Moderate	Similar
Good place for couples	Moderate	—	High	Similar
No extra $ payment for singles	Moderate	Similar	High	+
Can arrange last minute	Moderate	Similar	Moderate	Similar
No worry about your looks	Moderate	Similar	Low	Similar
Dance and drink till late	Moderate	Similar	High	+
People not wild	Moderate	—	Low	Similar
Have vacation romance	Moderate	—	High	Similar
Lots of sports to do	Low	Similar	High	+
Good place to go alone	Low	+	High	+
All paid in advance	Low	Similar	High	+
All in walking distance	Low	Similar	Moderate	+
Learn, improve skills	Low	Similar	Moderate	+

[a]*Question asked:* I would like to know how you feel about certain benefits derived from a vacation. I am going to read you a list of phrases. Could you rate on a scale of one to ten (with one being the lowest) how important these benefits are to you.

[b]*Question asked:* I would like to know how well you think Club Med delivers certain vacation benefits. I will read you a list of benefits. Could you rate on a scale of one to ten (with one being the lowest) how good you think Club Med is at delivering these benefits.

[c]Judgment categories for Key Prospects were determined as follows for both importance of benefits and ratings of Club Med:

Importance category (or Club Med rating category)	% of Key Prospects rating a benefit (or Club Med) at 9 or 10 on a ten-point importance scale
Very high	At least 65%
High	50–64.9%
Moderate	30–49.9%
Low	Less than 30%

[d]Key Members and Key Prospects are categorized as "similar" if their scores (% choosing 9 or 10 on the ten-point scale) are within 10 percentage points of each other. A "+" means that Key Members' ratings were more than 10 percentage points higher; a "−" means they were more than 10 points lower.

EXHIBIT 12 Quantitative Study: Impressions of Club Med Members
(% rating "Describes Most People")

Most people are:[a]	Agreement by Key Prospects[b]	Compared to Key Prospects, Key Members tend to agree		
		More	Similar[c]	Less
In their 30s	Strong			X
Active	Moderate	X		
Americans	Moderate			X
Self-confident	Moderate		X	
Successful	Moderate		X	
Professionals	Moderate		X	
Swinging singles	Moderate			X
Intelligent	Moderate	X		
Interesting	Disagree	X		
Good-looking women	Disagree		X	
Good-looking men	Disagree		X	
Sports experts	Disagree		X	
Just interested in sex	Disagree		X	
Immature women	Disagree		X	
Immature men	Disagree		X	
Couples	Disagree			X
Secretaries	Disagree			X
Rich	Disagree			X

[a]*Question asked:* I would like to have your impression of the people who vacation at Club Med.
Please indicate which of the following items describe most people who vacation at Club Med. Multiple answers are permitted.

[b]Agreement categories were determined as follows:

Agreement category	% of Key Prospects agreeing
Strong	At least 65%
Moderate	35–64.9%
Disagree	Less than 34.9%

[c]"Similar" means that the percentage of Key Members who agreed with the statement was within 10% of the percentage of Key Prospects who agree.

EXHIBIT 13 Quantitative Study: Booking Behavior for Last Club Med Visit

Booked Through	Key Members %
Club Med	16
Travel agent	82
*Reasons Club Med not used**	
Unaware could use, didn't know how/where	26
More convenient	21
Needed advice, had complex arrangements	13
Habit	11
Know, trust agent	7
No advantage	2
Don't know why not	17

*Multiple answers were permitted.

EXHIBIT 14 Quantitative Study: Perception of Comparative Cost of a Club Med Vacation

Compared to other places, the cost at Club Med is:	Key Prospects %	Compared to Key Prospects, Key Members are
Very low	2	0
Fairly low	0	+ 9
Moderate	57	+ 6
Fairly high	39	−14
Very high	2	− 1

Note: Four percent of Key Prospects thought a Club Med trip was more expensive than it really was.

EXHIBIT 15 Quantitative Study: Perceptions of Things Included in Cost

The basic cost covers:[a]	Key Prospects[b]	Compared to Key Prospects, Key Members' perceptions are		
		Higher	Similar[c]	Lower
Nighttime entertainment	Very high	X		
Sports instruction	Very high	X		
Most sports equipment	Very high	X		
Wine at meals	High	X		
Ski lifts	High	X		
Books and games	High	X		
Sightseeing tours[d]	High	X		
Air transportation	Moderate	X		
Tips[d]	Moderate			X
Drinks at bar[d]	Low			X

[a]Seven items are not listed. Key Prospects and Key Members agree that meals+, exercise classes+, maid service, and ground transportation+ are included in the basic cost while a high percentage of each group believe that food between meals is not included.

[b]Percentages of Key Prospects who believe that the cost covers the item fall into the following categories:

Very high	At least 80%
High	70–79.9%
Moderate	30–69.9%
Low	Less than 30%

[c]Key Prospects and Key Members are categorized as "similar" if their perceptions are within ten percentage points of each other.
[d]Items not included in the basic cost

EXHIBIT 16 Quantitative Study: Activities and Services of High Interest to Key Prospects

Key for own room	Private rooms for singles
Variety of dinner menu	Choice of restaurant
Food/beverages all hours	Phone in room
Flexible mealtime hours	

Note: These seven items were selected from a list of 64 activities (ranging from jazz concerts to 24-hour room service to supervision for children). They were the only ones for which more than 70% of Key Prospects reported that they were "very interested." None of the seven were currently offered at the majority of Club Med villages. Key Members were much less interested (by 15 to 60 percentage points) in these activities.

EXHIBIT 17   Summary of Data on Other Club Members

Other* Club Members have fairly low future visit intentions. They do not think they belong at Club Med and also do not think that status and money are unimportant at Club Med.

They are disenchanted with Club Med. Their alienation is not related to whether they are first-time visitors or repeaters, to whether they visit in season or out of season, or to the degree of Club Med knowledge. Their alienation *is* highly related to:

- The vacation attitudes and benefits sought in that they have more interest in doing things on their own and have more interest in seeing and doing new things.

- The fact that they are less receptive to the essence of Club Med since they have less interest in fun, sociability, activities, and internationality and are less willing to give up privacy and services.

- Their experience at the Club in that many benefits they consider important to a vacation are not delivered by Club Med to their satisfaction (for example, independence, smooth operations, spontaneity, activities they like), and they did not feel they belonged at the Club.

- Their expectations are not being met.

*To be defined as "Other" Club Member (as opposed to "Key"), a member had to have said that he or she probably or definitely would not consider a Club Med vacation in the near future.

EXHIBIT 18   The Travel Agent Study (Summer 1983)

Cost: $1,000 (plus travel and administrative expenses),–performed by a student full-time for a summer project so he received no salary.

Purpose: To discover how travel agents felt about Club Med and how to improve Club Med's working relationship with them.

Sample:
- Some large and some small travel agencies in terms of Club Med sales.
- Geographically diverse–six cities: New York, Houston, Atlanta, Los Angeles, Philadelphia, Chicago.
- Three groups emerged:
    Those with an increase in sales over the last year
    Those with a decrease in sales over the last year
    Those with no sales in 1983 but some in 1982

Methodology: First, ten personal interviews were conducted with travel agents in New York to develop the questionnaire. Then, 170 personal interviews were held with travel agents in the six cities.

Findings:
1. Reported number of people recommended to Club Med by the travel agent in the past 6 months:

17%–none	18%–20 to 40
21%–1 to 10 people	35%–more than forty
9%–11 to 19	

2. Eighty-five percent of the agencies found the Club Med product easy to sell.
3. The Club Med concept of an all-inclusive vacation was ranked best by 84% of the agencies when compared with the firms the agencies ranked as their top three competitors.
4. The Club Med brochure was considered superior to that of the competition by 90% of the travel agents.
5. There is still much misperception about Club Med's activities: In the midwest area especially, it is considered as a singles place with a wild reputation.
6. There is a lack of familiarity with the Club Med concept–some think there is too much structure and regimentation.
7. Sixty-five percent of the travel agents have never visited a Club Med village.
8. Travel agents did not feel there was a need to increase the number of sales representatives' visits.

EXHIBIT 19 The Destination Study (November 1983)

Cost: Minimal out-of-pocket costs, aside from Club Med and advertising agency staff time.

Purpose: The study helps determine geographically where certain cities' inhabitants went when they traveled abroad and how many went from each city. In this way, Club Med could follow the path of least resistance. For example, if New Yorkers tended to go to Mexico on vacation, there was no point in wasting resources promoting the packages for Tahiti vacations to them.

Sample: Club Med received data on arrivals and departures from 20 cities to destinations similar to Club Med village locations. This data helped determine which prime markets to focus on in the short term, which packages to sell in certain cities, and which cities were potential future markets.

Source: Civil Aeronautics Board of the United States.

Product Policy

One of the unique features of global companies is their potential for transferring proven product and brand concepts across national markets. As such, the opportunity exists for developing truly global product policies that create the conditions for repeating in every market the same superior performance experienced in their countries of origin. But inherent in this potential is a risk. The risk has to do with overlooking significant local market differences that negate the viability of international product and brand transfers. Predictably, questions relating to global product policy are the source of a constant tug-of-war between headquarters and country management. The former tends to look for opportunities to streamline product and branding practices across national organizations; the latter tends to focus on those local market features that make the application of a global policy impractical. Effectiveness of global policymaking often hinges on how well these different perspectives are accommodated in the final decisions.

ISSUES

The two cases in this section deal with different aspects of product policy. The first case, Colgate-Palmolive: Cleopatra, involves a less-than-successful transfer to Canada of a product idea that has proved itself in France. The case issues have to do with the wisdom of the transfer and whether the problem lies with how the transfer has been implemented. The second case, Nabisco Brands, Inc.–Cipster, raises the question of what benefits a company can expect from developing regional or global brands. Related to this question is the issue of the role of headquarters in bringing about international brand conformity and how this role might run counter to local management practices.

LEARNING POINTS

The student can expect the following learning points from the analysis and class discussion of the cases in this section:

- Skills in international consumer and competitive analysis for a new product;
- Practice in diagnosing product line and product positioning problems;
- Skills in making decisions based on research data;
- Recognition of the opportunities and problems in developing sound regional or global branding policies;
- Insights into the respective role and contribution of headquarters and country management in developing effective product policies, including branding.

7 COLGATE-PALMOLIVE: CLEOPATRA

The Canadian launch extravaganza in February 1986 began with cocktails served by hostesses dressed like Cleopatra, the queen of ancient Egypt. Then followed a gala dinner with a dramatic, multimedia presentation of the new brand, ending with the award-winning commercial and these words:

> Today the memory comes alive,
> a new shape rises up, a new texture,
> a new standard of beauty care
> worthy of the name it bears,
> Today the memory frozen in ancient stones comes alive . . .
> Cleopatra.

Each of the retailer guests had received an exclusive, golden, three-dimensional pyramid invitation to the launch, and expectations were high. The retailers were sick of discounted brands, all basically the same, and were looking for something different and exciting. Finally, the new soap Cleopatra was revealed to the audience of nearly 1,000—a huge turnout by Canadian standards—and the response was overwhelmingly positive.

So enthusiastic was the audience, that by the end of the evening the Colgate-Palmolive salespeople had received orders for 2,000 cases. Bill Graham, the divisional vice president of marketing for Canada, and Steve Boyd, group product manager, agreed that the night had been a grand success and that Cleopatra's future looked very rosy.

THE FRENCH EXPERIENCE WITH CLEOPATRA

Cleopatra soap was first introduced in France in November 1984. By May of the following year, the brand had reached an amazing market share of 10%, despite its

This case was prepared by Professor Sandra Vandermerwe, with the assistance of J. Carter Powis (MBA, IMI 1988–89). Copyright © 1990 by the International Institute for Management Development (IMD), Lausanne, Switzerland. Not to be used or reproduced without permission.

23% price premium compared with other brands. In fact, Colgate-Palmolive's biggest problem was keeping up with demand. By the end of 1985, market share shot up to 15%. Cleopatra had actually become the number one brand in France.

Cleopatra's success in France received a great deal of publicity within the organization. Encouraged by the experience, the Global Marketing Group, situated in New York, set out to find other markets for the product. They reasoned that if Cleopatra had worked well in France, it should do likewise elsewhere in the world.

Canada, especially French-speaking Quebec, seemed like an obvious choice to the Global Marketing Group. At the annual update meeting in New York, the group strongly recommended to the Canadian management that a test be done in Canada to see if Cleopatra was a proposition for them.

THE REACTION OF THE CANADIAN SUBSIDIARIES TO CLEOPATRA

The idea of a market test for Cleopatra was greeted with mixed feelings by the Canadians. Some managers, such as Stan House, assistant product manager, were enthusiastic, especially because they knew that Steve Boyd, group product manager for Canada, was convinced it would work. In Boyd's opinion, Canada could show the people in New York that the same formula would do as well or even better than in France.

Other managers, like Ken Johnson, were more skeptical. They resented having a brand thrust on them. Johnson believed that what Canada really needed was a strong "national" brand, and he doubted that Cleopatra could ever be that.

Nonetheless, a decision was made to proceed and test the Canadian market. One fundamental question had to be answered: Was there reasonable certainty that Cleopatra would be accepted by consumers in Quebec? Two types of research, both conducted in Toronto, tried to answer that question. The first study was among a "super group" of articulate professional women, specially chosen and brought together for the event. They were introduced to the product, its price, and the advertising; then they were asked to discuss their likes and dislikes openly. On balance, the results were positive; the women seemed to like the soap and the concept.

The second research study used more typical consumers; these people were exposed to the proposed advertising for Cleopatra and then were asked whether they would buy it. Fifty percent said they would. They were also given a bar of soap to try at home and were phoned a week later for their reactions. Sixty-four percent of the group who used the soap said they would buy Cleopatra as soon as it was available on the shelves.

The research confirmed the feelings of Boyd and most of the marketing team in Toronto that Cleopatra could indeed be a winner. Immediately, plans were made for an early launch the following year.

The Canadian marketing team was determined not to allow Cleopatra to go to war with all the other brands. They felt something had to be done to reverse the negative profit trends that had been brewing in the industry for some time. This was the ideal opportunity. They would position Cleopatra as the premium-quality, premium-priced soap and differentiate it from all the others. They wanted to avoid having a price war at all costs.

SOME BACKGROUND ON COLGATE-PALMOLIVE CANADA

Colgate-Palmolive, a multinational consumer packaged goods corporation operating in 58 countries, marketed a variety of personal care and household products worldwide. With annual sales of $5.7 billion, many of its brands were global leaders. For example, Colgate toothpaste was number one and Palmolive soap was number two in the world in their respective markets.

The Canadian subsidiary opened its doors in 1912, and since then had grown into a $250-million-a-year corporation. Together with two competitors, Procter & Gamble and Lever (both $1-billion subsidiaries of their parent companies), they dominated the aggressive and innovative personal care and household market sectors in Canada.

Colgate-Palmolive Canada manufactured and marketed a wide range of personal care and household products inside Canada and also supplied brands to the United States and Puerto Rico. The major products marketed in Canada were as follows:

Personal care products	Household products
Colgate toothpaste	Palmolive liquid soap
Colgate toothbrushes	Palmolive automatic dishwasher soap
Colgate mouth rinse	ABC detergent
Halo shampoo	Arctic Power detergent
Irish Spring soap	Fab detergent
Palmolive soap	Baggies food wrap
Cashmere Bouquet soap	Ajax cleanser
Cleopatra soap	Ajax all-purpose liquid cleanser

The Colgate-Palmolive head office and manufacturing facility were both located in a building in Toronto. Sales offices were in each of the six major regions across Canada, namely the Maritimes, Quebec, Ontario, the Prairies, Alberta, and British Columbia.

Marketing was organized at the head office under a product management system, whereby each person was responsible for a brand or group of brands and reported to a group product manager who, in turn, was responsible to the vice president of marketing (see Exhibit 1). The brand managers made decisions on all aspects of marketing planning and execution, from market research to consumer and trade promotion. The product managers made sure that their brands received the needed resources from the head office.

THE STATE OF THE CANADIAN SOAP MARKET

In 1986, the soap market in Canada was worth $105 million to manufacturers. This revenue figure was projected to grow by 4 to 5% in the years ahead. The Canadian soap market was probably one of the most competitive in which Colgate-Palmolive competed—a fact that even the average consumer could see each time he or she turned on a television set or opened a magazine.

The competition would continue at the store level, where limited shelf space was at a premium. Because of the intense competition, retailers were all-powerful. They literally could pick and choose with whom to do business. Inside the store, a brand's fate was in their hands; they decided what to promote, which prices to cut, and how to allocate shelf space.

Competition was extremely fierce for some of the following reasons:

1. Volume growth in the market had slowed and coincided with the growth of the Canadian population (1.0–1.5% annually). No further rapid expansion was expected.
2. The only method of survival for the many new brands and new variants of existing brands was to steal share from other products in the market.
3. Competition from no-name and private label products had increased.
4. Technological advances were slowing, and relaunches were increasingly "cosmetic" in nature (new color, new fragrance, etc.).
5. Consumers had a group of "acceptable" brands that they were willing to purchase (usually 3 or 4 in number). Buying decisions within this group were based on price. There were 15 mainstream brands, along with 20 to 25 minor ones, fighting to become one of these "acceptable" choices.
6. Trends toward larger bundle packs had developed (more than one bar of soap packaged and sold as a unit), reducing the number of purchases each consumer made during the year. For example, in the skin care segment, twinpacks (two bars sold together) were becoming the norm, whereas the refreshment segment was dominated by three- and four-packs, and the utility segment by four-, five-, and six-packs.
7. Competition was based on price, as there were no real competitive advantages or meaningful differences among most brands, and because of increased pressure from the retail trade to meet competitive deals and prices.
8. Liquid soaps had entered the market and held an 8% share. Based on current consumer reaction, the maximum share was not expected to grow beyond 10% in the future.

For most consumers, "a soap is a soap is a soap," with few perceivable differences among brands. Bombarded by advertising in every conceivable type of media, consumers mainly bought the "acceptable brands" on price. Therefore, becoming and staying an "acceptable brand" was where the ongoing competitive battle among the various brands took place.

The soap market was divided into three distinct groups: the skin care segment, the refreshment segment, and the utility segment (see Exhibit 2). The skin care market was the largest of the three segments, which were split as follows:

	1985 (%)	1986 (%)	1987 (%)
Skin care	37.3	38.4	38.8
Refreshment	34.9	33.4	32.3
Utility (price)	27.8	28.2	28.9

Exhibit 3 contains details of market share for each of the three large companies and their competitors. Although there were at least 15 mainstream brands (Exhibit 3), only 4 had managed to create a really distinctive niche.

In the skin care segment, Dove had been advertised for years as the facial soap. It had a loyal customer base, mainly because of its unique formulation and moisturizing capabilities. Low on additives and scent, it was seen as the "Cadillac" of this segment and was priced accordingly.

Ivory was an "institution" in the Canadian soap market, with its 100-year heritage and ever-powerful "I use it because my mother used it" pure soap positioning. The market leader, it successfully competed in all three markets.

Irish Spring, made especially for men, did well in the male market as a refreshment soap, although females used it as well. Consumers associated its strong scent and high lathering capability with cleaning strength.

Zest was also positioned in the refreshment segment. Seen as the "family brand that gets you cleaner than soap," it was low in additives and perfume. It especially appealed to people in "hard water" areas of the country. Its detergent formulation allowed it to make special claims against other brands, such as "it rinses clean and doesn't leave a soapy film."

THE QUEBEC MARKET

Quebec is Canada's second largest province in population and the largest in geographical size. The 6.7 million people (or 26% of Canada's total population) are clustered throughout the southern portion of this immense region, which is 2.5 times the size of France.

Unlike the other nine provinces whose populations are of British ancestry, Quebec has a population that came originally from France. In fact, over 80% of the 2.3 million households in Quebec list French as their mother tongue. Needless to say, with this unique culture, marketing strategies sometimes differ from those used in the rest of the country.

Quebec accounts for 28% of the Canadian soap market volume and is, therefore, slightly overdeveloped in proportion to the country's total population. The major brands and their positions in the Quebec market are similar to those throughout the rest of Canada. The exceptions are Zest, which does poorly because Quebec is mainly a soft-water market, and Lux, which has done extremely well due to its strong European image.

THE CANADIAN CLEOPATRA MARKETING STRATEGY

Cleopatra looked like an excellent prospect for Canada. Not only was it a premium quality product in all respects, but it complemented Colgate-Palmolive's Canadian product line and had a past history of success. If launched, the product line would include Irish Spring, well positioned and strongly niched in the refreshment segment; Cashmere Bouquet, performing well in the utility segment; Palmolive soap, positioned as the all-family skin care bar; and Cleopatra, the premium quality skin care brand worthy of competing with the segment leader, Dove.

After considering these facts as well as the positive research results from the two analyses, Colgate-Palmolive decided to launch Cleopatra as the "premium quality, premium priced beauty soap." The marketing team, however, decided that it would not be financially feasible to launch Cleopatra like any other soap, where ultimately its success would be determined by its ability to compete on price. Although the marketing team knew the risks, they wanted to avoid having to rely on retailers and being forced to offer large trade allowances and discounts. They wanted the demand to come directly from the consumers, by generating their interest in Cleopatra through strong media and consumer promotions.

This approach was very different from the industry norm, where manufacturers traditionally paid large sums of money to retailers just to get the product listed in their "accounts order books." Then, manufacturers would have to pay even more in discounts and allowances to have a showing in the retailers' weekly advertising fliers. Once management decided to forgo these payments, it was critical for the company to make the best possible media and consumer promotion schedule for the launch.

The company set an ambitious objective: a 4.5% market share for 1986; 100% distribution of the product with retail accounts; maximum shelf presence, defined as the same number of facings as the current segment leader Dove; proper shelf positioning, which meant being next to Dove; and, finally, maintaining Cleopatra's premium pricing strategy.

To make the strategy work, especially since targets were based on an 11-month first year, the company knew it had to get both consumers and salespeople enthusiastic about the brand. Therefore, it was essential to generate excitement from day one. The promotion had to be very powerful. In fact, it had to be so good that consumers would demand the brand and force retailers to stock it. That meant the emphasis would be on advertising. Television was chosen as the most obvious way to focus resources and create an impact and instant awareness among the target group—women between the ages of 18 and 49. The campaign, which the marketing team wanted to be "an event," began the first week in May.

The budget was set to make Cleopatra the number one spender in the entire soap market. The objective was clear to all: ensure that Cleopatra gets the most "share of voice" in its category in Quebec, which amounted to 15%. In other words, for every 100 minutes of advertising for soaps, 15 minutes would go to Cleopatra.

The Quebec TV commercial (see Exhibit 4) was the same one used in France, with one or two minor and hardly noticeable modifications. This commercial, shot in Rome on a very elaborate set, had been one of the most memorable aspects of the French marketing strategy. The feedback from consumer research in France had been particularly positive, and the commercial had received a number of awards for excellence.

Equally important in the marketing strategy was sales promotion, always popular with the average Canadian consumer. Since the team's research had established that 64% of the market would buy Cleopatra after trying it at home, the first and foremost aim was to be sure that people tried it. Thus the promotion campaign, scheduled to run from May to October, centered on the product being tried. Approximately 250,000 households in Quebec received free bar coupons that could be exchanged for a free bar of soap at the nearest store. All stores were fully informed.

There was also the "Cleopatra Gold Collection and Sweepstakes Promotion," which offered consumers a wide range of popular and fashionable costume jewelry at very reasonable prices. For example, one could send for a necklace and earrings that cost only $12.99. Consumers who bought the jewelry received forms and were automatically entered into the grand prize draw, a chance to win a Cleopatra-style, 14-karat gold necklace worth $3,500. Research among current brands on the market showed that mail-in offers and sweepstakes were very successful with consumers, and management had high hopes that this promotion would stimulate interest in the brand. The promotion began in August and ended with the draw in early January 1987.

Since Cleopatra had been positioned as the premium quality brand in soap, no discounts were offered. Single cartons were packed 48 to a case, at a price of $41.71. Cleopatra's pricing strategy was to be higher than Dove, historically the most expensive brand. (Comparative prices are shown in Exhibit 5.)

The product itself had been developed in France, with no changes made for the Canadian market. As it turned out, Cleopatra was the finest quality soap made by the company in Canada. Its unique formulation contained the best ingredients, including the equivalent of 15% beauty cream, which delivered a rich, creamy lather and was noticeably soft on the skin.

The perfume, blended in France, was said "to produce an unforgettable fragrance." The soap was also carved into a special shape to make it easy to hold and use. The Cleopatra logo was stamped on the ivory-colored bar—another differentiating feature intended to convey quality, luxury, and prestige. The bar was slightly larger than the French product, to conform with the other Canadian brands.

Each bar of soap came in its own gold-colored laminated carton, a difference from being wrapped in paper as in France. The laminated material was unique in that it not only reflected light, which made it stand out against the other brands on the shelves, but it also prevented the perfume from escaping.

THE RESULTS OF THE CANADIAN LAUNCH

Due to the launch, sales had started off with a bang. On the first evening alone, 67% of the first month's objectives had been achieved. But from then on, the brand started missing its targets.

Steve Boyd had warned his team not to expect an instant miracle. After all, the Quebec soap market was one of the most competitive, and it took time to establish a brand. As the retail trade had been so positive at the launch, he felt sure that things would eventually pick up. The results, however, continued to be discouraging well into the first year. Cleopatra simply was not selling and could not seem to reach the explosive growth everyone was anticipating and expecting to be "just around the corner."

After 13 weeks, the advertising commercial had created an awareness of 63%, the highest in the skin care segment. At that time Camay was at 49%; Dove, 24%; and Aloe and Lanolin, 13%. By the end of 1986, Cleopatra had achieved its "share of voice target"—that is, the number one position in advertising intensity in Quebec. By the end of the promotion period, the free bar coupon had been distributed to households throughout Quebec, and 21% of the coupons had been redeemed. The sweepstakes, however, had been disappointing: only 1,500 people had entered by the December deadline.

Market share reached only 0.9%, peaking in October/November at 1.8%, compared to the 4.5% goal. Sales, which were expected to reach $3,775,000, were only $755,000. Instead of a $389,000 positive contribution to sales, contribution was negative $442,000. (The performance figures for 1986 and for the first three months in 1987 are shown in Exhibit 6. The financial losses of 1986 and the first part of 1987 are presented in Exhibit 7.) Distribution also fell short of expectations, and presence and shelf positioning gradually deteriorated (see Exhibit 8). The sales force, however, did manage to restrict any discounting of the brand.

Over the first year, some small-scale research had been done in stores to determine consumer reaction, but nothing else had taken place. By January 1987, it was clear that some serious market research was needed, and a full-blown tracking study was commissioned.

Two panels from Quebec were chosen: a random sample of 204 consumers and an oversample of 99 Cleopatra "triers." Over 90 questions were asked to obtain key information on brand awareness, usage, brand ratings, likes and dislikes, advertising recall, and trial information (see Exhibits 9–14).

THE DILEMMA OVER CLEOPATRA'S FUTURE

Steve Boyd fumbled with his papers as he listened to Bill Graham, divisional vice president for marketing Canada, say, "I can't understand it. It was a star performer in France. The French loved it, and Quebec is, after all, part of the French culture. Why has the brand flopped so badly?" Boyd knew that for Cleopatra to succeed as a major brand in Quebec and perhaps in all of Canada, as the Global

Marketing Group had first suggested, he had to react quickly to rectify the situation. But how?

The research results on Cleopatra lay on the table. Product Manager Ken Johnson and Assistant Product Manager Stan House had been over the research with Boyd to try and solve the Cleopatra riddle. But they could not agree about what should be done. Johnson wanted to scrap the brand. He said that Cleopatra was just plain wrong for Canada and should never have been launched there in the first place. He believed there was no point in letting more good money chase a loser. House was adamant that what the brand needed was time. He accused Johnson of being shortsighted and impatient. It was, he believed, totally unrealistic to expect a new brand to succeed overnight, and Cleopatra had only been on the market a little over a year. With a sizable investment and some patience, House believed they could recreate momentum and achieve a target of 4.5% market share.

The Global Marketing Group in New York was convinced that there was nothing wrong with the brand but that implementation had been poor. They proposed rethinking the basic strategy and suggested that perhaps Cleopatra should not be positioned as a skin care product at all, competing head on with Dove. A smaller niche might be more sensible.

Boyd knew that he had three options:

- Admit defeat and discontinue the brand.
- Continue the strategy with minor modifications if necessary, and try to get a 4.5% market share by giving it more time and support.
- Alter the strategy or even the product itself.

Boyd could not help feeling that he should try to find a way to make Cleopatra work. Giving up would be such a shame. Yet, with retailers literally pulling the brand off the shelves, did he really have a choice?

EXHIBIT 1 Marketing Department Structure

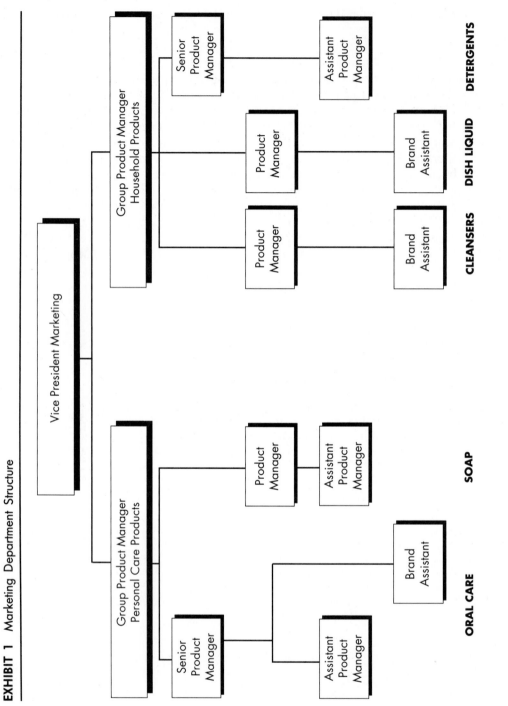

Note: Vice President Marketing reports to the General Manager of Colgate-Palmolive Canada, who, in turn, reports to the divisional Vice President of the Colgate-Palmolive Company, based in New York.

EXHIBIT 2 Market Segments and Brand Advertising Claims, 1986

Segment	Brand	Advertising copy claim
Skin care	Dove	For softer, smoother skin, try Dove for 7 days
	Camay	Skin care as individual as you are
	Caress	The body bar with bath oil
	Cleopatra	New soap: rich as a cream, sensual as a perfume
	Aloe & Lanolin	Good for skin because it has natural ingredients
	Palmolive	Not advertised
Refreshment	Zest	Zest leaves you feeling cleaner than soap
	Coast	Coast picks you up and pulls you through the day
	Irish Spring	Fresh fragrance, double deodorancy
	Dial	You will feel clean and refreshed all day long
Utility (price)	Jergens	Not advertised
	Woodbury	Not advertised
	Cashmere Bouquet	Not advertised
	Lux	Not advertised
-------	Ivory*	Ivory is 99 44/100 pure soap

Source: Colgate-Palmolive Canada.

*Ivory competes with different creative executions in each of the three segments.

EXHIBIT 3 Category Market Shares (Quebec)

	1985	1986	1987 YTD*
Colgate-Palmolive			
Irish Spring	6.2	6.0	6.5
Palmolive	3.7	3.6	6.4
Cashmere Bouquet	3.3	3.4	2.8
Cleopatra	0.0	0.9	1.1
Total:	13.2	13.9	16.8
Lever			
Lux	4.3	6.0	8.3
Dove	7.1	9.6	10.8
Caress	1.5	1.7	2.9
Other	3.9	2.7	1.2
Total:	16.8	20.0	23.2
Procter & Gamble			
Ivory	28.2	24.9	22.9
Zest	4.9	6.1	4.7
Coast	5.6	5.5	6.4
Camay	6.4	5.3	2.6
Other	0.1	0.1	0.1
Total:	45.2	41.9	36.7
Jergens			
Aloe & Lanolin	2.4	3.2	2.6
Woodbury	0.3	0.8	1.4
Jergens	5.4	5.4	5.4
Total:	8.1	9.4	9.4
Canada Packers			
Dial	2.4	2.4	3.2
Other	0.1	0.0	0.0
Total:	2.5	2.4	3.2
Other	14.2	12.4	10.7

Source: Colgate-Palmolive Canada.

Note: Market share is calculated on an equivalent case basis.

*Year end is the October/November share period. Therefore, 1987 YTD (year-to-date) is made up of two bimonthly share periods: December/January and February/March.

EXHIBIT 4 Television Commercial

The name is linked with the secrets of beauty

. . . rich as a cream,

Cleopatra, eternal woman, holder of all secrets.

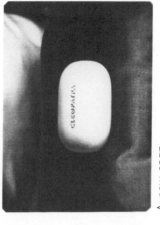

A new soap . . . .

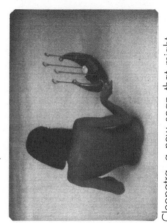

Cleopatra, a new soap that might well change the face of the world.

Cleopatra, Queen of Egypt.

cream and perfume . . . .

sensual as a perfume . . . .

EXHIBIT 5 Price and Trade Discount Structure

	Cleopatra	Dove
Case size*	48 × 140g	48 × 140g
Case price	$41.71	$39.72
Unit cost	0.87	0.83
Regular selling price	1.29	1.19
Off-invoice allowance	—	3.00
Deal unit cost	—	0.77
Feature price	—	0.99

Note: The average manufacturer's price for Cleopatra was 87 cents per single bar, compared with an average manufacturer's price of 31 cents per single bar for all toilet soaps.

*Dove is also available in a twinpack
(24 × 2 × 140g case size)

EXHIBIT 6 Performance to Date (Quebec)

	1986											1987		
	Feb.	Mar.	Apr.	May	June	July	Aug.	Sep.	Oct.	Nov.	Dec.	Jan.	Feb.	Mar.
Shipments (cases):														
Forecast (000s)	3.0	5.0	5.0	15.0	15.0	6.0	5.0	10.0	7.0	9.0	10.5	8.0	7.5	7.5
Actual (000s)	3.6	3.0	0.4	2.5	2.1	1.3	0.6	0.9	1.3	0.7	1.7	1.9	0.9	1.2
% Achieved	120	60	8	17	14	22	12	9	19	8	16	24	12	16
Market share[a]	0.1		0.7		1.1		1.7		1.8		1.1		1.1	
Distribution[b]	44		51		65		68		69		69		72	
Out-of-Stocks[c]	4		3		5		2		3		1		4	

Source: Colgate-Palmolive Canada.

[a]Bimonthly market share is calculated on an equivalent case basis (i.e., all brands' case packs are made equivalent based on weight, and market share is then calculated as a percentage of this base).

[b]Bimonthly percentage of accounts in Quebec where the brand is listed.

[c]Bimonthly percentage of accounts in Quebec where, at the time of audit, the brand was sold out.

EXHIBIT 7 Profit and Loss Statement (000)

		Actual 1986	1st Quarter 1987
Sales	$	755	167
Margin[a]	$	477	108
	%	63.2	64.8
Trade[b]	$	53	12
	%	7.0	7.2
Consumer[c]	$	401	34
	%	53.1	20.3
Media[d]	$	465	94
	%	61.6	56.3
Total expenditures	$	919	140
	%	121.7	83.8
Contribution[e]	$	(442)	(32)
	%	(58.5)	(19.2)

Source: Colgate-Palmolive Canada.

[a]Includes direct product costs, freight/warehousing, etc.

[b]Includes all expenditures directed to the retail trade.

[c]Includes all consumer promotion expenditures.

[d]Includes costs of developing a commercial, plus air-time.

[e]Contribution toward allocated overheads and operating profit.

EXHIBIT 8 Shelf Position

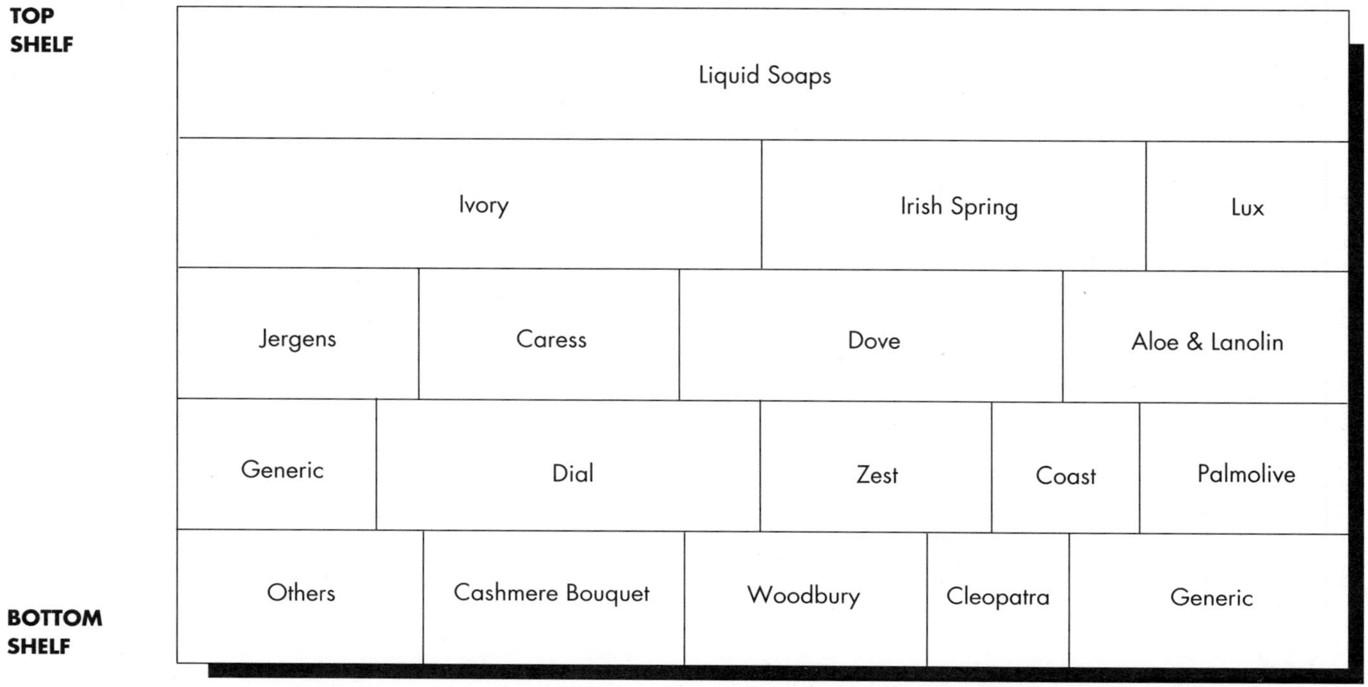

TOP
SHELF

Liquid Soaps	Irish Spring	Lux	
		Aloe & Lanolin	
Ivory	Dove	Coast	Palmolive
		Zest	
	Caress		Cleopatra
Jergens	Dial	Woodbury	Generic
	Generic	Cashmere Bouquet	
	Others		

BOTTOM
SHELF

Typical 12-foot Soap Section: 1st Quarter, 1987

Source: Colgate-Palmolive Canada.

EXHIBIT 9 Consumer Research on Brands (Quebec)

	Brands (total random sample)[a]				
	Aloe & Lanolin	Camay	Cleopatra	Dove	Palmolive
Brand awareness (%)[b]	54.4	98.5	73.5	99.5	96.1
Brand in-home (%)[c]	3.5	15.2	6.9	23.9	7.4
Ever tried (%)[d]	12.3	86.3	14.2	83.5	65.2
Brand used[e]					
All of the time (%)	1.5	8.3	2.9	12.3	3.9
Most of the time (%)	0.5	3.9	1.5	5.4	3.9
Occasionally (%)	7.4	47.6	8.8	46.6	36.3
Stopped using (%)	2.9	26.5	1.0	19.2	21.1

Source: Tracking study, Colgate-Palmolive Canada.

[a]Total random sample—204 respondents.

[b]Question: Have you ever heard of _____?

[c]Question: What brands do you have in your home now?

[d]Question: Have you ever tried _____?

[e]Question: Do you use _____? If yes, would you say you use it all of the time, most of the time, or occasionally? If no, did you use _____ at some time in the past?

EXHIBIT 10 Consumer Research on Best Brands (Quebec)

Brands best for...[a] Brand	Being good value for money		Being mild and gentle		Having a rich, creamy lather		Having a pleasant fragrance		Moisturizing your skin		Suitable for the whole family		Leaving skin soft and smooth	
	Total sample[b]	Cleo triers[c]	Total sample	Cleo triers	Total sample	Cleo triers	Total sample	Cleo triers	Total sample	Cleo triers	Total sample	Cleo triers	Total sample	Cleo triers
Aloe & Lanolin	11	2	31	9	8	0	13	0	27	2	13	1	19	1
Camay	40	11	31	7	50	9	53	13	28	7	32	10	41	10
Cleopatra	10	30	8	33	27	51	21	53	15	31	6	23	20	49
Dove	26	13	53	29	63	31	51	16	39	20	49	21	68	24
Palmolive	36	18	20	5	12	5	19	9	9	3	43	19	19	4
All	26	10	5	5	19	2	29	5	2	4	6	5	5	8
None	22	7	28	8	8	0	6	2	38	19	25	12	15	2
Don't know	33	8	28	3	17	1	12	1	46	13	30	8	17	1

Source: Tracking study, Colgate-Palmolive Canada.

Note: The two sets of data are from separate panels (i.e., the 99 Cleopatra triers are not included in the total random sample of 204 respondents).

[a]Question: Which of these five brands ———, ———, or ——— is best for "Being good value for the money" (for example).

[b]Total random sample = 204 respondents.

[c]Cleopatra trier sample (people who have tried Cleopatra in the last 6 months) = 99 respondents.

EXHIBIT 11 Consumer Research on Attitudes Toward Cleopatra

	% of triers[a]
Likes Cleopatra[b]	
The smell/good/nice/pleasant/perfume	29
Makes a lot of suds/foam/suds well	26
Mild perfume/light	22
Miscellaneous	21
Softens skin/soft for skin/leaves skin smooth	20
It's mild/good for skin/the mildness	19
The smell/perfume lasts/leaves nice smell on skin	12
It's creamy/creamier	11
The fresh smell/refreshing	10
It's soft/as silk/like satin/like milk	7
Dislikes Cleopatra[c]	
Price too high	20
Too strong a smell/contains too much perfume/harsh	17
Too harsh a soap/not mild enough	12
It melts too fast	10
The smell/the smell left on skin	7
Irritates the skin/burns skin/too much perfume	6
Dries the skin	5
Miscellaneous	5
Doesn't suds enough/not enough foam	3
Doesn't moisturize skin	3

Note: Only the 10 most frequent responses are shown here.

Source: Tracking study, Colgate-Palmolive Canada.

Note: For many French Canadians, the level of perfume is perceived to vary directly with the cleaning strength and harshness of the product.

[a]Cleopatra trier sample (people who have tried Cleopatra in the last 6 months) = 99 respondents.

[b]Question: Given that you have tried Cleopatra, what are your likes and/or dislikes of the brand?

[c]42 respondents had no dislikes.

EXHIBIT 12 Consumer Research, Usage

Questions asked of users[a]	% of respondents
Do you plan on buying Cleopatra again?	
Regularly	27
Occasionally	66
No intention to buy again	7
Do you use Cleopatra every day?[b]	
Yes	41
No	59
What part of the body do you use Cleopatra on?	
Face only	3
Body only	76
Face and body	21
Who uses Cleopatra in your household?	
Yourself only	65
Others	35
How often do you use Cleopatra?	
Regularly	33
Occasionally	67

Source: Tracking study, Colgate-Palmolive Canada.

[a]Questions asked of those who have tried Cleopatra in the last 6 months (Cleopatra trier sample = 99 respondents).

[b]Showers outnumber baths 4 to 1 in the province of Quebec.

EXHIBIT 13 Consumer Research, Advertising

	% of respondents[b]
Main point recall[a]	
It's a beauty soap/soap for women	22
It's perfumed/contains perfume	18
It's mild/a mild soap/mild as milk	16
Contains cream/milk/oils	15
Cleopatra/beauty linked together	14
Cleopatra/Egyptians linked together	14
It suds well/lots of lather	10
Fresh smell/it's refreshing	8
Smells good/nice	5
Makes skin soft/smoother skin	5
Note: Only the top 10 responses are shown here.	
Reaction to Cleopatra after seeing advertising[c]	
Positive	41
Negative	13
No reaction	46
Intention to try Cleopatra after seeing advertising[d]	
Yes	37
No	63

Source: Tracking study, Cleopatra-Palmolive Canada.

Note: Questions c and d were asked of those in the total random sample who had seen the advertising but who had not tried Cleopatra at the time of the study.

[a]Question: Do you recall Cleopatra advertising? If yes, what were the main points of the ad?

[b]Number of respondents out of the total random sample who recalled Cleopatra advertising = 128.

[c]Question: What is your reaction to Cleopatra?

[d]Question: Do you intend to try Cleopatra?

EXHIBIT 14 Consumer Research, Trial

Reasons for not trying Cleopatra?*	% of respondents
Not available where I shop	29
Haven't needed any soap	21
Too expensive	19
Happy with my present brand	19
Has too much perfume in it	16
I don't think about it	10
Miscellaneous	9
Waiting to get a coupon	6
It's new	4
Don't know	4

Source: Tracking study, Colgate-Palmolive.

Note: Only the top 10 responses are shown here.

*Question: Why haven't you tried Cleopatra soap? (Asked of those who have seen the advertising and had originally intended to try the brand.)

8 NABISCO BRANDS, INC.– CIPSTER

In November 1985, Aldo Osti, area president, Europe, Nabisco Brands, Inc., was reviewing some notes he had made to himself regarding a potential new product launch being planned by Saiwa Biscuits, one of the company's Italian operations. He was trying to reach decisions regarding several strategic concerns with this new product, along with some possible organizational changes that would affect the product and its management.

Following several successful years as the head of Nabisco's Italian operation, Osti had been appointed president of the European operations in 1976. Presently, he was responsible for the overall operations of Nabisco's companies throughout southern Europe, which included France, Italy, Spain, and Portugal. He reported to the executive vice president of Nabisco Brands International in the U.S. corporate office.

Headquartered in Paris, Osti had adopted an operating philosophy of decentralization, forcing the decisions for operations, marketing, and planning down to the local and subsidiary managers. He had maintained this organizational arrangement in the belief that those executives closest to the operations were best able to judge individual market trends and to implement strategies appropriate to the specific requirements of local conditions. One result of this style of management was that Osti had a very lean European headquarters staff, consisting of only one financial executive, one staff executive, two secretaries, and himself.

Over the last several months, Osti had conducted informal discussions with the executives of Saiwa regarding a further extension of the company's successful potato-formulated snack product, Cipster (pronounced "chipster") (see Exhibit 1 for a photograph of the product). After several years of spectacular growth, the brand's sales seemed to be leveling out. Since the product was already dominant in its narrow niche in the Italian snack market, it seemed most reasonable that future

This case was prepared by Professor Robert F. Young. Copyright © 1986 by the International Institute for Management Development (IMD), Lausanne, Switzerland. Not to be used or reproduced without permission.

growth could be obtained only with new product introductions. Accordingly, Osti had encouraged his Italian associates either to look for new product ideas for the brand or to plan for brand extensions.

Recently, Luigi Capurro, Saiwa's newly appointed director of marketing, had an informal discussion with Osti about some plans he was formulating to introduce a corn-based snack product under the Cipster label. These plans had not been formalized, nor had specific budgetary authorizations been requested. However, Osti thought that some preliminary guidance was appropriate at this time because he did not want the senior management at Saiwa to proceed through the lengthy process of developing written plans and requests if there would be major obstacles to the launch of the new product. Also, if he could raise and perhaps resolve major strategic issues through informal discussions at this preliminary stage, Osti thought he could avoid a lot of rework and delay during the more formal planning and budgeting process.

NABISCO BRANDS, INC.

Nabisco Brands, Inc. was one of the oldest and largest purveyors of packaged food products in the world. Headquartered in New Jersey, Nabisco Brands operated 170 manufacturing plants in 35 countries and had distribution in over 100 countries. In 1985, its worldwide sales were expected to exceed $6 billion, with Europe contributing about 15% of the total. Created in 1981 by the merger of Nabisco, Inc. and Standard Brands, Inc., Nabisco Brands' product line was diverse and included such well-known brands as Oreo cookies, Planters peanuts and snacks, Ritz crackers, Fleischmann's margarine, Belin biscuits, Baby Ruth candy, and Milk Bone dog food.

In the second half of 1985, Nabisco Brands was acquired by R. J. Reynolds Corporation, the large U.S.-based tobacco and food processing firm. One result of this merger was that Aldo Osti had recently been given the added responsibility for the Del Monte family of canned fruits and vegetables within those countries listed above. Del Monte was an old and well-established brand that had been acquired by R. J. Reynolds in the early 1970s.

NABISCO BRANDS' OPERATION IN ITALY

The Saiwa Biscuit Company of Genoa, Italy, had been acquired by Nabisco in 1965. Operated as an autonomous subsidiary, it had grown successfully in recent years and had returned attractive profits to the parent. Among the major products manufactured and sold throughout Italy by Saiwa were crackers, cookies, chocolate-covered biscuits, sugar wafers, and snacks. In 1985, it was expected that Saiwa's sales would be approximately 180 billion Italian lira.*

A second operating arm of the firm in Italy was Nabisco SpA, headquartered in Milan. This firm was run separately from Saiwa, with its own chief executive, manu-

---

*At the time this case was written, US $1.00 = 1,700 Italian lira.

facturing facilities, and sales force. As in other Nabisco subsidiaries, the president of Nabisco SpA had total responsibility for the organization's profits and sales growth.

Nabisco SpA processed and marketed an array of brands. Some of these were typical of Nabisco brands found in many other countries, such as Ritz crackers and Planters peanuts and snacks. Other products were unique to Nabisco SpA in Italy—for example, Catari pizza mix and Montania herbal tea. The total sales of Nabisco SpA would be about 60 billion lira in 1985.

Another Nabisco company, Del Monte Italy, had become Osti's responsibility only within the last few months. This firm concentrated on canned fruits and vegetables and in 1985 was expected to achieve a sales volume in Italy of 50 billion lira.

LAUNCH OF CIPSTER

In 1971, Saiwa successfully launched Cipster, an extruded potato-based snack product. The product is made by mixing potato flakes, starch, salt, and coloring. In mix form, the product is extruded in a manner similar to the process used to manufacture spaghetti. The resulting rolls are cut, dried, and then fried briefly in cooking oil. After further drying, the product is ready to be packaged.

The product was introduced with heavy spending on dramatic television advertising that proclaimed, "It's a potato. No, it's Cipster." The idea was to position Cipster as a "non-potato chip" snack against the category leader, potato chips. Initially, the company spent one lira on television advertising for every lira of sales. Such advertising pressure created almost overnight recognition of the brand and helped the sales force achieve very broad distribution.

In its initial years, the product was well received by a broad segment of the population. Cipster was consumed by youngsters as an afternoon snack, as well as by adults with a cocktail or aperitif. In 1975, Saiwa began concentrating most of its merchandising for the product on teenagers and young adults. The product was portrayed as "fun" for active, social people. By 1981, this positioning was further enhanced by television commercials using fast rock music. In 1985, this particular "fun" image development was continuing, along with a secondary theme of Cipster as the "non-potato chip."

The results of this effort by Saiwa were impressive. By 1985, the estimated sales of Cipster were 17.1 billion lira, and the brand represented about 18% (by tonnage) of the extruded snack market in Italy (see Exhibit 2 for sales history). Also, the brand's contribution to profits was above the corporate average.

THE ITALIAN SNACK MARKET

The Italian snack market had experienced substantial growth during the last five years (see Exhibit 3). Although all three major product segments had participated in this growth, extruded snacks had clearly grown the fastest (see Exhibits 4 and 5). Within the extruded snack segment, corn-based products had been the dominant form (see Exhibit 6). Also, it was apparent that the majority of sales within the extruded snack segment were from the sale of small bags (less than 40 grams) (see Exhibit 7). The distribution of extruded snacks was dominated by the traditional grocery store (see Exhibit 8). Consumer research indicated that there was a fairly high consumption rate of snacks in the Italian market (as shown in Exhibit 9).

CIPSTER'S POSITION IN THE SNACK MARKET

It was Luigi Capurro's opinion that Cipster, in its present form, had limited future growth potential. One reason for this was that Cipster had achieved a high share of market within its narrow segment, the extruded potato-based snack market. Currently, the brand had about 65% of the volume (in tons) in this particular niche. It was Capurro's opinion, even though there was no research to support his contention, that although Cipster competed with the higher-volume, corn-based products, consumers did not see the brand as being a direct substitute for other products. Thus, he thought that in its present form Cipster's incursion into the more voluminous corn-based segment could not be seen as a significant growth potential.

At the retail level, Cipster was priced significantly higher than the corn-based product (see Exhibit 10). This was mostly due to the more expensive raw material that had undergone substantial price increases in recent months. It was thought that this price differential was a further inhibitor to the product's growth prospects. Capurro reasoned that this was particularly true in Cipster's case because of the impulse nature of the snack market.

Presently, Cipster was bought primarily for consumption in the home. Despite its appeal to young people and teens, the product had achieved only limited success in penetrating the small bag, single-serving segment. Only 20% of Cipster's sales were in this package size, although about 70% of the unit volume of the snack category was sold in bags. Sales in this package form were dominated by potato chips. Also, it was believed that within the extruded product area, the corn-based product had been more successful in small bags due to its lower price.

As a result of the analysis that led to his conclusion regarding limited growth opportunity, Capurro was informally considering several strategic alternatives. He was suggesting that the Cipster brand strength might be used to launch a new product within the corn-based segment. Such a product would utilize existing equipment and have a texture similar to the potato-based product. Its color, taste, and price would be the product's principal distinguishing characteristic.

Although the new product could be produced with minimal new capital investment, the marketing investment for such a brand extension might be substantial. Capurro's tentative plan was to employ the strong Cipster brand recognition and market the product under that consumer franchise. He estimated that by utilizing such a widely recognized brand name, Saiwa would have to spend about 10 billion lira on advertising a corn-based product within the first two years.

The alternative of creating a totally new brand name and identity would probably cost about 20 billion lira. This second alternative also had the drawback that Saiwa would end up with two separate brand names competing for the same consumer usage occasion.

On a per unit basis, a corn-based extruded product could be produced for an estimated 60% of the direct manufacturing costs (variable manufacturing plus manufacturing overhead) of the present potato-based product. It would be sold by Saiwa's existing sales force through essentially the same wholesale and retail channels as the potato-based product. There would be, however, additional effort placed on obtaining distribution in kiosks and through various street vendors in order to penetrate more deeply into the impulse-orientated bag snack market.

Along with these tentative ideas for the new product, Capurro was proposing that the 1986 plan for the present Cipster product be a maintenance marketing program. To save funds for the eventual launch of the corn-based product, he was suggesting an advertising and promotion expenditure of about 1.2 billion lira. This money would be used primarily to stimulate trial use among teens and young adults. The emphasis would be on a series of sales promotions, such as contests, games, premiums, and point-of-purchase price reductions. Limited television and billboard advertising would also be aimed at the teen market.

Capurro estimated that about 2.5 billion lira was the amount that a brand such as Cipster would normally spend on marketing communications during a year. Thus, there was some risk in reducing the advertising effort, especially in light of the recent increase in the advertising effort of the major competitors.

OSTI'S VIEW OF THE PROPOSED STRATEGY

As Osti was reviewing the proposed Cipster strategy, he had reached several tentative conclusions. It appeared to him that, with a reasonable level of advertising support, a new corn-based Cipster had the potential to reach the break-even point within the second year after its introduction and be profitable in the third. However, the new product's effects on the sales of the current potato-based Cipster were difficult to determine. Osti thought that the sales and profitability of that product would probably go down. But, it was uncertain how fast that would happen and to what extent the profits would erode.

In addition to the plans for Cipster in Italy, Osti was also considering several broader strategic changes that could potentially affect that product's strategy, as well as the way in which the company would be organized to market it. As has been stated, Osti had consistently believed in the many benefits of the highly decentralized marketing decision making that had been practiced by Nabisco in its European operations. Nevertheless, some emerging trends had made him think that perhaps more central coordination would be called for in the future.

Recently, substantial publicity had been given to a concept called "globalization of markets." Some writers and marketers throughout the world (and especially in Western Europe) contended that a common (or global) consumer culture was emerging. Many Europeans were traveling with increasing frequency to other countries. They observed other cultures and local consumer habits. In addition, it was speculated that pan-European television, with its attendant advertising, would soon be a fact of life. Already homes in border areas and those wired for cable (still a little less than 10%) were receiving broadcasts from other parts of Europe. This pan-European television would mean that viewers not only would be exposed to alternative life-styles on a regular basis, but also would be watching commercials from several different countries.

It was argued that this cultural binding, both of consumers' brand knowledge and life-styles, would justify the development of common brand marketing efforts throughout Europe. It was suggested that marketers approach the entire Western European market as a single entity. Pan-European (or global) brand names, package designs, advertising, and promotional programs were being called for.

In addition to these cultural trends, several economic factors were encouraging Osti to consider a pan-European approach to the firm's marketing programs. In many of the firm's operating divisions there were major brand opportunities that would require substantial investment in marketing tools such as television commercials and innovative packaging. When this investment was weighed against the size of the market opportunity in just one country, such "up-front" spending often could not be justified. However, if these investments were compared with the revenue opportunity for all of Europe, the marketing plan sometimes became economically attractive.

Along with considering the validity of pan-European branding programs, Osti was in the process of reviewing with his key operations people a concept he called "centers of manufacturing excellence." It seemed that Nabisco should be consolidating some of its far-flung factory operations. In the current arrangement, each country manufactured its own products. Thus, for instance, Saiwa made all of its own products for its home market in its several factories throughout Italy. The same was true of the companies in France, Spain, and so forth. In each situation, there was virtually no exporting to other major markets.

With the advent of more technology in the food processing business (still a far cry from a "high-tech" business, however), it seemed reasonable that the factories should begin to specialize. Thus, perhaps one of Nabisco's French operations, Belin, might make all of the crackers ("biscuits") for the many Nabisco sales organizations throughout Europe; in the same vein, the Italian factory would make all of the extruded snack products. Such specialization would allow each factory to concentrate on a fewer number of technologies, focus on a limited number of products, and achieve operating efficiencies. Although there were no definite plans for implementing this manufacturing strategy, Osti was confident that this scheme or a similar one would be a reality within only a few years.

One of the strategic alternatives that had emerged from these considerations was the idea of establishing Planters as an umbrella snack brand or "family brand" for all of Nabisco's products in that category throughout Europe. This would mean using the name Planters on all packaging and with all advertising and promotional effort for snack products. In addition, if this concept were adopted, it seemed reasonable that the familiar deep blue that had come to be identified with the brand would become the dominant color on all packages.

Planters is synonymous with peanuts in North America. In fact, it is one of the most widely recognized consumer brands in the United States. In addition to peanuts, the American operation of Nabisco had recently been successful in expanding the Planters brand to encompass a wide range of snack products. The widely recognized blue package and the Mr. Peanut logo were being used to market various snacks, including cheese balls, pretzel sticks, and corn chips.

While not as well known in Europe, the Planters brand was gaining momentum. For example, starting from a small base, Nabisco's operations in Germany had doubled the Planters peanut volume over the last several years. Planters peanuts were sold in all the countries under Osti's supervision, but in none of them was the brand franchise "well known."

In addition to the arguments just presented, Osti was eager to initiate the concept of pan-European brands to alter the trend toward brand proliferation. It had been his observation that most of the operating companies tended to develop a new brand for each new product that was introduced. This required that each new brand carry the financial burden of its own unique brand development. If a "family brand," such as Planters for snacks, could be established, there were obvious economic advantages in the areas of advertising and promotion.

The use of a pan-European family brand for snacks also had the potential benefit of supporting more professional advertising development. Generally, the greater the financial contribution generated by a brand, the more money would be available for the development of advertising materials. Normally, a low-volume brand could not support the best efforts of the leading European advertising agencies. Although such agencies might agree to work on a low-volume brand because of their desire to develop relationships with Nabisco, their best creative talent would probably not be assigned. A high-volume umbrella brand, such as the one Osti envisioned for Planters, would certainly justify the best of the advertising profession.

Osti saw the launch of a "new" Cipster product as a potential opportunity to begin the broadening of the Planters brand family. It was perhaps possible to widen Nabisco's snack franchise by incorporating successful products under the Planters brand umbrella in Italy initially and then throughout Europe. Cipster could be the first such move in that direction.

At the time of the case, only one other firm was attempting to build a pan-European snack brand. Bahlsens, a well-established biscuit (cookies) brand in Germany, was trying to broaden its franchise to encompass a wide range of snack products—peanuts, extruded snacks, and sweet biscuits. In peanuts, Bahlsens was well established only in France, Switzerland, Austria, and Germany. Its biscuit line had long been established in Germany, but only recently had the firm attempted to move into other markets with Bahlsens biscuits.

Of course, there were examples of companies that had achieved success with pan-European or global brands in other categories. The most frequently mentioned companies were Coca-Cola and Marlboro. However, the extent to which these cases applied to a pan-European snack brand was uncertain.

At present, the Planters brand name was the responsibility of Nabisco Italy SpA. This company, which reported directly to Osti, was operated independently like all other Nabisco companies. Although the firm did sell Planters peanuts throughout Italy, the volume for that product was only about 2.5 billion lira.

OSTI'S DECISIONS

Thus far Osti had taken one step in operationalizing his ideas on pan-European brands. He had been instrumental in establishing a New Product Coordinating Committee, consisting of executives from both the southern European operations (his area of responsibility) and from Nabisco Northern Europe (which reported to another executive). The purpose of this group was to review the operating companies' new product plans, encourage the flow of information between the various companies, and promote pan-European brand programs where possible. One operating rule that had emerged from this committee was that any totally new brand would be developed in such a way that it could be sold by any of Nabisco's European firms if they so chose. Thus far, the committee had not become involved in the marketing programs of existing brands. (Both Planters and Cipster would be considered existing brands.)

It appeared to Osti that several alternatives regarding Cipster were open to him. Obviously, he could encourage Capurro and his associates to proceed with their ideas for a corn-based product similar to Cipster under the Saiwa label. Another course of action would be to allow the corn-based product development to continue and transfer its marketing responsibility to Nabisco SpA in Milan. A third choice was to instruct his operating executives that henceforth the Planters marketing program in Italy would be the responsibility of Saiwa. This alternative would probably also mean moving the operational responsibilities for Planters to the Genoa-headquartered Saiwa from the Milan-based Nabisco SpA.

As he was thinking through these choices, Osti was keenly aware that he had two very fine general managers in place in the two operating companies in Italy. Both had performed well, and Osti was eager to avoid anyone "losing face" with his decision.

The total snack market in Western Europe was the equivalent of several hundred million dollars. In organizing a consolidated approach to this market, what type of decisions would have to be made, and what form should the organization take? If he were to operationalize his ideas about a pan-European snack brand called "Planters," Osti wondered if this move would require more centralized marketing planning and control from his Paris office. For instance, would some direction be needed when decisions had to be made regarding which names (Nabisco, Saiwa, Planters, Cipster) would be on the package and how much prominence was to be given to each? Osti remembered well how he had fought for three years to obtain complete cooperation from the operating companies regarding the adoption of a common design and typeface for the distinctive Nabisco trademark and colophon on the package of the firm's products.

For many years Osti had encouraged his general managers to be both responsible for their operations and independent in their decision making. Was the implementation of pan-European branding going to "backfire" on him and create more interorganizational conflict than it might be worth? He also wondered whether introducing the Planters brand on top of a widely recognized name such as Cipster, along with the adoption of blue packaging in place of the present distinctive red package, might only serve to confuse current Cipster customers. Many consumers in Italy knew and liked Cipster by Saiwa.

EXHIBIT 1 An Advertisement for Cipster

Italian/
Rough
English
Translation

Croccantelle/
Crispy

Patatose/
Potatoes

Son/
Are

Le/
The

Favolose/
Marvelous

Allegre/
Happy

Sfogliantine/
Snacks

Croccantelle, patatose, son le Cipster favolose.

Cipster Saiwa. Allegre sfogliatine di patate.

EXHIBIT 2 Cipster's Recent Sales History

	1982	1983	1984	1985 (est.)
Tons	1,371	1,474	1,401	1,462
Lira (billion)	9.9	13.2	14.9	17.1

EXHIBIT 3 Sales of Snacks in Italy, 1981–1985 (in tons)

1981	1982	1983	1984	1985 (est.)
27,400	28,900	31,130	33,400	36,400

EXHIBIT 4 Product Segments in the Italian Snack Market, 1981–1985 (% of tons)

	1981	1982	1983	1984	1985 (est.)
Potato chips	65	63	59	58	56
Savory snacks	20	20	21	20	20
Extruded snacks	15	17	20	22	24
	100	100	100	100	100

EXHIBIT 5 Sales of Extruded Snacks in Italy (in billion lira)

1981	1982	1983	1984	1985 (est.)
34.5	46.0	64.9	88.3	114.0

EXHIBIT 6 Extruded Snacks—Percent by Type (% of tons)

	1984	1985
Popcorn	5.4	5.2
Corn-based	67.2	69.1
Potato-based	27.4	25.7
	100	100

EXHIBIT 7 Sales of Extruded Snacks—Percent by Package Size (% of tons)

	1984	1985
Less than 40 grams (small bags)	57.5	54.5
40–130 grams (large bags & medium-sized cartons)	34.5	36.5
130+ grams (large cartons)	8.0	9.0
	100	100

EXHIBIT 8 Extruded Snacks—Sales by Outlet Type (% of tons)

	1984	1985
Supermarkets	13.3	14.0
Superettes	10.9	13.5
Traditional grocery stores	49.3	50.2
Bar/Kiosk	26.5	22.3
	100	100

EXHIBIT 9 Snack Consumption (% of population over 16 years old)

Consumption	Potato chips	Savory snacks	Extruded snacks
Within last 7 days—winter	18.9	11.5	6.9
Within last 7 days—summer	23.5	11.9	7.5
Every 2–3 days—winter	5.0	5.5	4.0
Every 2–3 days—summer	7.7	7.2	4.4

EXHIBIT 10 Relative Retail Prices of Extruded Corn-based and Extruded Potato-based Snack Products (indexed prices)

	Potato-based	Corn-based
October 1984	1.35	1.10
October 1985	1.52	1.10

Communication

Marketing communication is often a local activity. Yet under certain conditions, a global strategy can benefit from international coordination among local communication activities. One such condition is the desirability of establishing a common positioning platform for a brand marketed in a number of countries. Another condition involves the need to have a coherent and consistent communication policy for global accounts—those clients who themselves coordinate their purchases among their local country organizations and who would not be served as well under a decentralized communication policy. Nevertheless, even where global considerations prevail, a corporate communication policy should not be so rigid as to prevent local organizations from experimenting with innovative communication practices—innovations that when successful could become the raw material for future global policy norms.

ISSUES

The three cases in this section deal with two elements of marketing communication: media advertising and personal selling. The first case, Hertz Autovermietung GmbH (A), describes the background to Hertz's German operation and management's decision to seek the help of a local advertising agency in revitalizing the company's marketing strategy. The second case, Hertz Autovermietung GmbH (B), provides details of the advertising campaign that led to a strengthening of the company's market position in Germany. The third case, Grasse Fragrances SA, examines the challenges of managing an effective sales force in a global company and explains how manage-

ment practices may have to be adapted to changes that cut across individual country markets.

LEARNING POINTS

The student can expect the following learning points from the analysis and class discussion of the cases in this section:

- Practice in customer and competitive analysis toward identifying opportunities for strategic repositioning;
- Skills in evaluating elements of an advertising campaign and the fit of those elements with customer and competitive reality;
- Exposure to issues of client–agency relationship;
- Insights into the role of personal selling and sales management practices in implementing a global marketing strategy;
- Exercise in making sales management decisions to reflect broad global changes in the selling environment.

9 HERTZ AUTOVERMIETUNG GMBH (A)

Niels Grothgar, president of Eggert Werbeagentur,[1] Dusseldorf, West Germany, was pondering the facts discussed during his meeting on Friday, June 2, 1982, with Ian Jenkins, vice president of sales and marketing for Hertz Europe. Jenkins had requested that the agency review the marketing strategy of the German subsidiary, Hertz Autovermietung GmbH, and make recommendations that could stimulate profitability and growth. As president of a large national agency, Grothgar was intrigued by the thought of serving a sizable international client, yet his knowledge of the rental business suggested that an in-depth market analysis was required before recommendations could be made.

COMPANY BACKGROUND

Hertz, a subsidiary of RCA Corporation, had had operations in West Germany since 1958. By 1973, it had over 200 locations, partly corporate-owned and partly independent agencies that rented Hertz-owned cars to the public on a commission basis. As the largest market shareholder in 1973, with over 10% share in a market that had more than 1,800 car rental firms, Hertz Germany had experienced a consistent growth of 20% per year during the early 1970s. This growth and size had enabled Hertz to reach a favorable position in the large replacement market (60% of volume).[2] The company made new car purchases from larger dealerships in return for rental business when a dealer's customer was having a car repaired. Hertz also benefited significantly from business travel and airport rentals through an agreement with Lufthansa. In addition, the firm had seen considerable growth in the truck rental business, placing it in a strong competitive position in that sector.

This case was prepared by Professor Per V. Jenster. Copyright © 1990 by the International Institute for Management Development (IMD), Lausanne, Switzerland. Not to be used or reproduced without permission. Certain figures in this case have been disguised for proprietary reasons.

   1. *Werbeagentur* means advertising agency.

   2. The replacement market refers to the demand for rental cars in situations where the renter's own car is being repaired.

With the oil crisis of 1973–1974, the German rental business spiraled into a slump—car-free Sundays, little business travel, and greater use of public transportation, such as Germany's effective train system. Hertz Germany was ill-prepared for this turn of events, as the company had a fleet oriented toward the larger and more gas-consuming cars, inadequate cost-control procedures, and large fixed assets. Under pressure from New York headquarters, the country manager was replaced by Volvo's German marketing manager. After six months, the contrast between German and American management styles and differences of opinion led to another change in leadership of Hertz Germany. This time, headquarters chose a small team of highly successful young Americans to turn the unprofitable situation in West Germany around. Despite the differences in cultural background, this team was well received in the German organization, and over the course of three months a number of decisions were implemented. One of the major decisions was to dismantle the agency network and close many corporate locations. Through proactive decision making, the number of Hertz locations was reduced to 50 corporate-owned outlets, situated mainly in large airports and large city centers. In addition, the team closed the firm's van operation. By 1976, Hertz West Germany showed profits and healthy key ratios, although on a much smaller asset base.

One executive commented:

> The closure of many locations resulted in significant savings, but caused substantial loss of business. For example, we closed the Hertz location in the small town of Heilbronn without considering that it was the headquarters of Maizena and Fiat Germany. This meant that we not only lost the local traffic, but also business from these headquarters coming and going to Frankfurt Airport. In addition, their executives stopped using our services in other locations as well. It didn't help that we also lost the renewal of the Lufthansa agreement.

Hertz Germany's competitors survived the oil crisis somewhat better than Hertz, partly because of Hertz's decisive action. InterRent, a subsidiary of Volkswagen, took direct advantage of Hertz's situation and offered most of Hertz's network the opportunity to become InterRent agents. It also assumed most of Hertz's van business.

By 1982, Hertz had 65 locations, including a few franchise arrangements. (See Exhibit 1 for organizational information on Hertz Germany.) Franchise operations differed from independent agency locations in that the franchisors owned the cars and received only marketing and billing services from Hertz Germany in return for royalty fees. Although Hertz had rebuilt some of the replacement business, the 1981–1982 downturn in the German economy made it difficult to realize any growth and avoid financial losses. In fact, the recession made it hard for Hertz to sell its used cars (the car fleet was normally renewed every 6 to 9 months), a problem that affected the company's ability to retain good relationships with the car dealerships. The average age of vehicles hired out by larger agencies was under 6 months for cars and 12 months for vans. On average, fleet costs were an estimated 25% of revenue for the major agencies. Replacement with new models tended to occur annually rather than after a certain mileage. The Gesamtverband der Kraftfahrzeug Vermieter Deutschland (Association of Motor Vehicle Rental Companies) estimated that new vehicle purchases by car rental operators accounted for about 7% of the total German new car market.

THE CAR RENTAL MARKET[3]

By 1982, the West German car rental business was defined as follows in Table 1:

TABLE 1 The West German Car Rental Market

	1982*	1983 (est.)
Rental fleet (000 units)	55.0	60.5
passenger cars	45.0	50.0
commercial vehicles	10.0	10.5
Turnover (DM million)	1,600	1,800
% private usage	0.18%	19%
Number of firms	1,350	–
Investment in vehicles (DM billion)	1.5	1.6
Average turnover/firm (DM million)	1.2	1.5

Source: Bundesverband der Autovermieter Deutschland/Euromonitor.
*Annualized data.

More than half the rental turnover accrued by car rental firms was from the traditional "money-spinner" of the industry—the "Unfall-Ersatzwagen-Geschäft," or accident replacement business. This business existed because insurance companies were obliged to provide a suitable replacement car or van to any customer inconvenienced by an accident until the damaged car was satisfactorily repaired. There had been, however, a noticeable decline in the relative significance of this business during the preceding years, due to three major influences:

■ The cost-cutting tactics of many insurance companies since the mid-1970s had discouraged customers who were entitled to rent a replacement car from doing so by providing a minor monetary compensation to the customer for not renting a replacement vehicle.
■ Many repair shops, during and since the recession, were reducing the average repair time for vehicles damaged in accidents.
■ The national accident rate over the past years had declined due to shorter average distances driven annually and generally higher driving standards.

The estimated percentage breakdown of revenues for the various vehicle rental sectors in 1982 was as follows:

3. Based on the Euromonitor report, *Car Rental in West Germany.*

Car hire	
accident replacement	54%
business requirements	12
personal and leisure	10
other	6
Light vans and trucks	18
Total	100%

The business market increased throughout the recession and was expected to see a further upturn, largely owing to a general growth in air travel. Car rentals to tourists and for personal travel also seemed to be growing. Car rentals to visiting American tourists (an important target market) had been slack during the weak dollar period of 1980/81, but had risen appreciably and were expected to continue to increase.

One other market sector was van rentals to firms seeking temporary replacement vans when their own trucks had an accident or breakdown and to private individuals who had to move large loads such as household goods. Van rentals had risen appreciably over the past few years. Operators had also sought to stimulate activity in this sector by discovering new market niches, such as camper vans. These had become immensely popular with tourists, as well as with firms that required, for example, a mobile office on a building site or at a trade fair.

Hertz competed against InterRent, Avis, Autohansa, Sixt, Eurocar, and approximately 1,350 smaller firms. Advertising was largely based on name recognition and functionality. In contrast to rental firms in the United States and the United Kingdom, German rental firms made little use of television advertising because the restricted air time imposed by federal and state laws made the impact-to-cost ratio unfavorable. Other options were billboards and newspaper and magazine advertisements. In addition, firms used posters and illuminated signs, especially at transport centers, such as major railway stations and airports. (Exhibit 2 shows the total advertising expenditures for the German industry. Exhibit 3 depicts the 1981 media schedules for the major competitors. Exhibits 4 and 5 display the annotated advertising strategy for the major competitors and selected ads.)

Each major car rental firm offered a range of car models and equipment (e.g., radios). Although firms made few attempts to differentiate the products, they did try to vary prices to reflect local conditions. In general, various methods were used to calculate rental rates, but essentially, engine size and type of vehicle were the determining factors. Rates and methods of calculating charges varied somewhat from company to company, and most major firms required a deposit or a credit card. The use of a credit card ensured a greater degree of control over the customer, who after all, was leasing a high-value product at a relatively low price.

By 1982, the general price situation in the car rental industry was influenced by a slight increase in rates, but at the same time, more rebates were being offered. Hertz and Avis had the highest prices, and InterRent offered the lowest prices among the major rental companies. Although competition was controlled primarily through differentiated pricing strategies for various parts of the car rental service (i.e., rates for mileage, insurance, return charges), there were only slight variances in the final price, as various tariff systems caused the industry to avoid price wars.

If one were to break down the different business elements which, when combined, constituted the rental firm's offer to a customer, the cost structure in Table 2 would be representative:

TABLE 2 Cost Structure of Car Rental Firms

	Fleet management	Car control	Outlet management	Marketing	Booking and sales	Customers
Large international firms						
Normal	30%	13%	35%	5%	17%	100%
Discount	30	8	35	2	2	75
Small rental firms						
Normal	35	5	30	1	4	75

In addition, arrangements were made for major customers to receive special discount rates of 30 to 40%, as well as other benefits for their employees who rented cars. Overall reductions reached 50% in some cases. To attract the requisite number of customers, the larger firms were usually forced to locate main branches in expensive locations, such as airports and city centers. To limit buildup of fixed costs, some firms tried to diversify into fleet management services for major corporations.

CAR RENTAL CUSTOMERS

According to a STERN "Up-market Target Group" survey, 14% of German adults claimed to have used a rental car during the previous three years (with 7 to 8% of all adults doing so within the last year). The share of rental car users was about one-third lower among women than men. (The major findings from a survey done for a consortium of companies within the car rental industry are shown in Exhibit 6. Exhibit 7 shows the results of an Omnibus survey of usage profiles, and Exhibit 8 depicts the STERN survey of selection criteria for rental car users.)

The German market in 1982 was characterized by a small user group (5% of the population over 18 years of age) and little repeat business (only 1% of the population rented a car more than once a year). Although, in the Federal Republic, there was fairly even distribution among social groups in the replacement sector (accidents could affect anyone), the overall rental pattern of business customers over the past few years was understandably important to the car rental companies. It is also worth noting that one-third of all business rentals were made to visitors to Germany, and 60% of all repeat business rentals were believed to take place at airports.

Within the tourist rental sector, two-thirds of the rentals were to foreigners, and only one-third to Germans. There was also a marked seasonal rise in replacement vehicle rentals during the winter, with an additional peak over the summer holiday period. Monday, incidentally, was the most important day for rental car companies, owing to the incidence of accidents on weekends.

One marketing research study concluded that customers had little "interest and involvement" in the industry and were generally unable to differentiate the basic product. Many customers viewed the car rental process as awkward and unpleasant, and the product as rather expensive. Because customers perceived little difference among firms, brand decisions were made primarily by habit or chance. In this respect, a comparison between Hertz and InterRent in name recognition, both spontaneous and prompted, revealed the following data:

	Spontaneous name recognition	Prompted name recognition
Hertz	17%	46%
InterRent	49	82

This particular report also concluded that no distinctive Hertz image existed except that of a "big, international, American company." In contrast, InterRent's image was "the biggest German (national) firm with a substantial truck fleet," and Avis was considered the "biggest worldwide, international firm."

COMPETITION IN THE CAR RENTAL MARKET

Since 1970, the total number of car rental firms operating in West Germany had steadily declined, from approximately 2,000 to 1,350 in 1982. The overwhelming majority of these were small independent firms that operated at a purely local level; for them renting cars was generally an ancillary activity to vehicle repair and sales. These local operators were not generally "geared up" for business travelers. Most of their turnover came from accident replacement rentals, and they had suffered from the contraction of this market. Their relative inflexibility, the debilitating effects of insurance companies' cost-cutting on the industry, and increasing competition from the multinational rental leaders also contributed to the decline in the total number of rental companies. Nevertheless, the small firms as a whole still accounted for about half of all vehicle rental turnover in West Germany.

Six large international firms were active in the German car rental industry, and all had experienced an increase in volume and revenues, as can be seen in Table 3.

In addition, there were approximately 30 regional car rental operators of some importance. However, 40% of all turnover was made by the six largest firms (Table 4).

TABLE 3 Volume and Revenue of Large International Firms

Firm	Market share (%)	Number of locations	Number of representatives	Number of models	Number of cars (000)	Number of trucks
InterRent	15.7	330	27	20	7.5	3,400
Avis	7.5	85	31	21	3.8	700
Autohansa	5.1	213	–	44	3.2	600
Hertz	3.4	58	27	17	2.5	50
Sixt	1.5	–	–	27	2.0	300
Europcar	3.2	90	22	24	2.3	300
All others	61.9	550	–	–	25.7	5,600

TABLE 4 Turnover of the Major Rental Companies (estimates in DM millions)

Company	1975	1976	1977	1978	1979	1980	1981
InterRent	92	117	140	178	200	220	232
Avis	50	60	70	80	95	105	115
Autohansa	40	45	51	58	70	72	102
Hertz	36	26	28	30	35	47	54
Sixt	–	–	–	15	16	18	20
Europcar	–	–	32	40	40	45	–

The airport market statistics differed from the national market share in the following respects:

	Airport market (%)	National market (%)
InterRent	17.6	15.7
Avis	22.6	7.5
Hertz	20.7	3.4
All others	39.1	73.4

Franchise arrangements were starting to emerge, and experts considered this business an important area of growth for industry leaders.

Car leasing as part of the rental business also differed in importance and critical success factors for the various major players. InterRent, because of Volkswagen's own leasing operation, did not lease cars. With years of market presence, Avis achieved a significant share of 20 to 25% of its unit volume from leasing, whereas leasing was only a minor marketing factor for Hertz. Banks, other financial institutions, and many car companies were expected to increase their commercial presence in this sector. (As part of an analysis of the strengths and weaknesses of various competitors, the findings of an outside consulting firm are summarized in Exhibit 9.)

EXHIBIT 1   Organization Chart

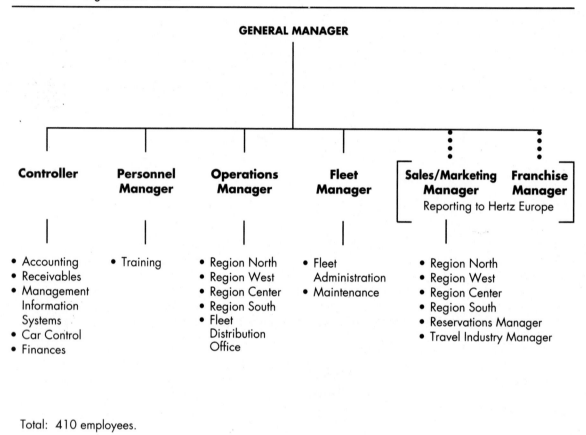

GENERAL MANAGER

Controller

- Accounting
- Receivables
- Management Information Systems
- Car Control
- Finances

Personnel Manager

- Training

Operations Manager

- Region North
- Region West
- Region Center
- Region South
- Fleet Distribution Office

Fleet Manager

- Fleet Administration
- Maintenance

Sales/Marketing Manager   **Franchise Manager**

Reporting to Hertz Europe

- Region North
- Region West
- Region Center
- Region South
- Reservations Manager
- Travel Industry Manager

Total: 410 employees.

EXHIBIT 2 Total Advertising Expenditures

Year	1,000 DM	Modification to the year before (%)	Daily newspapers 1,000 DM	%	Consumer magazines 1,000 DM	%	Trade magazines 1,000 DM	%	TV 1,000 DM	%	Radio 1,000 DM	%
1976	7,500	–	3,385	45	3,737	50	81	1	–	–	297	4
1977	9,106	+21	4,262	47	4,584	50	122	2	19	0	118	1
1978	12,822	+41	6,086	47	6,210	48	245	2	149	1	131	1
1979	11,679	– 9	3,999	34	6,885	59	148	1	–	–	647	6
1980	10,556	–10	4,515	43	4,906	46	224	2	–	–	911	9
1981	14,630	+39	6,968	48	5,574	38	606	4	–	–	1,483	10

EXHIBIT 3 Media Schedules, 1981

Account	Hertz	Autohansa	Avis	Fly + Drive (Lufthansa + Avis)	Europcar	InterRent
	681,897.–	618,222.–	1,218,260.–	1,331,537.–	879,649.–	8,164,527.–
TV	–	–	0.9 %	–	–	6.2 %
Radio	–	4.0 %	–	–	–	11.2 %
Print magazines	22.0 %	15.5 %	15.1 %	100 %	44.2%	39.5 %
Print newspapers	78.0 %	80.5 %	84.0 %	–	55.8 %	43.1 %
Magazines						
Auto Motor Sport		12 ×	3 ×			
Capital		1 ×		8 ×		4 ×
Impulse		1 ×				
Manager Magazine		1 ×		8 ×		4 ×
Spiegel	2 ×	12 ×	4 ×	12 ×	7 ×	12 ×
ADAC				1 ×		
Wiwo				12 ×		
Hör Zu	2 ×					
Stern	2 ×					7 ×
BamS						20 ×
Gong						4 ×
Merian						1 ×
Quick						7 ×

Source: Schmidt + Pohlman.

EXHIBIT 4 Competitive Advertising Strategies

InterRent

Advertising expenditure: 1981: DM 8,164,527.– (3.5% of turnover)

Media: National magazines
 National dailies
 Local dailies
 Radio

Campaign: National campaign for cars and trucks

Comments: InterRent tries to advertise all kinds of business and to all target groups within the campaign.
 InterRent emphasizes friendliness, safety, reliability, helpfulness, involving (and motivating) their employees.
 InterRent changed the slogan from being the *biggest* car rental company to a more familiar positioning: "InterRent is *your* car rental company."

Avis & Lufthansa

Advertising expenditure: 1981: DM 1,331,537.– (1.3% of turnover)

Media: National magazines

Campaign: National campaign for cars

Comments: Avis and Lufthansa focus their attention on businessmen who fly frequently.
 They market excellent cooperation and a highly developed reservations system.

Avis

Advertising expenditure: 1981: DM 1,218,260.– (1.1% of turnover)

Media: National magazines
 National dailies
 Local dailies

Campaign: National campaign for cars

Comments: Avis proves to be a reliable rental company for all events.
 Avis addresses itself to all target groups.
 Avis proposes possible opportunities for car rental to create new demand.
 Ads in local dailies recommend the local Avis phone number for car rentals.

(continued)

EXHIBIT 4   (continued)

Europcar

Advertising expenditure: 1981: DM 879,696.– (1.9% of turnover)

Media: National magazines
   National dailies
   Local dailies

Campaign: National campaign for cars

Comments: Europcar presents itself as an international car rental company with a reliable organization.

   All target groups are considered.

EXHIBIT 5   Examples of Ads

EXPERIENCE AMERICA BY CAR: A GREAT VALUE

Do you plan on touring the United States—by car, of course? Then our special "America on Wheels" rate is exactly what you need!

Your Hertz car will be ready upon arrival, reserved 7 days ahead of your departure date for at least a 7-day trip. For example, you can rent a Ford Escort for only US $89,00 a week.

We guarantee the "America on Wheels" rate until March 31, 1984, in each of our 800 Hertz agencies in the USA and Canada.

You pay only a very small fee when returning your Hertz car to an agency not more than 500 miles from the original rental office, regardless of your total mileage. Included in this package deal are discounts at 350 Holiday Inn Hotels in the United States of America and Canada.

Ask for our "America on Wheels" special brochure available through your travel agent. The coupons for your reservations can be sent directly to our central reservations Hertz office, or you can call one of the following numbers:

Berlin 030-2618077;   Hannover 0511-514509;
Düsseldorf 0211-357021;   München 089-558211;
Essen 0201-770404;   Nürnberg 0911-232367;
Frankfurt 0611-730404;   Stuttgart 0711-225161.
Hamburg 040-2801201;

*You will find all our rates for other U.S. states and Canada listed in the "America on Wheels" brochure. The "America on Wheels" rates are valid from April 1, 1983, until March 31, 1984. Governmental and local taxes are not included. A price supplement could be charged for the high season.

Please send me a free copy of your Hertz brochure "America on Wheels." Hertz "America on Wheels," P.O. Box 11 08 43,6000 Frankfurt/Main 1.

Name _____

Address _____

_____

AMERICA
ON WHEELS   HERTZ

Amerika mit dem Auto erleben- äußerst preiswert.

Planen Sie eine Entdeckungsreise durch Amerika – natürlich mit dem Auto?

Dann ist unser Spezial-Tarif "America on Wheels" genau das Richtige.

Ihr Hertz-Wagen steht bei Ihrer Ankunft bereit, wenn Sie 7 Tage vor Abreise für mindestens 7 Tage reservieren. Zum Beispiel können Sie in Florida* schon für US $89,00 eine Woche lang einen Ford Escort mieten.

Die "America on Wheels"-Tarife garantieren wir bis zum 31. März 1984 für insgesamt 800 Hertz-Stationen in USA und Kanada.

Übrigens: Bei Ihrem Hertz-Wagen zahlen Sie nur geringe Rückführgebühren, wenn der Rückgabeort weiter als 500 Meilen von der Anmietstation entfernt ist, und zwar unabhängig von den während Ihrer Entdeckungsreise gefahrenen Meilen. Und außerdem erhalten Sie bei 350 Holiday Inn Hotels in USA und Kanada einen Nachlaß auf die normalen Zimmerpreise.

Detaillierte Informationen über das Hertz Sonderprogramm "America on Wheels" enthält die gleichnamige Broschüre, erhältlich bei Ihrem Reisebüro und direkt bei Hertz durch Einsenden des anhängenden Coupons, bzw. auf Anfrage beim Zentralen Hertz Reservierungsbüro unter einer der folgenden Telefonnummern:

Berlin 030-2618077;   Hannover 0511-514509;
Düsseldorf 0211-357021;   München 089-558211;
Essen 0201-770404;   Nürnberg 0911-232367;
Frankfurt 0611-730404;   Stuttgart 0711-225161.
Hamburg 040-2801201;

*Tarife für andere US Staaten und Kanada enthält die Broschüre "America on Wheels." Die "America on Wheels"-Raten gelten vom 1. April 1983 bis 31. März 1984. Staatliche und lokale Steuern sind nicht inbegriffen. Ein Hochsaisonzuschlag kann erhoben werden.

Bitte senden Sie mir ein Gratisexemplar der Hertz Broschüre "America on Wheels." An: Hertz "America on Wheels," Postfach 11 08 43, 6000 Frankfurt/Main 1.

Name_____

Adresse_____

AMERICA ON WHEELS.   **Hertz**

HO /4   Hertz vermietet Ford und andere gute Wagen.

(continued)

EXHIBIT 5 (continued)

Weil wir wissen, was Sie wollen.

interRent Autovermietung iR

interRent iR
Die internationale Autovermietung
The International car renting company

Zu Ihrer persönlichen Sicherheit: Die Neuen des Modelljahres 84. Audi 200 Turbo, Golf II, Ford Sierra und z. B. der Mercedes 190E, garantieren einen Fuhrpark mit fortschrittlicher Technik. Alle bieten mit modernstem Fahrwerk ein Höchstmaß an technischer Sicherheit.

Der superschnelle Audi 200 Turbo auch mit ABS, dem elektronischen Antiblockier-Bremssystem.
Zu Ihrer rentablen Sicherheit: Gemeinsam mit dem ADAC vereinbarte Vertragsbedingungen. Zuverlässiger und freundlicher Service an über 300 Vermiet-stationen in Deutschland. Bedarfsorientierte Tarife mit einer Vorteilsregelung zu Ihren Gunsten bei der Abrechnung. Viel Leistung für den Mietpreis – denn wir wissen, was Sie brauchen.
Das nennen wir interRentabel. Nehmen Sie uns beim Wort.

For your own personal security; the new 1984 models—Audi 200 Turbo, Golf II, Ford Sierra, and Mercedes 190E—offer a choice in advanced technology cars. All of them offer maximum security!
The speedy Audi 200 Turbo with ABS offers electronic brakes system.

Reliable security and friendly service from more than 300 agencies in Germany. Discount rates in your favor when paying the bill. Great performance and good rates because we know what you need. We name it "InterRentabel." Trust us!

EXHIBIT 6 Usage Rate of the Total Population

	Population in %	Index figures	
		Car rented more than 1 time	Car rented at least 1 time
Total	100		
Sex			
Men	45.8	137	125
Women	54.2	68	78
Age			
20–29 years	16.2	88	188
30–39 years	15.2	221	162
40–49 years	19.2	114	115
50–59 years	14.6	149	70
60–69 years	12.3	36	34
70 years +	11.1		
Household net income (monetary unit: DM/month)			
up to 1,000	4.2	20	125
1,000–1,500	9.3	16	67
1,500–2,000	14.9	28	90
2,000–2,500	19.5	114	103
2,500–3,000	14.1	112	101
3,000–3,500	38.0	91	122
3,500–4,000	(38.0% =	27	116
4,000–5,000	3.000 upwards)	216	138
5,000 +		381	179
Occupation			
Company owners + freelancers	0.9	789	567
Owners of small and middle-sized companies	6.0	265	116
Top executives + civil servants in key positions	3.4	756	479
Other executives + civil servants	37.9	67	88
Skilled workers	13.8	51	102
Other workers	16.2	78	69
Farmers	2.0	0	33
Unemployed	19.8		
Education			
Primary school	64.6	70	72
Middle school	24.6	72	162
Secondary school grad.	5.6	214	136
University	5.2	574	168

Source: Omnibus Industry Survey, 1982.

EXHIBIT 7 Usage Rate
(% of car rentals within the last 12 months)

People with a driver's license	Total rented	Cars	Trucks
Sex			
Women	7	5	2
Men	7	5	2
Age			
up to 34 years	8	4	3
35–54 years	8	7	2
55+	3	3	0
City size			
0–5,000 inhabitants	6	6	0
5,000–19,999	3	1	2
20,000–99,999	8	5	3
100,000+	10	7	3
Education			
Primary school with apprenticeship	1	1	–
Primary school without apprenticeship	5	3	2
Middle school/technical school	7	5	3
Secondary school/university	18	14	4
Household Income			
(DM monthly)			
0–1,999	5	3	2
2,000–2,499	4	2	3
2,500–2,999	6	3	3
3,000+	10	9	2
Profession			
Company owner/freelancer	21	19	1
Top executive/civil servant	20	14	9
Other executive/civil servant	6	4	2
Skilled worker	2	1	2
In training	7	4	3
Unemployed	7	4	2
Pensioner	3	2	1

Source: Omnibus Survey, 1982, Sample Institute.

EXHIBIT 8 Criteria Governing the Selection of a Car Rental Firm, by Age, 1982

	Up to 29	30–39	40–49	50 & Over
Projection (000s)	162	726	924	793
Sample	251	1,124	1,430	1,227
Percentage shares	100	100	100	100
Hire-car used in last 3 years				
Yes	19	18	14	10
No	81	82	86	90
Selection criteria important				
High standard of maintenance	16	16	12	9
Fast service	17	16	12	9
Clean car	13	13	11	9
Tariff	18	14	10	7
Proximity to pick-up point	14	13	11	7
Flexibility of staff	11	11	8	8
Insurance	11	11	9	5
Pre-booking	10	10	9	6
Extent of branch network	8	9	7	5
Fly-and-drive option	7	7	7	4
Credit card	7	6	5	3
Reputation	7	5	5	3
Range of marques	6	3	4	4
Variety of vehicles	4	3	3	3

Source: STERN, Up-Market Target Groups 2.

EXHIBIT 9 Analysis of Competitors' Strengths & Weaknesses

Company	Strengths	Weaknesses

Hertz Autovermietung GmbH, Frankfurt	International network
	Reservation system worldwide
	Low-mileage cars
	Special offers
	   Rapid/Autocheck system
	   VIP Club
	   Taco Bonus System
	   Europswap System
	   Weekend tariffs
		Merely no advertising activities
		Changing actions in marketing and sales
		Weak distribution net
		   Locations
		   Sales team
		High price level

InterRent Autovermietung GmbH, Hamburg	Active sales policy
	Number of locations
	Biggest network in Germany
	Strong, effective, trained sales force
	Treatment of all business sectors and target groups
	Cooperations
	   ADAC
	   Railway
	   Dollar Rent-A-Car
	Efficient computerized systems
	Big fleet of vehicles
		No worldwide presence
		Tendency to scatter the resources

Avis Autovermietung GmbH, Frankfurt	International company
	Dense location network
	Well-trained staff
	Frank information policy
	Cooperation with Lufthansa
	   Fly & Drive
	Special offers
	   Avis Express
	   Minute Service
	   Special tariffs
		Divided advertising campaign

Autohansa Gesellschaft für Autovermietung GmbH, Frankfurt	Cooperative concept of enterprise Enterprising partners Flexibility In-client service Dense location network Lower price level	Limited international activities National coordination problems Low integrated appearance as one company
Europcar Deutschland GmbH	Concentration of activities on the European market Lower price structure	Low international activities Few sales activities

10 HERTZ AUTOVERMIETUNG GMBH (B)

As he reviewed his firm's work for Hertz Autovermietung GmbH, Niels Grothgar, president of Eggert Werbeagentur (an advertising agency in Dusseldorf, West Germany), was pleased with the results. Others were pleased as well. Hertz's market share had improved significantly in an otherwise tough market. In addition, the German advertising industry had acknowledged Eggert's creative approach with the prestigious EFFI award (selective advertising copies are shown in Exhibit 1). In some sense, Eggert's solution had added a completely new outlook to the German auto rental industry. As he re-read the description of the campaign that Eggert had submitted to the EFFI competition,[1] Grothgar began to think about how his firm should help Hertz when the competition started to react.

MARKETING SITUATION 1982[2]

Sales and Advertising

Limited rate of use: 5% of all drivers rent a car only once a year; only 1% rent several times a year.

Three different segments rent cars:

- accident/spare car (60% of market share value)
- business (30% of market share value)
- private (10% of market share value)

The market had been stagnant since 1979. Altogether there were 2,000 car rental firms, but big national firms covered 40% of the market. By 1982, Hertz had

This case was prepared by Professor Per V. Jenster. Copyright © 1990 by the International Institute for Management Development (IMD), Lausanne, Switzerland. Not to be used or reproduced without permission.

1. The following material is adapted from the submission to the EFFI competition by the R. W. Eggert Advertising Agency Ltd.

2. Based on data collected from Omnibus 1982 (licensed drivers), group discussions with persons renting a car for business and personal reasons, and interviews with Hertz's important clients and travel agencies.

a stagnating market share value of 5%, fourth place after the market leader InterRent (13.6%), Avis (9%), and Autohansa (7.3%). This meant that the market position of Hertz in Germany did not reflect its international importance—Hertz was number one worldwide, and Avis was number two. Hertz had no obvious objective or rational product advantages over other competitors. The package was the same quality as that offered by all the firms.

Consumers

The car rental business was considered by consumers to be of low interest, and renting a car was recognized as an expensive and complicated process. In addition, there was no perceived difference in the services offered by various firms. Therefore, the choice was made by chance or by habit.

Hertz was very poorly known (17%/46% response from all drivers) in comparison to the market leader, InterRent, (49%/82%).

In a comparison of image among the competitors, Hertz offered the least clear product. The only perception was "international," "American," and "big."

InterRent was seen as the "biggest car rental enterprise with a high density of stations, a big crew of trucks." Avis was positioned as "number one all over the world" and was considered "an international company."

THE NEW MARKETING STRATEGY

Decision Focus

Summary of all segment information on business travelers:

- Target group with high frequency of car rental and low price orientation.
- Compared to the market leader InterRent, Hertz had the largest recognition in this segment of all target groups. Could be perceived as the specialist for business travelers.

Strategic Goal

Hertz's goal was to reach the leading position in the "business travel" segment. By 1984, Hertz hoped to be positioned ahead of Avis and InterRent in the airport rental market.

Strategic Positioning

Hertz had to differentiate itself as the specialist for business travelers through:

- Creation of rational and perceptible advantages as "overall superiority in servicing and providing innovative offers."
- Creation of emotional (psychological) advantages that identify the company with excellent service and prestige identification.

ADVERTISING GOALS

Hertz's strategic objective of advertising was to create a new, distinct "brand." Hertz wanted to be established as a car rental enterprise that fulfills the wishes of business travelers better than any other firm.

Hertz's image goals were to place emphasis on the following areas:

- Offering special deals for business travelers and heavy users;
- Making professional transactions (faster, surer, more comfortable);
- Being international, big;
- Being used by professional business travelers *only*.

ADVERTISING STRATEGY

Target Group

- Demographic description: business travelers who had an above-average income.
- Psychological profile: prestige-oriented business travelers who liked to "show off" their status and achievements.

Copy Strategy

Advantage   Hertz was to be the appropriate partner for the successful, professional business traveler.

Reason Why   To meet the needs of the business traveler, Hertz offered professional service using the latest and best cars and equipment, a computerized reservations system, and international experience.

Creative Strategy

The remaining task was to find a creative way to transform Hertz's image to attract and motivate the business traveler. The target group had to be able to identify with Hertz.

To accomplish this, Hertz needed to have a brand that would clearly appeal to business travelers and, at the same time, communicate the superiority of the company's services. To fulfill this goal, the term "Business Class" was created. With the global expression, "Business Class," two different demands could be simultaneously satisfied:

- *The psychological need for prestige and professionalism.*   Hertz placed the business traveler in a position of high value. The business traveler who reserved a Hertz "Business Class" car could then consider himself or herself in an especially ambitious professional class.

■ *The need to justify business conduct rationally.* As part of its creative strategy within the car rental industry, Hertz developed innovative services, providing a high level of comfort for business travelers to prove its superiority. By offering better car equipment and more efficient systems for reservations and payment, Hertz differentiated itself from the competition.

MEDIA STRATEGY

Target Group

Demographic   Business travelers, specifically independent or self-employed, highly placed employees with an above-average income (DM 3,000 net monthly).

Psychological   Ambitious and status oriented.

Media Mix

To increase the amount of contact with the specific target group in magazines and national newspapers as well as radio (radio transmitter for drivers).

Allocation of media		Budget
Magazines	60%	1983–DM 3.2 million
Newspapers (national)	15	1984–DM 2.3 million
Radio	25	

Timing

Media activities were to be concentrated during the period from January to July and again from September to December, with a pause during vacation periods.

The highest budget allocation was to be spent in the first quarter as follows: Increase the number of messages at the beginning of the year with double-page spreads in magazines rather than half pages in newspapers.

RESULTS

The Hertz campaign started in January 1983. Prior to this date, no nationwide advertising had been undertaken for a long time. Meanwhile, the competitors had had ongoing nationwide image campaigns.

Development: Market Share and Turnover

In 1984, Hertz achieved its goal of being the leader in airport car rental.

Airport car rental market, 1984

Hertz	25.7%
InterRent	19.6
Avis	24.6

Overall market value

	Before the start of the campaign (1982)	January 1983— start of the campaign	January 1984
Hertz	5.0%	7.7%	9.1%
InterRent	13.6	15.6	15.4
Avis	9.0	9.3	9.4
Autohansa	7.3	8.5	8.2

In 1983, Hertz experienced a 20% increase in annual turnover, even though the market as a whole showed a slight reverse motion. The 1984 turnover increase was 30% over 1983.

Development of Image

Two evaluation surveys were initiated in January 1983 (before the start of the campaign) and in October 1984. Interviews were conducted with 300 business travelers.

Wave: Before the Start of the Campaign In the image evaluation, Hertz was consistently placing third behind InterRent and Avis.

Wave: After 22 Months of Advertising Hertz was positioned in second place after InterRent; Avis was in third place. In the following areas, which corresponded to Hertz's overall objectives, Hertz had even better results than InterRent:

- responsive to the needs of business travelers
- exclusivity and prestige
- active internationally

Qualitative Evaluation of the Campaign

The Hertz campaign was considered superior to the competition in the following areas:

- Clearly effective in communicating a service-oriented message;
- Clearly directed toward its target—the business traveler;
- Visually attractive—provides a friendly and lively atmosphere.

EXHIBIT 1 Selected Advertisements

Wenn Sie jetzt bei Hertz einsteigen, fahren Sie Business-Class.

| Business-Tarif für unbegrenzte Kilometer* | Verkehrsfunk-Decoder | Stereo-Cassettenradio | Näh-Set Erfrischungstücher | Deutschlandkarte | Regenschirm |

Wer geschäftlich viel unterwegs ist, hat Streß genug. Deshalb sollte Ihnen ein Autovermieter nicht bloß ein zuverlässiges Auto bieten, sondern auch möglichst vieles zu Ihrer Entlastung beisteuern.

Was das für uns konkret heißt, sehen Sie, wenn Sie einen Blick in die neue Hertz Business-Class werfen. Zunächst einmal finden Sie in allen Fahrzeugen viele Dinge, die Ihre Geschäftsreise angenehmer machen.

Angefangen vom Verkehrsfunk-Decoder, der vor Engpässen warnt, bis hin zum Näh-Set, das Ihnen knopflose Besprechungen erspart. In einigen Fahrzeugen sorgt ein Stereo-Cassettenradio für angenehme Unterhaltung. Außerdem bietet Ihnen die Business-Class spezielle, für Sie besonders günstige Business-Tarife. Zum Beispiel einen festen Tagespreis für unbegrenzte Kilometer* (einschließlich kompletter Versicherung und Mehrwertsteuer).

Ein modernes Computer-System garantiert schnelle, unbürokratische Abwicklung. Von der Reservierung bis zur Abrechnung. Damit Sie sicher weiterkommen. Weltweit.

Buchen Sie bei Ihrem Reisebüro oder über unser zentrales Hertz-Reservierungsbüro unter folgenden Telefonnummern:
Berlin 0 30-2 61 80 77 Düsseldorf 02 11-35 70 21 Essen 02 01-77 04 04 Frankfurt 06 11-73 04 04 Hamburg 0 40-2 80 12 01 Hannover 05 11-51 45 09 München 0 89-55 82 11 Nürnberg 09 11-23 23 67 Stuttgart 07 11-22 51 61 Wien 02 22-73 15 96 Zürich 01-2 41 80 77 Telex Frankfurt 4 14 991

Fahren Sie Business-Class.
Hertz vermietet Ford und andere gute Wagen.

See translation on page 227.

(continued)

EXHIBIT 1   (continued)

Immer mehr Geschäftsleute entdecken ihr Herz für Hertz. Woran das wohl liegen mag?

| Verkehrsfunk-Decoder | Stereo-Cassettenradio | Näh-Set Erfrischungstücher | Deutschlandkarte | Regenschirm | Business Club-Karte |

Mag sein, daß die überaus schnelle Reservierung durch unseren Zentralcomputer zu Komplimenten anregt. Schließlich erhalten Sie in kürzester Zeit die Bestätigung für die gewünschte Wagenklasse.

Es könnte natürlich auch die reizvolle Ausstattung unserer Wagen sein, die manchen Manager zum Hertz-Verehrer macht. Denn wo sonst bekommt man automatisch jedes Fahrzeug mit Stereo-Cassettenradio, Deutschlandkarte, Schirm, Näh-Set und und und…

Und dann gibt es da noch diejenigen, die den Erfolg der Business-Class nicht zuletzt dem Charme unserer Damen am Counter zuschreiben. Es soll sogar schon Herren gegeben haben, die sich trotz schnellster Abwicklung noch einige Augenblicke länger bei uns aufgehalten haben. Was wir natürlich für ein Gerücht halten.

Am besten, Sie gehen der Sache selbst mal auf den Grund. Auf einer Fahrt mit Herz. Pardon, mit Hertz.

Buchen Sie über Ihr Reisebüro oder über unser zentrales Reservierungsbüro unter folgender Telefonnummer: 01 30/21 21 bundesweit zum Ortstarif, aus Frankfurt: 73 04 04. Weitere Reservierungen möglich unter Zürich 01-2 41 80 77 und Wien 02 22-73 15 96. Telex Frankfurt 414 991.

Fahren Sie Business-Class.
Hertz vermietet Ford und andere gute Wagen.

See translation on page 227.

EXHIBIT 1 (page 225)

WHEN YOU GET INTO A HERTZ CAR, YOU DRIVE BUSINESS-CLASS

RADIO SENDER—DECODER
STEREO-CASSETTE RADIO
SEWING KIT
REFRESHING COTTON TISSUES
MAP OF GERMANY
UMBRELLA

Business travelers who are always on the move are stressed enough. Therefore, a car rental company should offer a reliable and comfortable car.

When you look at the new Hertz-Business car, you will find in all the vehicles many features that will make your business trip more comfortable.

To start with, you will find a traffic decoder that will warn you of busy roads and a sewing kit that will save you the embarrassment of a missing button. In several cars you will find a stereo radio and cassette recorder for pleasant entertainment.

In addition, the Business-Class offers you special daily business rates, with unlimited mileage, including full insurance coverage and value-added tax (VAT).

An up-to-date computer system eliminates red tape and guarantees quick, efficient service—from reservation to billing.

With these Business-Class features, you will go farther—worldwide.

Travel Hertz Business-Class

Hertz offers Ford and other quality cars

EXHIBIT 1 (page 226)

MORE AND MORE BUSINESSMEN AND BUSINESSWOMEN DISCOVER A HEART FOR HERTZ. WHAT IS IT ALL DUE TO?

It might be that the extremely quick reservation service through our central computer deserves compliments. In just a short time, you will get the confirmation on your desired car.

Hertz's popularity, of course, could also be due to what Hertz cars offer. For where else does one automatically obtain a car with a stereo radio and cassette recorder, a map of Germany, an umbrella, a sewing kit, and so forth?

Some Hertz customers are more fascinated by the charm of the hostesses behind the counters. In fact, in spite of Hertz's rapid service, some business travelers have tried to prolong the moment.

The best way for you to judge Hertz is to try us yourself. Drive with Heart. Discover Hertz.

Book with your travel agent.

11 GRASSE FRAGRANCES SA

Grasse Fragrances, headquartered in Lyon, France, was the world's fourth largest producer of fragrances. Established in 1885, the company had grown from a small family owned business, selling fragrances to local perfume manufacturers, to a multinational enterprise with subsidiaries and agents in over 100 countries.

Jean-Pierre Volet, Grasse Fragrances' marketing director, had devoted the last few years to building a strong headquarters marketing organization. In February 1989, he was returning to France after an extensive trip, touring Grasse sales offices and factories and visiting key customers. As the Air France flight touched down in Lyon Airport, Volet was worried about what he had learned on the trip. "Our sales force," he thought, "still operates much as it did several years ago. If we're going to compete successfully in this new environment, we have to completely rethink our sales force management practices."

THE FLAVOR AND FRAGRANCE INDUSTRY

Worldwide sales of essential oils, aroma chemicals, and fragrance and flavor compounds were estimated to be around $5.5 billion in 1988. Five major firms accounted for almost 50% of the industry's sales. The largest, International Flavors & Fragrances, Inc. of New York, had 1988 sales of $839.5 million (up 76% from 1984), of which fragrances accounted for 62%. The company had plants in 21 countries, and non-U.S. operations represented 70% of sales and 78% of operating profit.

Quest International, a wholly owned subsidiary of Unilever, was next in size, with sales estimated at $700 million, closely followed by the Givaudan Group, a wholly owned subsidiary of Hoffman-LaRoche, with sales of $536 million, and Grasse Fragrances, with sales of $480 million. Firmenich, a closely held Swiss family firm, did not disclose results, but 1987 sales were estimated at some $300 million.

This case was written by Professor H. Michael Hayes. All names, including the company name, have been disguised. Copyright © 1989 by the International Institute for Management Development (IMD), Lausanne, Switzerland. Not to be used or reproduced without permission.

Grasse produced only fragrances. Most major firms in the industry, however, produced both fragrances and flavors (i.e., flavor extracts and compounds used mainly in foods, beverages, and pharmaceutical products). Generally, the products were similar. The major difference was that flavorists had to match their creations with their natural counterparts, such as fruits, meats, or spices, as closely as possible. On the other hand, perfumers had the flexibility of using their imaginations to create new fragrances. Perfumery was closely associated with fashion and encompassed a wide variety of choice; scented products had to be dermatologically safe. Development of flavors was more limited, and flavored products were required to meet strict toxicological criteria because the products were ingested.

Markets for Fragrances

Although the use of perfumes is as old as history, not until the 19th century, when major advances were made in organic chemistry, did the fragrance industry as it is known today emerge. Use of fragrances, once restricted to perfumes, expanded into other applications. In recent years manufacturers of soaps, detergents, and other household products have significantly increased their purchases of fragrances and have represented the largest single consumption category. Depending on the application, the chemical complexity of a particular fragrance, and the quantity produced, prices could range from less than FF 40 per kilogram to over FF 4,000.[1]

Despite its apparent maturity, the world market for fragrances was estimated to have grown at an average of 5 to 6% during the early 1980s, and some estimates indicated that sales growth could increase even more during the last half of the decade. New applications supported these estimates. Microwave foods, for instance, needed additional flavorings to replicate familiar tastes that would take time to develop in a conventional oven. In laundry detergents, a significant fragrance market, the popularity of liquids provided a new stimulus to fragrance sales, as liquid detergents needed more fragrance to achieve the desired aroma than powders. Similarly, laundry detergents designed to remove odors as well as dirt also stimulated sales because they used more fragrance by volume.

The New Buying Behavior

Over time, buying behavior for fragrances, as well as markets, had changed significantly. Responsibility for the selection and purchase of fragrances became complex, particularly in large firms. R&D groups were expected to ensure the compatibility of the fragrance with the product under consideration. Marketing groups were responsible for choosing a fragrance that gave the product a competitive edge in the marketplace, and purchasing groups had to obtain competitive prices and provide good deliveries.

Use of briefs (the industry term for a fragrance specification and request for quotation) became common. Typically, a brief would identify the general charac-

1. In 1988, $1.00 = approximately FF 6.00.

teristics of the fragrance and the required cost parameters. The brief would also provide an extensive description of the company's product and its intended strategy in the marketplace. Occasionally, a fragrance producer would be sole sourced, generally for proprietary reasons. Usually, however, the customer would ask for at least two quotations, so competitive quotes were the norm.

GRASSE FRAGRANCES SA

Background

The company was founded in 1885 by Louis Piccard, a chemist who had studied at the University of Lyon. He believed that progress in the field of organic chemistry could be used to develop a new industry—creating perfumes—as opposed to relying on nature. Using a small factory on the Siagne River near Grasse, the company soon became a successful supplier of fragrances to the leading perfume houses of Paris. Despite the interruptions of World Wars I and II, the company followed an early policy of international growth and diversification. Production and sales units were first established in Lyon, Paris, and Rome. In the 1920s, the company headquarters was moved to Lyon. At that time, the company entered the American market, first establishing a sales office and then a small manufacturing facility in the United States. Acquisitions were made in the United Kingdom, and subsequently the company established subsidiaries in Switzerland, Brazil, Argentina, and Spain.

Faced with increased competition and large capital requirements for R&D, plant expansion, and new product launches, the Piccard family decided to become a public company in 1968. Jacques Piccard, eldest son of the founder, was elected president, and the family remained active in the management of the company. Assisted by the infusion of capital, Grasse was able to expand its business activities in Europe, the United States, Latin America, and the Far East.

In 1988, total sales were $450,000,000, up some 60% from 1984; 40% of sales came from Europe, 30% from North America, 15% from Asia/Pacific, 10% from Latin America, and 5% from Africa/Middle East. In recent years, the company's position had strengthened somewhat in North America.

By the end of 1988, the company had sales organizations or agents in 100 countries, laboratories in 18 countries, compounding facilities in 14 countries, chemical production centers in 3 countries, and research centers in 3 countries. Employees numbered 2,500, of whom some 1,250 were employed outside France.

Products

In 1988, the company's main product lines were in two categories:

- Perfumery products used for perfumes, eau de cologne, eau de toilette, hair lotion, cosmetics, soaps, detergents, and other household and industrial products.

- Synthetics for perfume compounds, cosmetic specialities, sunscreening agents, and preservatives for various industrial applications.

According to Piccard:

> From the production side, flavors and fragrances are similar, although the creative and marketing approaches are quite different. So far we have elected to specialize in just fragrances, but I think it's just a matter of time before we decide to get into flavors.

Following industry practice, Grasse divided its fragrances into four categories:

- Fine Fragrances
- Toiletries and Cosmetics
- Soaps and Detergents
- Household and Industrial

MARKETING AT GRASSE

In 1980, Jean-Pierre Volet was appointed marketing director after a successful stint as country manager for the Benelux countries. At the time, the headquarters marketing organization was relatively small. Its primary role was to make sure the sales force had information on the company's products, to send out samples of new perfumes that were developed in the labs, usually with little customer input, and to handle special price or delivery requests. As Volet recalled:

> In the 1940s, 1950s, and 1960s, most of our business was in fine fragrances, toiletries and cosmetics. Our customers tended to be small and were focused in local markets. Our fragrance salesman would carry a suitcase of 5-gram samples, call on the customer, get an idea of what kind of fragrance the customer wanted, and either leave a few samples for evaluation or actually write an order on the spot. It was a very personal kind of business. Buying decisions tended to be based on subjective impressions and the nature of the customer's relation with the salesman. Our headquarters marketing organization was designed to support that kind of selling and buying. Today, however, we deal with large multinational companies who are standardizing their products across countries, and even regions, and who are using very sophisticated marketing techniques to guide their use of fragrances. Detergents and other household products represent an increasing share of the market. When I came to headquarters, one of my important priorities was to structure a marketing organization which reflected this new environment.

The marketing organization in 1988 is shown in Exhibit 1.

In addition to directing the normal administrative activities such as field sales support, pricing, and budgeting, Volet had built a fragrance creation group and a product management group. More recently, he had established an international account management group.

The fragrance creation group served as a bridge between the basic lab work and customer requirements. It also ran the company's fragrance training center, used to train both its own sales force and customer personnel in the application of fragrances. The product management group was organized in the four product categories. Product managers were expected to be knowledgeable about everything that was going on in their product category worldwide and to use their specialized knowledge to support field sales efforts as well as to guide the creative people. It was Volet's plan that international account managers would coordinate sales efforts.

Field sales representatives in France reported to Piccard through Raoul Salmon. Salmon was also responsible for the activities of the company's agents, who were used in countries where the company did not have subsidiaries or branches. In recent years, the use of agents had declined, and the company expected the decline to continue.

Outside France, field sales were the responsibility of Grasse country managers. In smaller countries, country managers handled only sales, thus operating essentially as field sales managers. In other countries, where the company had manufacturing or other nonselling operations, the norm was to have a field sales manager report to the country manager.

The company relied extensively on its field sales force for promotional efforts, customer relations, and order-getting activities. There were, however, two very different kinds of selling situations. As Salmon described them:

> There are still many customers, generally small-scale, who buy in the traditional way where the process is fairly simple. One salesperson is responsible for calling on all buying influencers in the customer's organization. Decisions tend to be based on subjective factors, and the sales representative's personal relations with the customer are critically important.
>
> The other situation, which is growing, involves large and increasingly international customers. Not only do we see that people in R&D and marketing as well as in purchasing can influence the purchase decision, but these influencers may also be located in a number of different countries.

In either case, once the decision had been made to purchase a Grasse fragrance, the firm could generally count on repeat business, as long as the customer's product was successful in the marketplace.

On occasion, however, purchase decisions were revised, particularly if Grasse raised prices or if the customer's product came under strong competitive price pressure, thus requiring the customer to consider a less expensive fragrance.

The Quotation Procedure

For small orders, the quotation procedure was relatively simple. Popular fragrances had established prices in every country, and the sales force was expected to sell at these prices.[2] In some instances, price concessions were made, but they required management approval and were discouraged.

---

2. Subject to approval by marketing headquarters, each Grasse producing unit established a transfer price for products sold outside the country. Country prices were established, taking into account the country profit objectives and the local market conditions. Transfer prices were usually established for a year. Adjusting transfer prices for fluctuations in exchange rates was a matter of ongoing concern.

For large orders, the norm was to develop a new fragrance. Increasingly, customers would provide Grasse with extensive information on their intended product and its marketing strategy, including the country or countries where the product would be sold. To make sure the fragrance fit the customer's intended marketing and product strategy, Grasse was expected to do market research in a designated pilot country on several fragrances, sometimes combined with samples of the customer's product. According to Volet:

> Once we have found or developed what we think is the best fragrance, we submit our quotation. Then the customer will do his own market research, testing his product with our fragrance and with those of our competitors. Depending on the outcome of the market research, we may get the order at a price premium. Alternatively, we may lose it, even if we are the low bidder. If, on the other hand, the results of the market research indicate that no fragrance supplier has an edge, then price, personal relationships, or other factors will influence the award.

Because of the extensive requirements for development and testing, headquarters in Grasse was always involved in putting a quotation together, and close coordination between headquarters and the branch or subsidiary was vital. When buying influencers were located in more than one country, additional coordination of the sales effort was required to ensure that information obtained from the customer was shared and to have a coherent account strategy.

Coordination of pricing was also growing in importance. Many large customers manufactured their products in more than one country and looked for a "world" price rather than a country price. In these situations, country organizations were expected to take a corporate view of profits, sometimes at the expense of their own profit statements. The lead country—that is, the country in which the purchasing decision would be made—had final responsibility for establishing the price. Increasingly, however, this price had to be approved at headquarters in Lyon.

Submitting quotations in this environment was both complex and expensive. According to Volet:

> Receiving a brief from a customer starts a complex process. We immediately alert all our salespeople who call on various purchasing influencers. Even though the brief contains lots of information on what the customer wants, we expect our salespeople to provide us with some additional information.
>
> The next step is for our creative people to develop one or more fragrances which we believe will meet the customer's requirements. They are aided in this effort by our product managers, who know what is going on with their products worldwide. If additional information is needed from the customer, our international account people will contact the appropriate salespeople.
>
> After creating what we think is the right product or products, we may conduct our own market research in a country designated by the customer. This is usually done under the direction of our product manager, working closely with our market research people. Throughout this process, our sales force is expected to stay in close touch with the customer to give us any changes in his thinking or any competitive feedback. Based on the results of this effort, we then submit our proposal, which gives the customer the price, samples, and as much product information as possible.

With some customers, there is little further sales effort after they receive our quotation, and the buying decision is made "behind closed doors." In other instances, we may be asked to explain the results of our research or to discuss possible modifications in our product and, sometimes, in our price. Frequently we find that the customer is more concerned with our price policy (i.e., how firm the price is and for how long) than with the price quoted at the time of the brief.

When you make this kind of effort, you obviously hate to lose the order. On the other hand, even if we lose, the investment made in development work and market research is likely to pay off in winning another brief, either with the original customer or with another customer.

International Accounts

In 1988, about 50% of the firm's business came from some 40 international accounts. Looking to the future, it was expected that the number of international accounts would grow, and some estimated that by 1994 as much as 80% of the firm's business would come from international accounts.

As of 1988, 18 to 20 international accounts were targeted for coordination by international account managers (IAMs) in Lyon. The principal responsibility of each IAM was to research assigned customers on a worldwide basis and put that knowledge to use in coordinating work on a brief. The remaining international accounts were followed in Lyon, but coordination was a subsidiary responsibility. In either case, it was the view at headquarters that coordination was critical. As Volet described it:

> We rely extensively on account teams. European teams may meet as often as once a quarter. Worldwide teams are more likely to meet annually. For designated accounts, the IAM takes the lead role in organizing the meeting and, generally, coordinating sales efforts. For others, the parent account executive (the sales representative in the country selling the customer component with the greatest buying influence) plays the lead role. In these situations, we hold the parent account executive responsible for all the IAM's daily coordinating work with the customer. We also expect him to be proactive and already working on the next brief long before we get a formal request.
>
> Here in Lyon, we prepare extensive worldwide "bibles" on international accounts, which are made available to all members of the team. We also prepare quarterly project reports for team members. Our next step will be to computerize as much of this as possible.

Sales Management Practices

In 1988, sales force management practices were not standardized. Selection, compensation, training, organization, and so forth were the responsibility of subsidiary management. Even so, a number of practices were similar.

Sales representatives tended to be compensated by a salary and bonus system. A typical minimum bonus was 1.5 month's salary, but it could range up to 2.5 month's salary for excellent performance. The exact amount of the bonus was discretionary with sales management, and the bonus could reward a number of factors.

Sales budgets were established from estimates made by sales representatives for direct orders—that is, orders that would be placed by their assigned accounts. These estimates were developed from (1) expectations of sales volume for fragrances currently being used by customers, in which case historical sales were the major basis for the estimate, and (2) estimates of sales of new fragrances. Although historical sales of currently used fragrances were useful in predicting future sales, variations could occur. Sales activity of the customer's product was not totally predictable. In some instances, customers reopened a brief to competition, particularly when the customer was experiencing competitive cost pressures.

Predicting sales of new fragrances was even more difficult. Customers' plans were uncertain, and the nature of the buying process made it difficult to predict the odds of success on any given transaction. Grasse Fragrances, nevertheless, relied heavily on these estimates. The sum of the estimates was expected to add up to the company budget for the coming year. When this was not the case, sales managers were expected to review their estimates and increase them appropriately.

The company had recently introduced, companywide, its own version of management by objectives. Each sales representative was expected to develop a personal set of objectives for negotiation with his or her sales manager. Formal account planning, however, had not been established, although some subsidiaries were starting the practice.

Sales training had two components. Product knowledge tended to be the responsibility of headquarters, which relied heavily on the fragrance training center. Selling skills, however, were principally the responsibility of the subsidiary companies.

Selection practices were the most variable. Some subsidiaries believed that company and product knowledge were key to selling success and so tended to look inside the company for individuals who had the requisite company and product knowledge and who expressed an interest in sales work. Others believed that demonstrated selling skills were key and so looked outside the company for individuals with good selling track records, preferably in related industries.

SALES MANAGEMENT ISSUES

A number of sales management practices were of concern, both in headquarters and in the subsidiaries.

Influence Selling

Ensuring appropriate effort on all buying influencers was a major concern. According to Salmon:

> Our sales representatives understand the importance of influence selling, but we have no formal way of recognizing their efforts. A number of our large accounts, for instance, have their marketing groups located in Paris, and they have lots of influence on the buying decision. If we win the brief, however, purchasing is likely to take

place in Germany or Spain or Holland, and my sales representative will not get any sales credit.

In a similar vein, Juan Rodriquez, sales manager for a group of countries in Latin America, commented:

We have a large account that does lots of manufacturing and purchasing in Latin America but does its R&D work in the United States. The customer's people in Latin America tell us that without strong support from R&D in the United States, it is very difficult for them to buy our fragrances. The sales representative in New York is certainly aware of this, but his boss is measured on profit, which can only come from direct sales in the United States, so he's not enthusiastic about his sales representative spending a lot of time on influence business.

In some instances, the nature of the buying process resulted in windfalls for some sales representatives. Commenting on this aspect, Salmon observed:

It can work the other way as well. Our Spanish subsidiary recently received an order for 40 tons of a fragrance, but the customer's decision to buy was totally influenced by sales representatives in Germany and Lyon. Needless to say, our Spanish subsidiary was delighted, but the people in Germany and Lyon were concerned as to how their efforts would be recognized and rewarded.

Although there was general recognition that influence selling was vital, it was not clear how it could be adequately measured and rewarded. As Salmon pointed out:

In some instances (e.g., the order in Spain) we're pretty sure about the amount of influence exerted by those calling on marketing and R&D. In other instances, it is not at all clear. We have some situations where the sales representative honestly believes that his calls on, say, R&D are important but, in fact, they are not. At least not in our opinion. If we come up with the wrong scheme to measure influence, we could end up with a lot of wasted time and effort.

Incentive Compensation

Compensation practices were a matter of some concern. The salary component was established at a level designed to be competitive with similar sales jobs in each country. Annual raises had become the norm, with amounts based on performance, longevity, and changes in responsibility. The bonus component was determined by the immediate manager, but there was concern that bonuses had become automatic. Still further, some held the view that the difference between 1.5 and 2.5 times the monthly salary was not very motivating, even if bonus awards were more performance driven.

Sales representatives expected some level of bonus, whether merited or not, and there was concern that any change could cause morale problems. At the same time, there was growing recognition of the increasing importance of team selling.

Overall responsibility for compensation practices was assigned to Claude Larreché, director of human resources. According to Larreché:

Some of our sales managers are interested in significantly increasing the incentive component of sales force compensation. It has been my view, however, that large incentive payments to the sales force could cause problems in other parts of our organization. Plus, there seems to be considerable variation in country practice with regard to incentive compensation. In the United States, for instance, compensation schemes which combine a fixed or salary component and an incentive component, usually determined by sales relative to a quota, are common. To a lesser degree, we see some of this in Europe, and somewhat more in southern Europe, but I'm not sure that we want to do something just because a lot of other companies are doing it.

We're also thinking about some kind of team incentive or bonus. But, this raises questions about who should be considered part of the team and how a team bonus should be allocated. Should the team be just the sales representatives, or should we include the IAMs? And what about the customer service people without whom we wouldn't have a base of good performance to build on?

Allocation is even more complicated. We're talking about teams comprised of people all around the world. I think it is only natural that the local manager will think his sales representative made the biggest contribution, which could result in long arguments. One possibility would be for the team itself to allocate a bonus pool, but I'm not sure how comfortable managers would be with such an approach.

Small Accounts

Despite the sales growth expected from international accounts, sales to smaller national accounts were expected to remain a significant part of the firm's revenues and, generally, had very attractive margins. According to one country sales manager:

> With the emphasis on international accounts, I'm concerned about how we handle our smaller, single country accounts. Many of them still buy the way they did 10 and 20 years ago, although today we can select from over 30,000 fragrances. Our international accounts will probably generate 80% of our business in the years to come, but the 20% we get from our smaller accounts is important and produces excellent profits for the company. But I'm not sure that the kind of selling skills we need to handle international accounts is appropriate for the smaller accounts. Personal and long-term relationships are tremendously important to these accounts.

Language

In the early 1980s, it had become apparent to Grasse management that French would not serve as the firm's common language. In most of its subsidiary countries, English was either the country language or the most likely second language. With considerable reluctance on the part of some French managers, it was decided that English would become the firm's official language. Personnel in the United States and the United Kingdom, few of whom spoke a second language, welcomed the change. There were, however, a number of problems. As the Italian sales manager said:

> We understand the need for a common language when we bring in sales representatives from all over Europe or the world. And we understand that English is the

"most common" language in the countries where we do business. All of my people understand that they will have to speak English in international account sales meetings. What they don't like, however, is that the Brits and Americans tend to assume that they are smarter than the rest of us, simply because we can't express ourselves as fluently in English as they can. It's totally different when my people talk to someone from Latin America or some other country, where English is their second language, too.

A related problem is the attitude that people from one country have towards those of another. This goes beyond language. Frequently, our people from northern Europe or North America will stereotype those of us from southern Europe or Latin America as disorganized or not businesslike. My people, on the other hand, see the northerners as inflexible and unimaginative. To some extent, these views diminish after we get to know each other as individuals, but it takes time and there is always some underlying tension.

Language also influenced decisions on rotation of personnel. It was Volet's view that there should be movement of sales managers and marketing personnel between countries. Still further, he felt that sales representatives who aspired to promotion should also be willing to consider transfers to another country or to headquarters in Lyon. As he pointed out, however:

Customer personnel in most of our international accounts speak English. Hence, there is a temptation to feel that English language competency is the only requirement when considering reassignment of sales personnel. In fact, if we were to transfer a sales representative who spoke only English to Germany, for instance, he would be received politely the first time, but from then on it would be difficult for him to get an appointment with the customer. It has been our experience that our customers want to do business in their own language, even if they speak English fluently.

An exception might be an international account whose parent is British and which transfers a lot of British personnel to another country. Even here, however, there will be lots of people in the organization for whom English is not a native tongue.

Therefore, we require that our salespeople speak the language of the country and are comfortable with the country culture. Local people meet this requirement. The real issue is getting all, or most, of our people to be comfortable in more than one language and culture.

Sales Training

One of the most perplexing issues was what, if any, changes to make with regard to sales training. At headquarters, there was considerable sentiment for standardization. As Volet put it:

I really don't see much difference in selling from one country to another. Of course, personal relations may be more important in, say, Latin America or the Middle East than in Germany, but I think that as much as 80 to 85% of the selling job can be harmonized. In addition, it's my view that our international accounts expect us to have a standardized sales approach. Sales training, therefore, should be something we can do centrally in Lyon.

This view was supported by those in human resources. According to Claude Larreché, director of human resources:

> We no longer see ourselves as a collection of individual companies that remit profits to Lyon and make technology transfers occasionally. Our view of the future is that we are a global company that must live in a world of global customers and markets. I think this means we must have a Grasse Fragrances culture that transcends national boundaries, including a common sales approach, i.e., this is the way Grasse approaches customers, regardless of where they are located. A key element in establishing such a culture is sales training here in Lyon.

Others disagreed with this point of view, however. Perhaps the most vociferous was the U.S. sales manager:

> I understand what Jean-Pierre and Claude are saying, and I support the notion of a common company culture. The fact is, however, that selling is different in the United States than in other parts of the world. Not long ago, we transferred a promising sales representative from Sweden to our office in Chicago. His sales approach, which was right for Sweden, was very relaxed, and he had to make some major adjustments to fit the more formal and fast-paced approach in Chicago. I don't see how a sales training program in Lyon can be of much help. Plus, the cost of sending people to Lyon comes out of my budget, and this would really hit my country manager's profits.
>
> In fact, I think we ought to have more flexibility with regard to all our sales management practices.

As Jean-Pierre Volet waited for his bag at the Lyon Airport, he wondered how far he should go in making changes with regard to the sales force. Whatever he did would be controversial, but he was convinced some changes were necessary.

EXHIBIT 1 Partial Organization Chart

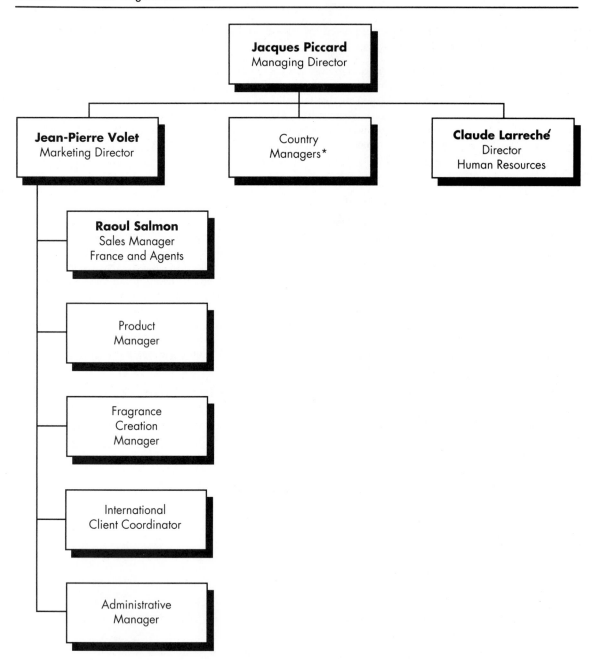

Jacques Piccard
Managing Director

Jean-Pierre Volet
Marketing Director

Country
Managers*

Claude Larreché
Director
Human Resources

Raoul Salmon
Sales Manager
France and Agents

Product
Manager

Fragrance
Creation
Manager

International
Client Coordinator

Administrative
Manager

* In France, all major functions (e.g., marketing, manufacturing, R&D) reported to Jacques Piccard. In most countries outside of France where the company did business, a subsidiary company was established, headed by a country manager. All company activities in each country reported to the country manager. In some countries, generally small countries, the company did business through agents who reported to Raoul Salmon.

Distribution

Distribution is often thought of as a local market concern for the reason that in the past, channel structure and behavior have tended to be different in different country markets. Similar trends in many developed countries, however, are slowly changing this picture. One such trend in many product categories is concentration among members of the wholesale and retail trade. That means more traded volumes are being channeled through fewer entities, with a resulting shift in channel power in favor of the members of the trade. Another trend is the emergence of multinational or even global channels of distribution, with purchasing policies coordinated across different local markets. Such trends are making distribution an area of increasing concern for regional and global marketers.

ISSUES

The two cases in this section deal with the issues of international distribution from the perspectives of industrial and consumer goods companies. Leykam Mürztaler AG, a maker of high-quality paper, is observing developments among its European paper merchants (distributors of paper), which comprise its main channel of distribution. Management is wondering if a more effective branding policy might help with the growing role and influence of the trade in the market. In the second case, Jordan A/S, a relatively small company with an extensive global market reach, is concerned with the consolidation of trade in its major markets. Management is wondering if its current niche strategy and innovative distribution policy need to be modified for the company to survive.

LEARNING POINTS

The student can expect the following learning points from the analysis of cases in this section:

- Recognition of the role and function of channels of distribution in a firm's regional or global marketing strategy;
- Insights into distribution channel power and factors contributing to it or changing it over time;
- Appreciation for the role of private branding and how this practice may contribute or detract from manufacturer's own brand;
- Understanding of the elements of effective worldwide distribution for a low-interest yet global product;
- Exposure to the problems and opportunities of a small company distributing its products globally.

241

12 LEYKAM MÜRZTALER AG

In February 1989, Dr. Gertrude Eder, marketing manager for Leykam Mürztaler AG, was reviewing a problem that had occupied her a great deal during the past few months. Although Leykam Mürztaler, like the paper industry in general, had been doing well in recent years, it was Eder's opinion that the company should think about ways to strengthen its ability to prosper, as industry growth had inevitably begun slowing down. In particular, she was considering what recommendations to offer the executive board regarding the firm's branding strategy.

COMPANY BACKGROUND

The past few years had been good ones for the Leykam Mürztaler Group. Paralleling the industry's increased sales, the firm's total sales had risen from ASch 4,842 million[1] in 1983 to ASch 7,100 million in 1988, an increase of 47%. For Leykam Mürztaler AG, the principal operating component of the group, 1988 revenues had reached ASch 6,300 million, an increase over 1986 sales of 41%, enhanced by the successful start-up of a new production line and by above-average growth in demand for high-grade, coated woodfree printing papers, the firm's main sales segment.

Leykam Mürztaler AG, together with its predecessor companies, had been a producer of paper for over 400 years. Headquartered in Gratkorn, Austria, the firm produced coated woodfree printing paper and newsprint, with integrated pulp production. Principal mills and offices were located at Gratkorn and Bruck, Austria. Export sales offices for coated woodfree paper were headquartered in Vienna.

In 1988, woodfree papers represented approximately 80% of sales, newsprint, 13%, and pulp, 7%. Twenty-two percent of revenues came from Austria, 56% from Western Europe, and 22% from exports to the rest of the world (including Eastern

This case was written by Professor H. Michael Hayes. Copyright © 1989 by the International Institute for Management Development (IMD), Lausanne, Switzerland. Not to be used or reproduced without permission.
    1. In December 1988, ASch 12.48 = $1.00.

Europe). The highest share of exports was for coated woodfree papers at approximately 90%.

(Production volumes in 1987 and 1988 are shown in Exhibit 1.) The large increase in production of printing and writing paper in 1988 (to 340,900 tons) reflected successful selling of the output of the new coated woodfree paper machine at Gratkorn, with a capacity of 138,000 tons per year. The decline in pulp production reflected a change in product mix. External sales of pulp were declining as the company's pulp production was further integrated into the company's own paper production.

With the addition of the new production line, the company had become the European market leader in coated woodfree papers, with a market share of 8 to 10%. In December 1987, the supervisory board approved a project to establish a new production line at Bruck to produce mechanical coated printing papers (LWC) for magazines, catalogues, and printed advertising materials. Planned capacity was 135,000 tons, to be put into operation at the end of 1989.

Despite the increased level of investment, financial results were very good. In 1987, the last year for which complete financial details were available, profit was down slightly from the previous year (see Exhibit 2), reflecting the greatly increased depreciation charges associated with the new paper machine and the decision to use the reducing-balance method of depreciation for it and for some other equipment. Cash flow, however, was close to an all-time record, results were "clearly better than originally forecast," and operating profits were near the top of the European woodfree paper producers, on a percentage-of-sales basis. Preliminary indications were that financial results for 1988 would be better still.

The company marketed its coated products under its MAGNO series brand (e.g., MAGNOMATT, MAGNOPRINT, MAGNOMATT K), principally through wholly owned merchants in Austria and other merchants throughout Western Europe. In addition, it sold to other kinds of merchants in Austria as well as to some printers and publishers directly. Paper merchants were contacted by sales representatives in Vienna and Gratkorn, by sales subsidiaries in Germany, Italy, and France, and by sales agents in other European countries. Some of its products were sold on a private brand basis to certain large merchants.

Although Leykam Mürztaler served paper markets on a worldwide basis and planned to enter the LWC market, this case focuses on coated woodfree papers for printing applications in Western Europe.

THE PULP AND PAPER INDUSTRY

Despite its maturity, the pulp and paper industry in Western Europe[2] was undergoing major change. For example, the industry was characterized by high break-even volumes; small fluctuations in demand could significantly impact profits, and there was some evidence that capacity was outgrowing demand. Despite the

2. Western Europe included the countries in the European Community, plus Finland, Norway, Sweden, Austria, and Switzerland.

sophistication of the paper-making technology, product differentiation was increasingly difficult to achieve. Some papermakers were integrating backward to control the cost or assure the supply of pulp. Others were integrating forward, buying paper merchants to gain better control of marketing. Still others were integrating horizontally to achieve a more complete product line.

Other changes were affecting the industry as well. Customers were being merged, acquired, or reorganized, thus changing established purchasing patterns. Changes in advertising were impacting traditional usage patterns. Paper merchants were merging to gain economies of scale. Some were emphasizing private brands to reduce their dependence on papermakers. Markets were fragmenting, as new, small businesses were forming at a record rate. Consumption patterns were also changing. In Europe, consumption ranged from 233kg per capita in Sweden to 60kg per capita in Portugal, but growth rates ranged from a high of 29.4% in Greece to a low of 2.4% in Denmark. There was some uncertainty about the implications of Europe's move toward a true common market in 1992, although trade barriers were not a significant factor in the industry.

Printing and Writing Paper

In the pulp and paper industry, the major, high-growth segment was printing and writing papers. Both coated and uncoated papers were produced from mechanically or chemically processed pulp to form four broad categories: coated woodfree, mechanical coated,[3] uncoated woodfree, and mechanical uncoated. To be defined as coated, a paper had to have a surface coating of at least 5 grams per square meter (gsm).

Coated woodfree papers represented the highest quality category, in terms of printability, gloss, feel, ability to reproduce color, and many other characteristics. Grades of coated woodfree papers were not precisely specified, but the industry had established further categories such as cast-coated, art paper, standard, and low-coated. (See Exhibit 3 for categories and prices.) The standard grade represented the bulk of sales. Within this category, however, there were many gradations—the amount of whiteness, brightness, stiffness, and other characteristics. Leykam Mürztaler competed principally at the high end of the standard grade but was planning to enter the art paper segment also.

Coated woodfree was the smallest printing and writing paper segment (17.8% of total consumption), but it was also the most dynamic, with an average growth rate of 8.4% from 1980 to 1987. Expectations were that 1988 consumption would exceed 3 million tons.

Markets for Printing and Writing Paper

Principal markets for printing and writing paper were magazines (33%), direct mail (17%), brochures and general print advertising (15%), copy paper (11%), other

---

3. Mechanical coated was designated LWC or MWC, depending on the weight, although the dividing line was not precise.

office paper (9%), and books (5%). For coated woodfree papers, it was estimated that advertising, direct and indirect, accounted for 85 to 90% of consumption.[4]

On a country-by-country basis, however, the variation in the mix of advertising expenditures was significant. In the United Kingdom, for instance, the bulk of advertising expenditures went to newspapers and TV, whereas in Germany, advertising expenditures were split somewhat evenly among newspapers, magazines, catalogues, and direct mail.[5] Major uses for coated woodfree papers included direct mail, brochures, annual reports, and so forth. The dynamic growth of coated woodfree papers in recent years was largely fueled by the rapid increases in "nonclassical" advertising. Changes in this mix could significantly affect country consumption patterns for coated woodfree papers.

Despite cost pressures and shifts in individual markets and end uses, coated woodfree papers were benefiting from demand for more and better four-color printing, as advertisers sought ways to improve the impact of their messages.

THE PRINTING INDUSTRY

The vast majority of orders for coated woodfree paper were placed by printers, either with the merchant or directly with the mill. In some instances, however, for very large orders, the order would be placed by either the printer or the publisher, depending on which seemed to have the stronger negotiating position with the supplier.

Selection of paper grade and manufacturer was a complex process that varied significantly according to end use, size of order, and sophistication of both the printer and the specifier or user. Almost without exception, the printer had the final say in the selection of paper and could significantly influence the grade of paper as well. The final user (i.e., the advertiser, ad agency, publisher, mail-order house, etc.) influenced paper selection, particularly with respect to grade, and could also influence selection of make, subject to final agreement by the printer.

For the printer, key paper characteristics were printability and runability. Surface characteristics, whiteness, and brightness were also important. Price was always important, especially when the user had to decide between two suppliers with similar offerings or when paper costs represented a significant portion of the total cost of the printed product. Complaint handling, emergency assistance, and speed and reliability of delivery were key service components. Sales representative knowledge was also important. Within limits, the relative importance of decision criteria varied from one country to another. In Italy and the United Kingdom, for instance, price and quality tended to be equally important, whereas quality and service factors tended to dominate importance rankings in Switzerland. Some favoritism was shown producers for patriotic reasons, but seldom at the expense of quality or price.

4. ECC International, Limited, 1987.
5. Papis Limited.

The user or specifier considered many of the same characteristics as the printer. Printability and delivery were usually at the top of the list, but the major concern was the paper's suitability for the particular advertising message, within the constraints of the overall advertising budget.

Despite the apparent similarity of products offered by different mills, there was substantial variation in runability, which could be determined only by actual trial. According to one printer:

> The final test is how well the paper prints on our presses. This is a matter of "fit" between paper, ink, and press characteristics. We find there are variations between papers that meet the same specifications, which can only be determined by actual trial. This is not cheap, as a trial involves printing 3,000 sheets. Because the paper characteristics cannot be completely specified, we like the idea of a mill brand. One time we tested two merchant brands that we thought were different. Then we found out that the paper came from the same mill, so we really wasted our time on the second test.
>
> Once we have selected a paper, it is critically important that its quality be consistent. Most suppliers are pretty good. Except for obvious flaws, however, we find they tend to want to blame problems on the ink or the press.

Over the past several years, the number of printers remained relatively constant, at about 15,000 to 20,000, with decreases from mergers and acquisitions offset by a growth in instant print outlets. In the last 10 years, the number of commercial print customers doubled to over 500,000, half of whom used instant print outlets.

As the number of small businesses and the use of desktop publishing continued to grow, it was suggested that within 10 years traditional printers would perhaps handle only longer-run, full-color work. Monochrome and spot-color work would be produced in customers' offices, with the paper-buying decision being made by people with little knowledge about paper or printing.[6] In-plant printing, however, was not expected to have a significant impact on the coated woodfree market.

PAPER MERCHANTS

Printers and publishers were reached in two principal ways: direct sales from the mill and sales from the mill through merchants, either independent or mill-owned. Direct sales were more common for high-volume products sold in reels, such as newsprint and LWC magazine paper. The pattern of distribution was influenced by characteristics of the transaction (see Exhibit 4), and the pattern varied significantly from one country to another (see Exhibit 5). For coated woodfree papers, it was estimated that 70 to 80% of sales went through merchants.

As with all wholesalers, stocking to provide quick delivery in small quantities was a principal merchant function. Fragmentation of the fastest-growing market segments (business and small printers) had decreased the average order size and increased demand for a wide choice of paper grades, making it more difficult for mills to access these customers directly.

6. By BIS Marketing Research Limited.

In warehousing, larger merchants had introduced expensive computer-controlled bar code systems, which reduced delivery times and the cost of preparing orders for delivery. Electronic interchange of information between merchants and their suppliers and larger customers was predicted to be the norm within the next few years. Merchants in the United Kingdom were spearheading an initiative to achieve industry standards for bar codes throughout Europe.

Changes in end-user profiles and new customer needs had forced merchants to expand the scope of their activities and customer support functions. As a result, the merchants' role broadened to include a number of additional services, including technical advice on paper choice and broader printing problems.

Private branding, supported by advertising, had long been used by some merchants to differentiate their products and service. Some large merchants had also invested in testing apparatus, similar to that found in mills, to check conformance to specifications and to support their desire to become principals, with full responsibility for product performance.

Merchant margins varied with location, type of sale, and nature of the transaction. For sales from stock, margins ranged from a low of 12% in Italy and 15% in Germany to 25% in France and Switzerland. Margins reduced to about 5%, or less, when a merchant acted as the intermediary solely for invoicing purposes.[7] (A typical income statement for a paper merchant is shown in Exhibit 6.)

Patterns of merchant ownership also varied from one country to another (see Exhibit 7). In the United Kingdom, for example, Wiggins Teape, a paper producer established in 1780, became a merchant in 1960 when existing merchants resisted introducing carbonless copy paper in the market. The company opened a network of offices to stimulate demand and to provide technical support for the product. Between 1969 and 1984, the company acquired control of several major merchants operating in the United Kingdom, France, Belgium, Italy, and Finland. In 1984, sales of $480 million made Wiggins Teape the largest merchant in Europe.

On the other hand, Paper Union, one of the two largest merchants in Germany (turnover of $142 million and market share of 12% in 1984), was an independent merchant. It was formed in the early 1960s, from three smaller merchants, in an attempt to reach the critical size of 100,000 tons per year. Due to low margins in Germany, Paper Union had emphasized reduced operating costs and consistent, fast delivery. Plans were being made, however, to introduce further services and advertising in an attempt to add value and increase customer awareness.

The move toward company-owned merchants was not without controversy. According to one independent merchant:

> We believe that independent merchants are very much in the best interest of paper mills. We're aware, of course, that many mills are integrating forward, buying merchants in order to maintain access to distribution. It is our view, however, that this will cause a number of problems. No one mill can supply all the products that a merchant must offer. Hence, even mill-owned merchants must maintain relations with a number of other mills, who will always want to supply their full range of products to

7. The European Printing and Writing Paper Industry, 1987, IMD Case No. GM 375.

the merchant, including those which compete with the parent mill. This will create serious tensions and frequently will put the merchant in the position of having to choose between corporate loyalty and offering the best package to the customer. The parent can, of course, impose restrictions on the merchant with respect to selling competing products, but the sales force would have serious problems with this.

Our strong preference is for exclusive representation of a mill. This is particularly important where there are strong influencers, such as advertisers, to whom it is important for us to address considerable promotional effort. Also, when we are an exclusive merchant, we provide the mill with extensive information on our sales, which allows the mill to do market analysis that both we and the mill find very valuable. We certainly would not provide this kind of information if the mill had intensive distribution. In a country like Switzerland, we can give the mill complete geographic and account coverage, so it's not clear to us why the mill needs more than one merchant. In our view, intensive distribution creates a situation where there is much more emphasis on price. While this first affects the merchant, it inevitably affects the mill as well.

If we do sell for a mill that has intensive distribution, we prefer to sell it under our brand, although we identify the mill, in small print. This is somewhat an historical artifact, going back to the days when mills did not attempt to brand their products, but if we're going to compete for business with another merchant, selling for the same mill, we feel having our name on the product helps us differentiate ourselves from the competitor.

At the same time, we should point out that we don't sell competing brands. There are about five quality grades within standard coated woodfree, and we handle two to three brands.

One industry expert predicted significant changes in distribution patterns.[8]

Looking to the future, it is predicted that there will be an increase in the number of paper grade classifications, moving from 4 just a few years ago to 20 or more. There will be an increasing number of different types of middlemen and distributors, and merchants will move into grades traditionally regarded as mill direct products (e.g., newsprint and mechanical grades) to bring these grades to the smaller customers.

Just as we have seen a technological revolution hit the traditional printing industry, we must now see a marketing revolution hit the traditional paper industry. Selection of the correct channel of distribution and the development of an active working relationship with that channel will be vital.

COMPETITION IN COATED WOODFREE PAPERS

In varying degrees, Leykam Mürztaler encountered at least 10 major European firms in the markets it served in Europe. Some, like KNP and Zanders, competed principally in coated woodfree papers. Others, like Stora and Feldmühle, produced a wide range of products, from coated woodfree papers to tissue to newsprint.

There was considerable variation in competitive emphasis among producers. Zanders, for instance, generally regarded as the highest quality producer, produced mostly cast-coated and premium art paper, competed only at the top end of the

8. From a paper presented by BIS Marketing Research Limited.

standard coated range, and was relatively unusual in its extensive use of advertising. Hannover Papier was particularly strong in service, offering fast delivery. PWA Hallein, which had tended to emphasize price over quality, had recently improved its quality but was keeping prices low in an apparent effort to gain market share. Arjomari, the biggest French producer, owned the largest merchant chain in France and had recently purchased merchants in the United Kingdom and southern Europe. It had recently entered the premium art paper segment, generally regarded as difficult to produce for. Burgo, a large Italian conglomerate, concentrated principally on the Italian market. (See Exhibit 8 for a report on the image of selected suppliers.)

Rapid growth in the coated woodfree market had stimulated capacity additions by existing producers and was also stimulating conversion of facilities from uncoated to coated. Nordland of Germany, for instance, switched 100,000 tons of capacity from uncoated to coated by adding a coater in October 1988. Although the company was excellent in service, there was, however, some question about its ability to produce high quality.

Branding was a relatively new aspect of the industry. All the major producers had established brand names for major products or grades. To date, however, only Zanders had actively promoted its brand to the trade or to advertisers.

MARKETING ACTIVITIES

Marketing activities at Leykam Mürztaler were divided between the sales director, Wolfgang Pfarl, and the marketing manager, Gertrude Eder. Pfarl, a member of the executive board, was responsible for pricing, as well as for all personal selling activities, both direct and through merchants. Eder was responsible for public relations, advertising and sales promotion, and marketing research. As a staff member, she reported to Dr. Siegfried Meysel, the managing director.

COATED WOODFREE PRODUCTS AND MARKETS

In coated woodfree papers, Leykam Mürztaler offered a comprehensive product line of standard coated papers under the MAGNO brand, for both sheet and web offset printing. These papers were produced in a wide variety of basic weights, ranging from 80 to 300 grams per square meter, depending on the particular application. The firm targeted the high-quality end of the standard coated category by offering higher coat weights, better gloss and print gloss, and better printability.

Using Austria as its home market, Leykam Mürztaler focused its principal efforts on countries in Europe. The majority of sales revenues came, in roughly similar amounts, from Austria, Italy, France, and the United Kingdom, with somewhat higher sales in Germany. Belgium, Holland, Switzerland, and Spain were important but smaller markets.

The firm also sold in a number of other countries, including the United States. Penetration of the U.S. market by the European paper industry had been assisted by the favorable exchange rates during the early 1980s. The firm's policy, however, was to maintain its position in different countries despite currency fluctuations. As Gertrude Eder explained:

> We believe our customers expect us to participate in their markets on a long-term basis and to be competitive with local conditions. This may cost us some profits in the short term, as when we maintained our position in the United Kingdom despite the weak pound, but now that the pound is strong again, this investment is paying off. If we had reduced our presence when the exchange rate was unfavorable, it would have been very difficult to regain our position.

Channels of Distribution

Over the years, Leykam Mürztaler had sold most of its output through merchants. To some degree the method of distribution was influenced by the country served, as the firm tended to follow the predominant trade practice in each country. In Switzerland, Germany, and the United Kingdom, the company conducted all its business through merchants. In France, Italy, and Austria, there was a mixed pattern of distribution, but with a strong merchant orientation.

Merchants were carefully selected, and the firm did business only with stocking merchants who competed on service rather than price. In some countries (e.g., Holland), the company used exclusive distribution, but this was not the normal pattern. Eder explained:

> As a large producer, we have a volume problem. In the larger countries, one merchant simply can't sell enough product for us; plus we believe it is risky to commit completely to one merchant.

Similarly, Wolfgang Pfarl commented:

> In Germany, for instance, we could go to one merchant only, but to get the volume of business we need would require going into direct business with some nonstocking merchants, and that is something that neither we nor our stocking merchants want to happen.

To date, the trend toward mill ownership of merchants had not adversely affected the firm's ability to get good merchant representation. There was some concern, however, that with changing patterns of mill ownership, some merchants might be closed off in the future to firms like Leykam Mürztaler.

Service was also seen as a key to merchant relations. In this connection, the firm felt its computerized order system and new finishing facilities at the Gratkorn mill provided great service capability and gave the firm a competitive advantage. The mill was highly automated, permitted flexibility in sheeting and packaging, and was able to handle the total output of the new paper machine. As the mill superintendent put it:

> From a production standpoint, the ideal scenario is one in which we can run one grade of paper all year and ship it to customers in large reels. Reality is that meeting customer needs is critical, and I believe we have "state-of-the-art competence" in our ability to meet a tremendous variety of customer requirements efficiently.

Pricing

Pricing practices in the paper industry had a strong commodity orientation; for coated woodfree papers, industry prices tended to serve as the basis for arriving at transaction prices. (See Exhibit 3 for information on industry prices and paper grades.) For sales to merchants, Leykam Mürztaler negotiated price lists, using the industry prices as a starting point, with final prices taking paper quality and other relevant factors into account. Price lists then remained in effect until there was a change in industry price levels. Routine orders were priced from the established price list. Large orders, however, usually involved special negotiation.

According to one Leykam Mürztaler sales manager:

> We have some interesting discussions with our merchants about price. The customer knows we make a high-quality product, so his principal interest is in getting it at the lowest possible price. In Europe there is no uniform classification of coated papers, as there is in the United States and Japan, so a standard approach is to try to get me to reclassify my product to a lower grade, and so a lower price. To some extent, though, my customer's preoccupation with price simply reflects price pressures he is experiencing from his customers. Still, it is frustrating because we believe we offer a lot more than just price and a good product. But I think we do a good job for the firm in getting the highest price possible.

Branding

In recent years, Leykam Mürztaler had followed the industry practice of branding its principal products. It did, however, supply products to certain merchants for private branding, a practice that was established when mill branding was not the norm. In 1988, some 30% of sales carried a merchant brand, largely reflecting the volume from Germany and the United Kingdom, where private branding was customary. Recently, however, the firm had started to identify most of its products by using a typical Leykam Mürztaler packaging, even for private labels.

Brands had been promoted primarily by the sales force, in direct contact with customers, using brochures and samples and by packaging. More recently, a series of superb visual messages was commissioned, using the theme "Dimensions in Paper" to suggest ways that high-quality paper combined with printing could produce more effective communication. The script accompanying the visual messages was designed to appeal to both the advertisers, with emphasis on communication, and printers, with emphasis on paper finish, touch, color, absorption, contrast, and other key paper characteristics. On a limited basis, these messages had appeared in selected magazines and in brochures for customers. (See Exhibit 9 for a copy of a MAGNOPRINT promotional piece.)

There was general agreement within the firm that more emphasis needed to be placed on branding as a way to achieve product differentiation and to convey the desired high-quality image. There was less agreement on how much to spend promoting the brands or how to deal with merchants who were now buying Leykam Mürztaler products for sale under the merchants' labels. According to Eder:

Over the past few years we designed the corporate logo and corporate graphics and established blue, black, and white as the colors for all corporate communication. We have worked hard to establish a consistent presentation of our corporate identity. Feedback from customers and the sales department indicates that this has helped improve our visibility and image. Nevertheless, we are currently spending considerably less than 1% of sales on advertising. Zanders, on the other hand, a firm of about our size, has been spending a lot of money on advertising for years and, as a result, has better visibility than we do, particularly with advertising agencies, as well as an enviable reputation for quality and service.

I don't know what the right number is for us, but we will need to spend substantially more if we are to establish the kind of brand awareness and image we desire. I think that to have any significant impact would take a minimum of ASch 3–4 million for classical advertising (i.e., advertising in trade publications, in various languages) and ASch 8–10 million for promotions, including brochures, leaflets, and trade fairs. In Western Europe we have to advertise in at least four to five languages, and sometimes more. In addition, the nature of the ads varies. In private brand countries, our ads emphasize the company name and focus on the "Dimensions in Paper" theme as well as the company's experience and modern production facilities. [See Exhibit 10 for a typical ad.] In other countries we emphasize the MAGNO brand.

We are convinced that printers want to know what mill brand they are buying. Also, we believe that there is some subjectivity in selecting paper, particularly by the advertiser, and we want to convince the advertiser that his message will come across better on Leykam Mürztaler paper.

The decision on supplying Leykam Mürztaler products for private branding was even more complex. As Pfarl commented:

I understand the position of the merchants who want to offer a private brand. The fact remains, however, that it is the mill that determines product characteristics and is responsible for meeting specifications. It is really a question of who is adding the value. In my view the merchant ought to emphasize those things which he controls, such as local stocks, good sales representation, and service. Putting a merchant label on paper produced by Leykam Mürztaler misrepresents the value-added picture. Don't get me wrong. Our firm strongly believes in merchants. In fact, we avoid direct business wherever there are strong stocking merchants. It's just that we think mills and merchants have distinct roles to play, and they should not be confused.

Currently, we will still produce for a merchant's label, but we have started to insist that it also is identified as Leykam Mürztaler. The merchants aren't very happy about this, but we think it's the right thing to do.

Nevertheless, the situation with respect to existing merchants was difficult. As one of the senior sales managers said:

We have been supplying some of our merchants with paper to be sold under a private label for a long time, and they have invested substantial sums of money in establishing their own brands. I completely support the company's position on this, but I don't know how we can get the practice to change. If we insist on supplying products only under our own brand, there are a lot of competitors who would, I think, be happy to step in and take over our position with some merchants. If we can't convince a merchant to switch over to our brand, we could lose a lot of business, in one or two instances as much as 6,000 tons. On the other hand, if we aren't uniform on this, we will not be able to really exploit the potential of developing our own brands.

In addition to questions about branding policy, it was not clear how to capitalize on increased brand preference, if indeed it were achieved. As Pfarl said:

> We might want to think in terms of higher prices or increased share, or some combination. Exactly what we would do could vary from market to market.

Personal Selling

Contact with merchants and with large, directly served accounts in Europe was mainly made by the company's own sales force, headquartered in Vienna, by sales representatives in subsidiary companies in Germany, Italy, and France, and by sales agents in other markets (e.g., the United Kingdom). Direct sales representatives numbered 20. Including clerical staff, Leykam had some 60 individuals in its sales department, most of whom had direct contact with customers.

The major activity of the sales force was making direct calls on large customers and on merchants. In addition, sales representatives made occasional calls on a merchant's customers, generally accompanied by the merchant's sales representative. Objectives usually included negotiating long-term contracts, "selling" the existing product line, introducing new products, and reviewing customer requirements for products and service.

It was the firm's belief that its sales force was a major asset and that sales representatives could significantly influence relations with merchants. A major objective for all Leykam Mürztaler representatives was to do everything possible to develop close relations with assigned merchants. According to Pfarl:

> The average age of our sales force is between 35 and 40, and most of the individuals have spent their entire career in sales with Leykam Mürztaler. They are really committed to serve the customer, with on-time deliveries or any other aspect of our relationship, and the customer really respects their high level of service. In addition, they are good negotiators and represent Leykam effectively during contract negotiations. They do not need to be technical experts, but they make sure that our technical people provide technical information as required. Also, they monitor shipping performance, make presentations to merchants, and may make joint customer calls with merchant sales representatives.

Mathias Radon, one of the Vienna-based sales managers, made the following comments:

> In total we call on about 100 merchants in Europe. I work with our sales offices in Italy, France, and Belgium and handle 5 merchants personally in the United Kingdom, in cooperation with our representative there. I call on the merchants two to three times a year and have extensive phone contact with our sales offices and representatives from Vienna. In general, the customer wants to talk about quantity, price, and service. We have conversations about private labeling. The new merchants would like us to give them private labels, but I think they know they can't get it. On the other hand, the ones to whom we are currently providing private labels don't want to

give it up. The problem varies from country to country. In France, for instance, it's not such a big problem.

One of my objectives is to encourage more stock business versus indent (merchant orders for direct mill shipment to the customer). This means we have to give them better service and provide backup stocks. Some merchants handle mill brands that compete directly with Leykam Mürztaler, but most tend to do this under a private label.

From time to time we work to develop a new merchant, but generally we work on building long-lasting relationships with existing merchants. We encourage trips by merchant personnel to the mill. I will make short presentations to merchant sales representatives when I call on the merchant, but generally they are pretty knowledgeable about paper. We've tried contests and other incentives with merchants and are still thinking about it, but I'm not sure if that's what we should do. From a quality standpoint, I try to stress whiteness, opacity, printability/runability, and consistency. Lots of customers ask for lab figures, but I don't think you can rely just on lab reports. We have trial print runs every week by an independent printer to check our consistency. I think most printers feel the same way.

We tend to have lots of small problems rather than any one large problem. Branding, for instance, pricing, friction when we appoint a new merchant, and country variations with regard to ways of doing business. I think branding will be important in all countries, but how we capitalize on it may have to vary.

After-Sales Service

Problems in printing could arise due to a number of circumstances. There might be variations or flaws in the paper or in the ink. Presses could develop mechanical problems. Even changes in temperature and humidity could negatively affect printing quality. Because of the complexity of the printing process, the cause of a problem was not always clear, and reaching an equitable settlement could be difficult.

When problems did arise, the printer turned to the merchant or mill for technical advice and frequently wanted financial compensation for lost production. According to Wolfgang Pfarl:

> When the printer encounters a production problem, it is important for us to be able to give him technical advice and work with him to solve the problem. Sometimes the sales representative can do this. More often, we have to involve one of our technical people from the mill. All too often, however, the printer is just looking for someone to compensate him financially, and we have to be very tough or we're likely to find ourselves paying for a lot of other people's mistakes.

Future Issues

Looking to the future, the firm was focusing its attention on managing "through the business cycle." As Wolfgang Pfarl put it:

> Our real challenge is to strengthen our market position in Western Europe. Most of our coated woodfree paper goes into advertising. We have seen extraordinary growth in this market in the last few years, but we have to expect there will be a significant

downturn in one or two years and that advertisers will then look intensely at their costs. In many cases this means the printer will suggest a lower-cost grade as a substitute for coated woodfree. Our task is to differentiate MAGNO from the generic category and position it as "a paper for all seasons," so to speak. In other words, we want our customers to think of MAGNO as the "right" paper for high-quality advertising, separately from coated woodfree.

In general, this means strengthening our corporate identity, being partners of the strongest merchants, and encouraging our merchants to support the MAGNO brand.

In a similar vein, Gertrude Eder commented:

This is a business where the impact of the business cycle is made worse by the tendency of merchants to overstock in good times and understock in bad times. Our objective, I think, should be to position Leykam as the last mill the merchant or printer would think of canceling in a downturn.

EXHIBIT 1 Highlights of the Development of the Leykam Mürztaler Group

	1987	1988	%
Production (in tons)			
Printing and writing papers	272,900	340,900	+24.9
Newsprint (Bruck)	98,200	99,200	+ 1.0
Paper total	371,100	440,100	+18.6
Chemical pulp	209,500	204,500	− 2.4
Mechanical pulp	30,900	32,100	+ 3.9
Deink pulp	58,900	62,700	+ 6.4
Total sales (gross, in ASch millions)			
Leykam Mürztaler AG	5,234	6,300	+20.4
Export share	4,056	5,100	+25.7
Exports in %	78	81	—
Leykam Mürztaler Group	5,906	7,100	+20.2
Capital expenditure and prepayments for fixed assets (in ASch millions)	1,418	1,500	+ 5.8
Cash flow (in ASch millions)	1,020	1,500	+47.1
Employees (excluding apprentices) as of 31 December	2,825	2,865	+ 1.4

Source: Annual Report.

EXHIBIT 2 Financial Results

	1983	1984[a]	1985[b]	1986	1987
Total sales (gross, in ASch millions)	4,842	5,367	5,420	5,187	5,906
Export sales (ASch millions)	2,973	3,413	3,537	3,331	4,062
Export share of Leykam Mürztaler AG (%)	69	72	74	74	78
Capital investment (ASch millions)	313	253	444	2,461	1,518
Total depreciation (ASch millions)	374	344	337	476	1,064
thereof: reducing balance depreciation (ASch millions)	—	—	—	125	674
Cash flow (ASch millions)	373	1,025	959	871	1,020
Profit for the year (ASch millions)	1	422	81	101	67
Personnel expenditure (ASch millions)	1,096	993	1,046	1,076	1,231
Number of employees (excluding apprentices) as of 31 December	2,918	2,424	2,364	2,578	2,825
Dividend and bonus (ASch millions)	—	54	81	101	67
%	—	4+4	4+8	4+8	8

Source: Annual Report.
[a]excluding Niklasdorf Mill.
[b]excluding Frohnierten Mill from 1 April 1985.

EXHIBIT 3 Prices per Ton (in $) of Woodfree Printing and Writing Papers in Western Europe (2nd quarter 1987 delivered)

Grade	West Germany	United Kingdom	France	Netherlands
Cast-coated, sheets	2,734	2,324	2,588	2,480
Art paper, sheets	1,897	1,660	1,837	1,736
Standard, sheets	1,283	1,212	1,235	1,166
Standard, reels	1,199	1,145	1,169	1,091
Low-coated, sheets	1,172	1,130	1,136	1,066

Source: EKONO Strategic Study, September 1988.
Note: Cast-coated paper was estimated to represent 5% of the coated woodfree market; art paper, 7–8%; standard-coated, 70%; and low-coated, less than 20%. Within the standard-coated category, actual transaction prices could vary as much as 25% as a function of quality and as much as 10% due to competition or other factors.

EXHIBIT 4 Transaction Characteristics: A Comparison of the Roles of Manufacturers and Merchants

Characteristics	Manufacturer	Merchant
Order size (kg)	>1,500	200–500
Items carried	Small	2,500–5,000
Fixed costs	High	Low
Stock level (kg)	>2,000/item	500–1,750
Delivery	Often slow	24 hours
Service	None	Possible
Cash flow	Low	Low

Source: The European Printing and Writing Paper Industry, 1987.

EXHIBIT 5 Market Shares per Distribution Channel (%)

| Form of distribution | Country | | | |
	United Kingdom	France	Germany	Italy
Paper mills	48	50	59	80
Mill-owned merchants	} 52	50	—	} 20
Independent merchants		—	41	

Source: The European Printing and Writing Paper Industry, 1987.

EXHIBIT 6 Typical Income Statement: Paper Merchant (%)

Sales	100
Cost of goods sold	75
Contribution	25
Other costs	23
Net profit	2
Depreciation	.5
Cash flow	2.5

Source: The European Printing and Writing Paper Industry, 1987.

EXHIBIT 7 Paper Merchants: Ownership and Concentration per Country

Country	Merchants totaling 80% of country sales	Ownership
Sweden	2	Mill-owned
Denmark	3	Mostly mill-owned
Netherlands	5	Mill-owned
Belgium	5	Mill-owned
Switzerland	5	Mostly mill-owned
Austria	2 (70%)	Mill-owned
France	6	Mill-owned
West Germany	7	All independent
United Kingdom	Few big and many small ones	Partly mill-owned Mostly independent

Source: Paper Merchanting, the Viewpoint of Independent Merchant.

EXHIBIT 8 Major Mill Reputation

Company	Comments on reputation
Zanders (Germany)	Mercedes Benz in coated woodfrees Excellent service Strong promotion Marketing activities have also been directed to advertising agencies, which can influence choice of brand.
Leykam Mürztaler	Reliable supplier Good service
Arjomari (France)	Strong positions in France due to its own merchants
Condat (France)	Good and stable quality
Feldmühle (Germany)	Stable quality Rapid deliveries and good stocking arrangements
KNP (Netherlands)	Flexible supplier, also accepts small orders Good service
PWA Hallein (Germany)	Competes with price
Scheufelen (Germany)	Good and stable quality Reliable deliveries
Stora Kopparberg (Sweden)	Reliable deliveries Quality and service OK

Source: EKONO Strategic Study, September 1988.

EXHIBIT 9 MAGNOPRINT Promotional Piece (text)

Dimensions of sound

photographed for Leykam-Mürztaler by Willi Langbein, Vienna.

Only when looking at the picture more closely does one realise how the artist interprets "dimensions of sound".
It is not the tuning fork that produces the sound but the impact of the melting metal on the water surface.

With this extraordinary photographic interpretation of the "sound" dimension we can not only demonstrate the outstanding quality of MAGNOPRINT but also the reproduction of the finest colour shades, the brilliance of the print; or, for example, the smoothness of the paper which brings out the contrast between the metallic light effects and the dark, calm water surface in the best possible way.

MAGNOPRINT

For the highest demands in printing.
The woodfree high-gloss double-coated MAGNOPRINT is among the most widely used brands of Leykam-Mürztaler and is mainly used for art printing, ambitious advertising and annual reports. Areas of application which fully bring out the qualities of MAGNOPRINT:

- *high-gloss and smoothness*
- *brilliant printed results*
- *high-contrast reproduction*
- *snow-white – therefore exact colour reproduction, even in the most delicate shades.*

The Magno range for the highest demands:

- *woodfree coated papers and boards*
- *velvet or high-gloss finish*
- *sheets and reels*
- *substance range 80 gsm up to 300 gsm.*

DIMENSIONS IN PAPER

(continued)

EXHIBIT 9   (continued)

EXHIBIT 10 Company Advertisement

VERSO
NUOVE DIMENSIONI

TOWARD NEW DIMENSIONS
The picture symbolizes the new Leykam dimensions realized through launching of the large PM9 machine for the production of glossy woodfree paper.

"Verso nuove dimensioni" – La fotografia simboleggia le nuove dimensioni Leykam, realizzate con l'avviamento della nuova grande continua PM 9 per la produzione di carta patinata senza legno. Dimensioni nella carta e' il nuovo slogan della Leykam Mürztaler AG.

DIMENSIONI NELLA CARTA "Dimensions in Paper" is the new catch-phrase of Leykam Mürztaler AG.

13 JORDAN A/S

Knut Leversby, managing director of Jordan A/S, took a good deal of pride in the certificate on his office wall in Oslo. In Norwegian, it proclaimed Jordan "Company of the Year 1986," as judged by a broadly composed jury and the journal *Næring-srevyen*. The jury had stressed Jordan's ability to conquer market positions, especially in an international context. Four years later, in January 1990, Leversby remained proud of the award, but his internal compass guarded against pride turning into complacency. As Jordan's CEO, he knew better than anyone the strategic challenges his company was facing. Jordan was a small company among multinational consumer goods giants like Unilever and Colgate-Palmolive. Furthermore, consumer goods was, more and more, a game that turned on volume, threatening to overwhelm smaller competitors.

Jordan had prospered by focusing its foreign strategy on mechanical oral hygiene products, mainly nonelectric toothbrushes, but also dental floss and dental sticks. By combining high product quality with an innovative distribution strategy, Jordan had successfully defined and defended its niche to become the number one toothbrush maker in Europe, and number four worldwide.

Nevertheless, Leversby was not sure that past tactics would carry Jordan in the post-1992 world of the European Community (EC). Increasingly, competition came from trade retailers and major multinationals, both of which had significantly greater resources than Jordan.

Jordan's retailers, mainly food-based mass retailers, were becoming increasingly concentrated to achieve economies of scale in purchasing and logistics. Larger scale also increased the bargaining power of retailers with suppliers on prices and trade terms. More and more, these trade terms included on-time delivery of increasingly smaller order lot sizes, as retailers implemented and refined just-in-time (JIT) systems.

This case was prepared by Research Associate David H. Hover, under the supervision of Professors Per V. Jenster and Kamran Kashani. The case was partially based on research by IMD Research Associates Dana Hyde and Mark E. Brazas and Peter O'Brien of the Industrial Development Authority of Ireland, and is part of IMD's institutional research project, Managing Internationalization. Copyright © 1991 by the International Institute for Management Development (IMD), Lausanne, Switzerland. Not to be used or reproduced without permission.

Retail chains were also increasing their cross-border activity, often via acquisitions or strategic alliances, as they prepared for the "single European market" of 1992. Consequently, they tended to favor pan-European brands for volume and ease of handling. Larger retailers could also contract production of "own label" products to compete with manufacturers' brands. In fact, about 13% of Jordan's sales came from contract production of these private labels. Leversby was concerned that Jordan's private label business might be cannibalizing name-brand sales and/or diluting the carefully built Jordan-brand image.

Concentration was also under way among the European toiletries manufacturers that performed contract distribution for Jordan. Leversby was especially concerned about the recent acquisitions of some of these distributors by multinational consumer goods companies. For example, in 1985, Procter & Gamble had acquired Richardson-Vicks, which distributed Jordan products in Italy and several other European countries. Quality distributors like Richardson-Vicks were very difficult to replace.

COMPANY BACKGROUND

Jordan was founded by Wilhelm Jordan, a man familiar with hard times. Born in Copenhagen in 1809, he was the eldest of 11 children raised by his widowed mother. Leaving home at an early age, he apprenticed himself to one of the master comb makers of Hamburg. In 1837, Wilhelm Jordan moved to Christiania, Norway, with two fellow comb makers to start a modest workshop destined to become the largest brush factory in Europe. When Wilhelm Jordan decided to manufacture brushes as well as combs (then made from cow horn), he personally recruited his workers from the best brush makers of Hamburg, moving them and their families to Christiania, as Oslo was then known.

During the late 19th and early 20th centuries, the Jordan company distinguished itself as a social pioneer. Despite frequent labor unrest in Norway, the Jordan factory never experienced a strike. In 1910, the company set up a pension fund wholly financed by profits. Considering the conditions of the time, Jordan was a good place to work, a fact reflected in the long-term employment and loyalty of its workers. Throughout Jordan's history, advancement from the shop floor was common; Per Lindbo, Knut Leversby's predecessor as managing director, began his career with Jordan as a 15-year-old on the production line. During World War II, Jordan gave financial support to workers who went underground to avoid forced labor conscription and otherwise resisted the Nazi occupation. A Jordan publication issued in 1987 to commemorate 150 years of company history referred to the internal "culture," strongly influenced by the founder's faith in the individual human being. For the employee with skill and the will to make the effort, the opportunity to accept the challenges was there, irrespective of formal education and qualifications.

Another continuous thread in Jordan's history was its commitment to product excellence. Brush making was a skilled worker's trade, and in 1989, Jordan still produced handcrafted "jewelry brushes" as nostalgia items. More important, the company continually invested in advanced technologies to maintain its competitive ability.

Jordan began producing toothbrushes in 1927 under the leadership of Hjalmar Jordan, grandson of the founder. By 1936, the company had captured half of the Norwegian market. In 1958, Jordan began to take a serious interest in exports, realizing that the oral hygiene field was largely underdeveloped. Jordan's subsequent success was evident. By 1988, foreign sales of dental products provided over 60% of Jordan's revenues. (See Exhibit 1 for financial information on Jordan and Exhibit 2 for Jordan's 1989 sales budget. Exhibit 3 is an organization chart.) The company's sales for 1989 reached NKr 330 million;[1] 44.6% of sales were made in Norway, 32.2% in the balance of Europe, and 10.0% in the rest of the world. The remaining 13.2% consisted of private label sales to other markets.

MANAGEMENT CHALLENGES

In the early 1980s, Jordan suffered a period of reduced earnings. The succcess that Jordan achieved in increasing exports led to overemphasis on marketing and sales at the expense of financial performance. Steps were taken to reemphasize the importance of financial results. Companywide financial targets were set at 18% return on assets with 16% return on sales and were communicated directly to employees. In addition, efficiency measurements were established for the individual foremen to help them identify their contribution to the overall profitability objectives of the company. Monthly reports and annual reviews for production looked at labor hours per unit, scrap rates, absentee rates, energy usage, and other measures of efficiency. Other reports for general distribution included weekly sales figures, profitability analysis, and accounts receivable.

The renewed emphasis on financial and efficiency measures made employees at all levels realize that the company was dependent on the successful interaction between production and marketing. This reorientation of company values had a direct impact on performance. Sales more than doubled between 1979 and 1989, and employment stayed flat at 450 after falling from 700 between 1979 and 1982. The work force reduction resulted from Jordan's policy to increase productivity through mechanization. The reduction was, however, achieved without major employee displacement. With government aid, older workers were retired, and approximately 80 workers were pensioned. Ongoing efforts in manufacturing managed to achieve productivity improvements in the range of 6 to 8% per year.

Downsizing remained a priority in 1989. The personnel department spent a considerable amount of time helping people leave the company. New people, however, were hired occasionally as needed, particularly in marketing. Jordan had achieved the reputation of being a good company for international marketing. A few individuals took advantage of Jordan, staying with the company only long enough

1. Note: Exchange rates had fluctuated widely in recent years. Approximate values for the Norwegian kroner were: NKr 1.00 = FF 0.88 = US $0.16 = £0.09.

to learn its methods and techniques before leaving and joining another company. Internationally minded employees were in high demand in Norway.

THE COMPETITIVE ENVIRONMENT IN 1989

Jordan's products were marketed in more than 85 countries worldwide; 1.4 billion toothbrushes were bought in 1989. (As Exhibit 4 indicates, toothbrush replacement rates varied considerably among countries.) Japan was the largest consumer of toothbrushes, both in total volume and on a per capita basis. Whereas Japanese consumers purchased an average of 3.2 toothbrushes per year, Irish consumers, for example, replaced their toothbrushes about once every two years. (Jordan's market share in major markets is provided in Exhibit 5. Information on Jordan's major competitors is provided in Exhibit 6, and key brands are listed in Exhibit 7.)

During the 1930s, Jordan had competed on quality, and its success had made Jordan-style quality an industry standard for toothbrushes. The company recognized that, as producing brushes was not a very difficult process, the battle of the future would not be about product development or production technology but rather about consumer marketing. As a result, Jordan shifted its focus toward product presentation and being responsive to end-user demands. Jordan concentrated its efforts on developing marketing techniques that reached the customer in the store, where most toothbrush purchase decisions were made. Through careful attention to point-of-sale promotions, packaging, and product design, Jordan was able to establish and maintain a strong market presence.

In the increasingly competitive consumer product market, volume was a precondition for survival. Consequently, during the mid-60s, Jordan considerably reduced its product lines (which included brushes, combs, toys, and wooden soles for footwear). The slimmed-down product portfolio concentrated on products with volume-related potential. From that time onward, oral hygiene products became increasingly important to Jordan's success.

Jordan's cost structure was probably not typical for the industry for two reasons. First, Norwegian labor costs were high. Hourly wages in Holland and Scotland, for example, were 70% and 30%, respectively, of the Norwegian rate. Manufacturing labor accounted for about 20% of the ex-factory sales price for toothbrushes. Second, as a small company with a nice strategy, Jordan did not have the financial or personnel resources for marketing and distribution that its large competitors had. Marketing expenses were generally allocated evenly between Jordan and the distributors in each country. Still, Jordan was limited in its ability to compete in some areas.

Jordan's experiences in the United Kingdom illustrated the problems Leversby expected to see develop in the rest of Europe. Although the United Kingdom had been one of Jordan's first export markets, the company's success there had been uneven. Despite repeated attempts, Jordan had been unable to secure ongoing distribution in several of the large retail chains. It was a perplexing problem. Retailers demanded that manufacturers support their products with advertising, which Jordan management felt was unnecessary given the impulsive nature of toothbrush purchases. In one case, a retailer wanted Jordan to spend £2 million on advertising, almost twice the company's annual budget for promotions in the United Kingdom. For comparison, the following data, taken from trade journals, shows the 1988 toothbrush advertising budgets in the United Kingdom for several of Jordan's competitors.

Company	Brand of toothbrush	Advertising budget
Unilever	Mentadent P Professional	£1.0 mn
Gillette	Oral-B	£1.5 mn
Johnson & Johnson	Reach	£2.0 mn

Because Jordan would not meet the retailers' advertising demands, retailers frequently placed Jordan products on lower shelves where the company's point-of-sales promotions were less effective. Naturally, under these conditions, sales could not meet expected levels, and so retailers would pull the line off the shelves entirely. Because of these difficulties, Jordan had only 4% of the U.K. market in 1987. (Exhibit 8 shows a comparison of the leading brands and distributors in the United Kingdom.)

Some large retail chains increasingly demanded listing fees before they would stock a particular item. For example, one large French chain required FF 150 per store per variant for a similar product. The total listing fee for an initial introduction of 10 product variants in 1,200 stores would cost FF 1,800,000. On the other hand, Jordan's relative scarcity of resources had led to the creative (and highly successful) use of marketing and distribution alliances, a key factor in the company's success.

By contractual agreement, most transactions between Jordan and its distributor and licensee partners were dominated in Norwegian kroner. The few exceptions included transactions with affiliates in developing countries and in Holland, which used U.S. dollars and Dutch guilders, respectively. The policy was a convenience. It was not Jordan's intention to push the foreign-exchange risk onto its overseas partners. If its affiliates or distributors stopped making money due to exchange-rate exposure (or any other reason), Jordan would soon lose them as partners. Jordan did not make currency denomination an issue in contract negotiations. Experience had shown that it was better to avoid involving the finance managers of the distributors, since "they would start to make all kinds of funny arrangements."

RETAIL DISTRIBUTION

Toothbrush distribution varied from country to country. In France, for example, 83% of 1987 volume was accounted for by the grocery trade and 17% by pharmacists; in the Netherlands, the comparable figures (1986) were 62% and 38%, respectively. Overall, however, pharmacists were losing ground to food-based retailers.

A second significant industry trend was the increasing concentration of the European grocery trade. Hypermarkets were getting a growing market share, along with organized retail groups, which pooled their member stores' purchases and supply. European supermarkets were more likely to be chain members, and retail outlets were generally getting larger. Although there continued to be some variation among countries, the share of food turnover by the top 10 food-buying organizations in West Germany had reached 81%; in the United Kingdom, the figure was 66%; for France, 62%, compared to only 36% in the United States.

For the end user, a larger-sized retailer meant not only lower prices but also a wider range of product choices. For the retailer, size meant more bargaining power with suppliers on prices, packaging, and other product characteristics, as well as payment terms, order lot sizes, and delivery times. The size of the new stores was a significant factor in managing distribution; one Euromarché hypermarket in France, for example, sold the same volume of toothbrushes as did 260 Norwegian stores.

The retail price of toothbrushes also varied from country to country for a number of reasons, including distributor and retailer margins. For the product category, retailer margins across Europe averaged 35% of the final consumer price. Country differences, however, could be significant; margins in France were about 25%, whereas U.K. retail margins reached 60% in some cases. Large retail chains and hypermarkets considered 30% the target margin in the product category. Wholesaler and distributor margins averaged 10 to 15% although country differences could also be substantial. In Spain, distributor margins ranged as much as 20 to 25%, while margins in the United Kingdom averaged about 10%. Manufacturers' coverage of sales, marketing, and overhead expenses was approximately 30% of the final retail price.

Jordan management expected that the EC's 1992 plan and European integration would further concentrate the European retail distribution trade. As competition rose, closures, acquisitions, and strategic alliances would accelerate. Carrefour, the leading French hypermarket chain, had already allied with Castorama, the leading French do-it-yourself chain, normalizing relations after a previous Carrefour takeover attempt. The prospect of 1992 was also stimulating increased cross-border activity in retail distribution, in contrast to the previous tendency of retail multiples to operate entirely within their domestic markets.

Coinciding with retail concentration was the increasing sophistication of retailers in obtaining and using market information. Retailers were highly aware of consumer preferences, competitive products, and market opportunities. Processing this market information had been enhanced by point-of-sale scanner systems that evaluated product contribution per increment of shelf space. Armed with analytical data closely tied to their own bottom line, retailers were increasing their demands on suppliers' sales representatives for changes in packaging, pricing, and other product attributes. As retailers became more aware of the changing market, product and package life cycles were getting shorter. Also, retailers were increasingly using JIT, which reduced their inventories but put a heavier logistical burden on suppliers to deliver smaller orders with less lead time.

JORDAN'S EXPORT DEVELOPMENT

Jordan began to take a serious interest in exports in 1958 when the European Free Trade Association (EFTA) and EC were in their formative stages. According to Leversby, the primary motivation for developing exports was that "4 million Norwegians did not consume enough toothbrushes to keep the company moving!" Jordan's initial exports, however, were vacuum cleaner brushes rather than toothbrushes. Choosing Great Britain as its first market because "they spoke the language," Jordan was disappointed with the results. The company realized that building a profitable business as a subcontractor was a difficult task.

The company, however, saw toothbrushes as an underdeveloped market, characterized by low usage rates and an increasing awareness of dental hygiene, with clear volume-related potential. With toothbrushes, Jordan could also take advantage of its dominant domestic market position to support developing overseas operations.

The strategy adopted by Per Lindbo, who was then managing director, and Leversby was simple and inexpensive. Jordan asked distributors to cover product launch expenses in return for sharply discounted prices on toothbrushes. Because the toothbrushes were of good quality and were supported by Jordan's marketing acumen, distributors found this offer attractive. It also allowed Jordan to enter new markets without substantial cash commitments.

Exports of toothbrushes were first made to Denmark, where Jordan entered into a distribution contract with the pharmaceutical company Astra. Denmark was chosen because of its physical proximity, cultural similarities, and the small size of the market. Later, due to Danish import restrictions, a factory was established in Copenhagen. The Danish factory assembled parts supplied by the Oslo factory. Jordan continued to diversify its export markets by expanding the Astra partnership to include Astra-Wallco in Sweden and Finland. Jordan toothbrushes were introduced in the Netherlands in 1963, with 240,000 units sold in two and a half months. In 1964, Switzerland, Belgium, and France were added to the export map, as Jordan became more confident in working with distributors and new markets.

A major boost to Jordan's initial export moves was a partnership with the large German consumer goods company, Blendax Werke, started in 1961. A license contract allowed Blendax to produce and market Jordan-designed toothbrushes in West Germany under the Blend-A-Med name. This arrangement with Blendax was still operational in 1989, making West Germany the only country in Europe where the Jordan brand name was not used. The relationship with Blendax was very important to Jordan in the competitive West German market. Leversby did not relish the idea of having to go it alone if something should happen to Blendax.

Export Strategy

Jordan's international strategy had a number of key elements. First, the company consciously and persistently pursued a niche policy, sticking to mechanical oral hygiene products. Shortly after Jordan went international, it selected one product only—toothbrushes—for export. Since then, the company had enlarged its foreign product line to include dental floss and dental sticks (interdental cleaners made from wood), but mechanical dental care remained Jordan's export business focus. The company's sales budget for 1989 estimated that 97% of its dental product volume would be exported.

Jordan deliberately shunned the toothpaste market. Entering it would put Jordan into a larger and, therefore, more visible competitive arena, inhospitable to companies of Jordan's size. (About 80% of all oral hygiene sales were toothpaste.) Moreover, Jordan had neither experience nor any particular strength in this arena.

Second, international expansion was conducted step by step, one country at a time. Jordan's modus operandi involved getting to know the culture of a particular target country and making an assessment of the market. If conditions looked promising, the company would begin to search for a local distributor, possibly collaborating with a local advertising agency. This process could take between one and two years. Given the right "chemistry" with a distributor, marketing would begin, with Jordan being introduced as an international rather than a Norwegian brand.

Third, Jordan fielded its own sales force only in the Norwegian market. Foreign sales were handled entirely by local distributors. There were several reasons for this policy. Overseas sales forces would overstretch Jordan's resources. Moreover, with only a limited product range to offer retailers, Jordan had no real distribution strength. Finally, an independent sales force would challenge well-developed distributors on their own ground. Instead, as Leversby put it, "Company management traditionally viewed limited marketing resources as an advantage. We continued to think small by gradually building all new export markets through distributorships and working arrangements with established, successful firms." The development of local distributors as active partners was crucial to the success of this strategy.

Resources

Similarly, Jordan tried to conserve its resources by limiting its capital expenditures. In 1988, 30% of Jordan toothbrushes sold were produced by licensed subcontractors in eight different countries, including Venezuela, Thailand, and Syria. Relative to direct foreign investment, licensing was an efficient way for Jordan to avoid tariff barriers. Even the high perceived value of Jordan products did not allow the company to remain profitable when import duties were as high as 60 to 80%, as was the case in some countries.

Direct foreign investment was made only when market factors dictated it. Jordan opened a factory in Holland in 1988 as a manufacturing bridgehead within the EC, anticipating the abolition of intra-EC trade barriers scheduled for 1993. (Norway was not an EC member.) The Dutch plant was also used to separate private brand production from Jordan brand. Private brand production ran in small lots, requiring many changeovers. To optimize the volume-based manufacturing technologies available at the Norwegian plants, private label production was done almost entirely in Holland. The proximity of the Dutch plant to the major private label customers also facilitated integration with the JIT requirements of these companies. The decision to manufacture in the Netherlands was heavily influenced by the Dutch government's offer to provide 35% of the plant cost. Other important factors included the sales volume available in the Dutch market, as well as tax, culture, and language issues.

Despite Jordan's successes, the company had not been able to enter markets at will. In Great Britain, the changing nature of the retail industry had disproportionately increased buyer power for the time being. High listing fees demanded by mass retailers exceeded the returns Jordan believed could be achieved. The situation in the United States was different; in Leversby's words, it was "a big black hole." Despite the attractiveness of its size, the U.S. market presented more risks than Jordan management was willing to undertake. Jordan, however, had not excluded the market and had actually begun working with an American company. In general, Jordan's managers believed that more attractive opportunities existed in countries with low toothbrush usage rates and limited penetration by competitors. Erik Foyn, finance director, emphasized "we cannot succeed in all markets; we must be selective."

Private Label

Jordan management also faced the problem of how to balance the Jordan brand and the private label parts of the company. Although the private label business provided only 13% of Jordan's sales, there was considerable debate about how this business fit into the company's future.

The private label business was organized as a separate company, Sanodnet, under the leadership of Mr. Juliussen, a member of the general management team. To distinguish the private label from the Jordan brand, Jordan used different toothbrush designs. The private label business had a diverse customer base, including Colgate-Palmolive and Safeway, the American retail chain.

Jordan's management was acutely aware of the problems associated with having two similar competing brands in one company. Cannibalization of the carefully built branded sales by the private label products was one such problem. It was possible to have two Jordan products next to each other on shelves—one Jordan brand and one Jordan-designed and -manufactured private label. For retailers and distributors, this could cause a conflict of interest between Jordan-made private label products carrying the retailer's or distributor's name and the Jordan brand. As one distributor commented, "I don't mind Jordan's private label business, but why do they have to be so good at it?"

International Management Issues

Control over the operations of licensees was also a major issue for Jordan. Because the company operated under the Jordan brand name throughout the world, it was felt that quality had to be uniform. Engineers were dispatched from Norway annually to inspect licensee plants, and product samples were sent to Oslo on an ongoing basis to ensure that standards were being met. Production volumes were controlled by supplying at least one part of the final product from Norway, usually the back of the package. Foreign accounts were relatively easy for Jordan to track as there was usually only one distributor per country.

Expansion into Greece

By the summer of 1988, Greece was one of the few European countries where the Jordan brand name was not known. Management believed that entering the Greek market was a logical step toward consolidating the company's position in Europe.

Preliminary market research, using readily available sources such as government statistics, trade journals, country reports, and Nielsen data, confirmed original suspicions that Greece was an attractive opportunity, characterized by low usage rates and underdeveloped competition. More comprehensive research, including extensive discussions with various distributors, retailers, and consumers, was carried out before securing a distributor. The interviews, besides giving Jordan management a first-hand account of local business practices, also allowed management to evaluate numerous potential in-country partners.

In Greece, as in many markets, it quickly became apparent that Jordan would have to work closely with the retail trade to create a new selling environment. Traditionally, Greek retailers kept toothbrushes behind the counter, forcing customers to ask for assistance, thus giving the store clerk a significant role in product selection. Jordan's competitive strategy relied on the impulsive nature of toothbrush purchases, which dictated that the products be readily visible to the customer.

To introduce the trade to Jordan's marketing concept, the company held two presentations for interested distributors. More than 250 representatives attended these meetings. The concept behind point-of-purchase displays was explained, samples were demonstrated, and results in similar countries were presented.

After selecting a partner, Jordan made a successful launch in the Greek market. Jordan's first-year target was for 5% of the market. The company's first shipment, equal to 1.6% of the total market, sold out in less than a month.

CONCLUSION

During 30 years of exporting, Jordan management had consistently relied on its knowledge of country markets and its ability to develop relations with experienced and qualified distributors. This had not always been easy. The changing European retail and economic environment implied that Jordan would face many more challenges in the future.

The consolidation of competitors in the industry, including the purchase of Jordan's local distributors by large multinationals, was straining the company's resources. The Jordan family, however, wanted to keep their company. Despite a number of attractive offers, the company was looked on as the family inheritance, as well as a prestigious institution in Norway for well over 150 years. The greater financial and distribution power that would come from a merger would be beneficial, but "after 12 months the spirit would be gone," Leversby explained.

Despite the challenges facing his company, Leversby was optimistic about the future. "Fortunately, we have a long way to go."

EXHIBIT 1   Selected Financial Results (millions of Norwegian kroner)

	1986	1987	1988
Income Statement			
Operating revenues	265.0	307.0	321.0
Operating expenses:			
depreciation		(14.0)	(15.6)
other		(240.0)	(257.5)
Total operating expenses	(226.4)	(254.0)	(273.1)
Net operating revenues	38.6	53.0	47.9
Net financial income (cost)	(8.3)	(2.0)	1.2
Extraordinary items	1.3	(8.7)	2.2
Profit before allocations to funds and taxes	31.6	42.3	51.3
Allocations	(15.8)	(11.8)	(12.6)
Taxes	(7.4)	(15.4)	(21.2)
Net profit	8.4	15.1	17.5
Balance Sheet			
Cash	31.9	55.2	81.5
Accounts receivable	42.8	35.8	52.9
Inventory	23.6	24.4	28.3
Total current assets	98.3	115.4	162.7
Long-term investments	10.8	12.9	14.2
Property, plant and equipment	124.1	129.6	144.5
Total fixed assets	134.9	142.4	158.7
Total assets	233.2	257.9	321.4
Current liabilities	71.1	75.0	98.4
Long-term liabilities	61.1	57.0	66.2
Untaxed reserves	79.7	91.5	106.7
Minority interests	–	–	0.8
Shareholders' equity	21.3	34.4	49.3
Total liabilities and shareholders' equity	233.2	257.9	321.4
Return on assets	18.0	23.4	18.2
Cash ratio	14.6	20.2	28.0
Equity ratio	43.3	48.8	48.5

Source: Jordan.

EXHIBIT 2 Sales Budget, 1989 (total: 330 million kroner)

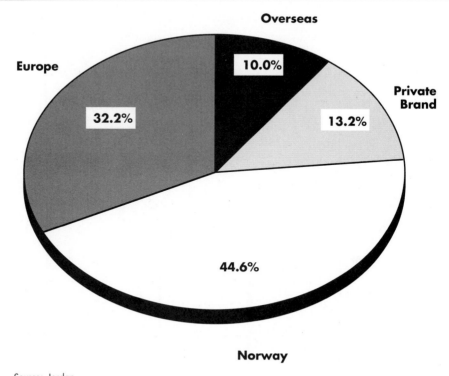

Overseas

Europe

Private Brand

32.2%

10.0%

13.2%

44.6%

Norway

Source: Jordan.

274

EXHIBIT 3 Organization Chart, June 1989

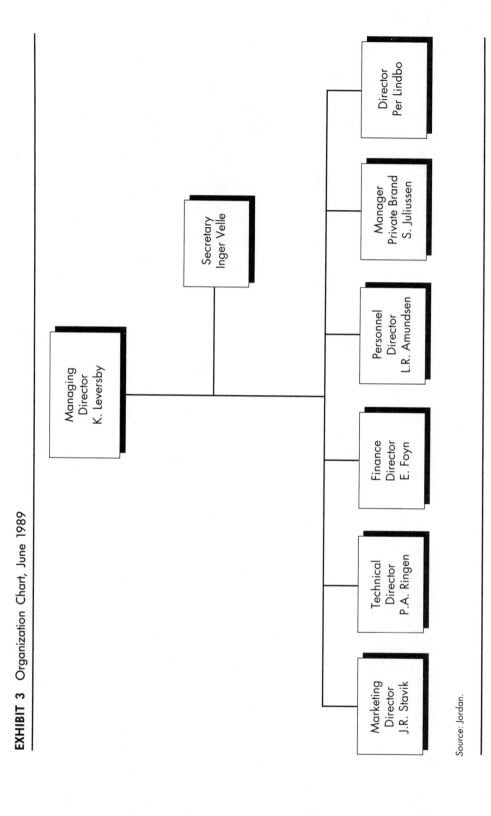

Source: Jordan.

EXHIBIT 4 The World Market for Toothbrushes, 1985 (data unavailable for some countries)

	Unit Sales	
Country	Total (millions)	Per capita
Japan	360.0	3.2
North America		
United States	300.0	1.4
Canada	25.0	1.1
Western Europe		
United Kingdom	53.0	0.9
Italy	38.1	0.7
France	36.0	0.7
Spain	15.8	0.4
Sweden	15.0	1.8
Netherlands	12.4	0.9
Switzerland	11.0	1.7
Denmark	7.2	1.4
Norway	5.8	1.4
Finland	4.3	0.9
Belgium	4.2	0.4
Ireland	2.0	0.6
South America		
Brazil	90.0	0.7
Colombia	21.0	0.7
Argentina	10.0	0.4
Venezuela	6.8	0.4
Chile	4.2	0.3
Australia	10.0	1.5

Source: EIU/Trade sources.

EXHIBIT 5 Jordan Market Share by Country, 1987

Country	Market share (%)
Norway	90
Finland	70
Denmark	48
Netherlands	50
Belgium	30
Ireland	28
Sweden	20
Iceland	20
Portugal	13
Spain	16
Canada	15
France	15
Italy	3
Switzerland	4
United Kingdom	4

Source: Jordan.

EXHIBIT 6 Selected Financial and Operating Statistics of Major Competitors, 1987 ($ millions)

Company/ Nation	Sales		Net income	Return on assets (%)*	Employees
	Total	% Toothbrush			
Lion Corp. (Japan)	2,451	20.3	41	4.8	4,892
Gillette (U.S.)	3,167	4	230	19.5	30,100
Unilever (Netherlands/ U.K.)	31,279	.002	1,407	7.6	294,000
Johnson & Johnson (U.S.)	8,012	.5	833	19.2	78,200
Colgate-Palmolive (U.S.)	5,648	1.6	204	16.5	24,700
Anchor Brush Co. (U.S.)	50	+50	N/A	N/A	1,150
Jordan (Norway)	46	69.7	2	23.4	475
Procter & Gamble (U.S.)	17,163	.01	327	3.6	73,000

Source: Jordan, Advertising Age, Annual Reports.
*Operating profit/total assets

EXHIBIT 7 Major Brand Competitors, 1987

Company	Major toothbrush brands
Lion	Lion
Gillette	Oral-B, Dr. West
Unilever	Gibbs, Signal, Mentadent, Pepsodent, DX, FSP
Johnson & Johnson	Micron, Reach, Prevent, Tek, Alcance
Colgate-Palmolive	Colgate, Dentagard, Defend, Tonigencyl
Anchor	Various private labels
Jordan	Jordan, private labels
Procter & Gamble	Blendax
Addis	Wisdom

Source: Jordan, Annual Reports.

EXHIBIT 8 British Toothbrush Market, 1989

Brand	Distributor	Number of sales representatives	Market share(%)	Average consumer price
Jordan	Alberto Culver	10	2.5	99p
Wisdom	Addis/Wisdom	20	26.3	99p
Mentadent	Elida Gibbs	N/A	1.9	£1.19
Oral-B	Oral-B (Gillette)	11	22.4	£1.09
Reach	Johnson & Johnson	15	7.0	99p

Source: Jordan.

Pricing

Local pricing takes on a global dimension when price levels in some markets impact sales levels in others. Such spillover effect, referred to as parallel trade or gray market, is of concern for a growing number of product categories. When parallel trade is an issue, some degree of central coordination of pricing becomes inevitable. Yet certain factors can complicate any such coordination, among them differences in price sensitivity in different markets, divergent country management objectives and potential for internal conflicts, and local government policies and attitudes.

When competitors are global, their pricing practices elsewhere may help explain their policies in any one local market. Experience and lessons learned in some countries could thus be used more effectively to counter competitive moves in others.

ISSUES

The issues in pricing are viewed in this section from the perspectives of companies in two different industries. The first company, Pharma Swede, is scrutinizing its current decentralized pricing policy to avoid significant losses in revenues, profits, or damage to its reputation. The impetus for management's reexamination of the policy is the upcoming European liberalization of trade in pharmaceutical products and the prospects of massive parallel trade if the policy is left unchanged. The second company, Philip Morris KK, is battling a global competitor that is using price to win market share in Japan. Management is looking at a number of options and wondering if the company's experience in Europe can help with the situation in Japan.

LEARNING POINTS

The student can expect the following learning points from the analysis and class discussion of the cases in this section:

- Understanding the different objectives of skimming vs. penetration pricing strategies and assessing their potential impact in a single country, a region, or worldwide;
- Practice cost and profitability analysis toward determining viable prices;
- Insights into the role of local governments in influencing pricing decisions;
- Exercise in relating pricing decisions to the broader regional or global marketing strategy;
- Skills in formulating competitive action plan as a response to a rival's price challenge.

278

14 PHARMA SWEDE: GASTIRUP

Early in 1990, Bjorn Larsson, adviser to the president and the head of Product Pricing and Government Relations for Pharma Swede, in Stockholm, Sweden, was reviewing the expected consequences of the economic integration of the European Community (EC) and the creation of a single market on Gastirup in Italy.

Gastirup was a drug used in the treatment of ulcers. Since its introduction in Italy in 1984, this innovative product had achieved considerable success in its category of gastrointestinal drugs. However, success had come as a result of pricing the drug at a significant discount below the prevailing prices for the same product in the rest of Europe. Higher prices would have disqualified Gastirup from the government reimbursement scheme, the system by which the state health insurance agency reimbursed patients for pharmaceutical expenditures. The government-negotiated prices for Gastirup in Italy were more than 40% below the average European price.

Bjorn Larsson was concerned that, with the anticipated removal of all trade barriers in Europe, Gastirup would fall victim to massive parallel trading from Italy to the higher-priced countries in the region. Furthermore, with the increased coordination among government health insurance agencies, also foreseen in the years following 1992, price differences among EC countries were expected to narrow. This likely development highlighted the need for a consistent pricing policy throughout Europe.

As head of Product Pricing and Government Relations, Bjorn Larsson was responsible for recommending actions that top corporate and local Italian management should take to avert potential annual losses for Gastirup, projected to be in the $20 to $30 million range. Among the alternatives being considered, the most extreme was to forego the large and growing Italian market altogether and

This case was prepared by Professor Kamran Kashani, with the assistance of Research Associate Robert C. Howard. This case was developed with the cooperation of a company that wishes to remain anonymous. As a result, certain names, figures, and facts have been modified. Copyright © 1991 by the International Institute for Management Development (IMD), Lausanne, Switzerland. Not to be used or reproduced without permission.

concentrate the product's sales elsewhere in Europe. The Italian market for Gastirup had grown to $27 million in recent years and accounted for 22% of European sales. Another option was to remove Gastirup from the Italian government reimbursement scheme by raising the prices to levels close to those prevailing in the higher-priced countries. This action would most likely reduce the drug's sales in Italy by as much as 80%. Still another alternative was to take legal action in the European Court of Justice against the Italian government's reimbursement scheme and the related price negotiations as barriers to free trade. Finally, the company could take a "wait and see" attitude, postponing any definitive action to a time when the impact of 1992 was better known.

COMPANY BACKGROUND

Pharma Swede, formed in 1948 in Stockholm, Sweden, concentrated solely in pharmaceuticals. In 1989, the company employed over 2,000 people and earned $50 million on sales of $750 million, distributed among its three product lines: hormones (20%), gastrointestinal products (50%), and vitamins (30%). Gastirup belonged to the gastrointestinal product category and, as of 1989, accounted for roughly $120 million of Pharma Swede's sales. (See Exhibit 1 for a breakdown of Pharma Swede's sales.)

International Activities and Organization

As of December 1989, Pharma Swede had wholly owned subsidiaries in 11 countries in Western Europe, where it generated 90% of its sales. The balance of sales came from small operations in the United States, Australia, and Japan.

Due to high research and development costs, as well as stringent quality controls, Pharma Swede centralized all R&D and production of active substances in Stockholm. Partly as a result of these headquarters functions, 60% of the company's expenditures were in Sweden, a country that represented only 15% of sales. However, the politics of national health care often required the company to have some local production. Consequently, a number of Pharma Swede's subsidiaries blended active substances produced in Sweden with additional compounds and packaged the finished product.

Pharma Swede had a product management organization for drugs on the market (see Exhibit 2). For newly developed drugs, product management did not begin until the second phase of clinical trials, when decisions were made as to where the new products would be introduced and how. (See Exhibit 3 for the different phases of a new product's development.) Besides country selection, product management at headquarters examined different positioning and price scenarios and determined drug dosages and forms. It had the final say on branding and pricing decisions, as well as on basic drug information, including the package leaflet that described a drug's usage and possible side effects. As one product manager explained, the marketing department in Stockholm developed a drug's initial profile and estimated its potential market share worldwide. It was up to local management, however, to adapt that profile to their own market.

As an example, in 1982, headquarters management positioned Gastirup against the leading anti-ulcer remedy, Tomidil, by emphasizing a better quality of life and 24-hour protection from a single tablet. To adapt the product to their market, the Italian management, with the approval of Stockholm, changed the name to Gastiros and developed a local campaign stressing the drug's advantages over Tomidil, the oral tablet that had to be taken two or three times a day.

As a rule, headquarters limited its involvement in local markets. It saw its role as one of providing technical or managerial assistance to country management, who were responsible for profit and loss.

Product Pricing and Government Relations

The Product Pricing and Government Relations Department, located at headquarters, was a recently established function within the company. It prepared guidelines for subsidiary management to use in negotiating drug pricing and patient reimbursement policies with local government agencies. The department was divided into Government Relations and Product Pricing. Those in Government Relations followed ongoing political events and prepared negotiating positions on such issues as employment creation through local production.

The role of Product Pricing, headed by Bjorn Larsson, was to determine the optimum price for new products. An "optimum" price, Bjorn explained, was not necessarily a high price, but a function of price-volume relationships in each market. An optimum price also reflected the cost of alternatives, including competitive products and alternative treatments like surgery, and the direct and indirect costs to society and the government of nontreatment. Each of these criteria helped to quantify a product's cost-effectiveness or, as government authorities saw it, its treatment value for money.

Using cost-effectiveness data in price negotiations was a recent development in the pharmaceutical industry and corresponded to the increasing cost consciousness among public health authorities. Economic exercises that were initially performed in Stockholm to measure a drug's treatment and socioeconomic benefits were repeated with local authorities during negotiations. In Larsson's opinion, the latest measure of "nontreatment cost" was becoming an important factor. He explained that a thorough understanding of the direct and indirect costs of an illness had come to play a key role in whether or not a government was willing to pay for a product by granting it reimbursement status, as well as the magnitude of that reimbursement. According to industry observers, the task of marketing to governmental agencies had become crucial in recent years, as public agencies were scrutinizing drug prices more carefully. (See Exhibit 4 for an overview and further description of the Product Pricing and Government Relations Department.)

THE PHARMACEUTICAL INDUSTRY

As of 1989, approximately 10,000 companies worldwide competed in the $180 billion pharmaceutical industry. Industry sales were concentrated in North America, Western Europe, and Japan, with the 100 largest companies in these areas accounting for nearly 80% of all revenues. Western Europe alone accounted for an estimated 25% of total volume.

The industry classified pharmaceutical products according to how they were sold and their therapeutic status. In the first instance, pharmaceutical sales were classified into two categories, prescription and over-the-counter (OTC). Prescription drugs, with four-fifths of all pharmaceutical sales worldwide and a 10% annual growth rate, could be purchased only with a doctor's prescription. These drugs were branded or sold as a generic when original patents had expired. OTC drugs were purchased without a prescription; they included both branded and generic medicines such as aspirin, cough syrups, and antacids. At Pharma Swede, prescription drugs accounted for more than 90% of total sales.

Prescription drugs were also classified into therapeutic categories, of which gastrointestinal was the second largest, representing 15% of industry sales. Within the gastrointestinal category, there were a number of smaller segments, such as anti-ulcer drugs used to control and treat digestive tract ulcers, anti-diarrheics, and laxatives. In 1989, the prescription anti-ulcer drug segment was valued at $7 billion worldwide and growing at 18% a year, faster than the total prescription market.

In parallel with worldwide trends, several factors were expected to play a role in shaping the future of the European pharmaceutical industry. Among these were an aging population, rising R&D and marketing costs, greater competition from generics, and government cost controls.

Aging Population

Europe's stagnating population was gradually aging. The segment of the population over 55 years old was forecast to grow and account for between 33 and 40% of the total by the year 2025—up from less than 25% in the mid-1980s. During the same period, the segment under 30 years of age was forecast to drop from about 40 to 30%. The "graying of Europe" was expected to have two lasting effects on drug consumption. First, low growth was projected in the sales of drugs normally used by children or young adults. Second, drug companies marketing products for age-related diseases, such as cancer, hypertension, and heart ailments, could expect growing demand.

Rising R&D and Marketing Costs

Research and development expenses included the cost of identifying a new molecule and all the tests required for bringing that molecule to the market. Generally, for every 10,000 molecules synthesized and tested, only one made it through the clinical trials to the market. Product development costs were estimated to average $120 million per drug, from preclinical research to market introduction. Industry estimates for R&D expenses averaged around 15% of sales in the late 1980s, with some companies spending as much as 20% of sales on new drugs. Research into more complex diseases like cancer, as well as lengthy clinical trials and government registration processes, had recently raised these costs.

Marketing costs had also increased due to a general rise in the level of competition in the industry. In the early 1980s, pharmaceutical firms spent, on average, 31% of sales on marketing and administrative costs. By 1987, the ratio had increased to 35% and was still rising. Some companies were reported to have spent unprecedented sums of $50 to $60 million on marketing to introduce a new drug.

Growth of Generics

Generic drugs were exact copies of existing branded products for which the original patent had expired. "Generics," as these drugs were known, were priced substantially lower than their originals and were usually marketed by some firm other than the inventor. Price differences between the branded and generics could be as large as 10:1. Depending on the drug categories, generics represented between 5 and 25% of the value of the total prescription drug market in Europe, and their share was expected to grow. For example, in the United Kingdom, sales of generic drugs had grown to represent an estimated 15% of the total national health budget and were forecast to reach 25% by 1995. In line with efforts to contain costs, governments in many parts of Europe were putting increased pressure on physicians to prescribe generics instead of the more expensive branded drugs.

Government Role

Governments, one of the strongest forces influencing the pharmaceutical industry in Europe, in conjunction with public and private insurance agencies paid an average of two-thirds of health care costs. In Italy, for example, 64% of all prescription pharmaceutical expenditures were covered by the public health care system. In Germany, France, and the United Kingdom, the respective shares were 57%, 65%, and 75%. These percentages had risen considerably throughout the 1960s and 1970s.

European governments were facing two opposing pressures: to maintain high levels of medical care while trying to reduce the heavy burden placed on the budget for such expenditures. Influence on pharmaceutical pricing, according to industry experts, had become an increasingly political as well as economic issue.

Not surprisingly, government agencies seeking to reduce health insurance costs encouraged the use of generics. In fact, before the advent of generics and official interventions, well-known branded drugs that had lost their patents in the 1970s, such as Librium or Valium, often maintained up to 80% of their sales for several years. In contrast, by the late 1980s, it was more likely that a drug would lose nearly 50% of its sales within two years after its patent expired.

THE DRUG GASTIRUP

Ulcers and Their Remedies

Under circumstances not completely understood, gastric juices—consisting of acid, pepsin, and various forms of mucus—could irritate the membrane lining the stomach and small intestine, often producing acute ulcers. In serious cases, known as peptic ulcers, damage extended into the wall of the organ, causing chronic inflammation and bleeding. Middle-aged men leading stressful lives were considered a high-risk group for ulcers.

Ulcers were treated by four types of remedies: antacids, H-2 inhibitors, anticholinergics, and surgery. Antacids, containing sodium bicarbonate or magnesium hydroxide, neutralized gastric acids and their associated discomfort. Some of the more common OTC antacid products were Rennie and Andursil. In contrast, H-2 inhibitors such as ranitidine reduced acid levels by blocking the action of the stomach's acid-secreting cells. Anticholinergics, on the other hand, functioned by delaying the stomach's emptying, thereby diminishing acid secretion and reducing the frequency and severity of ulcer pain. Only in the most severe cases, when ulceration had produced holes in the stomach and when ulcers were unresponsive to drug treatment, was surgery used.

In 1989, the world market for nonsurgical ulcer remedies was estimated at $8 billion, with most sales distributed in North America (30%), Europe (23%), and Japan (5%). Worldwide, H-2 inhibitors and OTC antacids held 61% and 12% of the market, respectively.

The Oral Osmotic Therapeutic System

Gastirup, introduced in 1982 as Pharma Swede's first product in the category of ulcer remedies, used ranitidine as its active ingredient. As of 1982, ranitidine was available as a generic compound, having lost its patent protection in that year. The U.S.-based Almont Corporation was the original producer of ranitidine and its former patent holder.

What distinguished Gastirup from other H-2 inhibitors, including ranitidine tablets produced by Almont and others, was not its active ingredient, but the method of administration called the oral osmotic therapeutic system (OROS). In contrast to tablets or liquids taken several times a day, the OROS medication was administered once a day. Its tablet-like membrane was specially designed to release a constant level of medicine over time, via a fine laser-made opening. By varying the surface, thickness, and pore size of the membrane, the rate of drug release could be modified and adapted to different treatment needs. Furthermore, the release of the drug could be programmed to take place at a certain point in time after swallowing the tablet. Consequently, drug release could be timed to coincide with when the tablet was in the ulcerated region of the upper or lower stomach. (See Exhibit 5 for a diagram and brief description of the OROS.)

Drugs supplied via OROS had certain advantages over other drugs. First, because of a steady release of the medicine, they prevented the "high" and "low" effects often observed with the usual tablets or liquids. Furthermore, the time-release feature also prevented overfunctioning of the liver and kidneys. In addition, because drugs contained in an OROS had to be in the purest form, they were more stable and had a prolonged shelf life. Pharma Swede management believed that drugs administered by OROS could lead to fewer doctor calls, less hospitalization, and reduced health care costs for insurance agencies and governments.

Because OROS was not a drug per se but an alternative method of drug administration, it was sold in conjunction with a particular pharmaceutical substance. By the end of 1989, Pharma Swede was marketing three drugs using OROS. Gastirup was the company's only OROS product in the gastrointestinal category; the other two were in the hormones category. The management of Pharma Swede characterized the use of OROS as an attempt to introduce product improvements that did not necessarily rely on new molecules but on new "software," leading to improved ease of use and patient comfort.

Ranitidine, the active ingredient in Gastirup, was not made by Pharma Swede, because of its complex manufacturing process and the fact that since 1982 it was available from a number of suppliers both inside and outside Sweden. Gastirup OROS tablets were manufactured by the company in Sweden; final packaging, including insertion of the drug information sheet, was done in a number of European countries, including Italy.

Patent Protection

OROS was developed and patented by the Anza Corporation, a U.S. company that specialized in drug delivery systems. In Europe, Anza had applied for patents on a country-by-country basis. Patent protection was twofold: OROS as a drug delivery system and OROS used with specific drugs. The more general patent on OROS was due to expire in all EC countries by 1991. The second and more important patent for Gastirup covered OROS's containing ranitidine. This latter patent, exclusively licensed to Pharma Swede for Europe, would expire everywhere on the continent by the year 2000.

Although Pharma Swede sold more than one OROS product, it had an exclusive license from Anza only for the ranitidine-OROS combination. Over the years, a number of companies had tried to develop similar systems without much success. To design a system that did not violate Anza's patents required an expert knowledge of membrane technology, which only a few companies had.

Competition

Broadly speaking, all ulcer remedies competed with one another. But, Gastirup's primary competition came from the H-2 inhibitors in general, and from ranitidine in particular. Since 1982, when ranitidine joined the ranks of generics, it was produced by a number of companies in Europe and the United States. Despite increased competition, ranitidine's original producer, the U.S.-based Almont Corporation, still held a significant market share worldwide.

Almont had first introduced its Tomidil brand in the United States in 1970. After only two years, the product was being sold in 90 countries, capturing shares ranging between 42 and 90% in every market. Tomidil's fast market acceptance, considered by many as the most successful for a new drug, was due to its high efficacy as an ulcer treatment and its few side effects. The drug had cut the need for surgery in an estimated two-thirds of the cases. Pharma Swede also attributed Tomidil's success to centralized marketing, planning, and coordination worldwide; high marketing budgets; and focused promotion on opinion leaders in each country. Although Almont was not previously known for its products in the ulcer market and the company had little experience internationally, Tomidil's success helped Almont grow into a major international firm in the field.

In the opinion of Pharma Swede management, Tomidil's pricing followed a "skimming" strategy. It was initially set on a daily treatment cost basis of five times the average prices of antacids on the market. Over time, however, prices were reduced to a level three times those of antacids. After 1982, the prices were cut further to about two times those of antacids. In 1990, competing tablets containing ranitidine were priced, on average, 20% below Tomidil for an equivalent dosage. In that year, Tomidil's European share of drugs containing ranitidine was 43%.

Pharma Swede management did not consider antacids and anticholinergics as direct competitors because the former category gave only temporary relief, and the latter had serious potential side effects.

Gastirup's Sales Results

Gastirup's sales in Europe had reached $120 million by the end of 1989, or 7% of the ethical anti-ulcer market. (See Exhibit 6 for a breakdown of sales and shares in major European markets.)

PRICING OF GASTIRUP

Gastirup was premium priced. Its pricing followed the product's positioning as a preferred alternative to Tomidil and other ranitidine-containing tablets by improving the patient's quality of life and providing 24-hour protection in a single dosage. While competitive tablets had to be taken two or three times daily, the Gastirup tablet was needed only once a day. The risk of forgetting to take the medicine was thus reduced, as was the inconvenience of having to carry the drug around all the time. Because of these unique advantages, substantiated in a number of international clinical trials, management believed that using Gastirup ultimately resulted in faster treatment and reduced the need for surgery. Gastirup was priced to carry a significant premium over Tomidil prices in Europe. The margin over the generics was even higher. (See Exhibit 7 for current retail prices of Gastirup and Tomidil across Europe.)

Pharmaceutical Pricing in the EC

Drug pricing was a negotiated process in most of the EC. Each of the 12 member states had its own agency to regulate pharmaceutical prices for public insurance reimbursement schemes. From a government perspective, pharmaceuticals were to be priced in accordance with the benefits they provided. Although the pricing criteria most frequently cited were efficacy, product quality, safety, and patient comfort, European governments were putting increasing emphasis on "cost-effectiveness," or the relationship between price and therapeutic advantages. Among diverse criteria used by authorities, local production of a product was an important factor. As a result of individual country-specific pricing arrangements, there were inevitably widespread discrepancies in prices for the same product across Europe.

For new products, price negotiations with state agencies began after the drug was registered with the national health authorities. Negotiations could last for several years, eventually resulting in one of three outcomes: no price agreement, a partially reimbursed price, or a fully reimbursed price. In the event of no agreement, in most EC countries the company was free to introduce the drug and set the price, but the patient's cost for the product would not be covered by health insurance. In many EC countries, a drug that did not receive any reimbursement coverage was at a severe disadvantage. Partial or full reimbursement allowed the doctor to prescribe the drug without imposing the full cost on the patient. Any price adjustment for a product already on the market was subject to the same negotiation process.

Once agreement was reached on full or partial reimbursement, the product was put on a reimbursement scheme, also called a "positive list"—a list from which doctors could prescribe. Germany and the Netherlands were the two exceptions within the EC employing a "negative list"—a register containing only those drugs that the government would not reimburse. Drugs on the reimbursement list were often viewed by the medical profession as possibly better than nonreimbursed products. (See Exhibit 8 for a summary of price setting and reimbursement practices within the EC.)

Pricing Gastirup in Italy

Pharmaceutical pricing was particularly difficult in Italy. Health care costs represented 8% of the country's gross domestic product and one-third of the state budget for social expenditures. Government efforts to contain health care costs resulted in strict price controls and a tightly managed reimbursement scheme. Italy was considered by Pharma Swede management as a "cost-plus environment" where pricing was closely tied to the production cost of a drug rather than its therapeutic value.

In May 1982, Pharma Swede Italy submitted its first application for reimbursement of Gastirup . The submitted retail price was $33 per pack of ten 400-milligram tablets. On a daily treatment cost basis, Gastirup's proposed price of $3.30 compared with Tomidil's $1.35. Although priced 25% lower than the average EC price for Gastirup, Italian authorities denied the product admission to the positive list. They argued that Gastirup's therapeutic benefits, including its one-a-day feature, did not justify the large premium over the local price of Tomidil, which was already on the reimbursement scheme. Tomidil and another generic ranitidine-containing brand were produced locally, while Gastirup was to be manufactured in Sweden and only packed in Italy.

Despite the rejection by authorities, Pharma Swede chose to launch Gastirup in Italy without the reimbursement coverage. Management hoped to establish an early foothold in one of Europe's largest markets. Hence, early in 1983, Gastirup was introduced in Italy under the brand name Gastiros, at a retail price of $37 for a pack of 10 units. This price translated to a daily treatment cost of $3.70, or 16% below the EC average retail price of Gastirup and nearly three times that of Tomidil in Italy.

The response of the Italian market to Gastiros was better than management had expected. Following an intensive promotional campaign aimed at the general practitioners, sales reached $500,000 a month, or 2% of the market. Meanwhile, the number of requests for reimbursement received by the Italian health care authorities from patients and doctors was growing daily. Management believed that these requests were putting increased pressure on the authorities to admit the product to the positive list.

In a second round of negotiations, undertaken at the initiative of management nine months after the launch, Pharma Swede Italy reapplied for reimbursement status based on a price of $31 per pack of 10 units. This price represented a daily treatment cost of $3.10 and was 30% below the EC average. Once again the price was judged too high, and the request was rejected. In November 1984, management initiated a third round of negotiations, and in April 1985, Gastiros was granted full reimbursement status at $24 per pack, a price that had not changed since.

Gastirup's Italian sales and market share among H-2 inhibitors grew substantially following its inclusion in the reimbursement scheme. By 1989, factory sales had reached $27 million, representing a dollar share of 7% of the market. Gastirup was Pharma Swede Italy's single most important product, accounting for nearly a quarter of its sales.

In Italy, as in other countries, Pharma Swede distributed its products through drug wholesalers to pharmacies. Typical trade margin on resale price for pharmacies was 30%. Gastiros' factory price to wholesalers of $15 per pack of 10 tablets had a contribution margin of $3 for the Italian company, which paid its parent $1 for every 400-milligram tablet imported from Sweden. The transfer price was the same across Europe. In turn, the parent company earned $0.70 in contribution for every tablet exported to its local operations. The variable cost of producing the tablets included raw materials and the licensing fees paid to Anza.

LIFTING THE TRADE BARRIERS

As 1992 drew closer, Pharma Swede management believed that two important issues affecting the European pharmaceutical industry would be manufacturing location and drug pricing. In the past, many of the cost-constraint measures taken by authorities had, by design or coincidence, an element of protectionism and represented national trade barriers. For example, local authorities might refuse a certain price or reimbursement level unless the sponsoring company agreed to manufacture locally. Under current EC regulations, such actions were considered barriers to trade and were illegal.

As a countermeasure to such barriers, companies could take legal action against local agencies at the European Court of Justice. With the support of the European Federation of Pharmaceutical Industries Associations (EFPIA), drug firms could sue the agencies for violating the EC regulations. Although the EFPIA had won 12 cases over the preceding decade, litigation processes sometimes lasted up to seven years and the results were often partial and temporary in value. Nonetheless, industry participants were relieved that, after 1992, the element of local production linked to price negotiation would disappear.

Since December 1988, under a new EC regulation called the Transparency Directive, government pricing decisions were open to review by the pharmaceutical companies. The directive served to eliminate any interference with the free flow of pharmaceutical products within the community caused by price controls or reimbursement schemes. It required state agencies to explain how they set drug prices in general as well as in each case. If not satisfied, companies that believed they had been discriminated against could appeal a ruling on price, first to local courts, thereafter to the EC Commission, and, ultimately, to the European Court of Justice.

In addition, the new law required that agencies act quickly when a new drug was approved for sale or when a company asked for a price adjustment. On average, it had taken Pharma Swede one year to reach agreement on a price for a new product. Price adjustments for old products, on the other hand, had taken as long as two years because of delays by local authorities.

Another development related to the creation of a single European market was the expected harmonization in pharmaceutical prices and registration systems among member states. Bjorn Larsson and others in the industry believed that, across Europe, pharmaceutical price differences would narrow in a two-stage process: initially as a result of the transparency directive, and thereafter as part of a more comprehensive market harmonization. Bjorn thought that harmonization was a gradual process and that the completion of a single European market would occur between 1995 and 2000 at the earliest.

Aside from a narrowing of the differences in drug prices, possible outcomes for the post-1992 environment included a pan-European registration system and harmonized health insurance. Some observers predicted that a harmonized drug registration system would be put in place sometime between 1992 and 1995, although the exact form it might take remained open. Pharma Swede management believed it was unlikely that such a system would discriminate against non-EC firms. Harmonization of national health insurance systems, a longer-term consequence of 1992, was not expected before 1995. Industry analysts believed that, in the interim, the states would continue to press for cost containment on a national basis. Private pan-European insurance offerings, on the other hand, were expected to increase with deregulation and the completion of the internal market.

THE PROBLEM

Prior to 1992, Europe's parallel trade in pharmaceutical products had been limited to less than 5% of industry sales. Each country had local language packaging and registration requirements that tended to restrict or prohibit a product's acceptance and distribution in neighboring markets. Furthermore, according to some Pharma Swede managers, products produced in certain countries, such as Italy or France, suffered a poor quality image in other markets, such as Germany and England. National sentiments aside, distributors seeking to capitalize on parallel imports had to have approval from local authorities, which often implied repackaging to meet local requirements.

Where parallel imports had been a minor problem in the past, they posed a serious challenge to drug firms, including Pharma Swede, in the post-1992 environment when such trade would be protected by law. Hans Sahlberg, the company's product manager for gastrointestinal drugs, explained that government insurance agencies were already examining price and reimbursement issues on a Europeanwide basis. For drugs already on the market, it was only a matter of time before authorities reimbursed on the basis of the lowest priced parallel import. As an example, this implied that Gastirup, priced at $2.40 per tablet in Italy and $5.40 in Germany, would be reimbursed in Germany at the lower price of imports from Italy. If this proved true, West German revenue losses from Gastirup alone could amount to $17 million on current sales. Furthermore, if a system should emerge after 1992 mandating a single EC price, Pharma Swede would have to revamp its entire price-setting policy.

MANAGEMENT OPTIONS

With the upcoming changes in Europe, Gastirup's pricing discrepancies had become a source of major management concern. If not carefully managed, Bjorn and his colleagues believed that the company could lose money, reputation, or both. (See Exhibit 9 for relative prices of Gastirup in Europe.)

In looking for options to recommend to top management at headquarters and at the Italian operation, Bjorn and his staff developed four alternatives. The first, and the most extreme option, was to remove Gastirup from the Italian market completely and to concentrate sales elsewhere in Europe. This action would be in defense of prices in the more profitable markets. This alternative was not Bjorn's first choice, as it implied sales revenue losses of $27 million. It also went counter to Pharma Swede's policy of marketing all its products in every European country. Bjorn feared that such a move would lead to heated discussions between headquarters and local management in Italy. It could even seriously damage the company's public reputation. "How," asked Bjorn, "could Pharma Swede, an ethical drug company, deal with public opinion aroused by the apparently unethical practice of denying Gastirup to the Italian market?"

As another alternative, Bjorn could suggest removing Gastirup from the reimbursement scheme by raising prices to levels closer to the EC average. Such action would place Gastirup in the nonreimbursed drug status and lead to an estimated 80% loss in sales. Since the magnitude of this loss was nearly as great as in the first option, headquarters did not believe the Italian management would be any more receptive. Moreover, if Gastirup were removed from the reimbursement scheme, both the product and the company might lose credibility with the medical profession in Italy. According to Bjorn, many doctors perceived the drugs on the reimbursement list as "economical" and "really needed."

Nonetheless, shifting the drug to nonreimbursement status would shift the financing burden from the government to the patient, thus coinciding with the Italian government's view that patients should assume a greater financial role in managing their health. With an increased emphasis on cost containment, such a proposal was liable to appeal to Italian authorities. Bjorn expected full support for this proposal from managers in high-priced markets whose revenues were jeopardized by low-priced countries such as Italy.

There was, however, a possibility that changing the reimbursement status might backfire. Hans Sahlberg recalled a case in Denmark where, after removing a class of cough and cold drugs from reimbursement, Danish authorities came under pressure from a group of consumer advocates and were forced to reverse their decision. If Pharma Swede requested that Gastirup be removed from the Italian reimbursement scheme and the government were forced to reverse that position, the company's public image and its standing with local authorities might be damaged.

Still, a third option was to appeal to the European Commission and, if necessary, start legal action before the European Court of Justice. As Bjorn explained, the artificially regulated low drug prices in Italy placed higher-priced imported drugs at a disadvantage and, hence, acted as a barrier to the free movement of pharmaceutical products. Since the EFPIA had sued and won a similar case against Belgium, Bjorn believed that Pharma Swede might have a good case against the Italian government. But as much as Bjorn might want to pursue legal action, he recognized the risks inherent in using a legal mechanism with which Pharma Swede had no prior experience.

Headquarters management, on the other hand, looked favorably at this option, as it provided the opportunity to settle "once and for all" the conflict with the Italian government over pharmaceutical pricing. Local management, however, feared that any legal action would create resentment and sour the atmosphere of future negotiations. At any rate, legal action could take several years and might even jeopardize Gastiros' status in Italy as a reimbursed drug.

A fourth option entailed taking a "wait and see" attitude until the full effects of 1992 became better known. Bjorn explained that for the next two to three years, governments would continue to concentrate on price controls. After 1992, pressure for harmonization would reduce differences in drug prices, though it was impossible to project the direction the prices might take. As an estimate, the Product Pricing and Government Relations staff had calculated that uniform pricing translated to an EC-wide general decrease of 10% in drug prices, although prices in Italy would probably rise by about 15%. Thus, for the next few years, management at Pharma Swede could monitor the changes within the EC and prepare as carefully as possible to minimize any long-term price erosion. Bjorn felt this option argued for vigilance and "having all your ammunition ready." But he was not sure what specific preparatory actions were called for.

CONCLUSION

With the integration of Europe in sight, top management was deeply concerned about the impact that the changing regulatory environment might have on Pharma Swede's operations. Gastirup was the first product to feel the effects of harmonization, but it would not be the last. A decision on Gastirup could set the pace for the other products. In evaluating the alternative courses of action for Gastirup, Bjorn had to consider their likely impact on several stakeholders, including the country management in Italy, the management in high-priced countries and at headquarters, the Italian and EC authorities, and the medical profession at large. Bjorn was not sure if any course of action could possibly satisfy all the parties concerned. He wondered what criteria should guide his proposal to the company president, who was expecting his recommendations soon.

EXHIBIT 1 Pharma Swede Sales (in $ millions)

Product line	1987	1988	1989
Hormones	90	130	150
Vitamins	175	205	225
Gastrointestinal	200	290	375
Total	465	625	750

EXHIBIT 2 Partial Organization Chart

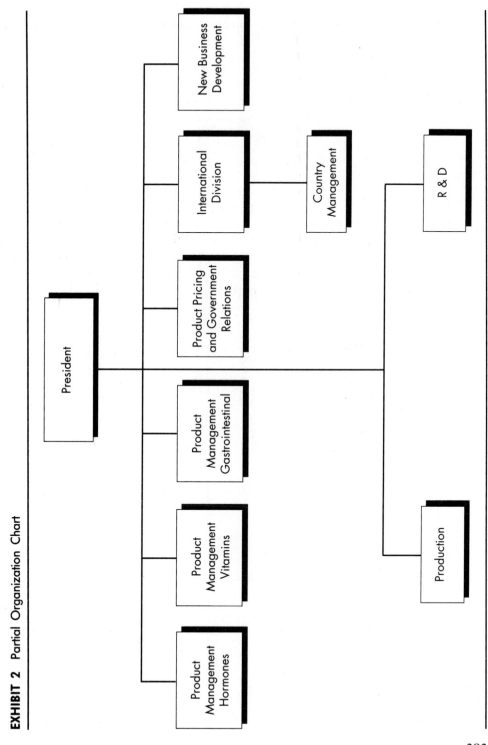

EXHIBIT 3 The Development of a New Drug

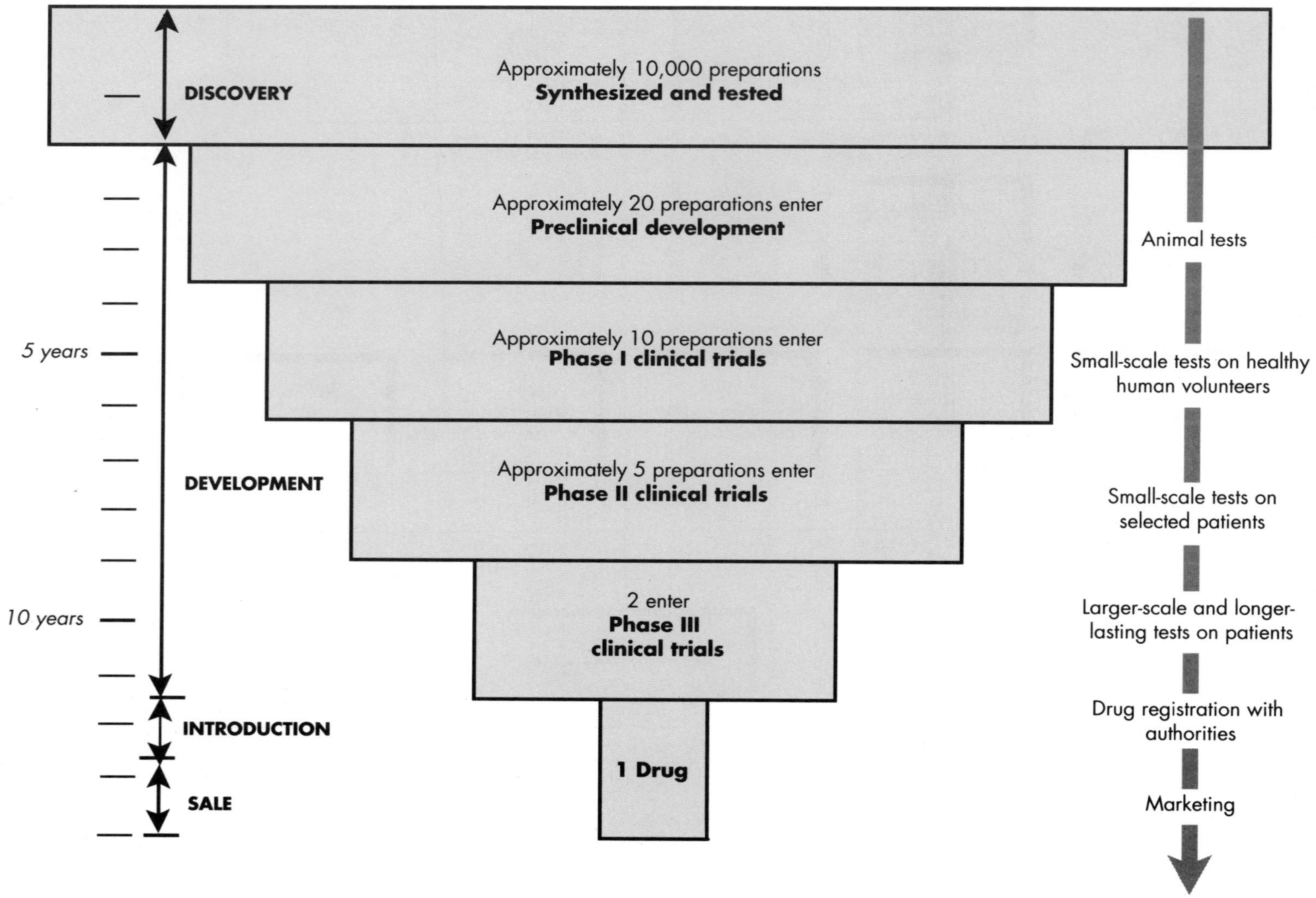

Animal tests

Small-scale tests on healthy human volunteers

Small-scale tests on selected patients

Larger-scale and longer-lasting tests on patients

Drug registration with authorities

Marketing

Approximately 10,000 preparations **Synthesized and tested**

Approximately 20 preparations enter **Preclinical development**

Approximately 10 preparations enter **Phase I clinical trials**

Approximately 5 preparations enter **Phase II clinical trials**

2 enter **Phase III clinical trials**

1 Drug

DISCOVERY

DEVELOPMENT

INTRODUCTION

SALE

5 years

10 years

EXHIBIT 4   Product Pricing and Government Relations Department

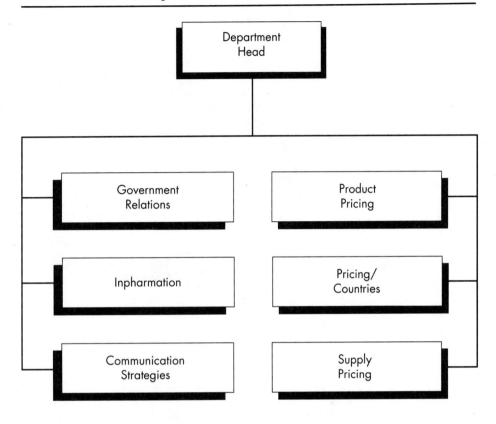

The Government Relations Group observed and recognized potential political problems for the division. When necessary, the group developed counterstrategies and oversaw their implementation.

During drug development, the Product Pricing Group worked to secure drug registration, using economic and social data.

Inpharmation gathered and managed all pharmapolitical information, on both a national and international basis.

Pricing/Countries oversaw and helped build a favorable negotiating environment for pricing decisions.

The Communication Strategies Group advised the division on product strategies and proposed communications programs.

Supply Pricing was responsible for administering prices and managing relationships with Pharma Swede's distributors.

Source: Company records.

EXHIBIT 5 The Oral Osmotic Delivery System

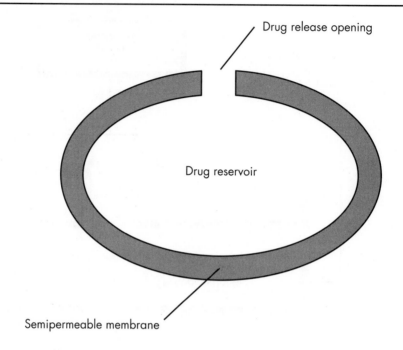

Drug release opening

Drug reservoir

Semipermeable membrane

Although OROS looked like a normal tablet, the system used osmotic pressure as a source of energy for the controlled release of active substance. Water, present throughout the body, passed through the semipermeable membrane as long as the reservoir contained undissolved substances. An increase in reservoir pressure, caused by the influx of water, was relieved by releasing drug solution through the opening. Up to 80% of the drug was released at a constant rate; the remainder, at a correspondingly declining rate. To guarantee the accuracy of the system, the opening had to comply with strict specifications. Hence, a laser was used to bore a hole through the membrane, in such a way that only membrane was removed, without damaging the reservoir.

Source: Company records.

EXHIBIT 6 Sales and Market Shares in Major European Markets (1989 sales in $ million)

Countries	Total market[a] (100%)	Gastirup (% share)	Tomidil (% share)	Others[b] (% share)
Belgium	41	2 (5%)	16 (39%)	23 (56%)
France	198	15 (8%)	61 (31%)	122 (61%)
Germany	318	30 (9%)	51 (16%)	237 (75%)
Italy	394	27 (7%)	110 (28%)	257 (65%)
Netherlands	81	8 (10%)	25 (31%)	48 (59%)
Spain	124	5 (4%)	11 (9%)	108 (87%)
Sweden	34	10 (29%)	5 (15%)	19 (56%)
United Kingdom	335	18 (5%)	97 (29%)	220 (66%)
All Europe	1,620	120 (7%)	486 (30%)	1,014 (63%)

[a]All ethical anti-ulcer remedies
[b]Includes branded and generic drugs

EXHIBIT 7 Retail Prices in Europe: 1989 Daily Treatment Cost

Countries	Gastirup ($)	Tomidil ($)	Gastirup/ Tomidil(%)
Belgium	3.86	2.47	+56
Denmark	5.96	3.94	+51
France	3.69	2.12	+74
Germany	5.31	3.54	+50
Greece	3.43	2.36	+45
Italy	2.40	1.35	+78
Netherlands	5.66	3.11	+82
Portugal	3.13	2.24	+40
Spain	4.03	2.82	+43
Sweden*	5.91	4.22	+40
United Kingdom	5.40	3.10	+74

*Not a member of the EC.

EXHIBIT 8 Price Setting and Reimbursement in the EC

Countries	Price setting	Reimbursement

Ireland	No price control for new introductions.	Positive list (prescription recommended)
		Inclusion criteria:
		   efficacy/safety profile
		   cost-effectiveness profile

	Prices of prescription drugs are controlled through PPRS (Pharmaceutical Price Regulation Scheme).
	Control is exercised through regulation of profit levels.
		Positive list for NHS prescriptions (National Health Service)
		Inclusion criteria:
		   therapeutic value
		   medical need

Belgium	Price control by the Ministry of Health on the basis of cost structure.	Positive list (Ministry of Health)
		Inclusion criteria:
		   therapeutic and social interest
		   duration of treatment
		   daily treatment costs
		   substitution possibilities
		   price comparison with similar drugs
		Co-payment: 4 categories (100%, 75%, 50%, 40%)

Greece	Price control by the Ministry of Health based on cost structure (support of local industry appears to be of importance).	Positive list (IKA, Social Security Ministry).

Portugal	Price and reimbursement negotiations with the Ministry of Health and Commerce based on:
	   local prices
	   lowest European prices
	   therapeutic value
	   cost-effectiveness
		Positive list
		Inclusion criteria:
		   therapeutic value
		   international price comparison
		   cost-effectiveness

Spain	Price control based on cost structure.	Positive list (Social Security system)
		Inclusion criteria:
		   efficacy/safety profile
		   cost-effectiveness

France	No control for nonreimbursable products.
	Price negotiations with the Ministry of Health for reimbursed products.
		Positive list (Transparence Commission and Directorate of Pharmacy and Pharmaceuticals, within the Ministry of Health)
		Inclusion criteria:
		   price
		   therapeutic value
		   potential market in France
		   local R&D
		Co-payment: 4 categories:
		   nonreimbursable
		   40% of retail price
		   70% of retail price
		   100% of retail price

(continued)

EXHIBIT 8 (continued)

Countries	Price setting	Reimbursement

Luxembourg	Price control by the Ministry of Health. Prices must not be higher than in the country of origin.	Positive list
		Inclusion criteria:
		   therapeutic value
		   cost-effectiveness

Italy	Price control for reimbursed drugs by CIP (Interministerial Price Committee), following guidelines of CIPE (Interministerial Committee for Economic Planning) based on cost structure.	Positive list (Prontuario Terapeutico Nazionale) National Health Council Reimbursement criteria: therapeutic efficacy and cost-effectiveness innovation, risk-benefit ratio and local research also considered.

West Germany	No direct price control by authorities.	Negative list. Reference price system since January 1989.
		Principles:
		   Drugs will be reimbursed only up to a reference price.
		   Patient pays the difference between the reference and retail prices.
		Co-payment: DM 3 per prescribed product (1992: 15% of drug bill)

Netherlands	No price control by authorities.	Negative list. Reference price system since January 1988.

Denmark	Price control based on:
	   cost structure
	   "reasonable" profits
		Positive list
		Inclusion criteria:
		   efficacy/safety profile
		   cost-effectiveness profile

EXHIBIT 9 Relative Retail Prices of Gastirup

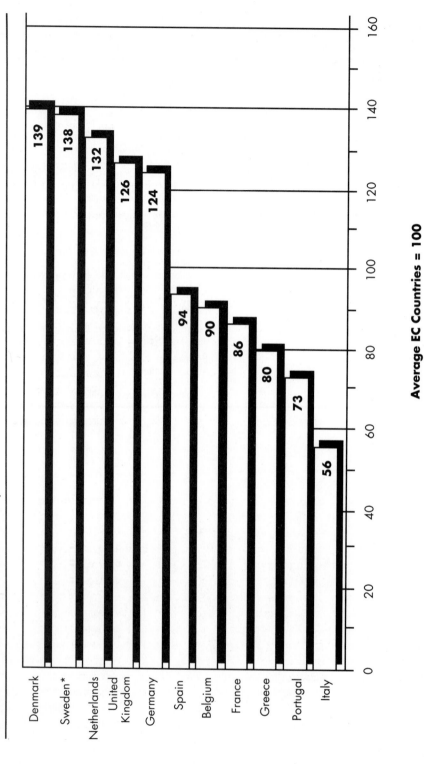

Denmark — 139
Sweden* — 138
Netherlands — 132
United Kingdom — 126
Germany — 124
Spain — 94
Belgium — 90
France — 86
Greece — 80
Portugal — 73
Italy — 56

Average EC Countries = 100

* Not a member of EC

15 PHILIP MORRIS KK

On January 7, 1988, Leonard D. Spelt, marketing manager of Philip Morris KK (PMKK), had gathered his marketing team at the PMKK headquarters in Tokyo to discuss the recent decision of competitor R. J. Reynolds to introduce a ¥200[1] cigarette brand in the Japanese market. After having reviewed and discussed all the options available, Spelt had returned to his office to ponder the alternatives that had surfaced during one of the most exhausting meetings he had ever had in Tokyo.

COMPANY BACKGROUND

Based in New York City, Philip Morris Companies Inc. was the largest and most diversified tobacco, food, and beverage company in the United States and one of the three largest in the world. With an operating income of $4.2 billion out of operating revenues of $27.6 billion for fiscal year 1987 (see Exhibit 1), Philip Morris Companies Inc. was ranked 10th in size among the U.S. Fortune 500 industrials.

Since its early days in 1847, when Philip Morris, Esq. first opened a tobacco shop on Bond Street in London, Philip Morris' core business had focused on the tobacco industry. In 1902, Philip Morris & Co. Ltd. was incorporated in the United States (in New York) by Gustav Eckmeyer, Philip Morris' sole agent for importing and selling the English-made cigarettes in the United States since 1872. In 1919, a new firm owned by American shareholders acquired the U.S. Philip Morris Company and incorporated it in Virginia under the name Philip Morris & Co. Ltd., Inc., which in turn became Philip Morris Incorporated in 1955.

The present organization had been set up in 1985 when the corporate framework of Philip Morris Incorporated was restructured to form Philip Morris Companies Inc., a holding company located in New York City. In 1988, Philip Morris Companies Inc. was still concentrating mainly on the tobacco industry. The two core companies, Philip Morris USA and Philip Morris International, were

This case was written by Professor Dominique Turpin. Copyright © 1989 by the International Institute for Management Development (IMD), Lausanne, Switzerland. Not to be used or reproduced without permission.
1. Average exchange rate in 1987, ¥145 = $1.00.

accounting for 27% and 25%, respectively, of Philip Morris Companies Inc.'s total operating revenues in 1987. In the 1980s, Philip Morris Companies Inc. also made major diversification moves into the food industry by acquiring Oscar Mayer in 1981 and then General Foods Corporation in November 1985. In 1970, Philip Morris Companies Inc. had also acquired the world's second-largest brewer, the Miller Brewing Company, which currently accounted for 10% of total operating revenues (see Exhibit 2). Financial services and real estate were the fourth major business activity of Philip Morris Companies Inc., representing 2% of total operating revenues.

Several of Philip Morris' cigarette brands, such as Marlboro, were among the most popular in the world. Originally introduced in 1924 as an unfiltered cigarette, Marlboro had rapidly become Philip Morris' flagship cigarette brand after being repositioned in 1955 as a full-flavored cigarette for men. Supported by the first Marlboro cowboy advertising campaign, its red and white package soon became familiar. In 1987, despite a decline in the total consumption of cigarettes in the American market, Marlboro had gained market share in the United States for the 23d consecutive year to approach a 25% share of the U.S. cigarette market. Worldwide, Marlboro also continued to be the best-selling cigarette brand since 1971.

The success of leading full-priced brands—for example, Benson & Hedges, Merit, Virginia Slims, Parliament, Lark, Chesterfield, and Philip Morris—also reinforced Philip Morris' leading position in the world tobacco industry. Philip Morris International's products were sold in more than 160 countries around the world. In free competition markets,[2] Philip Morris International enjoyed leading market share. For example, in the European Community (EC), Philip Morris' aggregate market share for tobacco exceeded 20%.

Developing established brands and introducing new ones had traditionally been Philip Morris Companies Inc.'s strategy for increasing volume and market share worldwide. In particular, Philip Morris International had seen great potential in Asia, where lowered trade barriers in several markets had recently allowed Philip Morris brands to compete more effectively with products marketed by local government monopolies. Since Philip Morris' share in most international cigarette markets was far below its U.S. level, Philip Morris executives believed there was considerable room for future growth in this part of the world.

PHILIP MORRIS KK

Philip Morris had been present in Japan since the early 1950s, using Mitsui & Co., the trading company of the giant Mitsui Group, as the agent for importing its cigarettes into Japan. Its competitor, R. J. Reynolds, had designated Mitsubishi Corporation, the trading company of the Mitsubishi Group, as its import agent. In Japan, the products of Philip Morris' diversified businesses, like General Foods and

---

2. Markets without state monopolies.

Miller, were managed separately from PMKK through joint ventures with local companies.

As tobacco in Japan was a government monopoly until 1985, Mitsui & Co. was basically handling Philip Morris cigarettes on behalf of the monopoly corporation. In the late 1970s, Philip Morris entered into an association with Nissho Iwai, another large Japanese trading company, when Nissho Iwai acquired the distributorship for Liggett & Myers Tobacco Co. in Japan. Liggett & Myers was an independent American tobacco company, producing the cigarette brands Lark, L&M, and Eve. In the early 1970s, Philip Morris had acquired the rights to produce and distribute Liggett & Myers' products outside the United States. Following Nissho Iwai's acquisition of Liggett & Myers' distributorship in Japan, Philip Morris KK (PMKK) renegotiated the distribution of all its tobacco products with Mitsui & Co. and Nissho Iwai. As a result of the new agreement, Mitsui & Co. became the exclusive distributor of all PMKK's brands in eastern Japan, and Nissho Iwai became PMKK's sole distributor in the western part of Japan. With the liberalization of the Japanese tobacco industry in 1985, PMKK was established as a wholly owned subsidiary of Philip Morris Companies Inc.

PMKK developed all of Philip Morris' marketing activities in Japan. PMKK's tasks also included initiating and coordinating product development and production of cigarettes with the United States. Jack Howard, vice president of PMKK, expected to continue importing Philip Morris products as long as the parameters for the cigarette industry in Japan remained as they presently were. More than ever in 1988, production costs for the tobacco industry in Japan were higher than those in the United States. Moreover, since the manufacture of cigarettes in Japan was still the monopoly of Japan Tobacco Inc. (JTI), PMKK did not plan to consider manufacturing locally in the near future.

At this stage in the company's development, PMKK's objective was to grow as fast as possible by offering consumer products of the highest quality and maintaining a good balance between market share and profitability. A major objective for PMKK was also to retain and expand its dominant share in the fast-growing imported segment. In terms of product diversification, Jack Howard believed that "this had to be put into context gradually." Howard said:

> We want to build a good durable image for franchises which we can then expand over time. Therefore, we want to concentrate on a few good franchises that can be developed. Obviously, there will be new franchises coming on the market, and each of the existing franchises can also be expanded. Lark is a good example of franchise diversification. We now have this brand in various formats and sizes, which were introduced into the market over time.

THE TOBACCO INDUSTRY

In 1988, the world tobacco industry (90% cigarettes) included free markets (e.g., West Germany, the Netherlands, England, and some developing countries); state monopolies (e.g., Austria, Spain, and most socialist countries); and officially free markets, where customs or administrative regulations limited access to foreign products (e.g., the United States, Canada, France, and South Africa). The majority of cigarette consumption (60%) occurred in the free world, with the Communist countries accounting for the other 40%. The world's leading four tobacco producers were China (960 billion units), the United States (682 billion units), the USSR (380 billion units), and Japan (320 billion units). During the last 20 years, the world tobacco industry had doubled; the 1988 volume was estimated at 5.2 trillion units.

The international market had gradually become an oligopoly. Five major companies—Philip Morris, Brown & Williamson (an affiliate of British American Tobacco Co.), R. J. Reynolds, American Tobacco Co., and Rothman International (also known as Tobacco Exporters International or TEI)—represented 80% of total free market sales volume (see Exhibit 3). With more than a decade of external pressure from antismoking campaigns and internal pressure for growth, the six largest multinational companies had become increasingly diversified, moving into paper, food and beverages, cosmetics, packaging, financial services, real estate, and so forth.

THE JAPANESE TOBACCO MARKET

Japan was the second-largest tobacco market in the non-Communist world; in 1987, 308 billion cigarettes at a total retail value of ¥3 trillion were sold (a decline of 6% in volume and 20.5% in value over the previous fiscal year). Although smoking was declining among Japanese adult males,[3] the 62.5% rate of smokers was among the highest in the developed world. As S. Katayama, a PMKK group brand manager, explained:

> Japan offers great opportunities for international tobacco companies. Not only will no one tell you to put out your cigarette at a bar or restaurant, but the practice of keeping a cigarette box and matching table lighter in the meeting rooms of many Japanese companies is a tradition still being maintained.

Among females, only 12.5% claimed to be smokers. Experts, however, believed the figure was much higher, as many female smokers were reluctant to admit to public researchers that they smoked.

The Japanese cigarette market, just as in Europe or in the United States, was experiencing growth in flue-cured tobacco products and a decline in the dark tobacco sector. Flue-cured tobacco was a bright yellow tobacco to which flavoring ingredients were added to create distinctive aromas. Flue-cured tobaccos could be divided into several types; among the blond tobacco variety American blended and straight Virginia were the most common. Most cigarettes sold in the United States and Europe were the American blended variety. However, in the United Kingdom and in most Commonwealth countries, the straight Virginia tobacco products were overwhelmingly the most popular. The Japanese consumer's taste was somewhere

---

3. Over 20 years old.

between these two varieties. The really distinctive feature of Japanese cigarettes, however, was the traditional charcoal filter imposed over time by the Japan Tobacco Inc. monopoly. These charcoal filters were made of tiny, porous charcoal spheres that reduced the tar and nicotine while giving a smoother taste and aroma.

Until recently, international tobacco firms had traditionally commanded only a marginal share of the Japanese market. Despite a 1972 license agreement with Japan Tobacco and Salt Public Corporation (JTS) to manufacture Marlboro cigarettes, Philip Morris had never achieved in Japan the significant size that it had typically enjoyed in free markets. High import duties (up to 350% in 1978) and the government monopoly had meant that Japan was practically a closed market for foreign tobacco manufacturers.

Before the market was liberalized in the early 1980s, PMKK had been confronted by a number of tariff and nontariff barriers. Jack Howard had found that restricting the distribution of cigarette products to a given number of retailers had seriously limited the potential of PMKK's business. He also believed that the high duties imposed on imported cigarettes had forced PMKK to increase its prices to the point of being priced out of most of the market, as the Japanese consumer was not willing to buy a given product at any price.

Under pressure from the United States since 1978 to accelerate the opening of its market, Japan had started in the early 1980s to revamp its tobacco industry. In April 1985, JTS' monopoly was removed and, as a private company, became Japan Tobacco Inc. (JTI). As part of the Japanese program to liberalize the tobacco market, retailers were allowed to handle tobacco imports and to receive the same 10% margin on imported as on domestically made cigarettes. Moreover, import duties had been eliminated by April 1987, and promotional activities, including advertising, were being permitted up to a limit of 6,300 GRPs[4] per brand family for TV advertising. As a result, international tobacco firms saw their sales jump two and a half times to 32 billion cigarettes in 1987 and their market share grow from 2.0% in 1984 to as high as 8.4% in a mere three years (see Exhibit 4).

The rapid success of international tobacco companies in Japan could be explained by their careful consideration of the Japanese market. Most sales representatives used by the trading companies to distribute foreign tobacco products in Japan were being paid by the international tobacco companies. By listening to advice from their sales force, foreign producers were able to develop products especially tailored for the Japanese market. For example, Winston and Camel brands did not have a charcoal filter in the United States, but they did in Japan. The nicotine and tar content of Kent Mild and Philip Morris Lights were kept at the same level as in Mild Seven Lights, the competing domestic brand. Another part of the foreign companies' strategy had been to keep the retail margin on foreign cigarettes higher than on Japanese cigarettes. Although retail margins were set at 10% of the retail price, the higher price of foreign cigarettes enabled retailers to receive a higher contribution. In S. Katayama's opinion, this was one reason that foreign cigarettes

---

4. GRP (gross rating point) equaled the sum of all airings of a program or spot announcement during a given time period. For example, a once-a-week program constantly recording a 15% rating (15% of TV homes) received 60 GRPs for a four-week period.

had become more competitive at the distribution stage. Moreover, Katayama believed that foreign cigarettes had a "high-class" image among Japanese consumers. He believed that this image, coupled with good marketing and large advertising expenditures, was the key success factor that had helped foreign tobacco firms gain a quick share of the Japanese market.

Japan Tobacco Inc.

After the privatization of JTI in April 1985, the presidency of JTI was assumed by Minoru Nagaoka, a former vice minister in the Ministry of Finance (the most powerful position in Japan's public administration). In December 1987, JTI's sales were predicted to drop 2.3% for the previous term (ending March 31, 1988) to ¥2,875 trillion, and current profits were expected to dip sharply by 20% to ¥85 billion. "Japan Tobacco is following a rocky path," President Nagaoka stated.

In response to this situation, JTI had mobilized its 2,700 sales personnel in a desperate attempt to fight back. The company had recently increased its advertising budget from 13% of sales to 20.5%, comparable to the 20% on sales without excise taxes expended on average by most international competitors. During 1986–1987, JTI had also introduced 30 new products, compared with 27 during the preceding five-year period. As a result, Japanese consumers were able to watch TV commercials that showed a female revue at the Crazy Horse in Paris, where the dancers used their legs to spell out the letters LIBERA, one of the company's newest brands. Another commercial depicted happy American college students on campus, smoking JTI's Mild Seven FK cigarettes. JTI had also changed its marketing strategy by focusing less on traditional "mom and pop" shops and more on large national retailers.

JTI's major handicap in competing with foreign brands was that it had to use a domestic tobacco leaf that cost three to five times more than an imported leaf. JTI was required by law to purchase Japan's entire domestic production of tobacco (¥200 billion in fiscal year 1986). Since the same amount of imported tobacco would cost only ¥70 billion, JTI was spending an extra ¥130 billion a year to abide by a political decision made by the Japanese government to protect domestic farmers. JTI was permitted to import roughly one-third of its tobacco from abroad. The imported tobacco was subsequently blended with domestic tobacco.

Ever since the tobacco industry monopoly had been eliminated in Japan, JTI's share of market had steadily declined. However, Kazue Obata, special adviser in the marketing and planning section of JTI, had predicted in a recent press interview that Japan would not experience a serious penetration of foreign tobacco, as had happened in France or Italy, where international tobacco firms had gained shares of 40% and 30%, respectively. Obata argued that Japanese employees were striving for higher sales and were not like the Italians and French who "had no loyalty." He also maintained that JTI's experience with Philip Morris' Marlboro brand had taught the company much about American blend tobacco. "We know the market intimately," he said.

In the meantime, Philip Morris had been able to maintain its share at around 60% of the total imported foreign tobacco market. At the end of 1987, JTI still commanded 91% of the cigarette market; PMKK was a distant second, with a 5.2% share of market (see Exhibit 5). Although JTI's market share was still comfortably large, some industry analysts believed that JTI would be under pressure to close one of its 32 factories whenever it lost two points of market share to the competition. However, Leo Spelt felt that the relationship between the loss of market share and the closing of factories was much more complex than that.

Other Competitors

With JTI as the dominant manufacturer and distributor of cigarettes in Japan, competition in the imported markets clearly came from the other major international tobacco manufacturers: Brown & Williamson (B&W), R. J. Reynolds (RJR), American Tobacco Company, and Tobacco Exporters International (TEI). At the end of 1987, these four groups, together with Philip Morris, commanded 99% of the imported cigarette segment in Japan. In the imported brands market, PMKK commanded a 62% market share of this segment by the end of 1987, followed by B&W and RJR, with a 25% and 9% market share, respectively (see Exhibit 4).

The three largest international competitors—Philip Morris, B&W, and RJR—were competing mainly in the ¥220 or ¥250 segments with some of their traditional international brands: Kent, Lucky Strike, and John Player Special (JPS) for B&W; Salem, Camel, Winston, and More for RJR. JTI, on the other hand, had a broader product line, with one brand in the ¥200 segment (Hi-Lite) and one in the ¥130 segment (Echo). (See Exhibits 6–8.)

Distribution of Cigarettes in Japan

The distribution of cigarettes in Japan remained almost unchanged after the monopoly was lifted from the Japanese market. Unlike U.S. distributors, distributors in Japan were not easily chosen, and all shops selling tobacco had to be licensed. Moreover, supermarkets could not use tobacco as a specialty product for big sales, offering a lower price than usual. Haiso, the company associated with JTI for distribution of tobacco in Japan, continued to distribute PMKK's products to the retailers through five regional operating companies. These wholesaling companies were in turn serving a total of 260,755 licensed retailers. Stores selling only tobacco, as well as liquor and grocery stores, each represented roughly 14% of total retail cigarette sales in Japan.

A major characteristic of the Japanese tobacco market was the importance of vending machines. In 1987, there were more than 1.6 million vending machines installed along Japanese streets (more than one machine for every 100 inhabitants), distributing almost everything from canned coffee, beer, and whiskey to batteries, newspapers and magazines, and even Bibles. The 428,000 vending machines installed in restaurants, bars, and so forth, as well as the ones along the streets, were used exclusively to distribute cigarettes. They accounted for 40% of all cigarettes sold in Japan. Typically, vending machines were owned by retailers (tobacco and/or liquor stores, restaurants, hotels, newsstands, etc.), although manufacturers also leased or gave away some machines.

Each cigarette vending machine had 6 to 25 columns. Typically, retailers would arrange the cigarettes in the columns according to brand popularity. Generally, a retailer with a 12-column machine would place the 12 best-selling brands in the 12 columns. Since JTI dominated the cigarette market, distributors for foreign manufacturers had to convince retailers to allocate enough columns to them for their respective brands. Given the frequent difficulties in gaining adequate space, some distributors would buy columns by offering free products or financial incentives to major tobacco retailers.

In addition to importing, Mitsui & Co. and Nissho Iwai employed a sales merchandising force of slightly over 500 people whose function was to merchandise PMKK's products at the retail level. In other words, Haiso acted only as a distributor, and Nissho Iwai, Mitsui & Co., and PMKK acted as partners in marketing, advertising, and merchandising. Competitors had a similar sales force, ranging from 2,700 sales representatives for JTI to 200 sales reps each for B&W and RJR.

PMKK'S PRODUCT LINE

The Japanese cigarette market could be segmented in many different ways (sex, imported versus domestic brands, cigarette lengths, etc.). PMKK, however, relied primarily on two major dimensions: price and flavor (i.e., tar and nicotine content). (See Exhibits 9–11 for marketing information.)

In January 1988, PMKK was distributing three major brands. For many years, Lark had been PMKK's best-selling brand (Exhibit 12). To meet smokers' changing tastes, PMKK had progressively extended the Lark line, adding Lark Milds KS (King Size), Lark Milds 100's, and Lark Super Lights. Lark Milds KS was now the best-selling imported brand in Japan. At the end of 1987, the Lark family represented 56% of PMKK's cigarette sales in Japan, and PM, PMKK's second best-selling brand, accounted for another 24%. Parliament represented 11% of PMKK's share of sales volume. The Marlboro family was produced under license by JTI, but it did not account for a significant share of the Japanese market (see Exhibit 13).

Despite PMKK's success with light and mild cigarettes in Japan, Philip Morris had never introduced any new product in the ¥200 segment. Moreover, the 5% share of the Japanese market gained by Hi-Lite, the only brand in this price segment (launched by JTI), was declining (see Exhibit 13). In addition, with the new year approaching, there was little time for the PMKK marketing team to investigate the overall implications of the new ¥200 segment.

The RJR Challenge

Through retailers, PMKK first heard rumors in the middle of November 1987 about a new brand introduction by RJR, but not until December 15, 1987, did Leo Spelt receive confirmation of RJR's decision to introduce Islands Lights in Japan at ¥200 as of February 1, 1988. Immediately, PMKK's marketing department decided to evaluate possible alternatives to counter the RJR initiative. That same day, a time schedule was made for potential development of a new product, including packaging, research, and commercial production. PMKK executives were not familiar with RJR's Islands Lights brand, since this brand had never been introduced in the United States or in any other market. It seemed, therefore, that Islands Lights was either a code name for an existing RJR brand or a completely new brand tailored for the Japanese market.

Because of the adjective "Lights," Spelt and PMKK brand managers assumed that Islands Lights would be positioned in the low-tar segment in Japan to compete with other light and mild cigarette brands. (Tobacco manufacturers were using either the adjective "light" or "mild" to label low-tar cigarettes, but no particular definition had been attached to either word.) In Japan, as in other industrialized markets, the low-tar segment had been growing more rapidly than other segments, as smokers increasingly considered high-tar cigarettes less healthy.

In 1987, the low-tar segment accounted for 34% of the total cigarette market in Japan. By comparison, the full-flavor (16 mg +) and the medium-tar (11.1 – 16 mg) segments, representing 15% and 51% of the market, respectively, were slowly declining 1 to 2% a year. The ultra low-tar segment (below 6 mg) was quite stable, with 0.10% of the cigarette market in Japan (see Exhibit 11).

After having received confirmation of RJR's decision to introduce Islands Lights in Japan, Spelt and the other marketing executives had tried to determine RJR's motivations and the objectives of its strategic move into the ¥200 segment. In Spelt's view, RJR had been less successful than other international tobacco firms in the Japanese market. Its Camel brand, launched in 1983 by RJR Japan, had never achieved a significant market share in Japan. Moreover, in 1987 its Winston Lights brand had been ruined overnight by a report from Japanese authorities that Winston Lights contained traces of an herbicide. This instant blow to RJR meant that Salem, a menthol cigarette, was that company's only successful brand in Japan.

Spelt had almost no information on how much RJR would spend on advertising and promotion to launch Islands Lights, but judging from his own experience in Japan, he estimated that the launch would require about $20 million, with a potential payback period of two to three years (quite short by industry standards; over five years is typical).

The Alternatives

During their meeting with Spelt, members of the marketing team had outlined the various alternatives for PMKK:

1. *Join forces with JTI.* Since RJR's launch of Islands Lights on February 1, 1988, had been confirmed, various options had been reviewed. George R. Austin, president of PMKK, had considered meeting with K. Katsukawa from JTI to discuss the ¥200 issue as well as a possible import licensing agreement for Philip Morris' L&M Milds brand. This idea had been triggered by PMKK's reluctance to compete directly with RJR in a price segment that meant smaller margins. Moreover, to dis-

tribute a new ¥200 segment in vending machines would mean convincing the owners either to grant Philip Morris one additional column in their machines or to have Philip Morris lose a column containing a more expensive, higher contribution brand.

2. *License L&M Milds to JTI.* L&M Milds, which belonged to Philip Morris through its agreement with Liggett & Myers (an independent American tobacco manufacturer), was one brand being considered for licensing to JTI as part of PMKK's countermove against the RJR initiative. Philip Morris International had introduced L&M in West Germany, where it had achieved a market share of 1.3% in 1987. In the United States, L&M's share under Liggett & Myers in this same year was 0.3%.

George R. Austin was not sure how JTI would respond to his proposal, since two obstacles had to be overcome. First, producing L&M Milds under license would force JTI to import more American tobacco leaves, which would mean having to renegotiate its import policy with the Japanese authorities. Second, JTI management would also have to negotiate for the support of JTI labor union leaders, who had a strong voice in JTI. Austin had proposed that JTI equally share the costs of launching this new brand by having PMKK handle all advertising and promotional costs. George Austin believed that this licensing agreement could benefit both JTI and PMKK by providing an estimated additional $1 million per month to JTI and a break-even position for PMKK.

If JTI were to decline Austin's offer, PMKK could possibly launch a new brand alone. However, this new product would have to be imported from the United States with the technical modifications necessary to meet the tastes of Japanese consumers.

3. *Launch L&M Milds in Japan, replicating a launch in West Germany.* Philip Morris had launched L&M in West Germany in 1982, following a competitive move in 1980 from Reemtsma, a local tobacco manufacturer. Until the end of the 1970s and the early 1980s, Reemtsma had been the leader in the German cigarette industry. Then the company steadily began losing market share. One of its brands, Ernte, was seriously affected by competition from Marlboro. German discount chains, locked into heavy competition among themselves, had added generic brands of cigarettes to their product lines. These generics were being marketed about 25% below the prevailing price level for nationally advertised brands, which were retailing from DM 3.80 to DM 4.00.[5] To counter this market trend, Reemtsma launched a new brand named "West" in 1980. The advertising and packaging were clearly aimed at the market for Marlboro cigarettes. However, despite an expenditure of DM 150 million, the West brand had captured only 0.4% share of the market by the end of 1982. After losing that battle, Reemtsma decided to cut the price of its West brand even more, from DM 3.80 to DM 3.30. This time, West's market share grew rapidly, reaching 5% within a three-month period.

Philip Morris Germany followed West's dramatic increase with concern, since it definitely affected Philip Morris' leading brands. The company chose L&M because

5. In 1982, U.S. $1 = DM 1.8.

all the other brands in the German market were either too small or too narrow in appeal. At only DM 3.00 for a pack of 19 cigarettes, L&M was the lowest priced national brand on the market. It was advertised as an international brand and was supported with readily available media. In order to enhance the brand's image, only box packs were used. L&M was first introduced in the southern part of Germany, where it rapidly achieved a 15% market share, thus becoming the second best-selling brand after Marlboro. L&M was later launched in the northern part of Germany.

By mid-1983, other major cigarette marketers had also reacted. L&M was no longer the only low-priced brand on the market. All major brands had lost market share to new low-priced competitors that had appeared everywhere. When one major competitor rolled back its prices from DM 3.80 to DM 3.50 for its leading brand, others, including Philip Morris, followed. L&M and other low-priced brands lost appeal, and consumers switched back to national brands. In 1987, L&M had 1.3% of the German market, a 0.2% loss over the previous year. In 1987, leading brands, including Philip Morris' Marlboro, regained their dominant positions, and price levels stabilized. At the end of the German cigarette war, Philip Morris had regained its former competitive position, albeit at a somewhat lower price level than before. The overall cost of launching L&M was $10 million.

While reflecting again on the German episode, Spelt believed that the German price war and its successive price cuts had had major financial repercussions for Philip Morris in Germany. In Tokyo, Spelt wanted to minimize the financial risk linked to a potential price war in Japan. Spelt wondered whether the L&M advertising concept currently being used in Germany could work in Japan as well, if PMKK decided to introduce L&M in the Japanese market. In any case, however, PMKK could not use any TV commercial from Germany since tobacco advertising on television had been banned there. Moreover, Spelt felt that L&M as a brand had two major weaknesses: L&M was difficult for Japanese consumers to pronounce, and the name would not mean anything in Japan.

4. *Launch Cambridge in Japan.* Cambridge, a Philip Morris brand of cigarettes made with a flue-cured tobacco, was also being considered as a launch possibility in the ¥200 segment. Cambridge could easily be pronounced by Japanese consumers, and the name had more potential for identification. However, Cambridge had not been successful in the U.S. market. Sold as a generically priced product, Cambridge had been positioned in the low-price segment with the help of discount coupons. In the United States, the product was advertised in newspapers and magazines but was not supported by image advertising. As a result, no advertising concept could be imported for use on Japanese television. Although Leo Burnett Kyodo Co. Ltd., one of the international advertising agencies under contract with PMKK, had its office in the same building as PMKK, Akio Kobayashi, a PMKK brand manager, described getting approval for a new advertising campaign as a "nightmare" and "too risky." Kobayashi said:

> Any new advertising concept must be approved by Philip Morris' Asian headquarters in Hong Kong and then by the head office in New York City. Developing an effec-

tive advertising and promotional campaign in just three weeks is a big risk that PMKK should avoid. By rushing too fast, we could easily blow up the whole thing.

5. *Reduce price of Philip Morris Superlights.* During the meeting, Kobayashi suggested that PMKK reduce the price of either Philip Morris Lights or Philip Morris Superlights from ¥220 to ¥200. In Mr. Kobayashi's view, repositioning one of these two brands was the quickest and safest way to respond to the Islands challenge. However, pricing issues on tobacco products had to be cleared first with the Japanese government, and it typically took 30 to 60 days to obtain government approval.

6. *Consider other alternatives.* Two other options were discussed during the meeting. The first option was for PMKK to undercut RJR by launching L&M or Cambridge at ¥180 for a pack of 20 cigarettes. The exchange rate between the dollar and the yen during fiscal year 1987 had been favorable to imports into Japan, and a ¥180 price would still leave PMKK with a positive profit margin.

The second option was for PMKK to offer L&M or Cambridge at ¥200 for a pack of 22 cigarettes or ¥220 for 25. Although some retooling in the U.S. manufacturing facilities would be required, Philip Morris had the production capacity to implement this option. "Players" was the only brand sold in the United States with 25 cigarettes in a pack, and its success had been limited. Larger packs would not be a problem for distribution in Japan, however, since Japanese vending machines could handle both the 22- and 25-pack sizes.

Leo Spelt's task now was to review all the alternatives discussed during one of the most animated meetings he had ever attended during his career at PMKK. It was also important that decisions regarding the marketing program be resolved quickly. For example, how should the company allocate the sales force, what advertising methods would be adequate, should soft or hard packs be used, and what kind of retail margins and distribution costs should be considered (see Exhibit 14)? The one point on which everyone had agreed was that any new product launched by PMKK in Japan must be a winner.

EXHIBIT 1 Financial Data (in $ million except per share amounts)

	1987	1986	1985
Operating revenues	$27,695	$25,409	$15,694
Net earnings	1,842	1,478	1,255
Earnings per share	7.75	6.20	5.24
Dividends per share	3.15	2.475	2.00
Funds from operations per share	11.73	9.28	7.41
Increase over prior year (%)			
Operating revenues	9.0	59.2	15.6
Net earnings	24.7	17.7	41.3
Earnings per share	25.0	18.3	44.6
Dividends declared per share	27.3	23.8	17.6
Operating revenues[a]			
Philip Morris USA	$ 7,576	$ 7,053	$ 6,611
Philip Morris International Inc.	7,068	5,638	3,991
General Foods Corporation	9,946	9,664	1,632
Miller Brewing Company	3,105	3,054	2,914
Other	—	—	816
Total	$27,695	$25,409	$15,964
Income from operations[a]			
Philip Morris USA	$ 2,683	$ 2,366	$ 2,047
Philip Morris International	631	492	413
General Foods Corporation	722	741	120
Miller Brewing Company	170	154	132
Philip Morris Credit Corporation[b]	51	55	23
Mission Viejo Realty Group Inc.[b]	21	18	12
Other	19	(8)	45
Total	$ 4,297	$ 3,818	$ 2,792
Amortization of goodwill	104	111	32
Total income from operating companies[c]	$ 4,193	$ 3,707	$ 2,760

Compounded average annual growth rate (%)	1987–1982	1987–1977
Operating revenues	19.0	18.2
New earnings	18.7	18.6
Earnings per share	20.0	18.7

Summary of Operations			
Operating revenues	$27,695	25,409	$15,964
United States export sales	1,592	1,193	923
Cost of sales:			
Cost of products sold	11,264	11,039	6,318
Federal excise taxes	2,085	2,075	2,049
Foreign excise taxes	3,331	2,653	1,766
Income from operating companies	4,193	3,707	2,760
Interest and other debt expense, net	685	770	308
Earnings before income taxes	3,348	2,811	2,329
Pretax profit margin	12.1%	11.1%	14.6%
Provision for income taxes	$ 1,506	$ 1,333	$ 1,074
Net earnings	1,842	1,478	1,255
Earnings per share	7.75	6.20	5.24
Dividends declared per share	3.15	2.475	2.00
Weighted average shares	238	239	240
Capital expenditures	$ 718	$ 678	$ 347

(continued)

EXHIBIT 1   (continued)

	1987	1986	1985
Annual depreciation	564	514	367
Property, plant, and equipment (net)	6,582	6,237	5,684
Inventories	4,154	3,836	3,827
Working capital	1,396	1,432	1,926
Total assets	19,145	17,642	17,429
Long-term debt	5,222	5,945	7,331
Total debt	6,378	6,912	8,009
Deferred income taxes	1,288	994	872
Stockholders' equity	6,823	5,655	4,737
Funds from operations	2,789	2,214	1,775
Net earnings reinvested	1,093	888	776
Common dividends declared as % of net earnings	40.6%	39.9%	38.1%
Book value per common share	$ 28.83	$ 23.77	$ 19.85
Market price of common share high-low	124½–72⅝	78–43⅞	47⅝–31
Closing price year-end	85⅜	71⅞	44⅓
Price/earnings ratio year-end	11	11	8
Number of common shares outstanding at year-end	237	238	239
Number of employees	113,000	111,000	114,000

Source: Philip Morris Companies Inc., Annual Report 1987.

Note: Certain amounts appearing in the prior years' consolidated statements of earnings have been reclassified to conform with the current year's presentation.

[a]Income from operating companies is income before corporate expense and interest and other debt expense, net.

[b]Represents equity in net earnings of these unconsolidated subsidiaries.

[c]Composed of The Seven-Up Company, of which substantially all the operations were sold in 1985. General Foods Corporation was acquired in November 1985. Accordingly, consolidated results shown above include the operating results of General Foods Corporation after October 1985.

EXHIBIT 2 Diversification of Philip Morris Companies Inc.

This is Philip Morris

Tobacco

Food

Beer

EXHIBIT 3 Worldwide Cigarette Industry, Unit Volume Estimates (millions)

	1980	1981	1982	1983	1984	1985	1986	1987
Total world industry	4,474,400	4,571,000	4,583,800	4,563,700	4,700,000	4,850,000	4,975,000	5,118,000
U.S. industry	620,500	638,100	614,000	597,000	599,700	594,700	583,500	571,000
World minus United States	3,853,900	3,932,900	3,969,800	3,966,700	4,100,300	4,255,300	4,393,060	4,547,000
Philip Morris total	429,550	448,742	447,107	449,458	469,805	488,468	506,835	540,780
United States	191,191	199,436	204,429	204,677	211,575	213,590	214,573	215,559
International	238,359	249,306	242,678	244,781	258,230	274,878	292,262	325,221
British American Tobacco total	548,900	563,200	550,000	522,500	522,000	543,000	554,000	542,500
United States	84,490	87,750	83,180	68,520	67,990	70,700	67,970	62,740
International	464,410	475,450	466,820	453,980	454,010	472,300	486,030	479,760
R. J. Reynolds total	283,710	295,280	289,390	271,620	274,440	274,900	278,020	284,290
United States	201,710	207,180	208,790	187,520	189,740	188,100	188,320	185,390
International	82,000	88,100	80,600	84,100	84,700	86,800	89,700	98,900
American Tobacco total	106,005	95,515	87,265	85,455	81,295	79,500	77,000	79,500
United States	66,630	59,770	55,350	51,500	47,250	44,800	41,810	39,440
International	39,375	35,745	31,915	33,955	34,045	34,700	35,190	40,060
Rothman total	162,011	158,866	154,183	151,400	145,700	138,500	133,000	134,400
United States	500	500	500	500	500	400	500	400
International	161,511	158,366	158,683	150,900	145,200	138,100	132,500	134,000
Japan Tobacco & Salt total	304,500	308,208	310,100	307,400	307,100	304,500	296,500	280,000
Liggett & Myers USA	14,350	15,450	17,900	28,600	34,000	29,200	22,730	20,280
Lorillard USA	60,200	57,560	54,360	55,000	48,900	48,100	47,440	46,970

EXHIBIT 4 Japan Market

	1983	1984	1985	1986	1987
Total market					
Sales volume (billions sticks)					
Industry	311.7	312.5	310.5	309.2	307.6
Domestic	306.4	306.1	303.3	298.6	281.7
Import	5.4	6.4	7.3	10.6	25.9
Share of market (%)					
Domestic	98.3	98.0	97.7	96.6	91.6
Import	1.7	2.0	2.3	3.4	8.4
Import segment					
Sales volume for non-Japanese companies (millions sticks)					
PMKK	4,241	4,766	5,391	7,945	16,077
B&W	316	335	430	829	6,203
RJR	584	827	951	1,171	2,364
Rothman (TEI)	101	160	282	330	369
AT	62	77	97	264	663
Share of market in the imported segment (%)					
PMKK	79.0	74.8	74.4	74.7	62.0
B&W	5.9	5.3	5.9	7.8	23.9
RJR	10.9	13.0	13.1	11.0	9.1
Rothman (TEI)	1.9	2.5	3.9	3.1	1.4
AT	1.1	1.2	1.3	2.5	2.6

Source: Philip Morris KK, 1987.

Key: PMKK   Philip Morris KK
B&W   Brown & Williamson (British American Tobacco/BAT)
RJR   R. J. Reynolds
TEI   Tobacco Exporters International (Rothman International)
AT   American Tobacco

EXHIBIT 5   Japan Pricing: Share of Market (SOM) by Price Category and Manufacturer, 1987 (%)

¥/pack	JTI	PMKK	B&W	RJR	AT	TEI	Others	Total market
70	0.36	—	—	—	—	—	—	0.36
90	0.14	—	—	—	—	—	—	0.14
110	3.41	—	—	—	—	—	—	3.41
120	0.40	—	—	—	—	—	—	0.40
130	3.10	—	—	—	—	—	—	3.10
140	1.31	—	—	—	—	—	*	1.31
150	0.15	—	—	—	—	—	—	0.15
180	—	—	—	—	—	—	—	—
200	5.00	—	—	—	—	—	*	5.00
220	64.65	1.26	1.49	0.19	0.10	—	*	67.69
230	—	—	—	—	—	—	*	*
240	12.13	—	0.08	—	*	—	*	12.22
250	0.37	2.84	0.42	0.45	*	*	*	4.10
260	0.46	—	*	—	0.05	—	—	0.51
270	—	—	0.01	—	—	—	*	0.01
280	0.01	1.07	*	0.05	*	0.08	*	1.22
290	—	—	—	—	—	—	*	*
300	0.02	—	—	0.06	—	—	*	0.08
320	—	—	—	—	—	*	*	*
350	—	0.03	—	—	—	0.01	*	0.04
380	—	—	—	—	—	*	—	*
400	—	—	—	*	—	—	—	*
550	—	—	—	—	—	—	*	*
600	—	—	—	—	—	—	*	*
650	0.06	—	—	—	—	—	—	0.06
Total	91.52	5.21	2.00	0.75	0.21	0.11	0.09	99.89

Source: Philip Morris KK, 1987.

Notes:

1. Sum of SOM by manufacturer in the above table does not add up to 100% due to unknown volume by brands that are sold independently.

2. Sum of SOM by price category and by manufacturer is not necessarily equal to total figure due to rounding.

3. ¥110 and ¥120 brands for JTI are sold in 10s, while ¥650 brands are sold in 50s by JTI. Also, ¥70 brands are "promotion packs."

4. * denotes numbers that are too small.

5. —denotes no participation.

EXHIBIT 6 Competitive Profile in Japan, 1987

Philip Morris main brands	Price/¥	Sales volume (bn)	Estimated sales revenues* (¥ bn)	Share of volume (%)
Lark Milds KS	250	5.55	19.81	34.51
PM Super Lights	220	1.63	4.72	10.14
Lark KS	250	2.11	7.53	13.12
Parliament 100s	280	1.81	7.67	11.26
PM Lights	220	2.24	6.49	13.93
Lark Super Lights	250	0.86	3.07	5.35
VSL Menthol	250	0.46	1.95	2.86
Lark Milds 100s	280	0.56	2.37	3.48
Others		0.86	3.07	5.35
Total		16.08	56.68	100.00

Source: Philip Morris KK, 1987.

*Sales revenues equal retail price minus taxes, distribution fee, and retailer's margin.

Key: PM   Philip Morris
     VSL   Virginia Slims Lights
     KS   King Size

EXHIBIT 7 PMKK Brand Mix Development in Japan

Philip Morris main brands	1982	1983	1984	1985	1986	1987
Lark Milds KS	33.3	33.3	35.4	37.0	31.6	34.5
Lark KS	38.9	33.3	25.0	22.2	16.4	13.1
Lark Superlight KS	—	—	—	1.8	5.1	5.3
Lark Milds 100s	—	—	10.4	9.3	6.4	3.5
Lark Deluxe Mild 100s	—	—	—	1.8	1.3	0.6
Other Lark	8.3	9.5	8.3	5.7	3.8	2.5
Total Lark	80.5	76.1	79.1	77.8	64.6	59.5
PM Superlights	—	—	—	—	—	10.1
PM Lights	—	—	—	—	12.6	13.9
Total Philip Morris	—	—	—	—	12.6	24.0
Parliament 100s (soft)	8.3	11.9	16.7	18.6	16.4	11.3
Parliament KS	—	2.4	2.1	1.8	1.3	1.2
Total Parliament	8.3	14.3	18.8	20.4	17.7	12.5
VSL Menthol	—	—	—	1.8	3.8	2.9
VSL Regular 20s	—	—	—	—	—	0.5
Total VSL	—	—	—	1.8	3.8	3.4
Other	11.2	9.6	2.1	—	1.3	0.6
Total PMKK (%)	100.0	100.0	100.0	100.0	100.0	100.0

Source: Philip Morris KK, 1987.

Key: KS   King Size
     PM   Philip Morris
     VSL   Virginia Slims Lights

EXHIBIT 8 Competitors in Japan, 1987

	Price ¥	Sales volume (bn)	Estimated sales revenues[a] (¥ bn)	Share of volume (%)
R. J. Reynolds				
Main brands				
Salem Lights	250	0.91	3.20	38.56
Camel KS	250	0.13	0.45	5.51
Winston KS	220	0.18	0.51	7.63
More	250	0.14	0.49	5.93
Others		1.00	2.22	42.37
Total		2.36	6.87	100.00
Japan Tobacco Inc.				
Main brands				
Mild Seven	220	80.51	259.89	28.59
Mild Seven Lights	220	41.41	133.67	14.70
Seven Stars	220	30.52	98.52	10.84
Caster	220	22.29	71.95	7.91
Cabin Milds	240	18.29	67.20	6.49
Hi-Lite	200	15.38	42.79	5.46
Hope 10s (10 sticks)	110	10.28	33.18	3.65
Echo	130	8.34	21.81	2.96
Libera Milds	220	2.71	8.75	0.96
Peace Lights	240	3.98	14.62	1.41
Marlboro Family[b]	240	1.45	5.33	0.51
Others		46.49	150.07	16.52
Total		281.65	907.78	100.00
Brown & Williamson				
Main brands				
Kent Milds	220	3.80	10.93	61.29
Lucky Strike	250	1.29	4.58	20.81
JPS Charcoal	220	0.26	0.75	4.19
Kent 100s	250	0.11	0.46	1.77
Others		0.74	2.62	11.94
Total		6.20	19.34	100.00

[a]Sales revenues equal retail price minus taxes, distribution fee, and retailer's margin.
[b]Produced by JTI under license from Philip Morris.

EXHIBIT 9   Japan Sales by Price Segmentation, 1987

¥ Price/pack*	Jan. 1987	Feb. 1987	Mar. 1987	Apr. 1987	May 1987	June 1987
Units in millions						
Premium (¥280 + above)	264.29	203.12	384.62	388.37	370.64	351.64
High (¥221 − ¥279)	3,519.31	3,568.15	4,416.16	4,641.09	4,549.77	4,347.39
Medium (¥220)	14,813.43	16,087.65	18,701.70	18,209.16	18,716.02	18,265.79
Low (below ¥220)	2,214.13	2,308.74	2,622.77	2,613.76	2,700.83	2,610.38
Unknown	0.00	0.00	0.00	0.00	0.00	0.00
Total	20,811.16	22,167.65	26,125.25	25,852.39	26,337.26	25,575.19
Share of market (%)						
Premium (¥280 + above)	1.27	0.92	1.47	1.50	1.41	1.37
High (¥221 − ¥279)	16.91	16.10	16.90	17.95	17.28	17.00
Medium (¥220)	71.18	72.57	71.58	70.44	71.06	71.42
Low (below ¥220)	10.64	10.41	10.04	10.11	10.25	10.21
Unknown	0.00	0.00	0.00	0.00	0.00	0.00
Total	100.00	100.00	100.00	100.00	100.00	100.00

Source: Philip Morris KK, 1988.

*All pack sizes other than 20s are treated as equivalent to 20s.

EXHIBIT 10   Japan Market: Imported Segment by price, 1987

¥ Price/pack*	Jan. 1987	Feb. 1987	Mar. 1987	Apr. 1987	May 1987	June 1987
Units in millions						
Premium (¥280 + above)	260.03	198.33	379.39	383.17	359.43	335.77
High (¥221 − ¥279)	505.07	417.54	773.15	1,058.41	1,156.77	1,103.76
Medium (¥220)	122.78	114.71	312.91	656.71	912.15	919.82
Low (below ¥220)	0.00	0.00	0.00	0.00	0.00	0.00
Unknown	0.00	0.00	0.00	0.00	0.00	0.00
Total	887.88	730.58	1,465.45	2,098.29	2,430.48	2,359.35
Share of imported segment (%)						
Premium (¥280 + above)	29.29	27.15	25.89	18.26	14.79	14.23
High (¥221 − ¥279)	56.89	57.15	52.76	50.44	47.59	46.78
Medium (¥220)	13.83	15.70	21.35	31.30	37.53	38.99
Low (below ¥220)	0.00	0.00	0.00	0.00	0.09	0.00
Unknown	0.00	0.00	0.00	0.00	0.00	0.00
Total	100.00	100.00	100.00	100.00	100.00	100.00

Source: Philip Morris KK, 1988.

*All pack sizes other than 20s are treated as equivalent to 20s.

July 1987	Aug. 1987	Sept. 1987	Oct. 1987	Nov. 1987	Dec. 1987	Year to date 1987	Year to date 1986	% Variance
394.63	384.71	373.08	387.75	357.35	467.87	4,328.06	3,338.04	29.66
4,639.58	4,649.80	4,460.34	4,235.65	4,052.54	5,419.59	52,499.38	50,080.79	4.83
19,332.16	19,122.07	19,624.55	17,767.73	16,964.25	22,247.71	219,852.21	221,314.02	−0.66
2,734.45	2,749.51	2,608.20	2,474.06	2,353.26	2,932.41	30,922.51	34,471.85	−10.30
0.00	0.00	0.43	0.37	0.17	0.24	1.22	0.00	100.00
27,100.82	26,906.09	27,066.60	24,865.57	23,727.57	31,067.83	307,603.37	309,204.70	−0.52
1.46	1.43	1.38	1.56	1.51	1.51	1.41	1.08	0.33
17.12	17.28	16.48	17.03	17.08	17.44	17.07	16.20	0.87
71.33	71.07	72.50	71.46	71.50	71.61	71.47	71.58	−0.10
10.09	10.22	9.64	9.95	9.92	9.44	10.05	11.15	−1.10
0.00	0.00	0.00	0.00	0.00	0.00	0.00	0.00	0.00
100.00	100.00	100.00	100.00	100.00	100.00	100.00	100.00	

July 1987	Aug. 1987	Sept. 1987	Oct. 1987	Nov. 1987	Dec. 1987	Year to date 1987	Year to date 1986	% Variance
376.73	360.23	353.23	371.88	337.73	439.32	4,155.23	3,305.97	25.69
1,219.39	1,195.12	1,191.90	1,202.98	1,098.74	1,421.95	12,344.78	6,143.09	100.00
1,057.80	1,058.76	1,101.78	1,076.83	922.51	1,167.32	9,424.09	1,185.85	100.00
1.73	1.54	2.49	2.49	6.29	7.33	24.00	0.00	NA
0.00	0.00	0.43	0.37	0.17	0.24	1.22	0.00	100.00
2,655.64	2,615.66	2,649.83	2,654.56	2,365.44	3,036.17	25,949.32	10,634.91	100.00
14.19	13.77	13.33	14.01	14.28	14.47	16.01	31.09	−15.07
45.92	45.69	44.98	45.32	46.45	46.83	47.57	57.76	−10.19
39.83	40.48	41.58	40.57	39.00	38.45	36.32	11.15	25.17
0.06	0.06	0.09	0.09	0.27	0.24	0.09	0.00	NA
0.00	0.00	0.02	0.01	0.01	0.01	0.00	0.00	0.00
100.00	100.00	100.00	100.00	100.00	100.00	100.00	100.00	

EXHIBIT 11 Japan Sales by Flavor Segmentation 1987

Flavor	Jan. 1987	Feb. 1987	Mar. 1987	Apr. 1987	May 1987	June 1987
Units in millions						
Full flavor (16 MG+)	3,232.08	3,338.52	3,879.62	3,908.45	3,978.57	3,826.84
Medium (11.1–16)	11,084.96	11,771.90	13,821.82	13,567.31	13,828.22	13,281.11
Low (6–11)	6,462.58	7,032.87	8,376.85	8,329.25	8,485.31	8,424.68
Ultra low (below 6)	20.80	16.48	36.31	34.41	30.03	28.32
Unknown	10.74	7.87	10.65	12.97	15.13	14.23
Total	20,811.16	22,167.65	26,125.25	25,852.39	26,337.26	25,575.19
Share of market by flavor (%)						
Full flavor (16 MG+)	15.53	15.06	14.85	15.12	15.11	14.96
Medium (11.1–16)	53.26	53.10	52.91	52.48	52.50	51.93
Low (6–11)	31.05	31.73	32.06	32.22	32.22	32.94
Ultra low (below 6)	0.10	0.07	0.14	0.13	0.11	0.11
Unknown	0.05	0.04	0.04	0.05	0.06	0.06
Total	100.00	100.00	100.00	100.00	100.00	100.00

Source: Philip Morris KK, 1988.

EXHIBIT 12 Top 20 Brand Family Evolution

\	1981		1982		1983		1984	
	Brand	Share of market (%)	Brand	Share of market (%)	Brand	Share of market (%)	Brand	Share of market (%)
1.	M. Seven	37.54	M. Seven	41.47	M. Seven	43.99	M. Seven	44.20
2.	S. Stars	17.07	S. Stars	15.64	S. Stars	13.83	S. Stars	12.93
3.	Hi-Lite	10.96	Hi-Lite	9.52	Hi-Lite	8.04	Cabin	6.98
4.	Hope	5.71	Hope	5.18	Cabin	5.04	Hi-Lite	6.95
5.	Echo	5.17	Cabin	5.09	Hope	4.81	Caster	6.87
6.	Cabin	4.08	Echo	4.71	Caster	4.42	Hope	4.45
7.	Peace	3.34	Peace	3.15	Echo	4.22	Echo	3.75
8.	Cherry	3.28	Cherry	2.62	Peace	3.06	Peace	3.06
9.	Partner	2.89	Partner	2.56	Wakaba	2.03	Wakaba	1.78
10.	Wakaba	2.42	Wakaba	2.23	Cherry	2.02	Cherry	1.58
11.	Lark[b]	0.95	Lark[b]	1.01	Partner	1.72	Lark[b]	1.24
12.	Mine	0.91	Tender	0.97	Lark[b]	1.15	Partner	1.09
13.	Shinsei	0.84	Mine	0.89	Tender	0.79	Mine	0.60
14.	Tender	0.67	Shinsei	0.72	Mine	0.73	Tender	0.56
15.	Just	0.63	Ministar	0.54	Shinsei	0.64	Shinsei	0.54
16.	Ministar	0.57	Just	0.46	Ministar	0.50	Sometime	0.52
17.	Current	0.48	Champagne	0.44	Sometime	0.46	Ministar	0.45
18.	Mr. Slim	0.38	Sometime	0.40	Just	0.33	Mr. Slim[b]	0.30
19.	Sometime	0.33	Current	0.37	Mr. Slim	0.32	Parliament[b]	0.27
20.	Hitone	0.32	Mr. Slim	0.36	Hitone	0.26	Just	0.27

Source: PMKK Segmentation Analysis.
Note: Unless otherwise noted, brands are of the Marlboro family (produced by JTI under license from Philip Morris).
[a]JTI brand.
[b]Philip Morris brand.
[c]B&W brand.

July 1987	Aug. 1987	Sept. 1987	Oct. 1987	Nov. 1987	Dec. 1987	Year to date 1987	Year to date 1986	% Variance
4,048.67	4,033.21	3,873.11	3,660.54	3,465.94	4,401.48	45,647.03	49,035.83	−6.91
13,935.83	13,698.58	13,293.79	12,204.17	11,593.03	15,208.47	157,289.19	172,683.48	−8.91
9,068.54	9,130.12	9,853.71	8,951.70	8,621.56	11,398.18	104,135.36	87,183.95	19.44
31.31	29.44	30.08	29.29	25.32	32.73	344.52	239.94	43.59
16.48	14.74	15.91	19.87	21.72	26.97	187.27	61.51	100.00
27,100.82	26,906.09	27,066.60	24,865.57	23,727.57	31,067.83	307,603.37	309,204.70	−0.52
14.94	14.99	14.31	14.72	14.61	14.17	14.84	15.86	−1.02
51.42	50.91	49.12	49.08	48.86	48.95	51.13	55.85	−4.71
33.46	33.93	36.41	36.00	36.34	36.69	33.85	28.20	5.66
0.12	0.11	0.11	0.12	0.11	0.11	0.11	0.08	0.03
0.06	0.05	0.06	0.08	0.09	0.09	0.06	0.02	0.04
100.00	100.00	100.00	100.00	100.00	100.00	100.00	100.00	100.00

1985		1986		1987	
Brand	Share of market (%)	Brand	Share of market (%)	Brand	Share of market (%)
M. Seven	44.41	M. Seven	45.92	M. Seven[a]	43.21
S. Stars	12.06	S. Stars	11.53	S. Stars[a]	10.58
Caster	8.41	Caster	7.72	Caster[a]	7.73
Cabin	7.31	Cabin	7.33	Cabin[a]	6.85
Hi-Lite	6.07	Hi-Lite	5.56	Hi-Lite[a]	5.00
Hope	3.94	Peace	4.27	Peace[a]	3.87
Echo	3.36	Hope	3.75	Hope[a]	3.44
Peace	3.08	Echo	3.01	Lark[b]	3.10
Wakaba	1.58	Lark[b]	1.67	Echo[a]	2.71
Lark[b]	1.31	Wakaba	1.42	Kent[c]	1.43
Cosmos	1.30	Cherry	0.97	Wakaba[a]	1.30
Cherry	1.24	Cosmos	0.83	P. Morris	1.26
Partner	0.81	Sometime	0.65	Sometime	0.90
Sometime	0.58	Partner	0.54	Libera[a]	0.88
Mine	0.54	Mine	0.47	Cherry[a]	0.78
Tender	0.49	Parliament	0.45	Parliament	0.67
Shinsei	0.43	Tender	0.42	Cosmos[a]	0.66
Ministar	0.42	Shinsei	0.42	Marlboro	0.49
Parliament[b]	0.35	Ministar	0.38	L. Strike[c]	0.43
Mr. Slim	0.28	P. Morris[b]	0.34	Tender	0.42

EXHIBIT 13 Japan Market Facts: Top 20 Brands

Family share of market (%)	1981	1982	1983	1984	1985	1986	1987
1. Mild Seven	37.54	41.17	43.99	44.20	44.41	45.92	43.21
2. Seven Stars	17.07	15.64	13.83	12.93	12.06	11.53	10.58
3. Caster	——	0.10	4.42	6.87	8.41	7.72	7.73
4. Cabin	4.08	5.09	5.04	6.98	7.31	7.33	6.85
5. Hi-Lite	10.96	9.52	8.04	6.95	6.07	5.56	5.00
6. Peace	3.34	3.15	3.06	3.06	3.08	4.27	3.87
7. Hope	5.71	5.18	4.81	4.45	4.07	3.75	3.44
8. Lark[a]	0.95	1.01	1.15	1.24	1.31	1.67	3.10
9. Echo	5.17	4.71	4.22	3.75	3.36	3.01	2.71
10. Kent[b]	0.07	0.05	0.04	0.04	0.04	0.05	1.43
11. Wakaba	2.43	2.23	2.03	1.78	1.58	1.42	1.30
12. Philip Morris[a]	——	——	——	——	0.01	0.34	1.26
13. Sometime	0.33	0.40	0.46	0.52	0.58	0.65	0.90
14. Libera	——	——	——	——	——	——	0.88
15. Cherry	3.28	2.62	2.02	1.58	1.24	0.97	0.78
16. Parliament[a]	0.08	0.11	0.19	0.26	0.35	0.45	0.67
17. Cosmos	——	——	——	0.30	1.30	0.83	0.66
18. Marlboro[c]	0.12	0.15	0.14	0.09	0.09	0.21	0.49
19. Lucky Strike[b]	——	——	——	——	0.04	0.12	0.43
20. Tender	0.67	0.97	0.79	0.56	0.49	0.42	0.42

Source: Philip Morris KK, 1987.

Note: Top 20 brand family ranking list is based on 1987 performance. Unless otherwise noted, names belong to JTI's brand families.

[a]PMKK brand.

[b]Belongs to B&W's brand.

[c]Belongs to Philip Morris but is being produced and distributed in Japan by JTI under license from Philip Morris.

EXHIBIT 14 Sales Revenue per 1,000 Sticks, 1987 (PMKK estimates)

Philip Morris	¥220	¥250	¥280	
	× 50	× 50	× 50	
	11,000	12,500	14,000	
Retail margin	1,100	1,250	1,400	
Excise tax	6,572	7,253	7,934	
Distribution	430	430	430	
	¥2,898	¥3,576	¥4,236	
Brown & Williamson	¥220	¥250	¥280	
	× 50	× 50	× 50	
	11,000	12,500	14,000	
Retail margin	1,100	1,250	1,400	
Excise tax	6,572	7,253	7,934	
Distribution	450	450	450	
	¥2,878	¥3,547	¥4,216	
R. J. Reynolds	¥220	¥250	¥280	
	× 50	× 50	× 50	
	11,000	12,500	14,000	
Retail margin	1,100	1,250	1,400	
Excise tax	6,572	7,253	7,934	
Distribution	480	480	480	
	¥2,848	¥3,517	¥4,186	
Japan Tobacco Inc.	¥130	¥200	¥220	¥240
	× 50	× 50	× 50	× 50
	6,500	10,000	11,000	12,000
Retail margin	650	1,000	1,100	1,200
Excise tax	3,135	6,118	6,572	7,026
Distribution	100	100	100	100
	¥2,615	¥2,782	¥3,228	¥3,674

Source: Philip Morris KK, 1987.

Global Marketing Programs

The primary role of marketing programs is to bring under a coherent strategy the various policy decisions such as product policy, communication, distribution, and so forth. It is often the synergy among the constituent elements rather than the individual decisions themselves that determines a program's potential for success. The synergy comes from the internal consistency among the various marketing decisions. When synergy exists, individual decisions interplay to reinforce each other toward their common strategic goal. It is therefore important to view a program in its entirety and to evaluate it not only for its fit with the external market and competitive forces but also for its internal consistency among its building blocks.

ISSUES

Two cases provide the opportunity to examine the issues related to formulating marketing programs for regional or global markets. The first case, Swatch, portrays a successful strategy looking for an "encore." Management is reexamining the key elements of the original marketing program to decide if major changes are called for. The second case, Volvo Trucks Europe, depicts the changes that are taking place in the company's most important sales region and raises the issue of how a competitive strategy could be devised to deal with them. Accordingly, management is wondering how to overcome the company's traditional multidomestic practices in Europe and what roles should be assigned to headquarters and local organizations in deciding the elements of a pan-European marketing strategy.

LEARNING POINTS

The student can expect the following learning points from the analysis and class discussion of the cases in this section:

- Practice in formulating effective marketing strategy, including segmentation and positioning;
- Skills in integrating individual marketing decisions into a comprehensive global or regional strategy;
- Exercise in revitalizing a proven marketing program through possible redefinition of brand concept and line extension;
- Exercise in defining the respective roles and contribution of headquarters and local management to the formulation and implementation of a regional or global marketing program;
- Insights into the problems inherent in implementing a coordinated panregional marketing program from the starting base of multidomestic autonomy and fragmented decision making.

16 SWATCH

It was mid-1986 and Chris Keigel had only recently returned from military service to become European marketing manager for Swatch, the new watch concept that had revolutionized the watch industry and brought Swiss watchmaking out of a 40-year slump. He knew that Swatch management in Biel, Switzerland, was concerned about maintaining sales growth and agreeing on long-term international strategy. Existing watch brands were renewing their strategies, and new competitors inspired by Swatch were mushrooming worldwide. Keigel had been requested to gather background information for an upcoming top management meeting called to arrive at a consensus on the very concept of Swatch, its international positioning, and its viable product line extensions.

COMPANY BACKGROUND

Swatch watches were manufactured by ETA SA, a century-old Swiss watch movement firm and a subsidiary of SMH (Société Micromécanique et Horlogère), the world's second-largest watchmaking concern after the Japanese firm, Seiko. SMH was formed from a merger in 1983 between ASUAG (Allgemeine Schweizer Uhrenindustrie) and SSIH (Société Suisse pour l'Industrie Horlogère), Switzerland's two largest watch manufacturers, both rescued from bankruptcy by the major Swiss banks. In addition to Swatch, the SMH product line included the well-known brands Omega, Longines, Tissot, and Rado. Swatch AG was a subsidiary set up in 1984 to handle the international marketing of Swatch watches. Its Executive Committee was composed of President E. T. Marquardt, Vice President American Operations Max Imgrüth, Vice President Continental Operations Felice A. Schillaci, and Vice President Australasian Operations H. N. Tune.

This case was prepared by Helen Chase Kimball, Research Associate, under the supervision of Christian Pinson, Associate Professor, Institut Européen d'Administration des Affaires (INSEAD). It was in part inspired by a report prepared by R. J. Burnett, INSEAD MBA student. Certain proprietary data have been disguised. Copyright © INSEAD/CEDEP 1987. All rights reserved.

WATCH TECHNOLOGY

Until the late fifties, all watches were mechanical—that is, spring-powered—with movements comprising 100 or more parts. In 1957, the first electric watch was marketed in the United States. A few years later, the American firm Bulova developed a tuning-fork watch, battery-powered and accurate to within one minute per month. The quartz electronic watch was invented in Switzerland in 1968 and first marketed in the United States by Hamilton. It improved accuracy to unheard-of levels. The quartz watch display was either of the traditional "analog" type, with hands moving around a face, or "digital," with numbers appearing in a frame. Table 1 gives a rough description of the components of four watch types.

TABLE 1 Major Components of Four Watch Types

	Mechanical	Tuning fork	Quartz digital	Quartz analog
Energy source	Hairspring	Battery	Battery	Battery
Time base	Balance spring	Tuning fork	Quartz crystal	Quartz crystal
Electronic circuit	—	Simple	Integrated circuit	Integrated circuit
Transmission	Gears	Gears	Gears	Stepping motor/gears
Display	Hands	Hands	Numbers	Hands

The first digital watches used either light-emitting diodes (LEDs) or a liquid crystal display (LCD), which consumed less energy. By 1986, most quartz digital watches had LCDs. The switch to quartz was spectacular: 98% of all watches and movements produced in 1974 were mechanical, and only 2% were quartz, but in 1984 the breakdown was 24% mechanical and 76% quartz.

THE WATCH INDUSTRY

Watchmaking was first developed in Switzerland by Swiss goldsmiths and French Huguenots fleeing religious persecution during the Reformation. During the Industrial Revolution, the Swiss industry branched into a two-tier system with component manufacturing separate from watch assembling. Swiss watchmakers were masters of precision workmanship, and "Swiss made" became synonymous with quality. By 1970, however, the Swiss contribution to world watch production had dropped considerably. This trend continued into the eighties, as less expensive and more accurate quartz watches and movements, mainly from Japan and Hong Kong, flooded the market. In 1985, 39% of watches and movements were from Japan, 22% were from Hong Kong, and only 13% were from Switzerland (see Table 2).

TABLE 2 Estimated Breakdown of World Watch Production (in million of watches and movements)

	World production	Switzerland (%)	Japan (%)	Hong Kong (%)	USA (%)	Rest of world (%)
1948	31	80	—	—	—	20
1970	174	43	14	—	11	32
1975	218	34	14	2	12	38
1980	300	29	22	20	4	25
1985	440	13	39	22	0.4	25

Source: Federation of the Swiss Watch Industry.

Starting in the 1950s, the production operations of the major American firms (Timex, Bulova, and Hamilton) gradually shifted overseas. By 1986, domestic production was considered virtually nil. Although Switzerland's estimated contribution to American import volume decreased from 99% in 1950 to 4% in 1984, the percentage of import volume from Asia increased from 10% in 1970, primarily from Japan, to 92% in 1984, mostly from Hong Kong.

The Japanese industry was highly concentrated with the two major firms, Hattori Seiko and Citizen; both stressed the development of automated production lines and maximum vertical integration of operations. Compared with the multitude of Swiss watch brands, the combined product lines of these two, plus Casio, the third major Japanese watchmaker, did not exceed a dozen brands. In contrast, the industry in Hong Kong was highly fragmented, with several manufacturers producing 10 to 20 million watches per year, and hundreds of small firms producing less than 1 million annually. These firms could not afford to invest in quartz analog technology, but with virtually no barriers to entry for watch assembly, they produced complete analog watches from imported movements and modules, often Swiss or Japanese. Design costs were also minimized by copying Swiss or Japanese products. The competitive advantages of the Hong Kong firms were low-cost labor, tiny margins, and the flexibility to adapt to changes in the market.

The spectacular rise of the Japanese and Hong Kong watchmaking industries, particularly in the middle- and low-price categories, was primarily due to the rapid adoption of quartz technology, a drive to achieve a competitive cost position through accumulation of experience, and economies of scale. Whereas in 1972 the digital watch module cost around $200, the same module cost only $.50 in 1984. The Asian watch-making industry had been ensuring a chronic state of world oversupply, mainly in the inexpensive quartz digital range. This had been the cause of a number of bankruptcies and had influenced watch manufacturers to turn to the quartz analog market where added value was higher. Since, in contrast to quartz digital technology, quartz analog technology was available only within the watch industry, the hundreds of watch assemblers scattered throughout the world were increasingly dependent on the three major movement manufacturers: Seiko, ETA, and Citizen.

THE WATCH MARKET

According to one industry analyst, the European Organization for Economic Cooperation and Development (OECD) member countries represented about 30% of total world watch sales volume; the United States, approximately 20 to 30%; and the Japanese market, about 10%. Estimated annual market growth was approximately 4%.

Industry experts estimated 1984 wristwatch purchases in the United States to be 90 to 95 million units, a 400% increase over 10 years. By 1985, Americans were buying a new watch once every 2 years, compared with once every 6 to 10 years a decade earlier. However, the U.S. market was considered to be near saturation, with an average of 3.5 watches per owner. Buying habits had also changed in Europe, with the 8- to 20-year-old age group representing nearly half of all watch sales in 1985. When commenting on buying habits, industry experts pointed out that the industry was increasingly committed to the quartz analog, stressing the different meanings the digital and the analog had for the consumer (Exhibit 1). Some of the more expensive Swiss watch manufacturers, however, seemed to believe in a future trend back to mechanical watches.

The watch market was generally divided into five retail price segments (Table 3). Swiss watches fell mostly in the mid- to expensive price ranges. To protect its mid-price niche, Seiko had adopted a multibrand strategy, offering cheap watches under the Lorus, Pulsar, and Phasar brands, with more expensive watches under the Credor, Seiko, and Lassale names.

TABLE 3 Watch Industry Price Segments, 1984

Segment	Retail price (SF)	% units	% value	Examples
A	8–30	60	10	Hong Kong LCDs, some cheap mechanicals
B	30–100	15	15	Swatch, Timex, Casio, Guess, Lip, Lorus, Jaz, Dugena, Junghans, Yéma, Pulsar, Hamilton
C	80–250	20	45	Tissot, Seiko, Citizen, Casio, Lip, Yéma, Jaz, Pulsar, Dugena, Junghans, Bulova, Hamilton, Herbelin
D	120–450	4	15	Omega, Longines, Eterna, Seiko, Citizen, Certina, Rado, Movado, Bulova
E	450+	1	15	Rolex, Piaget, Cartier, Audemars Piguet, Certina, Rado, Lassale, Ebel

Source: Compiled from records of the Federation of the Swiss Watch Industry.
Note: $/Swiss Franc 1984 exchange rate = 2.20.

DEVELOPMENT OF SWATCH

In 1978, Ernst Thomke joined ETA SA as president after proving his success in the marketing department of Beecham Pharmaceuticals. He had been an apprentice in the production division of ETA before earning a Ph.D. in chemistry and a medical degree. In early 1980, after considering the sorry state of the Swiss watch industry,

Thomke concluded that the future was in innovative finished products, aggressive marketing, volume sales, and vertical integration of the industry. Quartz analog technology was more complex than digital, but because ETA was known for the technology it possessed in the production of high-priced, ultra-thin "Delirium" movements, Thomke decided to develop a "low-price prestige" quartz analog wristwatch that could be mass-produced in Switzerland at greatly reduced cost.

Two ETA micromechanical engineers who specialized in plastic injection molding technology, Jacques Müller and Elmar Mock, were given the challenge of designing a product based on Thomke's concept. The process required inventing entirely new production technology using robots and computers for manufacture and assembly. By 1981, a semiautomated process had been designed to meet Thomke's goal of a 15 SF ex-factory price, and seven patents were registered. The watch's movement, consisting of only 51 instead of the 90 to 150 parts in other watches, was injected directly into the one-piece plastic case. The casing was sealed by ultrasonic welding instead of screwed, precluding servicing. The watch would simply be replaced and not repaired if it stopped. The finished product, guaranteed one year, was shock resistant, water resistant to 100 feet (30 meters), and contained a three-year replaceable battery.

In April 1981, Thomke took his idea to Franz Sprecher, a marketing consultant who had worked at Nestlé before setting up his own consulting firm. As background for ETA's project, Sprecher studied prestige products like perfumes, successful mass market brands like "Bic," and both designer and ready-to-wear fashion. He worked closely with advertising agencies in the United States on product positioning and advertising strategy. In addition to coming up with the name "Swatch," a snappy contraction of "Swiss" and "watch," this research generated the idea of downplaying the product's practical benefits and positioning it as a "fashion accessory that happens to tell time." Swatch would be a second or third watch used to adapt to different situations without replacing the traditional "status symbol" watch.

Product Launch

Thomke arranged to have Swatch distributed in the United States by the Swiss Watch Distribution Center (SWDC) in San Antonio, Texas, an American firm in which ETA held a minority interest and whose chairman, Ben Hammond, had been instrumental in setting up and building Seiko distribution in the southwestern states. Swatch was test marketed in December 1982 at 100 Sanger Harris department stores in Dallas, Salt Lake City, and San Diego without any advertising, public relations, or publicity. The original test product line consisted of 12 rather conventional watches in red, brown, and tan. Opinions on test results were mixed, but the ETA team continued undaunted. Swatch was officially launched in Switzerland in March 1983, and then gradually worldwide. Exhibit 2 shows the fall 1983 collection as pictured in sales brochures.

Max Imgrüth, a graduate of the State University of New York's Fashion Institute of Technology, took over as president of SWDC in April 1983, and arranged a second test market in December 1983, through both the Zale jewelry chain in Dallas and the New York department store Macy's, with television support created by Swatch's advertising agency, McCann-Erickson. Test market conclusions were that most of the watches in the 1983 fall/winter collection were not acceptable for the U.S. market. Imgrüth recalled:

> Nothing happened. I tried to figure out what was wrong. The product was not very distinctive. It was not just the ad, it was the watches. It was too close to the traditional watch. First of all it was its positioning, second the product, third pricing, fourth advertising. Basically, I ran down the marketing mix.

Imgrüth became increasingly involved in product design and local adaptation of Swatch communication. In early 1984, he was appointed president of the newly created American subsidiary Swatch Watch USA. The American pricing strategy was modified, and a direct sales force was organized to replace SWDC that year. Managers hired to run Swatch Watch USA included Vice President Operations Don Galliers, formerly in the watch strap business, and Marketing Manager/Creative Director Steve Rechtschaffner, 27, a former member of the U.S. freestyle skiing team with experience in sales promotion. Exhibit 3 gives the perceived advantages and disadvantages of Swatch, in four countries, in December 1984.

Launch Price

Initially there were three prices for the Swiss launch: SF 39.90 for a model with only two hands, SF 44.90 for three hands, and 49.90 SF for three hands and a calendar display. In the United States, however, Swatch was first marketed at seven price points, ranging from $19.95 to $37.50. Consumers did not seem to understand why certain watches cost more than others, so American prices were reduced to three in 1984: $25, $30, and $35. In 1986, one Swatch retail price was set throughout the world, based on the price in the United States of $30. Exhibit 4 presents the results of a survey on perceptions of Swatch retail prices in four countries.

From the start, Thomke and Sprecher had decided that product contribution would have to be sufficient to finance massive promotional communication. Manufacturing costs had been reduced substantially, and wholesaler and agent margins could be decreased a bit. Retail margins would have to be kept high enough to motivate retailers. Table 4 gives a comparison of costs and margins in 1982 to 1983 for traditional, moderately priced Swiss and Japanese watches, low-priced Hong Kong watches, and Swatch.

Product Line

Two Swatch collections of 12 different models each were marketed per year—one collection in the spring and the other in the fall. Styles were based on four major target groups, geared to social behavior and trends: "classic," "hi-tech," "sports," and "fashion." Collections were designed by Käthi Durrer and Jean Robert in Zurich, with fashion consultants in New York, Milan, and Paris. At first there was only one large-size model, enabling mass production. In 1984, a smaller size was added. Limitation of sizes to these two enabled substantial reductions in production

TABLE 4 Breakdown of Low- to Moderately Priced Watch Costs and Margins

	Swiss (%)	Japanese (%)	Hong Kong (%)	Swatch (%)
Retail price = 100%	100	100	100	100
(Retail margin)	(50)	(55)	(50)	(45)
Wholesale price	50	45	50	55
(Wholesale/agent margin)	(25)	(16)	(18)	(11)
Ex-factory price	25	29	33	44
(Contribution)	(4)	(12)	(3)	(24)
Manufacturing cost	21	17	30	20

Source: Company records.

costs. Variations in the collections were made possible through face and watchband graphics and style. In the spring of 1984, Max Imgrüth decided to name individual watches (e.g., "Pinstripe," "Black Magic," "McSwatch," "Dotted Swiss") and tie each collection in with specific themes, starting with the "Skipper" line of sailing-inspired sport watches. Subsequent themes ranged from "Street Smart" paisleys and plaids to "Kiva" American Indian designs. Exhibit 5 illustrates selected watches from the 1984–1986 collections.

By fall 1984, Swatch management realized that a continuous system for pretesting the 80 to 100 models presented by the designers for each collection was essential for constant collection renewal. Sprecher commented:

> The strategy should be to create best-sellers. This doesn't mean keeping the same collection for five years but improving the collection by identifying weak models and knowing whether to revamp them or create new models that will be leaders.

The collection illustrated in Exhibit 6 and including the three scented "Granita di Frutta" models,[1] was pretested in December 1984. Test results, presented with the actual ex-factory sales figures for the collection, revealed no significant differences between the four countries involved.

Distribution

Until the mid-1970s, most medium- and high-priced watches were sold through jewelry and specialty shops. The Swiss watchmakers, later followed by Seiko, had always placed emphasis on after-sales service and set up dealerships allowing jewelers to take up to 250% markups. As prices slipped, however, a gray market[2] developed, fired by a drive for volume and a lack of control over distribution channels.

In the United States, Swatch watches were sold primarily in "shop-in-shops" in upscale department stores, some specialized watch retailers, sports shops, and

1. A line of aromatic Swatches geared to the teenage consumer and consisting of pastel pink, blue, and yellow watches emitting strawberry, mint, and banana fragrances; it represented 80% of sales in the United States for the first two months of 1985.
2. Parallel importing and distribution through unauthorized channels.

boutiques; in Europe, Swatch was sold by the few existing upscale department stores but mostly by traditional jewelers and some specialized sports, gift, and fashion boutiques, mail-order houses, and duty-free shops (see Exhibit 7). In France, as part of his launch strategy, the Swatch distributor Raymond Zeitoun, previously with Seiko, persuaded the prestigious jeweler Jean Dinh Van on Rue de la Paix in Paris to sell Swatch for a few days. When the jeweler accepted "for the fun of it" and sales boomed, others followed suit. Zeitoun spoke of Swatch in France:

> Granted, it's an item without much of a margin, but the profession has to change and widen its horizons. The advantage of Swatch is that it brings a lively atmosphere and a younger clientele to the store.

Discounting by distributors was not allowed, and the trade was warned to keep an eye out for counterfeits (see Exhibit 8). Swatch Watch USA spent close to $1 million in 1984 to buy back Swatches displayed at less than the set price. Don Galliers recalled:

> We purchased 80 to 85% of the gray market watches. Counterfeits appeared in 1985. We set up an international brand protection program with a very sophisticated information network. All new styles were copyrighted, counterfeiters caught at the source and "confusingly similar" watch marketers taken to court. If we were spending $16 to $18 million a year on advertising, we could spend a couple of million to protect the brand.

Merchandising was considered fundamental and included sales promotional activities designed to catch the consumer's eye. Backed by 2-meter "maxi-Swatches," expensive and carefully designed display racks were "colorblocked" — that is, arranged in rows of color. In-store videos played pop or rock music, and sales brochures were available in ample supply. In all countries, parties for the trade were organized for each collection launch to create a feeling of a "Swatch Club," encouraging retailers to give Swatch prime window space and exposure in spite of lower margins. One of Swatch's selling points with distributors was its very low return rate[3] (e.g., 0.3% in 1984 compared with the industry average of 5%), which virtually eliminated after-sales service problems and customer dissatisfaction.

In general, the attitude of the distributors toward Swatch watches was very positive with the few negative comments limited to low profit margin, production-related delivery problems, skepticism about long-term success, and lack of distributor exclusivity. Galliers commented on Swatch's distribution strategy in the United States:

> Swatch's success was built on limited distribution. We should not sell more than 5 million Swatches in the United States in any single year, to keep it rare, in demand. You can't always get what you want so when you see it you'd better buy it. For a trendy article like this, if you accelerate too much into the market you risk making it become a fad.

3. Percentage of watches returned on warranty.

Product Line Extensions

While Swatch's major competitors—Seiko, Citizen, and others—were diversifying into other applications of electronics and "superwatches," complete with televisions, computers, or health-monitoring systems, Swatch, mainly through the initiative of Swatch Watch USA, had moved into a range of accessories and ready-to-wear apparel (Table 5) designed to express a "Swatch" life-style (Exhibit 9). One of the reasons given for expanding into accessories and apparel was the need to fill the available space in the shop-in-shops. "Funwear" and "Fungear," manufactured in Hong Kong and the USA, were designed by Renée Rechtschaffner, Steve Rechtschaffner's wife and the winner of a Swatch-organized contest at the Fashion Institute of Technology. By the last quarter of 1985, nonwatch items accounted for one-third of Swatch sales in the United States. (Aided awareness scores for Swatch accessories available only in the United States are presented in Exhibit 10.)

TABLE 5 Swatch Clothing and Accessories

Date	Product	Description	Retail price ($)
Fall 1984	Swatch Guard	Protective, decorative device for watches	3
Fall 1984	Maxi-Swatch	2-meter Swatch wall clock	150
Spring 1985	Shields	Sunglasses	35
Spring 1985	Chums	Eyeglass holders	5
Spring 1985	Signature line	Umbrellas, T-shirts, sweats with watch graphics	12–38
Spring 1985	Gift set	Keyholder and Swiss penknife	45
Spring 1985	Paraphernalia	Italian pens, stationery items, key rings, safety razors	7–15
Fall 1985	Fungear line	Knapsacks, belts, bags	10–65
Fall 1985	Funwear line	Unisex casual wear (pants, tops, sweats, shirts, shorts, skirts) linked to watch themes	12–65

Fashion retailing in the United States was stimulated by six "market weeks" per year to launch each new season (i.e., spring, spring-summer, summer, back-to-school, fall-winter, holiday) and to introduce products to retailers nationwide. At Swatch Watch USA, preparation of each market week began almost a full year in advance. Market and sales analyses, fashion forecasts, and theme development (watches and accessories), covering approximately two months for each season, were followed by gradual decisions and presentations on design, color, prints, prices, quantities, range, advertising, public relations, and promotion throughout the rest of the year. Coordination of production and delivery with "fickle fashion" was tricky business that relied on very short lead times. Perpetual innovation was also difficult to maintain. Don Galliers commented:

We don't have the flexibility of the traditional watch industry where if you miss it this year you can launch it next year. We also don't have the normal 18-month development time to field the watch after a one-year design time. Our whole cycle is built on the concept that every six weeks there is something new at the Swatch counter.

In the spring of 1986, under license from the Coca-Cola Company, the American subsidiary also started marketing a line of Coca-Cola watches. They contained traditional ETA, not Swatch technology quartz movements, and did not bear the name Swatch.[4]

Communication

Thomke and Sprecher had adopted a global communication strategy for Swatch to establish a distinctive brand personality. The company issued strict directives on use of the Swatch logo, baselines, layout, and the Swiss cross. The Swatch communication budget covered advertising/store promotion and public relations/special events. Local agencies were in charge of public relations, promotion, publicity, and special events, including contests, concert tours, and sports events. McCann-Erickson in Zurich was in charge of all advertising designed for local adaptation in different countries through the use of voice-overs for TV and cinema commercials (Exhibit 11) and strips of copy in the respective languages for print ads (Exhibit 12). Roger Guyard, regional manager for France, explained:

> We want to have a global image with the same image in England as in Australia. Where we are different from the others is in our launch events and promotions, adapted to each country and each population.

The Swatch communication target audience was described by McCann-Erickson in Zurich as "all men and women between 15 and 39 years of age, particularly between 20 and 29, opinion leaders/trend-setters, extroverts who were nonetheless group-dependent, young fashion wearers, and both active and passive sports fans." For Felice Schillaci, vice president continental operations, Swatch was "a brand for the young at heart, no age group, no 18 to 29—it's a state of mind, an attitude."

Public Relations

Heavy emphasis was placed on testimonials and endorsements by opinion leaders as well as on special events, including sponsoring musicians and artists, exhibitions, and competitions at which gadgets, leaflets, and Swatch magazines were distributed (Exhibit 13). Swatch promotion was often unsolicited, such as when Lady Diana wore not only her husband Prince Charles's watch at a polo match but also two Swatches, just when Swatch was introducing the idea of man-size watches for women and "multiple Swatch accessorizing." Swatch also benefited from massive publicity through the press. According to Elmar Mock:

> Management's stroke of genius was not to hide its engineers. We were on great terms with the newspapers who created an advertising effect, quite naturally, without the slightest solicitation.

4. Another SMH subsidiary, Endura SA, manufactured private label and promotional watches with conventional movements.

Limited edition watches were launched with elaborate parties. The first was designed by Kiki Picasso and distributed to 100 celebrities at a cocktail party in Paris. There was the diamond-studded "Limelight" ($100) available in both Europe and the United States. Then there were the Breakdance watch ($30) and four watches designed by New York artist Keith Haring ($50 each), marketed only in the United States. Swatch's French public relations agency claimed that the strategy behind these serial watches was to manage the production-related scarcity by "creating a frenzy through rarity." Organization of advertising and events revolved around developing a "Swatch cult." In 1984, for instance, Max Imgrüth organized a celebrity advertising campaign through a photographer in California who persuaded a number of stars to be in Swatch ads in exchange for a Rolex or Piaget gold watch. Lauren Hutton, Donna Mills, Lee Majors, and Ivan Lendl were among those who participated.

Advertising

Swatch advertising and promotion budgets are presented in Exhibit 14, along with industry media expenditure in the United States. Don Galliers explained that Switzerland had a strict policy whereby roughly 30% of the product's retail price would go to advertising. Swatch advertising relied primarily on films for television and cinema (Exhibit 14). Print ads, accounting for approximately one-third of total advertising expenditures, were used worldwide to reinforce awareness of each collection and current trend themes. They ran from April to June and from September to December every year. Swatch print media plans included sport, fashion, and avant-garde magazines (e.g., *Vogue, Elle, Cosmopolitan, Sports Illustrated, L'Equipe, Rolling Stone, The Face, City*), magazines geared to the young (e.g., *Just 17, Jacinte, Mädchen, Seventeen*), and occasionally, general news publications (e.g., *Stern, Der Spiegel, Figaro Magazine, Tiempo*).

Swatch Watch USA had an in-house department that adapted the McCann ads and created its own ads (Exhibit 15). Imgrüth commented on global advertising:

> We adapted the spots in a way that made sense, different wording, cut them a little bit with McCann here, knowing full well that what the Swiss wanted to achieve, a brand created and sent in directly from Switzerland, was impossible. A watch is not consumed like Coca-Cola. It is not a daily need. This is emotional, and you have to play local emotions.

Felice Schillaci explained that the loyal Swatch customer in the United States fell in the 10 to 16 age bracket. Reliable data on the Swatch buyer profile in Europe were not available, but buyer age group brackets in the United Kingdom were estimated to be 20% under 18, 40% between 18 and 24, 30% between 25 and 34, and 10% over 34. Management in the United States believed that if consumers were caught at an early age, they would stick with Swatch as they grew up, and the enthusiasm they generated would rub off on those older. By 1986, in New York City and Los Angeles, where Swatch awareness was at a maximum, Swatch Watch USA had limited television commercials to MTV[5] to avoid oversaturation. A firm specializing in TV and radio youth audience surveys conducted an analysis for Swatch of American consumers, based on interviews in 15 cities and including reactions to a random sample of eight Swatch ads (Exhibit 16). Scores for recall of Swatch advertising in five countries are presented in Exhibit 17.

SWATCH'S COMPETITION

When Swatch management was asked to define the competition, responses varied. Swatch was generally credited with having opened up a new market niche (Exhibit 18). By 1986, however, the market was flooded with Swatch imitations, some bearing similar brand names (e.g., Watch, Watcha, Swiss Watch, Smash, Swatcher, A-Watch, La-Watch, P-Watch, Q-Watch, Zee-Watch), as well as counterfeits using the brand name Swatch. Many Swatch imitations were produced in Hong Kong or Taiwan for distribution in the United States, Europe, or other major markets. Many of these looked strikingly similar to Swatch, and some were even similar in quality and very price competitive; the company was involved in a long series of legal proceedings to fight off the competition.

Timex, one of the companies worst hit by the LCD watch glut, had launched a line of colored fashion watches called "Watercolors," priced slightly below Swatch. Timex was also rumored to be preparing a new advertising campaign for its "Big-Bold-Beautiful" fashion watch line for women, introduced in the summer of 1986 and targeted to an age group older than Swatch's. According to one industry expert, the Timex range did not seem to have any "winners," at least in Europe.

Seiko's Lorus line was expanded in 1984 to include "Swatch-like" fashion models, priced lower than Swatch, and doing well when they had special design features. The first solar-powered wristwatch was also launched under the Lorus brand name in 1986. Competitors wondered, however, if Seiko was really committed to competing with Swatch, since nonwatch activities (e.g., personal computers, printers, and audio and video equipment) were to be increased to 30% of worldwide sales by 1989. Don Galliers summarized the challenge in the United States:

> If you want to take a significant market share away from the existing well-established brand, you have to spend three times the amount of advertising that brand spends. To kick us where we hurt worse, in delivery and depth, they'll have to build up $75 million worth of initial inventory, in addition to the $100 million investment in production facilities. That's one hell of an investment!

Citizen apparently did not think it necessary to launch a Swatch-like product, preferring instead to focus on its specialization, digitals, and technically sophisticated watches. At first, Casio, specializing more specifically in calculators and extremely price-competitive multifunction digital watches, did not jump on the Swatch bandwagon either. In 1986, however, when the shift from digital to analog

5. A music video cable TV station watched primarily by 12–24-year-olds.

watches became apparent, Casio launched "Color Burst," a line of quartz analog fashion watches, waterproof to 50 meters, retailing at less than the price of a Swatch watch. Sales were reported to be rather disappointing.

Swatch management claimed that only the very large firms could compete with ETA on price and that smaller firms undercutting Swatch on price were left with virtually no margin to compete with Swatch's intensive communication. Swatch refused to enter into a price war with its competitors. According to Jacques Irniger, ETA marketing manager, Swatch spent more than double the watch industry's average "ad spend" for a single brand: "Competitors can copy our watch but not our media spend. They will also have trouble duplicating some of Swatch's promotional stunts." Examples of "Swatch-like" fashion watches with limited market response were the "Twist" by Accurist and the "American Graffiti" watch by Gillex in the United Kingdom. According to Ernst Thomke, "In an era when superbly accurate quartz watches sell for $10, the key is not technology but image." (Exhibit 19 presents Swatch's image in five countries in 1986.)

Brands explicitly positioned as fashion accessories varied from one country to another, and it was difficult to obtain a global view of the situation as well as market share data to determine the relative threat presented by such brands. Designer watches (e.g., Gucci, Dior, Givenchy, Nina Ricci, Yves Saint Laurent, Ralph Lauren, Calvin Klein, Guy Laroche, Lanvin, Hermes, and Benetton), although often in a different price range from Swatch (see segments C and D in Table 3), were a growing trend, and the actual concept of "fashion watch" did not appear clear in consumers' minds. Responses to the survey question "Please tell me all the brands of fashion watches you can think of" included such diverse brands as Timex, Swatch, Bulova, Citizen, and Rolex. Franz Sprecher's definition of a fashion watch was "a watch not only colorful but with accessorizing potential and meaning, a statement of the fashion trends at a specific period of time."

In Europe, moderately priced fashion watches included Kelton, an inexpensive French watch brand launched by Timex in the early sixties. After initial rejection by the traditional jewelers' network, Kelton had been very successfully distributed through mass distribution channels. The breakdown of Kelton sales in France was estimated to be 45% from "tabacs" (registered tobacconists), 30% from supermarkets, and 25% from department and variety stores. Kelton was also distributed in the United Kingdom, Portugal, and Italy. Prices ranged from FF 99 to FF 320. K'Watch, Kelton's response to Swatch, launched in June 1984, was priced from FF 249 to FF 270. Kelton brand awareness was very high in France, and it had a young, inexpensive, active and fashionable image. Philippe d'Herbomez, Kelton's marketing manager, commented:

> When you think about the Swatch strategy, you realize that the product was launched on the Kelton concept: "Vous vous changez, changez de Kelton" (Time to change, change your Kelton!), but the consumer more readily changes his Swatch than his Kelton since with every new Swatch collection the previous ones become virtually obsolete. When Swatch was launched, Kelton was no longer very fashionable and had become expensive in comparison with Asian watches. The 1987 Kelton collection is a series of new lower-priced products. Our distribution is wearing thin also, so we plan

to open up new outlets and invest in communication with emphasis on our well-known, successful slogan.

Other fashion watches had mushroomed in the wake of the Swatch success. The M-Watch, an inexpensive (SF 38), traditional quartz watch containing ETA movements, was launched by Mondaine in Zurich at the same time as Swatch and was distributed by the Swiss supermarket chain Migros. In May 1984, the French firm Kiplé launched "Kip'Marine," priced from FF 210 to FF 440 and distributed through supermarkets, stationers, tabacs, and variety stores.

In October 1984, Dr. Konstantin Theile, ETA's marketing manager during the development of Swatch, left ETA to launch the new brand TIQ (Time Inter Corporation AG). This new, nonplastic, leather-strapped, silent, and repairable waterproof quartz watch priced at SF 70 to SF 150 targeted an "optimistic, individualistic, fashion-conscious consumer" aged 25 to 35 but one slightly more conservative than the Swatch consumer. Production costs were three times those of Swatch, and TIQ granted the usual margin to the trade. Distribution was through upscale department stores, established jewelers, and fashion boutiques. To quote Theile:

> Not everybody wants to wear a noisy, irreparable plastic watch. It is frustrating to become attached to your watch only to find out that your model cannot be repaired and is no longer available.

By early 1985, the French firm Beuchat had introduced a series of metal- and plastic-strapped watches with original and fun faces: a sports line illustrating 27 different sports; a "crazy" line, including a face with hands turning counterclockwise; and a "corporations" line illustrating different professions. Distribution was the same as Swatch, and prices were slightly higher. Beuchat's plans were to expand into promotional watches starting with BMW. Under license from Club Méditerranée, the French firm Harckley CDH had launched waterproof metal and plastic quartz watches distributed worldwide through selective channels. Prices were also slightly higher than Swatch. Harckley did not invest in advertising for the "Club Med" watch, but point-of-sale promotion included an aquarium display containing a submerged watch.

The American firm Le Jour started testing a $49 kaleidoscope-color fashion watch called "Sixty" in 1986. Sales, mainly through department stores, were reportedly encouraging. In the spring of 1986, a Swiss entrepreneur launched "The Clip," a clip-on, waterproof, shock-resistant, silent, and repairable quartz watch designed to be worn "anywhere except on the wrist" and sold through the same distribution channels as Swatch. Launched in Switzerland at SF 40 and SF 50, The Clip was introduced in France, Spain, West Germany, and the United Kingdom in the summer and would roll out to the United States in the fall. E. A. Day, managing director of Louis Newmark, the Swatch distributor in the UK, commented:

> It is too early to discuss the future of The Clip. It does appear to sell well when promoted, but once the promotion ends, sales drop back dramatically.

In the summer of 1986, the Swiss firm SAMEL SA had introduced "Sweet-zerland," a water-resistant quartz watch that snapped in and out of interchangeable elastic terrycloth wristbands in different colors, with a 2-year battery, priced at $40. Distribution was through jewelry stores, fashion boutiques, accessory and sports shops, perfumeries, and upscale department stores in Europe, as well as in the United States through a California subsidiary.

Sekonda, an English firm importing watches from the USSR and Hong Kong, launched a new line of fashion watches in 1985, under the brand names "Spangles," "Phantom," and "Nostalgia." Prices ranged from £15 to £20. A mechanical watch named "Hotline," with style variations on the dial and strap, appeared in West Germany and Switzerland in 1986. It was explicitly aimed at preteenage groups and retailed mainly in department stores for DM 30. Other fashion watches in roughly the same price category as Swatch included Avia, Alfex, Orion, Zeon, Video Clip, and Hip-Hop.

THE MEETING

Chris Keigel checked the fashionable collection of Swatches on his wrist. It was time to make major decisions for the future of Swatch, and the meeting with Thomke, Marquardt, Imgrüth, and Sprecher was approaching fast. He perused the sales figures (see Exhibit 20). Keigel knew that Swatch guards and shields, the Paraphernalia line, and the Coca-Cola watches yielded profit margins exceeding that of Swatch watches, whereas those of the other items in the U.S.-extended product line did not. Apparel profit margins had dropped, and sales were lagging behind forecasts. Swatch management knew that the transport and other costs involved in importing this line to Europe might put prices out of line, especially since the clothing was designed specifically for the American market. He also knew that Max Imgrüth was pushing for six collection changes per year but remembered hearing Franz Sprecher advocate a more conservative approach:

> We can't just announce "Here comes our collection" to the trade. We are an accessory, we are not making fashion. What is most important is what the consumer will think. Are we really enough of a fashion product in the eyes of the consumer to make a planned line extension into fashion wear? If Calvin Klein, Ralph Lauren, or Benetton make a watch, that works because they are established fashion firms, but I have never seen it work the other way around. There is a lot of competition in the department stores, whole floors of T-shirts, so where is our expertise?

EXHIBIT 1   A Semiotic Comparison of Digital and Analog Watches

Digital	Analog
Time is represented by a sign.	*Time is represented by a symbol.*
The focus is on	*The focus is on*
the instant	length of time
numerical code	a pictorial code
discontinuity	continuity
linearity and periodicity	circularity and cyclical character
Signification	*Signification*
The time display is precise.	Time display is imprecise.
Time is imposed.	Time can be negotiated.
Monosemy—only one meaning.	Polysemy—several meanings.

Source: Adapted from Michel-Adrien Voirol "Un Problème d'Evolution du Produit Horlogère," in "Les Apports de la Sémiotique au Marketing et à la Publicité," IREP Seminar, 1976.

EXHIBIT 2   Swatch International Launch Collection

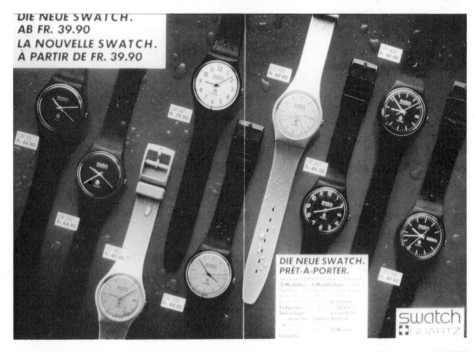

EXHIBIT 3   Perceived Advantages and Disadvantages of Swatch in 1984

	Total (n = 800)	United States (n = 200)	France (n = 200)	Great Britain (n = 200)	West Germany (n = 200)
Positive features					
pretty shape	34.5[a]	34.0	33.5	20.0	50.5
amusing, original	28.6	9.0	31.5	28.0	46.0
waterproof	28.4	37.5	29.5	29.5	17.0
fashionable, modern	24.5	7.5	30.5	24.0	36.0
pretty, varied colors	22.6	31.0	13.5	18.5	27.5
strong, resistant	22.1	24.5	27.5	24.5	12.0
can be worn by anyone	16.0	30.5	9.0	12.5	12.0
quality watches	14.8	28.0	8.0	4.0	19.0
low price	14.5	3.5	32.0	5.0	17.5
can be worn anywhere	12.6	13.5	13.5	11.0	12.5
Negative features					
uncomfortable plastic strap	16.0[b]	13.5	13.0	17.5	20.0
too fashionable, too modern	10.3	2.0	6.5	9.5	23.0
looks like a gadget, a toy	9.9	3.5	10.0	8.5	17.5
does not match all styles of dress	8.4	1.0	4.0	14.0	14.5
fragile	8.1	0.5	12.0	3.0	17.0
too sophisticated face	7.4	6.0	3.0	8.5	12.0
too much plastic	6.6	1.0	7.5	—	18.0
too noisy	3.6	—	12.5	1.0	1.0

Source: Delta International Market Study, December 1984.

[a]Percent of respondents indicating this feature in response to the question: "What, in your opinion, are the advantages of Swatch watches in comparison with other watches?"

[b]Percent of respondents indicating this feature in response to the question: "And what would be their disadvantages?"

EXHIBIT 4 Actual and Perceived 1986 Retail Prices of Swatch

France Actual price = FF 250					West Germany Actual price = DM 65				
Perceived price (FF)	Total n = 200	Buyers n = 66	Potential buyers n = 99	Non-buyers n = 35	Perceived price (DM)	Total n = 200	Buyers n = 67	Potential buyers n = 74	Non-buyers n = 59
< 100	10	2	11	20	< 20	3	3	—	7
100–150	9	2	12	14	21–40	11	6	12	14
151–200	17	8	23	17	41–60	38	27	42	44
201–250	41	74	32	3	61–80	39	58	34	22
251–300	7	9	5	9	81–100	7	4	8	8
301–400	4	3	4	3	101–200	3	2	3	3
> 400	2	3	1	3	> 200	1	—	1	2

United States Actual price = $30					United Kingdom Actual price = £24				
Perceived price ($)	Total n = 290	Buyers n = 99	Potential buyers n = 140	Non-buyers n = 51	Perceived price (£)	Total n = 202	Buyers n = 68	Potential buyers n = 83	Non-buyers n = 51
< 20	8*	3	9	16	<10	4	—	4	12
21–30	57	62	56	49	11–15	10	3	14	14
31–40	26	25	26	25	16–20	39	44	36	35
41–50	6	7	6	2	21–25	22	38	16	12
51–60	2	3	2	2	26–30	8	4	10	12
> 60	1	—	1	2	31–35	1	1	1	2
					36–40	2	—	4	2
					> 40	1	1	—	—

Source: Qualitest A.G. Market Study, Zurich, August 1986, and company records.

*Percent of total responses to the question: "All the [Swatch] watches have the same price—could you estimate that price?"

EXHIBIT 5   Selected Watches From the 1984–1986 Collections

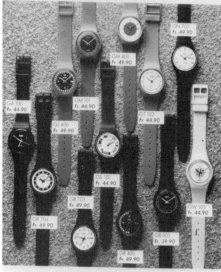

Spring/Summer 1984

GRANITA DI FRUTTA
Spring/Summer 1985

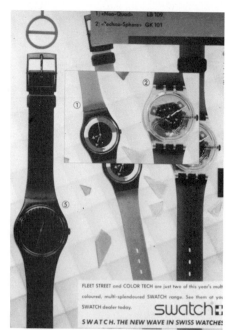

COLOR TECH
Fall/Winter 1985/86

(continued)

EXHIBIT 5 (continued)

DEVIL'S RUN

KIVA

JELLYFISH

CALYPSO BEACH

EXHIBIT 6 Preferences, Purchase Intentions, and Sales Data for 1985 Spring/Summer Swatch Collection (France, West Germany, Great Britain, United States)

| Swatch Code | Most preferred models[a] | | | Least preferred models[b] | Purchase intentions[c] | | | | Ex-factory sales worldwide (000 units) |
| | Total (n = 800) | Men (n = 400) | Women (n = 400) | Total (n = 800) | For self | | | Gift | |
					Total (n = 800)	Men (n = 400)	Women (n = 400)	Total (n = 800)	
GB 101	41.1	63.3	19.0	2.0	33.6	57.0	10.3	27.0	147
GA 102	36.1	58.8	13.5	3.9	28.4	48.5	8.3	26.0	149
LB 106	20.6	6.5	34.6	1.5	16.6	2.8	30.6	18.3	140
LM 104	20.4	3.3	37.6	2.3	18.1	1.0	35.3	21.0	70
GM 401	19.0	24.8	13.3	3.1	15.9	21.3	10.5	15.0	67
LW 104	18.3	3.8	32.8	3.5	15.1	1.3	29.1	16.6	246
LA 100	17.4	6.5	28.3	1.4	15.1	3.3	27.1	17.3	207
GN 401	17.3	31.8	2.8	4.3	15.1	28.3	2.0	11.8	63
GB 705	13.3	22.8	3.8	8.5	10.5	19.3	1.8	7.8	106
GW 104	12.9	11.8	14.0	7.9	8.0	5.8	10.3	9.9	221
GB 706	10.3	16.3	4.3	10.0	7.5	12.5	2.5	8.0	121
GK 100	9.9	11.5	8.3	48.9	6.3	7.3	5.3	8.0	286
GT 103	9.8	9.3	10.3	5.1	5.6	5.0	6.3	6.8	53
LT 101	9.5	1.8	17.3	3.1	7.1	0.3	14.0	10.3	53
LB 107	6.9	1.8	11.8	6.8	5.5	0.5	10.3	5.6	88
LW 107[d]	6.1	1.0	11.3	27.5	4.5	0.8	8.3	7.1	322
GJ 700	5.8	7.3	4.3	37.4	3.6	4.5	2.8	4.4	104
LN 103	4.1	0.8	7.3	2.6	3.3	—	6.5	5.6	64
LW 105[d]	3.9	0.8	7.0	17.3	3.0	0.3	5.8	4.6	213
GM 701	3.9	5.0	2.8	22.3	2.8	4.0	1.5	2.3	108
GB 403	3.5	4.5	2.5	13.9	2.5	3.5	1.5	2.9	78
LW 106[d]	2.4	0.8	4.0	27.1	1.5	—	3.0	3.1	152
LS 102	1.8	1.0	2.5	28.9	1.1	0.3	2.0	2.1	107
LB 105	1.5	0.8	2.3	5.0	1.3	0.8	1.8	1.6	118
LB 104	1.1	0.5	1.8	3.5	0.6	0.3	1.0	2.3	125

Source: Delta International Market Study, December 1984, and company records.

[a]Percent of total responses to the question, "Here are a number of new Swatch watches. They come in two sizes, standard and small. Which are the three you like best?"

[b]Percent of total responses to the question, "Which are the three watches you like least?" Responses were virtually the same, regardless of sex.

[c]Percent of total responses to the question, "Would you consider buying such a watch for yourself or as a gift?"

[d]"Granita di Frutta": 69.9% of those interested in these models as gifts claimed the recipient would be a girl under 15 years of age.

EXHIBIT 6 (continued)

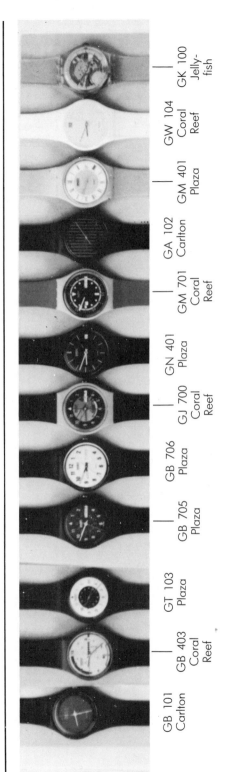

GB 101
Carlton

GB 403
Coral
Reef

GT 103
Plaza

GB 705
Plaza

GB 706
Plaza

GJ 700
Coral
Reef

GN 401
Plaza

GM 701
Coral
Reef

GA 102
Carlton

GM 401
Plaza

GW 104
Coral
Reef

GK 100
Jelly-
fish

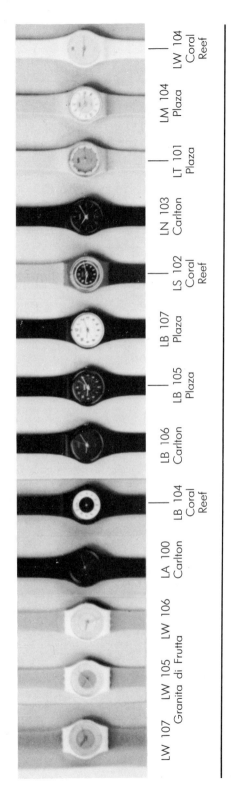

LW 107
LW 105
Granita di Frutta
LW 106

LA 100
Carlton

LB 104
Coral
Reef

LB 106
Carlton

LB 105
Plaza

LB 107
Plaza

LS 102
Coral
Reef

LN 103
Carlton

LT 101
Plaza

LM 104
Plaza

LW 104
Coral
Reef

351

EXHIBIT 7 Swatch Distribution Channels

Channel	Switzerland		United Kingdom		France		West Germany		United States	
	1985	1986	1985	1986	1985	1986	1985	1986	1985	1986
Department stores	10[a]	10	6	9	3	11	19	22	82	71
Jewelers	85	78	87	78	95	79	73	59	3	2
Sports shops	—	—	0.1	0.1	—	—	6	16	1	2
Fashion shops	5	12	6	12	—	—	2	4	6	12
Others[b]	—	0.2	0.4	0.5	2	10	—	—	8	14
Total number of stores (including branches)	590	511	1,708	1,273	2,634	2,266	1,030	511	6,437	4,634

Source: Company records.

[a]Percent of total number of outlets.

[b]Gift and card shops, drug stores, college bookstores, military exchanges, catalogues, etc.

EXHIBIT 8 Example of Swatch Counterfeit Alert Program

NOT ALL WRIST WATCHES BEARING THE SWATCH⊹ NAME ARE THE **REAL McCOY!**

1 NOTE THE DIFFERENCE BETWEEN A **SWATCH®** AND A CLEVER PHONY: THE **REAL** SWATCH®HAS THREE PLASTIC DIVISIONS AT THE HINGE — THE **PHONY** ONLY HAS **TWO!**

SWATCH®

PHONY

2 **REAL** SWATCH®WATCHES HAVE BATTERY HATCHES LOCATED **OFF-CENTER-** **PHONY** SWATCH WATCHES HAVE **CENTERED** HATCHES!

BE A **SWATCH®-WATCHDOG!**

DON'T ACCEPT A PHONY AS A **WARRANTY RETURN!**

EXHIBIT 9 Swatch Accessories and Apparel (U.S.A.)

SIGNATURE LINE

FUNWEAR AND FUNGEAR

EXHIBIT 10 Aided Awareness of Swatch Accessories (U.S.A.), 1985

	Total sample (n = 895)	Age		
		12–18 (n = 219)	*19–24* (n = 234)	*25–34* (n = 442)
Shields	17*	43	13	8
Bags	16	37	12	8
T-Shirts	15	36	13	6
Guards	11	27	10	4
Gift sets	9	20	10	3
Chums	8	20	6	3
Beach boxes	8	18	4	5
Maxi Swatch	8	17	7	3
Pocket knives	6	15	5	2
Pens and pencils	6	13	3	3
Razors	3	5	3	1

Source: "Attitude and Awareness of Swatch in Various Markets" Study, McCann-Erickson, July 1985.

*Percent of respondents indicating this accessory in response to the question: "Please tell me which of the following Swatch accessories you are aware of."

EXHIBIT 11   Swatch International TV Commercials

"HERO"—1983 LAUNCH CAMPAIGN

"Watch! Swatch! La Nouvelle Swatch! Swatch, Swiss quartz, water-resistant, shock-resistant, imported from Switzerland. It's come a long way since the cuckoo clock. Swatch, the new wave in Swiss watches."

"NEW CUT II"—1984

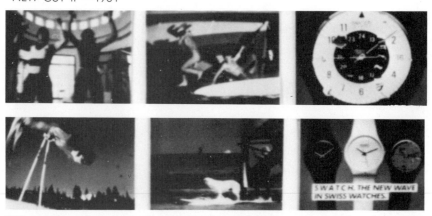

"Watch! Swatch! La Nouvelle Swatch! Portable Swiss quartz watches that are more than water-resistant, shock-resistant: Swiss watches that are more than precise. These days it's fashion that makes us tick. Swatch, the new wave in Swiss watches!"

(continued)

EXHIBIT 11 (continued)

"STREETLIFE"—1986

"Swatch! (Swatch. . .) Always different, always new! (Swatch!) Fashionable (Swatch!), water-resistant, shock-resistant, Swiss-made (Swatch!). Swatch, the·new wave in Swiss watches!"

EXHIBIT 12   International Adaptation of Swatch Print Ads

FRANCE

WEST GERMANY

CANADA

NORWAY

EXHIBIT 13 Major Special Events Organized or Sponsored by Swatch

Date	Country	Event
March 1984	Germany	13-ton giant Swatch on Commerzbank building, Frankfurt
April 1984	France	"Urban Sax" saxóphonist group at the Eldorado Theater in Paris to celebrate launch; first Swatch Magazine
August 1984	United States	Ivan Lendl U.S. Tennis Open
September 1984	United States	World Breakdancing Championship: The Roxy, New York
September 1984	France	First street art painting show with the French artists Les Frères Ripoulin, Espace Cardin Theater, Paris
November 1984	United States	The Fat Boys music sponsorship, Private Eye's, New York, to introduce "Granita di Frutta" to the trade
October 1984– January 1985	United States	New York City Fresh Festival: breakdancing, rapping, graffiti artists
January 1985	United States	World Freestyle Invitational/Celebrity Classic, Breckenridge, Colorado
March 1985	France	IRCAM "copy art" show, Paris; limited edition (119) Kiki Picasso design watches; second Swatch Magazine
Spring 1985	United States	Hi-fly freestyle windsurfing team sponsorship
May 1985	England	Second street art painting show, Covent Garden, London, with Les Frères Ripoulin and English street artists
June 1985	Switzerland	Art fair in Basel; third street art painting show with 50 European artists
Summer 1985	Sweden	Oestersjö Rallyt (Segal-Rallye)
September 1985	France	Cinema festival, Pompidou Center, Paris, with Kurosawa's film, "Ran"; Mini City Magazine
September 1985	France	"Le Défilé": Jean-Paul Gaultier & Régine Chopinot fashion/dance show, Pavillon Baltard, Paris
September 1985	England	Andrew Logan's Alternative Miss World, London
October 1985	Belgium	"Mode et Anti-Mode" fashion show, Brussels
Fall 1985	United States	Thompson Twins concert tour sponsorship
November 1985	Spain	Swatch launch party, the Cirque, Barcelona
November 1985	United States	Limelight launch party, Los Angeles (for trade)
November 1985	International	Freestyle World Cup sponsorship
November 1985	Japan	Giant Swatch in Tokyo for launch of Swatch
January 1986	United States	Fashion show: Private Eye's, New York (for trade)
January 1986	United States	Pierre Boulez orchestra concert tour

(continued)

EXHIBIT 13 (continued)

Date	Country	Event
January–November, 1986	England	"Time & Motion Competition," Royal College of Art, London
February 1986	England	Feargal Sharkey tour
February 1986	France	First World Freestyle Ski Championships, Tignes
February–March 1986	Germany	Swatch Freestyle World Cup, Oberjoch
March 1986	Switzerland	"Arosa" Freestyle skiing weekend with retailers
March 1986	Austria	"Exposa" jewelry fair with Swatch balloons
March 1986	France	"Waterproof Paris": Daniel Larrieux's subaquatic ballet performance
April–October 1986	Canada	Giant Swatch, Swiss Pavilion, Expo 86, Vancouver
May–September 1986	Sweden	Swatch Funboard Cup sponsorship
June 1986	France	Fourth street art painting show; fourth Swatch Magazine
June 1986	Italy	"Sssswatchgala Mailand," launch event
July 1986–February 1987	Switzerland	First International Swatch Freestyle Youth Camp, Zermatt
July 1986	International	Second Himalaya Super Marathon sponsorship
July 1986	Netherlands	Drachenflug Festival sponsored by Swatch

(continued)

EXHIBIT 13 (continued)

JAPAN

FRANCE

SWITZERLAND

"Swatch-like" stand
under a tent - BEA '84

WEST GERMANY

UNITED STATES

EXHIBIT 14A Swatch Advertising Budget (thousand Swiss francs)

Country	Launch	1983	1984	1985	1986
Switzerland	March 1983	459	620	964	1,107
United Kingdom	March 1983	922	2,398	2,398	2,767
West Germany	September 1983	2,275	4,132	2,706	2,706
United States	September 1983		9,480	32,838	33,404
Austria	January 1984		244	429	472
France	April 1984		2,610	2,423	2,583
Belgium	April 1984		199	295	307
Netherlands	May 1984		148	430	369
South Africa	September 1984		301	133	92
Australia	September 1984		562	883	984
Norway	October 1984			243	246
Sweden	October 1984			571	615
Denmark	March 1985			151	184
Finland	May 1985			236	246
Japan	October 1985			na	na
Spain	October 1985			1,230	2,460
Italy	June 1986				3,524

Note: "Advertising" includes production of ads, media spending, in-store programs, etc.

EXHIBIT 14B Swatch Public Relations/Special Events Budget (thousand Swiss francs)

Country	Launch	1983	1984	1985	1986
Central promotion budget			3,690	4,920	6,150
Switzerland	March 1983			258	184
United Kingdom	March 1983			369	633
United States	September 1983			3,978	886
West Germany	September 1983			300	209
Austria	January 1984		29	29	37
France	April 1984		898	1,204	1,291
Belgium	April 1984		139	253	246
Netherlands	May 1984		118	209	260
South Africa	September 1984		18	31	49
Australia	September 1984			86	123
Norway	October 1984			47	80
Sweden	October 1984			77	209
Denmark	March 1985			*	61
Finland	May 1985			*	37
Japan	October 1985			na	na
Spain	October 1985			492	1,599
Italy	June 1986				1,458

Source: Company records (disguised data).
Note: This budget includes music and sports promotions, special events, etc.
*Paid for by distributor.

EXHIBIT 15A   Selected Swatch TV Commercials in the United States

"FAT BOYS"—1985

"Swatch'" (opera music) "Oh, Fat Boys, where *are* you?" "Brrr, Swatch-up, ha ha ha, Swatch-up, tell the hands on the Swatch, oh the sister and the Swatch is water- and shock-resistant. Brrr, Swatch-up, Swatch-up. The new wave in Swiss watches, Swatch!"

"FUNWEAR AND FUNGEAR"—1986

"Swatch! Swatch! Funwear and fungear."

EXHIBIT 15B   Selected Swatch Print Ads in the United States

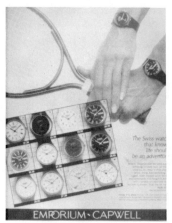

Spring 1983

Fall 1983

Christmas 1984

Spring 1985

Summer 1986

Summer 1986

(continued)

EXHIBIT 15B (continued)

(continued)

EXHIBIT 15B (continued)

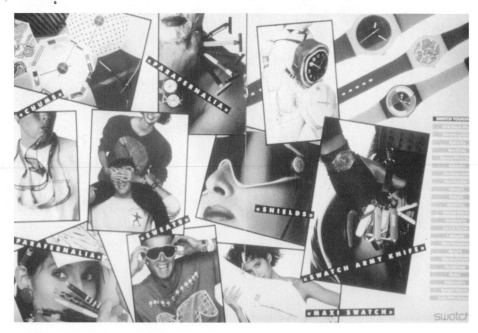

EXHIBIT 16   A Psychographic Segmentation of Consumers in the United States

Age	Children (6–10)	Teeny boppers (11–15)	Young teen rockers (11–15)	Students (11–15)
Profile/interests	TV: "Jem" rock cartoon, "Nikelodeon." Males: He-man, Transformers, G.I. Joe. Females: Care Bears.	Almost 100% female. Middle-middle/upper class, suburban, click-oriented, very fashion conscious: trendy, outrageous style, favor So. Calif. over Europe/NYC look. Like partying, dancing, hanging-out at malls. Music: breezy pop love songs, New Wave. Main hero: Madonna.	80% male, 20% female. Middle-upper/middle class, suburban, mall-creatures, macho, heavy-metal look. Hard rock concerts, partying (but isolated, not in cliques). Main heros: Stallone, Schwarzenegger, Iron Maiden ("Madonna is useless").	50% male, 50% female. Middle-lower/middle class, very conservative, like professional and participation sports. Music: no allegiance to type of music or artist.
Media	Network TV, MTV.[a]	MTV-crazy, fashion magazines, Top-40 radio.	AOR[b] radio, critical MTV watchers.	Network TV, AM radio.
Shopping habits	Dependent on parents. Stores: department stores, malls, etc.	Heavy consumers. Stores: department stores, record stores, malls.	Not shopping oriented. Stores: record stores, department stores, malls.	Consider shopping a function not an event. Stores: Sears, K-Mart, chain drug stores.
Reactions to Swatch	42% awareness (of which 4% ownership, 76% interest in teeny bop models). Consider it "cool," something the big kids wear. Parents' interests: durability, price, large face numbers, traditional styles, models that won't become unfashionable.	Very positive—provides a sense of identity—is a life-style magnifier but becoming too commonplace, boring. Line extensions: negative. Too expensive, not cool, "Swatch is not a clothing line, but a rock 'n roll timepiece."	High awareness due to visibility in schools but strong negative bias: Swatch represents teeny bopper life-style, "price too high for a piece of plastic." Only 16% wear watches but 72% desire to purchase Swatch if positioned right (NB: are currently undersymboled).	Price and function outweigh fashionability. Swatch too wild for their life-style yet potential interest to "fit in" (80% unawareness of traditional styles).

(continued)

[a]MTV = a leading national "basic cable" TV music TV station.
[b]AOR = album-oriented rock.

EXHIBIT 16 (continued)

Age	Transitionaries (22–32)	Older casuals (22–43)	Weekend hippies (33–43)
Profile/interests	Conservative, social climbers. Like wildness (as observers, not participants), competitive sports. Music: "intelligent" rock 'n roll.	The hidden mainstream, ultra-conservative, very family-oriented, fast-food patrons, socially inactive, disinterested in fashion. Music: traditional.	Mellowed former hippies. Look like but hate being called Yuppies; still subscribe to basic 60s principles. Music: mood music, "New Age" movement.
Media	Females: fashion magazines. Males: Time, Newsweek, Sports Illustrated. Not MTV (only 16% regular viewers).	Network TV. Local newspapers (even National Enquirer-type tabloids).	Cable TV (critical viewers) but no MTV, radio (as background music). Weekend newspaper supplements, traditional magazines (i.e., Time, Newsweek, etc.)
Shopping habits	Pro-American but respectful of foreign-made goods; appreciate quality/value; balance between fashion and conservatism. Stores: major mainstream department stores (91% source of potential Swatch purchase for 76% aware).	Traditional brands (e.g., Timex, Bulova, Casio for watches).	Heavy shoppers, appreciate quality products. Stores: upscale department stores (I.Magnin, Saks) for females. Mainstream department stores for men.
Reactions to Swatch	Positive: consider it a great leisure tool, like its durability, disposability, price, reliability. Line extensions: high awareness but overpriced for females, not really credible for males.	Watches are functional. Awareness: 12% aided. 4% unaided.	High awareness, but 43% of those aware have never seen one. Cheap, teen-item image; but like functionality, light weight, durability. Line extensions: overpriced, not functional, too gaudy. High awareness of competing brands.

(continued)

Source: Compiled from a Burkhard, Abrams, Douglas, Eliot market study, 1986.

EXHIBIT 16 Results (continued)

"Since we got Swatch, dad's really cookin' and our weiners taste better too!"

1. Liked by teeny boppers, too "young teeny" for all others. "Camp" humor was appreciated but considered too like "MTV parents." The caption was considered humorous but the visual too unrealistic for adult parents.

SWITCH TO SWATCH

THE CRAZY NEW WAVE IN SWISS WATCHES.

2. Good idea, poorly executed, not credible. The sports car was positive for males but the model was too unrealistic, too slick. "Race drivers would not wear three watches." The caption was felt to evoke the potential decline of the Swatch trend. The car was considered too European and sophisticated.

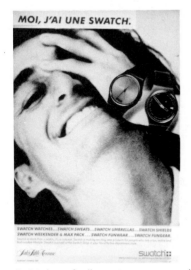

MOI, J'AI UNE SWATCH.

SWATCH WATCHES...SWATCH SWEATS...SWATCH UMBRELLAS...SWATCH SHIELDS
SWATCH WEEKENDER & MAX PACK ... SWATCH FUNWEAR ... SWATCH FUNGEAR

swatch::

3. Males of all ages except trendies felt the foreign language caption was counterproductive to the need for Swatch to move away from European "New Wave" clichés.

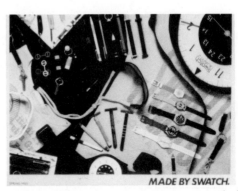

MADE BY SWATCH.

4. These items were of interest to a *very* fashion-conscious minority. The ad tended to reinforce the trend aspect of the Swatch look, a major concern for potential buyers. Most respondents wouldn't buy a Swatch pen or razor.

(continued)

EXHBIT 16 (continued)

5. The Thompson Twins tend to reinforce the young teen image. Use of another group, still appreciated by the teens but more accessible to older, potential, and existing Swatch customers (e.g., Transitionaries, Preppies, and Rockers), was advised.

6. The "collection" concept appealed to most teen females but: (1) What is it and what does it mean? (2) This concept aroused suspicion mostly among 16–32 age males that it was a ploy to push sales of Swatch nonwatch gear.

7. There is limited awareness of Keith Haring outside New York, but the ad tested well since most people like animation.
Only complaint: "too disco."

8. 43% of respondents recognized Bruce Jenner, but he was considered too "goody-goody," even for young teen female prior fans.

EXHIBIT 17 Aided Recall of Watch Advertisements

Brand	United States				Switzerland				United Kingdom			
	Total (n = 290)	Buyers (n = 99)	Potential buyers (n = 140)	Non-buyers (n = 51)	Total (n = 212)	Buyers (n = 90)	Potential buyers (n = 87)	Non-buyers (n = 35)	Total (n = 202)	Buyers (n = 68)	Potential buyers (n = 83)	Non-buyers (n = 51)
Swatch	67*	79	66	47	78	88	70	74	50	56	53	39
Omega	6	9	6	—	19	22	17	14	5	10	—	8
Rolex	31	32	25	45	20	29	10	23	17	16	22	12
Seiko	35	35	36	29	16	22	6	23	30	35	28	27
Cartier	14	7	16	25	16	22	10	11	11	12	13	6
Timex	41	37	46	35	4	3	2	11	23	26	19	24
Gucci	16	17	15	16	—	—	—	—	—	—	—	—
Citizen	18	17	21	12	5	3	3	11	15	18	18	6
Pulsar	11	12	14	—	—	—	—	—	—	—	—	—
Bulova	10	6	12	14	—	—	—	—	—	—	—	—
Casio	10	14	11	—	6	7	5	6	11	15	11	6
Longines	11	12	11	12	15	18	9	20	3	6	4	—
Guess	14	18	12	14	—	—	—	—	9	13	10	4
Tissot	8	12	7	—	50	50	45	60	4	4	6	—
A-Watch	10	10	13	—	—	—	—	—	—	—	—	—
K'Watch	—	—	—	—	—	—	—	—	—	—	—	—
M-Watch	—	—	—	—	13	18	6	20	—	—	—	—
Club Med	—	—	—	—	—	—	—	—	—	—	—	—
Dugena	—	—	—	—	—	—	—	—	—	—	—	—
Kiplé	—	—	—	—	—	—	—	—	—	—	—	—
Lorus	4	—	4	—	—	—	—	—	—	—	—	—
Yéma	—	—	—	—	—	—	—	—	—	—	—	—

Source: Compiled from a Qualitest A.G. study, Zurich, August 1986.

Note: No figure indicates that the brand was not listed on the card.

*Percent of total responses to the question, "Which of the watches on this list have you seen or heard advertised recently?"

(continued)

EXHIBIT 17 (continued)

	France				West Germany			
Brand	Total (n = 200)	Buyers (n = 66)	Potential Buyers (n = 99)	Non-buyers (n = 35)	Total (n = 200)	Buyers (n = 67)	Potential buyers (n = 74)	Non-buyers (n = 59)
Swatch	50	62	46	34	67	70	69	61
Omega	15	—	—	—	19	18	24	14
Rolex	30	17	12	17	34	31	39	31
Seiko	30	32	30	26	31	30	36	25
Cartier	—	—	—	—	—	—	—	—
Timex	21	23	23	9	22	24	26	15
Gucci	—	—	—	—	—	—	—	—
Citizen	58	64	56	49	—	—	—	—
Pulsar	4	3	5	—	6	16	—	—
Bulova	—	—	—	—	—	—	—	—
Casio	11	11	10	14	—	—	—	14
Longines	—	—	—	—	13	13	11	—
Guess	—	—	—	—	—	—	—	—
Tissot	—	—	—	—	12	14	11	10
A-Watch	—	—	—	—	—	—	—	—
K'Watch	4	6	3	—	—	—	—	—
M-Watch	—	—	—	—	—	—	—	—
Club Med	5	6	2	9	—	—	—	—
Dugena	—	—	—	—	15	15	15	15
Kiplé	11	12	10	9	—	—	—	—
Lorus	—	—	—	—	—	—	—	—
Yéma	14	17	12	14	—	—	—	—

Source: Compiled from a Qualitest A.G. study, Zurich, August 1986.

Note: No figure indicates that the brand was not listed on the card.

*Percent of total responses to the question, "Which of the watches on this list have you seen or heard advertised recently?"

EXHIBIT 18 A Perceptual Map of Swatch and Other Leading Brands in West Germany

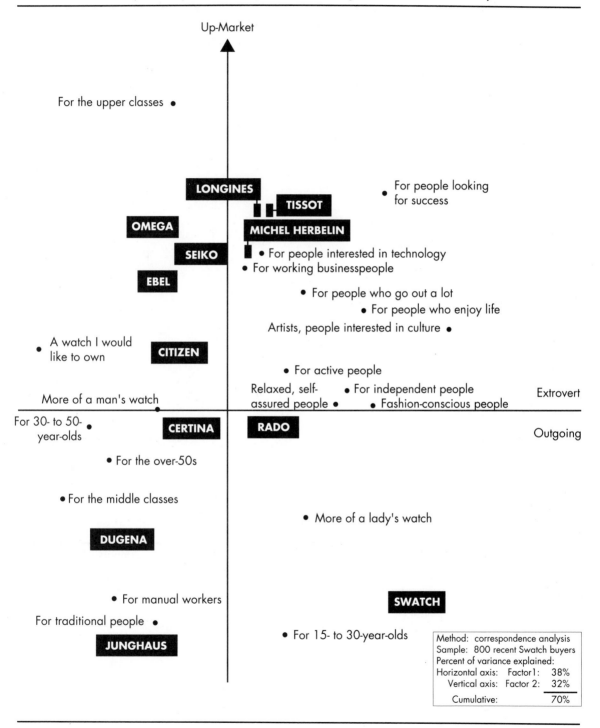

Up-Market

For the upper classes •

LONGINES

TISSOT

• For people looking for success

OMEGA

MICHEL HERBELIN

SEIKO

EBEL

• For people interested in technology
• For working businesspeople

• For people who go out a lot
• For people who enjoy life

Artists, people interested in culture •

• A watch I would like to own

CITIZEN

• For active people

More of a man's watch

Relaxed, self-assured people •

• For independent people
• Fashion-conscious people

Extrovert

For 30- to 50-year-olds •

CERTINA

RADO

Outgoing

• For the over-50s

• For the middle classes

• More of a lady's watch

DUGENA

• For manual workers

For traditional people •

SWATCH

JUNGHAUS

• For 15- to 30-year-olds

Method: correspondence analysis
Sample: 800 recent Swatch buyers
Percent of variance explained:
Horizontal axis: Factor 1:   38%
Vertical axis: Factor 2:   32%
Cumulative: 70%

EXHIBIT 19 Image of Swatch, 1986

	Switzerland				United Kingdom	
	Total (n = 212)	Buyers (n = 90)	Potential buyers (n = 87)	Non-buyers (n = 35)	Total (n = 202)	Buyers (n = 68)
Swatch:						
Is Swiss made	39*	43	37	31	15	13
Is reasonably priced	36	44	34	20	32	32
Is a sports watch	33	31	39	23	24	28
Is continuously introducing new models (colors, dials)	32	30	37	26	14	10
Is a watch for all occasions (business, sports)	30	37	32	9	31	35
Is a highly fashionable watch	25	27	31	9	37	35
Is mainly for young people	17	17	18	11	27	25
Is waterproof	15	16	16	9	10	10
Is the ideal present	14	17	16	—	11	15
Has good ads	10	13	7	11	8	6
Is a trendy watch	8	4	8	17	22	16
Is a high-quality watch	7	9	6	3	29	32
Is a quartz watch	6	4	7	9	3	1
Is shockproof	5	4	7	—	10	9
Attracts attention	3	2	3	3	24	25
I would like to own more than one.	1	1	1	—	1	1

Source: Qualitest A. G. Study, Zurich, August 1986.
*Percent of total responses to the question: "Which three statements on this card can you think of as the most important ones in describing Swatch?"

EXHIBIT 20A Swatch Sales (thousand units or Swiss francs)

Country	1983		1984		1985		January–August 1986	
	Units	SF	Units	SF	Units	SF	Units	SF
World	1,319	27,901	4,496	114,057	10,168	284,832	8,321	209,954
United States	135	NA	1,242	42,475	4,659	16,7562	3,817	102,824
Switzerland	NA	NA	1,032	23,451	924	21,707	595	14,585
France			399	8,910	756	17,710	667	14,824
England	NA	NA	455	7,140	762	14,288	524	9,694
West Germany	NA	NA	202	4,514	712	17,152	587	16,837
Japan					141	3,374	18	646

EXHIBIT 19   (continued)

| United Kingdom | | France | | | | West Germany | | | |
Potential buyers (n = 83)	Non-buyers (n = 51)	Total (n = 200)	Buyers (n = 66)	Potential buyers (n = 99)	Non-buyers (n = 35)	Total (n = 200)	Buyers (n = 67)	Potential buyers (n = 74)	Non-buyers (n = 59)
17	14	13	12	14	11	21	25	11	29
34	27	24	30	19	26	16	15	16	15
23	22	43	52	37	43	44	51	47	31
23	6	30	29	31	29	50	61	53	32
25	33	23	18	25	23	18	21	23	8
41	31	18	15	21	14	33	19	39	41
22	37	38	23	44	49	40	30	30	63
8	14	8	15	5	3	8	9	14	—
8	10	23	26	26	9	12	18	14	2
8	12	5	8	4	3	16	9	20	19
30	18	29	21	28	43	10	3	4	24
23	33	6	9	4	6	6	6	4	8
6	—	8	5	9	9	8	13	4	7
5	20	9	12	5	14	5	6	8	—
25	20	14	11	14	17	15	12	12	22
—	—	11	15	10	3	1	2	1	—

(continued)

EXHIBIT 20B   Extended Product Line Sales (thousand units or U.S. dollars)

| Item | 1984 | | 1985 | | January–August 1986 | |
	Units	$	Units	$	Units	$
Swatch Guards	7	10	3,617	4,280	2,637	3,721
Chums	13	26	104	226	24	6
Bags			224	2,497	134	1,042
Shields			141	2,418	87	1,381
Knives			263	1,236	4	20
Clocks			4	248	1	77
Umbrellas			181	1,606	109	359
Apparel			620	6,279	1,898	18,877
Paraphernalia			387	1,175	440	464
Coca-Cola watches					194	3,392

Source: Company records (disguised data).

EXHIBIT 19   (continued)

	United States			
	Total (n = 290)	Buyers (n = 99)	Potential buyers (n = 140)	Non- buyers (n = 51)
Swatch:				
Is Swiss made	16	16	16	14
Is reasonably priced	26	31	24	18
Is a sports watch	28	30	26	27
Is continuously introducing new models (colors, dials)	19	20	20	12
Is a watch for all occasions (business, sports)	14	16	16	8
Is a highly fashionable watch	25	27	24	25
Is mainly for young people	16	12	13	33
Is waterproof	17	22	16	10
Is the ideal present	12	12	14	6
Has good ads	16	8	21	20
Is a trendy watch	25	16	27	35
Is a high-quality watch	20	28	16	12
Is a quartz watch	6	6	7	4
Is shockproof	8	10	7	6
Attracts attention	34	35	35	31
I would like to own more than one.	6	9	5	—

17 VOLVO TRUCKS EUROPE

In early May 1989, Ulf Selvin, vice president of marketing, sales, and service for Volvo Truck Corporation, Europe Division (VTC Europe), was deep in thought. European Community (EC) directives aimed at creating a single internal EC market by the end of 1992 were reshaping the truck market in Europe. Truck buyers' sales support and service needs and demands were changing and becoming more pan-European. Competition was growing fiercer and increasingly pan-European as well.

Recently, VTC Europe had undertaken a number of programs aimed at bringing diverse regional practices into greater harmony. As Selvin reviewed the progress of these early initiatives in pan-European marketing, he had two questions in mind. First, what elements of VTC's marketing practices in Europe should be targeted for central coordination and, by implication, what others should be left for country management to decide independently? Possible decision areas and candidates for tighter regional control were truck market segmentation, product design and specifications, pricing, distribution, communication, sales and service support, and information systems. Second, how should any attempt at regional marketing be implemented? Of concern here were the critical steps that management would need to take in order to make the transition from multidomestic practices to "Euro-marketing" possible. These steps might include, but not be limited to, changes in the European organizational structure, marketing information systems, and human resource policies.

COMPANY BACKGROUND

Volvo Truck Corporation (VTC) was a wholly owned subsidiary of AB Volvo. Headquartered in Göteborg, Sweden, Volvo was the largest industrial group in the Nordic region. Established in 1927 as an automobile manufacturer, the company gradually expanded its production to include trucks, buses, an extensive range of

This case was prepared by Tammy Bunn Hiller under the supervision of Professor J. J. Lambin, Louvain University (Louvain-la-Neuve, Belgium) and Dean of Lovanium International Management Center (La Hulpe). Copyright © Lovanium International Management Center.

automotive components, and marine, aircraft, aerospace, and industrial engines. Beginning in the late 1970s, Volvo diversified into the food industry, finance, and the oil, fruit, and chemicals trade to increase the group's opportunities for growth and profitability and to counteract economic fluctuations. Volvo's structure and organization were characterized by decentralization and delegation of responsibility. Its myriad operations were united by the shared values of quality, service, ethical performance, and concern for people and the environment. The group's products were marketed around the world, with almost 90% of sales in 1988 occurring outside Sweden. Volvo's sales and net income totaled Swedish kronor (SEK) 96,639 million and SEK 4,953 million, respectively, in 1988, up from 1987 levels of SEK 92,520 million and SEK 4,636 million, respectively.

The first Volvo truck was manufactured in 1928. It was an immediate success and was met with high demand. Volvo's truck production expanded rapidly in the 1930s and 1940s. The profits from truck building financed the company's total operations for most of its first 20 years. Not until the late 1940s did Volvo's automobile production become more than marginally viable. By the late 1960s, however, the situation had reversed. Despite market leadership in Sweden and the rest of Scandinavia, Volvo's truck operations had become unprofitable due to heavy competition in new export markets, combined with problems with state-of-the-art truck models, which were placing severe stresses on Volvo's design and service departments. The truck business had become a drag on the company's automobile operations. Management contemplated divesting Volvo's truck operations but instead decided to form a separate truck division (VTC).

The creation of VTC marked the beginning of major investment in and continued expansion and profitability of Volvo's truck operations. During the 1970s and 1980s, VTC replaced its entire product line with new models and intensified its marketing efforts in international markets. Between 1979 and 1986, VTC became the first truck manufacturer to win the coveted "Truck of the Year" award three times. In 1981, VTC acquired the truck assets of the White Motor Company in the United States and formed the Volvo White Truck Corporation. In 1987, Volvo White joined with General Motors' heavy truck division to form a joint venture, the Volvo GM Heavy Truck Corporation, with Volvo as the majority shareholder with responsibility for management.

VTC's truck production grew dramatically between 1970 and 1980, from 16,300 to 30,200 trucks. By 1988, production had doubled to 60,500 units. During the 1980s, VTC's share of the world market for trucks in the heavy class—gross vehicle weight (GVW) of greater than 16 tons—doubled to 11%, and VTC became the world's second-largest producer of heavy trucks. In both 1987 and 1988, demand for Volvo trucks exceeded VTC's production capacity.

In 1988, VTC sold (delivered) 59,500 trucks worldwide. Exhibit 1 shows the breakdown of VTC's 1987 and 1988 unit sales (deliveries) by market area. The two largest markets were Western Europe and North America, which accounted for 52% and 36% of sales, respectively. Almost 90% of unit sales were in the heavy class. VTC earned SEK 2,645 million on sales of SEK 22,762 million in 1988, which represented 34% of Volvo's 1988 operating income, up from 14% in 1986. Exhibit

2 contains graphs of VTC's sales, operating income, return on capital, and capital expenditure and development costs for the years 1984 through 1988.

VTC's organization chart is shown in Exhibit 3. Separate divisions were responsible for the manufacture and marketing of trucks in Europe, overseas, the United States, and Brazil. Trucks were produced in 10 Volvo-owned assembly plants. Of the 60,500 trucks manufactured by VTC in 1988, 20,000 were produced in the United States, 17,200 in Belgium, 14,400 in Sweden, 3,700 in Scotland, 3,200 in Brazil, 1,500 in Australia, and 500 in Peru. VTC's trucks were sold through a network of 850 dealers operating with 1,200 service workshops in over 100 countries.

The product development division was responsible for the design and development of global truck concepts and components. It had development departments in Sweden, the United States, Belgium, the United Kingdom, Brazil, and Australia. About 6% of turnover was invested in product development annually.

VTC EUROPE

VTC Europe was responsible for the production and marketing of Volvo trucks in Europe. The Western European market for heavy trucks grew 13% in 1988, to 175,000 vehicles, based on new truck registration statistics. Despite full capacity utilization of its plants, VTC Europe was unable to keep pace with the market growth. Its share of the Western European heavy truck market declined from 14.3 to 14%. The Western European medium truck market (10 to 16 tons GVW) grew by 4.5% in 1988, to 42,000 vehicles. Volvo's share of this market declined from 10.6 to 9.0%. Exhibit 4 shows a comparison of new Volvo truck registrations and market shares by European country for 1987 and 1988.

Early 1989 registration figures indicated that Volvo was regaining lost share in Europe in both the heavy and medium truck markets, as shown in Exhibit 5. VTC Europe began 1989 with a large delivery backlog. The division dramatically improved its delivery precision between January and March 1989, moving from 56 to 80% of trucks being delivered within one week of scheduled delivery. However, delivery precision varied widely by country. As of March 1989, it ranged from 54% in Spain to 94% in Austria and Finland.

Distribution System

Two layers in the distribution system separated Volvo truck factories from Volvo truck customers. Each country's distribution network was headed by an importer that was responsible for marketing, sales and service of Volvo trucks, parts distribution, and the creation and maintenance of a dealer network within its country. Of VTC Europe's 15 importer organizations, only four—Austria, Spain, Portugal, and Greece—were independent importers. The other 11 were Volvo-owned. Importers purchased trucks from VTC Europe's corporate headquarters and sold them within their countries to the Volvo truck dealers, who in turn sold them to Volvo truck customers. VTC's European dealer network included approximately 400 dealers and 800 service points. Almost all dealers were independent, although a few were Volvo-owned. All dealers were dedicated—that is, they sold only Volvo brand trucks.

The normal distribution network was rarely circumvented. Almost all sales were conducted through a dealer. VTC Europe headquarters sold directly to end customers only when selling to the governments of state-controlled countries like the USSR. Similarly, importers bypassed their dealers infrequently. For example, the only customer to whom Belgium's importer made direct sales was the Belgian army.

As a matter of course, importer organizations were headed and staffed by local nationals, although in a few cases, a Swedish manager had headed an importer temporarily, during the transition from independent to Volvo-owned importer organizations. Historically, importer managers were never transferred to work in the Swedish headquarters or in the importer organizations of other countries.

As one VTC Europe manager stated, "Importers are responsible for their country—period." Each importer's management was evaluated and rewarded on the sales volume, market share, and profit earned within its country. Importers negotiated transfer prices for the trucks they purchased from VTC Europe headquarters. These transfer prices varied from country to country. Importers had the responsibility to set the prices at which they sold trucks to their dealers. Prices to dealers and, consequently, prices to truck buying customers, varied considerably by country, depending on local competitive pressures. For example, Belgium had no national truck producer. Consequently, the Belgian importer priced Volvo's trucks significantly higher than did the French importer which faced fierce competition from a local manufacturer.

Marketing Communications Programs

Prior to 1987, importers had complete control of the design and execution of marketing communications programs within their countries. In early 1987, Roger Johansson, marketing support manager for VTC Europe, developed a corporate communication platform. His objective was twofold. First, he hoped to encourage consistency in the visual presentation and underlying message of sales promotion and advertising materials across Europe, so as to enhance the total impact on customers of Volvo truck communications. Second, he aimed to improve the efficiency and cost-effectiveness of production of advertising and sales support materials. According to the communication platform, sales promotion and advertising activities were to be divided among all levels of the marketing organization— headquarters, importers, and dealers—based on which level was best suited for a given activity.

The platform was designed to remain in effect through 1989. Every three years, a new communication platform was to be introduced. The platform did not dictate the actual content of messages that importers and dealers could use in their communications. Instead, it encouraged creativity in designing messages that took account of local circumstances, as long as the thinking behind the messages was consistent throughout Europe. Consistency was also encouraged by a visual identity program that strictly specified the logotypes, emblems, symbols, colors, typefaces, and layouts that were authorized for use throughout the marketing organization. Responsibility for complying with the precepts of the communications platform and visual identity program rested with the management of each importer organization.

Personal selling occurred almost solely at the dealer level. Each importer ran its own training programs for its salespeople. In addition, a state-of-the-art training facility in Göteborg was used to train both importer and dealer management whenever a new Volvo truck product was introduced. Importers and dealers were taught the features of the new truck, how those features translated into benefits for the potential buyers, and how to determine the bottom line impact the new truck would have on the potential buyer's profit and loss statement.

Service Systems

In addition to selling trucks, Volvo dealers maintained and repaired them. Each dealer was responsible for designing its local service system to suit its customers' needs. Each importer was responsible for coordinating service on a national level and ensuring consistency in dealer service offerings throughout its country. Volvo's service philosophy was based on the principle of preventive maintenance. Volvo dealers offered their customers service agreements with fixed prices for maintenance service and repair. Trucks that operated internationally could participate in Volvo Action Service Europe, which provided 24-hour assistance throughout Europe in the event of a breakdown. Volvo offered a DKV/Volvo credit card to its customers, which could be used at most Volvo repair facilities in Western Europe and at thousands of gas and service stations.

Volvo's service systems were not consistent across Europe. Service agreements made with a dealer in one country were not automatically valid at service centers in another country. Even when they were honored, prices for the same service or part often differed dramatically across countries, as did parts availability. Opening hours of service centers varied within and among countries, and the work habits and quality of mechanics differed significantly from country to country. According to importer management in Belgium, few Volvo truck owners used the DKV/Volvo credit card when traveling internationally. A customer explained why:

> We do not use the DKV card anymore, except for fuel. Outside Belgium, we do not have the same discount, sometimes we find a difference of up to 22% in exchange rate, and sometimes the card is simply not accepted.

According to Jean de Ruyter, after-sales manager of Volvo's Belgian importer, repairs made outside of a Volvo truck owner's home country typically resulted in a communication nightmare involving discussions between the customer, the repairing dealer, the importer, the customer's local dealer, and the importer in the customer's home country.

Market Segmentation

Historically, VTC Europe had segmented its market solely on the basis of GVW. It divided the European truck market into three segments: heavy trucks (greater than 16 tons GVW), medium trucks (7 to 16 tons GVW), and light trucks (less than 7 tons GVW). Volvo did not produce trucks for the light truck market. Medium-duty trucks were further split into a 10- to 16-ton market, where Volvo had a truck range across Europe, and into a 7- to 10-ton market, where Volvo sold a model in selected markets. Therefore, marketing management ignored this segment and emphasized the heavy truck segment in which Volvo had achieved the bulk of its success, concentrating on tractors for international transport.

Marketing Information Systems

VTC Europe did not have a standardized method of forecasting sales across Europe. Each importer developed its annual sales forecast using its own forecasting technique. The importers' forecasts were sent to VTC Europe's marketing planning and logistics department, which used them as a starting point for making a total forecast. Forecasts were used for production planning and for long-term capacity planning. In both 1987 and 1988, several importers underestimated annual sales by as much as 25%, leading VTC Europe to underestimate its total sales substantially.

VTC Europe's marketing planning and logistics department conducted market research and market analysis. Market research included both Europewide and individual country surveys. Much of the research was qualitative, intended to reveal how Volvo was performing relative to competitors. Results were shared with importer marketing managers. The department regularly tracked new truck registration statistics to try to discern market trends. It bought competitive production figures in order to learn the kinds of trucks Volvo's competitors were building. The department also tracked Volvo's production, delivery precision, turnover rate, and market share by country.

In addition to research conducted by headquarters, importers commissioned market research in their own countries as needed. Most importer-initiated market research was conducted on a project-by-project basis rather than on a recurrent basis. There was no standardized method of gathering data across countries.

THE EUROPEAN TRUCK MARKET

Between 1970 and 1988, truck sales made by Western European manufacturers grew at a compound annual rate of almost 1%. During that time, however, there were two exaggerated cycles. Sales boomed in the 1970s, peaking in 1979 at 422,000 trucks (3.5 tons GVW and larger). In the early 1980s, depression in Western Europe combined with a collapse in demand from Middle East and African export markets. Sales bottomed out at 333,000 vehicles in 1984. Between 1984 and 1988, the Western European truck industry made a strong recovery. In 1988, sales reached 485,000 trucks. As Exhibit 6 shows, market growth was propelled by expansion in the heavy (greater than 16 tons GVW) and light (3.5 to 7.5 tons GVW) truck segments. Sales of medium-sized trucks (7.5 to 16 tons GVW) appeared to be in long-term decline. In 1988, approximately 310,000 new trucks (3.5 tons GVW and larger) were registered in Western Europe.

In 1950, there were 55 independent truck manufacturers in Western Europe. In 1989, there were 11. During the 1980s, several structural changes occurred in the European truck market. The most significant ones took place in the United Kingdom. Since the 1930s, both Ford and General Motors had based their European truck manufacturing in the United Kingdom. In 1986, Ford entered into a strategic alliance with Iveco, the truck subsidiary of Italy's Fiat, which led to the formation of Iveco-Ford. Ford ceded management control of its U.K. operations and marketing to Iveco. A few months later, General Motors (Bedford brand trucks) withdrew completely from truck manufacture in Europe after failed attempts to buy Enasa, MAN, and Leyland Trucks. The state-owned Leyland Trucks was losing more than $1 million per week, when, in 1987, the U.K. government wrote off Leyland's substantial debts in order to facilitate its merger with the Dutch truck maker, DAF. DAF received 60% of the equity of the merged company and effective control. The Rover Group received the remaining 40% equity stake.

In continental Europe, structural changes were less dramatic. West Germany's Daimler-Benz, the market leader in Western European truck sales, reduced production capacity in the early 1980s. The other West German truck manufacturer, MAN, had been heavily reliant on Middle East markets. The 1983 cancellation of a half-completed contract with Iraq left MAN financially crippled in the early 1980s. MAN's management fought off a takeover attempt by General Motors, completely reorganized the company, concentrated on building up market presence in Western Europe, and regained profitability. In 1984, Iveco closed its unprofitable Unic truck plant in France, making RVI, the truck subsidiary of Renault, the sole truck producer in France. During the 1980s, RVI underwent a severe rationalization (cost-reduction) program. By 1987, it was profitable for the first time since its formation in the mid-1970s. Enasa, Spain's only independent truck producer, entered into a joint venture with DAF for the development of a modern truck cab range that was introduced in 1987. Both of Sweden's truck manufacturers, Volvo and Saab-Scania, survived the recession in very good shape without restructuring in Europe.

There was no common classification of trucks throughout Western Europe. Although the definition of the truck market varied by country, each country maintained new truck registration statistics that industry members used to calculate market shares. In 1988, the top five truck manufacturers accounted for almost 75% of total Western European truck sales (greater than 3.5 tons GVW). Daimler-Benz (23.7%) was the market leader, followed by Iveco (20.6%), RVI (11.4%), DAF (9.4%), and Volvo (9.0%). In the two segments in which Volvo competed, heavy trucks and medium trucks (10 to 16 tons GVW only), Volvo was number two and number four in the Western European market, respectively, as shown in Exhibit 7. In 1988, the market leaders by individual country were as follows: DAF (Leyland) in the United Kingdom, Daimler-Benz in West Germany, RVI in France, Iveco in Italy, Enasa in Spain, DAF in the Netherlands, Volvo and Daimler-Benz in Belgium, and Volvo in Sweden, Denmark, Finland, and Norway.

Impact of 1992

The campaign to turn the 12 member countries of the European Community (EC) into one barrier-free internal market by the end of 1992 was known as "1992." The community's goal was to create a market of 322 million people in which the free movement of goods, services, people, and capital was ensured. Among the 286 legislative reforms designed to fulfill this objective were ones aimed at liberalizing road haulage in the EC. Already, transport delays at customs posts had been shortened by the January 1, 1988 introduction of a "Single Administrative Document," which replaced the plethora of individual country documents previously required for inter-EC border crossings. Historically, inter-EC transport was strictly limited by a system of quotas that restricted the number of trips that haulers of one country could make into other EC countries in a given year. In June 1987, the EC member nations agreed to increase these quotas by 40% per year in 1988 and 1989 and to abolish all road transport quotas to EC and non-EC destinations by January 1, 1993. As a result of these two measures, industry analysts expected a 30 to 50% increase in inter-EC trade by the year 2000.

The EC supported unrestricted cabotage—that is, the freedom for a trucker registered in one EC country to collect and deliver loads between two points inside a second EC country. EC member states had not reached agreement on allowing unrestricted cabotage, but the EC was pushing for agreement and implementation by the end of 1992. In 1989, restrictions on cabotage were partially responsible for 35% of all trucks traveling empty on EC roads. Unrestricted cabotage would give trucks more flexibility to contract short hauls on their return trips, which would enable them to avoid returning from a long trip with an empty truck.

Trucking companies had already begun to vie for position in the EC's post-1992 transport market. Industry analysts expected concentration in the road haulage industry via mergers, acquisitions, and strategic alliances, particularly among fleets specializing in international traffic. Many observers believed that medium-sized fleets would be squeezed out in favor of small, specialized haulers and large, efficient international haulers. Most believed that the scramble for business would result in a major shake-up of the EC transport industry, after which there would likely be fewer total competitors and, perhaps, a smaller total market for heavy trucks.

The implications for European truck manufacturers were several. Inter-European transporters had already begun to demand that truck producers supply consistent systems of service and sales support across Europe. As 1992 approached, pressures to harmonize both truck and parts prices throughout Europe would probably increase, as large fleet owners attempted to negotiate Europe-wide prices. In addition, "artificial" differences in truck product standards—that is, unique product standards that were designed solely to protect national markets—would likely disappear over time. Eventually, new trucks might be built to "Eurospecifications," in contrast with the existing situation in which "every European country had two unique possessions—a national anthem and a brake system standard." As large trucking companies became increasingly international, the loyalty of their truck buyers to locally produced vehicles would likely wane. Competition between truck producers was expected to intensify, as was concentration within the industry.

VTC EUROPE'S MOVES TOWARD PAN-EUROPEAN MARKETING

Market Segmentation and Sales Forecasting

In 1984, VTC Europe took over its previously independent Belgian importer. Throughout the early 1980s, VTC had experienced heavy price competition and low profitability in Belgium. To develop a sound marketing strategy designed to increase the profitability of VTC's Belgian operation, and at the same time satisfy VTC's customers, André Durieux, then marketing manager of VTC Belgium, commissioned an outside consultant, Professor Robert Peeters of the Université Catholique de Louvain, to perform a brand image study in the Belgian truck market. Peeters designed and executed a quantitative survey of a representative sample of truck owners in Belgium.

The first objective of the study was to conceive a truck market segmentation scheme that would help Belgian management target the right customer groups in order to increase the profitability of its sales. The study also aimed to discover the criteria that truck owners used when choosing a make of truck and, for each criterion, the position that Volvo and each of its competitors held in owners' minds. A third goal of the study was to determine the marketing mix through which VTC Belgium could send the right message to its target segments in ways that would best reach them and influence them to buy Volvo trucks.

One of the outcomes of this research was the development of a truck industry segmentation scheme that Belgian management used in reshaping its marketing strategy. In 1987, Pol Jacobs, VTC Belgium's current marketing and business development manager, commissioned a follow-up study to assess the impact of Volvo's post-1984 marketing efforts on brand image in Belgium and to reveal any changes that had occurred in the makeup of the market by segment. Comparing the results of the second survey with those of the first showed that the pattern of Volvo's penetration of different market segments in Belgium had changed significantly between 1984 and 1987. Between 1984 and 1989, VTC Belgium improved its profitability almost tenfold. Jacobs was convinced that the use of Peeters' segmentation scheme as a starting point from which to design Volvo's marketing strategy for Belgium had contributed to VTC Belgium's success.

Peeters and Jacobs had also worked together to develop an econometric forecasting model, the intent of which was to improve the accuracy of Belgium's short term (less than two years) sales forecasts. In 1989, the model was being tested in both Belgium and the United Kingdom. Ulf Norman, VTC Europe's manager of marketing planning and logistics, was supportive of expanding the model's use throughout Europe if it proved successful and reliable in both the United Kingdom and Belgium.

The VETD Project

In late 1988, Selvin organized the "Volvo Euro Truck Dealer" (VETD) project. Its steering committee was made up of two VTC Europe headquarters service managers and five importer after-sales and service managers (from Belgium, France, Italy, the Netherlands, and the United Kingdom). Chaired by John de Ruyter, the steering committee was charged with establishing the project's objectives; coordinating the working process of the project between VTC, Volvo Parts Corporation (VPC), Volvo Dealer Facilities (VDF), and the importers; organizing and providing education for the importers; advising VTC and VPC in policy matters relating to the project; allocating specific tasks to work groups; and motivating all parties involved to take an active part in the project.

By the end of March 1989, the VETD steering committee had established the project's objectives and the procedures that were to be followed at the importer level to realize those objectives. The fundamental objective of the VETD project was to create a common Volvo truck environment at all Volvo dealers in the EC (Switzerland and Austria were included in the project even though they were not EC members). The desired Volvo environment was translated into specific "Euro Dealer Standards," which applied to the external, internal, and service environments of all Volvo dealers. The importers were charged with evaluating their existing dealerships, establishing an action plan for each dealer, and following up on action plans.

Both the objectives and the importer working procedures were presented to VTC Europe's importer truck division managers in April 1989. Each manager was directed to appoint within his or her organization a VETD staff that included one specialist who would be responsible for the project. The next step would be taken in June, when the importer's newly appointed VETD specialists were scheduled to be trained.

The Eurofleet Task Force

Around the time that the VETD project was initiated, Selvin created a "Eurofleet" task force composed of the truck division managers of each of VTC Europe's six largest importers and a headquarters liaison. The purpose of the task force was for the importers to work together to satisfy the needs of VTC's international fleet customers. Through May 1989, the Eurofleet task force had operated unsystematically, attending to each issue individually as it arose.

Pan-European Management Training

Selvin had selected 200 VTC importer and headquarters managers throughout Europe to attend a three-day training seminar at the Lovanium International Management Center in Belgium. The purpose of the seminar was for the managers to think through and discuss the changes that were occurring in the European truck industry due to "1992" and the impact of those changes on VTC's business. Managers were to be trained in groups of approximately 35. The groups were to be cross-sectional, made up of managers from different countries and from different functional areas in order to foster the interchange of ideas and cooperation throughout the organization. The first seminar had been conducted in March 1989. The second one was scheduled for June 1989.

THE FUTURE OF PAN-EUROPEAN MARKETING IN VTC EUROPE

Selvin strongly believed that any attempts to move VTC Europe toward pan-European marketing would require the full support of both headquarters and importer management. Importer managers would not likely support a pan-European strategy that conflicted with their local interests or that was perceived as being dictated from Sweden. Therefore, Selvin was convinced that it was crucial to involve managers from throughout the organization in the development and successful implementation of any future steps toward pan-European marketing.

The remaining question was what future steps were needed, both at the headquarters and country levels, to help with the transition from fragmented local practices toward panregional marketing. Specifically, Selvin wondered what changes in the formal organization of the European division might be called for. He was also wondering what other changes, including marketing planning and information systems, as well as human resource policies, might facilitate this important, yet challenging, transition at VTC Europe.

EXHIBIT 1 Sales (Deliveries) of Volvo Trucks by Market Area and Size

	Number of trucks delivered			
Market area	1987		1989	
Europe		29,300		31,600
North America		13,200		21,500
White Autocar/WHITEGMC	11,100		19,800*	
Volvo	2,100		1,700	
Latin America		3,300		3,300
Middle East		500		700
Australia		400		800
Other markets		1,000		1,600
Total		47,700		59,500
of which <16 tons GVW	6,500		6,500	
of which >16 tons GVW	41,200		53,000	

*Includes GM's product line.

EXHIBIT 2   VTC Financial Trends, 1984–1988

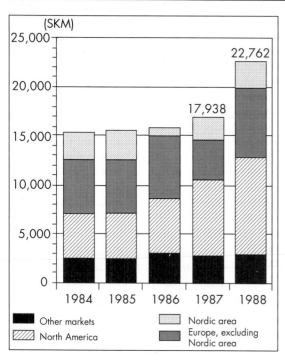

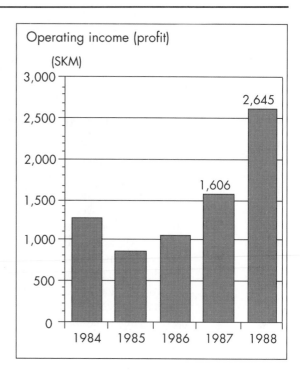

Operating income (profit)

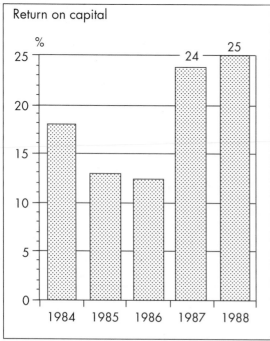

Return on capital

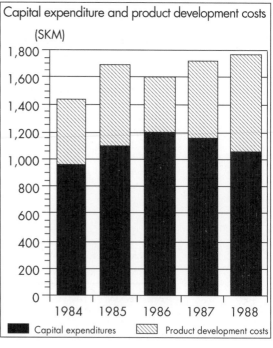

Capital expenditure and product development costs

EXHIBIT 3 VTC Organization Chart

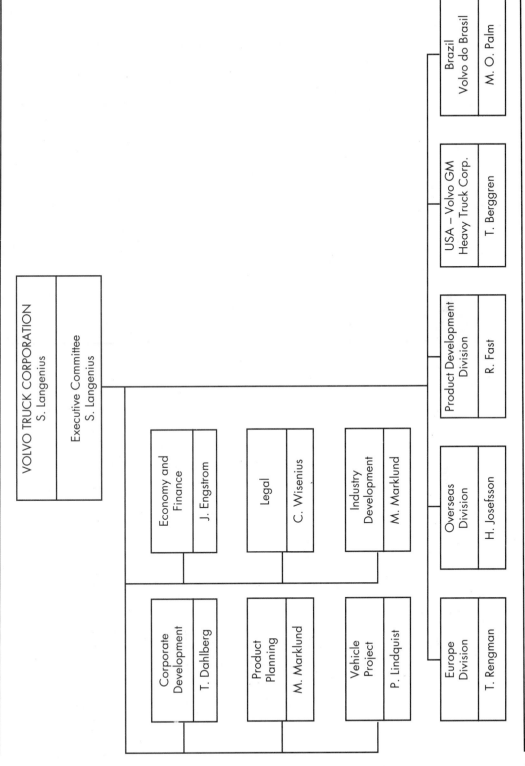

EXHIBIT 4 VTC Europe Sales (Registrations) and Market Share by Country, 1987 and 1988

Market	GVW class[b] (tons)	Number of new Volvo trucks registered[a]		Market share (%)	
		1987	1988	1987	1988
Great Britain	> 10	5,720	6,610	15.5	15.4
France	> 9	4,340	4,580	10.9	10.3
Sweden	> 10	2,970	3,030	50.9	53.7
The Netherlands	> 10	2,140	2,070	17.7	16.4
Italy[c]	> 9	1,490	1,780	6.5	6.8
Spain	> 10	1,010	1,700	6.5	8.4
Belgium	> 10	1,600	1,600	21.6	20.1
Portugal	> 10	1,020	1,280	29.9	27.1
Denmark	> 10	1,310	1,130	29.8	33.0
Finland	> 10	1,060	1,120	32.2	32.4
West Germany	> 10	950	1,030	3.0	3.2
Norway	> 10	1,280	800	40.6	37.5

[a]According to official registration statistics.
[b]Countries differ as to how they group their registration statistics by weight.
[c]Preliminary information.

EXHIBIT 5 Total Market New Truck Registrations and Volvo Market Share by Country

Market	For year ending month[a]	Total market registrations > 16 tons	Volvo market share >16 tons (%)	Total market registrations 10–16 tons	Volvo market share 10–16 tons (%)
Sweden	3/89	5,541	51.5	938	74.1
Denmark	2/89	2,317	34.7	1,379	42.6
Finland	2/89	3,827	30.3	609	34.3
Norway	3/89	1,064	45.1	203	51.9
Great Britain	2/89	39,637	19.6	5,942	8.8
Eire	1/89	1,782	14.2	672	1.4
Germany	2/89	28,157	4.2	5,593	2.4
Europe I	2/89[b]	83,962	18.1	14,851	14.8
France	3/89	35,921	11.3	8,371	7.3
Belgium	3/89	7,838	21.7	1,568	19.4
Luxembourg	12/88	385	31.9	86	19.8
Netherlands	1/89	9,419	16.0	1,489	22.0
Italy	2/89	27,198	7.5	13,328	2.0
Austria	2/89	3,751	14.5	1,072	7.8
Switzerland	12/88	3,349	15.4	476	19.7
Portugal	2/89	3,752	37.3	1,758	5.4
Spain	3/89	19,227	9.7	2,959	7.5
Greece	12/88	88	28.4	76	36.8
Israel	3/89	764	45.5	284	35.2
Europe II	2/89[b]	111,537	12.4	29,150	7.4
Europe total (excl. Israel)	2/89[b]	195,263	14.4	44,288	9.6

[a]The most current registration information available was used for each market.

[b]Markets with late information on registrations were estimated as of 2/89 for Europe I, Europe II, and Europe total.

EXHIBIT 6   Western European Truck Manufacturers' Sales by Truck Size

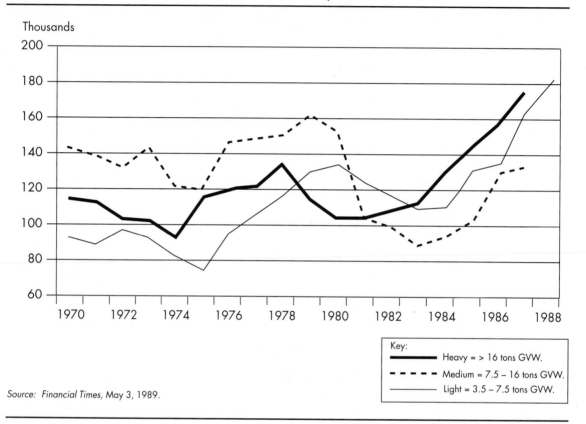

Thousands

Source: Financial Times, May 3, 1989.

Key:
Heavy = > 16 tons GVW.
Medium = 7.5 – 16 tons GVW.
Light = 3.5 – 7.5 tons GVW.

EXHIBIT 7 Western European Truck Market Shares by Manufacturer, Based on New Truck Registrations

Manufacturer	Market Share > 16 tons GVW		Market Share 10–16 tons GVW	
	1987 (%)	1988 (%)	1987 (%)	1988 (%)
Volvo	14.3	14.0	10.6	9.0
Damlier-Benz	20.1	18.9	23.9	23.7
Iveco	12.8	13.6	24.9	27.6
RVI	11.9	12.3	14.3	16.3
DAF	10.8	11.6	8.0	8.7
Scania	12.4	11.0	1.3	0.8
MAN	8.5	8.3	6.2	5.0
Pegaso	4.2	4.7	1.7	0.6
ERF	1.6	2.1	0.0	0.0
WRIGT	1.7	2.0	1.0	1.0
EBRO	0.0	0.0	2.0	2.7
Other	1.7	1.5	6.1	4.6

PART THREE

IMPLEMENTING GLOBAL STRATEGY

From Global Vision to Management Action

Why is implementation an issue in global marketing? In any discussion of global marketing, implementation deserves its full share of attention for several reasons. First, as a general rule, implementation is always an issue whenever a broad strategic vision is to materialize through specific management actions. Even the best strategies do not by themselves guarantee success: They need to be *put* into action before results can follow. Ensuring that the management actions taken throughout an organization closely follow the prescribed strategy is no simple task. Its complexity has to do with, among other things, merging often conflicting short-term objectives and long-term goals, forging widespread management support for the strategy and its required actions, and making sufficient resources available for the activities that need to take place. Keeping a strategy on track is a constant management preoccupation.

Second, implementing a strategy on a *global* scale is still more complex than dealing with national markets, for the reason that strategy makers are almost always away from the local scenes where the action is supposed to take place. The distance separating the decision makers and others is not only physical. A center-dominated decision-making process, as global marketing tends to be, has to live with the inherent difficulties of bringing about and coordinating actions of managers who are separated geographically by thousands of miles and who, in addition, live in different cultural settings.

Third, in trying to implement their global schemes, strategists often have to work through highly intricate organizational structures that span product lines, functions, and geographic units to exert influence on people and resources over which they do not have direct control.

Finally, to make the implementation task still more difficult, global strategies often call for major changes in the way marketing activities are performed. The changes frequently mean having to move away from traditional local autonomy toward an increased level of cross-market coordination. Experienced global strategists are only too aware of the obstacles that such a shift in the decision-making process puts on the path to implementation.

This introduction to Part Three examines the different facets of implementation in a global marketing context. It attempts to show how the success or failure of a global strategy can often be traced to a marketer's skills in moving from vision to action, or the strategy's implementation. To begin our discussion, consider the following illustration:

In the mid-1980's, two U.S.-based computer companies embarked on a strategy to standardize aspects of their marketing activities in Europe. Digital Equipment Corporation (DEC) aimed to standardize its sales management practices in 17 regional subsidiaries. Business Electronic Systems (BES), a disguised name for one of DEC's competitors, attempted to install a standardized software-house cooperation scheme in all of its eight European country operations. For both companies, it was their first experience with coordinated regional marketing. Management in both companies gave their newly announced programs adequate internal visibility. The top regional executives at DEC and BES publicly underscored the importance of the pan-European initiatives for the future of their companies. Total country-level autonomy, they said, would have to be selectively given up in favor of streamlined panregional marketing. In both cases, the center-led initiatives immediately ran into opposition from local country managers who saw their autonomy threatened. But, the similarity between the two cases ends here.

At DEC, where the standardized sales management program was conceived to help upgrade the productivity of the company's sales force of 2,500, the initiative gradually won the support of local managers. The two factors that helped to win them over were tangible results from a pilot test organized by the regional head office and persistent attention to the program by the headquarters manager charged with its implementation. The pilot test, with its measurable impact in reducing sales force cost per order, was specifically designed to show the skeptics that the proposed standardized system could actually deliver what it promised. The test results were highly publicized throughout the European sales organization. In addition, by monitoring progress at every step, those responsible for implementing the program made sure that their scheme received needed priority from subsidiary officials. The coordinating sessions for country sales managers were particularly helpful. These meetings, called regularly by the headquarters sponsors of the program, highlighted the payoffs from using the system and provided a forum for dealing with common problems. The sessions also proved to be valuable tools for taking a creative solution produced in one market and spreading it to the 16 other markets. In just two years time, the program had met or surpassed most of its initial targets in Europe and was being expanded to other field operations, including the service organization.

The experience with the software-house cooperation program at BES was decidedly different. The standardized program, formulated to help the company penetrate the small and medium-sized accounts—BES's weakest segment—required a big change in sales force operations. For this segment, the sales force would no longer exert total control on the hardware and software sold to prospective clients, but rather it had to participate in joint decision making with a software house that had direct access to the accounts. From the very beginning, it was clear to the strategists at headquarters that the success of their new scheme depended almost entirely on how well the sales force carried out its new assignment. Despite this awareness, the program and its progress never received the monitoring that was needed for its implementation. Responsibility for overseeing the project kept changing hands at the center, which impeded implementation and led to confusion. Partly as a result of switches in program management, efforts to monitor progress and take remedial action dwindled. Also, in the absence of a communication channel for sharing and building on subsidiary experiences, each country organization was obliged to find its own solutions to problems common to many. Thus, the wheel was reinvented every time. Finally, many country sales managers resented having to implement an unpopular program. Without any visible support from headquarters, some gave up; others grudgingly carried on. The program was terminated three years later due to poor performance.

The contrasting experiences of DEC and BES show the paramount role that the quality of implementation can play in the success of global marketing. Without skillful management of this process, even the best strategies can succumb to an organization's inertia or to management's other priorities.

FACETS OF GLOBAL IMPLEMENTATION

Implementing global strategy is a multifaceted process that involves managing a complex set of relationships across a far-flung organization. Issues that make an impact on the quality of implementation can be structural, process-related, and managerial. Structural issues are those that pertain to the formal definition of responsibilities and reporting relationships in an international organization. An organization's formal structure influences its ability to perform certain tasks, including global marketing. As a result, some structures are better suited to implementing global decisions than others. Process-related issues, on the other hand, include those related to the methods and tools of implementation. These processes can influence a global program's outcome by influencing the quality of decision making at every step, from initial program formulation to its launch, communication, and follow-up throughout the formal organization. Finally, managerial attributes and behavior have a great deal of influence on how well certain decisions are accepted by the larger organization. These qualities include skills in cross-cultural communication and interpersonal behavior. The three facets of global implementation are discussed in greater detail in the following sections.

STRUCTURAL ISSUES

It is rare to find a major global company that has not changed its management structure at least once in the past decade. The changes have been, for the most part, in response to the forces of globalization highlighted earlier in the introduction to Part One. The new structures were created to upgrade the company's ability to compete in an increasingly complex and interdependent global marketplace. To cite only one example, Philips, the Dutch consumer and industrial electronics giant, has repeatedly adjusted its traditionally fragmented international organization to cope with the challenges of its highly integrated global rivals from Japan. Management's aim has been to create a more streamlined structure in which new products reach their markets faster and savings from large-scale production are possible. Like Philips, other companies have been searching for organizational structures in which managers at headquarters, as well as those in the regional and local units, make better decisions and implement them more effectively.

To appreciate the impact of management structure on implementation, one needs to examine the different types of organizations and their features. Although no two organizations are alike, in their "pure" form most international corporate structures fall into one of four types: international division, geographic, product, or hybrids called matrix.

International Division Structures International division structures are often the choice of firms with narrow or related product lines. This structure is also common in companies that are in the early stages of their internationalization, where the home market accounts for the bulk of sales. In such a model, main corporate activities are organized around key business functions, such as manufacturing, finance, and R&D; alternatively, they are structured along product lines. Corporate activities are for the most part oriented toward the domestic market. The international activities are handled by an international division, hence the label; this division is responsible for the company's subsidiaries in other markets. Typically, the division head has a line responsibility and is accountable for the profitability of international markets. The division and its subsidiaries frequently enjoy a great deal of autonomy in managing their affairs. In larger firms, the international division may itself be organized geographically by regions. (See Exhibit 3.1 for an example of an international division organization alongside a functional domestic structure.)

Simplicity is the international division structure's most important virtue. The lines of authority and areas of responsibility are clear. The distinction between home market and international activities is equally clear. Strategy making and implementation are relatively easy in such a simple structure. Within this pattern's simplicity, however, lies a potential for future problems. As the international activities expand and as the product line grows in its diversity, the international division's structure soon exhausts its advantages. The international division managers, for example, may find themselves constantly having to negotiate for adaptations of products that are routinely developed in accordance with domestic needs. Or, when the foreign subsidiaries grow in size, their independence from the larger domestic organization may soon lead to duplication of activities at additional costs. Local independence may prove a major stumbling block when implementing a worldwide strategy. Moreover, the structural distinction between the larger home market and the smaller, though growing, international business may lead to a duality of managers, with the more qualified ones being assigned to the more visible domestic jobs. In many firms, this implicit duality has made international assignments far less attractive than domestic ones.

Geographic Structures Geographic structures represent a departure from the simple domestic–international distinction of the previous design. Here the world market is divided into several geographic regions, each responsible for a number of subsidiaries. The home market does not necessarily enjoy a special status because it constitutes or belongs to one of these geographic entities. A key assumption underlying this kind of structure is that regional markets are different enough to justify their own dedicated organizations. Regional heads are line managers responsible for results in their assigned geographic markets. They may be assisted by corporate staffs or, if the region's size of activities permits, they may provide their own internal services. (See Exhibit 3.2 for an example of a geographic structure assisted by corporate staff functions.)

Although geographic structures offer a more balanced orientation to world market opportunities than the international division structure, they, too, have their limitations. The geographic structure, for example, would be inappropriate for firms with diverse product lines, because the focus on national and regional markets tends to override the different strategic requirements related to products—their technology, production, marketing, and so forth. Similarly, a geographic structure may undermine implementation of a strategy that spans world markets. Regional managers, given their geographic orientation, tend to see more differences than similarities among the world markets. On the other hand, transfer of know-how and marketing practices inside the same region might be easier because of the geographic divisions and similarities that are likely to exist among neighboring markets. Such cross-fertilization is typically far more difficult to implement under an international division

EXHIBIT 3.1 International Division Structure

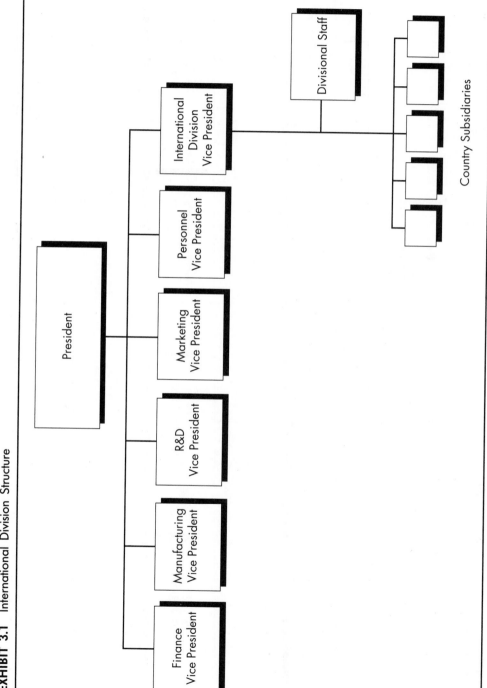

EXHIBIT 3.2 Geographic Organization Structure

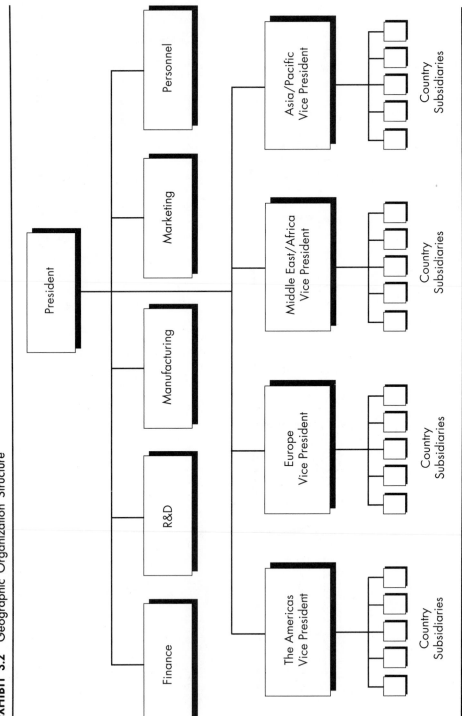

structure where the local companies enjoy a great deal of autonomy.

Product Structures Product structures tend to overcome some of the problems inherent in the previous two models—namely, a fragmented view of world markets and the subordination of product needs to geographic considerations. A product structure is especially useful when the number and diversity of products marketed worldwide are large. The key advantage of this structure is that it gives a group of line managers total control over the fate of a product line or a group of related products. The strategic business unit (SBU) managers, as product managers are sometimes called, typically have worldwide profit responsibility for their assigned lines. If a distinction is made between the home and international markets, it is done within each product organization and not for the entire firm. Country organizations may be grouped by area or region, but they report to the head of the product division. Product managers may be assisted by corporate staff functions, such as R&D and manufacturing. Or, if their size and scope of operations permit, product divisions would have these services internally. (See Exhibit 3.3 for an example of a product organization.)

A product organization with worldwide scope tends to be better prepared to deal with global trends than the previous two structures. Product division strategists have the mandate to monitor worldwide developments and respond accordingly. In their advanced form, product strategies may call for integration of activities and practices across geographic and country organizations. Implementing these strategies is helped by the fact that individual country units are integral to the division's global operation, and that local or regional autonomy, a feature of the previous two structures, is less of an issue in a worldwide product structure.

The major drawbacks of product structures have to do with the absence of synergy among product divisions, duplication of activities, and a potential tendency to ignore important differences among the various world markets. The question of synergy becomes a factor when the structure prevents transfer of people, knowledge, and technology among the different, yet related, product divisions. Implementing a strategy that builds on the promises of such cross-fertilization is often a Herculean task. Also, as self-sufficient business units, product structures tend to duplicate those services that could be shared across several lines. This duplication can extend all the way to country organizations where each product division maintains its own separate subsidiary in the *same* country. However, as product managers move toward developing an integrated global strategy, they can also fall into the trap of ignoring important differences among national and regional markets. This potential loss in responsiveness to international markets has been cited as one of the tendencies inherent in global product structures.[1]

Matrix Structures Matrix structures are a hybrid of product, geographic, and, to a lesser extent, functional organizations. They are the most common form of organizational design used by major global companies. A prominent feature of matrixes is their dual chain of command: Many managers report to two different bosses—one representing perhaps the product structure and the other a regional organization. (See Exhibit 3.4 for an example of a matrix organization.)

In theory at least, matrix structures facilitate a balanced influence of different perspectives on major decisions. For example, a global product strategy formulated by a matrix organization would be, by design, the output of the interaction between the worldwide product managers and the regional chiefs of geographic structure. Such a strategy would not only exploit worldwide commonalties among the different regions, but also recognize the major geographic market differences and incorporate them in its design. Similarly, regional plans would have input from the various product lines in addition to the region's own managers. Such an overlapping decision

EXHIBIT 3.3 Product Organization Structure

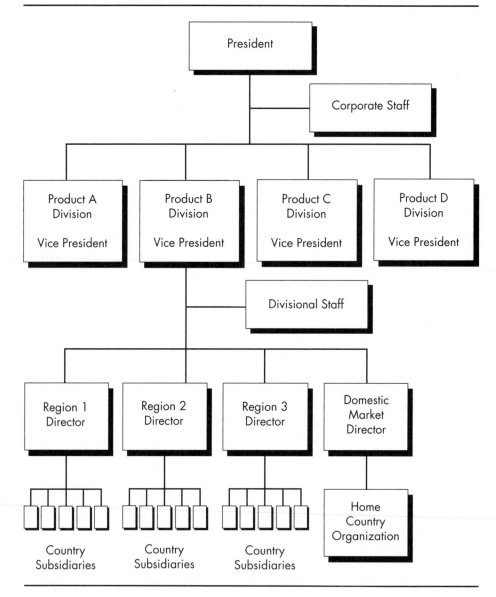

EXHIBIT 3.4 Matrix Organization Structure

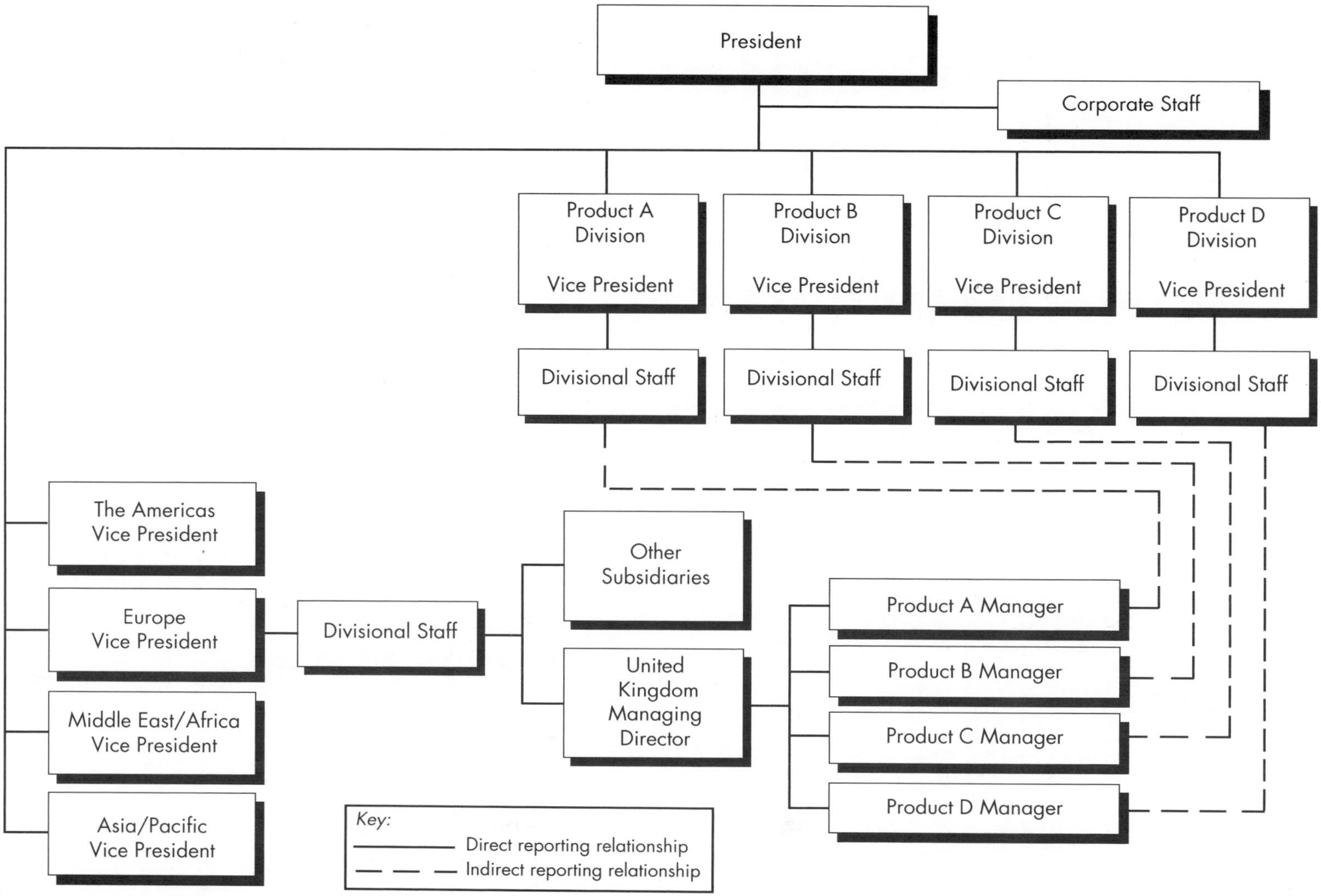

President

Corporate Staff

Product A Division — Vice President — Divisional Staff

Product B Division — Vice President — Divisional Staff

Product C Division — Vice President — Divisional Staff

Product D Division — Vice President — Divisional Staff

Product A Manager

Product B Manager

Product C Manager

Product D Manager

Other Subsidiaries

United Kingdom Managing Director

Divisional Staff

The Americas Vice President

Europe Vice President

Middle East/Africa Vice President

Asia/Pacific Vice President

Key:
——— Direct reporting relationship
- - - Indirect reporting relationship

process is of particular value to firms operating in diverse product and geographic markets.

Matrix organizations were once hailed as the answer to a growing need for strategic flexibility in global business. Because they incorporated several clusters of expertise—around products, geographic markets, and even functions—and looked at key issues from different angles, such organizations were considered the structural solutions to the complexity of global decision making. In practice, however, the matrix structures have fallen far short of that ideal. Instead, managers have complained about such impediments as role confusion, excessive meetings, and the slow speed of decision making. In the worst cases, implementation of strategic decisions has come to a standstill because of the built-in conflicts in the structure.

Despite these shortcomings, companies are not abandoning their matrix structures. Instead, attempts are being made to refine and simplify them. In some companies, although the parallel product and geographic market structures are maintained for a given line of business, one dimension is given priority over the other, thereby recognizing the special needs of that organization. Sony, for example, had a highly centralized structure where product divisions tended to dominate regional organizations. Recently, however, management of the larger zones such as the United States and Europe were accorded more weight in major strategic decisions. This shift has come in response to what Sony's top management sees as a need for "global localization" (also called "glocalization"), meaning a balanced emphasis between local responsiveness and global strategic imperatives. Likewise, IBM has lessened the traditionally strong influence of its product divisions in favor of country managers, some of whom have been assigned a broader regional responsibility for marketing programs targeted at certain segments. In other companies, such as General Electric, management has moved to simplify the interaction between product and geographic managers by removing certain management layers believed to be clogging the communication lines.

Regardless of how matrixes are refined, their inherent complexity puts special demands on strategy making and implementation. Managerial skills in resolving conflicts and negotiating, valuable in any organization, are important assets for operating effectively in a matrix.

A highly acclaimed recent study of the structural forms used by a number of U.S., European, and Japanese companies has concluded that an eclectic organizational concept called "transnational" might be better adapted than matrixes to the increasingly global strategies of firms.[2] The proposed transnational solution aims to overcome the major deficiencies of the traditional structural models by simultaneously promoting interdependence, dispersion, and specialization of assets and capabilities around a worldwide organization. Accordingly, the country organizations would not all play the same role in the global structure. Depending on their core skills, their contribution to an integrated global operation would differ. Also, the center's role in a transnational structure would be to create and maintain a flexible, yet integrated global network where efficient operations, local market responsiveness, and sharing of innovations are possible. The authors of this study maintain that the starting point in shifting to a transnational solution does not involve changing the formal structure of the firm. In fact, building on their observations of Japanese and European firms, they argue that any change in the formal shape of the organization should follow—and not precede—the more pervasive changes needed in management attitudes and perspectives, as well as managerial relationships and processes. Shifting lines and boxes around the formal organization chart, they correctly argue, does not by itself lead to an ideal structure.

PROCESS-RELATED ISSUES

Organizational structures are inert elements of strategy implementation. Though they can help or hinder moving from a strategic vision and a plan of action to targeted results, structures by themselves are no more than the hardware around which the living action takes place. What influences the live action are management processes, or the ways managers actually reach decisions and implement them. Unlike structures, which after being created tend to stay in place for years, management processes can be tailored at any time to fit the requirements of a given situation. Processes encompass a wide array of formal management tools and methods, including planning and target setting, performance measurement, management appraisal, and rewards. They also include informal processes such as the level and quality of interaction among decision makers and implementers, ways internal conflicts are recognized and resolved, and how broad-based support is built for certain actions. Together, the formal and informal processes help to determine the outcome of strategic decisions.

What puts process-related issues at the heart of global implementation is the often ignored fact that, in the majority of cases, global marketing involves departures from the traditional ways an organization has practiced its business. These departures require not only a borderless perspective on one's market, but also often a shift in the balance of influence on strategic decisions. For example, country marketing managers may find themselves having to sacrifice some of their autonomy in order to work with managers from other national markets to define standardized practices worldwide. Or, the headquarters management may find that the traditional center-led marketing initiatives are no longer necessary or appropriate when sufficient know-how and competence exist in regional markets. In both instances, a major change is in store for the organization, and those charged with implementation need to take into account the obstacles that such changes naturally generate.

A recent research study by the author on process-related issues has shown that, in implementing global marketing, organizational resistance to global decisions is endemic.[3] The more radical a departure from the past, the study shows,

the larger the obstacles are. However, by comparing the more and less successful attempts at global marketing, the study has also highlighted some of the "facilitators," or process tools, that global strategists can use to soften or even eliminate the impact of such resistance on implementation. The facilitators are program champions, "piloting," consultation, coordinating mechanisms, and allowance for exceptions.

Program Champions Managers who champion global marketing programs contribute a great deal to the adoption of those programs by the larger international organization. They do so by overcoming the implementation bottlenecks in the organization, both at headquarters and in the subsidiaries, and by gradually building up support for the global concept where it would otherwise be lacking. To illustrate with an example described earlier in this introduction, when Digital Equipment Corporation (DEC) tried to streamline its sales operations in Europe, top management gave the program to a project leader with considerable sales management experience. The project, which aimed to rationalize (streamline) sales management practices across the company's 17 European operations, was not popular with the country sales managers, who feared they would lose control. The program would have fallen an easy victim to local opposition if not for the constant presence and organizational skills of the project leader, who ensured that it received its fair share of attention from headquarters management as well as from those most likely to benefit from it—the country-level salespeople themselves. Using such vehicles as periodic and well-rehearsed interventions by the region's CEO vis-à-vis country heads, direct communication through cassettes and booklets with the local sales personnel, and quarterly progress meetings with all local managers responsible for the project's implementation, the program champion succeeded in neutralizing much of the resistance that could have blocked initial progress. Furthermore, as tangible results from the program began to appear, the program champion used these local successes to nudge the more reluctant countries along.

As this example illustrates, a program champion's facilitating role is often twofold: to overcome initial management resistance to the changes necessitated by the rationalization of marketing practices and to ensure continued management attention to the program and access to needed resources over time. Both tasks are important, especially in firms where management has traditionally had a multidomestic concept of its business, thereby allowing local management a great deal of autonomy.

Piloting   Positive results from formal testing of a global concept can help overcome much of any initial skepticism and, in doing so, speed up implementation. Henkel's experience with the global branding of Pattex is a case in point. When the central product management at Henkel, the leading German-based adhesives manufacturer, embarked on a strategy to bring many scattered adhesive products targeted at the do-it-yourself market under the umbrella of its well-known Pattex brand, many local managers "shook their heads" in disapproval. The move that aimed to place several new but underperforming adhesives under one strong global brand was too unconventional to be readily accepted by the subsidiaries. Headquarters' assertion that consumer behavior in the do-it-yourself market was similar everywhere failed to convince management in the subsidiaries. But local opposition subsided considerably following a pilot run of the concept in Henkel's three major markets: Germany, Austria, and Belgium. The success of the umbrella branding in these three different markets was glaring enough to convince the skeptics that the strategy was sound and had a chance to succeed. The subsequent launch of the umbrella brand in Europe and 20 other countries worldwide proved the concept was right: Today, Pattex is a leading adhesives brand, generating nearly one-half of its world volume from the previously underperforming products.

Henkel's experience and that of others show how piloting a concept can potentially facilitate implementation in three related ways: by educating local organizations about the anticipated benefits of standardization, by adding credibility to the overall global program, and by justifying enforcement of the global concept once it is launched. All three make this facilitator a particularly effective implementation tool.

Consultation   Although global marketing requires an element of central coordination, the study indicates that without subsidiary input into global decisions the risk of failing to implement those decisions is high. At issue here is the openness of the decision-making process to local management influence.

Polaroid's European advertising campaign for its innovative SX-70 camera shows what can go wrong when global decisions are made in the absence of genuine subsidiary management inputs. The campaign, modeled after successful U.S. introductory advertising, was conceived in the company's headquarters in Cambridge, Massachusetts, and relayed to the European management for implementation. As in the United States, the TV and radio campaign featured local language testimonials from the late Sir Laurence Olivier, who was not well known on the continent. (A country manager for one of Polaroid's major European markets declared later that he had difficulty understanding Sir Laurence's lines because of his strong English accent!) Furthermore, tight rules governed the advertising in other media, including print. Any deviations from the approved text had to be cleared with Cambridge. No local management ideas were sought in planning for the campaign; nor were they given much weight when offered. One country manager recalled that he spent his funds on the campaign not because he believed it would work but because he had to. The outcome: poor campaign results and disenchanted local managers who believed they could have spent their money more wisely.

Evidence from the study suggests that some degree of genuine local management involvement in global marketing decisions not only helps to facilitate implementation of those decisions; it actually improves the decisions as well. For example, consultation with country management was a constant feature of DEC's sales operations program cited earlier. The initial model, which had benefited by incorporating the best practices in individual subsidiaries, was further improved thanks to a steady stream of feedback from the experiences of local organizations. Thus, as time-consuming and even acrimonious as the consultation process may be, nothing can substitute for it as a process facilitator.

Coordinating Mechanism Given the need for a healthy "permeability" of the decision-making process by local management influences, a coordinating mechanism is indispensable for soliciting and channeling such field inputs. Headquarters-based coordination often fails as a mechanism because it is removed from the "front line." It tends to lose its responsiveness to changing local conditions and become insular over time. As an alternative, a number of companies use a "lead country" mechanism, in which one country management takes the lead in defining the standardized elements of a global marketing program for all other local organizations. Though this latter mechanism benefits from decisions being made close to the market—or at least one local market—it suffers from a common tendency to ignore input from other local organizations. The problem is often compounded when the lead country is also the home market for a successful marketing "formula."

To illustrate, when the Anglo-Dutch consumer products firm Unilever tried to repeat internationally its success in the United Kingdom with Domestos, the company's bleach-based household cleaner, headquarters assigned the job of creating a unified brand strategy to the product's originators, the U.K. management. However, what was finally proposed by the brand's lead market to the rest of the world was an almost exact copy of U.K.'s strategy. Pointing to a home-grown success, the lead market managers turned a deaf ear to requests from "follower" countries to make changes in the proposed reference mix. According to a headquarters executive, the prevailing attitude was, "It worked for us; it should work for you."

As later experience showed, what worked in the United Kingdom was unique to that market and could not be reproduced elsewhere. The problem was diagnosed only after a number of expensive false starts. Where Domestos seemed to have done better, the local management had significantly changed the reference mix, including the brand's U.K. positioning as a lavatory germ killer.

The more experienced firms in global marketing are gravitating toward a mixed multisubsidiary mechanism as a viable alternative to the single-perspective process of either headquarters-based or "lead-country" coordination. At Unilever, for example, pan-European decision making has recently been assigned to teams of marketing executives from key country organizations. Called EBGs, an acronym for European Brand Groups, each team has been taking the lead in developing a strategy for its assigned brand after accounting for the similarities and important differences among the various markets. Thus, no single perspective, including the one held by headquarters, prevails at the expense of others; the brand strategies begin and end with a pan-European vision. Similarly, at Polaroid a roundtable of country heads has been chosen as the mechanism for regional coordination and decision making in Europe. Meeting periodically and being hosted by different country managers, the multisubsidiary group has been a key vehicle for conceiving many successful pan-European initiatives.

Allowance for Exceptions Global marketing has a tendency of being implemented with an iron hand: Local organizations are often left with little choice but to go along with a scheme concocted elsewhere. The argument usually put forward by the headquarters marketers in favor of an unbending and uniform implementation of their global design is a persuasive one: To be true to their objectives, decisions must be enforced without exception or else nothing will remain of the global programs. There is an element of truth in this argument, but only an element. For most global marketing strategies, only a few variables are critical to their success, and others are not. For example, in the case of the Pattex umbrella branding cited earlier, the key ingredients for its success were uniform packaging and display units. Everything else was secondary. Or, in the case of DEC's streamlining its sales operations, only the key tasks were included in the standardization scheme; the others were left for local management to decide.

Thus, the success of global marketing often depends on how uniformly a short list of pivotal decisions essential to attaining the aims of the strategy are implemented. These critical decisions, and only these decisions, qualify for enforcement across the local organizations. By the same token, allowance must be made for exceptions, as implementing a long list of standardized practices just for the sake of international uniformity can be counterproductive.

Hence, there is room for local judgment and exceptions to global decisions, and such allowances should be built into program implementation. A manifestation of this principle is the guiding motto used by the top regional management of U.S.-based Johnson Wax in harmonizing their national marketing practices: "As unified as possible, as diversified as necessary."

MANAGERIAL SKILLS

"Right" management behavior, however defined, is the essence of effective implementation, and managerial skills in producing that behavior can have a direct impact on the fate of a strategy. Managerial skills play an even greater role in an international context because implementation is so much more complex. The complexity, as we have mentioned earlier, is a function of physical distances, cultural and language barriers, obstacles created by organizational structure, and the frequent need to influence without authority the routine actions of managers elsewhere in the worldwide organization. The implementation task is not made any easier by the necessity of having to balance the big global picture and its interests against individual country- or region-specific market needs.

What are the skills required of a global manager? The list of skills can be very long, but for the purposes of this discussion the essential competences are grouped into two interrelated categories: cross-cultural communication and interpersonal skills.

Cross-cultural Communication Skills   This first category of competences has to do with distortion-free interaction between people of different cultural heritages. Consider the letter written by Toshio Horie, a disguised name for the marketing manager of a Japanese food company operating in Indonesia, to his Indonesian colleagues upon his repatriation to Japan. On the surface, the letter, originally written in English and reproduced in Exhibit 3.5, speaks of Toshio's gratitude toward his Indonesian hosts, as well as his personal and company philosophy on what constitutes good work. But, at a more profound level, the letter reveals deep cultural roots that have no doubt influenced Toshio's attitude toward his assignment in Indonesia and also his relationship with local colleagues. To appreciate the influence of culture in this specific communication, the non-Japanese reader is invited to design his or her own farewell communication and compare it with Toshio's letter.

Ineffective cross-cultural communication has been blamed for routine misunderstandings in international business contacts. The phrase "We will study your proposal" may mean just that in the United States or Germany. But in other countries—for example, Japan or France—it may mean something quite different, such as, "We are not ready to talk any further about your

EXHIBIT 3.5 A Farewell Letter from Toshio Horie

August 6, 1990

Dear Colleague:

Through this letter I would like to thank you for your friendship and hospitality extended to me during my six years' stay in Indonesia. I am destined to leave Indonesia in a few days time because I have been assigned back to our head office, (name of the company) Tokyo, in July 1990.

During my assignment here, my main objective was to develop the working efficiency and ability of my staffs through perfect discipline in order to establish a good, modern system of management as can be proven by their fruitful contributions to the company and the achievement of good results of the Indonesian and Japanese staffs.

There can be no progress in our business without proper education and development of the human resources because, it not only serves as contributions to the company but also to release themselves from the traditional and conservative way of thinking.

So I am happy that I have done my best to create in our staffs the spirit of national pride and devotion to their religions but I hope they all could be united as (Company's name) staffs to work together to achieve the company targets.

Best of lucks to you all.

Regards.

Toshio Horie

New address:
Office: (address and telephone number deleted)
Home: (address and telephone number deleted)

Note: Reproduced verbatim with only names and addresses disguised or deleted.

proposal," or simply and politely, "No thanks, we are not interested."

Experts on cross-cultural communication have categorized most world cultures as either high or low context.[4] In high-context cultures what is *not* said can be as important as what is said. In France, Spain, Saudi Arabia, China, and Japan—examples of high-context countries—communication tends to be both direct and indirect. What is

verbally communicated is often of general orientation, approximations lacking fine details. Such cultures put more emphasis on nonverbal communication, including body language and physical distance between sender and receiver.

Low-context cultures, in contrast, put more emphasis on what is said than what is not. In the United States, Germany, Sweden, Switzerland, and the United Kingdom—examples of low-context countries—straightforward communication is considered good business behavior. Generalities are avoided, factual information is prized, and candid communication is respected. In dealing with counterparts from a high-context setting, unprepared low-context people often find themselves searching in vain for concrete meaning in what they hear. They also ignore or are distracted by nonverbal communication. To avoid misunderstandings, one expert says, "low-context communicators must learn to listen not only with their ears, but with their eyes as well."[5]

Cultural differences often override whatever commonalties may exist because of membership in the same organization.[6] With an unprecedented number of managers working outside their familiar home-country environment, cross-cultural problems have come to be recognized as real barriers to managerial effectiveness. Although quick remedies do not exist, companies are organizing training seminars to sensitize their managers to cultural differences across their global organization. Firms are also recognizing that extended and consecutive overseas assignments in different parts of the world are an essential ingredient for developing over time a pool of managers who are comfortable anywhere on the globe.

Ethical issues are a constant feature of cross-cultural encounters. Though ethical dilemmas are a facet of business life anywhere, what makes them acute issues in the international context is the fact that different cultures have different norms of ethical behavior. For example, while secret payments to individuals in a buying organization in return for purchase orders may be considered unethical and even illegal in certain parts of the world, they are an accepted way of life in many other cultures. The unethical act of "bribing" in the first instance may be construed as simply "returning a favor" and, hence, acceptable in the second context. The following are some common ethical dilemmas that face international managers:[7]

- Decisions on whether to pay secret commissions for "special services";
- Decisions about product or service quality, reliability, and safety;
- Tax evasion;
- Conflict between the demands of the organization, including superiors, and what the individual manager believes to be right;
- Conflict created by what the manager or the manager's organization considers as unacceptable conduct and the severe consequences of refusing to act in that manner.

Faced with such dilemmas, it is tempting to put one's own cultural norms above those of others and to act self-righteously. That is the easy way out of the dilemma, yet not always in the best interest of the parties involved. Such attitudes of ethical superiority are at the core of many recurring cross-cultural conflicts.

By the same token, it is equally easy and inappropriate to consider ethical norms as culture-bound and, thereby, to wash one's hands of making the fine judgment between ethical and unethical conduct. Such cultural relativism ignores the fact that, besides commercial interests, global business has a universal obligation to satisfy customer needs and contribute to the economic and social welfare of host countries. These overriding societal goals are the fundamentals by which global business can thrive. Doing business at any cost and by any standard runs counter to such fundamentals and is, in the long run, self-defeating.

An experienced international businessman has offered managers a two-step approach toward helping to resolve ethical dilemmas.[8] First, individuals must determine as precisely as possible their own personal rules of conduct. This exercise means looking back at past decisions, hence actions, as a guide for arriving at one's own actual values and norms. Next, managers should think about others who would be affected by the decision and how their interests might be weighed. This second step ensures that the welfare of all the stakeholders, including the direct and indirect parties, is taken into consideration. Though this approach might help in arriving at a more balanced resolution to an ethical issue, it will not make it any easier. The businessman warns:

> There is no simple, universal formula for resolving ethical problems. We have to choose from our own codes of conduct whichever rules are appropriate to the case in hand; the outcome of those choices makes us who we are.[9]

Interpersonal Skills The other set of managerial competences for effective implementation, interpersonal skills, encompasses a wide assortment of attributes. Those directly related to implementing global strategies may be classified as follows:

■ *Ability to influence others in an organization without the benefit of direct line authority.* This attribute includes being skilled at moving with relative ease up and down the company's far-flung organizational structure as well as sideways across geographic boundaries. It also includes being skilled at building "networks" of like-minded individuals and cooperative relationships, and at using the networks to accomplish specific tasks. Such skills are vital, especially when implementation involves a well-coordinated participation of managers from several parts of the global organization.

■ *Ability to resolve conflicts.* This skill belongs to the "survival kit" of any global marketer since implementation, as we have observed, is a mine field of organizational friction. The conflicts are at times built into the structure. For example, "turf wars" between product and geographic divisions are typical of the inherent tensions in a worldwide matrix organization. At other times, the conflicts are generated by the changes in marketing practices called for by a global scheme. Whatever their source, a marketer's ability to move around these obstacles has a direct bearing on the success of implementation.

■ *Negotiating skills.* Global marketers are often required to negotiate creative solutions to unavoidable problems of conflicting interests in the organization. Creative negotiated solutions —also called win-win strategies—can make a difference between success and failure in implementation.

■ *Ability to adapt to diverse cultural and language settings.* As the previous discussion has shown, overcoming the obvious and not-so-obvious pitfalls in cross-cultural communication can be an asset. Some global marketers are gifted with personality attributes that help them overcome the barriers, whatever the cultural contexts. Others will have to work hard at developing those critical interpersonal skills.

■ *Ability to endure and perform at high physical and emotional energy levels.* The complexity of the global implementation task puts a heavy burden on those responsible for its outcome. This burden is often manifested by high pressure and deadline-driven assignments, crowded agendas, and seemingly never-ending meetings and discussions in different parts of the world. Despite the widespread availability of electronic communication, global implementation still demands face-to-face interaction, which only extensive international travel can offer.[10]

To demonstrate the above managerial qualities in action, we return to the case of DEC, mentioned earlier in this introduction, and the implementation challenge faced by Jacques Morel, a disguised name for the young manager who was given the task of designing and implementing the firm's first standardized sales operations system in Europe. Jacques was chosen by DEC's regional president for his previous multinational experience in selling and sales management in France (his home country), the United Kingdom, and Italy. He was also selected because he spoke several European languages and had shown remarkable stamina in previous assignments.

The problems of concern to top management were the soaring selling costs per order and the declining sales force productivity. It was felt that a common and rationalized sales management system incorporating the best national practices would help improve sales force operations and make them more efficient across the continent. It was also recognized that any headquarters interference in the way local sales operations were organized and run would conflict with the tradition of leaving such matters in local hands.

Jacques' assignment was a difficult one. Though he had top management endorsement, his mission needed active support from the company's 17 subsidiaries to become a reality. His task was further complicated by the fact that as a member of the headquarters marketing staff function reporting to the regional president, he did not have any direct influence on regional or local sales activities since they were line operations. Early on, Jacques identified the powerful country general managers and their national sales officers as his staunchest adversaries. On the other hand, he believed the proposed simplification of sales operations, which could result in more time for customer contact and selling, might potentially win many sales personnel over to his side. The problem, however, was to get past the country-level general and sales managers and to sell his ideas from the bottom up.

A review of Jacques' actions in the months following his assignment highlights some of the interpersonal skills that he used to facilitate the implementation task and that proved instrumental to its success.

As a first step, Jacques traveled to a number of DEC subsidiaries with the announced intention of identifying, with the help of local managers, successful regional practices in sales management. Following these early consultations, a rationalized sales management model was conceived for Europe and was tested in one of DEC's smaller subsidiaries for six months to measure its impact on results. The pilot run proved highly successful.

By using a variety of internal media such as DEC's house organ, subsidiary-level management presentations, informational booklets, and even audio cassettes, Jacques broadcast the test's positive results throughout the regional organization.

The audio cassettes, describing the model and its potential benefits for salespeople, were sent to the 2,500 local sales personnel in a direct attempt to bypass the organizational hierarchies. Still, the choice of whether to adopt the model was left to country management.

With outspoken support from the regional head, Jacques managed to install within each country sales organization a new position, called sales operations manager (SOM). The SOM's sole function was to monitor key parameters of sales force productivity, such as customer-visit frequency, selling time spent per order, customer satisfaction, and so on. The SOMs reported directly to their local sales officer but had a dotted-line relationship with Jacques, who called them "his eyes and ears."

Through his now pan-European network of SOMs, Jacques began to build, for the first time, a valuable database of how sales forces performed across the continent. The fact that the early adopters of the model were doing measurably better than others was communicated to all country general managers and their sales officers. Jacques also began using the data to put pressure on the laggards. For example, he periodically presented to top regional and country management the best-to-worst country rankings in sales force productivity. Resistance to the model began to soften, and the number of countries adopting the proposed sales management system grew steadily.

By organizing quarterly meetings with SOMs, Jacques could underline the key elements of the pan-European model and encourage adoption where it was still not in practice. He also used these meetings to learn about common problems with the model's implementation, as well as the solutions country organizations had found to solve them. "They learned more from each other than from me," he recalled later.

Jacques avoided forcing the model on unwilling countries. Instead, he "let the results do the job." He zigzagged around Europe, continuously visiting the subsidiaries to hear about their problems and progress first hand. Personal selling, he believed, was part of the job.

In less than three years' time, all but two of the subsidiaries had adopted the global model and were reporting improved sales force productivity in addition to enhanced audited measures of customer satisfaction. DEC's success with its multi-country sales management program can be attributed as much to the global vision that led to its conception as to the interpersonal skills exercised in its implementation. This potent union of analytical capacity and managerial dexterity is what the challenge of global marketing is all about.

CASES IN IMPLEMENTATION

The cases following this introduction to Part Three deal with the challenges facing managers responsible for implementing strategy. They describe personal and managerial battles that need to be won in order to succeed. Such battles are external to an organization as well as internal. Externally, managers face market and competitive challenges to their business to which they must effectively respond; internally, they have to deal with people and organizational tensions that, if left unattended, could derail their strategy. The cases provide the student with realistic arenas to practice implementation in a global corporate setting and to experience its different facets, from structural to process-related to managerial. By touching on "real-life" challenges that global marketers routinely face, these cases are a useful closure to a discussion of issues in managing global marketing.

The first case series, Maschinenfabrik Meyer AG, describes a small semi-autonomous unit within a large corporate structure. Management is lobbying for the parent's support in implementing an ambitious global strategy. But, at the same time, management does not want to trade its current independence for the corporate help. Kao in Singapore, the next case, is about the personal dilemmas of a newly appointed Japanese country manager who finds himself torn between the conflicting demands of headquarters management and the marketing strategies of his local colleagues. The country manager has to decide how to resolve the conflict without compromising the future of his local operation. The final case series, Alto Chemicals Europe, raises the issues of managing strategic change and resolving conflict in a complex international corporate structure. Both the strategy and the human side of implementation are at stake.

The student can expect the following learning points from analyzing and discussing the cases in implementation:

- An integrative view of global marketing that combines strategic decisions with their prerequisites for implementation;
- Appreciation for structure- or process-related and managerial issues of marketing through the labyrinth of a complex worldwide organization;
- Skills in identifying structural and human obstacles to implementation *before* launching a global strategy;
- Practice in devising creative solutions to eliminate or minimize conflicts inherent in strategy implementation;
- Exposure to cross-cultural factors that can hamper global marketing.

Further Readings

Bartlett, Christopher A. "Building and Managing the Transnational: The New Organizational Challenge." In *Competition in Global Industries,* edited by M. E. Porter, 367–401. Boston: Harvard Business School Press, 1986.

Bartlett, Christopher A., and Sumantra Ghoshal. "Managing Across Borders: New Strategic Requirements." *Sloan Management Review* (Summer 1987): 7–17.

————. *Managing Across Borders: The Transnational Solution* (Boston: Harvard Business School Press, 1989), Chapters 8–11.

Cateora, Philip R. *International Marketing,* 6th ed. Homewood, Ill.: Irwin, 1987, Chapter 20.

Doz, Yves, and C. K. Prahalad. "Patterns of Strategic Control Within Multinational Corporation."

Journal of International Business Studies, (Fall 1984): 55–72.

Ferguson, Henry. *Tomorrow's Global Executive.* Homewood, Ill.: Dow Jones-Irwin, 1988, Chapter 7.

"ICI: Adapting the Structure to Suit the Times." *Management Europe* (October 1990): 15–16.

Jain, Subhash C. *International Marketing Management,* 3d ed. Boston: PWS-KENT, 1990, Chapters 18–19.

Kashani, Kamran. "Beware the Pitfalls of Global Marketing." *Harvard Business Review* (September–October 1989): 91–98.

———. "Why Does Global Marketing Work—Or Not Work?" *European Management Journal* (June 1990): 150–155.

Keegan, Warren J. *Global Marketing Management,* 4th ed. Englewood Cliffs, N.J.: Prentice-Hall, 1989, Chapters 18–19.

Locke, William W. "The Fatal Flaw: Hidden Cultural Differences." *Business Marketing* (April 1986): 65–76.

Ohmae, Kenichi. "Managing in a Borderless World." *Harvard Business Review* (May–June 1989): 152–161.

"Philips: 'Thinking Global, Acting Local.'" *Management Europe,* April 10, 1989, pp. 1–2.

Taylor, William. "The Logic of Global Business: An Interview with ABB's Percy Barnevik." *Harvard Business Review* (March–April 1991): 91–105.

"3M's Global Marketing Plan: How a New Package Helped Its Worldwide Reorganization." *Business International,* July 13, 1987, pp. 217–218.

Wiechmann, Ulrich E., and Lewis G. Pringle. "Problems That Plague Multinational Marketers." *Harvard Business School* (July–August 1979): 118–124.

Endnotes

1. See William H. Davidson and Philippe Haspesplage, "Shaping a Global Product Organization," *Harvard Business Review* (July–August 1982): 125–132.

2. See Christopher A. Bartlett and Sumantra Ghoshal, *Managing Across Borders* (Boston: Harvard Business School Press, 1989).

3. See Kamran Kashani, "Beware the Pitfalls of Global Marketing," *Harvard Business Review* (September–October 1989): 91–98.

4. This discussion is based on the works of Robert Moran, Professor of cross-cultural studies at American Graduate School of International Management. For a brief overview see, for example, Robert Moran, "Watch My Lips," *International Management* (September 1990): 77.

5. Ibid.

6. André Laurent, a researcher on cross-cultural communication, has observed the dominance of national cultures over corporate cultures. For reference to his work, see, for example, "Editor's Viewpoint," *Management Europe* (May 1990): 2.

7. The list is based on "Critical Ethical Incidents," prepared by Dr. Werner Ketelhohn and published by IMD, Lausanne, Switzerland, 1990.

8. See Sir Adrian Cadbury, "Ethical Managers Make Their Own Rules," *Harvard Business Review* (September–October 1987): 69–73.

9. Ibid., p. 69.

10. As an extreme example of heavy travel, an international marketing executive of Memorex Telex was reported to be traveling more than 250 days per year. The reason: "[not] to lose contact with the people, the business, and the customers," according to the executive. See "Marathon Man," *International Management* (July/August 1988): 30–32.

18 MASCHINENFABRIK MEYER AG (A)

In October 1983, Fred Oberli, managing director of Maschinenfabrik Meyer AG (MMD) in Deitingen, Switzerland, was considering the position of his small company within the evolving global membrane separation industry. MMD's involvement in the industry dated from 1980, when the company built its first prototype plants to separate emulsions, treat waste water, and purify drinking water. Membrane separation techniques were used in diverse applications for industry: desalinating seawater, treating industrial waste water, chemical separations, and food processing, such as whey removal in cheese production.

MMD management was now at the start of the 1984–1988 planning process. As part of that exercise, management was looking at the dynamics of the separation industry. In recent years, fast growth in the membrane-based separation market had attracted a large number of firms to the industry. By 1983, however, some of those firms had started to leave the industry. MMD management believed their departure was due to a lack of engineering competence in meeting stringent customer requirements. To survive and prosper, one executive believed, MMD had to secure a significant presence in specific growth segments and get access to international distribution and financing through its parent, Brown Boveri Corporation (BBC).

"BBC's organization is large and tangled," explained Oberli. He went on to explain:

> They are not used to bringing new technology to new markets—something that we have done and which the future of this company hinges on. So far we have managed to operate without any interference from our parent, and that's how this entrepreneurial management prefers to operate. Now we need their help to grow in an increasingly competitive international market. We need their distribution network and financing. But we are not yet ready to sacrifice our independence.

It seemed to Oberli that the five-year business plan for membrane separation was an excellent way to persuade BBC top management that MMD needed added

This case was prepared by Professors Kamran Kashani and Kurt Schaer, assisted by Research Associate Robert C. Howard. Copyright © 1989 by the International Institute for Management Development (IMD), Lausanne, Switzerland. Not to be used or reproduced without permission. Certain names and financial data have been disguised.

support. He hoped that the 1984–1988 plan he was about to prepare would accomplish this goal.

THE BROWN BOVERI CORPORATION

BBC was a major Swiss industrial company. In 1983, it had sales of close to SFr 10 billion, employed nearly 100,000 people worldwide, and spent almost 10% of sales on research and development. The diversity of BBC's activities was considered by management as a source of strength. As one member of top management put it, "We can do nearly everything." In 1983, the multinational company conducted business in 28 countries around the world. Its diverse activities were divided into four broad sectors: Power Generation, Power Distribution, Power Utilization, and Automation and Control.[1] (BBC's worldwide organization is shown in Exhibit 1.)

The BBC "Konzern" comprised four management groups, each with several companies. A six-member body, called the Konzern Management Committee, managed BBC's corporatewide activities. Each group was supervised by one member of the committee, and the remaining two members were responsible for technical strategy and finance and control, respectively. Organizationally, MMD was part of Automation and Control.

Superimposed on the corporate organization was a "horizontal" secondary organization aimed at "defining product/market strategies across the Konzern." In 1983, there were five business sector teams in the secondary organization: Power Generation, Power Transmission and Distribution, Power Utilization, Components and Products, and Electronics. A sector team, comprised of several smaller business area teams, was responsible for more specific activities in the corporation. For example, the Power Utilization sector had seven business area teams: Mining, Storage and Handling, Chemicals, Boilers, Mechanical Handling, Robotics, and Water Treatment. The Water Treatment team reflected BBC's broad interest in the water business, such as water purification and related products.

Within the Konzern it was felt that a great deal of autonomy and decision-making power rested at the individual company level and country organization. Both were operated as independent profit centers.

FROM PRODUCTION SATELLITE TO INDEPENDENT NEW BUSINESS

In the 1970s, MMD was a wholly owned captive supplier of turbochargers to BBC, a component that the parent used in the production of large diesel engines. Revenues from the internal sales of the company's only product enabled management to branch out into new areas outside current BBC activities. The new ventures, in return, provided compensation to MMD for the forecasted long-term decline in

1. The organization, management structure, and systems reflect the situation in 1983, before BBC's merger with ASEA to form ABB on January 4, 1988.

turbocharger production caused by changes in technology. The new businesses also permitted management to be less dependent on the larger BBC organization.

In the mid-1970s, MMD management began to search for markets outside of turbochargers. By the late 1970s, two markets were identified: membrane separation (referred to internally as *anlagenbau,* meaning process equipment in German) and automation. Neither business had any relation to turbochargers. The main impetus for both markets was that technical know-how within MMD's staff was available.

The automation business included small systems and robotics, as well as the engineering, manufacture, and installation of computer-controlled equipment for loading and unloading machine tools. The membrane separation business used membrane technology in a wide range of applications, such as water purification, enzyme processing, blood processing, and drug purification. A membrane, acting as a filter, was the key component in the system. This synthetic membrane acted to separate compounds by pore size, so that water and small molecules passed through and large molecules remained on the other side.

By the early 1980s, MMD had begun its metamorphosis from a captive producer of BBC turbochargers to a high-tech specialist in the automation and membrane separation industries. By 1983, sales in automation and membrane separation amounted to SFr 4.8 million each. Their combined contribution to total MMD sales was 40% and compensated for declining revenues in the turbocharger field (see Table 1). The contribution was projected to increase to 50% in 1984 and over 70% by 1988. This prospect was especially gratifying, as entry into these fields had been undertaken by MMD with only limited prior expertise in the requisite technologies.

TABLE 1　MMD Sales by Business Area (SFr in millions)

Business area/year	1980	1981	1982	1983
Turbocharger	21.5	18.2	15.8	14.4
Automation	1.0	2.3	3.5	4.8
Anlagenbau (Membrane separation)	0.5	2.0	3.8	4.8
Total	23.0	22.5	23.1	24.0

MMD executives were proud of the fact that the new businesses had been created with little assistance from BBC. MMD utilized its own finances and skilled labor and developed new expertise where necessary. In Oberli's words, "We have grown from a production satellite to an independently run yet wholly owned BBC subsidiary."

The rest of this case focuses on the developments related to membrane separation.

THE MEMBRANE SEPARATION INDUSTRY

Membrane Technology

Membrane separation occurred when molecules migrated through a porous synthetic material called a membrane. When the process was accelerated by applying pressure, it was called ultrafiltration (UF). In reverse osmosis (RO), pressure was applied to reverse the flow of solvent, a process that allowed concentration of impurities. Membranes used for RO had smaller pore sizes and required higher operating pressures than the more open membranes used in ultrafiltration. In general, UF was used for separating high-molecular weight substances, and RO for small molecules and/or ions.

Initial separation markets for membrane technology were secured at the expense of older, energy-intensive methods that membrane processes performed at a fraction of the cost. One example included the energy-intensive desalination of seawater to produce potable water. Membrane technology was also used to concentrate dilute solutions without the energy requirements of previous techniques. RO and UF membranes were only one component of larger processing systems that also included pipes, valves, pumps, meters, filters, and, most important, a high engineering content. Complete assemblies, referred to as "plants," varied in size and were mobile or stationary.

Industry Size and Segments

In 1982, the worldwide market for UF and RO was valued at $170 million and was forecast to reach nearly $1,800 million by 1990.[2] North America represented 50% of this market, Europe 35%, and Japan 10%, with Australia and New Zealand making up the balance. The industry covered a number of techniques by which mixtures of substances were purified and/or concentrated. (Exhibit 2 shows 1982 values and 1990 forecasts for major application segments. A more detailed listing of segments and applications, including customer information, can be found in Exhibit 3.) As the industry developed, the technology was expected to be used in new applications, particularly in biotechnology.

Competition

Membrane separation as a natural concept had been known for years, but synthetic membranes made of polymers did not emerge until the 1970s. Advances in polymer science made it possible to manufacture membranes with commercially viable product lines, able to withstand a number of industrial applications. Not surprisingly, many of the first companies to produce or use membrane technology were large chemical companies with polymer science know-how. Some of these companies manufactured only membranes, some designed and manufactured membrane-based systems, and still others did both.

As the membrane industry grew, it attracted a large number of smaller companies, usually installation suppliers concentrating on one or few applications. As of

2. In 1982, SFr 2.2 = $1.00.

1983, approximately 40 firms worldwide manufactured membranes for membrane separation systems. (Information on main players is summarized in Exhibit 4.)

By 1983, two types of players had emerged: a few large and well-established firms, such as DuPont and Alfa-Laval, and many smaller and still unproven start-ups. In the competition for orders, prices and process know-how were growing in importance. This development of the membrane industry in some ways resembled the development of the computer industry where application software was considered more important than hardware, which was increasingly becoming a commodity.

Many of the start-ups entering the industry in proven areas such as water treatment applications found themselves ill-prepared to handle the technical complexities involved in membrane separations. Moreover, their lack of financial resources did not position them to take advantage of growth in the industry as strongly as the big players. Among the approximately 40 competitors in the field, Oberli believed only half a dozen would remain serious contenders in the long run.

DuPont's membranes monopolized the desalination market. An industrywide qualification ranking awarded by consulting engineers also benefited DuPont, as such a ranking was difficult for small membrane producers to obtain. Abcor was known to compete on price, and DDS had strong finances and a firm presence in Scandinavia. Millipore, despite its strong financial base, was weak in industrial scale systems. Paterson Candy International had the reputation of being a world leader in RO but was known to have a small UF team. Rhone-Poulenc, based in France, had few sales outside its home territory.

Industry Cost Structure

The membrane separation industry drew on a number of other industries for components. Process hardware associated with membrane installations included pipes, valves, pumps, meters, and filters. Each separation problem had its own unique solution with different hardware configurations, and each demanded a high degree of process know-how.

From a production standpoint, the "membrane plant business" consisted of three distinct phases: systems engineering, component manufacturing and assembly, and on-site installation. Systems engineering might represent one-eighth of the cost of goods sold (CGS) for a standard application. Component manufacturing and assembly incurred approximately one-fourth of the CGS for the purchased membranes, one-fourth for other goods and materials purchased, and one-fourth for labor. On-site installation represented the remaining one-eighth of CGS.

Although these cost figures were merely indicative, they did reflect the cost structure of MMD when most drive motors, pumps, and measurement and control devices were bought outside. The company sourced most of its membranes from Desalination Systems Inc. (DSI), a small American producer. Design and production of the separation systems were done entirely in-house.

MMD's cost structure typified most producers that did not involve themselves in membrane development and manufacturing but provided complete installations. Companies could, however, elect or be forced to define the production scope of their businesses differently. For example, there could be cost considerations, such as local content requirements, that called for the installation work or part of the manufacturing to be done by third parties. In fact, a company could choose to concentrate only on engineering and membrane sales for both original installations and the periodic membrane replacements.

Of the approximately 70 contracts handled by MMD during the preceding year, most were total installations involving all three production phases. Ten of these were new process development projects, with six in water purification. The rest were in diverse applications.

Keys to Success

Industry observers maintained that a number of factors would be important to sustain a strong competitive position through the 1980s and into the 1990s, among them the following:

- Access to high-quality membranes and ability to stay abreast of innovation in membrane technology. Access could be limited for smaller players without strong links to major producers.
- Systematic buildup of process systems know-how.
- Enhanced productivity through the use of computerized engineering systems and modular components for tailor-made installations.
- Participation in the sale of membranes over the total life of an installation.

In addition, MMD management saw access to international distribution as a key to future success. Currently, MMD dealt with a heterogeneous group of industries and geographically scattered customers. Drinking water plants, for example, might be sold to local authorities in Algeria, to the Iraqi government for military camps, to private owners of a Greek island, or to international general contractors for hotel and hospital projects. Process water plants could be used in the electronics, food, chemical, and pharmaceutical industries across Europe.

Management believed that to acquire new business, execute projects, and service current and past customers across this wide range of markets, an international marketing and distribution organization with numerous resources and skills was required. Among these were personal contacts with local decision makers, in-depth industry knowledge, and application and technical know-how.

MMD IN THE MEMBRANE SEPARATION INDUSTRY

Products and Services

MMD's products and services covered the two broad UF and RO segments of the membrane separation industry. MMD's entry into the separation business followed the Swiss government's enforcement of environmental legislation on water being disposed of by automobile service garages. MMD solved the disposal problem by manufacturing emulsion plants to separate oil from the water used to clean cars. By 1983, membrane separation was organized into water and nonwater businesses, accounting for 30% and 70%, respectively. The water business had two product/ service areas: water purification and waste water treatment.

Water purification was further divided into drinking and industrial water and ultra-pure water. Drinking and industrial water plants were used to separate suspended solids, colloidal matter, and dissolved minerals from water. MMD's stationary and mobile water plants purified water from sea, brackish, river, and spring water sources. These plants were marketed to islands, remote settlements, hotels, construction sites, and factories. Plants for the production of ultra-pure water were based on ion exchange and RO processes. These plants were used to produce different qualities of ultra-pure water from sea, brackish, surface, spring, and tap water sources. The water produced could be used in boiler feed water supplies, cooling water supplies, and pharmaceutical processes.

Waste water treatment was further divided into emulsion and recycling. Emulsion separating plants were operated by UF and were used to treat oil/water emulsions from metal cutting, degreasing baths, and regional collecting dumps. Recycling plants were based on UF and RO. Recycling plants separated liquids and gases and then fed a stream back into the process for further treatment. Recycling was especially important in the foodstuffs, pharmaceutical, chemical, paper, and textile industries.

The nonwater business used the same membrane separation products and know-how but applied them to other markets. Examples included blood plasma concentration and methane separation from biogas. Thus, what MMD offered was a full product line that began with consulting engineering and extended to component selection, installation, and after-sales service. Plant installation, and particularly after-sales service, required access to high-quality membranes, most of which were currently supplied by Desalination Systems Inc. (DSI). Run by an inventive owner-manager, DSI ranked fourth among U.S. membrane producers, with sales of around $5 million.

New Business Development—The MMD Way

MMD management believed that the technology or hardware side of membrane separation was relatively standardized. Management thought that future growth depended on applying that technology to new areas, either through "experimental" or "joint development" work. The more "experimental" ideas were pursued in-house or at universities. Projects closer to current commercial uses were developed in conjunction with clients. Joint development projects began with an MMD inquiry or at the request of customers. Eager to pursue all opportunities, MMD had not turned away a single development project as of 1983.

Typically, each project called for the construction of a pilot plant to meet a customer's requirements. MMD guaranteed the quality of the output, based on a given type, and the quality of the input. In addition to output quality, a customer's typical concerns were volume of throughput, life and cost of membranes, and the front-end investment in the project. The financing of a pilot plant took many forms. For example, a customer could "rent" a plant during a test period and apply the rental fees to the eventual purchase. MMD's technical staff assigned to the project would monitor the system and make adjustments to comply with the guaranteed quality of output. MMD aimed for breakeven on each pilot plant, although this goal was not always achievable. A customer could cancel the order if the plant failed to meet output specifications.

Pricing

Each product and process development project was the responsibility of a task force of three people— one each from development, production, and marketing. Once a pilot plant was constructed and delivered, the same team would plan future projects for similar markets. These plans set forth several policy statements on applications, user targets, pricing, distribution, and advertising. For 1984, a total of SFr 750,000 was budgeted for new product and market development in membrane separation.

One member of management indicated that these development expenditures were partially recovered when completed systems were sold to customers, thus allowing future development projects to be financed. The payback period for investments in development and marketing varied from one application to another. In blood plasma separation, for example, where development and marketing investment amounted to SFr 100,000, a sales volume of between SFr 500,000 and SFr 1,000,000 (5 to 10 plant sales) was needed to recover the initial investment. For drinking water applications, where more intense competition meant lower contribution margins, a sales volume of SFr 5 million was needed to recover the initial investment of SFr 300,000 in process development alone.

Marketing and Sales Organization

Membrane separation was a separate profit center. (A partial organization chart appears in Exhibit 5.) The marketing manager reporting to Oberli assisted in identifying new application areas, conducting market studies, and formulating entry strategies. In addition, the marketing manager provided market information to the sales organization.

Sales were organized geographically, with each of MMD's five sales engineers responsible for one or more country markets. The sales organization was expected to grow in step with the growth in membrane separation sales. It was estimated that a minimum increase of SFr 2 million in sales was needed to support each additional sales representative.

Distribution

Distribution had become increasingly important to large-scale commercialization of membrane separation, especially in waste water treatment applications. Management believed the company had gained enough expertise in this area to meet a customer's requirements anywhere in the world. Distribution, therefore, was considered key to expansion.

Oberli explained that the general principle at BBC was "to use parent offices where possible." MMD had tried distributing its water treatment products through local BBC companies, with mixed results. By 1983, MMD management was dissatisfied with the support it had received from the BBC companies.

According to one spokesperson, a competent distributor, in-house or otherwise, had to have the following:

- A sales force that understood the water treatment business.
- A sales force with knowledge of local customers in a variety of industries where separation was a problem.
- People on hand with sufficient know-how in membrane separation to educate the customer and help design a system to meet the customer's requirements.
- The capability to sell, install, and service each project.
- Sufficient interest in MMD's products and processes to invest in local market development, at least in the initial years.

Investment in market development was considered particularly important as membrane separation technology was new and relatively unknown to many potential users. Mr. Vilen, sales engineer for Scandanavia and the United Kingdom, explained that once sales support was provided at the local level, "it's easy to prove membrane technology is economical and a total solution to the customer's water treatment problem." Vilen believed that a mix of "canvasing" potential market segments, following up leads, and maintaining contact with headquarters were the important functions of distribution. Like others in management, Vilen was disappointed with the support he had received from BBC offices in his geographic area.

MMD management attributed part of the distribution problem to BBC's organizational complexity. Given the relatively autonomous local operations, there was no top management instruction to local companies to sell MMD's products. Some local companies were only sales offices, whereas others had significant local production facilities. MMD found the smaller sales offices easier to work with than the larger manufacturing companies, although both served as local representatives of the entire BBC operation.

Added to the distribution problem was the fact that some local companies already had a water treatment sales organization that competed indirectly with membrane separation. These organizations reflected BBC's broad interest in the "water business," with a variety of products and services. Originally, BBC supplied electrical and electronic control installations for water treatment plants and municipal water distribution systems. Component sales such as ultraviolet lamps and water meters were another part of BBC's water business. The third part of BBC's water interest lay in turnkey plants such as irrigation projects. To the extent that BBC could couple the strengths of its "water business" with those of MMD, potential for mutual benefit existed from the "water business."

MMD's experience, however, indicated that the presence of representatives from the water business was not necessarily advantageous. Vilen explained that this local expertise sometimes contradicted the effort and that these representatives were oriented toward traditional but narrow market segments. MMD was particularly "allergic" to any news that a local company was handling competitive membrane separation products.

For a number of countries, MMD had trained a local BBC employee in membrane separation technology. This training, spread over a period of up to two years, was considered important to the local operation's effectiveness as MMD's distributor. In only a minority of cases, however, was management satisfied with the actual posttraining results.

Parallel to working through the parent sales or production companies, MMD had tried other schemes for distributing its membrane separation products. Among these were distribution through MMD's own representative offices, through third-party water treatment specialists, and via direct sales from Switzerland. The last alternative was considered expensive and pursued only occasionally. One manager pointed out that only when the local BBC office showed a lack of interest did his company resort to an alternative distribution channel. In a number of cases, the BBC companies reversed their decision when they learned of MMD's plans to work with a third party. (Exhibit 6 summarizes the exchanges between MMD and the BBC Spanish office as an example of one such reversal. Exhibit 7 shows the types of distribution channels used by MMD in different countries and management's assessment of their effectiveness.)

Sweden was an exemplary case among BBC companies distributing MMD's membrane separation products. In MMD management's view, the Swedish company had done exceptionally well with distribution due to the efforts of one local sales engineer. According to Vilen, "The man is traveling most of the time, making contacts in all possible industry segments and keeping us informed of his progress. Of course, the BBC name and his association with that company help."

Smaller BBC sales companies received a commission on MMD sales ranging from 3 to 10%, depending on the size of an order. Larger companies preferred to buy the products directly from MMD and price them independently. Third-party distributors' commissions also ranged from 3 to 10%. Estimates were that a minimum of SFr 2 million of orders was needed for a distributor to break even on MMD sales.

Membrane Separation: Bidding for 10% of a Growth Market

MMD's commitment to the water business was such that management expected it to account for over 70% of sales in membrane separation, from an existing 30%, and perhaps up to 25% of total company sales in 1984. Over the years, these shares might decline as other segments grew, but "water business" was still expected to at least double in volume and continue to represent the most important field of applications for membrane technologies. With so many variables to consider in the industry, MMD defined its product/market scope with the following points in mind:

- MMD would not produce the actual membranes but would concentrate on engineering, component production and assembly, and on-site installation of systems.
- MMD would not seek direct involvement in the United States nor, for the foreseeable future, in Far Eastern markets. The United States was the territory of MMD's membrane supplier, and the Far East was considered too far away for the close attention each project required.
- MMD would set a SFr 3- to 4-million size upper limit for any installation built on its own, which would reflect management's concept of a tolerable level of financial risk. Larger jobs might, however, be considered in cooperation with appropriate partners.
- MMD would pick and choose from the broad spectrum of membrane applications according to their potential and MMD's competitive strength. Thus, MMD expected to be active in the drinking and industrial water and ultra-pure water segments that represented 40% of the market. MMD also hoped to secure 10% of the SFr 300 million recycling applications segment anticipated by 1990.
- MMD would attain its sales objective through a combination of complete installations, engineering and parts manufacture, and the supply of purchased membranes.

Planning for the Future

For Oberli, the 1984–1988 planning exercise, the first to be undertaken by MMD, provided his company with an opportunity to win top-management support for the future direction of the membrane separation business. The 1984–1988 business plan could thus mark a turning point for membrane separation—one that would give MMD the means to win a healthy share of this fast-evolving global market. MMD executives knew that members of the Konzern Management Committee, the intended audience for the business plan, would decide on BBC support only after closely examining the key issues affecting the future prospects of the separation business. For that reason, he wanted the business plan to be a comprehensive one, addressing all the issues that were central to membrane separation's long-term viability.

With those thoughts in mind, Oberli poured a fresh cup of coffee and began to prepare the outline of the first business plan for membrane separation.

EXHIBIT 1 Konzern Organization

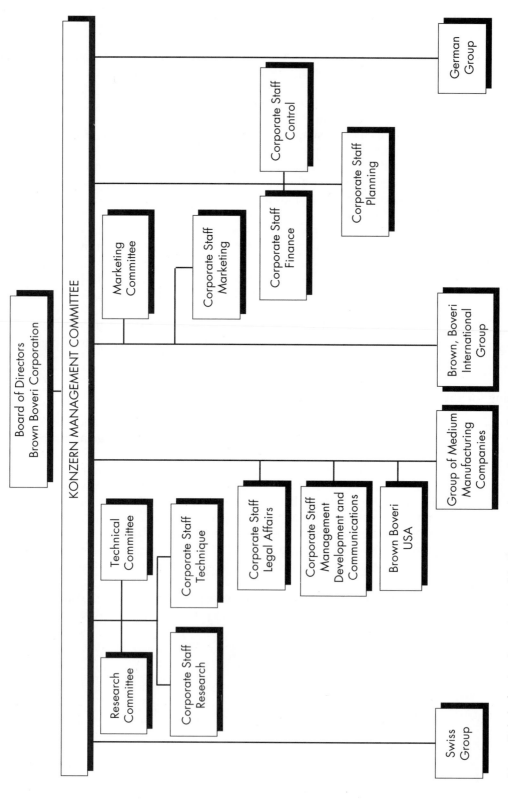

Note: Only the functional organization of the Konzern is shown. The individual companies' legal structure and the authority of their boards remain untouched.

EXHIBIT 2 Estimated Markets for Membranes, Modules, and Module-Related Equipment

Markets: Application segments	1982 ($ million)			Forecast 1990 ($ million)		
	U.S.	Rest of world	Total	U.S.	Rest of world	Total
Ultrafiltration						
laboratory use	9.0	6.0	15.0	39.5	26.3	65.8
process use	18.0	37.0	55.0	48.7	98.7	147.4
oil and gas wells	14.5	—	14.5	120.3	120.3	240.6
biotechnology	—	—	—	308.8	600.8	909.6
subtotal	41.5	43.0	84.5	517.3	846.1	1,363.4
Reverse osmosis						
waste water	27.4	48.6	76.0	154.3	172.6	326.9
seawater	1.3	4.8	6.1	9.6	35.0	44.6
biotechnology	—	—	—	15.8	17.2	33.0
subtotal	28.7	53.4	82.1	179.7	224.8	404.5
Combined total	70.2	96.4	166.6	697.0	1,070.9	1,767.9

Source: Company records.

Notes: Membranes were made in one of two forms. The more complex form was in the shape of spiral wound tubes or hollow fiber cylinders that were inserted into a supporting vessel. The complete assembly of fiber cylinder plus vessel was called a *membrane module* or module for short. Alternatively, membranes were manufactured in sheet form and inserted into a membrane cell. A membrane cell normally contained several membranes, differing in pore size. Figures cited above include the value of new and replacement membranes, modules and associated process hardware, engineering design, and installation.

The estimates exclude smaller segments such as nuclear waste water treatment, protein concentration, blood plasma separation, and various food applications.

EXHIBIT 3   Segmentation of the Membrane Separation Market

Segments	Potential applications	Typical customers	Primary geographic markets[a]	Key customer benefits[b]
Food				
Dairy	Whey concentration for protein recovery, Milk preconcentration	Cheese companies	F, DK, CH, D, USA	Higher yields, higher purity
Beverage	Alcohol removal from beer or wine	Breweries and vineyards	Diverse	Alcohol-free beer or wine
Chemical				
Electrochemical	Chlorine production	Basic chemicals manufacturers	Diverse	Pollution control
Pulp and paper	Process spent sulfite wastes	Paper mills	USA, Canada, N, S, SF	Pollution control
Miscellaneous	Paint/solvent recovery	Automobile manufacturers	Diverse	Environmentally safer
		Appliance manufacturers	Diverse	
Medical				
Dialysis	Blood fractionation, Toxin separation	Hospitals and research laboratories	Diverse	Purity
Pharmaceutical (Antibiotics, vitamins, amino acids, etc.)	Drug purification, Processing cell cultures	Pharmaceutical companies	Diverse	Purity
Biotechnology	Protein separation, Preconcentration of fermentation solutions, Recovery or recirculation of fermentation broths, Enzyme concentration, Cell separation	Biotechnology and pharmaceutical firms	Diverse	Throughput time, purity

(continued)

Sources: Company records; published information; ALFA-LAVAL: Filter Products Center Case prepared by Professor Jean-Pierre Jeannet, © 1983 by IMD.

[a]Identified as markets with the greatest immediate potential.

[b]In addition to overall cost and energy savings.

European market codes:
CH = Switzerland
 D = West Germany
DK = Denmark
 F = France
SF = Finland
 N = Norway
 S = Sweden

EXHIBIT 3   (continued)

Segments	Potential applications	Typical customers	Primary geographic markets[a]	Key customer benefits[b]
Water treatment				
Pure water	Steam power generation	Steam power stations, Engineering and consulting firms	Diverse	Purity, reduced pollution
	Removal of radioactive particles	Nuclear power plants	Diverse	Purity, reduced pollution
	Laboratory water	Various laboratories and hospitals	Diverse	Purity
	Semiconductor manufacturing	Electronics companies	USA, Japan	Purity
	Polluted stream cleanup, Sewage treatment	Municipal water authorities	Diverse	Purity
	Desalination	Municipal water authorities, Remote settlements	Diverse	Purity
Waste water	Oil/water emulsion separation	Steel rolling plants, Automotive garages	Diverse Diverse	Savings on waste disposal, Reduced pollution
	Ink/water emulsion separation	Ink manufacturers	Unknown	Savings on waste disposal, Reduced pollution
Gas separation				
Pollution control	Control smoke stack emissions	Steel mills, Paper mills	Diverse	Reduced pollution
Refining	Separate hydrocarbon gases at petrochemical refineries, retrieval of catalysts	Oil refineries	Diverse	Reduced pollution
	Separate oxygen from nitrogen	Specialty gas companies	Unknown	Purity

EXHIBIT 4 Main Players in the Membrane Separation Industry

Company	Location	Own membrane production	System producer	Primary segments	Active countries
Abcor	U.S.	na	+	Paint, oil/water	U.S., Europe, Australia, and COMECON*
Alfa-Laval	Sweden	–	+	Pharmaceutical, dairy, chloralkali, biochemical	Diverse
Allied	U.S.	+	+	Caustic soda, gas separation, waste water treatment	Unknown
Amicon	U.S.	+	+	Processing cell cultures	Unknown
Aqua-Chem	U.S.	na	+	Pulp and paper	U.S.
Asahi	Japan	+	+	Chlorine plants, automotive, semiconductor	Newly industrializing countries
DDS (Danish Sugar Co.)	Denmark	+	+	Hygienics, food and dairy, pharmaceuticals, beer industry, pulp and paper	Europe, U.S., Japan, Australia
Dow Chemical	U.S.	+	na	Gas separation, pure water	Diverse
DuPont	U.S.	+	+	Desalination, brackish water, gas separation, chlorine	Diverse
Membrana (subsidiary of Enka)	Germany	+	na	Unknown	Unknown
Millipore	U.S.	+	+	Lab scale UF, pharmaceutical, food, beverage, potable water, blood processing	Diverse
Mitsui	Japan	–	+	Unknown	Japan, SE Asia

Sources: Company records; published information.

*COMECON is an economic association of Communist countries.
na = not available or known
+ = yes (positive)
– = no (negative)

(continued)

EXHIBIT 4 (continued)

Company	Location	Own membrane production	System producer	Primary segments	Active countries
Monsanto	U.S.	na	+	Gas separation	Unknown
Nitto	Japan	+	+	Semiconductor, biotechnology, food, pure water	Japan, U.S.
Olsa	Italy	na	+	Water purification	Unknown
Osmonics	U.S.	+	+	Ultrapure water, automotive waste water, paint	U.S.
Paterson Candy International (PCI)	U.K.	+	+	Dairy, food, pure water, pulp and paper	Europe, Turkey, Iraq
Powell Duffryn Control	U.K.	na	+	Dewater solids, sludge thickening	Unknown
Rhone-Poulenc	France	+	+	Dairy/cheese, gas separation, pharmaceuticals	France, USSR
Rochem		+	+	Desalination, brackish water	Europe, Egypt, Mexico
Romicon (subsidiary of Rohm & Haas)	U.S.	+	+	Dairy, food, drug, waste water	Diverse
SFEC	France	na	+	None as of 1983	France
Stilmas	Italy	na	+	Water purification	Unknown
Toray industries	Japan	+	na	Semiconductor, pure water	Japan
UOP	U.S.	+	+	Beer industry, desalination, brackish water	U.S.

EXHIBIT 5 MMD'S Partial Organization Chart

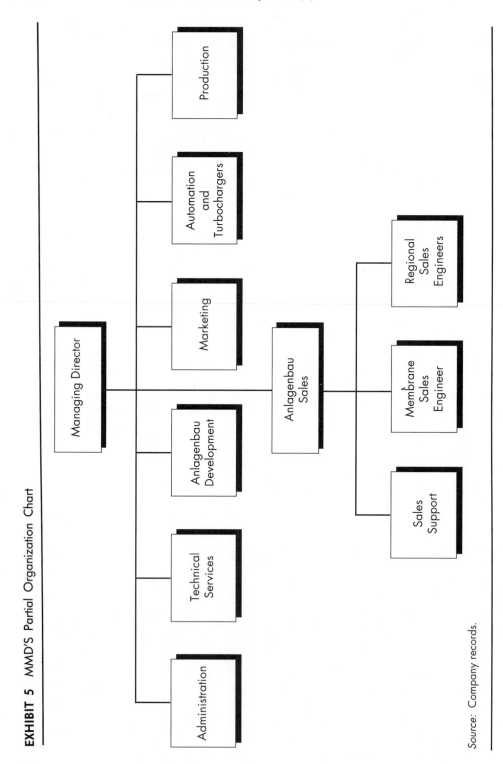

Source: Company records.

EXHIBIT 6 Chronology of Exchanges with Brown Boveri Espana SA

March 1980	Mr. Montes, managing director of BBC Spain, was invited to distribute in Spain.
August 1980	Montes declined to represent MMD in Spain because "well-established competitors (three identified) benefit from cost advantages through local production/parts supplies which are often required by customers." Other reasons included: ■ slow-moving legislation on environmental protection; ■ little enforcement of existing legislation to dissuade industries from using inadequate nonmembrane solutions.
March 1981	Oberli informed Montes that MMD was looking for a third-party representative; Spain would be advised of MMD's choice as soon as an arrangement was found. It was suggested that Spain consider competitive bidding for local-production subcontracts.
September 1983	Montes expressed interest in selling water purification plants, primarily for "pure" water. Oberli indicated MMD was already exploring two projects in Spain, yet cooperation remained possible if BBC Spain: ■ assigned one person full-time to water treatment; ■ agreed to train this person in Deitingen, with an eye to project management and local parts manufacture in Spain. Such cooperation could extend to other MMD product lines. Montes's response was expected for January 1984, and Oberli suggested a joint visit to spanish OEM as a next step.

EXHIBIT 7 MMD Distribution Channels

Distribution	Countries	Management assessment
Through BBC local companies	Netherlands*	Ineffective; Discontinued
	Finland*	Ineffective
	Sweden*	Effective
	Norway*	Ineffective
	Great Britain*	Ineffective
	Greece*	Effective
	Austria	Effective
	Algeria	Effective
	Denmark	Ineffective
	Italy*	Ineffective
Through MMD office	Germany	Effective
Direct from headquarters	Switzerland	Effective
	East Germany	Effective
	Yugoslavia	Effective
	Belgium	Effective
	Luxembourg	Effective
	Spain	Effective
Through third party representing BBC and MMD	Hungary	Effective
	Bulgaria	Too early to assess
	Poland	Ineffective

*Sales engineer trained by MMD.

19 MASCHINENFABRIK MEYER AG (B)

Fred Oberli glanced at the final copy of the 1984–1988 Planning Strategy for Maschinenfabrik Meyer AG (MMD). Although the plan was limited to membrane separation, similar plans were prepared for MMD's automation and turbocharger businesses. The framework for planning at MMD was developed by a consultant and hinged on a product-portfolio matrix. Businesses were positioned on the matrix relative to their market attractiveness and competitive strength. The membrane separation plan, shown in Exhibits 1–8, called for an increase in worldwide market share from 4% in 1983 to 10% by 1988, corresponding to sales of SFr 4.8 million and SFr 26 million, respectively. To meet these objectives, MMD management wanted BBC to provide SFr 12 million over the next five years for plant and equipment as well as for international distribution support. Without that assistance, however, management believed MMD would achieve only half its target sales in a fast-growing global market for membrane separation equipment and systems.

FUTURE CONCERNS

Oberli's vision as projected in the 1984–1988 Planning Strategy was clouded by the uncertainties surrounding BBC's financial support. The 1984–1988 plan set the direction he wanted MMD to take, provided increased financing was available. He commented:

> We need money not so much for product and process development, but for marketing. The development is self-financing. Where we need additional funds is for market development and distribution.

Oberli clarified this point with an example:

This case was prepared by Professors Kamran Kashani and Kurt Schaer, assisted by Research Associate Robert C. Howard. Copyright © 1989 by the International Institute for Management Development (IMD), Lausanne, Switzerland. Not to be used or reproduced without permission. Certain names and financial data have been disguised.

Take Egypt, for instance. A preliminary look at this market has cost us over SFr 10,000, including travel expenses. Next, we commissioned a formal market study. We estimate the study will cost us an additional SFr 40,000. Should we get serious about Egypt, a local salesperson would have to be hired and trained, which would mean an investment of SFr 200,000 to 300,000 for the first two years. And that's before the first order comes in. To this you can add front-end start-up investment, the costs of local promotion and additional management overhead in Deitingen. Furthermore, the Egyptian government requires local production, which means a local engineering capability has to be started from scratch. Now, my question is, who will pay for all this—MMD or the local BBC office? We simply don't have the funds to invest in every market that is promising. If the local BBC office invests all or part of the required funds, then what will happen to the commission structure?

According to Oberli, the 1984–1988 sales projections in membrane-based installations assumed limited help from BBC and local companies:

We are budgeting for 5% of what we see as the potential market in our segments. This means some SFr 13 million by 1988 and SFr 15 million by 1990. But if we receive the financing as well as the local cooperation we need, our sales projections are double the budgets. That's 10% of the market or SFr 26 million by 1988 and SFr 30 million by 1990.

One MMD manager explained that the lower projected sales figures were based on entry into 9 primary country and regional markets. The higher projections were based on entry into an additional 10 secondary markets.[1] The financing schemes Oberli considered were a one-time "development grant" from BBC, covering part of his requirements. Alternatively, he considered venture capital from outside the Konzern. He explained:

They don't like us to go out for venture capital. They want 100% equity ownership, but I know of other companies within BBC which have raised outside equity.

PREPARING FOR THE BOARD MEETING

Management considered the board meeting in November as a turning point. MMD's future performance in the membrane market depended on parent support. As Oberli prepared for the meeting, he wondered if he would win the board's approval for both the 1984–1988 membrane separation strategy as well as the long-term financial and marketing support. In his words:

The success of our membrane separation strategy depends on the BBC-MMD interface. If we get the financing and marketing support we need, then we have no real problems. We can always solve the development problems internally. But what's the use of having the technology without the distribution? Either BBC directs the local

1. The primary and secondary markets were identified as follows:
   Primary: Eastern Europe, Scandinavia, Switzerland, Austria, Algeria, Italy, Spain, Great Britain, Greece.
   Secondary: Central America, Colombia, Venezuela, Egypt, Sudan, Jordan, Mexico, South Africa, Morocco, Tunisia.

companies to give us the necessary support or it gives us the funds to invest in distribution directly. Without such tangible support, our sales can reach no more than half of our potential.

As part of the recent exercise, Oberli had sent an advance copy of the membrane separation business plan to board member Professor Schmidt. Schmidt was responsible for research and technology on a corporatewide basis and had been sympathetic to MMD's arguments in the past. Successful presentation and discussion of the plan by Schmidt to the full six-person board were key to securing BBC support and providing for MMD's survival.

EXHIBIT 1 Basic Strategy for Membrane Separation

Objective To be among the five leading competitors in membrane engineering in Europe, with annual orders of at least SFr 20 million by 1988, at a 10% profit.

To reach market share in excess of 10% by relevant product/market areas.

Business Scope Engineering, manufacturing, and installation of plants costing up to SFr 3 million for water purification (drinking and industrial water and ultrapure water) and waste water treatment (emulsion plants, recycling plants, and solids handling pumps) in addition to other applications.

Technology Applications of membrane engineering (ultrafiltration [UF] and reverse osmosis [RO]) and ion-exchange processes.

Development of modular designs incorporating such standard components as multilayer filters, recovery stations, vessels, control equipment, UF and RO units.

Computerized engineering systems and computer simulation for applications design and testing at limited cost.

Distribution Two-pronged approach through BBC representatives (opening contacts) and MMD sales engineers (consulting and selling).

Appropriate forms of cooperation for large projects in Europe and for selling to Eastern countries presenting special state-trading conditions.

In parallel with distribution of complete installations, creation of a product sales organization for small units, membrane (replacement) supply, resins, and miscellaneous components.

Production In-house production of key components, unless outside suppliers offer lower cost. Local sourcing of vessels and piping whenever possible. Assembly always under MMD responsibility.

Acquisition of or participation in a membrane company to ensure the necessary control over membrane production and supply.

EXHIBIT 2 Guiding Principles

1. Concentration of effort on selected product/market areas; allocation of financial, human, and physical resources according to priorities.

2. Balance diversification of risks.

3. Cooperation possibilities to be used when economically favorable.

4. Consistent pursuit of market and environment changes.

5. Full deployment of existing strengths (skills, finance, technical know-how), and avoidance/elimination of weaknesses (slowness, overorganization).

6. Steady and persistent approach to business development; adjustments only in response to fundamental change in conditions.

EXHIBIT 3 Situation Analysis and Objectives for Anlagenbau, 1984–1993

A Business Portfolio Perspective suggests the following grouping of the MMD product lines:

"Children"   Recycling installations

"Stars"   Garage waste water treatment
                Drinking and industrial water purification plants
                Ultra-pure water production
                Solids handling pumps
                Membrane sales

"Cows"   Emulsion separating plants

"Stars" that are destined to become "cows" need marketing/sales support; making "children" into "stars" requires special development effort.

The total picture shows good future potential and portfolio balance.

Availability of financial resources for development, capacity expansion, and marketing will be important.

High-quality standards must be maintained and cost-reduction potential fully exploited.

The goal for all MMD products is to reach market positions that permit maintaining a competitively viable market share in the long run (i.e., share of market approaching 10%, depending on specific conditions in product/market areas).

"The Basic Goal is Profit Optimization."

EXHIBIT 4 Product/Market Strategy for Drinking and Industrial Water Plants

Geographic Coverage: Algeria, Belgium, Italy, Denmark, Sweden, Norway, Finland, Netherlands, Great Britain, Switzerland, Austria, Germany, Poland, Hungary, Greece.

Basic Strategy

	Low	High	
High		X	
Market attractiveness	O		
Low			

Relative competitive advantage

O = Current

X = Target

Intensify acquisition of new customers
Achieve breakthrough in market
Capitalize on technical advantages over competition

Evaluation

Strengths and opportunities:

- Technical know-how and experience
- Synergies
- Reference installations
- Range of available membranes from DSI
- Financing

Weaknesses and threats:

- Sales organization
- Customer awareness
- Competition
- Outside assembly
- Economic stagnation
- Import restrictions

Business conditions

- Increasing needs due to
  environmental concerns
  economic development
  population increase
- 1984 Market for MMD segments estimated at SFr 120 million and growing to SFr 260 million by 1988.
- Current Market Share: 4% in current segments
  1984 objective: 7% in current segments
  1988 target: 10% in current segments

Action Planned

1. Reach market share goal using sales engineers to actively cover geographic territories, stress product features, and advertise as planned.
2. Attract offers using a basic unit with options.
3. Reduce costs with less expensive components.
4. Enhance cooperation with new partners to circumvent restrictions.

EXHIBIT 5 Product/Market Strategy for Ultra-Pure Water Plants

Geographic Coverage: Algeria, Belgium, Italy, Denmark, Sweden, Norway, Finland, Netherlands, Great Britain, Switzerland, Austria, Germany, Poland, Hungary, Greece.

Basic Strategy

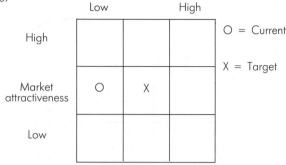

Intensify acquisition of new customers
Achieve breakthrough in market
Capitalize on technical advantages over competition

Evaluation

Strengths and opportunities:

- Technical know-how and experience
- Synergies
- Reference installations
- Range of available membranes from DSI
- Financing

Weaknesses and threats:

- Sales organization
- Customer awareness
- Competition
- Outside assembly
- Economic stagnation
- Import restrictions

Business conditions

- Increasing needs due to environmental concerns economic development population increase
- 1984 Market for MMD segments estimated at SFr 120 million and growing to SFr 260 million by 1988.
- Current Market Share: 4% in current segments
  1984 objective: 7% in current segments
  1988 target: 10% in current segments

Action Planned

1. Reach market share goal using sales engineers to actively cover geographic territories, stress product features, and advertise as planned.
2. Attract offers using a basic unit with options.
3. Reduce costs with less expensive components.
4. Enhance cooperation with new partners to circumvent restrictions.

EXHIBIT 6 Portfolio Graph of Membrane Separation, 1984/88 Targets

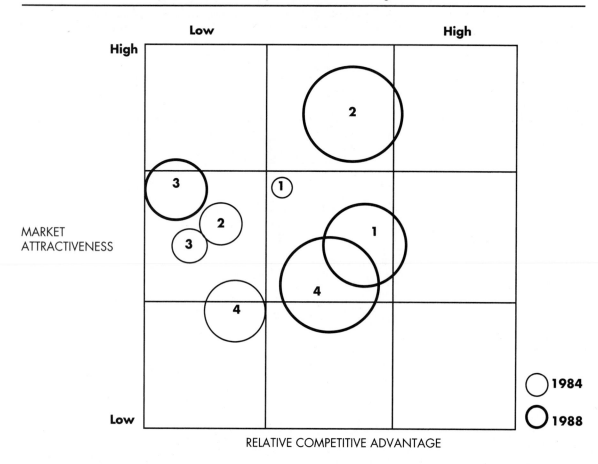

Code	Product Line (Type of Plant)	Countries	1984 (SFr mn)	1988 (SFr mn)
1	Emulsion separation:			
	Garage waste water treatment	Switzerland	0.3	1.8
	Other applications	Switzerland and rest of world	0.2	2.5
2	Drinking and industrial water	Others	1.3	8.7
3	Ultra-pure water	Others	0.9	5.2
4	Other applications		6.2	7.8
			8.9	26.0

EXHIBIT 7 Marketing Planning

Product Group	Markets	1984	1985
Drink, common use, and clean water plants	Egypt, Mexico, Venezuela, Colombia, Austria, Italy, Spain	Conclude market research, establish distribution where appropriate	Build up sales
	Holland, Bulgaria, East Germany, Czechoslovakia, Yugoslavia, West Germany	Carry out market research (preliminary to acquisition)	Decide on distribution system
	Morocco, Tunisia, Libya, Kenya, South Africa	Carry out market research	Conclusions on research
	Iran	Clarify ongoing financed project	
	Other African countries		Market research
Garage waste water plants	West Germany, Holland, U.K., Belgium, Austria, Denmark	Review environmental laws, select market(s)	Same as 1984

EXHIBIT 8 Strategy Requirements

Personnel Total employment is estimated to reach 300 in 1993. Over 10 years, a total of approximately 25 new management positions will need to be filled, 2 to 3 per year, preferably through internal recruiting. This requires hiring graduates from ETH (Swiss Federal Institute of Technology) or HTL (Engineering Schools).

Plant and Equipment No additional office facilities are required over the 10-year period. For 1989, expansion of the workshop facilities is necessary. A total of SFr 12 million will need to be invested over the next five years for expansion, replacement, and cost reduction.

Organization The present structure should meet the requirements of the coming years. However, wider use of computers will advance automation.

Distribution Detailed product/market strategies will guide the continuing development of a differentiated distribution system.

Production Sites MMD has no plans for production abroad.

United States Possible acquisition of DSI in the United States. Present plans do not assume completion of acquisition.

20 KAO IN SINGAPORE

As he sat at his desk one evening late in 1980, Toshio Takayama pondered uneasily over what he should do about Kao Singapore Private Limited, where he was the newly appointed director and representative of the Japanese parent, Kao Corporation. Kao was the leading soap and toiletries manufacturer in Japan. (See Exhibits 1–3 for data on Kao and its position in the Japanese economy.)

In September 1974, after Kao and its former agent in Singapore decided to terminate their business arrangements, Kao Singapore had been set up to take over the distribution of Kao products in Singapore. At that time, Kao sales in Singapore were only about S$2.4 million a year.[1]

By 1979, sales had grown to S$4.5 million; however, the Singapore operation had never made money. Already by 1976, cumulative loss was exceeding equity. Nevertheless, headquarters in Japan continued to hope that Singapore could be made into a model international operation. Hence, Kao Singapore was sustained through repeated injections of equity in 1977 and 1978. In addition, bank loans fully guaranteed by the parent were arranged to overcome cash flow difficulties. (See Exhibits 4–7 for financial data on Kao Singapore.)

Before Takayama was assigned to the Singapore company, he had had an interview with his mentor, Kozaburo Sagawa, who was then senior managing director of Kao Japan and chairman of Kao Singapore. Sagawa had stressed:

> The Singapore market, though small, is ideal to be a model international operation. The market is competitive, complex but manageable. We want to learn from this compact international operation and use the experience to develop our other larger international markets.
>
> However, the current performance of our operation in Kao Singapore is far behind our expectations. We want to experiment, to lead and be profitable in this market. We want to turn Singapore into a model Kao international market which our other markets can emulate.

This case was written by Professor Joseph D'Cruz. The information for the Appendix to the case was assembled by Professors Kamran Kashani and Dominique Turpin. Copyright © 1991 by the International Institute for Management Development (IMD), Lausanne, Switzerland. Not to be used or reproduced without permission.

1. In 1980, 1S$ (Singapore dollar) = U.S. $0.4670 and ¥105.54.

How to turn the Singapore operation into an international model had become Takayama's obsession. At the minimum, he knew that he must not only increase sales but also make the operation profitable. It was clear that Kao's problems in Singapore were not simple. There was severe competition from well-established multinationals like Procter & Gamble, Colgate-Palmolive, and Unilever, as well as from local manufacturers. Furthermore, Singapore was one of the world's most open markets and hence had products from virtually every corner of the world.

Takayama found that Kao's product lines were usually concentrated in the high-quality and relatively high-priced end of the market, while the Singapore market in general tended to be dominated by a wide range of lower-quality and lower-priced products. Knowing Kao's tradition of positioning its products as market leaders, Takayama was reluctant to adopt a low price strategy in Singapore to achieve brand leadership. On the other hand, Takayama wondered how Kao could become market leader in Singapore.

A proposal to launch Biore facial cleanser in Singapore lay on Takayama's desk. The proposal had been prepared by Chia Hock Hwa, the most senior local manager in Kao Singapore. Hwa was pressing for an immediate decision on Biore. However, Takayama knew that the officials at the Tokyo head office would be firmly opposed.

KAO CORPORATION IN JAPAN

Founded in 1890, Kao Corporation[2] had developed into Japan's leading cleaning products company for the household sector. Its first product, Kao toilet soap,[3] gave the company its direction, which it continued to follow thereafter. Early efforts were focused on fats and oils (tallow and coconut oil), the basic raw materials of the soap industry. Thus Kao's interest in organic chemistry began. Progressively, Kao began to emphasize research in surface and polymer sciences because of the role surface tension played in soap chemistry and the detergent industry. More recently, the corporation was engaged in research on skin physiology and other aspects of biological science, as part of an attempt to understand how the company's products worked on the human body. (See Exhibit 8 for details on R&D at Kao.)

In Kao, senior managers went about the company's business activities with an almost religious sense of dedication. This was reflected in the corporation's slogan, "A Clean Nation Prospers." It was generally accepted that it was the duty of every Kao employee to "strive hard to create products that will truly benefit people in their everyday lives."

Fulfilling this mission required more than emphasizing R&D. Early in its development, Kao made the strategic decision to develop and produce in-house, wherever possible, the essential ingredients that would affect the quality of its products. The corporation was not satisfied with merely mixing purchased raw

2. The company changed from its former name, Kao Soap Company Ltd., to Kao Corporation in July 1982.
3. This was a high-quality soap which, when launched in Japan, was the only soap that could claim "so high in quality that it can be used to cleanse your face." In fact, in Japanese the word *Kao* means "face."

materials to formulate finished products. Instead, it established laboratories to work on developing new materials that could be subsequently manufactured in the corporation's own plants as the raw materials for its finished products.

This strategy of vertical integration was later extended into the marketing system. Many toiletries and cosmetics manufacturers in Japan tended to rely heavily on the country's multistage wholesaling system to place their products in retail outlets. Kao, however, worked through a network of wholesalers who distributed Kao products exclusively. In many ways, these wholesalers operated like Kao branches. In fact, Kao sales representatives frequently worked from the wholesalers' premises. They would take orders for the wholesaler in addition to performing their regular jobs, which included promoting new products, doing administrative work with the trade (such as merchandising and handling complaints), and collecting information about competitors' activities. The close working relationship between Kao sales representatives and the wholesalers often strengthened the bonds between Kao sales managers and the owners/managers of the wholesalers. These exclusive Kao wholesalers were acutely aware of the advantages of distributing Kao products. They benefited not only from Kao's having wide product lines that were extremely popular with consumers, but also from the philosophy, style, and management system at Kao. Thus they were very eager to cooperate with Kao. Unlike other wholesalers, they were totally dedicated to that one company.

When Kao introduced its integrated Marketing Intelligence System (MIS), designed to track sales by product, region, and market segment, the wholesalers cooperated enthusiastically. They installed Kao data terminals in their offices and even allowed Kao sales representatives to enter their own orders. The MIS was used both to monitor sales and market trends and as a tool for market research. Kao market researchers frequently visited retailers, along with the wholesalers' sales representatives, to gather information directly from the trade. Kao was known to operate one of the most sophisticated trade intelligence systems in Japan.

Supplementing its trade intelligence, Kao developed an equally sophisticated system of consumer intelligence. An integral part of this system was a 24-hour "hot line" that consumers were encouraged to use if they had a complaint or any question about using Kao products. An on-line computer system assisted the hot-line staff answering queries. This system also recorded pertinent data from every call. Analysis of these data and other computerized data on market research served as the basis for monitoring consumer interests and identifying new product opportunities.

MANAGING CORPORATE R&D AT KAO

Kao managers firmly believed that R&D was an important element in the corporation's strategy. Kao operated 12 laboratories, employing about 1,700 people (roughly a quarter of the total employees) who worked in many different areas of science and technology. The corporation had developed a number of organizational devices and management processes in its R&D activities.

An example of the unique R&D operating style was the monthly R&D conference, usually attended by all members of top management and key R&D staff. These informal meetings were conducted like university seminars. Researchers reported on studies in progress and presented the results of their projects. The theoretical and practical implications of the research findings were openly discussed by the participants. During these meetings, researchers received prompt feedback on their projects from other researchers. They also benefited from the advice and encouragement that members of top management offered on the commercial implications of their work.

All R&D meetings at Kao were "open door"—that is, any interested employee could attend. It was a strictly observed rule, however, that visitors never spoke unless asked for their opinion. It was not unusual to find employees from sales and marketing at R&D meetings. Occasionally, these employees even brought along outside visitors—suppliers, customers, or academics. Visitors were often struck by the open and informal nature of these meetings. Kao managers believed that this informality encouraged individual creativity—a vital ingredient for maintaining the quality and momentum of the company's R&D.

This "open-door" practice gave Kao's R&D efforts tremendous flexibility and enabled the corporation to undertake large-scale interdisciplinary projects. Furthermore, the projects were usually undertaken in spacious, open office research laboratories where scientists and engineers from various disciplines worked together daily in close physical contact with each other. Kao's top management considered this type of environment essential for its R&D activities, as it facilitated integrated technological development.

The process of R&D was commonly referred to as "sowing seeds for improved products to better satisfy consumer needs." R&D was highly integrated with the corporation's various other components, especially marketing. The corporation's key technologies were continuously being applied in primary chemicals for new product development.

In developing and introducing new products, Kao closely observed a basic set of principles to ensure that the products would truly meet consumer needs:

- Is the new product truly useful to consumers and society?
- Is Kao's basic technology being fully utilized?
- Is the product's performance superior to that of similar products made by competitors, both in terms of quality and cost?
- Has the product recorded significant acceptance in consumer tests?
- Has the marketing communication plan been effectively formulated, so that accurate information on the product's value is received by every participant in the distribution channel (from the corporation to the consumer)?

Management would have to be fully satisfied with the responses to these questions before deciding to launch any product. Kao usually avoided the standard test marketing programs favored by its competitors before launching a new product. Instead, when basic requirements were fulfilled, Kao's products were often launched on a nationwide basis, mobilizing the entire sales force and wholesaling network to achieve rapid distribution. National advertising would then quickly follow.

DEVELOPMENT OF BIORE IN JAPAN

The development of Biore, a nonsoap facial cleanser, followed the typical strict but simple process of Kao's R&D. Its impetus came from analyzing data received by Kao's consumer hot line. These data showed that using soap to wash after removing facial cosmetics—the conventional method used by Japanese women—was not really effective. Consumers were asking Kao for a product that would give a cleaner wash. Laboratory tests confirmed that soap was not efficient for cleaning thoroughly after removing makeup for the reason that facial pores were often clogged with cosmetic pigments after using cleansing cream and paper tissues to remove makeup. Leaving pigments in the pores harmed the skin's natural mechanisms. Kao researchers concluded that a water-soluble product, gentle yet effective in cleansing delicate facial skin, was needed.

This challenge was solved by MAP, a neutral nonsoap-based chemical developed by Kao's organic chemists. "Biore" was formulated with MAP and blended with a subtle flowery perfume specially developed by Kao's fragrance researchers to complement the product's image as a gentle facial cleanser. It was decided to package the product in a plastic tube to emphasize its quality image. Recommended prices for consumers were ¥300 for the 60g size and ¥550 for the 120g size, substantially higher than an equivalent amount of soap.

Kao considered two factors when developing its positioning strategy for Biore. One element was cleansing ability. Competitive products were cleansing creams and facial and toilet soaps, mostly sold by cosmetic companies as part of a line of branded cosmetics.

The second element was the prevention of pimples. Since this was one of Biore's claims, it had to compete with the drug products positioned for treating pimples and acne. The major product in this category was Clearasil, an anti-acne cream marketed by Nippon-Vicks KK, the Japanese subsidiary of Richardson-Vicks, a U.S.-based multinational. Clearasil was marketed as a registered drug. Under Japanese law, registered drugs could be sold only through pharmacies. Hence, though Nippon-Vicks had extensive distribution of Clearasil at drug counters in retail outlets, its overall retail coverage was poor. Despite Clearasil's heavy advertising, its market share was small, as sales were limited to registered druggists only, where it held a dominant position.

Kao decided to avoid the constraints of being a registered drug product. Biore was positioned as a skin cleanser that also helped to prevent skin problems rather than as a product just to prevent or treat acne and pimples. Advertising focused on the benefits of a clean face, emphasizing the importance of thoroughly cleaning the face after the superficial removal of makeup. This approach contrasted sharply with Clearasil's hard-selling commercials that focused on pimple treatment. Biore's advertising also deliberately aimed to downplay the product's treatment role.

Because Biore was not registered as a drug, Japanese law allowed Biore to have a significantly broader retail coverage than Clearasil. Biore was sold widely by conventional toiletries retailers as well as at self-service toiletry counters in pharmacies. See Exhibit 9 for Biore's launch plan.

The product was an instant success, and a new category of facial cleansing cream was created.

KAO'S INTERNATIONAL OPERATIONS

Kao's first ventures outside Japan had been to search for raw materials. Coconut oil was an important raw material for many of the company's products, such as soaps, shampoos, and detergents. As it was important to have a reliable source of high-quality coconut oil, a major subsidiary was set up in the Philippines to produce coconut alcohols and their derivatives. Later, other subsidiaries were established in Spain, Mexico, and Indonesia to produce fatty acids, fatty amines, and other raw materials. These chemical subsidiaries also benefited from Kao's R&D efforts in Japan. For example, Kao developed a species of more productive coconut plant that matured more quickly and produced fruits at a lower height. In Japan, Kao also conducted extensive R&D in natural fats and oils, using the results in its overseas operations.

Other subsidiaries were established in Taiwan, Thailand, Hong Kong, Malaysia, Indonesia, the Philippines, and Singapore to produce and sell consumer products in overseas markets. Although initial efforts in these countries focused mainly on facilitating exports from Japan, Kao also emphasized the principle that subsidiaries' activities "contribute toward improving people's lives in the host countries." In every case, Kao tried to maintain close control of raw materials and the manufacturing process to ensure a consistently high-quality product.

In 1980, Kao began to expand marketing operations to developed countries. Overseas branches were established in the United States and West Germany, and plans were being made to set up branches in other countries. Progress was deliberately slow, partly because Kao's philosophy was to investigate the local consumer habits before introducing any fundamental product in a developed country. For example, when introducing a shampoo, the structure and physiology of hair in the targeted area would be carefully studied so that Kao's product formulations could be modified accordingly.

As the senior managing director, Kozaburo Sagawa was responsible for the major policy and strategy issues in Kao's international operation. At the same time, he was head of the Household Products Division to which the international counterpart reported.

Sagawa was a dynamic individual with a strong personality. Though some members of top management tended to be conservative in thought and action, Sagawa appeared to enjoy being different. He was known to use strong language and was reputed to have a fiery temper. However, he was generally respected for his creativity and ability to adopt a difficult course of action for the company's long-term benefit. For example, he received credit for the strong performance made by an unorthodox but successful joint venture business between Kao and Beiersdorf AG, a major German company. Sagawa had always been critical of Kao's foreign operations. Therefore, when international business was added to his portfolio, there was much speculation among Kao managers as to how he would improve things.

TAKAYAMA'S APPOINTMENT TO SINGAPORE

Sagawa was widely recognized as Takayama's mentor in the company. Takayama had joined Kao in April 1967 after graduating from Tohoku University. His first assignment had been in the Personnel Department where Sagawa was director. Although Sagawa was a chemist by training and had been Tokyo plant manager for six years, he had a keen interest in general management and particularly in strategic marketing. With his persuasive personality and strong interests in human relations, Sagawa had succeeded in creating a very dynamic personnel department.

Takayama, then a new employee, respected Sagawa not only because of his seniority but also for his dynamism. Sagawa often challenged, with great conviction, the wisdom of continuing traditional practices. Sagawa's revolutionary ideas occasionally caused friction intradepartmentally as well as within his own department. His fine achievement record, however, continued to earn strong support from most of his colleagues, particularly in top management. He aired his views openly and critically. He was hard on his staff, always demanding their best efforts in the shortest time possible. However, Sagawa had always been disposed kindly to Takayama, perhaps because Takayama was then only a trainee, but perhaps also because his open and straightforward behavior was similar to Sagawa's. Takayama himself felt that it was his persistence and old-fashioned patience that appealed to Sagawa.

In May 1968, Sagawa was appointed to the main board of the corporation. Three years later, he was promoted to the head of marketing operations. In June 1974, Takayama was transferred to the Chemical Division. He worked for another three years in the Chemical Division, responsible for the accounting and financial functions of two subsidiaries within the division. In September 1976, Sagawa requested Takayama's transfer to the Marketing Division. Takayama was made directly responsible for a line of French perfumed soaps and fragrance products for which Kao then acted as the sole agent in Japan. For reasons not clear to anyone, Takayama reported directly to Sagawa. That was unusual, for Takayama's new role was of no particular significance, and his position in the management hierarchy was in fact considerably lower than others who reported directly to Sagawa.

One day in February 1980, Sagawa called Takayama into his office. He explained that Kao's Singapore subsidiary was having difficult problems. For the past four years, sales had been growing but, despite financial support from the head office, the business did not appear to be viable.

He showed Takayama the following summary:

(Unit: S$000)	Kao's Operations in Singapore			
	1976	*1977*	*1978*	*1979*
Sales	2,517	1,967	2,642	4,497
Contribution margin (% of sales)	908 (36)	692 (35)	973 (37)	1,922 (43)
Overhead	1,206	890	1,163	1,965
Operating loss (% of sales)	298 (12)	198 (10)	190 (7)	43 (1)
Kao's subsidy in overhead	—	471	778	963
"Actual" loss (% of sales)	298 (12)	669 (34)	968 (37)	1,006 (22)
"Actual" breakeven sales level (% of actual sales)	3,350 (133)	3,889 (198)	5,246 (199)	6,809 (151)

Sagawa provided Takayama with more details:

Like Hong Kong, where we have been relatively successful, Singapore is a free and competitive international market. Because of Singapore's strategic position in the region, I want Kao to be successful there too. This can be done by applying correct marketing strategy and an appropriate management style.

You may be too young (Takayama was then 35) to take charge of an overseas company. However, I have to send someone to replace the current manager and I want you to go there. I don't want to hear anything from you about accepting this job, but do ask your wife if she will go with you to Singapore. That's all.

After seeing Sagawa, Takayama knew that his transfer to Singapore had been already decided. Sagawa was right. Not only was he young, he had never been outside Japan, let alone working in isolation in an overseas subsidiary. Though he was nervous, he felt he had to do what Sagawa instructed. Outwardly, he appeared confident. Inside, he knew this confidence was only because he felt that he had Sagawa's support. He was amused that Sagawa had said he should consult his wife. She knew Sagawa well, as she had previously been a secretary for a senior managing director in Kao. When Takayama mentioned the transfer to his wife, she calmly replied, "Is there a choice? If Sagawa-san says so, we have to go. Let's pack!" Next morning, Takayama sent a message to Sagawa, "My wife says yes."

Three weeks later Takayama was in Singapore experiencing his first overseas posting as a director of Kao Singapore. In the months that followed, as he struggled to understand the various problems confronting the subsidiary, he often wondered how such a short, simple meeting with Sagawa could have resulted in this dramatic change in his career and way of life.

When Takayama first arrived in Singapore, he knew that he faced a difficult situation. The outgoing Japanese director, Nagase, had reported regularly that sales were improving and that the operational activities were going well. However, the company was continuing to lose money, which was attributed to the high operational expenses. Although Nagase was eager to return to Japan and rejoin his family, he did spend a few days with Takayama to explain the Singapore crisis thoroughly. After Nagase's excellent briefing, Takayama felt that he understood the situation well, but he continued to feel uneasy since the reasons for the problems remained vague and confusing.

Before arriving in Singapore, Takayama had decided that, since this was his first working experience abroad, he should spend most of the first year observing and learning about the Singapore operations, its market and culture. When he had previously done business with the French in Japan, he had found it difficult to understand foreigners. He remembered the cultural differences between the French and the Japanese. Therefore, he assumed that the Singaporean way of thinking might also differ from the Japanese. Until he understood the local people, he felt that he should avoid speculating or imposing his ideas about what needed to be done. After meeting with Nagase, he felt even more strongly that his "observe first, do later" strategy was appropriate. With this in mind, he set about getting to know his local staff. He took an immediate liking to Chia Hock Hwa, a local manager. Board meetings with him were often "conducted" in the local "pubs."

Sagawa had told Takayama that he would be in Singapore for about four years. However, given the Singapore situation, Takayama estimated that it would need at least six or seven years to achieve something worthwhile during his term of stay. It would take one year to understand, the next two years to plan and experiment, and the last three years to set up a strategic plan. Takayama explained:

> I feel I should wait until the second or third year after I understand the local situation before trying out my ideas. At Kao, top management tends to say, "hurry up" or "do it now," but this Singapore situation reminds me of the old Japanese proverb, "haste makes waste." However, I am aware of my responsibility at Kao Singapore. Although I prefer to be an observer for at least the first year, I am prepared to accept the full responsibility from my first day in charge if things don't go well.

THE CRISIS OF KAO SINGAPORE

Kao's products had been sold in Singapore as early as 1965. At that time, Kao had appointed a sole distributor in Singapore—Boustead Trading Sdn. Bhd., then a major British-owned trading house with significant operations in Singapore and Malaysia, as well as in several other Southeast Asian countries. Boustead had a strong network and considerable experience distributing consumer goods in these countries. In fact, when Boustead took on the Kao line, it was already representing P&G (Procter & Gamble, a major competitor of Kao) besides other well-known brands such as Gillette, Ovaltine, Kellogg's, and Del Monte. However, under Boustead, growth of Kao sales in Singapore was slow. In 1975, Kao and Boustead agreed to terminate their Singapore trading arrangement. This was partly because Boustead was increasingly being pressured by P&G to decide between the two competing companies. Boustead chose P&G because it had a much larger volume of business than Kao. Despite this decision, Kao and Boustead parted on friendly terms; in fact, the two companies continued their shampoo joint-venture operation in Malaysia, which had started in 1972.

Instead of appointing another agent, Kao decided to set up its own operations in Singapore. Chia Hock Hwa was hired to run the operation. Chia had previously worked for Boustead, where he was responsible for sales of Kao, P&G, and Gillette products in Singapore. Chia found Kao's corporate philosophy attractive and was interested in building the new business. He felt confident that with hard work and financial support from Japan, the Singapore operation could be made highly successful.

At the start, overall responsibility for the Singapore office was given to a Kao manager, a Japanese named Akimi Suzuki, who had been the director of a newly established Kao joint venture in Indonesia. To ease communication and accommodate his family, he had been technically based in Singapore, returning there once a month. For the rest of the time, he traveled throughout Indonesia.

When Kao's Singapore office commenced business, its major products were laundry detergents and a few shampoo items. Since detergents were bulky, transportation from Japan was expensive. To overcome this problem, Kao had made an arrangement with UIC (United Industrial Corporation), a local competitor in Singapore, to manufacture the Kao detergents for the Singapore market. Kao supplied or specified the raw materials and packaging, set quality standards, and conducted regular quality checks. Despite difficulties implementing this arrangement, Kao believed it could be made to work well. This system enabled Kao to manufacture detergents in Singapore at a lower cost than importing them from Japan. Another advantage was that Kao did not have to make investments in production facilities. Chia tried hard to convince headquarters that Kao's detergent was not an appropriate product for the Singapore market, even with this arrangement. He explained repeatedly that the Singapore market differed from the Japanese market. In Japan, consumers had been using home washing machines for many years. They were quality conscious and willing to pay higher prices for better products. In Singapore, on the other hand, the market was acutely price conscious. Machines in the home were still relatively uncommon, and laundry was mainly washed by hand. Thus the market potential for high-priced, high-quality detergents was limited. Despite vigorous marketing efforts, sales of detergent products in Singapore remained small.

In a final attempt to increase the detergent business, Kao decided to launch a product at the lower end of the market. Sales increased somewhat, but the costs of selling grew even more rapidly.

At the same time, other nondetergent product lines were gradually being added, mainly hair care products imported from Japan. Sales of these new products grew significantly. Kao Singapore consciously limited itself to those household and basic toiletry products that were well established in Japan. To expand this business, Chia was constantly looking to Japan for new nondetergent products. In late 1976, Kao was persuaded to provide some funds to help advertise some of the new products.

Though sales of these products responded well to advertising, Kao headquarters was really more interested in promoting detergent products. Instructions were often being sent to Singapore to push detergent products more aggressively.

As Kao's Singapore business grew, headquarters decided that Singapore required a stronger senior management team than the prevailing arrangement. Accordingly, Teruyuki Nagase was sent from Japan in 1978 to be the full-time Japanese director. Nagase was new to overseas operations and was persuaded to operate the Singapore subsidiary along the line of the parent company in Japan. He emphasized detergents the same way as in Japan, obtaining more funds from Japan to advertise Kao detergent products. Chia managed to persuade Nagase to maintain the level of funds previously allocated for hair care products. Total sales then began to grow significantly; profitability increases, however, came mainly from sales of hair care products. Sales of detergent products also climbed, but the expenses for detergent sales grew at an even faster rate. As a result, Kao Singapore continued to incur losses.

With the newly available funds from Japan for advertising and promotion, Chia regained his confidence and optimism about Kao's future in the market. However, he said:

> We have got to be willing to do things differently. We are emphasizing the wrong products here. We must be sensitive to the environmental factors and move from a selling company to a marketing company. We must have a range of products that will give us steady growth based on both sales and profits.

Chia made no effort to hide his dissatisfaction with the detergent product line. He repeatedly complained about its low-priced positioning. On the other hand, he admitted that the Singapore market was price sensitive, and any attempt to move the Kao product line upscale was unlikely to be successful. Until laundry washing habits changed, high-quality detergents would not have a chance, he reasoned. At the same time, Kao had no opportunity to become a low-cost producer in Singapore, because its detergents were being manufactured by UIC, the only viable local detergent manufacturer. Thus Kao's costs would always be higher than UIC's, which had its own brand in the market. Chia was firmly convinced that detergents could not provide the base for a successful Kao business in Singapore.

When Takayama came to Singapore, Chia explained to him: "We will never make it with detergents. If we want to lead and be profitable here, we have to think of something else or forget the whole thing."

When Takayama reported Chia's opinion to headquarters, he received a sharp negative reaction:

> Our company has been built on soaps and detergents.[4] That is the base of our business in Japan, and that should also be the base of our business in Singapore. It is not wise to change a corporate strategy that has been so successful. Instead, you must convince your people in Singapore to think correctly about the importance of detergents. Don't you understand your role in Singapore?

4. At that time, about one-third of Kao's total sales in Japan were in detergent products.

BIORE FOR SINGAPORE

On one of his frequent visits to headquarters in Tokyo, Chia learned about the Biore development project at one of the open-door meetings. Chia was fascinated by the Biore idea. He was convinced that he had found the product that could turn Kao Singapore around and give it a new direction. However, Biore had become a controversial product at Kao; in a company that had been built on soap, many were skeptical of a nonsoap cleanser like Biore. One of Kao's long-time employees said:

> All these years we have been telling our customers that they should use our high-quality soap to clean their faces. Now, with Biore, we need to say soap is bad for the face. That's ridiculous. It is also extremely difficult to convince women to clean their faces with a chemical product in a tube.

Chia obtained a sample of Biore. When he tried it in his hotel room in Tokyo, he was amazed by its cleansing action. He was deeply impressed and convinced that Biore's unique properties would give Kao Singapore a real chance to develop and lead a new market. The more he studied the Biore proposition, the more he liked it. The Singapore market for cleansers was underdeveloped. The only major product sold as a facial cleanser was Dearland; it was manufactured in Taiwan and imported into Singapore by a local company. On his return, Chia bought a tube of Dearland. When he tried it, he was pleased to find that Biore clearly seemed to be a superior product.

Chia particularly liked the Biore idea because he felt that the product was capable of satisfying a need; it was effective and unique. He also realized that the product could be sold at a price high enough to sustain advertising. He said:

> With the higher margin, Biore is capable of making a significant contribution to fixed operating costs. This could turn the company into a profitable operation within a short period of time. In fact, Biore could also help project the company from a completely sales-oriented organization into a more strategy-directed consumer marketing company.

During his years working with Gillette and P&G, Chia had learned various aggressive marketing tools that he was eager to use but could not because the margins in the detergent business were so low. He felt Biore would give him this opportunity. Chia had gone further than thinking big about Biore. He had actually prepared a marketing plan to launch the product in Singapore. He then presented Takayama with a copy of his plan. (Elements of Chia's proposal are presented in the appendix at the end of the case.)

THE DILEMMA

Takayama stared at Chia's proposal recommending that Biore be launched in Singapore right away. Although he knew Chia was right, Takayama thought about his own decision to act only as an observer during the first year. He was also familiar with the attitude of the managers at headquarters in Tokyo. Facial cleansers were still new in Japan, and Biore was a new product category just created by Kao. The parent company had been built over the years on toilet soaps (launched in 1879), shampoos (1930s), detergents (1950s), laundry additives (1960s), and sanitary products (1975). Biore facial cleanser marked a challenging entry into the high-value-added cosmetics business. That was not an easy entry in Japan, where the established competitors in cosmetics were strong and well entrenched. Kao managers believed there was still much more to be learned about the facial cleanser business. Many regarded Biore as an experiment that could easily fail. The Biore product team, of course, was enthusiastic about the new product's prospects, sure that they had a winner. But they admitted that there were many uncertainties.

Takayama was at a loss about how to respond. He told Chia:

> We are not sure whether this new product will succeed or fail in Japan. If we fail in Singapore and they fail in Japan, we will be reprimanded for being impatient and not waiting for Japan's results to be known. If we succeed and they fail, we will have to withdraw the product from the market anyway, since it will be discontinued and no longer available. Introducing this product will work only if we all succeed, a situation that is uncertain at this point. The head office has instructed us to wait another two to three years. Furthermore, to launch this product now, we would need more advertising money from the head office. Even if we proceeded without their blessing, we would still have the problem of funds.

An integral part of Chia's proposal was his recommendation that Singapore should get out of the detergent business to free up the sales team for the Biore business. This recommendation was even more disturbing, and Takayama knew that the response from headquarters would be strong and sharp. Chia stubbornly upheld his stand. He told Takayama:

> Kao should get out of the detergent business in Singapore. We've not yet made and will never make a profit in detergents. Actually, we are only helping to build UIC's business. The opportunities for us here are in hair care and cosmetic products, not detergents.

Takayama could see the merits of Chia's proposal and was particularly impressed by Chia's calculations that "if only 10% of our sales in Singapore come from Biore, we will become profitable. For the same result, we would have to increase detergent sales six times."

Takayama also felt that this strategy might be the only way to fulfill Sagawa's goals to make the Singapore operation profitable and to start establishing Kao brands in leadership positions. On the other hand, he was afraid to take the risks that most of his colleagues in Japan were advising him to avoid. He knew that they were counting on him to proceed with building up the detergents business. Furthermore, he did not know the market well enough to be able to evaluate Biore's prospects in Singapore. Would Biore really do as well as Chia claimed?

As he pondered these questions, Takayama felt very alone and suddenly realized how much he missed his network of contacts at Kao. Takayama was well known and liked at Kao where so many different jobs had brought him into contact with a large number of people. After office hours, he often had met casually with his colleagues in bars and small restaurants. When something troubled him seriously, he would usually talk it over informally with several people. He had found that such dialogues would help him understand the various aspects of his problem and usually the appropriate solution would emerge.

In Singapore, Takayama was the only Japanese manager on the spot. He was alone with no opportunity to talk things over with his peers and superiors. It was then that he realized why Sagawa had insisted that he take his wife to Singapore. Though she knew little about business matters, her support and confidence in him were comforting, and he could talk to her in the traditional way. Even so, Takayama's confidence in himself was becoming increasingly shaken. Having to decide about Biore was the major cause of his depression. He looked again at Chia's proposal for Biore. How should he respond to Chia? Should he stay with his original strategy merely to observe during the first year? Should he call Sagawa to ask his advice? Or was this the opportunity he should seize to make a personal impact in the company?

Takayama noticed that his ashtray was filled to the brim and that he had run out of cigarettes. The time had come to act. He looked around the empty room and murmured to himself, "I will decide this by myself!"

EXHIBIT 1 Growth of Japanese Economy and Kao Corporation's Position in the Japanese Economy

| | Japanese Economy | | | | Kao Corporation | | | | | |
| | Nominal GNP | | Advertising expenditures | | Net sales | | Advertising expenditures | | | |
Year	(¥ bn)	Growth rate (%)	(¥ bn)	Growth rate (%)	(¥ mn)	Growth rate (%)	(¥ mn)	Growth rate (%)	% of sales	Rank in advertising expenditure
1965	33,602	13.3	334	-4.3	32,813	17.0	2,894	19.3	8.8	Unknown
1966	39,509	17.6	383	14.7	39,230	19.6	3,982	37.6	10.2	Unknown
1967	46,239	17.0	459	19.9	43,691	11.4	5,264	32.2	12.0	Unknown
1968	54,761	18.4	532	15.8	45,435	4.0	5,688	8.1	12.5	7
1969	64,920	18.6	633	18.9	50,179	10.4	6,223	9.4	12.4	8
1970	75,152	15.8	756	19.5	57,708	15.0	7,169	15.2	12.4	9
1971	82,806	10.2	787	4.1	66,131	14.6	8,920	24.4	13.5	5
1972	96,539	16.6	878	11.6	83,785	26.7	12,419	39.2	14.8	2
1973	116,679	20.9	1,077	22.6	116,189	38.7	14,791	19.1	12.7	2
1974	138,156	18.4	1,170	8.6	142,057	22.3	12,804	-13.4	9.0	4
1975	152,209	10.2	1,238	5.8	146,917	3.4	13,910	8.6	9.5	2
1976	171,153	12.4	1,457	17.7	161,056	9.6	17,742	27.5	11.0	2
1977	190,035	11.0	1,643	12.8	186,753	16.0	17,858	0.7	9.6	2
1978	208,781	9.9	1,846	12.4	214,246	14.7	20,431	14.4	9.5	2
1979	225,453	8.0	2,113	14.5	245,698	14.7	21,243	4.0	8.6	2
1980	245,163	8.7	2,278	7.8	252,438	2.7	22,052	3.8	8.7	2

Sources: 1. GNP: National Economic Accounting Annual Report by the Japanese Government, Economic Planning Agency.
2. Total Japanese Advertising Expenditures: Dentsu Japan Marketing/Advertising Yearbook by Dentsu Incorporated, Tokyo, Japan.
3. Kao figures: Company records.

EXHIBIT 2 Balance Sheet (¥ millions)

	Mar. 1976	Mar. 1977	Mar. 1978	Mar. 1979	Mar. 1980	Mar. 1981
Current assets	36,605	39,415	54,379	62,998	74,042	74,384
Fixed assets	40,154	40,944	46,687	67,193	108,407	97,866
(Tangible assets)	(31,540)	(31,714)	(36,732)	(50,213)	(84,281)	(70,609)
(Investments, others)	(8,614)	(9,230)	(9,955)	(16,980)	(24,126)	(27,257)
Total	76,759	80,359	101,066	130,191	182,449	172,250
Current liabilities	40,752	41,784	53,777	65,882	78,093	69,953
Long-term liabilities	12,897	7,667	13,271	25,216	56,330	48,845
Shareholders' equity	23,110	30,908	34,018	39,093	48,026	53,452
(Common stock)	(3,632)	(4,400)	(5,397)	(6,165)	(7,479)	(7,749)
(Legal reserves)	(4,261)	(9,229)	(9,377)	(11,538)	(16,790)	(19,731)
(Retained earnings)	(15,217)	(17,279)	(19,244)	(21,390)	(23,757)	(25,972)
Total	76,759	80,359	101,066	130,191	182,449	172,250

EXHIBIT 3 Profit and Loss Account (¥ millions)

	Apr. 1975– Mar. 1976	Apr. 1976– Mar. 1977	Apr. 1977– Mar. 1978	Apr. 1978– Mar. 1979	Apr. 1979– Mar. 1980	Apr. 1980– Mar. 1981
Net sales	146,917	161,056	186,753	214,246	245,698	252,438
Ordinary profit	4,422	6,127	7,377	9,797	8,835	8,880
Income before tax	4,243	5,988	7,089	9,269	8,149	9,233
Income after tax	2,059	2,749	2,930	3,304	3,619	3,885

EXHIBIT 4 Sales Amount by Product Category (S$000)

	Sept. 1975– Dec. 1975	Jan. 1976– Dec. 1976	Jan. 1977– Dec. 1977	Jan. 1978– Dec. 1978	Jan. 1979– Dec. 1979	Jan. 1980– Dec. 1980
Toilet soap	—	29	14	28	106	310
Shampoo and other hair care	211	359	431	945	1,878	2,980
Laundry detergent	818	2,082	1,248	1,249	1,664	1,717
Other detergents	5	14	249	389	805	769
Others	6	33	25	31	44	60
Total	1,040	2,517	1,967	2,642	4,497	5,836

EXHIBIT 5 Sales Contribution by Product Category (%)

	Sept. 1975–Dec. 1975	Jan. 1976–Dec. 1976	Jan. 1977–Dec. 1977	Jan. 1978–Dec. 1978	Jan. 1979–Dec. 1979	Jan. 1980–Dec. 1980
Toilet soap	—	1	1	1	2	5
Shampoo and other hair care	20	14	22	36	42	51
Laundry detergent	79	83	63	47	37	30
Other detergents	0.5	0.5	13	15	18	13
Others	0.5	1.5	1	1	1	1
Total	100	100	100	100	100	100

EXHIBIT 6 Balance Sheet (S$000)

	Dec. 1975	Dec. 1976	Dec. 1977	Dec. 1978	Dec. 1979	Dec. 1980
Current assets	553	110	412	686	1,547	2,010
Cash	359	1	3	5	4	27
Trade debtors	123	43	141	298	873	994
Inventories	60	41	235	300	511	527
Others	11	25	33	83	159	462
Fixed assets	62	140	129	153	197	405
Motor vehicles	57	129	115	130	164	370
Others	5	11	14	23	33	35
Total	615	250	541	839	1,744	2,415
Current liabilities	547	516	774	924	1,821	2,345
Trade creditors	372	183	401	461	1,110	1,305
Bank overdraft	—	213	272	314	398	480
Others	175	120	101	149	313	560
Shareholders' equity	68	(266)	(233)	(85)	(77)	70
Share capital	100	100	300	600	600	600
Revenue reserve	(32)	(366)	(533)	(685)	(677)	(530)
Total	615	250	541	839	1,744	2,415

EXHIBIT 7 Profit And Loss Account (S$000)

	Sept. 1975– Dec. 1975	Jan. 1976– Dec. 1976	Jan. 1977– Dec. 1977	Jan. 1978– Dec. 1978	Jan. 1979– Dec. 1979	Jan. 1980– Dec. 1980
Net sales	1,040	2,517	1,967	2,642	4,497	5,836
Cost of sales	842	1,609	1,275	1,669	2,575	2,934
Gross profit	198	908	692	973	1,922	2,902
Administration, selling expenses	83	432	619	848	1,121	1,609
Marketing expenses	151	774	271	315	844	1,121
Operating profit/(loss)	(36)	(298)	(198)	(190)	(43)	172
Nonoperating profit/(loss)	(1)	(33)	33	43	41	(25)
Profit/(loss) before taxation	(37)	(331)	(165)	(147)	(2)	147
Taxation	—	—	—	—	—	—
Profit/(loss) after taxation	(37)	(331)	(165)	(147)	(2)	147
Depreciation charged for the year	3	30	38	48	65	123
Kao Japan's Subsidy*	—	—	471	778	963	901

*For marketing activities not included in the above profit and loss account.

EXHIBIT 8 R&D at Kao Corporation

Laboratories	R&D activities
1. Wakayama First Laboratory	Fat and oil chemistry Organic chemistry Polymer science Manufacturing processes
2. Wakayama Second Laboratory	Specialty chemicals Lubricant additives Foundry chemicals
3. Tochigi First Laboratory	Biological science Skin physiology Organic chemistry
4. Tochigi Second Laboratory	Household products
5. Tochigi Third Laboratory	Hygiene products Technology of developing composite materials
6. Tokyo First Laboratory	Hair care products Color science Fragrances and flavors
7. Tokyo Second Laboratory	Skin care products Cosmetics
8. Kashima Laboratory	Fat and oil chemistry Edible oils and foods Fermentation and enzymes
9. Recording and Imaging Science Laboratories	Applied physics Information and electronic industries related products
10. Knowledge and Intelligence Science Institute	Computer science Information science
11. Production Technology Institute	Production technology systems
12. Kao Institute for Fundamental Research	Fundamental research in cooperation with domestic and foreign universities and research institutes

EXHIBIT 9 New Product Launch Plan for "Biore" Facial Cleansing Foam in Japan

Market Situation

1. Products currently used for facial cleansing are cleansing cream, facial soap, and toilet soap. The market shares of these products are 44%, 31%, and 25%, respectively. It is projected that the share of cleansing cream will grow considerably because of some changes observed in the facial cleansing habit of consumers.

2. The usage rate of cleansing differs among age groups:

Age group (year)	15–19	20–24	25–34	35–44	45–54	55–59
Usage rate	56%	70%	54%	48%	34%	28%

Heavy users are the young 20s, followed by high teens and older 20s or young 30s.

3. What are product benefits that consumers expect to get from cleansing cream?

	15–24 years (%)	25–39 years (%)
Gentle on skin/Less skin irritation by use	21	34
No tight feeling/Feel moisturized after use	22	23
Helps to prevent pimples	11	2

Though a good cleansing ability is the common expectation, there are differences in age groups. That is, high teens and young 20s expect gentleness on the skin and pimple prevention as well, while the other age groups show higher expectation on gentleness, even on delicate skin.

4. The market size of cleansing cream has been reported as follows:

1978	1979	1980
¥12 billion	¥13 billion	¥14 billion

The total market size of cleansing cream and facial soap is estimated to be approximately ¥25 billion in 1980.

"Biore" Facial Cleansing Foam

1. Biore performs differently compared to other existing facial cleansing products. It is gentle even on delicate skin. It does not leave a "tight" feeling but leaves the moisturized feeling even if it is repeatedly used in a day. It is also effective in preventing pimples.

2. Biore's main ingredient is MAP (Mono-Alkil Phosphate), which was developed by Kao's R&D. MAP is neutral and nonalkaline. It is totally different from soap. It is not harmful to the skin but is as gentle as water.

MAP's cleansing ability is as good as that of soap. While cleansing by soap washes away NMF (natural moisturizing factor) of the skin, MAP washes off dirt but retains NMF on the skin. This is why cleansing by soap leaves a "tight" feeling on the skin but not if cleansed by MAP.

Together with an antiseptic agent and an antiphlogistic agent, MAP also works effectively to prevent pimples.

(continued)

EXHIBIT 9   (continued)

"Biore" Marketing Objectives

1. To emphasize gentleness on the skin, less chances of skin troubles or irritation even with the frequent use of the product.
2. To create and encourage a new cleaner and gentler washing habit.
3. To achieve a good product distribution in the market and to secure a dominant position against existing competitor's products.

Note: Almost all of existing competitors' products are packed in a tube or a jar, and all are soap-based.

"Biore" Marketing Activities

1. To launch the product in March 1980.
2. Media advertisement:
   - To start in April using mainly TV and magazines.
   - To target females in 20s who are heavy users of cleansing cream and high teens who are concerned with pimple prevention.
   - To promote brand awareness, explain product characteristics, and encourage a new facial cleansing habit.
3. Product Distribution:
   - To achieve high product distribution, 85% and above at self-service outlets, 60% and above at pharmacies, and 50% and above at other types of outlets.
4. Product Sampling:
   - To carry out a sampling program to the targeted user group, and encourage trial usage of the product.

CASE 20 APPENDIX

New Product Launch Plan for "Biore" Facial Cleansing Foam

1. Singapore's Statistical Profile, 1980

General Statistics
Land area: 618 sq km
Climate: Temperature ranges from 24°C–31°C;
average rainfall is 2,326 mm
Population: 2,413,900, with an annual growth rate of
1.2%

Economic Statistics
GNP: S$22,216.7 million in 1980
Per capita GNP: S$9,204 in 1980
Economic growth rate: 10.2% in 1980
Labor force: 1.1 million at end of 1980, with
unemployment rate of 3%
Health: 3.5 hospital beds; 0.8 doctors per 1,000
population

Country Risk
The republic is dependent on general tranquillity in the
Southeast Asia region and is cushioned from outside
shocks through membership in ASEAN.

2. Objectives

Primary Objective The primary objective is to make
available to the public a neutral, nonsoap facial cleanser
to replace toilet soap commonly being used for facial
cleansing.

Problem The appearance of the paste is unattractive
and tends to harden in the tube. The Tochigi Laboratory of Kao is working toward a solution. However, if
no solution is forthcoming, the eventual switchover to
a liquid-type cleanser would eliminate this problem
altogether.

Opportunity Biore is the first-known available neutral
nonsoap cleanser that cleanses while reducing destruction of facial tissue to under 35%. Biore cleanses as well
as toilet soap and is gentle on the skin. No performance
equivalent is available in the market.

Short-term Tactic The 60g size enables trial usage with
subsequent upgrading to the more economical 120g
size. When appropriate, to market Biore in various
forms—e.g., regular and medicated, lotion and paste—
and to broaden its base to meet the varying requirements of consumers.

Long-term Strategy The long-term strategy is to market a range of economical facial and skin care products
to match the needs arising from the growing sophistication of consumers.

Corporate Goal The corporate goal is to reinforce the
corporate mission of "Clean, better living" by offering
a revolutionary, new, effective product and staying
ahead of competition.

3. Segmentation

Primary Objectives
- To develop the market based on a clear idea of
  response and characteristics of a specific market
  segment.
- To specialize and attain leadership in an
  identified segment.
- To be in a better position to focus on identified
  market opportunity.

Segment Description
Current leader in the identified segment has developed
this segment (both primary and secondary targets) rather extensively over the last 1½ years. Their product is
visibly inferior and highly priced, which provides Kao
with an opportunity to substitute our product. The
groundwork generally has already been laid by the
competitor.

Short-term Tactic The short-term tactic is to enlarge
the segment within the targeted groups by encouraging
family use of the product.

Target consumers	Primary target	Secondary target
Age	15–29 years	30–39 years
Marital status	Schoolgirls; single working women	Housewives
Income group (per month)	S$600–$1,499	S$800–$2,499
Family size	2–3	4
Literacy	English and Mandarin	Mandarin only
Shopping habits	Shopping centers and supermarkets	Supermarkets and groceries
Main media exposed	TV, cinema, radio, and magazine	TV, press
Residential type	Apartments	Terrace houses

Long-term Strategy The long-term strategy is to enlarge the segment by providing teenagers from 15–19 years of age with a medicated version that will contain a mild, yet effective, anti-pimple agent. This positioning strategy will effectively enlarge the segment.

Competitors in the Segment Competitive status is shown below.

Brand	Presentation	Market share (%)		Trend	Consumer price (100 g)
		Last year	This year (est.)		S$
Total		100	100	+0 -	
Dearland	Tube	26	16	*	7.90
Maggie	Tube	4	3	*	7.00
Meichi	Tube	1	1	*	6.50
Black Beauty	Tube	1	1	*	6.50
Aichi	Tube	1	0	*	6.00
Kose	Cake	15	11	*	4.80
Shiseido	Cake	10	10	*	6.00
Kanebo	Cake	11	14	*	5.50
Pias	Cake	5	6	*	6.00
Max Factor	Tube	9	6	*	12.00
Coty	Tube	8	5	*	14.00

Competitors in the Segment   Main competitors' activities are highlighted below.

Main brand	Advertising	Promotion	Distribution	Sales team	Main strategies	Main reasons for success	Estimated profitability
Dearland	Weak. Mainly magazine and press	Very strong in consumer schemes	Strong except in supermarkets	Very effective	Product guarantee Asian film star endorsement	First in market Effective promotions	45%
Kose	Weak. Mainly press	Nil	Only in cosmetic outlets	Poor	Umbrella effect	First in market Strong counter sales	125%
Max Factor	Weak. Only magazine	Nil	Only in cosmetic outlets	Good	Umbrella effect	Excellent packaging Strong studio activities	128%

4. Product Policy

Focus   The product acceptance was verified in the initial simulated store studies and other consumer tests.

Primary Objective   The primary objective is to position the product as a quality facial care product, with great emphasis placed on its unique ingredient, which revolutionizes facial cleansing yet reduces tissue destruction by 35%.

Short-term Tactic   The short-term tactic is to promote a habitual usage through positioning as one of the basic toilet necessities by constant association with the company's range of shampoo products.

Long-term Strategy   The long-term strategy is to promote a total Biore brand program of basic family facial and skin care.

5. Product Positioning

The product is to be positioned as basic a facial cleansing need as detergent is to laundry.

Market Share Considerations   Though the general strategy is to maximize market share, the measurement is relative to the leading competitor initially and overall market share subsequently. Profit is clearly to be secondary to market share and growth.

6. Unique Selling Point

Biore is a neutral, nonsoap facial cleanser that cleanses gently. It cuts tissue destruction by 35%.

7. Brand Name

The name "Biore" is adapted from "biological" and "refresh." Recent focus group interviews have again endorsed its acceptance, and brand recalls are significant. This is helped by the presentation on pack, color, shape, and position; in addition, only five alphabets are used. The corporate brand name "Kao" will be featured with the name Biore to help achieve quality assurance.

8. Competition

Focus   Though in the long term, the focus will be on the generic competitions—i.e., toilet soap—in the short term, the focus will be brand oriented, particularly in relation to "Dearland." The market share of this competitor is a significant strength, which must be recognized and monitored. A significant weakness is the competition's product quality and high-promotion spending. The resultant market share is hence expected to be built on a very fragile structure.

Primary Objective   The primary objective is to replace competitors' products, particularly Dearland, within the next 1½ years. There will be considerable shakeout, and remaining brands are expected to pull out.

Problem   Far too many brands and strong and virtually continuous promotion activities have resulted in heavy stock in trade.

Opportunity   Competitors' products are far inferior and poorly coordinated; their marketing efforts would not be cost effective in the long term, enabling the company to benefit from its efforts.

Short-Term Tactic   The short-term tactic is to avoid head-on collision with competition by concentrating on the vital self-service outlets in which competition is weakest. As these outlets consistently proved to have the quickest response to TV advertising and massive display, these activities are expected to be very rewarding.

9. Pricing

Primary Objective   Price is considered the next important element after the product. Prices are pegged to maximize volume usage and market share, without impairing the product image. As the perceived value is high, the economical price is expected to increase usage but not to a level to hurt acceptable profitability.

Problem   It is feared that the economical price in this semicosmetic segment may affect quality image.

Opportunity   Competitors are generally highly overpriced. Hence, the price advantage will enable Kao to encourage greater and more frequent usage.

Corporate Goal   The corporate goal is to enable the majority of working-class households to afford the product on a continuous basis.

Price Structure (60g)

	(S$)	%
Price to consumer (per tube)	3.90	
Price to consumer (per carton of 96 tubes)	374.40	
Price to trade*	300.00	100
Less: manufacturing and selling expenses	230.00	77
Company gross margin	70.00	23

*Trade margins are pegged at 5% higher than competition to secure their interest.

10. Distribution

Focus   Though various channels of distribution are available, the company's policy is direct sales to the retailers because it is the one closest to the consumers.

The focus will be on the supermarket and self-service, as these outlets offer quick response to promotional efforts and provide efficient communications to the consumers. As competitions are relatively weak in self-service outlets, top priority will be given to generate high volume through these high traffic outlets, with target achievement rebate incentive scheme.

11. Sales Operations

Focus   Sales personnel are seen as the representatives of the company. In addition to teaching selling skills, sales training must be aimed at familiarizing each sales representative with the company's operation, history, products, and policies, and the characteristics of market competition. The aim will be to ensure that sales personnel understand the reasons for the product and the role retailers can play in achieving consumer satisfaction.

Sales Contests and Motivation   Sales contests and motivation are to be aimed at achieving not only the sales targets but also the merchandising goals, and efforts to ensure adequate explanation and trade's understanding of the product concept and the overall marketing objectives.

Sales Force Size   Although the usual sales force will be covering the product, considerations should be given to increase it by another team of three for strategic coverage.

Sales Force Training   With the usual fortnightly sales training, the sales force should be reminded to try the products and to evaluate advertising schemes, including the creative work, and to report their personal findings. Briefs will regularly be made by the product executives to explain reasons for product development, promotion schemes, rationale, methodology, and results.

Sales Report   The daily report from the sales personnel should report as accurately as possible comments, criticisms, and praises they encountered each day. This will then be discussed in the monthly coordination meeting.

12. Advertising

Primary Objective The primary objective of advertising is to provide the optimum media mix and creativity to communicate the product attributes in achieving the desired responses.

Problem The major problem is stringent control and bureaucracy of the advertisement controlling body of the Ministry of Health.

Opportunity High reach and impact of television are seen as the major opportunity.

Specifics
Priority target audience:

- Schoolgirls and single working women 15–29.
- Housewives 30–39.
- Schoolboys and single working men 15–29.

Copy platform:

- "Gentle even on delicate skin" is the basic copy to be adopted.

- Neutral nonsoap cleanser that retains natural moisturizing factor of the skin.
- Refreshes and moisturizes the facial tissues.

Creative strategy:

- Soft sell, cheerful and pleasant, appealing to the rational emotion. The product in full color whenever possible.
- Appeal to rational motive for need to change from soap and to prompt purchase action.
- Communicate believable after-use refreshing feelings.

Media Strategy The strategy for the media mix is influenced to a large extent by the nature of the segment the product is positioned for. Within the media, identified priority is accorded to maximize reach at a continuous, year-round basis instead of the periodic impact/burst mode. The media budget is outlined in the following table:

Media	Budget	Desired impact
TV	S$110,000	Emotional communication of product attributes in general
Radio	30,000	Informative to young target group
Cinema	20,000	Emotional communication of product attributes specific to young target group
Magazine	30,000	Informative to young women and housewives
Newspaper	25,000	Informative to all in general
POP/Outdoor	35,000	Reminder reinforcement at point of purchase (POP)
Production	10,000	
Others	10,000	
Total	S$270,000	

13. Promotion

Focus Sales promotions are essentially short-term programs, implemented to stimulate sales. Emphasis should be directed at consumer promotion rather than promotion to trade.

Primary Objective The main aim of promotion is to reinforce greater awareness and understanding of the product attributes and to prompt trial purchases.

Promotion efforts must not be taken as a vehicle to generate sales.

Promotion schemes and budget

Consumer scheme	S$70,000
Trade scheme	60,000
Total	S$130,000

14. Marketing Research

Focus   The marketing research is aimed at providing specific studies of market opportunities, marketing effectiveness, and marketing problems. Marketing research procedure consists of five steps: problem definition, research design, field work, data analysis, and report preparation.

Primary Objective   Marketing research is the main component of the marketing information system linking the marketing division personnel with the external environment so as to guide and improve the planning, executing, and controlling functions within the marketing framework.

Problem   The major problem for marketing research is inadequate staff, aggravated by the lack of reliable and usable syndicated information.

Opportunity   The newly computerized internal accounting system enables complex correlations exercises to be carried out to improve quality of output.

Marketing Research Categories   The budget for marketing research is S$175,000. The breakdown of the various categories of marketing research is shown in the following table.

Product research	Sales and market research	Advertising research	Promotion research	Consumer research
Competitive product studies*	Market share analysis*	Media selection	Store audits	Consumer behavior and purchase pattern*
New improved formulation*	Sales analysis	Copy research*	POP materials analysis	Consumer response to the product survey
Product extension	Sales territory analysis	Scheduling analysis	Campaign analysis	Brand switch and consumer analysis
New packaging and color schemes*	Distribution analysis	Advertising recall surveys*		
	Depth of stock analysis			
	Repeat sales analysis			

*Cost borne by Kao in Tokyo.

First year budget		
Sales	S$1,725,000	100%
Less: cost of goods sold	1,328,000	77%
Gross margin	397,000	23%
Marketing expenditures:		
Advertising	270,000	16%
Promotion	130,000	7%
Marketing research	175,000	10%
Contribution after marketing expenditures	(178,000)	(10%)

21 ALTO CHEMICALS EUROPE (A)

Eberhard Graaff had held the position of headquarters marketing manager for stabilizers at Alto Chemicals Europe (ACE) for only two months when problems with subsidiary sales managers began to surface. It was December 1980 and the end of an eight-week period in which Graaff had spent time studying the industry and the company's several European subsidiary sales organizations to familiarize himself with the challenges of his new job. In the preceding week, Graaff had made a number of important decisions that would have long-term strategic implications for ACE's stabilizers business. He had informed the subsidiary sales organizations that the stabilizers, a category of chemicals used in making plastic products, were no longer to be sold based on low or even competitive prices, and that share gaining at the expense of profitability of sales was no longer an acceptable policy. The subsidiaries were also informed that headquarters marketing was to take on a more active role in setting prices and determining target sales volumes for the various subsidiaries.

Reactions to Graaff's decisions were quick to come from the field. Subsidiary sales managers were unanimous in their opposition to them. Expressions used by the managers to describe the new headquarters policies ranged from "unworkable" and "contradictory" to "theoretical" and "dictatorial." What the sales managers appeared to resent the most was the notion of having to subordinate in the future their own local judgment on sales matters to that of the headquarters. In the past, they had enjoyed relative autonomy in these areas.

Graaff was not overly perturbed by the negative reactions from the subsidiary sales organizations. He was, however, concerned with the steps needed to ensure sound implementation of the revised strategy for stabilizers.

This case was prepared by Professor Kamran Kashani. Copyright © 1986 by the Institute for International Management Development (IMD), Lausanne, Switzerland. Not to be used or reproduced without permission. All names and data have been disguised.

COMPANY BACKGROUND

ACE was the regional headquarters for Alto Chemicals Corporation's operations in Europe. Alto was a major North American-based multinational whose principal activities included production and marketing of commodity and specialty chemicals. With its headquarters and production facilities located in Switzerland and France, ACE accounted for more than a third of Alto's global production and sales volume.

Nine wholly owned subsidiaries, each serving one or more countries in Western Europe, reported to ACE.[1] The products produced and sold by the subsidiaries in the region ranged from finished compounds such as agricultural chemicals to "building blocks" used in the production of other products such as solvents, elastomers, and stabilizers.

ACE's headquarters organization was by product group. Five directors, each responsible for one or more products, reported to the company's president. Functions such as marketing, manufacturing, and planning were included under each product organization. Every director, in addition to having a regionwide product management responsibility, also supervised one or more of Alto's subsidiaries in Europe. The subsidiary managing directors, who reported to their assigned "associate" director, were in turn responsible for ACE's operations in their respective national markets. These included sales of all products produced in the region as well as any local production. The subsidiaries were typically organized by function.

The headquarters–subsidiary interaction was best described as a matrix relationship. The "dual boss system" was a common expression used to portray the dual sources of influence on product and subsidiary management.

STABILIZERS

Stabilizers were a category of chemicals used in the making of plastic products. When mixed with PVC (polyvinylchloride) resins and dyes, the stabilizers helped prevent in the finished product the breakdown of polymers caused by environmental factors such as temperature, light, and general aging. A plastic product not adequately treated with stabilizers was likely to become brittle and discolored over time. For example, the plastic covering of an electrical cable would lose its flexibility and disintegrate over time if it were not for the protective effect of stabilizers. Management estimated that close to 40% of all PVC uses in Europe were in applications requiring the addition of a stabilizer.

Product management had identified eight end-use and process segments for the stabilizer market. These segments produced a wide range of goods from plastic bags and upholstery to wall covering, cables, hoses, and shoes. Although the share of each segment in total market varied from one country to another, the three largest segments accounted for more than 50% of the market Europe-wide (see Exhibit 1).

1. Alto's subsidiaries operated in the United Kingdom, France, Belgium, West Germany, the Netherlands, Italy, Spain, Portugal, and Sweden.

In 1980, an estimated 600 thousand tons of stabilizers of all types, valued at approximately $600 million, were sold by the industry to approximately 1,100 plastic fabricators in Europe. This market was considered one of the most fragmented markets served by ACE. Stabilizers had experienced an annual growth rate averaging less than 3% in tonnage during the 1970s. The market was expected to remain stagnant, however, for most of the 1980s. As one member of product management explained:

> Stabilizers have matured as an industry. All potential applications have been discovered and we do not see any prospect for rapid growth among the existing uses.

The recessionary conditions prevailing in many European user industries during the last year were blamed for the 15% decline in total consumption from the 1979 level. The industry's unutilized plant capacity was estimated at about one-third.

More than 20 companies competed in the European stabilizer market. The four largest producers were Ciba-Geigy (Switzerland), ACE, Berlocher (W. Germany), and Lankro (United Kingdom); together, in 1980, they accounted for approximately one-half of the market. ACE management pointed out that most competitors had a home base where they were particularly strong. All companies, however, tried to sell their stabilizers regionwide.

The chemical properties of stabilizers produced by ACE differed from those made by others in Europe. The company's variety were referred to in the trade as "Tin" (Sn)—the generic name representing its chemical structure. Most of the stabilizers produced by competitors had a different structure and were generically referred to as "Barium" (Ba). Both varieties were general-purpose products with large end-use applications. Differences in properties, such as heat and light resistance, weathering, and oil absorption were considered by many in management to be minor between the two varieties. Although in theory, general-purpose stabilizers could be substituted for one another in most applications, in practice, plastic fabricators could not easily be switched from one type to another because the process technologies required were considerably different. Barium was by far the more commonly used stabilizer in Europe.

ENTRY STRATEGY

ACE's decision to enter the European stabilizers market was made in 1970. The original strategy called for a step-by-step penetration of the market toward a long-term market share objective of 20%, projected at 160 thousand tons by 1979. The major elements of the entry strategy are described in the following sections.

Market Exploration

As ACE did not have any working knowledge of the European stabilizer industry, the first few years after entry were to be spent exploring "the possibility of becoming a major fully integrated stabilizer supplier by 1980."

The long-term choice of stabilizers for ACE was to be tin, for which the company's European subsidiaries had ample feedstock—that is, the needed raw material. Beginning in 1970, however, ACE entered the market with barium purchased from European producers.

Third-Party Production

Due to the high level of start-up investment in production facilities, ACE's supply of barium initially, and of tin later on, was to be secured through production agreements with established European producers. A member of the management closely involved with supply negotiations referred to the process as "difficult—something you can do when you have a strong heart and a lot of guts." The company foresaw eventual European production once sufficient sales volume was attained.

Conversion

Barium was to be an entry product in Europe. ACE management intended to convert its customers to tin gradually. Conversion was to be encouraged through lower initial prices but also through assurances of better product performance. Initial discounts of 2 to 3% below barium prices were deemed necessary because conversion required changes in process and machinery that had to be justified economically.

Segmentation

Product management was keenly aware of the differences among various segments in the stabilizer market. For some, performance was more important than price; for others, the reverse held true. In wire and cables, for example, stabilizer costs were less than 2% of the total cost. As a result, these producers were less sensitive to price than those in flooring for whom the cost ratio was around 10%.

Size also played an important role. The large firms purchasing in excess of 500 tons per month paid lower prices than small and medium-sized firms purchasing one truck load or more at a time. The difference in price could be as large as 5%.

The entry strategy placed its sales emphasis on those segments for which price played a relatively more significant role. As one subsidiary sales manager explained:

> We had to get the attention of people when we first started up. We used the tools we had, and price was an important tool.

SELLING STABILIZERS

ACE's tin stabilizers, branded as Polystab, were sold through a specialized sales force in all the subsidiaries. The sales representatives were assisted in technical matters by staff from Technical Service, located in Geneva. The service was thought to be of particular importance for small and medium-sized clients who did not have an in-house service operation. Management believed that the specialized salespeople and the highly competent technical service, both unique in the industry, had allowed the company to gain and build in-depth knowledge of the various industries and processes using stabilizers.

For selling purposes, subsidiaries grouped the accounts according to the following classification:

1. *Base.* Regular Polystab customers mostly converted from barium.
2. *Strategic.* Important prospects; usually trend setters in their industry, currently using barium.
3. *Swing.* "In-and-out" customers; price oriented.

In 1980, the base accounts provided the bulk of Polystab sales. The strategic accounts, on the other hand, were key targets for conversion and, hence, long-term sources of sales. They required intensive attention from the management and often a highly technical type of selling. The swing accounts were usually converted, but could not be counted on as regular customers because of their low price orientation.

The task of converting from barium to tin fell on the sales force. The sales management pointed out that selling revolved around establishing tangible advantages for the client to justify the changes in equipment and process that were usually needed. They also mentioned that in certain applications conversion held only small benefits that were hard to demonstrate. In all cases, conversion was a time-consuming process. The product management estimated that it took on the average 18 months to convert an account. The actual time spent could vary from 6 months to several years. In every case, a minimum of 8 to 10 visits from the Technical Service staff in Geneva were required.

For all the subsidiaries, the proportion of selling time spent on conversion had declined since the mid-1970s. In one typical case, the sales force was spending in 1980 only a quarter of its time on conversion prospects, whereas in 1975 the ratio was close to 60%.

Since ACE was not the sole supplier of tin in the market,[2] most converted customers compared prices before placing an order—usually done on a monthly basis. The sales force, therefore, was intimately aware of the importance of price in making sales.

One subsidiary sales manager explained the buying behavior of stabilizer customers:

> The larger companies have a professional buying practice. They check with two or three regular suppliers and then place their order. The smaller firms, on the other hand, tend to contact a multitude of producers trying to negotiate a low price. They often wait till the middle or end of the month, hoping for a general deterioration in prices.

2. For all other producers, tin accounted for a minor share of their stabilizers sales as they did not have their own feedstock required for its production.

He added that barium producers were the price setters in the market and, therefore, a knowledge of their prices as well as those for tin was essential in selling:

> Prices do fluctuate during the month, depending on the level of demand and the producers' eagerness to sell their inventory. So timing is critical. When you set your prices high at the beginning of the month and you don't get an order by the tenth, you get pretty nervous. You can easily overreact and then destroy your average price level for the rest of the month.

Typically, about two-thirds of each month's sales were made in the first two weeks of the month.

A stabilizer sales representative in the subsidiaries had between 10 and 25 accounts to look after. A rep's days were spent partly in the office, preparing reports and reaching customers by phone, and partly on the road, visiting companies. Some sales managers insisted on a minimum of monthly visits to each account.

STABILIZER MARKETING ORGANIZATION

The marketing organization for stabilizers is shown in Exhibit 2. Partial job descriptions for key executives in the organization are given in Exhibit 3.

Graaff, who was new to the stabilizers organization, described the matrix structure as one built on "interaction and positive confrontation." Another executive, Peter Hansen, director for stabilizers, referred to the "dual boss system" as working well: "In the old days before the system arrived, the subsidiaries wouldn't even let us into their offices!" A sales manager with many years in the company also commented on the system: "The dual boss relationship can be useful or painful. It depends on the chiefs."

Headquarters marketing had profit responsibility for stabilizers. Graaff described the product line's profitability as a function of production costs, average prices received by the subsidiaries, and the total volume of sales. Subsidiary management, on the other hand, was held accountable primarily for the volume of sales generated in their market, in addition to the cost of selling and the level of receivables. Subsidiaries paid a transfer price for stabilizers sold in their market.

The performance of sales managers was evaluated jointly by the subsidiary managing director and headquarters marketing manager. Where a manager was responsible for sales of a number of products, a joint-performance appraisal would be undertaken for each line. Company executives pointed out that a superior overall performance could mean an increase in annual salary of up to 10% for the sales managers. This merit raise was said to be a "big carrot" and an important incentive.

Before Graaff joined stabilizer marketing, quarterly and annual sales quotas were used as bases for performance evaluation. Quarterly meetings in Geneva between the marketing and sales managers compared the progress in stabilizer sales against quotas.

By company policy, all ACE executives and members of the sales organization were compensated by a fixed salary. This policy also applied to the 10-person specialized stabilizer sales force in Europe whose salaries and performance evaluation procedures were determined at the subsidiary level.

EBERHARD GRAAFF

Eberhard Graaff had been with Alto for 15 years before being assigned to stabilizer marketing. A chemical engineer by training, he had filled various positions in Europe and the Far East as business analyst, design engineer, plant supervisor, and subsidiary sales manager. This was his first appointment in Geneva; his predecessor had recently retired from the company. In 1980, Graaff was 40 years old and the second-youngest member of the stabilizer marketing organization.

"We felt we needed a man with positive leadership," explained Peter Hansen, Graaff's immediate boss. Graaff's outstanding performance as sales manager in France was considered as one factor in his promotion to the marketing position. Graaff himself believed that his "tough name" in the company was also instrumental in his selection.

ACE executives were aware of the difficulties inherent in Graaff's new assignment. Hansen explained:

> The job of headquarters marketing is complicated not only by the different market and competitive conditions of each subsidiary, but also by the diversity in personalities and cultures of their management.

Hansen believed that the job required, in addition to marketing expertise, skills in establishing dialogue with the subsidiaries and in building a sales team.

STRATEGY REVISED

The stabilizer strategy set in motion in 1970 had achieved most of its objectives by 1980. ACE's stabilizer share in Western Europe was nearly 18%. Predictably, the proportion of barium in total company sales had declined over the years. As of mid-1979, tin stabilizers were being produced by the company's own facilities in France. In that year, the stabilizer sales force was calling on a total of 170 accounts in the region.

Graaff's first couple of months in the new job was spent visiting each of the nine subsidiaries and reviewing marketing and sales practices regionwide. By December, Graaff had identified the following problems regarding the current Polystab strategy as implemented in the field:

1. *Overreliance on price.* Selling was too price oriented; barium prices were matched or undercut by 2 to 3 percentage points, even for the converted tin accounts.

2. *Narrow market base*. Price-oriented selling had led to emphasis on those segments where it played an important role—that is, the larger companies and swing accounts.
3. *Low profitability*. Low prices in the region meant low profitability for the stabilizer business. The current regional average contribution margin of $40 per ton was deemed an unsatisfactory return for the recently completed facilities in France.
4. *Price discrepancies*. In the absence of central coordination, differences in subsidiary prices were encouraging the larger geographically diversified clients to buy their entire requirements from less expensive subsidiaries and transfer them for use to other subsidiary markets. Price differentials among subsidiaries were partly due to different average market prices in each country. Traditionally, for example, German stabilizer prices were a few percentage points above those of other European countries.

"The picture became rather clear to me," Graaff commented in the conclusions of his eight-week study:

> We are a volume-oriented organization, from here all the way down. This is a legacy of the original strategy which gave us a chance to compete in this market. So, as long as the quarterly sales quotas were met, nobody complained. And to meet the quotas, subsidiaries had a fairly open hand in setting prices. Headquarters price guidelines were only good for the first few days of each month. Afterwards, the sales pressure from the field forced the people in Geneva to give in, leading to low average prices for the whole month. This cycle would repeat itself 12 times a year.

Graaff was convinced that a revision of the successful stabilizer strategy was in order: "The product management and top ACE executives have been increasingly concerned with the return on our heavy investment in stabilizers facilities," he explained. "My understanding of this market leads me to believe that improved profitability is possible, provided we have the right segments and selling approach."

In December 1980, Graaff communicated in writing the following elements of the revised stabilizers strategy to the subsidiary sales managers and asked them to incorporate these into their future sales plans. A summary of the revised strategy follows:

1. *Nonprice selling*. Price to play a subsidiary role in selling; instead, emphasis to be placed on areas where ACE held a competitive edge such as expert sales force, superior technical service, and general corporate reputation for supplier reliability.
2. *New accounts*. Selling aimed at conversion of new accounts to receive added impetus; new accounts to come primarily from small and medium-sized firms and segments that were less price sensitive, such as wire and cable.
3. *Price leadership*. Discounting or merely "meeting barium prices" no longer an acceptable pricing policy for converted accounts; sales management

to watch for opportunities to initiate price leadership vis-à-vis other suppliers.

4. *Central coordination.* Geneva to take a more active part in setting price and volume targets for subsidiaries; the highly competitive low price markets to receive less sales emphasis than those enjoying higher average prices; headquarters coordination to aim at regional optimization.

The average price improvement was expected to yield immediate results. For the 1981–1982 planning period, Graaff was projecting a doubling of contribution margins to $80 per ton. In his communication to the sales organization, Graaff also mentioned that although he was willing to accept a slight short-term drop in sales due to price improvement, the longer-term objective remained a growth in volume. This, he maintained, was essential if the new stabilizers plant was to operate at an economical utilization rate.

SALES MANAGEMENT RESPONSE

Reactions from the field did not take very long to come. Communicating their sentiments to Graaff mostly by phone, the sales managers were unanimously against the announced changes in the business strategy. "To speak of price improvement at a time when the whole market is declining is just absurd," was a typical comment from the field. Another manager reacted: "Your strategy of improving both price and volume is unrealistic and contradictory." Still another commented: "The smaller accounts take the same amount of selling time as the larger ones. If we added these to our customer list, we would be running after more accounts for the same volume of sales. It wouldn't make sense." One other manager labeled the revised strategy "not market oriented, but rather inward looking."

Sales management also expressed concern regarding future relationship with the clients. One manager explained:

> We have gained our customer base through conversion and the promise of savings to the client. They did not scream when we gradually raised our prices to the barium level in the last few years. At least they know that they won't be paying more than their barium-using competitors. Now, if you were a user of barium for 25 years and I succeeded in converting you, how would you react if I came around a few months later and told you that from now on you will be paying a premium over their prices? You'd probably ask me: Whatever happened to the savings you promised? The money is in your pocket, not mine!

This executive added that problems of this kind would have a detrimental effect on sales force motivation.

Underlying most managers' complaints was another concern that the initiative in key decision areas was shifting away from subsidiaries and toward Geneva. One subsidiary sales manager explained what was felt by many:

So far, we have succeeded in stabilizers because of local initiative; and we knew our markets well enough to have the confidence of headquarters marketing. They trusted our best judgment. . . . We are professionals in this field and we should be allowed to harmonize our own performance. Headquarters can help by synthesizing and giving broad guidelines. That's all. Rigid rules go against management harmony.

IMPLEMENTATION

Graaff was not surprised with the sales organization's reactions to his proposals. He explained: "I was myself in the subsidiaries for a number of years, so I know how they'd feel."

Graaff intended to take steps toward implementing the strategy, which he believed was sound and consistent with market realities. "I am convinced the strategy will work," he said in defense of his decisions. He added:

> It aims at changing our customer mix, which in turn allows us some pricing leverage in the long run. It also aims at enlarging the base, which reduces our risk with a few large customers, and finally it takes a regional view of the stabilizers business, where all competitors and a number of customers are operating in more than one national market. A regional strategy gives us the flexibility of shifting our volumes toward those markets where we earn better margins.

Graaff did not minimize the implementation task ahead of him: "The job won't be easy, but I have always been sent into jobs with difficult problems." He added that, although he believed Hansen was in favor of improved profitability, he had not cleared with the director the specifics of his strategy and was certainly not going to ask for his help in implementing it in the field. "I am not the type who would seek advice from the boss on everything," he emphasized. "I have always followed the things I believe in."

EXHIBIT 1 Stabilizer Market Segments, 1979

	Sample products	Consumption (% of total)	Number of fabricators (estimate)
End-use segments			
Coated fabrics	Upholstery	17	180
Flooring	Cushion flooring, sheets/tiles	20	160
Wire and cables	Cables jackets and insulation	17	235
Compounds	Shoes	11	55
Process Segments			
Plastisole	Wall covering, gloves, balls	5	90
Calendering	Very broad: dresses, housing, etc.	13	180
Extrusion	Hoses	11	130
Injection molding	Shoes	6	70
		100%	1,100

EXHIBIT 2 Stabilizer Marketing Organization

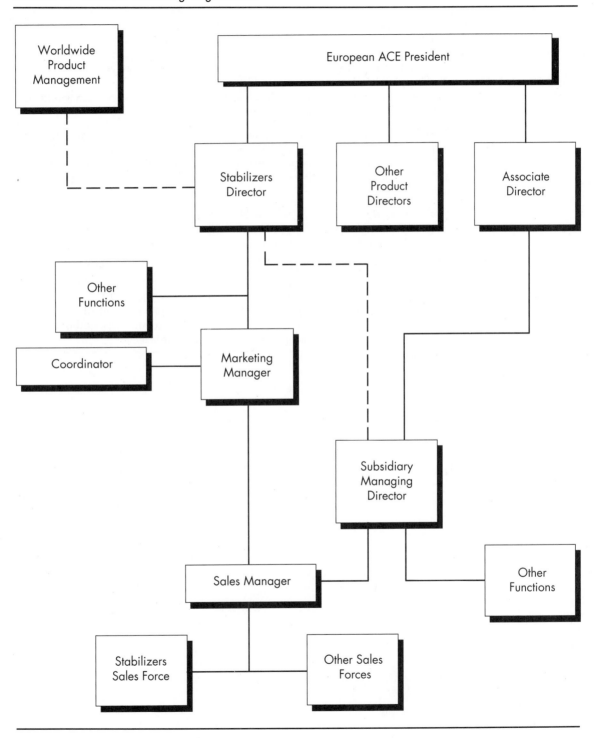

EXHIBIT 3 Partial Job Definitions

Director, stabilizers   Serves as regional product manager, responsible for all phases of the region's stabilizer business, including technology, manufacturing, marketing and supply, and transportation; establishes regional goals, objectives, plans, and action steps and works with worldwide product manager to assure that these are consistent with the worldwide plan and resources; responsible for proper execution of approved plans; must coordinate his or her conduct of business with and seek guidance from worldwide product line manager and the region president.

Stabilizers marketing manager   Responsible for all marketing activities within stabilizers; consults subsidiary marketing and sales personnel to develop the marketing inputs for the stabilizers business plan; responsible for proper execution of approved marketing plan and regionwide results; shares responsibility with subsidiary sales manager for development of sales staff.

Subsidiary managing director   Is accountable for all of the chemical businesses in the subsidiary; shares responsibility with each of the regional product line directors for planning and conduct of each of the businesses within the subsidiary.

Subsidiary sales manager   Shares responsibility with each of the regional product line marketing managers for planning and conduct of the businesses within the subsidiary; must play an important role in high-level contacts with key customers; will advise on overall strategy within the country, including the economic outlook as well as opportunities for new businesses; will encourage a close working relationship between sales personnel and the regional product line marketing managers.

ALTO CHEMICALS EUROPE (B)

In the first six months of 1981, Eberhard Graaff had undertaken a number of steps that he believed were necessary to implement the revised stabilizers strategy for Alto Chemicals Europe (ACE). He was reviewing the results to date with the purpose of deciding what to do next.

GRAAFF'S ACTIONS

The measures that Graaff had taken between January and June of 1981 are outlined in the following sections.

Headquarters Presentation

Early in January, Graaff invited the subsidiary sales managers to a planning meeting at which he presented the main elements of the revised strategy. Central "monitoring" on price and volume, in addition to new emphasis on smaller accounts for the less price-sensitive segments, was highlighted in the presentation. Graaff also emphasized that selling should become more technical in nature, with the focus on quality and performance arguments. The need for closer collaboration between the sales force and technical service staff was similarly underscored.

Monthly Meetings

Subsidiary sales managers were asked to meet monthly with Graaff at headquarters to set price and volume targets and review progress to date. Graaff later explained:

This case was prepared by Professor Kamran Kashani. Copyright © 1986 by the Institute for International Management Development (IMD), Lausanne, Switzerland. Not to be used or reproduced without permission. All names and financial data have been disguised.

"The meetings were necessary to better control the business but also give the subsidiaries a chance to talk to each other and see the whole picture."

Account Targets

Along with price and volume targets, the monthly meetings resulted in a "rolling list" of named accounts for each subsidiary's sales force to pursue. The accounts were segmented by size, end use, and whether they deserved a special effort for conversion. Accounts known for "price cutting" were left out of the list, even the larger ones. Some rules were established for division of the selling effort between old accounts and new ones.

Volume Redistribution

To improve average prices received in the region, lower sales targets were set for historically competitive markets such as The Netherlands. With higher target volumes for less price-oriented markets such as Germany, Graaff intended to shift the total volume toward the more profitable subsidiaries.

RESULTS TO DATE

Although Graaff considered the first six months too short a time to determine if the new strategy was effective, a few results were beginning to surface. The company had gained a number of new accounts among the medium-sized and smaller companies. This gain had been achieved despite the absence of discounts. On the other hand, several medium-sized and large accounts had been lost, some going to the competitors and others converting back to barium.

The overall impact on total volume of changes in the customer base was difficult to assess because industry sales had declined by about 8% during this period. Also, in some markets the contribution margins had increased slightly; in others they had not.

Meanwhile, the relationship between Graaff and the subsidiary sales managers had deteriorated significantly. The monthly meetings had often turned into shouting matches between the more outspoken sales managers and Graaff. The complaints voiced by the sales managers centered on the inherent wisdom of the new strategy and its impact on short-termed results. Typical among these complaints were the following:

> You show us numbers and ratios to argue why a higher price is better than a lower price. But the market doesn't have to follow your logic. Our customers don't understand our ratios; they don't even care. What they want is a lower price.

> For every key account I lose I have to run after several smaller ones.

> You are destroying what took me years to build.

CONCLUSION

Graaff did not enjoy his monthly encounters with the sales managers, but he was not overly concerned. He felt it was "part of the job." What was beginning to concern him, however, were signs that his boss was losing patience. On some recent occasions, Hansen had mentioned that sales force motivation should not be sacrificed for the sake of a strategy and that a more consensus-oriented approach might be more effective in winning subsidiary support. Evidently, some subsidiary managing directors had been in touch with him regarding complaints from the field.

Although agreeing with the merits of a consensus approach, Graaff was not totally convinced that it would work in this situation: "Consensus is fine. But at the end of the day someone has to make a difficult decision, and in this case that someone is me." A more profound concern of Graaff was whether Hansen really believed in what he was trying to accomplish. Graaff complained:

> There are times I think even Hansen doesn't believe the strategy is going to work. It's difficult to change things when people have been around a long time and used to a different thinking.

In spite of certain signs of unease, Hansen had not tried to stop Graaff. On the contrary, he had given him a free hand to proceed.

APPENDIX:

Country Facts Sheets

AUSTRIA

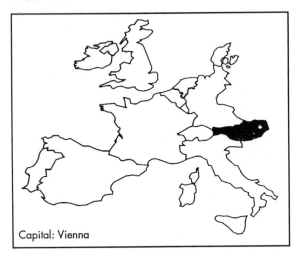

Capital: Vienna

Political Background

Austria, under the Hapsburg rulers, enjoyed for over 600 years an empire consisting of Hungary, Czechoslovakia, and Yugoslavia. After World War I, however, the empire was broken up. Austria was occupied by Germany from 1938 to 1945. Full independence was established in 1955 when the postwar occupation by the United States, the Soviet Union, the United Kingdom, and France was formally ended. Since then, this neutral country has enjoyed 40 years of consensus politics. Austria is a member of the UN, the OECD, the Council of Europe, and EFTA.

Population

Population	7.60 million
Annual population growth (1982–1988)	.07%
Urbanization	55.1%

Population structure (%):

Toddler (0–4)	5.7
Child (5–14)	11.9
Youth (15–24)	14.7
Adult (25–64)	52.7
Elderly (65 and over)	15.0

Ethnic diversity (%):

Austrian	96.0
Yugoslavian	2.0
Turkish	1.0
Other	1.0

Official language	German

Religions (%):

Roman Catholicism	89.0
Protestantism	9.0
Other	2.0

Divorce rate (per 1,000)	2.05

Economy

Gross domestic product (GDP) ($ billions)	127.2
Annual growth in GDP (1981–1987)	5.59%
Per capita GDP ($)	16,737
Savings rate	24.04%
Annual inflation rate	2.5%
Cost of living index (New York = 100)	105.2
Exchange rate (schilling/$)	13.18
Unemployment	3.75%
Personal income tax (top bracket)	62.0%

Life-style

Life expectancy	75.0 years
Hours of work per week	34.98
Annual number of vacation days	13.04

Consumer expenditures (% of total disposable income):

Food	23.6
Drink	3.2
Durables	5.5
Clothing	13.0
Services	5.1
Transport	17.4
Miscellaneous	11.8
Housing	20.4

Product ownership (per 1,000):

Number of telephones	384.0
Number of radios	530.0
Number of televisions	321.0
Number of cars	335.0
Number of newspaper subscriptions	362.0

Secondary schooling	79%
Advertising expenditures per capita	$100.80

BELGIUM

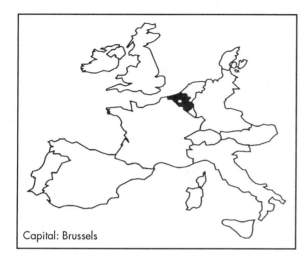

Capital: Brussels

Political Background

Belgium, a parliamentary monarchy, was established as an independent state in 1830. Flemings (Dutch-speaking) and Walloons (French-speaking) have officially recognized regional status. From 1970 to 1981, the government consisted of coalitions where few decisions were made. Since 1981, Mr. Martens has headed the eight coalition governments, with the economy as the major issue. Belgium is a member of the UN, the OECD, the Council of Europe, NATO, the WEU, Benelux, and, since 1921, has been linked with Luxembourg in the Belgium-Luxembourg Economic Union.

Population

Population	9.87 million
Annual population growth (1982–1988)	.1%

Population structure (%):

Toddler (0–4)	5.8
Child (5–14)	12.3
Youth (15–24)	14.2
Adult (25–64)	53.0
Elderly (65 and over)	14.7

Ethnic diversity (%):

Belgian	91.0
Italian	3.0
Moroccan	1.0
French	1.0
Dutch	1.0
Turkish	1.0
Other	2.0

Official languages	Dutch, French, German

Religions (%):

Roman Catholicism	96.0
Other	4.0

Divorce rate (per 1,000)	1.85

Economy

Gross domestic product (GDP) ($ billions)	152.39
Annual growth in GDP (1981–1987)	5.84%
Per capita GDP ($)	15,439
Savings rate	18.68%
Annual inflation rate	3.3%
Cost of living index (New York = 100)	99.9
Exchange rate (franc/$)	39.34
Unemployment	10.5%

Income distribution (% of total household income):

Lowest 20%	7.9
Highest 20%	36.0

Personal income tax (top bracket)	70.7%

Life-style

Life expectancy	75.5 years
Hours of work per week	33.0
Annual number of vacation days	24.3

Consumer expenditures (% of total disposable income):

Food	20.8
Drink	2.5
Durables	10.4
Clothing	14.4
Services	6.7
Transport	13.9
Miscellaneous	7.1
Housing	24.2

Product ownership (per 1,000):

Number of telephones	342.9
Number of radios	468.0
Number of televisions	301.0
Number of cars	339.0
Number of newspaper subscriptions	224.0

Secondary schooling	96%
Advertising expenditures per capita	$119.00

CANADA

Capital: Ottawa

Political Background

Canada, a parliamentary and federal monarchy, became independent from the United Kingdom in 1867. There have been some calls for separation of the mainly French-speaking province, Quebec, from the dominion. Politics has been controlled by two parties, the center left Liberals and the center right Conservatives. Since 1984, after 16 years of Liberal rule, Canada has been governed by the Conservatives under the leadership of Mr. Mulroney. Canada is a member of the UN, the Commonwealth, the OECD, NATO, and the Colombo Plan. It recently signed a Free Trade Agreement with the United States.

Population

Population	26.0 million
Annual population growth (1982–1988)	.87%
Urbanization	55%

Population structure (%):

Toddler (0–4)	6.9
Child (5–14)	14.0
Youth (15–24)	14.2
Adult (25–64)	53.5
Elderly (65 and over)	11.4

Ethnic diversity (%):

British	40.0
French	27.0
German	5.0
Italian	3.0
Other	25.0

Official languages	English, French

Religions (%):

Roman Catholicism	47.0
Protestantism	41.0
Judaism	1.0
Other	11.0

Divorce rate (per 1,000)	2.44

Economy

Gross domestic product (GDP) ($ billions)	486.5
Annual growth in GDP (1981–1987)	8.12%
Per capita GDP ($)	18,747
Exchange rate (C$/$)	1.18
Savings rate	18.53%
Annual inflation rate	5.2%
Cost of living index (New York = 100)	100.1
Unemployment	7.8%

Income distribution (% of total household income):

Lowest 20%	5.3
Highest 20%	40.0

Personal income tax (top bracket)	29.0%

Life-style

Life expectancy	76.2 years
Hours of work per week	38.8
Annual number of vacation days	17.0

Consumer expenditures (% of total disposable income):

Food	28.1
Drink	6.5
Durables	9.9
Clothing	10.9
Services	6.0
Transport	15.3
Miscellaneous	10.2
Housing	13.1

Product ownership (per 1,000):

Number of telephones	524.1
Number of radios	821.0
Number of televisions	479.0
Number of cars	427.0
Number of newspaper subscriptions	220.0

Secondary schooling	103%
Advertising expenditures per capita	$232.40

DENMARK

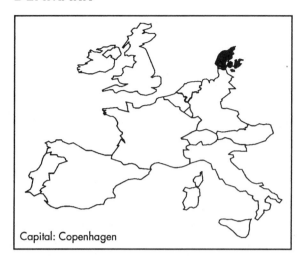

Capital: Copenhagen

Political Background

Similar to the Netherlands, Denmark, a parliamentary monarchy, was occupied by Germany in World War II. Since the end of World War II, politics has been characterized by shifting coalitions. Up to 11 parties vie for 179 seats. As a result, minority or coalition governments usually rule for up to two years before another election. Denmark is a member of the UN, the OECD, the Council of Europe, NATO, the EC, and the Nordic Council.

Population

Population	5.13 million
Annual population growth (1982–1988)	.03%
Urbanization	83.9%

Population structure (%):
Toddler (0–4)	5.4
Child (5–14)	11.6
Youth (15–24)	14.9
Adult (25–64)	52.6
Elderly (65 and over)	15.5

Ethnic diversity (%):
Danish	99.0
Other	1.0

Official language	Danish

Religions (%):
Lutheranism	96.0
Roman Catholicism	1.0
Other	3.0

Divorce rate (per 1,000)	2.83

Economy

Gross domestic product (GDP) ($ billions)	107.48
Annual growth in GDP (1981–1987)	7.67%
Per capita GDP ($)	20,952
Savings rate	15.49%
Annual inflation rate	4.5%
Cost of living index (New York = 100)	113.9
Exchange rate (kroner/$)	7.30
Unemployment	8.5%

Income distribution (% of total household income):
Lowest 20%	5.4
Highest 20%	38.6

Personal income tax (top bracket)	40.0%

Life-style

Life expectancy	76.2 years
Hours of work per week	38.0
Annual number of vacation days	20.7

Consumer expenditures (% of total disposable income):
Food	24.1
Drink	4.2
Durables	8.3
Clothing	11.2
Services	6.8
Transport	16.4
Miscellaneous	10.1
Housing	18.9

Product ownership (per 1,000):
Number of telephones	528.7
Number of radios	395.0
Number of televisions	371.0
Number of cars	306.0
Number of newspaper subscriptions	359.0

Secondary schooling	105%
Advertising expenditures per capita	$154.30

FINLAND

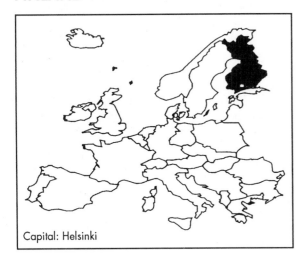

Capital: Helsinki

Political Background
Finland, a republic, declared its independence from the Soviet Union in 1917. Cordial relations with its neighbor have been maintained; a treaty of friendship was signed in 1948 and was revised in 1990. Consensus politics has ruled in Finland, a country with a large number of political parties. Finland is a member of the UN, the OECD, EFTA, and the Nordic Council.

Population
Population	4.95 million
Annual population growth (1982–1988)	.44%
Urbanization	59.8%

Population structure (%):
Toddler (0–4)	6.2
Child (5–14)	13.1
Youth (15–24)	13.3
Adult (25–64)	54.2
Elderly (65 and over)	13.2

Ethnic diversity (%):
Finnish	92.0
Swedish	7.0
Other	1.0

Official languages	Finnish, Swedish

Religions (%):
Lutheranism	90.0
Greek Orthodox	1.0
Other	9.0

Divorce rate (per 1,000)	1.93

Economy
Gross domestic product (GDP) ($ billions)	105.18
Annual growth in GDP (1981–1987)	10.24%
Per capita GDP ($)	21,248
Savings rate	22.58%
Annual inflation rate	6.6%
Cost of living index (New York = 100)	129.8
Exchange rate (markka/$)	4.27
Unemployment	4.75%

Income distribution (% of total household income):
Lowest 20%	6.3
Highest 20%	37.6

Personal income tax (top bracket)	74.8%

Life-style
Life expectancy	75.7 years
Hours of work per week	32.40
Annual number of vacation days	30.8

Consumer expenditures (% of total disposable income):
Food	28.9
Drink	5.2
Durables	7.3
Clothing	12.0
Services	8.2
Transport	16.2
Miscellaneous	9.1
Housing	13.1

Product ownership (per 1,000):
Number of telephones	479.8
Number of radios	987.0
Number of televisions	432.0
Number of cars	314.0
Number of newspaper subscriptions	532.0

Secondary schooling	102%
Advertising expenditures per capita	$357.20

FRANCE

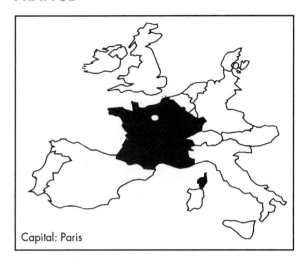

Capital: Paris

Political Background

France, under the leadership of Charles de
Gaulle, formed its Fifth Republic in 1958. Until
1981, the country was governed by the Conservative party. In 1981, however, the Socialist party,
under the leadership of François Mitterrand, who
still continues to lead today, took over. France is
a member of the UN, the OECD, the Council of
Europe, the Franc Zone, EC, the WEU, NATO, the
South Pacific Commission, and La Francophonie.

Population

Population	55.87 million
Annual population growth (1982–1988)	.42%
Urbanization	73.4%

Population structure (%):
Toddler (0–4)	6.9
Child (5–14)	13.3
Youth (15–24)	15.0
Adult (25–64)	51.0
Elderly (65 and over)	13.8

Ethnic diversity (%):
French	93.2
Algerian	1.5
Portuguese	1.4
Moroccan	.8
Italian	.6
Spanish	.6
Other	1.9

Official languages	French, Breton, Basque

Religions (%):
Roman Catholicism	76.0
Islam	3.0
Protestantism	2.0
Judaism	1.0
Other	18.0

Divorce rate (per 1,000)	1.95

Economy

Gross domestic product (GDP) ($ billions)	949.24
Annual growth in GDP (1981–1987)	7.69%
Per capita GDP ($)	16,990
Savings rate	19.59%
Annual inflation rate	3.4%
Cost of living index (New York = 100)	101.1
Exchange rate (franc/$)	6.36
Unemployment	10.25%

Income distribution (% of total household
income):
Lowest 20%	5.5
Highest 20%	42.2

Personal income tax (top bracket)	57%

Life-style

Life expectancy	76.6 years
Hours of work per week	38.7
Annual number of vacation days	28.2

Consumer expenditures (% of total disposable
income):
Food	21.1
Drink	2.1
Durables	7.4
Clothing	17.8
Services	4.2
Transport	24.1
Miscellaneous	6.4
Housing	16.9

Product ownership (per 1,000):
Number of telephones	439.7
Number of radios	860.0
Number of televisions	375.0
Number of cars	379.0
Number of newspaper subscriptions	599.0

Secondary schooling	95%
Advertising expenditures per capita	$124.20

GREECE

Capital: Athens

Political Background

After four centuries of Ottoman rule, Greece secured its independence in 1830. Civil war broke out after World War II. In 1967, a coup d'état occurred and the king was exiled; the military junta ruled until 1974. In that year, Greece was declared a republic, and a new constitution was introduced in 1975. Since that time, Greek politics has been dominated by the Panhellenic Socialist movement (the PASOK party) lead by Mr. Papandreou. In 1988–89, after suffering several reverses, the government fell, and several inconclusive elections followed. No majority or coalition government has taken over for the last 10 months. New elections were set for April 1990. Greece is a member of the UN, the OECD, the Council of Europe, NATO, and the EC.

Population

Population	10.01 million
Annual population growth (1982–1988)	.37%
Urbanization	58%

Population structure (%):
Toddler (0–4)	5.8
Child (5–14)	13.9
Youth (15–24)	14.8
Adult (25–64)	51.8
Elderly (65 and over)	13.7

Ethnic diversity (%):
Greek	95.0
Macedonian	2.0
Turkish	1.0
Muslim	1.0
Other	1.0

Official language	Greek

Religions (%):
Greek Orthodox	98.0
Islam	1.0
Other	1.0

Divorce rate (per 1,000)	.87

Economy

Gross domestic product (GDP) ($ billions)	52.49
Annual growth in GDP (1981–1987)	19.36%
Per capita GDP ($)	5,244
Savings rate	14.65%
Annual inflation rate	13.1%
Cost of living index (New York = 100)	92.0
Exchange rate (drachma/$)	164.49
Unemployment	7.3%
Personal income tax (top bracket)	50.0%

Life-style

Life expectancy	76.4 years
Hours of work per week	39.2
Annual number of vacation days	22.0

Consumer expenditures (% of total disposable income):
Food	15.9
Drink	2.2
Durables	11.7
Clothing	22.2
Services	2.9
Transport	18.0
Miscellaneous	8.0
Housing	19.1

Product ownership (per 1,000):
Number of telephones	346.9
Number of radios	406.0
Number of televisions	178.0
Number of cars	127.0
Number of newspaper subscriptions	121.0

Secondary schooling	88%
Advertising expenditures per capita	$29.90

IRELAND

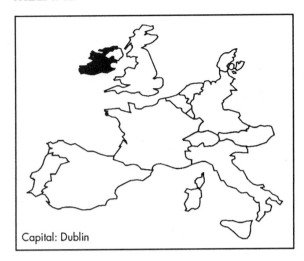

Capital: Dublin

Political Background
Ireland became independent from the United Kingdom in 1921 but has been a republic since 1949. In 1920, the British Parliament provided for six counties of the northeast (Ulster), to remain in the United Kingdom; the other 26 counties formed a separate state. The government has been led by either the Fianna Fail party or a coalition of the Fine Gael and Labour parties. There have been discussions with the United Kingdom concerning the possibility of combining with Northern Ireland in some form of permanent cooperation. Ireland is a member of the UN, the OECD, the Council of Europe, and the EC.

Population
Population	3.54 million
Annual population growth (1982–1988)	.29%
Urbanization	55.6%

Population structure (%):
Toddler (0–4)	8.8
Child (5–14)	18.9
Youth (15–24)	18.3
Adult (25–64)	43.7
Elderly (65 and over)	10.3

Ethnic diversity (%):
Irish	96.0
English and Welsh	2.0
North Irish	1.0
Other	1.0

Official languages	English, Irish

Religions (%):
Roman Catholicism	94.0
Protestantism	4.0
Other	2.0

Economy
Gross domestic product (GDP) ($ billions)	32.55
Annual growth in GDP (1981–1987)	8.08%
Per capita GDP ($)	9,194
Savings rate	18.63%
Annual inflation rate	3.8%
Cost of living index (New York = 100)	104.4
Exchange rate (I£/$)	.70
Unemployment	16.6%

Income distribution (% of total household income):
Lowest 20%	7.2
Highest 20%	39.4

Personal income tax (top bracket)	58.0%

Life-style
Life expectancy	75.1 years
Hours of work per week	41.10
Annual number of vacation days	22.1

Consumer expenditures (% of total disposable income):
Food	20.3
Drink	4.8
Durables	9.9
Clothing	14.5
Services	6.4
Transport	20.2
Miscellaneous	9.7
Housing	14.2

Product ownership (per 1,000):
Number of telephones	222.9
Number of radios	456.0
Number of televisions	249.0
Number of cars	199.0
Number of newspaper subscriptions	252.0

Secondary schooling	96%
Advertising expenditures per capita	$65.50

ITALY

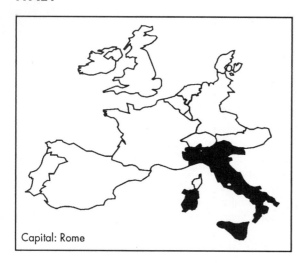

Capital: Rome

Political Background
Italy became a modern nation in 1859 when Garibaldi conquered Sicily and south Italy. After World War II, in 1946, Italy became a republic. A peace treaty concerning World War II was signed in 1947, and an agreement concerning the division of territory east of Trieste was made with Yugoslavia in 1975. Politics has been characterized by unstable coalitions usually lasting one year. Italy is a member of the UN, the OECD, the Council of Europe, NATO, the EC, and the WEU.

Population
Population	57.44 million
Annual population growth (1982–1988)	.23%
Urbanization	n/a

Population structure (%):
Toddler (0–4)	5.3
Child (5–14)	15.9
Youth (15–24)	11.8
Adult (25–64)	52.8
Elderly (65 and over)	14.2

Ethnic diversity (%):
Italian	98.0
Austrian	0.3
French	0.3
Other	1.4

Official language	Italian

Religions (%):
Roman Catholicism	83.0
Other	17.0

Divorce rate (per 1,000)	.29

Economy
Gross domestic product (GDP) ($ billions)	828.87
Annual growth in GDP (1981–1987)	12.05%
Per capita GDP ($)	14,430
Savings rate	20.90%
Annual inflation rate	6.7%
Cost of living index (New York = 100)	105.1
Exchange rate (lira/$)	1371.76
Unemployment	11.25%

Income distribution (% of total household income):
Lowest 20%	6.2
Highest 20%	43.9

Personal income tax (top bracket)	50.0%

Life-style
Life expectancy	76.3 years
Hours of work per week	39.0
Annual number of vacation days	24.6

Consumer expenditures (% of total disposable income):
Food	24.8
Drink	2.1
Durables	9.9
Clothing	13.3
Services	5.9
Transport	18.9
Miscellaneous	10.4
Housing	14.7

Product ownership (per 1,000):
Number of telephones	333.1
Number of radios	249.0
Number of televisions	404.0
Number of cars	392.0
Number of newspaper subscriptions	82.0

Secondary schooling	76%
Advertising expenditures per capita	$87.90

JAPAN

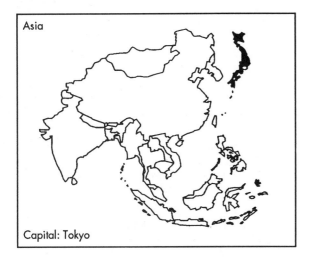

Asia

Capital: Tokyo

Political Background

Japan became a constitutional democracy in 1947 when the powers of the emperor were reduced. Since that time, until 1988, the Liberal Democratic party, a conservative political group, has dominated. Since 1988, the political scene has become more unstable due to several scandals; as a result, the Socialist party has gained support. Japan is a member of the UN, the OECD, and the Colombo Plan.

Population

Population	122.61 million
Annual population growth (1982–1988)	.58%

Population structure (%):

Toddler (0–4)	5.6
Child (5–14)	12.9
Youth (15–24)	15.4
Adult (25–64)	54.4
Elderly (65 and over)	11.7

Ethnic diversity (%):

Japanese	99.4
Korean	.6

Official language	Japanese

Religions (%):

Shintoism*	87.0
Buddhism*	73.0
Christianity	1.0
Divorce rate (per 1,000)	1.38

Economy

Gross domestic product (GDP) ($ billions)	2,843.43
Annual growth in GDP (1981–1987)	5.15%
Per capita GDP ($)	23,191
Savings rate	31.78%
Annual inflation rate	3.0%
Cost of living index (New York = 100)	159.6
Exchange rate (yen/$)	139.52
Unemployment	2.5%

Income distribution (% of total household income):

Lowest 20%	8.7
Highest 20%	37.5

Personal income tax (top bracket)	50.0%

Life-style

Life expectancy	78.8 years
Hours of work per week	41.30
Annual number of vacation days	16.1

Consumer expenditures (% of total disposable income):

Food	28.0
Drink	3.4
Durables	7.4
Clothing	12.0
Services	5.6
Transport	12.4
Miscellaneous	7.4
Housing	23.8

Product ownership (per 1,000):

Number of telephones	403.4
Number of radios	710.0
Number of televisions	562.0
Number of cars	230.0
Number of newspaper subscriptions	533.0

Secondary schooling	96%
Advertising expenditures per capita	$281.60

*A majority adhere to both Shintoism and Buddhism.

THE NETHERLANDS

Capital: Amsterdam

Political Background

The Netherlands, a parliamentary monarchy, was liberated from German occupation in 1945 at the end of World War II. It joined with Belgium and Luxembourg to form Benelux in 1960. The government has been characterized by shifting coalitions between the center right and center left. The Netherlands is a member of the UN, the OECD, the Council of Europe, NATO, the EC, and the WEU.

Population

Population	14.76 million
Annual population growth (1982–1988)	.52%
Urbanization	88.5%

Population structure (%):

Toddler (0–4)	5.8
Child (5–14)	12.0
Youth (15–24)	15.6
Adult (25–64)	53.7
Elderly (65 and over)	12.9

Ethnic diversity (%):

Netherlander	96.0
Turkish	1.0
Moroccan	1.0
Other	2.0

Official language	Dutch

Religions (%):

Roman Catholicism	36.0
Protestantism	27.0
Other	37.0

Divorce rate (per 1,000)	2.13

Economy

Gross domestic product (GDP) ($ billions)	228.29
Annual growth in GDP (1981–1987)	3.42%
Per capita GDP ($)	15,467
Savings rate	21.84%
Annual inflation rate	1.1%
Cost of living index (New York = 100)	92.8
Exchange rate (florin/$)	2.12
Unemployment	12.5%

Income distribution (% of total household income):

Lowest 20%	8.3
Highest 20%	36.2

Personal income tax (top bracket)	60.0%

Life-style

Life expectancy	77.5 years
Hours of work per week	40.20
Annual number of vacation days	34.7

Consumer expenditures (% of total disposable income):

Food	20.0
Drink	3.1
Durables	6.6
Clothing	23.3
Services	5.9
Transport	17.4
Miscellaneous	10.1
Housing	13.6

Product ownership (per 1,000):

Number of telephones	425.2
Number of radios	791.0
Number of televisions	449.0
Number of cars	337.0
Number of newspaper subscriptions	310.0

Secondary schooling	104%
Advertising expenditures per capita	$173.70

NORWAY

Capital: Oslo

Political Background
Norway, a parliamentary monarchy, became independent from Sweden in 1905. The country was occupied by Germany in World War II. Since the end of the war, the majority of the coalition governments formed have been Labor. The country is a member of the UN, the OECD, the Council of Europe, NATO, EFTA, and the Nordic Council.

Population
Population	4.20 million
Annual population growth (1982–1988)	.36%
Urbanization	70.7%

Population structure (%):
Toddler (0–4)	6.2
Child (5–14)	12.4
Youth (15–24)	15.6
Adult (25–64)	49.4
Elderly (65 and over)	16.4

Ethnic diversity (%):
Norwegian	98.0
Danish	0.3
U.S. Citizens	0.3
U.K. Citizens	0.2
Swedish	0.2
Pakistani	0.2
Other	0.8

Official language	Norwegian

Religions (%):
Lutheranism	88.0
Other	12.0

Divorce rate (per 1,000)	1.95

Economy
Gross domestic product (GDP) ($ billions)	91.18
Annual growth in GDP (1981–1987)	8.60%
Per capita GDP ($)	21,710
Savings rate	23.39
Annual inflation rate	4.8%
Cost of living index (New York = 100)	131.6
Exchange rate (kroner/$)	6.92
Unemployment	3.0%

Income distribution (% of total household income):
Lowest 20%	6.0
Highest 20%	38.2

Personal income tax (top bracket)	54.0%

Life-style
Life expectancy	77.4 years
Hours of work per week	29.70
Annual number of vacation days	22.8

Consumer expenditures (% of total disposable income):
Food	24.2
Drink	6.1
Durables	7.5
Clothing	14.6
Services	6.0
Transport	16.3
Miscellaneous	9.7
Housing	15.6

Product ownership (per 1,000):
Number of telephones	465.1
Number of radios	775.0
Number of televisions	319.0
Number of cars	364.0
Number of newspaper subscriptions	622.0

Secondary schooling	97%
Advertising expenditures per capita	$181.20

PORTUGAL

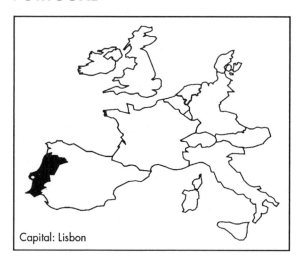

Capital: Lisbon

Political Background
A coup d'état in 1974 ended a one-party rule established since 1932, mostly under the dictator Salazar. At one time, Portugal was a significant colonial power; most of these territories, however, were given their independence during 1974–1975. Between 1976 and 1989, Portugal has experienced 11 coalition governments consisting of the Socialists, the Centrists, and the Democratic Alliance. Portugal is a member of the UN, the OECD, NATO, the Council of Europe, and the EC.

Population
Population	10.41 million
Annual population growth (1982–1988)	.79%
Urbanization	29.7%

Population structure (%):
Toddler (0–4)	6.5
Child (5–14)	14.7
Youth (15–24)	16.6
Adult (25–64)	49.3
Elderly (65 and over)	12.9

Ethnic diversity (%):
Portuguese	99.0
Angolan	0.2
Cape Verdean	0.1
Other	0.7

Official language	Portuguese

Religion (%):
Roman Catholicism	95.0
Protestantism	1.0
Other	4.0

Divorce rate (per 1,000)	.88

Economy
Gross domestic product (GDP) ($ billions)	41.70
Annual growth in GDP (1981–1987)	12.48%
Per capita GDP ($)	4,006
Savings rate	27.43%
Annual inflation rate	13.3%
Cost of living index (New York = 100)	83.9
Exchange rate (escudo/$)	158.96
Unemployment	6.5%

Income distribution (% of total household income):
Lowest 20%	5.2
Highest 20%	49.1

Personal income tax (top bracket)	68.0%

Life-style
Life expectancy	74.3 years
Hours of work per week	37.7
Annual number of vacation days	23.0

Consumer expenditures (% of total disposable income):
Food	23.3
Drink	2.0
Durables	7.6
Clothing	10.1
Services	5.2
Transport	14.6
Miscellaneous	7.5
Housing	29.7

Product ownership (per 1,000):
Number of telephones	160.0
Number of radios	170.0
Number of televisions	152.0
Number of cars	156.0
Number of newspaper subscriptions	59.0

Secondary schooling	52%
Advertising expenditures per capita	$23.80

SINGAPORE

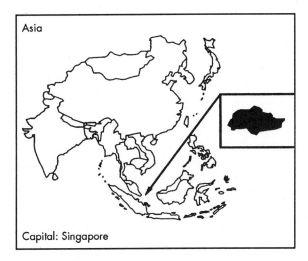

Asia

Capital: Singapore

Political Background
In 1965, Singapore, a republic, became independent from Malaysia. Previously, the country had been a separate U.K. colony until 1963 when it fell under the state of Malaysia. After 1965, the government has been dominated by the People's Action party with little opposition from the Democratic party. Singapore is a member of the UN, the Colombo Plan, the Commonwealth, and ASEAN.

Population
Population	2.65 million
Annual population growth (1982–1988)	1.18%
Urbanization	100%

Population structure (%):
Toddler (0–4)	7.9
Child (5–14)	14.9
Youth (15–24)	16.9
Adult (25–64)	54.7
Elderly (65 and over)	5.6

Ethnic diversity (%):
Chinese	77.0
Malayan	15.0
Indian and Sri Lankan	6.0
Other	2.0

Official languages	Chinese, Malay, English, Tamil

Religions (%):
Taoism	29.0
Buddhism	27.0
Islam	16.0
Christianity	10.0
Hinduism	4.0
Other	14.0

Divorce rate (per 1,000)	1.00

Economy
Gross domestic product (GDP) ($ billions)	23.87
Annual growth in GDP (1981–1987)	6.64%
Per capita GDP ($)	9,009
Savings rate	40.41%
Annual inflation rate	2.8%
Cost of living index (New York = 100)	90.8
Exchange rate (S$/$)	1.95
Unemployment	2.8%
Personal income tax (top bracket)	33.0%

Life-style
Life expectancy	73.8 years
Hours of work per week	49.00
Annual number of vacation days	17.2

Consumer expenditures (% of total disposable income):
Food and beverage	25.2
Clothing and footwear	10.3
Rent and utilities	12.1
Durables	12.1
Transport	14.4
Recreation and education	21.5
Health	4.4

Product ownership (per 1,000):
Number of telephones	339.5
Number of radios	272.0
Number of televisions	188.0
Number of cars	87.0
Number of newspaper subscriptions	277.0

Secondary schooling	71%
Advertising expenditures per capita	$76.80

SPAIN

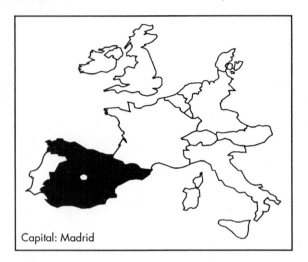

Capital: Madrid

Political Background

In 1936, a one-party state was formed by General Franco, but the king was restored in 1975 following Franco's death. Since then, a parliamentary monarchy has resulted with the Socialist party in power. There have been disputes with Morocco concerning Spanish North Africa and with the United Kingdom regarding Gibraltar. There are continuing internal tensions concerning the Basque, Catalan, and Galician minorities. Special autonomous communities were approved for the Basque and Catalan areas in 1979. Since 1980, the Socialists under Felipe Gonzalez have played a dominant role in Spanish politics. Spain is a member of the UN, the OECD, the Council of Europe, NATO, and the EC.

Population

Population	39.05 million
Annual population growth (1982–1988)	.46%
Urbanization	91.4%

Population structure (%):

Toddler (0–4)	6.3
Child (5–14)	14.1
Youth (15–24)	16.6
Adult (25–64)	50.0
Elderly (65 and over)	13.0

Ethnic diversity (%):

Spanish	73.0
Catalan	16.0
Galician	8.0
Basque	2.0
Other	1.0

Official languages	Spanish, Catalan, Galician, Basque

Religion (%):

Roman Catholicism	97.0
Other	3.0

Divorce rate (per 1,000)	.57

Economy

Gross domestic product (GDP) ($ billions)	340.10
Annual growth in GDP (1981–1987)	12.48%
Per capita GDP ($)	8,709
Savings ratio	22.02%
Annual inflation rate	6.6%
Cost of living index (New York = 100)	101.1
Exchange rate (peseta/$)	116.56
Unemployment	18.2%

Income distribution (% of total household income):

Lowest 20%	6.9
Highest 20%	40.0

Personal income tax (top bracket)	70.0

Life-style

Life expectancy	77.3 years
Hours of work per week	36.9
Annual number of vacation days	27.3

Consumer expenditures (% of total disposable income):

Food	23.0
Drink	1.8
Durables	7.7
Clothing	14.1
Services	5.2
Transport	16.2
Miscellaneous	8.2
Housing	23.8

Product ownership: (per 1,000):

Number of telephones	263.6
Number of radios	285.0
Number of televisions	257.0
Number of cars	240.0
Number of newspaper subscriptions	359.0

Secondary schooling	98%
Advertising expenditures per capita	$150.80

SWEDEN

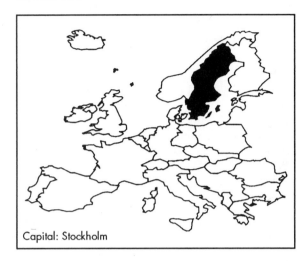

Capital: Stockholm

Political Background
Sweden, a parliamentary monarchy, was neutral during World War I and World War II and remains neutral today. The labor movement is strong in the country. Since 1932, the Social Democrats, left of center, have dominated Swedish politics (with one brief spell from 1976 to 1982 when the Conservatives were in power). The country is a member of the UN, the OECD, the Council of Europe, EFTA, and the Nordic Council.

Population

Population	8.44 million
Annual population growth (1982–1988)	.22%

Population structure (%):

Toddler (0–4)	5.6
Child (5–14)	10.9
Youth (15–24)	13.8
Adult (25–65)	51.4
Elderly (65 and over)	18.3

Ethnic diversity: (%)

Swedish	95.0
Finnish	2.0
Other	3.0

Official languages	Swedish, Finnish, Lapp

Religions (%):

Lutheranism	68.0
Atheism	30.0
Roman Catholicism	1.0
Other	1.0
Divorce rate (per 1,000)	2.27

Economy

Gross domestic product (GDP) ($ billions)	178.88
Annual growth in GDP (1981–1987)	9.74%
Per capita GDP ($)	21,195
Savings rate	17.98%
Annual inflation rate	6.3%
Cost of living index (New York = 100)	120.7
Exchange rate (kroner/$)	6.43
Unemployment	1.75%

Income distribution (% of total household income):

Lowest 20%	7.4
Highest 20%	41.7
Personal income tax (top bracket)	75.0%

Life-style

Life expectancy	77.8 years
Hours of work per week	36.20
Annual number of vacation days	27.5

Consumer expenditures (% of total disposable income):

Food	27.6
Drink	4.9
Durables	9.0
Clothing	19.5
Services	8.3
Transport	13.7
Miscellaneous	9.1
Housing	7.9

Product ownership: (per 1,000):

Number of telephones	657.1
Number of radios	858.0
Number of televisions	390.0
Number of cars	377.0
Number of newspaper subscriptions	521.0
Secondary schooling	83%
Advertising expenditures per capita	$178.80

SWITZERLAND

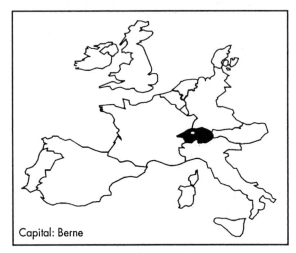

Capital: Berne

Political Background
Switzerland has been a republic of 23 cantons and has maintained neutrality since 1848. Each canton has a strong sense of independence, especially since four languages are represented. The federal government is represented by a seven-person Federal Council consisting of a co-alition of the major political parties. The country is a member of the OECD, the Council of Europe, and EFTA.

Population

Population	6.51 million
Annual population growth (1982–1988)	.1%
Urbanization	60.9%

Population structure (%):

Toddler (0–4)	5.8
Child (5–14)	10.6
Youth (15–24)	13.5
Adult (25–64)	54.8
Elderly (65 and over)	15.3

Ethnic diversity (%)

Swiss	86.0
Italian	4.0
French	2.0
Spanish	2.0
German	2.0
Other	4.0

Official languages	German, French, Italian, Romansch

Religions: (%)

Roman Catholicism	48.0
Protestantism	44.0
Other	8.0

Divorce rate (per 1,000)	1.76

Economy

Gross domestic product (GDP)($ billions)	183.69
Annual growth in GDP (1981–1987)	5.41%
Per capita GDP ($)	28,217
Savings rate	31.68%
Annual inflation rate	3.0%
Cost of living index (New York = 100)	111.47
Exchange rate (SFr/$)	1.62
Unemployment	.75%

Income distribution (% of total household income):

Lowest 20%	6.6
Highest 20%	38.0

Personal income tax (top bracket)	58.8%

Life-style

Life expectancy	77.6 years
Hours of work per week	42.40
Annual number of vacation days	23.5

Consumer expenditures (% of total disposable income):

Food	25.1
Drink	3.1
Durables	8.0
Clothing	15.1
Services	7.0
Transport	14.5
Miscellaneous	8.0
Housing	19.2

Product ownership: (per 1,000):

Number of telephones	535.1
Number of radios	367.0
Number of televisions	381.0
Number of cars	404.0
Number of newspaper subscriptions	387.0

Advertising expenditures per capita	$301.50

UNITED KINGDOM

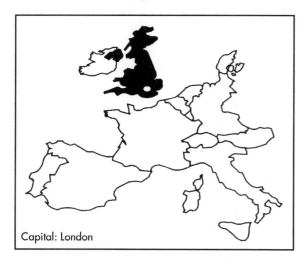

Capital: London

Political Background

The United Kingdom, a parliamentary monarchy, was formed in 1801 by a union of Great Britain and Ireland. In 1921, Southern Ireland formally separated from the United Kingdom, and Northern Ireland had a separate parliament until 1973. Since the end of World War II, the government has been formed by one of two parties—the Labour party or the Conservative party. The Conservatives, under the leadership of Margaret Thatcher, have been in power since 1979, pushing the country from a welfare state into a free market economy. The United Kingdom is a member of the UN, the OECD, the Council of Europe, NATO, the EC, the WEU, the Commonwealth, the Colombo Plan, and the South Pacific Commission.

Population

Population	57.08
Annual population growth (1982–1988)	.22%
Urbanization	87.7%

Population structure (%)
Toddler (0–4)	6.6
Child (5–14)	12.3
Youth (15–24)	14.7
Adult (25–64)	50.9
Elderly (65 and over)	15.5

Ethnic diversity: (%)
British	94.4
Indian	1.3
West Indian or Guyanese	1.0
Other	3.3

Official languages	English, Welsh

Religions (%):
Protestantism (Anglicanism, Presbyterianism)	57.0
Roman Catholicism	13.0
Islam	2.0
Other	28.0
Divorce rate (per 1,000)	3.20

Economy

Gross domestic product (GDP) ($ billions)	822.79
Annual growth in GDP (1981–1987)	8.78%
Per capita GDP ($)	14,415
Savings rate	17.21%
Annual inflation rate	7.3%
Cost of living index (New York = 100)	99.7
Exchange rate (£/$)	.62
Unemployment	8.5%

Income distribution (% of total household income):
Lowest 20%	7.0
Highest 20%	39.7
Personal income tax (top bracket)	40.0%

Life-style

Life expectancy	76.0 years
Hours of work per week	42.20
Annual number of vacation days	24.1

Consumer expenditures (% of total disposable income):
Food	21.9
Drink	4.0
Durables	7.0
Clothing	9.5
Services	6.9
Transport	17.8
Miscellaneous	8.5
Housing	24.4

Product ownership (per 1,000)
Number of telephones	409.4
Number of radios	993.0
Number of televisions	328.0
Number of cars	292.0
Number of newspaper subscriptions	411.0

Secondary schooling	85%
Advertising expenditures per capita	$211.80

UNITED STATES

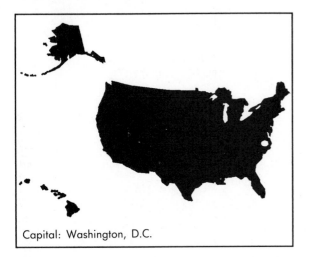

Capital: Washington, D.C.

Political Background
The United States, a republic, became independent from Great Britain in 1776. Originally there were 13 states; now there are 50, with the most recent additions Alaska in 1959 and Hawaii in 1960. The Democratic (center left) and Republican (center right) parties dominate U.S. politics. Since 1980, the United States has been governed by the Republican party under the leadership of Ronald Reagan and later George Bush. The United States is a member of the UN, the OAS, the OECD, NATO, the Colombo Plan, and the South Pacific Commission. It recently signed a Free Trade Agreement with Canada.

Population
Population	246.3 million
Annual population growth (1982–1988)	.97%
Urbanization	77%

Population structure: (%)
Toddler (0–4)	7.4
Child (5–14)	14.1
Youth (15–24)	14.5
Adult (25–64)	51.4
Elderly (65 and over)	12.6

Ethnic diversity (%):
English	21.8
German	21.7
Irish	17.7
Afro-American	9.2
French	5.7
Italian	5.4
Scottish	4.4
Other	14.1

Official language	English

Religions (%):
Protestantism	58.0
Roman Catholicism	38.0
Judaism	4.0

Divorce rate (per 1,000)	4.80

Economic
Gross domestic product (GDP) ($ billions)	4,847.30
Annual growth in GDP (1981–1987)	7.65%
Per capita GDP ($)	19,678
Savings rate	14.66%
Annual inflation rate	4.7%
Cost of living index (New York = 100)	100
Unemployment	6.2%

Income distribution (% of total household income):
Lowest 20%	5.3
Highest 20%	39.9

Personal income tax (top bracket)	29%

Life-styles
Life expectancy	76.3 years
Hours of work per week	41.0
Annual number of vacation days	13.1

Consumer expenditures (% of total disposable income):
Food	23.8
Drink	3.2
Durables	4.6
Clothing	12.7
Services	4.9
Transport	9.3
Miscellaneous	6.0
Housing	35.5

Product ownership (per 1,000):
Number of telephones	519.9
Number of radios	2,030.0
Number of televisions	785.0
Number of refrigerators	382.0
Number of cars	537.0
Number of newspaper subscriptions	267.0

Secondary schooling	100%
Advertising expenditures per capita	$480.20

WEST GERMANY

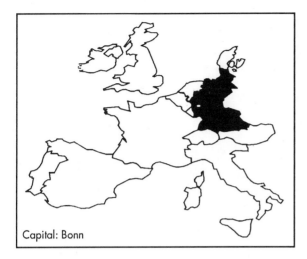

Capital: Bonn

Political Background*

West Germany is a republic formed in 1945 from the British-, French-, and U.S.- occupied zones of Germany after World War II. The Saar was returned by France in 1957. In 1972, East Germany and West Germany signed a treaty to settle differences between the two states. Politics has been dominated by the Christian Democratic party and the Social Democratic party. Germany is a member of the UN, the OECD, the Council of Europe, NATO, the EC, and the WEU.

Population

Population	61.20 million
Annual population growth (1982–1988)	−.12%
Urbanization	76.6%

Population structure(%):

Toddler (0–4)	6.4
Child (5–14)	13.4
Youth (15–24)	13.2
Adult (25–64)	53.9
Elderly (65 and over)	13.1

Ethnic diversity (%):

German	93.0
Turkish	3.0
Yugoslavian	1.0
Italian	1.0
Greek	1.0
Other	1.0

Official language	German

Religions (%):

Protestantism (mainly Lutheranism)	47.0
Roman Catholicism	44.0
Islam	2.0
Other	7.0

Divorce rate (per 1,000)	3.14

Economy

Gross domestic product (GDP) ($ billions)	1,201.8
Annual growth in GDP (1981–1987)	4.75%
Per capita GDP ($)	19,637
Savings rate	23.87%
Annual inflation rate	2.9%
Cost of living index (New York = 100)	86.1
Exchange rate (deutsche mark/$)	1.87
Unemployment	7.75%

Income distribution (% of total household income):

Lowest 20%	7.9
Highest 20%	39.5

Personal income tax (top bracket)	53.0%

Life-style

Life expectancy	75.7 years
Hours of work per week	40.1
Annual number of vacation days	29.9

Consumer expenditures (% of total disposable income):

Food	18.3
Drink	2.9
Durables	8.0
Clothing	16.9
Services	6.8
Transport	17.0
Miscellaneous	9.2
Housing	20.9

Product ownership (per 1,000):

Number of telephones	450.6
Number of radios	401.0
Number of televisions	360.0
Number of cars	428.0
Number of newspaper subscriptions	348.0

Secondary schooling	72%
Advertising expenditures per capita	$192.50

*East and West Germany were united in 1990 following upheavals in the formerly soviet-dominated countries in Eastern Europe.

NOTES TO COUNTRY FACTS SHEETS

Category	Year	Reference
Political Background		The World in Figures, 1987, *The Economist,* London.
Population		
Population	Mid-1988	*International Financial Statistics, 1989 Yearbook* and monthly issues, International Monetary Fund, Washington, D.C.
		Asian Development Bank, Manila, July 1989.
Population growth	Annual compound growth 1982–1988	*International Financial Statistics, 1989 Yearbook* and monthly issues, International Monetary Fund, Washington, D.C.
		Asian Development Bank, Manila, July 1989.
Urbanization: percentage of population in towns of 1,000–5,000 (depending on the country)	1980–1986	United Nations, *Demographic Yearbook, 1988,* New York, 1989.
Population structure	Estimates for 1990 by United Nations	United Nations, *World Population Prospects, 1988,* New York, 1989.
Ethnic diversity	1980–1985	The World in Figures, 1987, *The Economist,* London.
Religion	1980–1983	The World in Figures, 1987, *The Economist,* London.
Divorce rate	1982–1986	United Nations, *Demographic Yearbook, 1988,* New York, 1989.
Economy		
Gross domestic product	1988 in U.S. dollars	*International Financial Statistics, 1989 Yearbook* and monthly issues, International Monetary Fund, Washington, D.C.
		Economic Outlook, December 1989, Organization for Economic Cooperation and Development, Paris.
Annual nominal growth in gross domestic product	Annual compound percentage change, computed on a local currency basis, 1981–1987	*International Financial Statistics, 1989 Yearbook* and monthly issues, International Monetary Fund, Washington, D.C.
GDP per capita	1988	*International Financial Statistics, 1989 Yearbook* and monthly issues, International Monetary Fund, Washington, D.C.

(continued)

NOTES TO COUNTRY FACTS SHEETS (continued)

Category	Year	Reference
GDP per capita	1988	Economic Outlook, December 1989, Organization for Economic Cooperation and Development, Paris.
Domestic savings: gross domestic savings as a percentage of GDP	1987	National Accounts, 1988, Organization for Economic Cooperation and Development, Paris.
		Key Indicators of Developing Member Countries, July 1988, Asian Development Bank, Manila.
Annual inflation rate	October 1989	International Monitor of recent changes in taxation and living costs, 1989, PE-Inbucon, International Salary Research, Surrey, U.K.
Cost of living index: New York was the base city at 100.	October 1989	International Monitor of recent changes in taxation and living costs, 1989, PE-Inbucon, International Salary Research, Surrey, U.K.
Exchange rate	October 1989	International Monitor of recent changes in taxation and living costs, 1989, PE-Inbucon, International Salary Research, Surrey, U.K.
Unemployment	1988	Economic Outlook, December 1989, Organization for Economic Cooperation and Development, Paris.
		Asian Development Bank, Manila, July 1989.
Income distribution	1973–1981	Data derived from national surveys, conducted in different years and not always compatible.
Personal income tax	1988, 1989	Price Waterhouse, Individual Taxes—A Worldwide Summary, 1988.
		Survey of the Swedish Economy, *The Economist*, March 3, 1990, page 10.
Life-style		
Life expectancy	1990–1995	*World Population Prospects, 1988*, United Nations, New York, 1989.

(continued)

NOTES TO COUNTRY FACTS SHEETS (continued)

Category	Year	Reference
Hours of work per week	1987	*Yearbook of Labour Statistics,* International Labour Organization, Geneva, Switzerland.
Annual number of vacation days	1988	Price and Earnings Around the Globe, Union de Banque Suisse, 1988. Taken for a skilled mechanic with vocational training and about 10 years' experience with a large company in the metal industry.
Consumer expenditures	October 1989	International Monitor of recent changes in taxation and living costs, 1989, PE-Inbucon, International Salary Research, Surrey, U.K. For Singapore, *The Economist Book of Vital Statistics,* 1990.
Number of telephones per 1,000	1988	Siemens International Telephone Statistics, 1989.
Number of radios per 1,000	1983–1985	The World in Figures, 1987, *The Economist,* London, U.K.
Number of televisions per 1,000	1983–1985	The World in Figures, 1987, *The Economist,* London, U.K.
Number of cars per 1,000	1984–1985	The World in Figures, 1987, *The Economist,* London, U.K.
Number of newspaper subscriptions per 1,000	1982–1984	The World in Figures, 1987, *The Economist,* London, U.K.
Secondary schooling: percentage of relevant age group receiving full-time education.	1986	Economic Outlook, December 1989, Organization for Economic Cooperation and Development, Paris. World Development Report, 1988, World Bank, Washington, D.C. For some countries the enrollment ratio exceeds 100% because some students are below or above the country's standard primary school age.
Annual advertising expenditures per capita	1988	Starch INRA Hooper, *World Advertising Expenditures,* 23 Edition, New York.